The Psychology of Music

This is a volume in

ACADEMIC PRESS
SERIES IN COGNITION AND PERCEPTION

A Series of Monographs and Treatises

A complete list of titles in this series appears at the end of this volume.

The Psychology of Music

EDITED BY

Diana Deutsch

Department of Psychology
University of California, San Diego
La Jolla, California

 ACADEMIC PRESS, INC.

(Harcourt Brace Jovanovich, Publishers)

Orlando   San Diego   New York   London
Toronto   Montreal   Sydney   Tokyo

ACADEMIC PRESS, INC.
Orlando, Florida 32887

United Kingdom Edition published by
ACADEMIC PRESS, INC. (LONDON) LTD.
24/28 Oval Road, London NW1 7DX

Library of Congress Cataloging in Publication Data

Main entry under title:

The Psychology of music.

   (AP series in cognition and perception)
   Includes index.
   1. Music--Psychology. I. Deutsch, Diana.
II. Series.
ML3830.P9   781'.15   82-1646
ISBN 0-12-213560-1   AACR2

PRINTED IN THE UNITED STATES OF AMERICA

85 86 87 88   9 8 7 6 5 4 3 2

Contents

List of Contributors   xi
Preface   xiii

1. The Perception of Musical Tones
    R. A. Rasch and R. Plomp
     I. The Psychoacoustics of Music   1
    II. Perceptual Attributes of Single Tones   6
   III. Perceptual Attributes of Simultaneous Tones   14
    IV. Conclusion   21
         References   21

2. Exploration of Timbre by Analysis and Synthesis
    Jean-Claude Risset and David L. Wessel
      I. Timbre   26
     II. Timbre and the Fourier Spectrum: The Classical View   26
    III. The Shortcomings of the Classical Conception   29
     IV. Attack Transients   29
      V. Complexity of Sounds: Importance of Characteristic Features   30
     VI. Instrumental and Vocal Timbres: Additive Synthesis   30
    VII. Cross Synthesis and Voice Synthesis   34
   VIII. Additive Synthesis: Percussion Instruments   37
     IX. Substractive Synthesis   39
      X. Acoustic Modeling as a Synthesis Technique   41
     XI. The Importance of Context   42
    XII. Analysis-Synthesis as Fitting Acoustic and Perceptual Models to Data   44
   XIII. The Use of Analysis-Synthesis Models of Timbre   45
    XIV. Timbral Space   47
     XV. Conclusion   49
           Appendix: Signal Representations and Analysis-Synthesis Processes   50
           References   54

3. Perception of Singing
        Johan Sundberg

    I.   Introduction   59
   II.   Function of the Voice   60
  III.   Resonatory Aspects   62
   IV.   Phonation   76
    V.   Vibrato   82
   VI.   Pitch Accuracy in Singing Practice   89
  VII.   Phrasing and Emotion   91
 VIII.   Concluding Remarks   94
          References   95

4. Grouping Mechanisms in Music
        Diana Deutsch

    I.   Introduction   99
   II.   Grouping Principles   100
  III.   Two-Channel Listening to Melodic Sequences   101
   IV.   Channeling of Rapid Sequences of Single Tones   118
    V.   Voluntary Attention   127
   VI.   Conclusion   130
          References   130

5. The Listener and the Acoustic Environment
        R. A. Rasch and R. Plomp

    I.   Introduction   135
   II.   Methodology   137
  III.   Level Effects of Indirect Sound: Loudness   140
   IV.   Temporal Effects of Indirect Sound: Definition   141
    V.   Spatial Effects of Indirect Sound: Spaciousness   142
   VI.   The Compromise between Definition and Spaciousness   145
  VII.   Conclusion   146
          References   146

6. Rhythm and Tempo
        Paul Fraisse

    I.   Definitions   149
   II.   Rhythm and Spontaneous Tempo   151
  III.   Rhythmic Forms   157
   IV.   The Perception of Musical Rhythms   170
    V.   Conclusion   175
          References   177

7. Timing by Skilled Musicians
Saul Sternberg, Ronald L. Knoll, and Paul Zukofsky

    I.   Perception, Production, and Imitation of Fractions of the Beat   182
   II.   Perceptual Judgment of Beat Fractions   187
  III.   Production of Beat Fractions   198
  IV.   Imitation of Beat Fractions   207
   V.   A Shared-Process Model of the Perception, Production,
       and Imitation of Beat Fractions   212
  VI.   Further Analysis of Perceptual Judgment   215
 VII.   Further Analysis of Production   224
VIII.   Summary   229
       Glossary   231
       Appendix   231
       References   237

8. Intervals, Scales, and Tuning
Edward M. Burns and W. Dixon Ward

    I.   Introduction   241
   II.   Are Scales Necessary?   243
  III.   Musical Interval Perception   246
  IV.   Natural Intervals and Scales   255
   V.   Conclusions and Caveats   264
       References   265

9. The Processing of Pitch Combinations
Diana Deutsch

    I.   Introduction   271
   II.   Feature Abstraction   272
  III.   Higher Order Abstractions   282
  IV.   Alphabets and Hierarchies   287
   V.   Memory Systems   291
  VI.   Conclusions   311
       References   312

10. Melodic Processes and the Perception of Music
Burton S. Rosner and Leonard B. Meyer

    I.   The Perception and Classification of Two Archetypal Melodic Processes   317
   II.   Experimental Findings   326
  III.   Implications   339
       References   340

11. Structural Representations of Musical Pitch
Roger N. Shepard

I.   Introduction   344
II.   Unidimensional Approaches to Pitch   344
III. Potentially Multidimensional Approaches to Pitch   347
IV.   The Spatial Representation of Pitch   350
V.   Illustrative Analyses of Empirical Data   365
VI.   Discussion   369
      References   385

12. Musical Ability
Rosamund Shuter-Dyson

I.   Concepts of Musical Ability   391
II.   Correlational and Factorial Studies of Musical Ability   393
III. Musical Ability and Other Intellectual Abilities   404
      References   408

13. Melodic Information Processing and Its Development
W. Jay Dowling

I.   Introduction   413
II.   Development   415
III. Adult Memory   421
IV.   Contour versus Interval   427
V.   Summary   427
      References   428

14. Absolute Pitch
W. Dixon Ward and Edward M. Burns

I.   Introduction   431
II.   Genesis of AP   434
III. Measurement of AP   436
IV.   Stability of the Internal Standard   444
V.   Learning AP   445
VI.   The Value of AP   447
      References   449

15. Neurological Aspects of Music Perception and Performance
Oscar S. M. Marin

I.   Introduction   453

II.   Amusia   454
III. Auditory Agnosia and Verbal Deafness   462
IV.   General Comments   466
      References   473

16. Music Performance
John A. Sloboda

  I.   Introduction   479
 II.   The Nature of Performance Plans   480
III.   Acquisition of Performance Plans   483
 IV.   The Role of Feedback in Performance   488
  V.   Social Factors in Performance   491
 VI.   Summary   494
       References   494

17. Social Interaction and Musical Preference
Vladimir J.Konečni

  I.   Introduction   497
 II.   Effects of Social Stimulation on Aesthetic Choice   502
III.   Effects of Information Load and Arousing Nonsocial Stimulation
       on Aesthetic Choice   505
 IV.   Effects of Listening to Melodies Differing in Complexity on
       Emotional States and Social Behavior   507
  V.   Listeners' Sequencing and "Chunking" of Musical Materials
       and the Use of Music for Mood Optimization   511
       References   515

18. New Music and Psychology
Robert Erickson

  I.   Introduction   517
 II.   Music Theory and Music   519
III.   Understanding Tonality   520
 IV.   Music and Perceptual Streaming   523
  V.   Fused Sounds in Music   529
 VI.   Music Theory and Experimental Science   534
       References   535

       Index   537

List of Contributors

Numbers in parentheses indicate the pages on which the authors' contributions begin.

Edward M. Burns (241, 431), Department of Audiology and Speech Sciences, Purdue University, West Lafayette, Indiana 47907

Diana Deutsch (99, 271), Department of Psychology, University of California, San Diego, La Jolla, California 92093

W. Jay Dowling (413), Program in Psychology and Human Development, University of Texas at Dallas, Richardson, Texas 75080

Robert Erickson (517), Department of Music, University of California, San Diego, La Jolla, California 92093

Paul Fraisse (149), Laboratoire de Psychologie Expérimentale et Comparée, Université René Descartes, Paris, France

Ronald L. Knoll (181), Bell Laboratories, Murray Hill, New Jersey 07974

Vladimir J. Konečni (497), Department of Psychology, University of California, San Diego, La Jolla, California 92093

Oscar S. ·M. Marin (453), Department of Neurology, Good Samaritan Hospital and Medical Center, Portland, Oregon 97210

Leonard B. Meyer (317), Department of Music, University of Pennsylvania, Philadelphia, Pennsylvania 19104

R. Plomp (1, 135), Institute for Perception TNO, Soesterberg, The Netherlands, and Faculty of Medicine, Free University, Amsterdam, The Netherlands

R. A. Rasch (1, 135), Institute of Musicology, University of Utrecht, Utrecht, The Netherlands

Jean-Claude Risset (25), Faculté des Sciences de Luminy et Laboratoire de Mécanique et d'Acoustique, Marseille, France

Burton S. Rosner (317), Department of Psychology, University of Pennsylvania, Philadelphia, Pennsylvania 19104

Roger N. Shepard (343), Department of Psychology, Stanford University, Stanford, California 94305

Rosamund Shuter-Dyson[1] (391), Senior Lecturer in Psychology, Hatfield Polytechnic, Hertfordshire, England

John A. Sloboda (479), Department of Psychology, University of Keele, Keele, Staffordshire, England

Saul Sternberg (181), Bell Laboratories, Murray Hill, New Jersey 07974

Johan Sundberg (59), Department of Speech Communication and Music Acoustics, Royal Institute of Technology, S-100 44 Stockholm, Sweden

W. Dixon Ward (241, 431), Hearing Research Laboratory, University of Minnesota, Minneapolis, Minnesota 55455

David L. Wessel (25), Institute de Recherche et Coordination, Acoustique-Musique, Paris, France

Paul Zukofsky[2] (181), Bell Laboratories, Murray Hill, New Jersey 07974

[1]Present address: 6 Rectory Close, Tadley, Basingstoke, Hampshire RG26 6PH, England.
[2]Present address: Musical Observations, Inc., Port Jefferson, New York 11777.

Preface

The above words were written by Aristoxenus of Tarentum (ca. 320 B.C.) in the course of arguing that musical phenomena can be understood only through scientific investigation of human processing mechanisms. Reasonable as this view may seem to modern psychologists, it ran counter to the prevailing theoretical stance, based on Pythagorean doctrine, which has profoundly influenced the study of music throughout history. Most characteristic of this stance is a strong distrust of the evidence of the senses, together with the belief that music ought to be investigated by contemplation of numerical relationships alone. As Anaxagoras (ca. 499–428 B.C.) put it: "Through the weakness of our sense perceptions we cannot judge truth." And later as Boethius, the leading music theorist of the Middle Ages and a strong follower of Pythagoras, wrote in *De Institutione Musicae:* "For what need is there of speaking further concerning the error of the senses when this same faculty of sensing is neither equal in all men, nor at all times equal within the same man? Therefore anyone vainly puts his trust in a changing judgment since he aspires to seek the truth."

There are several good reasons that such a rationalistic position should have been adopted at the time and should have persisted for so long. One reason was a lack of understanding of the nature of sound. One can see that the inability to characterize a physical stimulus should have inhibited development of theories concerning how this stimulus is processed. A related problem was the lack of stimulus control, which made experimentation difficult. Another problem was the lack of mathematical techniques appropriate for the study of probabilistic phenomena.

These factors considered, it appears as no coincidence that the last decade has seen a sudden flowering of interest in the empirical study of music on the part of both psychologists and musicians. The nature of sound is now well understood, and the required mathematical techniques have been developed. Recent advances in computer technology have enabled investigators for the first time to generate complex sound stimuli with versatility and precision. It has thus become possible to explore such issues as auditory shape analysis, attentional mechanisms in music, the organization of memory for musical information, and so on, with the stimulus control required for tight experimentation. Researchers have been able to build on conceptual frameworks recently developed in other branches of psychology and in music theory. This same technological development has led composers to experiment with the computer as a compositional tool. In so doing, numerous questions in perceptual and cognitive psychology that are of both practical interest to composers and theoretical interest to psychologists have been raised. As a result of this developing interest on the part of both scientists and musicians, we are experiencing a rapid expansion of work in the area of musical processing; and perhaps more importantly, collaboration between musicians and scientists is a rapidly growing phenomenon.

The purpose of this volume is to draw together the diverse and scattered literature on musical processing that has accumulated particularly over the last decade. The work is intended as a reference source for all those interested in music and the way it is processed by the listener and the performer. It is also intended as a reference source for perceptual and cognitive psychologists, who will find in the study of music much that is of general interest to their fields. The volume may also be used as a text for courses in the psychology of music.

The volume opens with a chapter on *The Perception of Musical Tones*, by Rasch and Plomp, which surveys the classical psychoacoustical literature on tone perception, focusing on characteristics of particular relevance to music. The attributes of pitch, loudness, and timbre are examined, as are psychoacoustical phenomena that occur when tones are presented simultaneously, such as beats and roughness, combination tones, and consonance and dissonance. The authors also provide a useful summary of research methods in psychoacoustics.

Timbre perception is examined in depth by Risset and Wessel in *Exploration of Timbre by Analysis and Synthesis* (Chapter 2). The authors address several issues that are of importance both to perceptual psychology and to contemporary music. For example, How is it that we can identify the sound of an instrument regardless of its pitch or loudness? What types of information can be discarded in the synthetic replication of a sound without distorting perceived timbre? How are the timbres of different instruments perceptually related? By investigating such questions it has proved possible to modify timbres in intriguing ways, for example, to extrapolate a timbre beyond its instrument register or to create a sequence of timbres that progress regularly from one instrument type to another. As the authors note, this field of research is likely to have a profound impact on the development of new music.

Johan Sundberg's chapter on *The Perception of Singing* (Chapter 3) examines some closely related issues. For example, How are we able to hear a singer's voice against a loud or orchestral background? How do we manage to identify sung vowels even though these differ markedly from those in speech? Why do we perceive singing as a set of discrete pitches even though the fundamental frequency events are not discrete? These and other questions are expertly evaluated.

Consider what happens when we listen to a live performance by an orchestra. The mixture of sounds that reaches our ears is produced by many instruments playing in parallel. Somehow our auditory system is able to sort out this mixture of sounds, so that we may choose to listen to a particular instrument or to a particular melodic configuration. What are the mechanisms whereby such groupings are achieved? To what extent are they under voluntary control? These questions are explored in *Grouping Mechanisms in Music* (Deutsch, Chapter 4). It is also shown that under certain circumstances the listener may perceptually reorganize what he or she hears, so that striking illusions may occur. When this happens, the listener's perceptions may not accord with the intentions of the composer.

As implied in Berlioz's statement "There is no such thing as music in the open air," the enclosed space of the concert hall contributes much to the aesthetic quality of music, through the complex sound reflections to which it gives rise. Experiments on the subjective effects of different sound fields are reviewed by Rasch and Plomp in *The Listener and the Acoustic Environment* (Chapter 5). The results of such studies have important practical implications for the design of concert halls.

The next two chapters in the volume are concerned with temporal aspects of music. In Chapter 6 on *Rhythm and Tempo* Paul Fraisse thoroughly surveys a field which he has so ably pioneered, including a review of his own classical contributions. This chapter is complemented by an in-depth study on *Timing by Skilled Musicians*, by Sternberg, Knoll, and Zukofsky (Chapter 7). As the authors write, "During ensemble rehearsal and performance, players must judge, produce and imitate beat fractions. It is plausible that because of the requirement that players 'keep together,' performing experience would cause the three functions to become at least consistent with each other and probably accurate as well. Neither of these expectations was borne out by our experiments." The results of this unique study are particularly valuable; such eminent musicians as the composer and conductor Pierre Boulez and the violinist and conductor Paul Zukofsky were employed as subjects. Based on their findings, the authors propose an information-flow model of timing which also has general implications.

The next four chapters are concerned with abstract structures formed by pitch relationships in music. The large majority of musical cultures employ scales. In Chapter 8, *Intervals, Scales, and Tuning*, Burns and Ward explore the perception of musical scales in detail, focusing on the interval as the basic building block. The authors argue that the use of a small set of discrete pitch relationships in music is probably dictated by inherent limitations in our ability to transmit sensory information. Such limitations probably also account for the phenomenon of categorical perception of musical intervals, the evidence for which is thoroughly reviewed. Arguments for different tuning systems are explored, and the authors conclude that patterns of intonation used by musicians are primarily a function of their acquired ability to reproduce learned interval categories.

The *Processing of Pitch Combinations* (Deutsch, Chapter 9) examines how pitch information is internally represented at different levels of abstraction. At the lowest level, local features such as intervals and pitch classes are represented, as are global features such as contour. At the next higher level, such features are combined so as to give rise to perceptual equivalences and similarities between larger sets of pitches. At a yet-higher level, pitch information is mapped onto a set of highly overlearned alphabets and is retained in the form of hierarchies. A distinction is drawn between musical abstractions that result from passive "bottom-up" processes and those that are the result of hypothesis testing or are "top-down" in nature. The final section of the chapter is concerned with memory for pitch at these different levels of abstraction.

The internal representation of musical hierarchies is explored in an elegant collaborative study by Rosner and Meyer on *Melodic Processes and the Perception of Music* (Chapter 10). The authors argue, following Meyer's earlier theoretical work, that melodies often appear to be hierarchically structured in such a way that the type of patterning exhibited by a given melody differs from one hierarchical level to the next. The authors further hypothesize that "melodic patterns are classified by listeners, as well as music theorists, in terms of the organization of the highest level on which significant closure is created by the parameters that shape musical relationships." Using a concept identification task, the authors found that musically untrained listeners did indeed classify melodies in accordance with theoretical expectations.

The question of how pitch relationships within a musical system can best be represented has traditionally been the main focus of music theory. In his provocative *Structural Representations of Musical Pitch* (Chapter 11) Roger Shepard proposes that pitch in our tonal system be represented as a double helical structure requiring an embedding space of five dimensions. In arguing for this model, Shepard draws on recent empirical findings from psychology and psychoacoustics, as well as on considerations from tonal music.

The next four chapters consider musical ability from different points of view. In *Musical Ability* (Chapter 12) Rosamund Shuter-Dyson describes and critically evaluates different tests of musical ability. Various questions are then explored. For example, How does musical ability correlate with other intellectual abilities? How does musical ability develop with age? To what extent is musical ability a learned phenomenon and to what extent does it depend on training? Cases of exceptional musical ability are also described. This chapter should serve as a particularly useful reference for music educators.

The question of how the ability to process melodic information develops with age is explored in detail by Dowling in *Melodic Information Processing and Its Development* (Chapter 13). Dowling argues for a developmental sequence that begins with the infant's ability to match pitches and distinguish such gross features as contour, progresses to the young child's ability to recognize tonal scales and discriminate key changes, and arrives finally at the adult's ability to detect small differences in interval size. Dowling proposes that the same hierarchy of melodic features is manifest in adult musical behavior.

One intriguing example of unusual musical ability is the possession of absolute pitch. Ward and Burns discuss this phenomenon in depth in Chapter 14 (*Absolute Pitch*). Why is it that a few people possess absolute pitch, whereas most people do not? Is it innate, or is it acquired through experience, perhaps at a critical age? Is it an ability that tends to disappear through a process of unlearning? A detailed study of the processing capacities of one listener with absolute pitch is also presented.

Chapter 15 (*Neurological Aspects of Music Perception and Performance*) was written by Oscar Marin with two aims: first, to characterize the types of deficit in music perception and performance that are associated with damage to the nervous system and second, to use this information to elucidate the neuroanatomical basis of musical function in the normal case. Marin emphasizes that music is a highly complex function, so that simplistic views of how it is represented are bound to prove incorrect. This chapter also includes a discussion of the relationship between the neuroanatomical substrates of music and those of speech.

Instrumentalists will find Sloboda's *Music Performance* (Chapter 16) of particular interest. Sloboda emphasizes the importance of abstract structural representation to understanding how music is performed. Deviations from accuracy in expert performers can often be explained as serving to communicate musical structure to the listener. Experiments involving sightreading, memorization, and improvization are discussed with this theoretical framework.

Konečni's contribution on *Social Interaction and Musical Preference* (Chapter 17) stresses the important role played by music in everyday life. As the author writes, "a thorough understanding of aesthetic behavior cannot be achieved without examining how it changes as a function of its immediate social and nonsocial antecedents, concurrent cognitive and resultant emotional states." Furthermore, "both subtle and major changes in social behavior may occur as a function of listening to music." A set of laboratory experiments documents these arguments.

In the final chapter of the volume, *New Music and Psychology*, the composer and music theorist Robert Erickson presents a thoughtful evaluation of the relationship between the two disciplines. Erickson also outlines several questions raised by contemporary music that can usefully be approached using the methods of experimental psychology.

I am grateful to Michael Jordan for compiling the index, and I should like particularly to thank E. C. Carterette for his invaluable contribution in organizing the volume.

Diana Deutsch

1

The Perception of Musical Tones

R. A. Rasch and R. Plomp

I. The Psychoacoustics of Music 1
    A. Introduction 1
    B. Methodology 2
    C. The Ear as a Frequency Analyzer 4
II. Perceptual Attributes of Single Tones 6
    A. Pitch 6
    B. Loudness 10
    C. Timbre 12
III. Perceptual Attributes of Simultaneous Tones 14
    A. Beats and Roughness 14
    B. Combination Tones 17
    C. Consonance and Dissonance 19
IV. Conclusion 21
    References 21

I. THE PSYCHOACOUSTICS OF MUSIC

A. Introduction

The aim of research in music perception is to explain how we respond subjectively to musical sound signals. In this respect it is a part of psychophysics, the general denomination for scientific fields concerned with the relationship between the objective, physical properties of sensory stimuli in our environment and the subjective, psychological responses evoked by them. If the stimuli are of an acoustic nature, we speak of *psychoacoustics*. Psychoacoustics can be of a general, theoretical nature; it can also be applied to a certain class of auditory stimuli, such as music and speech. This chapter is devoted to *musical psychoacoustics*.

The most important topics of musical psychoacoustics are the subjective properties of musical tones (pitch, loudness, timbre) and the phenomena that occur when several tones are presented simultaneously, which is what usually happens in music (beats and roughness, combination tones, consonance and dissonance). We will focus our discussion on these topics. However, before we deal more extensively with them, some attention must be given to the methodology of psychoacoustics and to the frequency-analyzing power of the ear, a capacity that is fundamental to its perceptual functioning.

B. Methodology

Psychoacoustics is an empirical or, rather, experimental science. Observations from daily life and informal tryouts may be starting points for psychoacoustical knowledge, but the core of the scientific content is the result of laboratory investigations. In this respect it is an interdisciplinary field of research. Contributions have been made both by experimental psychologists and by physicists and acousticians.

A *psychoacoustical experiment* can be described most simply in a stimulus–response scheme. The *stimulus* is the sound presented to the subject. The experimenter requires the subject to give a *response*. The experimenter tries to discover the relationship between stimulus and response characteristics. Both stimulus and response are observable events. The subject is considered a "black box" that cannot be entered by the experimenter. Psychoacoustical research is often carried out without an attempt to explain the experimental results functionally in terms of sensory processes. Such attempts are made in research that is labeled *physiological acoustics*, a part of sensory and neurophysiology.

Our ears are very sensitive organs. Because of this, very accurate control of the stimulus variables is required in psychoacoustical experiments. Sound pressure level differences of less than 1 dB, time differences of a few msec, and frequency differences of less than 1 Hz can have a profound effect on the subjective response to a stimulus. It is impossible to obtain well-controlled psychoacoustic stimuli by manual means, like playing tones or chords on a musical instrument. The precision of the ear in distinguishing fine nuances is much greater than our ability to produce these nuances. As a rule, psychoacoustics makes use of electronic audio equipment that can produce sound stimuli according to any specification. In recent years it has become feasible to run the experiments under computer control. The computer can also be used for storage and analysis of stimuli and response data. Most problems concerning the production of the stimuli in psychoacoustical experiments may be considered solved. After the sound stimulus has been produced, it must reach the subject's eardrum with the least possible distortion. Usually high-quality headphones are used unless the spatial effect of the listening environment is involved. Background noises should be reduced, if not eliminated.

It is possible to have the subject describe his perception verbally. However, this response is often insufficient because our sensations allow much finer distinctions than our vocabulary does. Moreover, the use of words may differ from subject to subject. Because of this, in psychoacoustics most results are derived from responses made on the basis of a certain perception without direct reference to the perception itself. For example, if we have to indicate in which of two time intervals a sound has occurred, the response is a time indication based on an auditory sensation. A great deal of inventiveness is often required of the experimenter in designing his experimental paradigms.

The procedures used most often in psychoacoustical experiments are choice methods and adjustment methods. A single presentation of a sound event (one or more stimuli) to which a response must be made is called a *trial*. Using *choice methods*, the subject has to make, for each trial, a choice from a limited set of well-defined alternatives. The simplest case is the one with two alternatives, the *two-alternative-forced-choice* (2AFC). The insertion of the word "forced" is essential: The subject is obliged to choose. He must guess when he is incapable of making a meaningful choice.

For example, let us assume that the investigator is studying under what conditions a probe tone can be heard simultaneously with another, or masking sound. Each trial contains two successive time periods marked by visual signals. The masking sound is continuously present; the probe tone occurs in one of two time periods, randomly determined. If the probe tone is clearly detectable, the subject indicates whether it was presented in the first or in the second period. If the tone is not perceived at all, the subject must guess, resulting in an expectation of 50% correct responses. The transition from clearly detectable to not detectable tones is gradual. It is reflected by a gradual slope of the so-called *psychometric curve* that represents the percentage of correct responses plotted as a function of the sound pressure level of the target tone. The sound pressure level that corresponds to a score of 75% correct responses is usually adopted as the threshold for detection.

In order to arrive at an accurate estimate of the threshold, the experimenter varies sound pressure level of the tone for the successive trials. In the *constant stimuli* method the experimenter presents the tones according to a fixed procedure. The method of constant stimuli is time consuming because a number of trials are definitely supra- or infra-threshold and, therefore, do not give much information. Another class of choice methods, called *adaptive methods*, makes a more efficient use of trials. The experimental series is started with a certain initial value of the stimulus variable. One or more correct responses, depending upon the experimental strategy adopted, result in a change in the stimulus variable that makes it harder for the subject to make a correct choice. If the subject makes one or more false responses, the experimental task is facilitated. In this way, the value of the stimulus variable fluctuates around a certain value, which can be defined to be the threshold for perception.

Besides choice methods there is the *adjustment method*. The subject controls the stimulus variable himself, and he uses this control to find an optimal value. This method is not always feasible. The adjustment method is suitable for stimulus variables that allow an optimal quality in perception: the best pitch for a tone in a musical interval, the most comfortable loudness, the greatest similarity or dissimilarity, etc. The optimal adjustment behaves like a stable equilibrium between lower and higher, both suboptimal, adjustments. Adjustment methods have the advantage that the results can be derived directly from the adjusted value, and do not have to be derived indirectly from the psychometric curve.

C. The Ear as a Frequency Analyzer

Only by the ear's capacity to analyze complex sounds are we able to discriminate simultaneous tones in music. *Frequency analysis* may be considered the most characteristic property of the peripheral ear. The cochlea is divided over its entire length into two parts by the basilar membrane. In 1942 Von Békésy was the first to observe, with ingenious experimentation, that at every point along its length this membrane vibrates with maximum amplitude for a specific frequency. This finding confirmed the hypothesis, launched 80 years earlier by Helmholtz, that the cochlea performs a frequency analysis. Sound components with high frequencies are represented close to the base; components with low frequencies are represented near the apex of the cochlea. The frequency scale of the sound is converted into a spatial scale along the basilar membrane.

This capacity of the ear means that any periodic sound wave or *complex tone* is resolved into its frequency components, also called *partials* or *harmonics* (see Fig. 1). In mathematics the analogous procedure of determining the sinusoidal components of a periodic function is called *Fourier analysis*. In contrast with the theoretically perfect

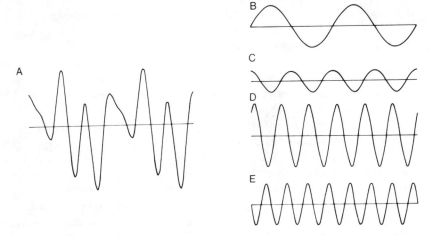

Fig. 1. The wave form A, a complex tone, is in fact the sum of the simple tones B-E. This is an illustration of Fourier's theorem that every vibration of frequency f can be analyzed mathematically into a series of sinusoidal vibrations with frequencies f, $2f$, $3f$, etc. These sinusoidal vibrations are called the harmonics.

Fourier analysis, the frequency-analyzing power of the ear is limited: Only the lower harmonics can be analyzed individually.

There are many ways of studying the extent to which the ear can separate simultaneous tones. Only two approaches will be considered here. The first method investigates how many harmonics (with frequencies nf, $n = 1, 2, 3, 4$, etc.) can be distinguished in a complex tone. This can be done by using the 2AFC procedure: The listener has to decide which of two simple (sinusoidal) tones—one with frequency nf, the other with frequency $(n \pm \frac{1}{2})f$—is also present in the complex tone. The percentage of correct responses varies from 100 for low values of n to about 50 for high values of n. Experiments along these lines have shown (Plomp, 1964) that, on the average, listeners are able to distinguish the first five to seven harmonics.

A quite different approach involves measuring the minimum sound pressure level necessary for a probe tone to be audible when presented with a complex tone. This is the so-called masked threshold; by varying the probe-tone frequency, we obtain the "masking pattern" of the complex tone. In Fig. 2 such a pattern is reproduced. The masking pattern of a complex tone of 500 Hz reveals individual peaks corresponding to the first five harmonics, nicely demonstrating the limited frequency-analyzing power of the ear.

The usual measure indicating how well a system is able to analyze complex signals is its bandwidth. The finding that the fifth harmonic can be distinguished from the fourth and the sixth means that the mutual distance should be a minor third or more. This distance constitutes a rough, general estimate of the bandwidth of the hearing mechanism, known in the psychophysical literature as the *critical bandwidth* (Fig. 3). A detailed review (Plomp, 1976) revealed that the bandwidth found experimentally is dependent on the experimental conditions. The values may differ by a factor of two.

In the lower frequency region (below 500 Hz) critical bandwidth is more or less constant if expressed in Hz. That means that musical intervals (frequency ratios) larger than the critical bandwidth at high frequencies may fall within the critical bandwidth at lower frequencies.

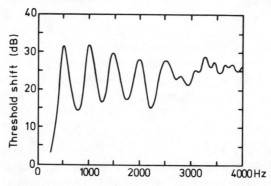

Fig. 2. Masking pattern of a complex tone consisting of the first 12 harmonics of 500 Hz (based on Plomp, 1964). Only the first five harmonics are analyzed by the ear.

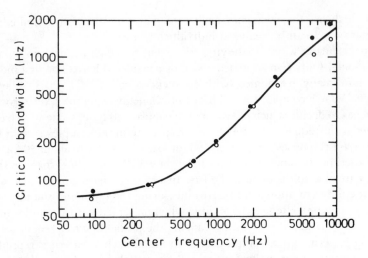

Fig. 3. Critical bandwidth as a function of frequency. This curve is a rough approximation only.

II. PERCEPTUAL ATTRIBUTES OF SINGLE TONES

A. Pitch

Pitch is the most characteristic property of tones, both simple (sinusoidal) and complex. Pitch systems (like the diatonic-chromatic and the 12-tone system) are among the most elaborate and intricate ever developed in Western and non-Western music. Pitch is related to the frequency of a simple tone and to the fundamental frequency of a complex tone. The frequency of a tone is a property that can usually be controlled in production and is well preserved during its propagation to the listener's ears.

For our purposes, pitch may be characterized as a *one-dimensional* attribute, i.e., all tones can be ordered along a single scale with respect to pitch (but see Chapters 8, 9, and 11, this volume). The extremes of this scale are *low* (tones with low frequencies) and *high* (tones with high frequencies). Sometimes tones with different spectral compositions (timbres) are not easily comparable as to pitch. It is possible that the clearness of pitch varies, for example, as a result of important noise components or inharmonic partials, or that the subjective character of the pitch varies, for example, when comparing the pitch of simple and complex tones. There are a number of subjective pitch scales:

1. The *mel* scale (see Stevens, Volkmann, & Newman, 1937). A simple tone of 1000 Hz has a defined pitch of 1000 mel. The pitch in mels of other tones with another frequency must be determined by comparative scaling experiments. A sound with a pitch subjectively twice that of a 1000 Hz tone is 2000 mel; "half pitch" is 500

mel, etc. Since there is no unambiguous subjective meaning of "a pitch half as high" or "double as high," the mel scale is a rather unreliable scale. It is not used very often.

(2.) The *musical pitch* scale (i.e., the ordinary indications C1, D1, . . . , C4, . . . , A4, etc.). These indications are only usable in musical situations.

(3.) The physical *frequency* scale in Hz. In psychoacoustical literature the pitch of a tone is often indicated by its frequency or, in the case of complex tones, by its fundamental frequency. Since the correspondence between frequency and pitch is monotonic, frequency is a rough indication of our pitch sensation. It must be realized however, that our perception operates more or less on the basis of a logarithmic frequency scale.

Pitch in its musical sense has a range of about 20 to 5000 Hz, roughly the range of the fundamental frequencies of piano strings and organ pipes. Tones with higher frequencies are audible but without definite pitch sensation. Low tones in the range of 10 to 50 Hz can have the character of a rattling sound. The transition from the perception of single pulses to a real pitch sensation is gradual. Pitch can be perceived after very few periods of the sound wave have been presented to the ear.

Simple tones have unambiguous pitches that can be indicated by means of their frequencies. These frequencies may serve as reference frequencies for the pitches of complex tones. The pitch sensation of complex tones is much more difficult to understand than the pitch of simple tones. As was discussed, the first five to seven harmonics of a complex tone can be distinguished individually if the listener's attention is drawn to their possible presence. However, a complex tone, as heard in practice, is characterized by a single pitch, the pitch of the fundamental component. This pitch will be referred to as *low pitch* here. In psychoacoustical literature this pitch is also known under a variety of other terms, such as periodicity pitch, repetition pitch, residue pitch, and virtual pitch. Experiments (Terhardt, 1971) have shown that the pitch of a complex tone with fundamental frequency f is somewhat lower than that of a sinusoidal tone with frequency f. The existence of low pitch of a complex tone raises two questions. First, why are all components of the complex tones perceived as a perceptual unit; that is, why do all partials fuse into one percept? Second, why is the pitch of this perceptual tone the pitch of the fundamental component?

The first question can be answered with reference to the Gestalt theory of perception. The "Gestalt explanation" may be formulated as follows. The various components of a complex tone are always present simultaneously. We become familiar with the complex tones of speech signals (both of our own speech and of other speakers) from an early age. It would not be efficient to perceive them all separately. All components point to a single source and meaning so that perception of them as a unit gives a simpler view of the environment than separate perception. This mode of perception must be seen as a perceptual learning process. Gestalt psychology has formulated a number of laws that describe the perception of complex sensory stimuli. The perception of low pitch of complex tones can be classed under the heading of the "law of common fate." The harmonics of a complex tone exhibit "common fate."

The second question can also be answered with the help of a learning process directed toward perceptual efficiency. The periodicity of a complex tone is the most constant feature in its composition. The amplitudes of the partials are subjected to much variation, caused by selective reflection, absorption, passing of objects, etc. Masking can also obscure certain partials. The periodicity, however, is a very stable and constant factor in a complex tone. This is reflected in the wave form built up from harmonics. The periodicity of a complex tone is at the same time the periodicity of the fundamental component of the tone. The perception of complex tones can be seen as a pattern recognition process. The presence of a complete series of harmonics is not a necessary condition for the pitch recognition process to succeed. It is sufficient that at least a few pairs of adjacent harmonics are present so that the periodicity can be determined. It is conceivable that there is a perceptual learning process that makes possible the recognition of fundamental periodicity from a limited number of harmonic partials. This learning process is based on the same experiences as those that led to singular pitch perception. Pattern recognition theories of the perception of low pitch are of relatively recent origin. Several times they have been worked out in detailed mathematical models that simulate the perception of complex tones (Goldstein, 1973; Wightman, 1973; Terhardt, 1974a; see also de Boer, 1976, 1977; Patterson & Wightman, 1976; Gerson & Goldstein, 1978; Houtsma, 1979; Piszczalski & Galler, 1979). It will probably take some time before the questions about the low singular pitch of complex tones are completely solved.

The classical literature on tone perception abounds with theories based on von Helmholtz's (1863) idea that the low pitch of a complex tone is based on the relative strength of the fundamental component. The higher harmonics are thought only to influence the timbre of the tones but not to be strong enough to affect pitch. However, low pitch perception also occurs when the fundamental component is not present in the sound stimulus. This was already observed by Seebeck (1841) and brought to the attention of the modern psychoacousticians by Schouten (1938). These observations led Schouten to the formulation of a *periodicity pitch theory*. In this theory pitch is derived from the waveform periodicity of the unresolved higher harmonics of the stimulus, the *residue*. This periodicity does not change if a component (e.g., the fundamental one) is removed. With this theory the observations of Seebeck and Schouten concerning tones without fundamental components could be explained. An attempt has also been made to explain the low pitch of a tone without fundamental ("the missing fundamental") as the result of the occurrence of combination tones, which provide a fundamental component in the inner ear. However, when these combination tones are effectively masked by low-pass noise, the sensation of low pitch remains (Licklider, 1954).

In musical practice complex tones with weak or absent fundamentals are very common. Moreover, musical tones are often partially masked by other tones. These tones can, however, possess very clear low pitches. Effective musical sound stimuli are often incomplete when compared to the sound produced by the source (instrument, voice).

Experiments in tone perception have pointed to a *dominance region* for pitch perception, roughly from 500 to 2000 Hz (Plomp, 1967; Ritsma, 1967). Partials falling in the dominance region are most influential with regard to pitch. One way of showing this is to work with tones with inharmonic partials. Assume a tone with partials of 204, 408, 612, 800, 1000, and 1200 Hz. The first three partials in isolation would give a pitch of "204 Hz." All six together give a pitch of "200 Hz" because of the relative weight of the higher partials, which lie in the dominance region. The low pitch of complex tones with low fundamental frequencies (under 500 Hz) depends on the higher partials. The low pitch of tones with high fundamental frequencies is determined by the fundamental because it lies in the dominance region.

Tones with inharmonic components have been used quite frequently in tone perception research. An approximation of the pitch evoked by them is the fundamental of the least-deviating harmonic series. Assume a tone with components of 850, 1050, 1250, 1450, 1650 Hz. The least-deviating harmonic series is 833, 1042, 1250, 1458, and 1667 Hz, which contains the fourth, fifth, sixth, seventh, and eighth harmonics of a complex tone with a fundamental of 208.3 Hz. This fundamental can be used as an approximation of the pitch sensation of the inharmonic complex (Fig. 4). Let us consider an inharmonic tone with frequency components of 900, 1100, 1300, 1500, 1700 Hz. This tone has an ambiguous pitch, since two approximations by harmonic series are possible, namely one with a fundamental of 216.6 Hz (the component of 1300 Hz being the sixth harmonic in this case) and one with a fundamental of 185.9 Hz (1300 Hz being the seventh harmonic).

If not all partials of a complex tone are necessary for low pitch perception, how few of them are sufficient? The following series of experimental investigations show a progressively decreasing number (see Fig. 5). De Boer (1956) worked with five harmonics in the dominant region; Schouten, Ritsma, and Cardozo (1962), with three;

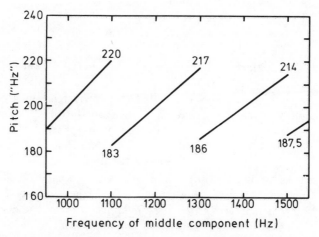

Fig. 4. Schematic diagram of the low pitch of a complex tone consisting of five (inharmonic) components 200-Hz apart. The horizontal axis represents the frequency of the middle component. This component is taken as the fifth, sixth, seventh, or eighth pseudo-harmonic partial of a complex tone with low pitch, which is indicated along the vertical axis. The figure in the graph indicate the "pitches" of the stimuli with ambiguous pitch.

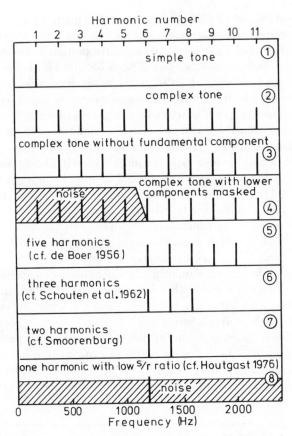

Fig. 5. Schematic diagram representing eight signals with the same low pitch.

Smoorenburg (1970), with two; Houtsma and Goldstein (1972), with one plus one—that is, one partial presented to each ear. In the latter case it is also possible to elicit low pitch perception. The authors concluded that low pitch was a central neural process not brought about by the peripheral sense organ (the ears). The last step in the series should be a low pitch perception evoked by one partial. That this is also possible has been shown by Houtgast (1976). The following conditions have to be fulfilled: The frequency region of the low pitch has to be filled with noise, the single partial must have a low signal-to-noise ratio, and attention has to be directed to the fundamental frequency region by prior stimuli. These conditions create a perceptual situation in which it is not certain that the fundamental is not there so that we are brought to the idea that it should be there by inference from earlier stimuli.

B. Loudness

The physical correlate that underlies the *loudness* of a tone is intensity, usually expressed as sound pressure level (*SPL*) in dB. Sound pressure level is a relative measure, expressed either relative to a zero level defined in the experimental situation or relative to a general reference sound pressure of 2×10^{-5} N/m^2. Sound pressure levels of performed music vary roughly from 40 dB for a pianissimo to about 90 dB for a full orchestral forte-tutti (Winckel, 1962). By means of electronic amplification higher levels are reached in pop concerts. These levels, sometimes beyond 100 dB, are potentially damaging to the ear in case of prolonged presentation (Flugrath, 1969; Rintelman, Lindberg, & Smitley, 1972; Wood & Lipscomb, 1972; Fearn, 1975a,b).

The subjective assessment of loudness is more complicated than the physical measurement of the sound pressure level. Several *loudness scales* have been proposed during the last decades. None of them, however, can be applied fully satisfactorily in all conditions. We give the following summary review:

1. The *sone* scale, a purely psychophysical loudness scale (Stevens, 1936). The loudness of a simple (sinusoidal) tone of 1000 Hz with a sound pressure level of 40 dB is defined to be 1 sone; a tone with double loudness is assigned the loudness of 2 sones, etc. In general, a sound of X sones is n times louder than a sound of X/n sones. The experimental determination of the relationship between the physical sound level and the psychophysical loudness is not very reliable because of the uncertainty of what is actually meant by "X times louder."

2. The *phone* scale, a mixed physical–psychophysical loudness scale with scale values expressed in dB and, therefore, termed *loudness level* (LL). The loudness level of a sound in phones is equal to the sound pressure level of a 1000 Hz tone with the same loudness. For tones of 1000 Hz the identity relation $SPL = LL$ holds. The loudness level of simple tones with other tones with other frequencies and of complex tones or other sounds (noises, etc.) is found by comparison experiments, which can be done with acceptable reliability. These comparisons may be used to draw contours of equal loudness as a function of, for example, frequency.

3. The *sensation-level* scale, also a mixed scale. Sensation level is defined as the sound pressure level relative to threshold level and, as such, is also expressed in dB. It may differ as a function of frequency or other characteristics of a sound but also from subject to subject.

4. In many papers on psychoacoustics no loudness indications are given. Instead, physical levels are mentioned. For the investigator this is the most precise reference and at the same time a rough indication of subjective loudness.

In the description of the relation between sound pressure level and loudness, a clear distinction must be made between sounds with all spectral energy within one critical band and sounds with spectral energy spread over more than one critical band. If all sound energy is limited to one critical band, the loudness L in sones increases monotonically with intensity I. The relation is often approached by the equation

$$L = kI^n$$

in which k and n are empirically chosen constants. A consequence of this relation is the rule that equal intensity ratios result in equal loudness ratios. Now, an intensity ratio is a fixed level difference (dB) so that the rule can also be formulated as follows: A certain loudness ratio corresponds to a certain level difference. Psychophysicists have been much interested in the level difference that results in doubling or halving loudness, and many experiments have been carried out to establish this. The outcomes of these experiments are disappointingly dissimilar. Stevens (1955) summarized all experiments known to him with the median value of 10 dB for doubling loudness, later (1972) modified to 9 dB. These values correspond to values of $n = 0.3$ and $n = 0.33$ for the exponent in the formula. It is also possible to interpret the subjective loudness judgment as an imaginary judgment of the distance to the sound source. In this theory (Warren, 1977) half loudness must correspond to double distance, which gives, in free field conditions, a decrease of 6 dB sound pressure level. Warren conducted experiments in which this value is indeed found.

The assessment of loudness is a complicated matter if sound energy is present in more than one critical band. This situation is the common one for musical tones, especially for chords, and music played by ensembles, choirs, and orchestras. Total loudness is greater than when the same amount of sound energy is concentrated within one critical band. A number of models have been proposed that intend to be simulations of the perceptual processes involved and the parameters of which have been assigned values in accordance with psychophysical experiments. Well known are the models by Stevens (1955), Zwicker, Flottorp, & Stevens (1957), Zwicker and Scharf (1965), and Stevens (1972). These models have also been applied to musical sounds, especially to organ tones (Churcher, 1962; Pollard, 1978a,b).

Although loudness variations play an important role in music, they are less important than pitch variations. The number of assignable loudness degrees in music is limited to about five, coded musically from soft to loud as pianissimo, piano, mezzo-forte, forte, and fortissimo. The definition of these loudness degrees is rather imprecise (Clark & Milner, 1964; Clark & Luce, 1965; Patterson, 1974). Judgment of musical loudness cannot have the degree of reliability and preciseness that is possible with the judgment of (relative) pitch, duration, tempo, etc. This is a consequence of the fact that the underlying physical dimension, intensity, is hard to control precisely. Sources of variation are encountered in sound production, in the fixed acoustic conditions of a room (absorption and thus attenuation by walls, floor, ceiling, etc.), in variable acoustic conditions (like the presence or the absence of an audience, the relative positions of sound source and listener, disturbing external noises), and in the audiograms of the listeners. In all the stages on the road from sound production to sound perception, sound pressure level is liable to be altered whereas frequency is not.

C. Timbre

Timbre is, after pitch and loudness, the third attribute of the subjective experience of musical tones. Subjectively, timbre is often coded as the function of the sound source or of the meaning of the sound. We talk about the timbre of certain musical instruments, of vowels, and of sounds that signify certain events in our environment (apparatus, sounds from nature, footsteps, the slapping of a door, etc.).

What are the physical parameters that contribute to the perception of a certain timbre? In a restricted sense timbre may be considered the subjective counterpart of the spectral composition of tones. Especially important is the relative amplitude of the harmonics. This view was first stated by Helmholtz over a century ago and is reflected by the definition of timbre according to the American Standards Association (Acoust. Terminology S1.1., 1960): "Timbre is that attribute of auditory sensation in terms of which a listener can judge that two steady-state complex tones having the same loudness and pitch are dissimilar." Recent research has shown that temporal characteristics of the tones may have a profound influence on timbre as well, which has led to a broadening of the concept of timbre (Schouten, 1968). Both onset effects (rise time, presence of noise or inharmonic partials during onset, unequal rise of partials, characteristic shape of rise curve, etc.) and steady state effects (vibrato, amplitude modulation, gradual swelling, pitch instability, etc.) are important factors

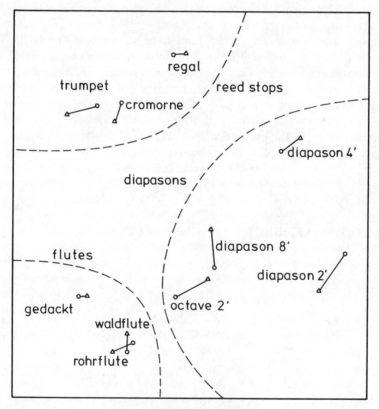

Fig. 6. Result of matching a two-dimensional perceptual timbre representation (circular symbols) of organ stops with the corresponding physical (spectral) representation (triangular) of the same sounds. The timbre scaling is the result of mulidimensional scaling applied to triadic comparison data. The physical scaling is based on a factor analysis of the spectral composition of the tones. The vertical dimension can be labeled as few versus many strong higher harmonics (based on Plomp, 1979).

in the recognition and, therefore, in the timbre of tones. Experiments (Clark, Robertson, & Luce, 1964; Berger, 1964; Saldanha & Corso, 1964) have shown that the identification of instrumental sounds is impaired when temporally characteristic parts of tones (especially the onsets) are removed.

Sounds cannot be ordered on a single scale with respect to timbre. Timbre is a *multidimensional attribute* of the perception of sounds. Dimensional research is highly time-consuming and is therefore always done with a restricted set of sound stimuli. The dimensions found in such an investigation are of course determined by the stimulus set.

Dimensional research of timbre leads to the ordering of sound stimuli on the dimensions of a timbre space. An example of such research is that by Von Bismarck (1974a,b). His stimulus set contained a large number (35) of tone and noise stimuli. The most important factors found by him can be characterized as follows: (a) *sharpness*, determined by a distribution of spectral energy that has its gravity point in the higher frequency region and (b) *compactness*, a factor that distinguishes between tonal (compact) and noise (not compact) aspects of sound.

In some investigations sound stimuli have been submitted to multidimensional scaling, both perceptual and physical. The physical scaling can be based on the spectral composition of the sounds, as was done in Plomp's (1979) experiments with tones from a number of organ stops. Figure 6 gives the two-dimensional representation of 10 sounds, both perceptual and physical. The representations correspond rather well, leading to the conclusion that in this set of stimuli the sound spectrum is the most important factor in the perception of timbre.

Other examples of dimensional research on timbre are the investigations by Plomp (1970), Wedin and Goude (1972), Plomp and Steeneken (1973), Miller and Carterette (1975), Grey (1977), and de Bruijn (1978).

III. PERCEPTUAL ATTRIBUTES OF SIMULTANEOUS TONES

A. Beats and Roughness

In this and the following sections we will discuss perceptual phenomena that occur as the result of two *simultaneous tones*. We will call the simultaneously sounding tones the *primary tones*.

We consider first the case of two simultaneous simple tones. Several conditions can be distinguished, depending on frequency difference (Fig. 7). If the two primary tones have equal frequencies, they fuse into one tone, in which the intensity depends on the phase relation between the two primary tones. If the tones differ somewhat in frequency, the result is a signal with periodic amplitude and frequency variations with a frequency equal to the frequency difference. The frequency variations are only slight and will not be considered here. The *amplitude variations*, however, can be

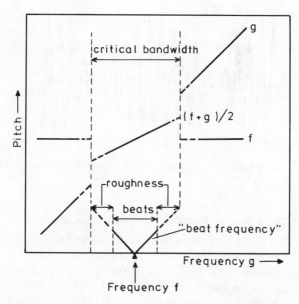

Fig. 7. Schematic diagram representing perceptual phenomena that may occur when two simple tones with a small frequency difference sound simultaneously. The frequency of one tone is set constant (f); the frequency of the other tone (g) varies along the horizontal axis (based on Roederer, 1975).

considerable and result in a fluctuating intensity and perceived loudness. These loudness fluctuations are called *beats*, if they can be discerned individually by the ear, which occurs if their frequency is less than about 20 Hz. A stimulus equal to the sum of two simple tones with equal amplitudes and frequencies f and g

$$p(t) = \sin 2\pi f t + \sin 2\pi g t$$

can be described as

$$p(t) = 2 \cos 2\pi\tfrac{1}{2}(g - f)t \times \sin 2\pi\tfrac{1}{2}(f + g)t$$

This is a signal with a frequency that is the average of the original primary frequencies, and an amplitude that fluctuates slowly with a *beat frequency* of $g - f$ Hz (Fig. 8). Amplitude variation is less strong if the two primary tones have different amplitudes.

When the frequency difference is larger than about 20 Hz, the ear is no longer able to follow the rapid amplitude fluctuations individually. Instead of the sensation of fluctuating loudness, there is a rattle-like sensation called *roughness*. Beats and roughness can only occur if the two primary tones are not resolved by the ear (that means, not processed separately but combined). If the frequency difference is larger than the critical band, the tones are perceived individually with no interference phenomena.

In musical sounds beats can occur with just noncoinciding harmonics of mistuned consonant intervals of complex tones. If the fundamental frequencies of the tones of

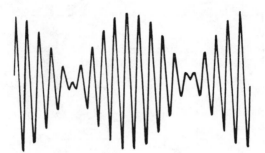

Fig. 8. Wave form arising from the superposition of two simple tones with a small frequency difference.

an octave (theoretically 1:2) or fifth (2:3) differ a little from the theoretical ratio, there will be harmonics that differ slightly in frequency and will cause beats. These beats play an important role when tuning musical instruments.

No psychophysical research has been done on mistuned intervals of complex tones, but to a certain extent psychophysical results found with two beating simple tones and with amplitude-modulated simple tones (see Fig. 9) can be applied to the perception of beating mistuned intervals of complex tones (Zwicker, 1952; Terhardt, 1968a,b, 1974b). The following relations can be stated. Thresholds vary with beat frequency. There appears to be a minimum at about 5 to 10 Hz. The threshold decreases when the sound pressure level increases. It is possible to define perceptual quantities called *beating strength* and *roughness strength* and to determine their values as a function of stimulus characteristics. Research following this line has shown that such a quantity increases with modulation depth and with sound pressure level. Moreover, there seems to be a modulation frequency giving maximal roughness (about 50 to 70 Hz).

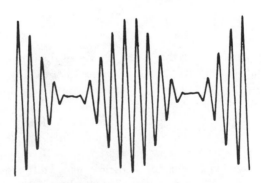

Fig. 9. Wave form that arises when a simple tone has been modulated in amplitude sinusoidally. This wave form is an example of complete modulation.

B. Combination Tones

Two simple tones at a relatively high sound pressure level and with a frequency difference that is not too large can give rise to the perception of so-called combination tones. These combination tones arise in the ear as a product of nonlinear transmission characteristics. The combination tones are not present in the acoustic signal. However, they are perceived as if they were present. The ear cannot distinguish between perceived components that are "real" (in the stimulus) and those that are not (combination tones). The combination tones are simple tones that may be cancelled effectively by adding a real simple tone with the same frequency and amplitude but opposite phase. This cancellation tone can be used to investigate combination tones.

The possible frequencies of combination tones can be derived from a general transmission function. Assume a stimulus with two simple tones:

$$p(t) = \cos 2\pi ft + \cos 2\pi gt$$

f and g being the two frequencies. Linear transmission is described by

$$d = ap + c$$

(a and c being constants). If transmission is not linear, higher order components are introduced:

$$d = a_1 p + a_2 p^2 + a_3 p^3 + \cdots$$

The quadratic term can be developed as follows:

$$
\begin{aligned}
p^2 &= (\cos 2\pi ft + \cos 2\pi gt)^2 \\
&= 1 + \tfrac{1}{2} \cos 2\pi 2ft + \tfrac{1}{2} \cos 2\pi 2gt \\
&\quad + \cos 2\pi(f+g)t + \cos 2\pi(f-g)t
\end{aligned}
$$

It can be seen that components with frequencies $2f$, $2g$, $f + g$, and $f - g$ are introduced in this way. Similarly, the cubic term can be developed:

$$
\begin{aligned}
p^3 &= (\cos 2\pi ft + \cos 2gt)^3 \\
&= \tfrac{9}{4} \cos 2\pi ft + \tfrac{9}{4} \cos 2\pi gt + \tfrac{1}{4} \cos 2\pi 3ft \\
&\quad + \tfrac{1}{4} \cos 2\pi 3gt + \tfrac{3}{4} \cos 2\pi(2f + g)t + \tfrac{3}{4} \cos 2\pi(2g + f)t \\
&\quad + \tfrac{3}{4} \cos 2\pi(2f - g)t + \tfrac{3}{4} \cos 2\pi (2g - f)t
\end{aligned}
$$

This term is responsible for components with frequencies $3f$, $3g$, $2f + g$, $2g + f$, $2f - g$, $2g - f$. The higher terms of the nonlinear transmission formula can be worked out analogously. The factors just preceding the cosine terms indicate the relative amplitudes of the components in their groups. Psychoacoustical research on combination tones has shown that the pitches of the combination tones agree with the frequencies predicted by nonlinear transmission (Plomp, 1965; Smoorenburg, 1972a,b; Hall, 1975; Weber & Mellert, 1975; Schroeder, 1975b; Zurek & Leskowitz, 1976). However, the correspondence between the relative amplitude predicted and the subjective loudness measured is far from perfect. Clearly, the phenomenon of combination tones

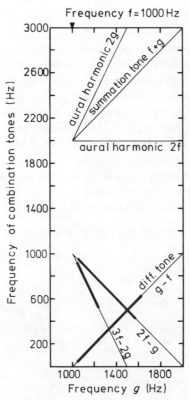

Fig. 10.   Frequency ranges over which particular combination tones can occur. The frequency f of the lower primary tone is 1000 Hz. The frequency of the higher primary tone (g) varies from 1000 Hz up to 2000 Hz. The thin lines correspond to the various theoretically possible combination-tone frequencies; the solid lines represent the combination tones found most often.

is more complicated than can be described in a simple formula. Moreover, there are individual differences, which should be expected since this is a distortion process. Experiments have shown (see Fig. 10) that the following combination tone frequencies are the most important: the so-called *difference tone* with frequency $g - f$ Hz, the *second-order difference tone* with frequency $2f - g$ Hz, and the *third-order difference tone* with frequency $3f - 2g$ Hz. The diagram illustrates that the combination tones are stronger for small frequency differences of the primary tones than for large differences; this indicates that the origin of combination tones is tightly connected with the frequency-analyzing process in the inner ear. It should be noted that the importance of *summation tones* (with frequency $f + g$) and the so-called *aural harmonics* (with frequencies $2f$, $3f$, etc., and $2g$, $3g$, etc.) is questionable. Although combination tones were discovered by musicians in musical contexts (Tartini and Sorge in the eighteenth century), their significance for music is not very high. They can be easily evoked by playing loud tones in the high register on two flutes or recorders or double stops on the violin. In a normal listening situation, however, their levels are usually too low to attract attention. Moreover, they will be masked by the tones of other (lower) instruments. Some violin teachers (following Tartini) advise the use of combination tones as a tool for controlling the intonation of double-stop intervals. Because audible combination tones behave more as simple tones in lower frequency regions than the complex tones to be intonated, a pitch comparison of combination tones and played tones should not be given too much weight.

C. Consonance and Dissonance

The simultaneous sounding of several tones may be pleasant or "euphonious" to varying degrees. The pleasant sound is called *consonant;* the unpleasant or rough one, *dissonant.* The terms consonance and dissonance have been used here in a perceptual or sensory sense. This aspect has been labeled *tonal consonance* (Plomp & Levelt, 1965) or *sensory consonance* (Terhardt, 1976), to be distinguished from consonance in a musical situation. Musical consonance has its roots in perceptual consonance, of course, but is dependent on the rules of music theory, which, to a certain extent, can operate independently from perception.

The perceptual consonance of an interval consisting of two simple tones depends directly upon the frequency difference between the tones, not upon the frequency ratio (or musical interval). If the frequency separation is very small or large (more than critical bandwidth—the tones not interfering with each other), the two tones together sound consonant. Dissonance occurs if the frequency separation is less than a critical bandwidth (see Fig. 11). The most dissonant interval arises with a frequency separation of about a quarter of the critical bandwidth: about 20 Hz in low-frequency regions, about 4% (a little less than a semitone) in the higher regions (Fig. 12). The frequency separation of the minor third (20%), major third (25%), fourth (33%), fifth (50%), and so on, is usually enough to give consonant combination of simple tones. However, if the frequencies are low, the frequency separation of thirds (and eventually also fifths) is less than critical bandwidth so that even these intervals cause a

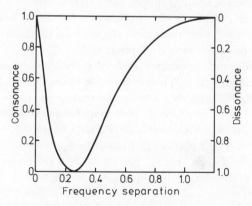

Fig. 11.   Consonance of an interval consisting of two simple tones as a function of frequency separation, measured relative to critical bandwidth (based on Plomp & Levelt, 1965).

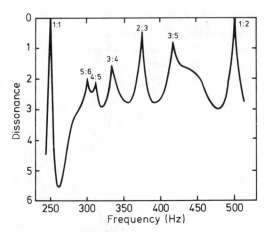

Fig. 12. Consonance of an interval consisting of two complex tones (with six harmonics). The lower tone (*f*) has a fundamental frequency of 250 Hz; the fundamental frequency of the higher tone is the variable along the horizontal axis. The consonance/dissonance values are predictions from the model of Plomp & Levelt (1965).

dissonant beating. For this reason, these consonant intervals are not used in the bass register in musical compositions.

The consonance of intervals of complex tones can be derived from the consonances of the simple-tone combinations comprised in them. In this case the dissonance is the additive element. The dissonance of all combinations of neighboring partials can be determined and added to give the total dissonance and, inversely, the total consonance of the sound. Sounds with widely spaced partials, such as clarinet tones (with only the odd harmonics) are more consonant than sounds with narrowly spaced partials. The composition of the plenum of an organ is such that the partials are widely spaced throughout the spectrum. Some mathematical models have been worked out that describe the dissonance of a pair of simple tones and the way in which the dissonances of partial pairs in tone complexes have to be added (Plomp & Levelt, 1965; Kameoka & Kuriyagawa, 1969a,b; Hutchinson, 1978). As far as can be decided, these models give a good picture of consonance perception.

The consonance of a musical interval, defined as the sum of two complex tones with a certain ratio in fundamental frequency, is highly dependent on the simplicity of the frequency ratio. Intervals with frequency ratios that can be expressed in small integer numbers (say, less than 6) are relatively consonant because the lower, most important components of the two tones are either widely apart or coincide. If the frequency ratio is less simple, there will be a number of partials from the two tones that differ only a little in frequency, and these partial pairs give rise to dissonance. It seems that intervals with the number 7 in their frequency proportions (7/4, 7/5, . . .) are about on the borderline between consonance and dissonance.

Experiments with inharmonic partials (Slaymaker, 1970; Pierce, 1966) have shown that consonance or dissonance is indeed dependent on the coincidence of partials and not necessarily on the simple frequency ratio between the fundamental frequencies (which is usually the cause of the coincidence).

If the number of partials in a complex tone increases or if the strengths of the higher harmonics (with narrow spacing) increase, the tone is perceived as more dissonant (compare the trumpet with the flute, for instance). However, the nth partial is required in order to make an interval with frequency ratio $n:m$ or $m:n$ relatively consonant. For example, if the fifth harmonic is absent, the usual beating (dissonance) of a mistuned major third (4:5) will be absent (see also Fig. 12).

Musical consonance in Western polyphonic and harmonic music is clearly based on perceptual consonance of complex (harmonic) tones. Intervals with simple frequency ratios are consonant. Intervals with nonsimple frequency ratios are dissonant. The way in which consonance and dissonance are used in music theory and composition varies considerably from one historical period to another.

IV. CONCLUSION

More than a century ago von Helmholtz published his classic volume *On the Sensations of Tone* (1863). The subtitle specifically indicates the intention of this study: "As a Physiological Basis for the Theory of Music." For Helmholtz the theory of music (as a compendium of rules that control composition and as such the musical sound stimulus) could only be understood fully if it could be shown that its elements had their origin in the perceptual characteristics of our hearing organ. Helmholtz's working hypothesis has been put aside by later investigators, both those who worked in music and those who worked in psychoacoustics. Several reasons for this can be given. First, before the introduction of electroacoustic means of tone production and control in the 1920s, it was not possible to carry out the necessary psychoacoustical experiments, while Helmholtz's observations proved to be insufficient in many ways. Second, it turned out that music theory has its own rules apart from the perceptual relevance of the characteristics of the sounds that it creates. Therefore, it is not clear, neither for the music theorist nor for the psychoacoustician, which aspects of music theory should be subjected to psychoacoustical research and which should not. Fortunately, in recent years much research has been initiated that is aimed at the investigation of the relationship between musical-theoretical and perceptual entities. For the time being, no complete view can be given, but there may come a time in which Helmholtz's ideas on the relation between the properties of our perceptual processes and the elements of musical composition can receive new, more complete and exact formulations than was possible a century ago.

REFERENCES

Berger, K. W. Some factors in the recognition of timbre. *Journal of the Acoustical Society of America*, 1964, *36*, 1888–1891.

Bismarck, G. von. Timbre of steady sounds: A factorial investigation of its verbal attributes. *Acustica*, 1974, *30*, 146-159.
Bismarck, G. von. Sharpness as an attribute of the timbre of steady sounds. *Acustica*, 1974, *30*, 159-172.
Boer, E. de. On the 'residue' in hearing. Dissertation, Amsterdam, 1956.
Boer, E. de. On the 'residue' and auditory pitch perception. In W. D. Keidel & W. D. Neff (Eds.), *Handbook of sensory physiology*. (Volume V, Auditory system, Part 3, Clinical and special topics) Berlin: Springer-Verlag, 1976. Pp. 479-583.
Boer, E. de. Pitch theories unified. In E. F. Evans & J. P. Wilson (Eds.), *Psychophysics and physiology of hearing*. New York: Academic Press, 1977. Pp. 323-335.
Bruijn, A. de. Timbre-classification of complex tones. *Acustica*, 1978, *40*, 108-114.
Churcher, B. G. Calculation of loudness levels for musical sounds. *Journal of the Acoustical Society of America*, 1962, *34*, 1634-1642.
Clark, M., & Luce, D. Intensities of orchestral instrument scales played at prescribed dynamic markings. *Journal of the Audio Engineering Society*, 1965, *13*, 151-157.
Clark, M. Jr., & Milner, P. Dependence of timbre on the tonal loudness produces by musical instruments. *Journal of the Audio Engineering Society*, 1964, *12*, 28-31.
Clark, M. Jr., Robertson, P., & Luce, D. A preliminary experiment on the perceptual basis for musical instrument families. *Journal of the Audio Engineering Society*, 1964, *12*, 199-203.
Evans, E. F., & Wilson, J. P. (Eds.), *Psychophysics and physiology of hearing*. New York: Academic Press, 1977.
Fearn, R. W. Level limits on pop music. *Journal of Sound and Vibration*, 1975, *38*, 591-592. (a)
Fearn, R. W. Level measurements of music. *Journal of Sound and Vibration*, 1975, *43*, 588-591. (b)
Flugrath, J. M. Modern-day rock-and-roll music and damage-risk criteria. *Journal of the Acoustical Society of America*, 1969, *45*, 704-711.
Gerson, A., & Goldstein, J. L. Evidence for a general template in central optimal processing for pitch of complex tones. *Journal of the Acoustical Society of America*, 1978, *63*, 498-510.
Goldstein, J. L. An optimum processor theory for the central formation of the pitch of complex tones. *Journal of the Acoustical Society of America*, 1973, *54*, 1496-1516.
Green, D. M. *An introduction to hearing*. Hillsdale, New York: Lawrence Erlbaum, 1976.
Grey, J. M. Multidimensional perceptual scaling of musical timbres. *Journal of the Acoustical Society of America*, 1977, *61*, 1270-1277.
Hall, J. L. Nonmonotonic behavior of distortion product $2f_1$-f_2: Psychophysical observations. *Journal of the Acoustical Society of America*, 1975, *58*, 1046-1050.
Helmholtz, H. von. *Die Lehre von den Tonempfindungen als physiologische Grundlage für die Theorie der Musik* (*Sechste Ausg.*). Braunschweig: Vieweg, 1913 (1st ed., 1863). Translated by A. J. Ellis as: *On the sensations of tone as a physiological basis for the theory of music*. London: Longmans, Green, 1885. (1st ed., 1875; reprint of the 1885 ed., New York: Dover, 1954).
Houtgast, T. Subharmonic pitches of a pure tone at low S/N ratio. *Journal of the Acoustical Society of America*, 1976, *60*, 405-409.
Houtsma, A.J.M. Musical pitch of two tone complexes and predictions by modern pitch theories. *Journal of the Acoustical Society of America*, 1979, *66*, 87-99.
Houtsma, A.J.M., & Goldstein, J. L. The central origin of the pitch of complex tones: Evidence from musical interval recognition. *Journal of the Acoustical Society of America*, 1972, *51*, 520-529.
Hutchinson, W., & Knopoff, L. The acoustic component of Western consonance. *Interface*, 1978, *7*, 1-29.
Kameoka, A., & Kuriyagawa, M. Consonance theory, Part I: Consonance of dyads. *Journal of the Acoustical Society of America*, 1969, *45*, 1451-1459. (a)
Kameoka, A., & Kuriyagawa, M. Consonance theory, Part II: Consonance of complex tones and its calculation method. *Journal of the Acoustical Society of America*, 1969, *45*, 1460-1469. (b)
Licklider, J.C.R. 'Periodicity' pitch and 'place' pitch. *Journal of the Acoustical Society of America*, 1954, *26*, 945.
Miller, J. R., & Carterette, E. C. Perceptual space for musical structures. *Journal of the Acoustical Society of America*, 1975, *58*, 711-720.
Patterson, B. Musical dynamics. *Scientific American*, 1974, *31*, 78-95.

Patterson, R. D., & Wrightman, F. L. Residue pitch as a function of component spacing. *Journal of the Acoustical Society of America*, 1976, *59*, 1450–1459.

Pierce, J. R. Attaining consonance in arbitrary scales. *Journal of the Acoustical Society of America*, 1966, *40*, 249.

Piszczalski, M., & Galler, B. A. Predicting musical pitch from component frequency ratios. *Journal of the Acoustical Society of America*, 1979, *66*, 710–720.

Plomp, R. The ear as a frequency analyzer. *Journal of the Acoustical Society of America*, 1964, *36*, 1628–1636.

Plomp, R. Detectability threshold for combination tones. *Journal of the Acoustical Society of America*, 1965, *37*, 1110–1123.

Plomp, R. Pitch of complex tones. *Journal of the Acoustical Society of America*, 1967, *41*, 1526–1533.

Plomp, R. Timbre as a multidimensional attribute of complex tones. In R. Plomp & G. F. Smoorenburg (Eds.), *Frequency analysis and periodicity detection in hearing*. Leiden: Sijthoff, 1970. Pp. 397–414.

Plomp, R. Auditory psychophysics. *Annual Review of Psychology*, 1975, *26*, 207–232.

Plomp, R. *Aspects of tone sensation*. New York: Academic Press, 1976.

Plomp, R. Fysikaliska motsvarigheter till klanfärg hos stationära ljud. In *Vår hörsel och musiken*. Stockholm: Kungl. Musikaliska Akademien, 1979.

Plomp, R., & Levelt, W.J.M. Tonal consonance and critical bandwidth. *Journal of the Acoustical Society of America*, 1965, *38*, 548–560.

Plomp, R., & Smoorenburg, G. F. (Eds.), *Frequency analysis and periodicity detection in hearing*. Leiden: Sijthoff, 1970.

Plomp, R., & Steeneken, H.J.M. Place dependence of timbre in reverberant sound fields. *Acustica*, 1973, *28*, 49–59.

Pollard, H. F. Loudness of pipe organ sounds. I. Plenum combinations. *Acustica*, 1978, *41*, 65–74. (a)

Pollard, H. F. Loudness of pipe organ sounds. II. Single notes. *Acustica*, 1978, *41*, 75–85. (b)

Rintelmann, W. F., Lindberg, R. F., & Smitley, E. K. Temporary threshold shift and recovery patterns from two types of rock-and-roll music presentation. *Journal of the Acoustical Society of America*, 1972, *51*, 1249–1255.

Ritsma, R. J. Frequencies dominant in the perception of the pitch of complex sounds. *Journal of the Acoustical Society of America*, 1967, *42*, 191–198.

Roederer, J. G. *Introduction to the physics and psychophysics of music*. New York and Berlin: Springer, 1974 (2nd ed., 1975).

Saldanha, E. L., & Corso, J. F. Timbre cues and the identification of musical instruments. *Journal of the Acoustical Society of America*, 1964, *36*, 2021–2026.

Schouten, J. F. The perception of subjective tones. *Proceedings of the Koninklijke Nederlandse Akademie van Wetenschappen*, 1938, *41*, 1083–1093.

Schouten, J. R., Ritsma, R. J., & Cardozo, B. L. Pitch of the residue. *Journal of the Acoustical Society of America*, 1962, *34*, 1418–1424.

Schouten, J. F. The perception of timbre. In *Report of the Sixth International Congress on Acoustics, Tokyo*, Paper GP-6-2, 1968.

Schroeder, M. R. Models of hearing. *Proceedings of the IEEE*, 1975, *63*, 1332–1350. (a)

Schroeder, M. R. Amplitude behavior of the cubic difference tone. *Journal of the Acoustical Society of America*, 1975, *58*, 728–732. (b)

Schubert, E. D. (Ed.) *Psychological acoustics*. Stroudsburg, Pennsylvania: Dowden, 1979 (Benchmark Papers in Acoustics 13).

Seashore, C. E. *Psychology of music*. New York: McGraw-Hill, 1938 (Reprint New York: Dover, 1967).

Seebeck, A. Beobachtungen über einige Bedingungen der Entstehung von Tönen. *Annalen der Physik und Chemie*, 1841, *53*, 417–436.

Slaymaker, F. H. Chords from tones having stretched partials. *Journal of the Acoustical Society of America*, 1970, *47*, 1569–1571.

Smoorenburg, G. F. Pitch perception of two-frequency stimuli. *Journal of the Acoustical Society of America*, 1970, *48*, 924–942.

Smoorenburg, G. F. Audibility region of combination tones. *Journal of the Acoustical Society of America*, 1972, *52*, 603–614. (a)

Smoorenburg, G. F. Combination tones and their origin. *Journal of the Acoustical Society of America*, 1972, *52*, 615–632. (b)

Stevens, S. S. A scale for the measurement of a psychological magnitude: Loudness. *Psychological Review*, 1936, *43*, 405–416.

Stevens, S. S. The measurement of loudness. *Journal of the Acoustical Society of America*, 1955, *27*, 815–829.

Stevens, S. S. Perceived level of noise by Mark VII and decibels (E). *Journal of the Acoustical Society of America*, 1972, *51*, 575–601.

Stevens, S. S., Volkmann, J., & Newman, E. B. A scale for the measurement of the psychological magnitude pitch. *Journal of the Acoustical Society of America*, 1937, *8*, 185–190.

Terhardt, E. Über die durch amplitudenmodulierte Sinustöne hervorgerufene Hörempfindung. *Acustica*, 1968, *20*, 210–214. (a)

Terhardt, E. Über akustische Rauhigkeit und Schwankungsstärke. *Acustica*, 1968, *20*, 215–224. (b)

Terhardt, E. Die Tonhöhe harmonischer Klänge und das Oktavintervall. *Acustica*, 1971, *24*, 126–136.

Terhardt, E. Pitch, consonance, and harmony. *Journal of the Acoustical Society of America*, 1974, *55*, 1061–1960. (a)

Terhardt, E. On the perception of periodic sound fluctuations (roughness). *Acustica*, 1974, *30*, 201–203. (b)

Terhardt, E. Ein psychoakustisch begründetes Konzept der musikalischen Konsonanz. *Acustica*, 1976, *36*, 121–137.

Terhardt, E. Psychoacoustic evaluation of musical sounds. *Perception & Psychophysics*, 1978, *23*, 483–492.

Tobias, J. V. (Ed.). *Foundations of modern auditory theory.* (Volumes 1 & 2) New York: Academic Press, 1970, 1972.

Warren, R. M. Subjective loudness and its physical correlate. *Acustica*, 1977, *37*, 334–346.

Weber, R., & Mellert, V. On the nonmonotonic behavior of cubic distortion products in the human ear. *Journal of the Acoustical Society of America*, 1975, *57*, 207–214.

Wedin, L., & Goude, G. Dimension analysis of the perception of instrumental timbre. *Scandinavian Journal of Psychology*, 1972, *13*, 228–240.

Wightman, F. L. The pattern-transformation model of pitch. *Journal of the Acoustical Society of America*, 1973, *54*, 407–416.

Winckel, F. W. Optimum acoustic criteria of concert halls for the performance of classical music. *Journal of Acoustical Society of America*, 1962, *34*, 81–86.

Wood, W. S. III & Lipscomb, D. M. Maximum available sound-pressure levels from stereo components. *Journal of the Acoustical Society of America*, 1972, *52*, 484–487.

Zurek, P. M., & Leshowitz, B. Measurements of the combination tones $f_2 - f_1$ and $2f_1 - f_2$. *Journal of the Acoustical Society of America*, 1976, *60*, 155–168.

Zwicker, E. Die Grenzen der Hörbarkeit der Amplitudenmodualtion und der Frequenzmodulation eines Tones. *Acustica*, 1952, *2*, Beihefte 125–135.

Zwicker, E., & Feldtkeller, R. *Das Ohr als Nachrichtenempfänger* (2nd Ausg.). Stuttgart: Hirzel, 1967.

Zwicker, E., Flottorp, C., & Stevens, S. S. Critical bandwidth in loudness summation. *Journal of the Acoustical Society of America*, 1957, *29*, 548–557.

Zwicker, E., & Scharf, B. A model of loudness summation. *Psychological Review*, 1965, *72*, 3–26.

Zwicker, E., & Terhardt, E. (Eds.), *Facts and models in hearing.* Berlin: Springer-Verlag, 1974.

2

Exploration of Timbre by Analysis and Synthesis

Jean-Claude Risset and David L. Wessel

I.	Timbre	26
II.	Timbre and the Fourier Spectrum: The Classical View	26
III.	The Shortcomings of the Classical Conception	29
IV.	Attack Transients	30
V.	Complexity of Sounds: Importance of Characteristic Features	30
VI.	Instrumental and Vocal Timbres: Additive Syntheses	30
VII.	Cross Synthesis and Voice Synthesis	36
VIII.	Additive Synthesis: Percussion Instruments	37
IX.	Substractive Synthesis	39
X.	Acoustic Modeling as a Synthesis Technique	41
XI.	The Importance of Context	42
XII.	Analysis–Synthesis as Fitting Acoustic and Perceptual Models to Data	44
XIII.	The Use of Analysis–Synthesis Models of Timbre	45
	A. Insight	45
	B. Information Reduction	46
	C. Possibility of Producing Variants	46
XIV.	Timbral Space	47
XV.	Conclusion	49
	Appendices	50
	A. Signal Representations and Analysis–Synthesis Processes	50
	B. A Synthesis Model Based on Perceptual Principles	53
	References	54

Copyright © 1982 by Academic Press, Inc.
All rights of reproduction in any form reserved.
ISBN 0-12-213560-1

I. TIMBRE

Timbre refers to the quality of sound. It is the perceptual attribute that enables us to distinguish among orchestral instruments that are playing the same pitch and are equally loud. But, unlike loudness and pitch, timbre is not a well-defined perceptual attribute. Definitions tend to indicate what timbre is not rather than what it is. Take as an example the following enigmatic definition provided by the American Standards Association (1960, p. 45): "Timbre is that attribute of auditory sensation in terms of which a listener can judge that two sounds similarly presented and having the same loudness and pitch are dissimilar."

The notion of timbral constancy or invariance is even vaguer than that suggested in the definitions of timbre as a basis for discrimination. It would seem that a form of timbral constancy is implied by the common observation that a sound source can be reliably identified over a wide variety of circumstances. For example, a saxophone is readily identified as such regardless of the pitch or dynamic it is playing. Furthermore, the saxophone remains a saxophone whether it is heard over a distortion-ridden pocket-sized transistor radio or directly in a concert hall. Thus, the question arises as to the physical correlates of this constancy. Is there a physical invariant or a characteristic feature mediating a given timbre?

The issue is not only academic: it has musical relevance, since the electronic and computer technology promises access to an unlimited world of timbres. One must, however, know how to evoke a given timbre; that is, how to describe it in terms of the physical structure of sound.

II. TIMBRE AND THE FOURIER SPECTRUM: THE CLASSICAL VIEW

Physicists have been performing analyses of musical instrument tones for some time. The goal of many of these acoustical analyses is to determine the physical correlates of tone quality.

Many results of such analyses have been published (Miller, 1926; Richardson, 1954; Meyer & Buchmann, 1931; Culver, 1956; Olson, 1967). The general conclusion of such studies was that musical sounds are periodic and that the tone quality is associated solely with the waveshape, more precisely with the Fourier spectrum of the waveshape. These early analyses were strongly motivated by the theorem of Fourier, which states that a periodic waveshape is completely defined by the amplitudes and phases of a harmonic series of frequency components (see Feynman, Leighton, & Sands, 1963, Chapters 21–25; Jenkins & Watts, 1968). But the claim, often known as Ohm's acoustical law, is that the ear is phase deaf. Put more precisely, Ohm's acoustical law states that if the Fourier representation of two sounds have the same pattern of harmonic amplitudes but have different patterns of phase relationships, a listener will be unable to perceive a difference between the two sounds, even though they may have very different waveforms (see Fig. 1)

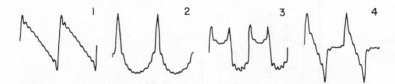

Fig. 1. The waves 1 to 4 correspond to tones generated with the same spectrum but with different phase relations between the components, these tones with quite different waveforms sound very similar (Plomp, 1976).

It has been argued that the ear is not actually phase deaf. It is indeed true that under certain conditions, changing the phase relationship between the harmonics of a periodic tone can alter the timbre (Mathes & Miller, 1947; Plomp & Steeneken, 1969); however, this effect is quite weak, and it is generally inaudible in a normally reverberant room where phase relations are smeared (Cabot, Mino, Dorans, Tockel, & Breed, 1976; Schroeder, 1975). One must remember, though, that this remarkable insensitivity to phase, illustrated by Fig. 1, only holds for the phase relationship between the harmonics of periodic tones.[1]

Thus, it would appear that timbre depends solely on the Fourier spectrum of the sound wave. The most authoritative proponent of this conception has been Helmholtz (Helmholtz, 1954). Helmholtz was aware that "certain characteristic particularities of the tones of several instruments depend on the mode in which they begin and end": yet he studied only "the peculiarities of the musical tones which continue uniformly," considering that they determined the "musical quality of the tone." The temporal characteristics of the instruments were averaged out by the early analyses (Hall, 1937); but since different instruments had different average spectra, it was believed that this difference in average spectrum was utterly responsible for timbre differences. This view is still widely accepted: a reputed and recent treatise like the Feynmann Lectures on Physics gives no hint that they may be factors of tone quality other than "the relative amount of the various harmonics."

Actually, even a sine wave changes quality from the low to the high end of the musical range (Köhler, 1915, Stumpf, 1926). In order to keep the timbre of a periodic tone approximately invariant when the frequency is changed, should the spectrum be transposed so as to keep the same amplitude relationship between the harmonics or should the absolute position of the spectral envelope be kept invariant? This question produced a debate between Helmholtz and Herman (cf. Winckel, 1967, p. 13). In speech, a vowel corresponds approximately to a spectrum with a given formant structure. A formant is a peak in the spectral envelope that occurs at a certain frequency, and which is often associated with a resonance in the sound source. This is the case for speech, and the formants can be related to resonances in the vocal tract.

[1]A varying phase can also be interpreted as a varying frequency. Also, dispersive media (for which the speed of propagation is frequency-dependent) cause inaudible phase distortion for periodic tones and objectionable delay distortion for nonperiodic signals (e.g., the high frequencies can be shifted by several seconds with respect to the low ones in a long cable, which makes speech quite incomprehensible).

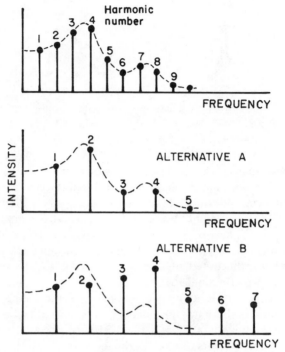

Fig. 2. This figure refers to an experiment by Slawson (1968) comparing alternative predictions of invariance in timbre under octave increases in fundamental frequency. The experiment rules out alternative B, that of the relative pitch or overtone theory, in favor of alternative A, that of the fixed-frequency or formant theory.

Indeed, in many cases a fixed formant structure gives a timbre that varies less with frequency than a fixed spectrum (Slawson, 1968; Plomp, 1976, pp. 107–110; Plomp & Steeneken, 1971).

Certain characteristics of the spectrum seem to induce certain timbral qualities. Brightness (or sharpness) relates to the position of the spectral envelope along the frequency axis. Presence appears to relate to strong components around 2000 Hz.

The concept of critical bandwidth, linked to the spectral resolution of the ear (Plomp, 1966), may permit a better understanding of the correlation between spectrum and timbre. In particular, if many high-order harmonics lie close together, that is, within the same critical bandwidth,[2] the sound becomes very harsh. Hence, for instance, antiresonances in the frequency response of string instruments play an important part to diminish the roughness of the tones. It may be more significant to

[2] The critical bandwidth around a certain frequency roughly measures the range within which this frequency interacts with others. The width of a critical band is about one third of an octave above 500 Hz and approximately 100 Hz below 500 Hz (cf. Zwicker & Scharf, 1965). It is an important parameter of hearing, which relates to spectral resolution (Plomp, 1964).

display spectra modified so as to take critical bands into account. This was done in some studies: the frequency axis is converted into so-called Bark units (1 Bark corresponds to the width of one critical band over the whole frequency range (Cf. Zwicker, 1961; Zwicker & Scharf, 1965: Grey & Gordon, 1978).

III. THE SHORTCOMINGS OF THE CLASSICAL CONCEPTION

So, for periodic tones, timbre depends upon spectrum. It has long been thought that musical tones were periodic, at least for most of their duration. Musical tones are often thought of as comprising three sections: attack, steady state, and decay. Note that Helmholtz and his followers considered that timbre is determined by the spectrum of the steady state. However, this conception suffers from serious difficulties. As we noted at the beginning of this article, musical instruments can be recognized even from a very poor recording, despite the fact that their spectra are radically changed by such distortion (Eagleson & Eagleson, 1947).

In fact, a normally reverberant room has an incredibly jagged frequency response, with fluctuations up to 20 dB, and this frequency response is different at every point in the room (Wente, 1935). Hence, spectra are completely changed in ways that depend on the specific location. However, when one moves in the room, the corresponding timbres are not completely upset as one would expect them to be if they depended only on the precise structure of the frequency spectrum.

Also, various methods of sound manipulation show that temporal changes bear strongly on tone quality. Removing the initial segment of notes played by various instruments impairs the recognition of these instruments, as noted by Stumpf as early as 1910 (Stumpf, 1926). Subsequently, tape-recorder manipulation (George, 1954; Schaeffer, 1966) has made it easy to demonstrate the influence of time factors on tone quality. For instance, playing a piano tone backwards gives a nonpiano-like quality, although the original and the reversed sound have the same spectra. However, temporal factors were not taken into account in most early analyses (cf. Hall, 1937): the analysis process could not follow fast temporal evolutions.

Recently, computer sound synthesis (Mathews, 1963, 1969) has made it possible to synthesize virtually any sound from a physical description of that sound. Efforts have been made to use the results of analyses of musical instrument tones that are to be found in treatises on musical acoustics as input data for computer sound synthesis. In most cases, the sounds thus obtained bear very little resemblance to the actual tones produced by the instrument chosen; the tones thus produced are dull, lacking identity as well as liveliness (Risset & Mathews, 1969). Hence, the available descriptions of musical instrument tones must be considered inadequate, since they fail to pass the foolproof synthesis test. This failure points to the need for more detailed, relevant analyses and for a more valid conception of the physical correlates of timbre. Clearly, one must perform some kind of "running" analysis that follows the temporal evolution of the tones.

IV. ATTACK TRANSIENTS

A few attempts have been made since 1930 to analyze the attack transients of instrument tones (Backhaus, 1932; Richardson, 1954). These transients constitute an important part of the tones—in fact, many tones like those from the piano or percussion instruments have no steady state. Yet their analysis has not produced much progress. The transients are intrinsically complex, and they are not reproducible from one tone to another, even for tones that sound very similar (Schaeffer, 1966). Most analyses have been restricted to a limited set of tones, and the researchers have tended to make generalizations that may be inappropriate even for different samples collected from the same instruments. These shortcomings have produced many discrepancies in the literature and cast doubt on the entire body of acoustic data.

V. COMPLEXITY OF SOUNDS: IMPORTANCE OF CHARACTERISTIC FEATURES

Sounds are often intrinsically complex. Musical instruments have a complex physical behavior (Benade, 1976); often the damping is low, and transients are long compared with note duration. Also, the tones are not generated by a standardized mechanical player, but by human musicians who introduce intricacies both intentionally and unintentionally. Even if a human player wanted to, he could not repeat a note as rigorously as a machine does. If he has good control of his instrument, he should be able to play two tones sounding nearly identical, but these tones can differ substantially in their physical structure. More often the performer will not want to play all notes the same way, and his interpretation of some markings depends upon his sense of style as well as upon his technique. All these considerations, which involve different disciplines—physics, physiology, psychology, physiology, esthetics—certainly make it difficult to isolate characteristic invariants in musical instrument sounds.

This points out the need to extract significant features from a complex physical structure. Also, one must be able to control through synthesis the aural relevance of the features extracted in the analysis. Only recently has this been possible.

We shall now give a brief review of recent work on exploration of timbre by analysis and synthesis.

VI. INSTRUMENTAL AND VOCAL TIMBRES: ADDITIVE SYNTHESIS

The study of trumpet tones performed in the mid-1960s by one the authors (Risset, 1966; Risset & Mathews, 1969) illustrates some of the points made above. We chose trumpet tones because we were experiencing some difficulties in synthesizing brass-like sounds with the computer. The tones synthesized with fixed spectra derived from the analysis of trumpet tones were unconvincing.

To obtain more data, we recorded musical fragments played by a professional trumpet player in an anechoic chamber. Sound spectrograms suggested that, for a given intensity, the spectrum has a formant structure; that is, it varies with frequency so as to keep a roughly invariant spectral envelope. The spectrograms gave useful information, although it was not precise enough. Thus, selected tones were converted to digital form and analyzed by computer, using a pitch-synchronous analysis (PISA program, Mathews, Miller, & David, 1961). Pitch-synchronous analysis assumes that the sound is quasi periodic; it yields displays of the amplitude of each harmonic as a function of time (one point per fundamental pitch period). The curved functions resulting from the analysis program were approximated with linear segments (see Fig. 3). These functions were then supplied to the MUSIC IV sound-synthesis program and the resulting synthetic tones were indistinguishable from the originals even when compared by musically skilled listeners. Hence, the additive synthesis model, with harmonic components controlled by piece-wise linear functions, captures the aurally important features of the sound.

Conceptually, the model is simple. The pitch-synchronous analysis yields a kind of time-variant harmonic analysis that is further reduced by fitting the linear segments to the amplitude envelope of each component. However, computationally this model is not very economical. Figure 3 shows that the functions can be quite complex and an estimation of the parameters must be performed for every tone. So further simplifica-

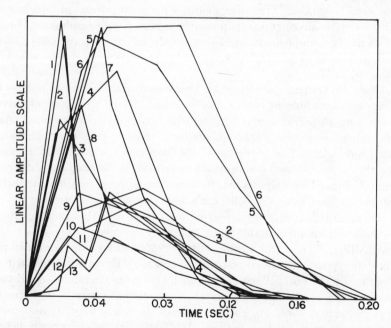

Fig. 3. This figure shows line-segment functions that approximate the evolution in time of 13 harmonics of a D4 trumpet tone lasting 0.2 sec. Functions like these, obtained by analysis of real tones, have been used to control the harmonic amplitudes of synthetic tones (Risset & Mathews, 1969).

tions of the model were sought. By systematic variation of the various parameters—one at a time—the relative importance of the parameters were evaluated. Whereas some parameters were dismissed as aurally irrelevant—for example, short-term amplitude fluctuations—a few physical features were found to be of utmost importance. These include the following: the attack time, with faster build-up of the low-order harmonics than the high-order ones; for certain tones, a quasi-random frequency fluctuation; and, most importantly, a peak in the frequency spectrum between 1000 and 1500 Hz and an increase in the proportion of high-order harmonics with intensity.

In fact, the latter property permitted us to abstract a simplified model of brasslike tones. Here only the amplitude function for the first harmonic was provided and the amplitude functions for the other harmonics were deduced as fixed functions of this first harmonic amplitude so that they increased at a faster rate. The specification was much more economical than the previous one and did not need to be precisely adjusted to yield the brasslike quality. Hence this property of an increase in spectral content with amplitude seems to be the most salient physical correlate of brass-tone quality. Beauchamp (1975) studied these nonlinear interharmonic relationships in cornet tones and ascribed the brass-like character to the type of nonlinear relationship between the different harmonics, which are all functions of the first one regardless of the general level. This relationship has been found later to have an acoustical basis (Benade, 1976, pp. 439–447: Backus & Hundley, 1971). This nonlinear property has been used to produce brass-like sounds with synthesizers, in which a voltage-controlled low-pass filter's cutoff frequency is increased with amplitude. This characteristic has also been implemented in a very simple, satisfying way, using Chowning's powerful technique of spectral generation by frequency modulation (Chowning, 1973; Morrill, 1977).

It was found in the trumpet-tone study that some factors may be important in some conditions and inaudible in others. For instance, details of the attack were more audible in long sustained tones than in brief tones. Also, it appeared that some listeners, when comparing real and synthetic tones, made their decision about whether a tone was real or synthetic on the basis of some particular property. For instance, they often assumed that the real tones should be rougher, more complex than the synthetic ones. This suggests that by emphasizing roughness in a synthetic tone, one could cause the listeners to believe it was a real tone. In his striking syntheses of brassy tones, Morrill (1977) has simulated intonation slips that greatly enhance the realistic human character of the tones. Similarly, in their study of string tones, Mathews, Miller, Pierce, and Tenney (1965, 1966) had included an initial random-frequency component, which corresponds to erratic vibration when the string is first set in motion by the bow. When exaggerated, this gives a scratchy sound strikingly characteristic of a beginning string player. Such idiomatic details, imperfections, or accidents (Schaeffer, 1966) are characteristic of the sound source, and the hearing sense seems to be quite sensitive to them. Taking this into account might help to give stronger identity and interest to synthetic sounds. Indeed, a frequency skew imposed on even a simple synthetic tone can help strongly endow it with subjective naturalness and identity. The pattern of pitch at the onset of each note is often a characteristic feature of a given instrument: the subtle differences between such patterns (e.g., a violin, a trombone, a singing voice) act for the ear as signatures of the source of sound.

The paradigm for the exploration of timbre by analysis and synthesis followed in the latter study has been much more thoroughly pursued by Grey and Moorer (1977a,b) in their perceptual evaluation of synthesized musical instrument tones. Grey and Moorer selected 16 instrumental notes of short duration played near E♭ above middle C. This pitch was selected because it was within the range of many instruments (bass clarinet, oboe, flute, saxophone, cello, violin, etc.); thus, the tones represented a variety of timbres taken from the brass, string, and woodwind families of instruments. The tones were digitally analyzed with a heterodyne filter technique, providing a set of time-varying amplitude and frequency functions for each partial of the instrumental tone. Digital additive synthesis was used to produce a synthetic tone consisting of the superposition of partials, each controlled in amplitude and frequency by functions sampled in time. Each of the 16 instrumental notes could appear in at least four of the five following conditions: (1) original tone; (2) complex resynthesized tone, using the functions abstracted from the analysis: (3) tone resynthesized with a line-segment approximation to the functions (4 to 8 line segments); (4) cut-attack approximation for some of the sounds; and (5) constant-frequencies approximation. In order to evaluate the audibility of these types of data reduction, systematic listening tests were performed with musically sophisticated listeners. The tones were first equalized in duration, pitch, and loudness. An AA AB discrimination paradigm was used. On each trial four tones were played, three of them identical and the fourth one different; the listeners had to detect whether one note was different from the others, to tell in which pair it was located and to estimate the subjective difference between this note and the others. The judgments were processed by multidimensional scaling techniques.

The results demonstrated the perceptual closeness of the original and directly resynthesized tones. The major cue helping the listeners to make a better than chance discrimination was the tape hiss accompanying the recording of the original tones and not the synthetic ones. The results also showed that the line-segment approximation to the time-varying amplitude and frequency functions for the partials constituted a successful simplification, leading to a considerable information reduction while retaining most of the characteristic subjectivity. This suggests that the highly complex microstructure in the time-varying amplitude and frequency functions is not essential to the timbre and that drastic data reduction can be performed with little harm to the timbre. The constant frequencies approximation (for tones without vibrato) was good for some tones but dramatically altered other ones. The importance of the onset pattern of the tones was confirmed by the cut-attack case.

A recent study by Charbonneau (1979) has demonstrated that the simplification can go even further for most of the tones studied by Grey and Moorer (namely short tones of nonpercussive instruments). The various envelopes controlling each harmonic are replaced by a single averaged envelope; for each harmonic, this curve is weighted in order to preserve the maximum amplitude for this harmonic; it is also warped in time

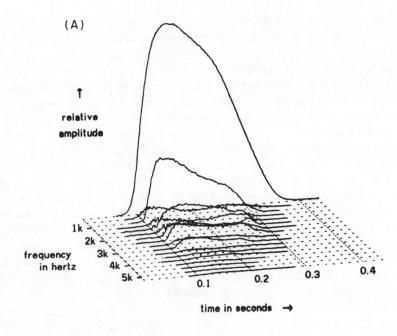

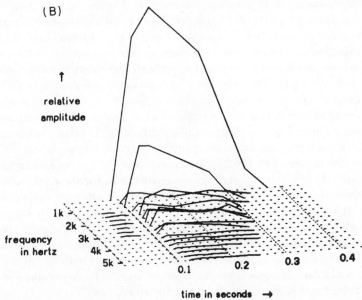

Fig. 4. (A): Time-varying amplitude functions derived from heterodyne analysis for a bass clarinet tone, shown in a three-dimensional perspective plot. (B): Line-segment approximation to the functions plotted in A. Both of these functions have been used to resynthesize the tone. Form B gives a considerable information reduction (Grey & Moorer, 1977).

in order to preserve the times of appearance and extinction of the various harmonics. While this is not a proper model for flute tones, it permits a good imitation for most of the other instruments.

Fletcher and his collaborators (Fletcher, Blackham, & Stratton, 1962; Fletcher & Bassett, 1978; Fletcher, Blackham, & Christensen, 1963; Fletcher & Sanders, 1967) studied the timbre of several instruments by analysis and synthesis, using an additive synthesis model. (The earlier of these studies did not use a computer but *ad hoc* analysis and synthesis devices.) A study of the quality of piano tones (1962) indicated that the attack time must be less than 0.01 sec, whereas the decay time can vary from 20 sec for the lowest notes to less than 1 sec for the very high ones. The variation of partial level versus time during the decay was highly complex and not always monotonic—the partials at time increase in intensity rather than decrease. However, the complexities of the decay pattern did not appear to be very relevant to the ear since the much simplified syntheses could sound similar to the original sounds. The study provided a major insight. It ascribed subjective warmth to the inharmonicity of the partials. The frequencies of the successive partials of a low piano tone are close to, but higher than, the frequencies of the harmonic series (to the extent that the 15th partial frequency can be 16 times that of the lowest one (Young, 1952). Now this slightly inharmonic pattern gives rise to a complex pattern of beats that induces a peculiar lively and warm quality. This is an important feature for low piano tones (and also for organ tones; cf. Fletcher *et al.*, 1963). Actually, many analyses have been performed on piano sounds (Martin, 1947). They have been used to devise electronic pianos (Dijksterhuis & Verhey, 1969) whose tone quality (while not fully satisfying) depends upon the simplified model abstracted from the analyses.

In a study of violin tones, Fletcher and Sanders (1967) investigated the slow frequency modulation (around 6 Hz) known as vibrato, showing that it also modulates the spectrum of the tone. They also pointed to two features that enhance naturalness if they are simulated in the synthetic tones: the bowing noise at the onset of the tone and the sympathetic vibrations coming from the open strings (the latter occur substantially only when certain frequencies are played).

Clark, Luce and Strong have also performed significant research on wind instrument tones by analysis and synthesis. In a first study (Strong & Clark, 1967a) wind instrument tones were synthesized as the sum of harmonics controlled by one spectral envelope (invariant with note frequency) and three temporal envelopes. (A more specific model was also sought for brass instruments, cf. Luce & Clark, 1967). Listeners were tested for their capacity to identify the source of the tones. Their identification was nearly as good as for real instrument tones, which indicates that this model grasps the elements responsible for the difference between the sounds of the different instruments. Incidentally, the probability of confusion between the tones of two instruments gives an indication of the subjective similarity between these tones; it has been used to ascertain the perceptual basis of the conventional instrument families (cf. Clark, Robertson, & Luce, 1964). The results suggest that some conventional families represent fairly well the subjective differentiations, especially the string and the brass family. A double reed family also emerged, comprising a tight subfamily (oboe and English horn) and a more remote member (the bassoon).

VII. CROSS-SYNTHESIS AND VOICE SYNTHESIS

In another study, Strong and Clark (1967b), in order to evaluate the relative significance of spectral and temporal envelopes, resorted to an interesting process: they exchanged the spectral and temporal envelopes among the wind instruments and asked listeners to attempt to identify these hybrid tones. The results indicated that the spectral envelope was dominant if it existed in a unique way for the instrument (as in the oboe, clarinet, bassoon, tuba, and trumpet); otherwise (as in the flute, trombone, and French horn), the temporal envelope was at least as important.

It should be noted that the above conclusions apply to wind instruments, which can have different temporal characteristics, although not very drastic ones. On the other hand, it is easy to verify by synthesis that a sharp attack followed by an exponential decay gives a plucked or percussive quality to any waveform. In this case, temporal cues tend to dominate over spectral ones.

One often speaks of cross synthesis to characterize the production of a sound that compounds certain aspects of a sound A and other aspects of a sound B. There are interesting possibilities for cross synthesis when sound production can be modeled as the combination of two relatively independent processes. In particular, a sound source can often be thought of as comprising an excitation that is transformed in ways that can be characterized in terms of a stable response (Huggins, 1952)—think of someone hitting a gong or blowing into a tube. The temporal properties of the sound are often largely attributable to the excitation insofar as the response depends on the structural properties of a relatively stable physical system; the spectral aspects result from a combination of those of the excitation and those of the response. (Huggins suggests that the hearing mechanism is well equipped to separate the structural and temporal factors of a sound wave.) A good instance is that of voice production (cf. Fant, 1960): the quasi-periodic excitation by the vocal cords is fairly independent of the vocal tract response, which is varied through articulation. Thus, the speech waveform can be characterized by the *formant* frequencies (i.e., the frequencies of the vocal tract resonances) and by the fundamental frequency (*pitch*) of the excitation— except when the excitation is noise-like (in unvoiced sounds like s or f).

A considerable amount of research on speech synthesis has demonstrated the validity of this physical model. It is possible to synthesize speech that sounds very natural. It remains difficult, however, to mimic the transitions in spectrum and frequency that occur in speech with enough accuracy and suppleness. In fact, while one can faithfully imitate a given utterance by analysis and synthesis, it is still difficult to achieve a satisfactory "synthesis by rule," whereby the phonetic elements (phonemes or dyads) would be stored in terms of their physical description and concatenated as needed to form any sentence, with the proper adjustments in the physical parameters performed automatically according to a set of generative rules. We cannot dwell at length here on this important problem; we can notice that the correlates of speaker's identity are multiple and the spectral quality of the voice as well as the rhythmic and intonation patterns are significant. At this time one cannot reliably identify speakers from their voiceprints as one can from their fingerprints (cf. Bolt, Cooper, David, Denes, Pickett, & Stevens, 1969, 1978).

The notion of independence between the vocal tract and the vocal cords is supported by an experiment by Plomp and Steeneken (1971); however, it has to be qualified for the singing voice. For high notes, sopranos raise the first formant frequency to match that of the fundamental in order to increase the amplitude (Sundberg, 1977). Specific features detected in the singing voice have been recently confirmed by synthesis in the work of Sundberg, Chowning, Rodet, and Bennett. Through certain processes of analysis (like inverse filtering or linear predictive coding—cf. Flanagan, 1972), one can decompose a speech signal to separate out the contributions of the vocal cords and the vocal tract. These processes made it possible for Joan Miller to synthesize a voice as though it were produced with the glottis of one person and the vocal tract of another one (cf. Mathews et al., 1961).[3] Actually, the source signal—due to the vocal cords—can be replaced by a different signal, provided this signal has enough frequency components to excite the vocal tract resonances (between, say, 500 and 3000 Hz). It is thus possible to give the impression of a talking (or singing?) cello or organ. Composers are often interested in less conspicuous effects, for instance in producing timbres from the combination of two specific tone qualities, using processes other than mere mixing or blending. This can be achieved through processes of analysis and synthesis—like the phase vocoder or the predictive coding process, or also through the reconstitution of the sounds through a certain model, like frequency modulation or additive synthesis. By physically interpolating the envelopes of the harmonics, Grey and Moorer (1977) have been able to gradually transform one instrumental tone into another one (e.g., a violin into an oboe) through monodic intermediary stages that do not sound like the mere superposition of a violin and a oboe.

VIII. ADDITIVE SYNTHESIS: PERCUSSION INSTRUMENTS

The above studies of timbre resorted to models of additive synthesis, whereby the sound was reconstituted as the superposition of a number of frequency components, each of which can be controlled separately. Such models require much information specifying in detail the way each component varies in time: hence, they are not very economical in terms of the amount of specification or the quantity of computations

---

[3]Impressive examples of voice synthesis and processing for musical uses have been demonstrated in particular by Bennett, Chowning, Moorer, Olive and Petersen. Compositions by Dodge, Olive, and Petersen using synthesized voices can be heard on record CRI SD 348, and on the album *New Directions in Music*, Tulsa studios.

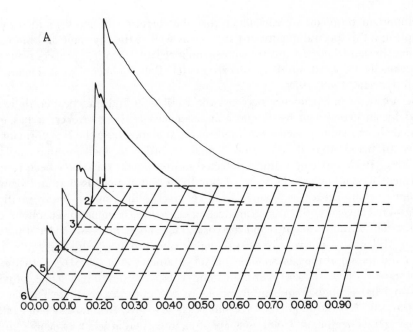

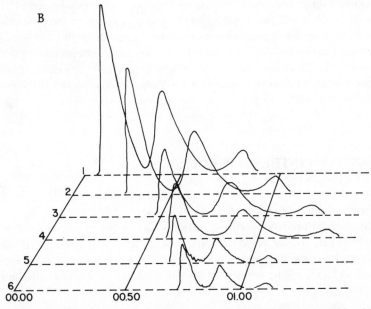

Fig. 5. Perspective plots of synthetic inharmonic tones: the vertical axis is amplitude, the horizontal axis is time, and the depth axis is frequency. In *A*, the sharp attack followed by a decay yields a bell-like tone. In *B*, the time-varying amplitude function yields a fluid nonpercussive tone, in which the components can be heard much better than in the fused bell-like tone. (In spite of the appearance of equal spacing, these tones have nonharmonic components.)

they require. However, as was stated, the information on the temporal behavior of the components can often be simplified. In addition, the development of the digital technology has made it possible to build special processors with considerable processing power, for instance, digital synthesizers that can yield in real time dozens of separate voices with different envelopes (Alles & Di Giugno, 1977); so additive synthesis is a process of practical interest, considering its power and generality. It is not restricted to quasi-periodic tones; in fact, it can be used to simulate the piano and percussion instruments (Risset, 1969; Fletcher & Bassett, 1978).

In percussion instruments, the partials are no longer harmonics: their frequencies, found from the analysis, are those of the modes of vibration excited by the percussion and can sometimes be predicted from consideration of theoretical acoustics. The synthesis can correspond to a considerably simplified model and still be realistic, provided it takes into account the aurally salient features. Fletcher and Bassett (1978) have simulated bass drum tones by summing the contribution of the most important components detected in the analysis—these were sine waves decaying exponentially, with a frequency shift downwards throughout the tone. The simulation was as realistic as the recorded bass drum tones. The authors noted, however, that the loudspeakers could not render the bass drum tones in a completely satisfactory way.

Timbre can often be evoked by a synthesis that crudely takes into account some salient properties of the sound. Bell-like tones can be synthesized by adding together a few sine waves of properly chosen frequencies that decay exponentially at different rates—in general, the higher the frequency, the shorter the decay time. Realism is increased by introducing slow amplitude modulation for certain components of the spectrum. Such modulations exist for real bells; they can be ascribed to beats between closely spaced modes because the bell does not have perfectly cylindrical symmetry.) Snare drums can also be imitated because the decays are much faster than for bells and the effect of the snares can be evoked by adding a high-pitched noise band (Risset, 1969). Bell-like or drum-like sounds synthesized this way can also be transformed morphologically by changing the envelopes controlling the temporal evolution of the components. Thus, for instance, bells can be changed into fluid textures with the some harmonic (or rather inharmonic)[4] content yet with a quite different tone quality (see Fig. 5).

IX. SUBSTRACTIVE SYNTHESIS

Whereas additive synthesis, used in most of the previous examples, builds up the tone as the sum of elementary components, subtractive synthesis consists of submitting a spectrally rich wave to a specific type of filtering, thus arriving at the desired tone by eliminating unwanted elements rather than by assembling wanted ones. Subtractive synthesis is better adapted to certain types of sounds. As was mentioned, the process of speech articulation consists of shaping the vocal tract so that it filters in a specific way the spectrally rich source signal produced by the vocal cords. In fact,

[4]cf. Inharmonique, in the record *Risset-Mutations* (INA-GRM AM 546 09).

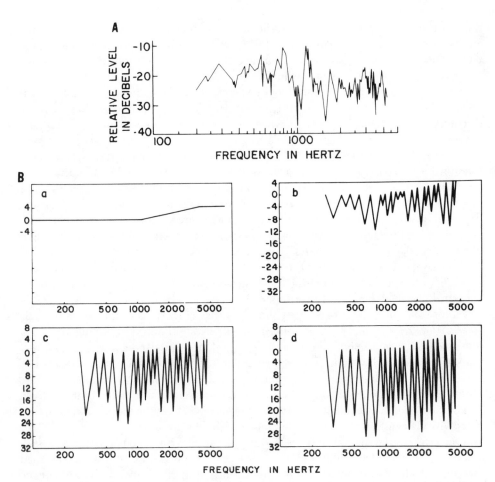

Fig. 6.   Relative frequency response: *A*, as measured in a real violin from sinewave excitation; *B*, as simulated in the electronic replication of the violin tone: from (a) to (d), the Q of the simulated resonances increases from a too low to a too high value (Mathews & Kohut, 1973).

linear prediction coding consists of adjusting the parameters of a recursive filter so as to minimize the difference between the original speech signal and the signal obtained by filtering a single, quasi-periodic pulse wave by this time-variant recursive filter (see below).

Another instance in which subtractive synthesis has proven most useful is the case of violin tones, as demonstrated by Mathews' electronic violin. Mathews and Kohut (1973) have studied the aural effect of the resonances of the violin box through electronic simulation. They have approximated the complex frequency response of a violin (which exhibits many peaks and minima—as many as 20 or more in the audible frequency range) with a set of electrical resonant filters (between 17 and 37). In this experiment, the vibration of the violin string near the bridge was converted into an electric signal by a magnetic pickup. This signal was approximately a triangular wave, as predicted by Helmholtz (Kohut & Mathews, 1971); hence, it consisted of a number of significant harmonic components whose amplitude decays regularly with the rank. This signal was then subjected to the complex filtering approximating the response of the box. It was possible to change the characteristics of that filtering by changing both the damping of the resonances and their distribution along the frequency axis. It was found that a violin-like tone could be achieved with 20 or 30 resonances distributed in the frequency range of 200–5000 Hz, either randomly or at equal musical intervals (see Fig. 6). The best tone was obtained with intermediate values of damping, corresponding to a peak-to-valley ratio of about 10 dB in the response curve of the resonant filter. With too small a damping, the sound was even but dull; with too great a damping, the sound was hollow and uneven in intensity for various pitches.

The experimental equipment constitutes an electronic violin, which has been used musically to obtain either violin-like tones (e.g., in a quartet by M. Sahl) or sounds of very different qualities, by changing the filter settings (e.g., in pieces by V. Globokar or M. Urbaniak).

This experiment has suggested to the authors that the specific quality of violin vibrato could be due to the interaction of the frequency modulation with the resonant peaks, producing a complex pattern of spectral modulation. Different harmonics are modulated in different ways, depending on the slope of the frequency response at the position of these harmonics. This can be verified by synthesis: the effect is not very sensitive to the parameters of a jagged frequency response. Imitative synthesis of violin tones (Schottstaedt, 1977) indicates that a good vibrato quality may be obtained in apparently simpler ways, not ensuring a truly fixed spectral envelope, but modulating the spectrum in a complex way, through a variant of Chowning's frequency modulation technique.

X. ACOUSTIC MODELING AS A SYNTHESIS TECHNIQUE

An ambitious approach for analysis and synthesis has been tried by Hiller and Ruiz (1971) in their work on the use of physical models for string sounds. The analytical study of the acoustic behavior of an instrument can lead to differential equations governing the motion of the vibrating elements. One can try to synthesize the sound by solving these differential equations. This approach is in a way the reciprocal of the one used in analog computers, in which one assembles a physical system with parameters governed by the equations to be solved. In the latter case the measurement of these parameters gives solutions to these equations. In the study of Hiller and Ruiz the resolution of the differential equations gives an approximation to the sound of the instrument. This approximation may be a good one if the differential equations embody a good physical model.

Now this method makes it easy to change at will the physical parameters of the model—to the extent of choosing completely unrealistic values (like negative stiffness) or transforming step-by-step a vibrating object into a different one—and to produce the corresponding sound. Unfortunately, in most cases the equations of motion provide only crude approximations to systems as complex as musical instruments, and even then the computations necessary to solve them are often overwhelming in that they require great numerical precision and a considerable amount of computing power. The development of faster computers and special fast processors may eventually make this method more conveniently usable, but at the moment it still appears difficult to apply (except for demonstration purposes). In fact, Ruiz has produced convincing demonstrations of the behavior of the violin string through the solution of the equations for motion. One may also mention here the use by Freedman (1967) of a model somewhat based on physical behavior, and also the relevance of some physical processes that have been used, if only in a schematic way, as the basis of a synthesis technique. We have already mentionned some of these processes, like nonlinear distorsion (Risset, 1969, #150, Beauchamp, 1975; Arfib, 1979; Le Brun, 1979). Weinreich (1977, 1979) has shown the contribution to the tone of the piano of the coupling between strings which are not exactly tuned to the same frequencies (this ensures the prolongation of the tone as well as a specific quality): he is currently applying this model successfully to the synthesis of piano-like tones.

XI. THE IMPORTANCE OF CONTEXT

The importance of a given cue depends on context. For instance, details of the attack of trumpet-like tones (especially the rate at which various partials rise) are more significant in long sustained tones than in brief or evolving tones (Risset, 1965, 1966). In the case of a very short rise time (as in the piano), the subjective impression of the attack is actually more determined by the shape of the beginning of the amplitude decay (Schaeffer, 1966). The acoustics of the room may also play an important role (Benade, 1976; Schroeder, 1966; Leipp, 1971). The sound of an organ, for instance, depends considerably upon the hall or church where it is located.

Most of the exploration of timbre by analysis and synthesis has focused on isolated tones, but music usually involves musical phrases. Throughout these phrases, the physical parameters of the tones evolve, and this evolution can obscure the importance of certain parameters which are essential for the imitation of isolated tones. Similarly, in the case of speech the parameters of isolated acoustic elements (e.g., phonemes) undergo a considerable rearrangement when the elements are concatenated to form sentences. The specification of simple and valid models of this rearrangement is the problem of speech synthesis by rule. The importance of prosodic variations throughout the sentence is obvious in speech; pitch bends and glides even subtle ones are also essential in music. In a musical context the evolution of various parameters throughout a phrase can be significant. The prosodic variation of one parameter may subjectively dominate other parameters in a musical phrase. So, it is essential to study musical prosody by analysis and synthesis. Actually, this appears to be the new frontier for exploration of analysis and synthesis. (One had to first understand the parameters of isolated tones to be able to describe how they evolve in a musical phrase.)

Currently, musical prosodic studies appear difficult since the phrasing is likely to depend upon the musical style. Its importance seems greater, for instance, in Japanese shakahachi flute playing than in Western instrumental playing. In the latter the music is built from fairly well-defined and relatively stable notes from which the composer can make up timbres by blending, whereas in the former the state of the instrument is constantly disrupted. Hence, a prosodic study on the shakahachi is interesting, even necessary, since the sound can only be described properly at the level of the phrase (A. Gutzwiller, private communication). Mathews has used the GROOVE hybrid synthesis system (Mathews & Moore, 1970), which permits the introduction of performance nuances in real time, to explore certain correlates of phrase, for instance the role of overlap and frequency transition between notes in achieving a slurred, legato effect. Using his algorithms for trumpet synthesis, Morrill is studying the correlate of phrasing in the trumpet. Grey (1978) has studied the capacity of listeners to distinguish between recorded instrumental tones and simplified synthetic copies when the tones were presented either in isolation or in a musical context (single- or multivoiced). He found that while multivoice patterns made discrimination more difficult, single-voice patterns seemed to enhance spectral differences between timbres, while isolated presentation made temporal details more apparent. This finding may relate to the phenomenon of *stream segregation* (Bregman & Campbell, 1971; McAdams & Bregman, 1979; see also Chapter 4, this volume), an important perceptual effect which can be described as follows: if a melodic line is made up of rapidly alternating tones belonging to two sets that are sufficiently separated, the single stream of sensory input splits perceptually into segregated lines. (Baroque composers, such as Bach, resorted to this interleaving of lines to write polyphonic structures for instruments capable of playing only one note at a time.) This segregation is helped by increasing the frequency separation between the lines. Recently, studies by van Noorden (1975) and by Wessel (1979) indicates that the influence of frequency separation on melodic fission has more to do with brightness—that is, with spectral differences—than with musical pitch per se, which appears to be linked with Grey's finding on single-voice patterns.

Chowning has recently performed synthesis of sung musical phrases that sound supple and musical. In addition to carefully tuning the tone parameters for each note, he has given due care to the change of musical parameters throughout the phrase. He has found that the parameters had to vary in ways that are to some extent systematic and to some extent unpredictable. These changes seem to be essential cues for naturalness. In fact, the musical ear may be "turned off" by a lack of variability in the parameters, which points to an unnatural sound for which even complex details may be aurally dismissed. One can hope to develop musical phrase synthesis "by rule," that is, to find rules for the change of musical parameters throughout the phrase that would yield musically acceptable phrases. In the course of this study Chowning has given strong evidence that the addition of the same vibrato and jitter to several tones enhances the fusion of these tones, a fact investigated by Michael McNabb and Stephen

McAdams (1982). Chowning's syntheses strongly suggest that the ear relies on such micromodulations to isolate voices among a complex aural mixture such as an orchestral sound.

In a complex auditory situation it often appears that one dominant feature can eradicate more subtle differences. The most striking aspect according to which the stimuli differ will be taken into consideration rather than the accumulation of various differences between a number of cues. Lashley (1942) has proposed a model of such behavior in which the dominant feature masks the less prominent features. This often seems to hold for perception in a complex environment. Certainly, in the case of musical timbre, which can depend on many different cues, context plays an essential role in assessing whether or not a given cue is significant.

XII. ANALYSIS-SYNTHESIS AS FITTING ACOUSTIC AND PERCEPTUAL MODELS TO DATA

Having described a number of significant studies of timbre by analysis and synthesis, we shall pause here to put these studies in a conceptual framework that will help us to understand possible applications of the analysis–synthesis approach.

A general scheme that we have found useful is shown in Fig. 7. The analysis–synthesis process begins with a sound that is to be modeled. In these general terms the analysis of a sound involves estimating the parameters of a model (for example, in the Fourier analysis model the frequencies, amplitudes, and phases of a set of sine wave components must be estimated). Once the parameters of the model have been estimated, the model can be driven with them to generate a synthetic version of the

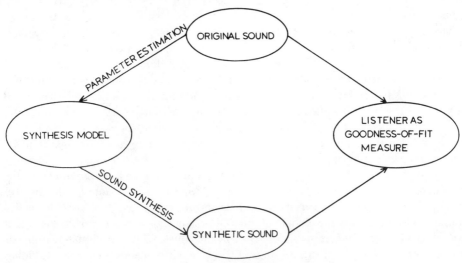

Fig. 7.   Conceptual framework of the analysis–synthesis process.

original sound. For our purposes the appropriate goodness-of-fit evaluation technique is to make auditory comparisons between the original sound and its synthetic replica. If the analysis–synthesis model captures the essential perceptual features of the sound in a thorough way, then the listener should be unable to distinguish the difference between the original and the synthetic version.

The above criterion of validity characterizes what we call a *perceptual model*, as opposed to an *acoustic model*: the latter would mimic the physical mechanisms that give rise to the sound whereas the former simulates the sound through processes that may well not reflect the way the sound is really produced, provided the aural result comes close enough to the original. As we have seen, a good acoustic model can also be a good perceptual model; but the physical behavior of the sound-emitting bodies is very complex, and acoustic simulations require simplifications such that they can rarely sound faithful to the ear. While hearing is very demanding in some respects, it is also very tolerant in other respects: perceptual models can concentrate on those features to which the ear is most sensitive.

Acoustical and perceptual models often represent waveshapes in terms of certain mathematical functions. In the appendix the reader will find some general notions about representations of signals and their utility. A workable and reasonably general perceptual model is also described.

XIII. THE USE OF ANALYSIS–SYNTHESIS MODELS OF TIMBRE

The models drawn from analysis–synthesis of timbre can be useful for several purposes: (1) providing of insight and understanding. (2) information reduction; and the (3) possibility of producing variants or modifications.

A. Insight

Analysis–synthesis provides insight into the perception of timbre, which displays highly specific features. Many of these features can perhaps be better understood from an evolutionary perspective, considering the ways in which hearing has adapted to provide useful information about the environment. For instance, hearing is very sensitive to changes: it is well equipped to be on the alert, which makes sense since sounds propagate far and around obstacles. Perhaps this is why the musical ear tends to reject steady sounds as dull and uninteresting. Hearing is very sensitive to frequency aspects, which are only rarely modified between the sound source and the listener. On the other hand, the ear is quite insensitive to the phase relations between the components of a complex sound, which is fortunate since these relations are smeared in a reverberant environment. Timbre is related to rather elaborate patterns that resist distortion (e.g., the relationship between spectrum and intensity in the brass). From these elaborate patterns, hearing has intricate ways to extract information about loudness and distance. Models of timbre shed light on our capacity to assign different sounds to the same source, for instance, recognition of a note as such regardless of the register in which it is playing. The models help us to to understand what properties form the basis of such categorization.[5] This understanding can be of importance in the fields of experimental music; a composer may want to confer some distinctive identity to certain artificial sounds.

B. Information Reduction

Usually we require that there should be many fewer parameters in the analysis–synthesis model than there are degrees of freedom in the data of the original signal. This is a form of data reduction. For example, consider a digitally sampled sound one second duration. If the sampling rate is 40,000 samples per second and if we wish to account for all these sample values in our model, then we could trivially simulate this signal with a model containing 40,000 parameters: however, a model with a reduced amount of information would be more practical. In fact, much research on speech analysis–synthesis (e.g., the channel vocoders) has been performed to try to find a coding of speech that would reduce the bandwidth necessary to transmit the speech signal (Flanagan, 1972). Such a coding would in fact be an analysis–synthesis model because the speech would be analyzed before transmission and resynthesized at the other end (see Appendix). Such systems have only occasionally been put into practical use since it is difficult to preserve a good speech quality and since the price of the transmission bandwidth has gone down substantially, so that the devices implementing analysis and synthesis at the ends of the transmission line would be more costly that the economized bandwidth. However, information reduction can work very well for certain types of sound, as we have already seen above (Grey & Moorer, 1977): linear predictive coding is an economical way to store speech and is now used in portable speaking machines.

C. Possibility of Producing Variants

If one manipulates the parameters before resynthesis, one will obtain modifications of the original sound and such modifications can be very useful. For instance, starting with a recording of a spoken sentence, one can change the speed by playing it on a variable-speed tape recorder; however, the pitch and the formant frequencies will also be changed, completely distorting the original speech. Now if one analyzes this sentence according to an analysis–synthesis process which separates glottal excitation and vocal tract response [e.g., channel vocoder, phase vocoder, linear predictive

[5]It seems clear that the identity of the timbre of an instrument such as the clarinet, whose high notes and low notes are physically very different, must be acquired through a learning process. It has been proposed that this learning process involves senses other than hearing; in particular, the experiments of Cadoz *et al.* (1981) aim at better understanding "motor" aspects of timbre perception, in particular how the gestural experience of producing a sound interacts with its perception.

coding (Flanagan, 1972; Moorer, 1978)], one can then alter the tempo of articulation independently of the pitch. Moorer has thus been able to slow down speech excerpts by a factor of 20 or more without loosing quality or intelligibility. This example shows the usefulness of analysis–synthesis in obtaining variants of the original sounds.

We shall distinguish here between two uses of sound modification: classical musical processing and expanding timbral resources. In classical musical processing the goal is to transform the sound so as to maintain timbral identity while changing pitch and/or duration (also possibly articulation and loudness). For instance, as mentioned above, linear predictive coding or phase vocoder analysis–synthesis permits the changing of pitch and speed independently. Also, as was discussed at the beginning of this chapter (see Fig. 2), it is often improper to keep the same spectrum when one changes pitch. It may also be necessary to change the spectrum as one changes loudness. Such changes are essential if one wants to use digitally processed real sounds (e.g., instrumental sounds) for music. Without resorting to analysis–synthesis processes, one can only perform rather superficial and often unsatisfying modifications of the sound. On the other hand, one should be aware that these processes are complex and difficult to implement, especially in real time. Even a fast digital processor can have difficulty in coping with the demands of real time if it has to perform analysis–synthesis processes.

In expanding timbral resources, the goal is different: to change certain aspects of the tone so as to modify the timbre while preserving the richness of the original model. Here again, analysis–synthesis processes are essential for allowing interesting timbral transformations (like cross-synthesis), interpolation between timbres (Grey & Moorer, 1977), extrapolation beyond an instrument register,[6] "perversion" of additive synthesis to produce sound paradoxes and illusions (Shepard, 1964; Risset, 1971, 1978a,b,c; Deutsch, 1975; Wessel & Risset, 1979), or transformation of percussive sounds into fluid textures while preserving their frequency content (see p. 39 above). The extension of the models can thus lead to the synthesis of interesting nonconventional timbres, which is a fascinating area open to musicians.

XIV. TIMBRAL SPACE

We have discussed perceptual models; we have also said that analysis–synthesis is useful in modifying timbres. In this respect it would be useful to have a good notion of the structure of the perceptual relationship between different timbres. This can be greatly eased by geometrical models provided by multidimensional techniques, which in effect provide displays of this structure. As was stated earlier by one of the authors: "A timbre space that adequately represented the perceptual dissimilarities could conceivably serve as a kind of map that would provide navigational advice to the composer interested in structuring aspects of timbre (Wessel, 1973)."

[6]This can be heard in *Studies for Trumpet and Computer* by Morrill (recording by Marice Stith, Golden Crest, recital series RE-7068).

One can indeed propose geometric models of subjective timbral space such that individual sounds are represented as points in this space: sounds judged very dissimilar are distant, and sounds judged similar are close. The models are not constructed arbitrarily, but by asking subjects to rate for many pairs of sounds the dissimilarities between the sounds of each pair and by submitting the dissimilarity data to multidimensional scaling programs. These programs—strictly devoid of preconceptions about the data—provide a geometrical model that best fits these data. The dimensions of the model can then be interpreted (e.g., by investigating the stimuli that are least, or most, differentiated along these dimensions).[7] Wessel (1973, 1978) and Grey (1975) have thus already provided models of timbral space for string and wind instrument tones. These models unveil two dimensions—one that differs within the instruments of a same family (e.g., cello, viola, violin) and which appears to relate to the spectral distribution of energy in the sound (cf. von Bismarck, 1974); and one that is the same within a family of instruments and which seems to be linked to temporal features like the details of the attack (Wessel, 1973; Grey, 1977).

The corresponding representations of timbral space tempt one to fill the space, to draw trajectories through it, like the timbral interpolations mentioned above. According to Grey (1975), "The scaling for sets of naturalistic tones suggest a hybrid space, where some dimensions are based on low-level perceptual distinctions made with respect to obvious physical properties of tones, while other dimensions can be explained only on the basis of a higher level distinction, like musical instrument families." The intervention of cognitive facets, such as familiarity and recognition, indicates that a fully continuous timbre space may not be obtainable. Nevertheless, subjective space models can propose new paths and new intriguing concepts, such as that of analogies between timbral transitions (Wessel, 1979), which may permit one to do with timbres something similar to melodic transposition with pitches. Resolving timbre, that "attribute" defined as neither pitch nor loudness, into dimensions may uncover new features or parameters susceptible to precise differentiation and appropriate for articulating musical structures.

For instance, multidimensional scaling of timbre often unveils a dimension correlated with the spectral energy distribution, hence with that aspect of timbre termed *brightness*. As Wessel (1979) has shown, this dimension is the one that can best articulate stream segregation (McAdams & Bregman, 1979). Here, isolating dimensions of timbres permits one to make predictions about the behavior of these timbres in context.

The timbre-space representation suggests relatively straightforward schemes for controlling timbre. The basic idea is that by specifying coordinates in a particular timbre space, one could hear the timbre represented by those coordinates. If these coordinates should fall between existing tones in the space, we would want this interpolated timbre to relate to the other sounds in a manner consistent with the

---

[7]From only quantitative judgments of dissimilarities between sounds, multidimensional scaling in effect unveils in what ways these sounds differ. Schaeffer failed to realize that in his criticism of the process as described by Babbitt (1965) [cf. Music and Technology (1971), pp. 77–78].

structure of the space. Evidence that such interpolated sounds are consistent with the geometry of the space has been provided by Grey (1975). Grey used selected pairs of sounds from his timbre space and formed sequences of interpolated sounds by modifying the envelope break points of the two sounds with a simple linear interpolation scheme. These interpolated sequences of sounds were perceptually smooth and did not exhibit abrupt changes in timbre. Members of the original set of sounds and the newly created interpolated timbres were then used in a dissimilarity judgment experiment to determine a new timbre space. This new space had essentially the same structure as the original space with the interpolated tones appropriately located between the sounds used to construct them. It would appear from these results that the regions between the existing sounds in the space can be filled out, and that smooth, finely graded timbral transitions can be formed.

The most natural way to move about in timbral space would be to attach the handles of control directly to the dimensions of the space. One of the authors examined such a control scheme in a real-time context (Wessel, 1979). A two-dimensional timbre space was represented on the graphics terminal of the computer that controlled the Di Giugno oscillator bank at I.R.C.A.M. One dimension of this space was used to manipulate the shape of the spectral energy distribution. This was accomplished by appropriately scaling the line-segment amplitude envelopes according to a shaping function. The other axis of the space was used to control either the attack rate or the extent of synchronicity among the various components. Overall, the timbral trajectories in these spaces were smooth and otherwise perceptually well behaved. To facilitate more complex forms of control, we need an efficient computer language for dealing with envelopes. The basic idea behind such a language is to provide a flexible control structure that permits specification, sequencing, and combination of various procedures that create and modify envelopes. These procedures would include operations like stretching or shortening duration, changing pitch, reshaping spectrum, synchronizing or desynchronizing spectral components, and so forth. With such a language it will be possible to tie the operations on the envelope collections directly to the properties of the perceptual representations of the material.

XV. CONCLUSION

As was explained above, the exploration of timbre by analysis and synthesis can serve several purposes: it provides insight into the physical parameters of the sound and the relevance of these parameters to the resulting timbre; it leads to simplified models that permit data reduction in the synthetic replication of the sound; and it uses models to perform transformations on the original sound, either from the point of view of classical musical processing (for instance, by independently changing pitch, duration, articulation, and loudness) or by expanding timbral resources (rearranging at will the complex variations abstracted from the analysis to obtain new and rich sounds).

Exploration of timbre by analysis and synthesis is difficult but rewarding. Since the development of analysis and synthesis devices, in particular the digital computer and its descendants, it has brought a better understanding of the physical correlates of timbre as well as recipes for new musical resources.

Although much remains to be done, these new possibilities available to musicians will probably increase the musical role of timbre. In classical Western music timbres were used mostly to differentiate musical lines. Later this linear organization was disrupted by Debussy, Varése, and others. Schoenberg's *Klangfarbenmelodie* associated different timbres to successive notes; Boulez submitted the succession of timbres to serial organization. With the control of timbre now made possible through analysis and synthesis, composers can compose not only with timbres, but they can also compose timbres: they can articulate musical compositions on the basis of timbral rather on pitch variations. It has been argued that timbre perception is too vague to form the basis of elaborate musical communication; however, as Mathews has remarked, there already exists an instance of a sophisticated communication system based on timbral differentiation; namely human speech.[8] Hence, it is conceivable that proper timbral control might lead to quite new musical architectures, and analysis and synthesis processes will be of much help in providing a great musical potential. This will require the acute ear of the musician, provided with some psychoacoustic know-how and with a good interactive environment that permits him or her to achieve fine timbre tunings and manipulations. Hence, the exploration of timbre by analysis and synthesis may become a basic musical endeavor.

APPENDICES

A. Signal Representations and Analysis–Synthesis Processes

Analysis–synthesis according to a given process implies estimating the parameters of a model of the sound. This model may or may not be adequate; it may or may not lend itself to a good imitation of the sound. For instance, Fourier series expansion is a useful tool for periodic tones, and Fourier synthesis, using the data of Fourier analysis, indeed permits one to synthesize a faithful copy of a periodic sound. However, as was explained above, most sounds of interest are not periodic; hence, Fourier series expansion is inadequate to replicate, for instance, a sound whose spectrum varies with time.

A sound can be mathematically described by the waveshape function $p(t)$, giving the acoustic pressure as a function of time. Mathematics tells us that reasonably regular functions can be analyzed in a number of ways, that is, in terms of one or another set of basic functions. This set is said to be complete if an arbitrary function can indeed be obtained as the proper linear combination of these basic functions. (This proper combination is unveiled by the analysis process that consists of estimat-

---

[8]As Moorer demonstrated by analysis and synthesis, speech can remain intelligible under certain conditions after removal of pitch and rhythmic information.

ing the parameters of the corresponding model.) For instance, Fourier's theorem states that any periodic function (of frequency f) can be expanded as a linear combination of the sine and cosine functions of frequencies f, $2f$, $3f$, . . ., so that this linear combination can be arbitrarily close to the periodic function. Hence, the set of sine and cosine functions of frequencies f, $2f$, $3f$, etc. is "complete" over the space of periodic functions of frequency f (cf. Panter, 1965; Rosenblatt, 1963).

Actually, the representation of nonperiodic signals in terms of basic functions usually requires an infinite number of basic functions so that the series expansion turns into a transformation. For instance, nonperiodic signals can be represented in terms of the so-called Fourier transform or Fourier integral, in which the discrete spectral components are replaced by a continuous amplitude spectrum; the discrete phases are also replaced by a phase spectrum. There are other transformations used for analysis–synthesis (e.g., the Walsh–Hadamard and the Karhunen–Loève transformations). Such linear expansion in terms of a basic set of signals is similar to the expansion of a vector in terms of a set of basic vectors; it is practical to use orthogonal transforms—that is, to use functions that form an orthonormal (and complete) set (cf. Harmuth, 1972).

The application of a given transform to a sound signal provides a representation of the signal that may be revealing and should make it possible to restore the signal by means of the inverse transform. Hence, representation of signals is closely linked to analysis–synthesis processes. Actually, the representation of signals purports both to characterize the information (bearing elements in the signal) and to describe in a simple way the effect of modifications of the signals (like those introduced by an imperfect transmission system or by a deliberate simplification of the signal).

Although we cannot go into much detail here, we would like to make several points:

1. Some analysis–synthesis processes and the corresponding representation are intrinsically limited to certain classes of signals. Others can be transparent if they are complete in the above sense—for instance, the Fourier or the Hadamard transform, the phase vocoder, the linear predictive coding scheme. However, the two latter schemes will permit one to reproduce the original signal only at the expense of a considerably detailed analysis, an information explosion instead of an information reduction. This can only be substantially simplified for certain classes of signals (quasiperiodic signals with relatively independent excitation and response mechanisms, like speech; for instance, linear predictive coding is efficient in simulating oboe sounds but poor for low clarinet sounds because eliminating the even harmonics is taxing for the filter). Indeed, much work on analysis–synthesis and signal transformation was originally directed toward efficient coding of speech information for economical transmission over technical channels (Flanagan, 1972; Campanella & Robinson, 1971; Schafer & Rabiner, 1975). It is also for certain types of signals that the representation of the signal will be most enlightening [but, for instance, phase vocoders' programs implemented by Moorer (1978) have permitted Castellengo to obtain useful information on nonharmonic "multiphonic" tones].

Similarly, Gabor's expansion of a signal into Gaussian elementary signals has been proven to be complete (Bastiaans, 1980). Hence, it can in principle produce exactly what Fourier or other types of synthesis can produce (cf. Gabor, 1947; Xenakis, 1971; Roads, 1978). The idiosyncrasies of different complete analysis–synthesis methods only appear in what they permit—or suggest—in a simplified, archetypal use.

2. The Walsh-Hadamard transform seems promising because it leads to operations that are easy to implement with digital circuits. However, from a psychoacoustical standpoint this transform is quite inappropriate. The basic functions do not sound elemental to the ear; they are spectrally very rich, and an approximated representation in those terms would lead to aurally unsatisfying results. The analysis–synthesis process does not deteriorate gracefully for the ear, and it has great difficulty in producing timbres that are not rich and harsh (for instance, it has trouble approaching a sine wave).

3. Fourier-type analysis (and synthesis) has been much criticized, often in a poorly documented way. Whereas Fourier series expansion is indeed inadequate for non-periodic sounds, there are more elaborate variants of Fourier analysis of great utility. The Fourier transform provides complete information of an amplitude spectrum and a phase spectrum; however, the latter characterizes the evolution of the signal in time in a way that is unintuitive and very hard to use. Since this evolution in time is very significant to the ear, one needs some kind of running analysis. This is obtained by calculating, as a function of time, the spectrum of the signal viewed through a specified *time-window* (also called *weighting function*), which at any time only shows the most recent part of the past values of the signal. Such representations are very useful: they have been used in several of the studies previously described. The sound spectrograph (Koenig, Dunn, & Lacey, 1946) implements this type of running analysis: Its windows are appropriate for a useful portrayal of speech sounds, but it often displays significant features of music as well (Leipp, 1971), even though the analysis is often too crude to provide data for a proper synthesis.

The significance of Fourier analysis has a multiple basis. There is clear evidence that the peripheral stages of hearing, through the mechanical filtering action of the basilar membrane, perform a crude frequency analysis with a resolution linked to the critical bandwidth (Plomp, 1964; Flanagan, 1972). The distribution of activity along the basilar membrane relates simply to the Fourier spectrum. Also, when the sound is quasi-periodic, the phase deafness of the ear (Fig. 1) permits a substantial reduction of information. One can also in this case take advantage of the concentration of energy at the harmonic frequencies to describe the sounds by the evolution in time of the amplitude of few harmonics. We have seen that such additive synthesis was a very useful model (cf. Risset & Mathews, 1969; Keeler, 1972; Grey & Moorer, 1977).

4. Global methods like frequency-modulation (Chowning, 1973) and nonlinear distortion or waveshaping (Arfib, 1979; Le Brun, 1979) are appealing because they provide powerful control over salient features of the spectrum in terms of few parameters: the amount of specification and processing is much reduced as compared with additive synthesis. However, strength is at the expense of generality. It is difficult with the global methods to achieve certain results unless one uses them in refined ways that can quickly become complex (cf. Schottstaedt, 1977).

B. Synthesis Model Based on Perceptual Principles

We now give a brief account of how synthesis procedures can provide for direct control over some essential perceptual attributes of timbre. The essential principle underlying these synthesis schemes is the decomposition of a musical signal into perceptual attributes that are, for the most part, perceptually independent of each other. The motivation is to provide a reasonably general but simple control scheme for additive synthesis as this form of synthesis is becoming more and more practical with advances in the development of high-speed digital-synthesis hardware.

1. Pitch Versus the Global Impression of the Spectral Envelope

Several studies (Plomp & Steeneken, 1971; Risset, 1978b,c) suggest that musical pitch and the global spectral energy distribution as perceptual attributes are reasonably independent of each other. This is true to a large extent for harmonic tones that tend to produce clear pitch percepts, but it is not true for inharmonic spectra whose ambiguous and otherwise multiple-pitch content depends on the spectral balance of the components. What we mean by independence is that it is possible to manipulate, for example, the placement and shape of formants without influencing the perceived pitch and conversely manipulate the pitch while keeping the perceived shape of the spectrum constant. The voice provides an example of such an independent control scheme that operates over a reasonably wide range of pitches and spectral shapes. A singer can sing the same pitch with a large variety of vowel qualities and can likewise maintain a constant vowel quality over a substantial range of pitches.

2. Roughness and Other Spectral Line-Widening Effects

Terhardt (1978) has provided evidence that our impression of roughness in sounds depends on an additive combination of independent spectrally distributed amplitude fluctuations. Consider the following example using a tone consisting of the three components: 400, 800, and 1600 Hz. Here the components are widely distributed (i.e., more than a critical bandwidth between them) and amplitude fluctuations of say 10% of the component amplitude at frequencies between 10 and 35 Hz contribute independently to the overall impression of roughness. The implication for synthesis is to provide for independent control of the amplitude fluctuations in different regions of the spectrum.

By *spectral line widening* we mean the spreading or smearing of energy around a spectral line. Such spectral line widening can be obtained by amplitude and/or frequency modulation of a sinusoid. Many instrumental timbres have noise-like effects in their attack transients and most often their spectral placement is essential to the timbre. For example, in the synthesis of string-like attacks the middle to upper spectral regions require more noise than the lower regions. It is to the synthesis model's advantage to allow for the independent placement of noise-like effects in separate spectral regions, which can be accomplished by widening the spectral lines in those regions.

3. Vibrato and Frequency Glides

Our impression of timbre is often strongly dependent on the presence of a vibrato or frequency glide and the synthesis procedure should provide for an easy application of these effects without disrupting the global spectral energy distribution. A frequency glide of an oscillator with a fixed spectrum results as well in a glide of the spectral energy distribution and thus violates the desired independence. Such independence has been accomplished in the glissando version of Shepard's illusion (Shepard, 1964) produced by Risset (1978b,c).

In our additive synthesis procedure we should be able to provide an overall spectral envelope that remains constant in spite of changes in the specific frequencies of the components. In addition, the model should provide for the independent placement of roughness and noise-like effects in separate regions of the spectrum again without violating the overall spectral envelope. These kinds of control can be accomplished fairly easily in most sound synthesis languages by the use of table-look-up generators, such as the VFMULT of the MUSIC V language. These generators allow one to store a spectral envelope function that is used to determine the sample-by-sample amplitude of a given component that could be executing a frequency glide. This technique works similarly for control of the spectral distribution of roughness or other line-widening effects. To obtain time-variant effects with these attributes, the spectral envelopes and roughness distributions are defined at successive and often closely spaced points in time, and interpolation is carried out between successive pairs of these functions.

REFERENCES

Allen, J. B., & Rabiner, L. R. A unified approach to short-time Fourier analysis and synthesis. *Proceedings of the IEEE*, 1977, *65*, 1558–1564.

Alles, H. G., & Di Giugno, P. A one-card 64-channel digital synthesizer. *Computer Music Journal*, 1977, *1* (n°4), 7–9.

American Standard Association. American Standard Acoustical Terminology, New York, 1960.

Appleton, J. H., & Perera, R. C., editors, *The development and practice of electronic music*. Prentice Hall, Englewood Cliffs, New Jersey, 1975.

Arfib, D. Digital synthesis of complex spectra by means of multiplication of non-linear distorted sine waves, *Journal of the Audio Engineering Society*, 1979, *27*, 757–768.

Babbitt, M. The use of computers in musicological research. *Perspectives of new music*, 1965, *3*, n° 2.

Backhaus, W. Einschwingvorgänge, *Zeitschrift für Technische Physik*, 1932, *13*, 31.

Backus, J. *The acoustical foundations of music*. Norton, New York, 1969.

Backus, J., & Hundley, J. C. Harmonic generation in the trumpet, *Journal of the Acoustical Society of America*, 1971, *49*, 509–519.

Bastiaans, M. J. Gabor's expansion of a signal into Gaussian elementary signals, *Proceedings of the IEEE*, 1980, *68*, 538–539.

Beauchamp, J. W. Analysis and synthesis of cornet tones using non linear interharmonic relationships. *Journal of the Audio Engineering Society*, 1975, *23*, 778–795.

Benade, A. H. *Fundamentals of musical acoustics*. London and New York: Oxford University Press, 1976.

Berger, K. W. Some factors in the recognition of timbre, *Journal of the Acoustical Society of America*, 1964, *36*, 1888–1891.

Blackman, R. B., & Tukey, J. W. *The measurement of power spectra from the point of view of communications engineering.* Dover, New York, 1958.

Bolt, R. H., Cooper, F. S., David, E. E. Jr., Denes, P. B., Pickett, J. M., & Stevens, K. N. Identification of a speaker by speech spectrogram. *Science,* 1969, *166,* 338-343.

Bolt, R. H., Cooper, F. S., David, E. E. Jr., Denes, P. B., Pickett, J. M., & Stevens, K. N. *On the theory and practice of voice identification.* National Research Council Washington, D.C., 1978

Boomsliter, P. C., & Creel, W. Hearing with ears instead of instruments. *Journal of the Audio Engineering Society,* 1970, *18,* 407-412.

Bregman, A. S., & Campbell, J. Primary auditory stream segregation and perception of order in rapid sequences of tones. *Journal of Experimental Psychology,* 1971, *89,* 244-249.

Bregman, A. S., & Pinker, S. Auditory streaming and the building of timbre. *Canadian Journal of Psychology,* 1978, *32,* 19-31.

Cabot, R. C., Mino, M. G., Dorans, D. A., Tackel, I. S., & Breed, H. E. Detection of phase shifts in harmonically related tones. *Journal of the Audio Engineering Society,* 1976, *24,* 568-571.

Cadoz, C., Luciani, A., Florens, S. L. Synthèse musicale par simulation des mécanismes instrumentaux et transducteurs gesteuls retroactifs pour l'étude du jeu instrumental. *Revue d'Acoustique,* 1981, *59,* 279-292.

Campanella, S. J., & Robinson, G. S. A comparison of orthogonal transformations for digital speech processing. *IEEE Transactions on Communication Technology,* 1971, COM-19, 1045-1050.

Charbonneau, G. Effets perceptifs de la réduction des données dans la perception du timbre. *C. R. Acad. Sci., Paris,* 1979, 289 B, 147-149.

Chowning, J. The synthesis of complex audio spectra by means of frequency modulation. *Journal of the Audio Engineering Society,* 1973, *21,* 526-534.

Clark, M. Robertson, P., & Luce, D. A preliminary experiment on the perceptual basis for musical instrument families. *Journal of the Audio Engineering Society,* 1964, *12,* 194-203.

Culver, C. A. *Musical Acoustics.* New York: McGraw Hill, 1956.

Deutsch, D. Musical illusions, *Scientific American,* 1975, *233,* 92-104.

Dijksterhuis, P. R., & Verhey, T. An electronic piano. *Journal of the Audio Engineering Society,* 1969, *17,* 266-271.

Eagleson, H. W., & Eagleson, O. W. Identification of musical instruments when heard directly and over a public address system. *Journal of the Acoustical Society of America,* 1947, *19,* 338-342.

Erickson, R. *Sound structure in music.* Berkeley, California: University of California Press, 1975.

Fant, G. *Acoustic theory of speech production.* Gravenhage: Mouton, 1960.

Feynman, R. B., Leighton, R. B., & Sands, M. *The Feynman lectures on physics,* Reading, Massachusetts: Addison-Wesley, 1963

Flanagan, J. L. *Speech analysis, synthesis and perception.* New York: Academic Press, 1972.

Fletcher, H., & Bassett, I. G. Some experiments with the bass drum. *Journal of the Acoustical Society of America,* 1978, *64,* 1570-1576.

Fletcher, H., Blackham, E. D., & Christensen, D. A. Quality of organ tones. *Journal of the Acoustical Society of America,* 1963, *35,* 314-325.

Fletcher, H., Blackham, E. D., & Stratton, R. Quality of piano tones. *Journal of the Acoustical Society of America,* 1962, *34,* 749-761.

Fletcher, H., & Sanders, L. C. Quality of violin vibrato tones. *Journal of the Acoustical Society of America,* 1967, *41,* 1534-1544.

Freedman, M. D. Analysis of musical instrument tones. *Journal of the Acoustical Society of America,* 1967, *41,* 793-806.

Gabor, D. Acoustical quanta and the nature of hearing. *Nature (London),* 1947, *159,* No. 4.

George, W. H. A sound reversal technique applied to the study of tone quality. *Acustica,* 1954, *4,* 224-225.

Grey, J. M. An exploration of musical timbre. Thesis, Stanford University, 1975.

Grey, J. M. Multidimensional perceptual scaling of musical timbres. *Journal of the Acoustical Society of America,* 1977, *61,* 1270-1277.

Grey, J. M. Timbre discrimination in musical patterns. *Journal of the Acoustical Society of America,* 1978, *64,* 467-472.

Grey, J. M., & Gordon, J. W. Perceptual effect of spectral modifications in musical timbres. *Journal of the Acoustical Society of America*, 1978, *63*, 1493-1500.

Grey, J. M., & Moorer, J. A. Perceptual evaluation of synthesized musical instrument tones. *Journal of the Acoustical Society of America*, 1977, *62*, 454-462.

Hall, H. H. Sound analysis. *Journal of the Acoustical Society of America*, 1937, *8*, 257-262.

Harmuth, H. *Transmission of information by orthogonal functions*. New-York. Springer, 1972.

Hiller, L. & Ruiz, P. Synthesizing musical sounds by solving the wave equation for vibrating objects—Part I. *Journal of the Audio Engineering Society*, 1971, *19*, 463-470.

Huggins, W. H. A phase principle for complex frequency analysis and its implication in auditory theory. *Journal of the Acoustical Society of America*, 1952, *24*, 582-589.

Jansson, E., & Sundberg, J. Long-term average spectra applied to analysis of music. *Acustica*, 1975/1976, *34*, 15-19, 269-274.

Jenkins, G. M., & Watts, D. G. *Spectral analysis and its applications*. San Francisco, California: Holden-Day, 1968.

Keeler, J. S. Piecewise-periodic analysis of almost-periodic sounds and musical transients. *IEEE Transactions on Audio & Electroacoustics*, 1972, *AU-ZO*, 338-344.

Koenig, W., Dunn, H. K., & Lacey, L. Y. The sound spectrograph. *Journal of the Acoustical Society of America*, 1946, *18*, 19-49.

Köhler, W. Akustische Untersuchungen. *Zeitschrift für Psychologie*, 1915, *72*, 159.

Kohut, J., & Mathews, M. V. Study of motion of a bowed string. *Journal of the Acoustical Society of America*, 1971, *49*, 532-537.

Lashley, K. S. An examination of the "continuity theory" as applied to discriminative learning. *Journal of General Psychology*. 1942, *26*, 241-265.

Le Brun, M. Digital waveshaping synthesis. *Journal of the Audio Engineering Society*, 1979, 27, 250-266.

Leipp, E. *Acoustique et musique*. Paris: Masson, 1971.

Luce, D., & Clark, M. Jr., Physical correlates of brass-instrument tones. *Journal of the Acoustical Society of America*, 1967, *42*, 1232-1243.

Martin, D. W. Decay rates of piano tones. *Journal of the Acoustical Society of America*, 1947, *19*, 535.

Mathes, R. C., & Miller, R. L. Phase effects in monaural perception. *Journal of the Acoustical Society of America*, 1947, *19*, 780-797.

Mathews, M. V. The digital computer as a musical instrument. *Science*, 1963, *142*, 553-557.

Mathews, M. V. *The technology of computer music*. Cambridge, Massachusetts: MIT Press, 1969.

Mathews, M. V., & Kohut, J. Electronic simulation of violin resonances. *Journal of the Acoustical Society of America*, 1973, *53*, 1620-1626.

Mathews, M. V., Miller, J. E., & David, E. E. Jr., Pitch synchronous analysis of voiced sounds, *Journal of the Acoustical Society of America*, 1961, *33*, 179-186.

Mathews, M. V., Miller, J. E., Pierce, J. R., & Tenney, J. *Journal of the Acoustical Society of America*, 1965, *38*, 912. (abstract only)

Mathews, M. V., Miller, J. E., Pierce, J. R., & Tenney, J. Computer study of violin tones. Murray Hill, New Jersey: Bell Laboratories, 1966.

Mathews, M. V., & Moore, F. R. Groove—a program to compose, store and edit functions of time. *Communications of the ACM*, 1970, *13*, 715-721.

Mathews, M. V., Moore, F. R., & Risset, J. C. Computers and future music. *Science*, 1974, *183*, 263-268.

McAdams, S. Spectral fusion and the creation of auditory images. In M. Clynes (Ed.) *Music, mind and brain: The neuropsychology of music*. Plenum: New York, 1982.

McAdams, S., & Bregman, A. Hearing musical streams. *Computer Music Journal*, 1979, *3*, No. 4, 26-43.

Meyer, E., & Buchmann, G. *Die Klangspektren der Musikinstrumente*. Berlin: 1931

Miller, D. C. *The Science of musical sounds*. New York: Mac Millan, 1926.

Moorer, J. A. Signal processing aspects of computer music: a survey. *Proceedings of the IEEE*, 1977, *65*, 1108-1137.

Moorer, J. A. The use of the phase vocoder in computer music applications. *Journal of the Audio Engineering Society*, 1978, *26*, 42-45.

Moorer, J. A., & Grey, J. Lexicon of analyzed tones.-Part I: A violin tone. *Computer Music Journal*, 1977, *1*, No. 2, 39-45. (a)

Moorer, J. A., & Grey, J. Part II: Clarinet and oboe tones. *Computer Music Journal*, 1977, *1*, No. 3, 12-29. (b)

Moorer, J. A., & Grey, J. Part III: The trumpet, *Computer Music Journal*, 1978, *2*, No. 2, 23-31.

Morrill, D. Trumpet algorithms for music composition. *Computer Music Journal*, 1977, *1*, No. 1, 46-52.

Music and Technology. UNESCO and *Revue Musicale*. Paris, 1971.

Olson, H. F. *Music, physics and engineering*. New York: Dover, 1967.

Panter, P. F. *Modulation, noise and spectral analysis*. New York: McGraw Hill, 1965.

Plomp, R. The ear as a frequency analyzer. *Journal of the Acoustical Society of America*, 1964, *36*, 1628-1636.

Plomp, R. *Aspects of tone sensation*. New York: Academic Press, 1976.

Plomp, R. Timbre as a multidimensional attribute of complex tones. In R. Plomp & F. G. Smoorenburg (Eds.) *Frequency analysis and periodicity detection in hearing*. Leiden: Suithoff, 1966.

Plomp, R., & Steeneken, J. M. Effect of phase on the timbre of complex tones. *Journal of the Acoustical Society of America*, 1969, *46*, 409-421.

Plomp, R., & Steeneken, J. M. Pitch versus timbre. *Proceeding of the 7th International Congress of Acoustics, Budapest*, 1971, *3*, 377-380.

Richardson, E. G. The transient tones of wind instruments. *Journal of the Acoustical Society of America*, 1954, *26*, 960-962.

Risset, J. C. *Journal of the Acoustical Society of America*, 1965, *38*, 912 (abstract only).

Risset, J. C. Computer study of trumpet tones, Bell Laboratories, Murray Hill, New Jersey, 1966.

Risset, J. C. *An introductory catalog of computer-synthesized sounds*, Bell Laboratories, Murray Hill, New Jersey, 1969.

Risset, J. C. Paradoxes de hauteur, *Proceedings of the 7th International Congress of Acoustics, Budapest*, 1971, 20 S 10.

Risset, J. C. Musical acoustics. In E. C. Carterette & M. P. Friedman, *Handbook of perception. (Volume IV, Hearing)* New York: Academic Press, 1978. Pp. 521-564. (a)

Risset, J. C. Paradoxes de hauteur. IRCAM Report No. 10, Paris, 1978 (with a cassette of sound examples). (b)

Risset, J. C. Hauteur et timbre. IRCAM Report No. 11, Paris, 1978. (with a cassette of sound examples). (c)

Risset, J. C., & Mathews, M. V. Analysis of musical instrument tones. *Physics Today*, 1969, *22*, No. 2, 23-30.

Roads, C. Automated granular synthesis of sound. *Computer Music Journal* 1978, *2*, No. 2, 61-62.

Rodet, X., & Bennett, G. Synthèse de la voix chanteé pour ordinateur. *Conferences des Journées d'Etudes du Festival du son, Paris*, 1980. Pp. 73-91.

Rodet, X. Time-domain formant-wave-function synthesis. *Proceedings of the NATO-ASI Meeting Bonas*, July 1979.

Roederer, J. G. *Introduction to the Physics and Psychophysics of Music*. London: The English Universities Press, 1974.

Rosenblatt, M. (Ed.), *Time series analysis*. New York: Wiley, 1963.

Saldanha, E. L., & Corso, J. F. Timbre cues and the identification of musical instruments. *Journal of the Acoustical Society of America*, 1964, *36*, 2021-2026.

Schafer, R. W., & Rabiner, L. R. Digital representations of speech signals. *Proceedings of the IEEE*, 1975, *63*, 662-677.

Schaeffer, P. *Traité des objets musicaux*. Paris: Ed. du Seuil, 1966. (with three records of sound examples)

Schottstaedt, W. The simulation of natural instrument tones using frequency modulation with a complex modulating wave. *Computer Music Journal*, 1977, *1*, No. 4, 46-50.

Schroeder, M. R. Complementarity of sound buildup and decay. *Journal of the Acoustical Society of America*, 1966, *40*, 549-551.

Schroeder, M. R. Models of hearing. *Proceedings of the Institute of Electrical and Electronics Engineers*, 1975, *63*, 1332-1350.

Shepard, R. N. Circularity of relative pitch. *Journal of the Acoustical Society of America*, 1964, *36*, 2346-2353.
Slawson, A. W. Vowel quality and mustical timbre as functions of spectrum envelope and fundamental frequency. *Journal of the Acoustical Society of America*, 1968, *43*, 87-101.
Strong, W., & Clark, M. Jr., Synthesis of wind-instrument tones. *Journal of the Acoustical Society of America*, 1967, *41*, 39-52. (a)
Strong, W., & Clark, M. Jr., Perturbations of synthetic orchestral wind instrument tones. *Journal of the Acoustical Society of America*, 1967, *41*, 277-285. (b)
Stumpf, C. *Die sprachlante*. Berlin and New York: Springer-Verlag, 1926.
Sundberg, J. The acoustics of the singing voice. *Scientific American*, 1977, *236*, 82-91.
Tenney, J. C. The physical correlates of timbre. *Gravesaner Blätter*, 7, Heft 26, 106-109.
Terhardt, E. Psychoacoustic evaluation of musical sounds. *Perception & Psychophysics*, 1978, *23*, 483-492.
Van Noorden, L. *Temporal coherence in the perception of tone sequences*. Eindhoven, Holland: Instituut voor Perceptie Onderzoek, 1975.
von Bismarck, G. Sharpness as an attribute of the timbre of steady sounds *Acustica*, 1974, *30*, 159-172.
von Helmholtz, H. *Sensations of tone*. 1877. English translation with notes and appendix by E. J. Ellis, New York: Dover, 1954.
Weinreich, G. Coupled piano strings. *Journal of the Acoustical Society of America*, 1977, *62*, 1474-1484.
Weinreich, G. The coupled motions of piano strings, *Scientific American*, 1979, *240*, No. 1, 118-127.
Wente, E. C. Characteristics of sound transmission in rooms. *Journal of the Acoustical Society of America*, 1935, 7, 123.
Wessel, D. L. Psychoacoustics and music: A report from Michigan State University. *Bulletin of the Computer Arts Society*, 1973, *30*.
Wessel D. L. Low dimensional control of musical timbre, IRCAM Report Paris No. 12, 1978 (with a cassette of sound examples).
Wessel, D. I. Timbre space as a musical control structure. *Computer Music Journal*, 1979, *3*, No. 2, 45-52.
Wessel, D. L., & Risset, J. C. *Les illusions auditives*. Universalia: Encyclopedia Universalis, 1979. Pp. 167-171.
Winckel, F. *Music, sound and sensation*. New York: Dover, 1967.
Xenakis, I. *Formalized music*. Bloomington, Indiana: Indiana University Press, 1971.
Young, R. W. Modes, nodes and antinodes. *Journal of the Acoustical Society of America*, 1952, *24*, 267-273.
Zwicker, E. Subdivision of the audible frequency range into critical bands. *Journal of the Acoustical Society of America*, 1961, *33*, 248.
Zwicker, E., & Scharf, B. A model of loudness summation. *Psychological Review*, 1965, 72, 3-26.

3

Perception of Singing

Johan Sundberg

I.	Introduction	59
II.	Function of the Voice	60
III.	Resonatory Aspects	62
	A. Female Singing	62
	B. Male Singing	69
	C. Voice Classification	73
IV.	Phonation	76
	A. Vocal Effort and Pitch	77
	B. Register	78
V.	Vibrato	82
	A. Background	82
	B. Perceptual Aspects	83
VI.	Pitch Accuracy in Singing Practice	89
VII.	Phrasing and Emotion	91
VIII.	Concluding Remarks	94
	References	95

I. INTRODUCTION

An understanding of singing perception may be developed from two different types of investigation. One type considers the acoustic property of singing, varies it systematically, and explores the perception of these variations. Such investigations are rare in singing research. Another type of investigation concerns the acoustic correlates of certain types of voices or phonations. The underlying typology of voices and phonations must be based mainly on aural perception. Consequently, even such investigations have perceptual relevance. Most of the investigations of singing have this type of perceptual relevance. However, research on the perception of singing is not as developed as is the closely related field of speech research. Therefore, the reader will not find an exhaustive presentation in this chapter. Rather he or she will find a presentation of different investigations only partly related to each other.

A confession on the part of the author of this chapter is in place here. Writing this chapter has been a bit embarassing, because so many references to the author's own work seemed motivated. As the reader might notice, it is difficult to be fully objective in the presentation of one's own investigations. However, as was just mentioned, there are comparatively few studies published on the perceptual aspects of singing.

When we listen to a singer there are a number of remarkable perceptual facts. For instance: How is it that we can hear the voice even when the orchestra is loud? How is it that we generally identify the singer's vowels correctly even though vowel quality in singing differs considerably from that which we are used to in speech? How is it that we can identify the individual singer's sex, register, and voice timbre when the pitch of the vowel lies within a range common to all singers and several registers? How is it that we perceive singing as sequence of discrete pitches even though the fundamental frequency events do not form a pattern of discrete fundamental frequencies? How is it that we hear a phrase rather than a sequence of isolated tones? These are some of the main questions that will be discussed in the present chapter. In order to understand the questions as well as the answers, it is necessary to have a basic knowledge of the acoustics of singing. We will therefore first briefly present what is known about this.

II. FUNCTION OF THE VOICE

The vocal organ consists of three basic components: (1) the respiratory system that provides an excess pressure of air in the lungs, (2) the vocal folds that chop the air stream from the lungs into a sequence of quasi-periodic air pulses, and (3) the vocal tract that gives each sound its final characteristic spectral shape and thus its timbral identity. These three components are referred to as respiration, phonation, and resonance or or articulation, respectively.

The chopped air stream (i.e., the *voice source*) is the raw material of all voiced sounds. It can be described as a complex tone composed of a number of harmonic partials. This implies that the frequency of the nth partial equals n times the frequency of the first partial, which is called the *fundamental*. The frequency of the fundamental (i.e., the fundamental frequency) is identical to the number of air pulses occurring in one second or, in other words, to the frequency of vibration of the vocal folds. The fundamental frequency determines the pitch we perceive in the sense that the pitch would remain essentially the same even if the fundamental sounded alone. The amplitudes of the voice-source partials decrease monotonically with rising frequency. As a rule of thumb, a given partial is 12 dB stronger than a partial located one octave higher. However, for low degrees of vocal effort the slope of this source spectrum is steeper than 12 dB/octave. On the other hand, the slope of the voice-source spectrum is generally not dependent on which voiced sound is produced.

Spectral differences between various voiced sounds arise when the sound from the voice source is transferred through the vocal tract (i.e., from the vocal folds to the lip opening). The reason for this is that the ability of the vocal tract to transfer sound is highly dependent on the frequency of the sound being transferred. This ability culminates at certain frequencies, called the *formant frequencies*. In consequence, those voice-source partials that lie closest to the formant frequencies are radiated from the lip opening at greater amplitudes than the other neighboring partials. Hence, the formant frequencies are manifest as peaks in the spectrum of the radiated sound.

The formant frequencies vary within rather wide limits in response to changing the position of the articulators (i.e., lips, tongue body, tongue tip, lower jaw, velum, and larynx). We can change the two lowest formant frequencies by two octaves or more by changing the position of the articulators. The frequencies of these two formants determine the identity of most vowels. The higher formant frequencies cannot be varied as much. They seem to be more relevant as personal voice characteristics. Thus, properties of vowel sounds that are of great importance to vowel identity can be described in a chart showing the frequencies of the two lowest formants, as is done in Fig. 1. Note that each vowel is represented by a small area rather than by a point in the chart. In other words, these formant frequencies may vary within certain limits without changing the identity of the vowel. This reflects the fact that a given vowel is normally observed to possess higher formant frequencies in a child or in a woman

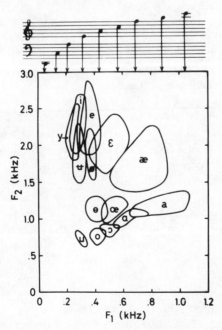

Fig. 1. Ranges of the two lowest formant frequencies for different vowels represented by their symbols in the International Phonetic Alphabet (IPA). Above, the scale of the first formant frequency is translated into musical notation.

than in a male adult. The reason for such differences lies in differing vocal tract dimensions, as will be shown later.

In singing, more or less substantial deviations are observed from the vowel ranges shown in Fig. 1. Indeed, a male opera singer may change the formant frequencies so much that they enter the area of a different vowel. For instance, in the vowel [i:][1] as sung by a male opera singer the two lowest formant frequencies may be those of the vowel [y:] according to Fig. 1. And in female high-pitched opera singing the formant frequencies may be totally different from those found in normal speech. Yet we tend to identify such vowels correctly. This shows that the frequencies of the two lowest formants do not determine vowel identity entirely. Next we will see how and why these deviations from normal speech are made in singing.

III. RESONATORY ASPECTS

A. Female Singing

1. Formant Frequencies

A soprano singer is required to sing at fundamental frequencies as high as 1000 or 1400 Hz. In normal female speech the fundamental frequency rarely exceeds about 350 Hz. The normal value of the first (and in some vowels even the second) formant frequency is far below 1000 Hz, as can be seen in Fig. 1. If the soprano were to use the same articulation in singing a high-pitched tone as in normal speech, the situation illustrated in the upper part of Fig. 2 would occur. The lowest partial in the spectrum (i.e., the fundamental) would appear at a frequency far above that of the first formant. In other words, the capability of the vocal tract to transfer sound would be optimal at a frequency where there is no sound to transfer. It seems that singers tend to avoid this situation. Instead they abandon the formant frequencies of normal speech and move the frequency of the first formant close to that of the fundamental. The main articulatory gesture used to achieve this tuning of the first formant is a change of the jaw opening, which is particularly effective for changing the first formant frequency (cf. Lindblom & Sundberg, 1971). This explains why female singers tend to change their jaw opening in a pitch-dependent manner rather than in a vowel-dependent manner, as in normal speech. The acoustic result of this maneuver is illustrated in the lower part of the same Fig. 2: The amplitude of the fundamental and hence the sound power of the vowel increases considerably. Note that this gain in sound power results from a resonatory phenomenon. It is obtained without increasing vocal effort.

Figure 3 shows formant frequencies measured in a soprano singing various vowels at varying pitches (Sundberg, 1975). As can be seen from the figure, the vowels maintain the formant frequencies of normal speech up to that pitch where the fundamental comes close to the first formant. Above that frequency the first formant is

---

[1]All letters appearing within [] are symbols in the International Phonetic Alphabet.

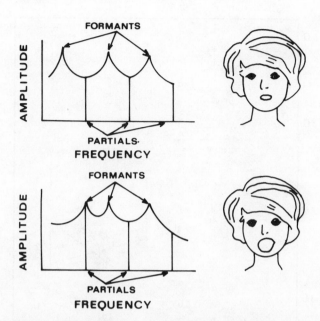

Fig. 2. Schematical illustration of the formant strategy in female singing at high pitches. In the upper case the singer has a small jaw opening. The first formant appears at a frequency far below the frequency of the lowest partial of the vowel spectrum. The result is a low amplitude of that partial. In the lower case the jaw opening is widened so that the first formant matches the frequency of the fundamental. The result is a considerable gain in amplitude of that partial (reprinted from Sundberg, 1977b).

raised to a frequency in the near vicinity of the fundamental. If the jaw opening is changed, the main effect observed is in the first formant frequency, but the higher formant frequencies also change to some extent. This is illustrated in Fig. 3: All formant frequencies change when the first formant starts to match the fundamental frequency.

2. Sound Intensity and Masking

As was mentioned above, the amplitude of the fundamental increases when the first formant is tuned to that frequency. This results in a gain in overall sound pressure level (SPL). The magnitude of the gain can be seen in Fig. 4, which shows the increase in SPL associated with the formant frequencies plotted in Fig. 3. We can see that the pitch-dependent choice of formant frequencies results in an amplitude gain of almost 30 dB in extreme cases. This corresponds to a thousandfold increase of sound power. A perceptually important conclusion is that the female singer will gain in loudness to a corresponding extent.

The singer's need for exceptionally high degrees of loudness is of course a consequence of the fact that opera singers are generally accompanied by an orchestra. The average SPL of an orchestra playing loudly in a concert hall is about 90 to 100 dB. This is much more than we can expect from a human speaker. The masking effect that

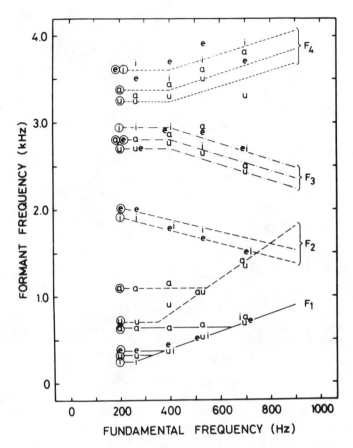

Fig. 3. Formant frequencies in the vowels indicated (IPA symbols) measured in a professional soprano singer singing at different fundamental frequencies. The lines show schematically how the formant frequencies are changed with fundamental frequency for the vowels indicated by the circled symbols (adapted from Sundberg, 1978b).

the orchestral sound will exert on a singer's voice is determined by the distribution of sound energy along the frequency scale. A long-time average spectrum of orchestral music shows the average of this distribution. Such a spectrum is shown in Fig. 5. It was obtained from the *Vorspiel* to the first act of Wagner's *Meistersinger* opera. The frequency scale is based on the mel unit, which is preferable when masking and spectral pitch are considered (cf. Zwicker & Feldtkeller, 1967). The graph shows that the strongest spectral components are found in the region of 400–500 Hz. The average spectrum level falls off more steeply toward higher frequencies than toward lower frequencies (Sundberg, 1972a).

The masking effect of a noise with the spectrum shown in Fig. 5 can be estimated from hearing theory (see Zwicker & Feldtkeller, 1967). Avoiding details, we may say that the masking effect will be greatest at those frequencies where the masking sound

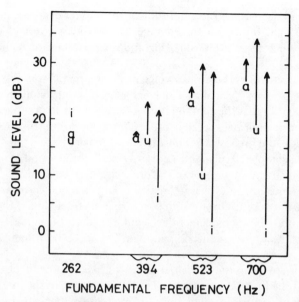

Fig. 4. The overall sound level of vowels indicated (IPA symbols) that would result at different fundamental frequencies if the formant frequencies were kept constant at the values observed for the fundamental frequency of 260 Hz in Fig. 3. The arrows show how much these sound levels increase when the formant frequencies are changed with the fundamental frequency in the way indicated by the noncircled vowel symbols in Fig. 3.

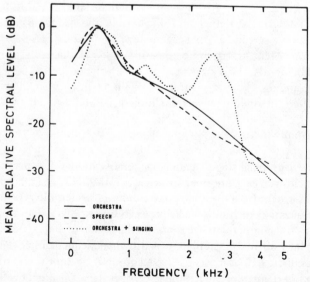

Fig. 5. Idealized long-time average spectra showing the mean distribution of sound energy in the "Vorspiel" of act 1 in Wagner's opera "Meistersinger" (solid line) and in normal speech (dashed line). The dotted line pertains to an opera singer singing with orchestra accompaniment (from Sundberg, 1977b).

is loudest and it will decrease as the amplitude of the masker decreases toward higher and lower frequencies. Thus, on the average, the masking effect of the sound of the orchestra will be greatest at 400–500 Hz and decrease toward higher and lower frequencies.

What types of spectra does the human voice produce, then? From Fig. 5 we can see that the long-time average spectrum of normal speech is very similar to that of the orchestra. This suggests that the combination of the sound of an orchestra with that of the human voice during normal speech is probably the most unfortunate one possible. If the sound level of the orchestra is considerably higher than that of the voice, the voice is likely to be completely masked. And, inversely, if the sound of the voice were much stronger (which is very unlikely), the orchestra may be masked. From this we can conclude that the acoustic characteristics of the human voice as observed in normal speech are not very useful for solo parts when combined with the sound of an orchestra. Therefore, these characteristics would need to be modified if both the singer's voice and the orchestral accompaniment are to be both loud and independently audible.

Let us now return to the case of female singing. The spectrum will be dominated by the fundamental if the first formant is tuned to the frequency of the fundamental. We would expect this to occur as soon as the fundamental frequency is higher than the normal frequency value of the first formant. This value is 300 to 800 Hz, depending on the vowel (see Fig. 1). From what was said about masking, we see that all vowels are likely to be masked by the orchestra as long as their first formant is below 500 Hz, approximately. This will be the case for all vowels except [a:, a:, æ:] sung at fundamental frequencies lower than about 500 Hz, which is close to the pitch B4. As soon as the fundamental frequency exceeds this value, it will be strong, and its frequency will be higher than that of the partial which is likely to be the strongest in the accompaniment. Summarizing, we can say that a female singer's voice can be expected to be masked by a strong orchestral accompaniment as soon as the vowel is not [a:, a; æ:] and the pitch is below B4. This seems to agree with the general experience of female voices in opera singing. They are rarely difficult to hear when they sing at high pitches, even when the orchestral accompaniment is loud.

3. Vowel Intelligibility

We have seen that female singers gain considerably in loudness by abandoning the formant frequencies typical of normal speech when they sing at high pitches. On the other hand, the formant frequencies are extremely important to vowel intelligibility. This poses the question of how vowel intelligibility is affected by high pitches in female singing.

One of the first to study this problem was the phonetician Stumpf (1926), although he probably was not aware of its acoustic background. Stumpf used one professional opera singer and two amateur singers. Each singer sang various vowels at different pitches, turning their backs to a group of listeners who tried to identify the vowels. The identifications were found to be better when the vowels were sung by the professional singer. These results are illustrated in Fig. 6A. The percentages of correct identifications dropped as low as 50% for several vowels sung at the pitch of G 5. The identification was far better for most vowels when the vowel was preceded by a consonant, particularly [t]. This shows that vowels are much easier to identify when they contain some transitions. Incidentally, this seems to be a perceptual universal: Changing stimuli are more easy to process than quasi-stationary stimuli.

Morozov (1965) studied intelligibility of syllables sung by professional singers (even males) as a function of fundamental frequency. According to his results, intelligibility drops below 80% correct identification above the pitch of E4 and B4 in male and female singers, respectively. At the pitches of C5 and C6 intelligibility has decreased to 50% and 10% correct identification for male and female singing, respectively. At the very highest pitches in female singing, all vowels tend to be perceived as an [a:] according to Howie and Delattre (1962). This appears to agree with results already mentioned on the formant frequencies in female high-pitched singing: The highest pitches would be sung with almost the same (i.e., maximum) jaw opening for all vowels; under such conditions the formant frequency pattern would be similar regardless of which vowel is intended by the singer. Nelson and Tiffany (1968), Scotto di Carlo (1972) and Smith and Scott (1980) all found that vowel intelligibility differed for different vowels sung at the same pitch. For instance, Nelson and Tiffany found that open vowels were harder to interpret correctly than closed vowels and diphthongs.

All these results on intelligibility of vowels and syllables sung at high pitches should be seen against the background of two different effects. One is that singers systematically deviate from the formant frequency patterns of normal speech. This deviation is likely to generate intelligibility problems, at least under certain experi-

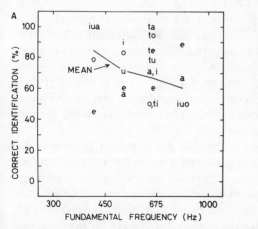
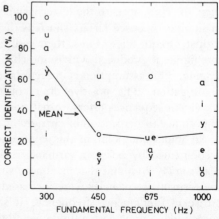

Fig. 6. (A) Percentages of correct identification of vowels (IPA symbols) sung by a professional singer according to Stumpf (1926). The solid line represents the average. Note that intelligibility increased when the vowels vowels were preceded by a [t]. (B) Corresponding values obtained by Sundberg (1977a) in an experiment with synthesized vibrato vowels, each of which had the same formant frequencies regardless of the fundamental frequency. The solid line represents the average.

mental conditions. The other effect is that in high-pitched vowels few partials are distributed over the frequency band that normally contains the information we needed to identify a sound as a specific vowel. Thus, a lack of information about vowel identity seems to arise when a vowel is sung at a very high pitch because of the low number of spectrum partials. This effect will certainly add to the score of failing intelligibility in tests like those we have discussed.

The question of how the female singer's deviations from the formant frequencies of normal speech affect vowel intelligibility was studied by Sundberg (1977a). A set of six vowels were synthesized (with vibrato) at different fundamental frequencies ranging from 300 to 1000 Hz. The formant frequencies were kept constant in each of the vowels. The sounds were presented to a group of phonetically trained listeners who tried to identify each of them as one of 12 given vowels. The results are shown on Fig. 6B. It can be seen in this figure that, on the average, vowel intelligibility decreased monotonically as pitch rose, although there were exceptions and minor variations. More important, though, is that the percentages of correct identification were much lower than those reported by Stumpf, using nonsynthetic vowels. A major difference between the synthetic vowels and the vowels used by Stumpf is that the first formant was presumably never lower than the fundamental in Stumpf's case. This being so, we may conclude that the pitch-dependent articulation in high-pitched female singing improves vowel intelligibility when compared to the case in which the formant frequencies are kept constant regardless of the pitch.

Smith and Scott (1980) studied the effect on vowel intelligibility of larynx height and consonantal environment as a function of pitch. Their results, which were based on material from a female singer, confirm that vowel identification is much simpler if the vowel is surrounded by consonants than when it is rendered in isolation. The results also showed that vowels sung with a raised larynx position are more intelligible than vowels sung with the lower larynx position, which their subject normally used in singing. A raised larynx shortens the vocal tract and, by consequence, raises the formant frequencies. Thus, their results suggest that high-pitched vowels are more intelligible if produced with somewhat higher formant frequencies than in normal singing. This assumption is in accordance with the findings of the Sundberg (1977a) investigation. The positive effect of transitions characterizing consonant-vowel-consonant sequences offers formal evidence for Stumpf's observation of the decisive importance to perception of changes in stimuli.

An important point in this connection is the fact that a rise in pitch *must* be accompanied by a rise in formant frequencies if vowel quality is to be preserved. Slawson (1968) found that maximum similarity in vowel quality was obtained when the formant frequencies were increased by 10% on the average for each octave increase in fundamental frequency. It should be noted that Slawson worked with speech-like sounds with a fundamental that never exceeded 270 Hz. In any case, our ears seem to expect a certain increase in the formant frequencies when the fundamental frequency is increased.

The difference in the percentage of correct identifications between Stumpf's and Sundberg's investigations may not necessarily depend solely on a difference in the formant frequencies. Other differences between synthetic and real vowels may very well have contributed. As was just mentioned, the beginning and ending of a sound are probably very revealing, and presumably the vowels in these two investigations differed in this respect also. Therefore, a direct comparison using well-defined synthetic stimuli is needed before we can draw safe conclusions as to whether or not the pitch-dependent choice of formant frequencies in high-pitched female singing really is a positive factor in vowel identification.

B. Male Singing

1. The "Singer's Formant"

The audibility problem appears rather different for a male singer than for a female singer. The reason for this lies in the difference in the fundamental frequency ranges. In normal speech the male voice centers around approximately 110 Hz whereas the female voice is about one octave higher. The top pitch for a bass, a baritone, and a tenor is generally E4 (330 Hz), G4 (392 Hz), and C5 (523 Hz), respectively. Consulting Fig. 1 once more, we find that most vowels have a first formant frequency that is higher than these top fundamental frequencies, at least in the cases of bass and baritone voices. The case in which the fundamental frequency is higher than the normal values of the first formant frequency will occur only in the upper part of the tenor and baritone ranges. Therefore, in male singing a pitch-dependent choice of the two lowest formant frequencies is not to be expected except in vowels with a low formant frequency sung at high pitches by tenors and baritones. Measurements by Sundberg (1973) and Cleveland (1977) support this.

The consequence of this seems to be that the male singers produce spectra that are on the average similar to the average spectrum of the orchestral accompaniment (see Fig. 5). Previously, we found that such a similarity in spectrum leads to maximum masking. On the other hand, we know that male voices can be heard readily even when the orchestral accompaniment is loud.

If vowel spectra of normal speech are compared with those produced by male opera and concert singers, at least one difference can be almost invariably observed. Sung vowels contain more sound energy than spoken vowels in the partials falling in the frequency region of 2.5–3 kHz, approximately. Thus, the spectrum envelope exhibits a more or less prominent peak in the high-frequency region. This peak is generally referred to as the "singer's formant" and it has been observed in most acoustic studies of male singing (see, e.g., Bartholomew, 1934; Winckel, 1953; Rzevkin, 1956; Sundberg, 1974; Hollien, Keister, & Hollien, 1978). Figure 7 provides a typical example.

The "singer's formant" has been studied from acoustical and perceptual points of view by Sundberg (1974). There are strong reasons for assuming that the "singer's formant" is an acoustic consequence of a clustering of the third, fourth, and fifth formant frequencies. If formants approach each other in frequency, the ability of the vocal tract to transfer sound increases in the corresponding frequency region. Hence,

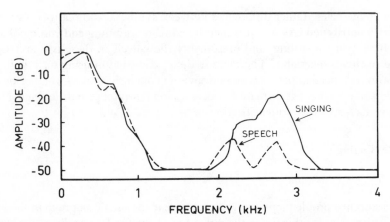

Fig. 7.   Spectrum contours (envelopes) of the vowel [u] spoken (dashed curve) and sung (solid curve) by a professional opera singer. The amplitudes of the harmonics between 2 and 3 kHz give a marked peak in singing as compared with speech. This peak is called the "singer's formant." It is typical for all voiced sounds in male professional opera singing (adapted from Sundberg, 1978a).

the spectrum envelope peak called the the "singer's formant" seems to be primarily a resonatory phenomenon. However, the amplitude of this peak does not seem to depend on one but on several formants and also, of course, on the source spectrum characteristics.

Formant frequencies are determined by the dimensions of the vocal tract, (i.e., by articulation). According to Sundberg (1974), an articulatory configuration that clusters the higher formants in such a way that a "singer's formant" is generated involves a wide pharynx that appears to result from lowering the larynx. Such lowering of the larynx is typically observed in male singers. Thus, the "singer's formant" can be interpreted acoustically and articulatorily. It should be mentioned that other articulatory interpretations have also been suggested (Hollien et al., 1978).

2. Audibility

Another question is why male opera singers add a "singer's formant" to their voiced sounds in singing. Probably the reason is perceptual. In a sound illustration contained in Sundberg (1977b), it is demonstrated that a singer's voice is much easier to discern against the background of a noise with the same average spectrum as the sound of an orchestra when the voice has a prominent "singer's formant". This effect is certainly associated with masking. The average spectrum of an orchestra culminates around 400–500 Hz and then decreases toward the higher frequencies (see Fig. 5). The mean spectral level at 2.5–3 kHz is about 20 dB below the level at 400–500 Hz. It seems to be an extremely good idea to enhance the spectrum partials in this frequency range. These partials are likely to be perceived without difficulty by the audience because the concurrence from the orchestra's partials is moderate at these high frequencies.

Another perceptual advantage of producing vowels containing a "singer's formant" has been suggested by Winckel (1953, and personal communication). It relates to the sound-radiation characteristics of the lip opening. It can be shown theoretically and has also been demonstrated by measurements (Flanagan, 1965) that low-frequency components scatter spherically from the lip opening while the radiation of the high-frequency components is more concentrated along the length axis of the mouth cavity. In other words, high spectrum partials are radiated sagitally with greater efficiency than lower partials. For a singer facing the audience, the sound radiated behind and above his head is probably lost on an opera stage because of the high sound absorption in the backstage area. The high-frequency components contained in the "singer's formant" are lost to a lesser extent as their radiation is more limited to the sagittal direction. Hence, the relative amplitude of the "singer's formant" would be greater compared to the lower partials when the sound reaches the audience. This would help the audience to discern the singer's voice against the background of the orchestral accompaniment. As yet, however, no attempts have been made to assess the magnitude of this effect. It may be mentioned here that many singers and singing teachers speak about "projecting" or "focusing" the voice as a requirement for the audibility of the voice in a large audience. These expressions appear to agree with the above reasoning that the singer's voice is radiated more efficiently in the sagittal direction if the voice contains a "singer's formant."

Before we leave masking problems, one more fact should be mentioned. There are two exceptions to the principle that we cannot hear sounds that fall below the masked threshold resulting from a louder, simultaneous sound. One exception is when the softer sound starts some fraction of a second earlier than the masker sound (cf. Rasch, 1978). The other exception applies to the situation when the masker sound is time varying. Plomp (1977) has demonstrated that we can hear a sound below the masked threshold provided that the masker signal is interrupted regularly. Under these conditions we can hear the signal continuously even in the presence of the masker. Both these cases might apply to the singer–orchestra combination. The orchestral sound, of course, varies in intensity. Given Plomp's results, it should not be necessary for the "singer's formant" to be heard all the time. It would be sufficient for it to be audible during the moments when the amplitude of the orchestral sound in this frequency region is low, provided that such moments are separated by sufficiently short time intervals.

As the "singer's formant" is a perceptually apparent characteristic of male singer voices, it is not surprising that it is recognized as an important timbral attribute among singers and singing teachers. In general, we invent names for such attributes. There seems to be a number of different names for the "singer's formant". Gibian (1972) synthesized vowels in which he varied the frequency of the fourth formant while the remaining formants were kept constant. An expert on singing found that the "placement in the head" of the tone was most "forward" when the fourth formant was 2.7 kHz, which was only .2 kHz above the third formant. Vennard, who was an eminent singing teacher and had a thorough knowledge of the acoustics of singing, simply speaks about "the 2800 Hz" that produces the "ring" of the voice (Vennard, 1967).

3. Modification of Vowel Quality

Just as in the case of female singing, male singing involves modifications of the vowel qualities characteristic of normal speech. The main articulatory background of these modifications is probably the lowering of the larynx and the widening of the pharynx required for the generation of the "singer's formant". These articulatory characteristics affect not only the third and higher formant frequencies but also the two lowest formant frequencies, which are critical to vowel quality, as was mentioned. Sundberg (1970) measured formant frequencies in vowels sung by four singers and compared these frequencies with those reported by Fant (1973) for nonsingers. As shown in Fig. 8, there are considerable differences here. For instance, the second

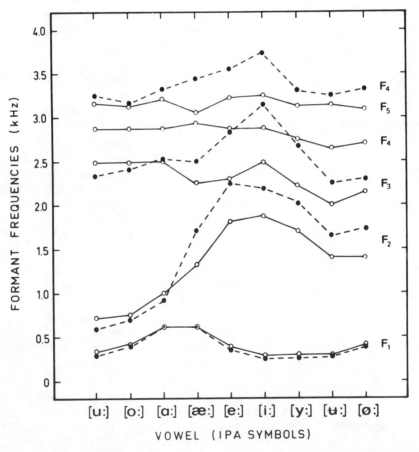

Fig. 8. Average formant frequencies in different vowels as produced by nonsingers (dashed curves) according to Fant (1973) and four male singers (solid curves) according to Sundberg (1970). Note that the fourth formant (F_4) in nonsingers is slightly higher in frequency than the fifth formant (F_5) in singing (reprinted from Sundberg, 1974).

formant does not reach as high a frequency in sung vowels as in spoken vowels. This is the acoustic consequence of a wide pharynx and a low larynx. As a result, some vowels do in fact assume formant frequencies typical of a different vowel in singing. This poses the same question as was posed for female singing: Can we really identify the sung vowels correctly?

Unfortunately, there is no formal evidence available to supply an answer to this question. (It will be recalled that the Morozov (1965) study concerns syllables, not isolated vowels.) On the other hand, the differences in quality between spoken and sung vowels are well known, at least to singers and singing teachers. Many singing teachers instruct their students to modify an [i:] toward a [y:], and [e:] toward an [œ], an [a:] toward an [a:], etc. (see, for example, Appleman, 1967). It is considered important that a vowel should not be *replaced by* but only *modified toward* another vowel. This must mean that the sung vowels do retain their vowel identity, although the two lowest formant frequencies are clearly "wrong." It is likely that a low value of the second formant frequency in front vowels can be compensated for by the presence of the "singer's formant."

In summary, we can say that the departures from the formant frequencies typical of normal speech lead to a modification of vowel quality. This modification is probably not sufficiently great to shift the vowel identity. With front vowels, part of the reason for this might be that the "singer's formant" compensates the effect from the too low frequency of the second formant. It seems likely that transitions associated with consonants are the most important factors for vowel identification.

Before we leave this subject, reference should be made to a study by Simon, Lips, and Brock (1972). It concerns the spectra of a vowel sung with differing timbres by a professional singer. These measurements show how properties of the spectrum vary when the singer mimics different types of singing with labels such as *Knödel*. It seems that formant frequencies explain many of these differences.

C. Voice Classification

1. Bass, Baritone, and Tenor Timbre

As we all know, singing voices are classified in terms of soprano, mezzosoprano, alto, tenor, baritone, bass. The main criterion for such classification is the pitch range available to the singer. If a singer's range is C3 to C5 (131–523 Hz), his classification is tenor. Pitch ranges of different voice classifications overlap to some extent. In fact, the range C4 to E4 (262–330 Hz) is common to all voices. Still, we rarely have any difficulty in deciding whether a tone in this range is sung by a male or a female singer, and often we can even judge the voice classification correctly.

Cleveland (1977) studied the acoustic background of this discrimination ability in the case of male singing. He presented five vowels sung at four pitches by eight singers classified as basses, baritones, or tenors to singing teachers who were asked to decide on the voice classification. The natural beginnings and endings of the tones were spliced out. The results revealed that the major acoustic cue in voice classification is the fundamental frequency. Incidentally, the same result was found by Coleman (1976) in a study of maleness and femaleness in voice timbre. The result is not very surprising if we assume that we rely mainly on the most apparent acoustic characteristic in this classification task. By comparing vowels sung at the same pitches, Cleveland found that the formant frequencies serve as a secondary cue. The trend was that the lower the formant frequencies, the lower the pitch range the singer is assumed to possess. In other words, low formant frequencies seem to be associated with bass singers and high formant frequencies with tenors. In a subsequent listening test Cleveland verified these results by presenting the same singing teachers with vowels synthesized with formant frequencies that were varied systematically in accordance with his results obtained from real vowel sounds.

Cleveland also speculated about the morphological background of these findings. As has been described, formant frequencies are determined by the dimensions of the vocal tract. These dimensions are smaller in children and females than in male adults, and the formant frequencies differ accordingly. As a longer tube resonator has lower resonance frequencies than a shorter tube, the formant frequencies produced by a male tend to be lower than those produced by a female for a given vowel. The female vocal tract is not simply a small-scale copy of the male vocal tract (Fant, 1973). The pharynx-to-mouth length ratio is smaller in females than in males. The acoustic consequence is that certain formant frequencies in certain vowels exhibit greater differences between sexes than others, as can be seen in Fig. 9 (see also Nordström, 1977). The greatest variations are found in the two lowest formant frequencies. In the same figure are shown the corresponding values that Cleveland found when he compared a tenor voice with a bass voice. There is a clear similarity suggesting a similar morphologic background in the tenor/bass case as in the female/male case. This

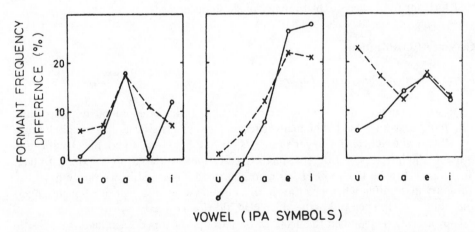

Fig. 9. Percentage differences between various voices in the first (left), second (middle), and third (right) formant frequency in the vowels indicated. Solid curves compare a tenor with a bass singer, according to Cleveland (1977). Dashed curves show the average over six languages of female nonsingers compared with male nonsingers according to Fant (adapted from Fant, 1975).

finding should be corroborated by X-ray measurements on a number of singers of differing voice classification. As yet, we can only hypothesize that tenors tend to have smaller pharynx-to-mouth ratios than basses.

An investigation by Dmitriev and Kiselev (1979) is of interest in this connection. It shows a clear correlation between the center frequencies of two peaks in a long-term average spectrum of voices of different classifications and the associated vocal tract length, particularly with regard to the center frequency of the higher of these two peaks, which would reflect the "singer's formant." The lower of the peaks, which occurs in the frequency range of about .4 to .9 Hz, would relate to the average frequency of the first formant.

In summary, experimental support has been found for the following conclusions. In voice classification the fundamental frequency seems to be the main acoustic cue. However, formant frequencies typically differ between bass, baritone, and tenor voices. These differences, which probably reflect differences in vocal tract dimensions as well as in the pharynx-to-mouth length ratios, serve as secondary cues in voice classification.

2. Alto and Tenor Timbre

Generally, there is a clear difference in timbre between alto and tenor voices. Since their pitch ranges overlap to a great extent, the fundamental frequency cannot always explain this difference. We have seen that tenor and bass voices differ with respect to formant frequencies in a way similar to that in which female and male voices differ. This suggests that with respect to formant frequencies a tenor voice is more similar to a female voice than a bass voice is. What, then, are the acoustic differences that account for the timbral differences between alto and tenor voices?

Ågren and Sundberg (1978) compared two alto and two tenor voices singing the same six vowels at the same pitches. Although the subjects in this study were too few to allow for general conclusions, and in spite of the fact that no perceptual evaluation of the results was attempted, the results of this investigation have perceptual relevance. Only the fourth formant frequency showed a consistent difference that could account for the considerable difference in timbre between the two voice types. This formant was observed to have a higher frequency in the alto voices than in the tenor voices. This means that the frequency distance between the third and fourth formants was smaller in the tenor voices. There was also a clear difference in the source spectrum: The amplitude of the fundamental was higher in the alto voices. As we shall see later, this might reflect the principle that the amplitude of the fundamental decreases toward the upper limit of a singer's pitch range. Obviously, the tenors sang in the upper part of their pitch range when singing at the same fundamental frequencies as the altos.

The smaller distance between the third and fourth formants in the tenor voices is not surprising. As was mentioned, it implies a stronger "singer's formant" in the tenor voices. This is in agreement with the finding of Hollien et al. (1978) that the "singer's formant" is more developed in male voices than in female voices.

The perceptually interesting point is the relationship between the "singer's formant" and roughness in timbre. First some words about roughness may be in order. With more extreme degrees of roughness we perceive a series of rhythmic pulsations, as in the case of a very low-pitched tone from a reed instrument, such as the bassoon. At the other extreme (i.e., with complete absence of roughness) the sound is completely smooth. A good example of this is the timbre of a sine wave. Against this background it seems intuitively reasonable to assume that male and female voices differ with respect to roughness.

Terhardt (1974) has studied the acoustical correlate of roughness. He revealed that roughness appears as soon as a spectrum contains at least two partials that (a) have high and reasonably equal amplitudes and (b) excite the same critical band of hearing. This critical band is a sort of analyzing bandwidth of the ear. It is about 100 Hz for center frequencies up to 450 Hz and approximately 20% of the center frequency for higher frequencies. Let us consider a harmonic spectrum with a fundamental frequency lower than 100 Hz. In this case, all adjacent partials are closer than 100 Hz. Therefore, any pair of adjacent partials will excite one critical band. As a consequence, any pair of partials may contribute to roughness. Let us next consider a harmonic spectrum with a higher fundamental frequency. In this case, all of the lowest five partials excite different critical bands because they are more than 20% apart in frequency. Hence, they cannot give rise to roughness. Roughness can occur in such spectra only if one or more pairs of higher partials have high and reasonably equal amplitude.

Let us now return to the alto/tenor case. In the pitch region of relevance, only pairs of partials above the fourth partial can give rise to roughness. If we take into account the fundamental frequency ranges of alto and tenor voices, this leads us to consider partials in the vicinity of the third formant, which is generally located around 2500 Hz. If the frequency distance between the third and fourth formant is on the same order of magnitude as the fundamental frequency, it is likely that these formants will enhance two adjacent partials and thus give rise to roughness. In the Ågren and Sundberg study (1978) the mean frequency distance between these formants in the six vowel sounds analyzed was found to be 785 Hz, (SD = 212 Hz) in the case of the two altos and 439 Hz (SD = 189 Hz) in the case of the two tenors. Thus, we find that this distance is of the same order of magnitude as the frequency separation between the partials only in the case of the tenor voices. Therefore, we would expect roughness from the tenor voices but not from the alto voices. It seems reasonably safe to assume that alto and tenor voices differ with respect to roughness because of the difference in the frequency distance between the third and fourth formants.

IV. PHONATION

Up to this point we have focused primarily upon resonatory phenomena (i.e., on characteristics associated with formant frequencies). In the present section some aspects on phonation will be presented (i.e., the behavior of the vibrating vocal folds and the acoustic properties of the resulting voice source).

A. Vocal Effort and Pitch

Voice-source characteristics change with vocal effort and with pitch as related to the pitch range of the individual voice. In normal speech the amplitudes of the higher overtones increase at a faster rate than the amplitude of the fundamental when vocal effort is increased while the reverse is true when pitch is raised (cf, e.g., Fant, 1960). Sundberg (1973) studied the voice source in two professional singers and found the amplitudes of the overtones above 1 kHz to increase at a faster rate than the lower overtones. This occurred not only when the vocal effort was increased, but also when pitch was raised.

In a later study Sundberg and Gauffin (1978) measured both the waveform and spectrum of the voice source in singers. They used an inverse filter technique, such as that of Rothenberg (1972), which allowed them to study the partials up to 1.5 kHz, approximately. The results showed that in this low-frequency part of the source spectrum, the amplitude relationship between the fundamental and the overtones changed with pitch rather than with vocal effort. When pitch was raised, the amplitudes of the overtones increased more than the amplitude of the fundamental. When vocal effort was increased, the amplitude of the fundamental was observed to increase at approximately the same rate as the SPL. As the SPL is mainly determined by the amplitude of the partial underlying the first formant, which was an overtone, the amplitude of the fundamental increased at about the same rate as the amplitudes of the overtones. However, the amplitudes of the source spectrum partials above 1.5 kHz would be expected to increase more rapidly than the amplitudes of the lowest source spectrum partials when vocal effort is increased. This can be inferred from the observations by Sundberg (1973) and Hollien *et al.* (1978) that the amplitude of the "singer's formant" increases faster than the SPL when vocal effort is raised. In addition to these findings Sundberg and Gauffin (1978) also found that "pressed" phonation is characterized by strong overtones as compared with the fundamental.

The above findings may explain why Ålgren and Sundberg (1978) found a stronger fundamental in the alto than in the tenor voices. In that investigation all subjects sang vowels at identical fundamental frequencies. Hence, the tenors sang in the upper part of their pitch range while the altos sang in the lower part of their pitch range. A similar reasoning can be applied whenever vowel sounds of voices with differing pitch ranges are compared under conditions of identity with respect to fundamental frequency (for instance, in Cleveland's (1977) investigation). It is likely that voice experts can hear if an individual phonates in the upper, middle, or lower part of his/her pitch range by listening to the voice timbre characteristics associated with the voice-source spectrum.

In summary, the dominance of the source spectrum fundamental is promoted by low and medium pitch. At high pitch and in pressed phonation the dominance of the fundamental is decreased. The amplitudes of the overtones above 1.5 kHz increase more rapidly than the overall SPL when vocal effort and pitch are raised.

B. Register

One phonatory aspect of singing which has been subject to a considerable amount of scientific effort, is register (see Large, 1972). Unfortunately, register terminology is rather choatic. On the other hand, there is general agreement that a register is a series of adjacent tones on the scale which (a) sound equal in timbre and (b) are felt to be produced in a similar way. Also, it is generally agreed that differences in register reflect differences in the mode of vibration of the vocal folds (see Hollien, 1974).

Several objections can be raised against this definition since it relies so heavily on subjective impression. Nevertheless, lacking a definition based on physiological facts, we accept it for the time. In trying to understand it, it is helpful to contrast two registers, namely the modal (normal) and the falsetto register of the male voice. These are two clear examples of different registers. In the female voice there are three main registers: chest, middle, and head. They cover the lowest, the middle, and the top part of the pitch range, respectively. However, many voice experts speak about modal and falsetto register both in male and female voices.

2. Female Chest and Middle Register

Large, mostly with various co-authors, has published a series of investigations concerning the acoustic characteristics of different registers. With respect to the physiological background of registers, Large, Iwata, and Von Leden (1970) found that tones sung in the chest register consume more air than those sung in the middle register. They conclude that the conversion of air stream to sound is more efficient in the chest registers.

Large and Shipp (1969) studied the influence of various parts of the spectrum on the ability to discriminate between the chest and middle registers. The material included the vowel [a:] sung by 12 singers at the pitch E4 (330 Hz). The quality of the vowel (but obviously not its timbre) and its acoustic intensity were kept approximately constant by the singers. A test tape was made in which the natural beginnings and endings of each tone were spliced out. The vowel sounds were presented with and without low-pass filtering at 1400 Hz to a jury of voice experts who were asked to classify them with respect to register. The results revealed that generally the registers were correctly identified when the vowels were unfiltered. When they were low-pass filtered, identification of register became more difficult, but it never dropped as far as the level of mere guessing. The authors concluded that the higher spectrum partials merely contribute to register differences. Large (1974) returned to this question in a later study. His results agreed with those of the previous investigation, but this time he studied the spectrum of the vowels more closely. The experiment showed typical differences between the registers in the amplitudes of the lower spectrum partials. By and large, the chest-register vowels were found to possess stronger high partials than the middle-register vowels. However, the differences were all very small. Large found that the results support the assumption that register differences reflect differences in the vocal fold vibrations.

Sundberg (1977c) studied the voice-source and the formant frequency characteristics underlying timbre differences between the chest and middle register in one soprano singer. The subject sang a vowel in both registers at the same pitches. The intensity was left to the subject to decide. The results revealed a considerable source spectrum difference in that the relative amplitude of the fundamental was more than 10 dB stronger in the middle register. This is much more than the small differences reported by Large (1974). Probably, the register difference was less pronounced in Large's subjects.

Sundberg (1977c) also found formant frequency differences between the registers, suggesting that the timbre differences between the registers may depend not only on voice source, but also on articulatory differences. In order to test this hypothesis, he synthesized pairs of vowels differing in either formant frequencies or source spectrum. A group of singing teachers were asked to identify the registers in these pairs of vowel sounds. The results confirmed that both formant frequencies and source spectrum may contribute to register identification. Thus, some of the spectral differences reported in the previously mentioned studies may have been due to formant frequency differences. We will return to this question later.

2. Male Modal and Falsetto Registers

A number of investigations into the differences between the modal and falsetto registers have been published. Although falsetto is rarely used in traditional Western singing—except, perhaps, in counter-tenor singing—the research in this field will be reviewed.

It has been shown that physiologically the vocal folds are longer, stiffer, and thinner in falsetto than in modal register. As a rule, the glottis is never completely closed in falsetto. This is in agreement with the finding of Large, Iwata, and von Leden (1972) that falsetto tones consume more air than comparable tones sung in modal register. On the other hand, complete glottal closure may occur in falsetto (see Fig. 35, frame F on page 71 in Vennard, 1967); and, inversely, incomplete glottal closure is sometimes observed in modal register phonation.

Part of the literature on falsetto and modal register focuses on the question of whether or not listeners can identify these registers from sustained, isolated vowel sounds. Even though difficulties sometimes arise, particularly when the vowels are sung by professional singers, the answer is generally found to be in the affirmative (see, for instance, Lerman & Duffy, 1970). A dependence on the subjects' voice training was also found, which is not surprising since singers are generally trained to blend registers (i.e., to reduce timbral differences between registers). An experiment by Colton and Hollien (1973) allowed for more detailed conclusions. They found vocal registers to be a multidimensional phenomenon: "Under normal conditions it is the combination of pitch, loudness, and quality that an observer utilizes to distinguish two vocal registers. When pitch and loudness are equalized, register discrimination becomes more difficult."

The study by Large *et al.* (1972) used vowels recorded under conditions of equality in pitch and acoustic intensity. Under these conditions the falsetto was found to produce weaker high overtones than the modal register. This agrees with the observation made by the same authors that more air is consumed in falsetto singing; the conversion of air stream into sound is less efficient in falsetto than in modal register.

Again equalizing pitch and acoustic intensity, Russo and Large (1978) compared the two registers perceptually and acoustically. Twelve expert listeners judged the similarity of pairs of tones sung in the different registers. The pairs considered most dissimilar in timbre differed mainly in (a) the amplitudes of the higher spectrum partials, which were lower in falsetto, and (b) the amplitude of the fundamental, which tended to be slightly greater in falsetto. Both these observations agree with spectral evidence collected from singers and nonsingers that Colton had published earlier (1972).

These studies have dealt with the amplitudes of spectrum partials. As we have seen, such amplitudes depend not only on the amplitudes that the partials have in the source spectrum, but also on the frequency separation between the partials and the formants. Thus, the relationships between amplitudes of individual partials and identification of registers are strongly influenced by the formant frequency differences between the spectra compared. Against this background it seems interesting to explore the properties of the voice source that characterize the registers.

Monsen and Engebretson (1977) studied the voice source in various types of phonation. To eliminate the formants, they used a reflectionless tube into which the subjects phonated. The resulting voice-source waveforms are open to question, probably because of phase distortion in the system they used. Such distortion does not, however, affect the amplitudes of spectrum partials. Hence, their results with regard to voice-source spectrum differences would represent reliable information.

They found that the slope of the spectrum envelope was much steeper in falsetto. In other words, the falsetto voice source was more dominated by the lower source spectrum partials. The data shown in Fig. 10 have been selected from the study of Sundberg and Gauffin (1978) mentioned earlier. The waveform is smoother in the falsetto register than in the modal register, and the amplitude of the source spectrum fundamental is much greater in falsetto. These results obviously agree qualitatively with those of Monsen and Engebretson.

On the other hand, Large and his co-authors mostly found very small differences with respect to the fundamental. There may be several reasons for this difference. One is the fact that all tones were sung with vibrato in the Large studies. As will be shown, this implies that the frequency of each partial varies, and a variation in the frequency of a partial leads to an amplitude variation. If spectra are compared, which have not been sampled at identical vibrato phases, errors can be expected. Such errors will be greatest for partials with frequencies close to the formants. In most of

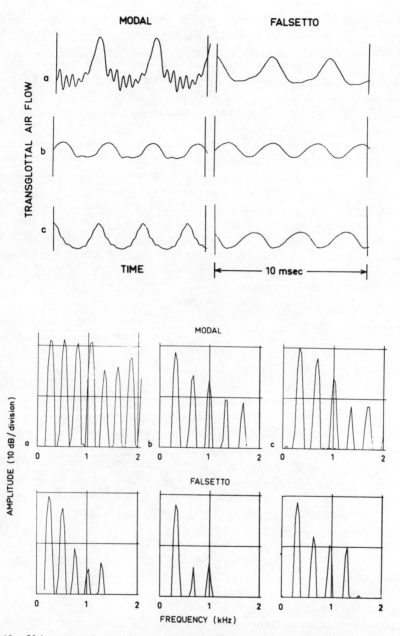

Fig. 10. Voice source characteristics in modal and falsetto register in three singers as determined by inverse filtering technique ad modum Rothenberg (1972). The upper series of curves shows the waveform and the lower series shows the corresponding spectrum boosted by 6 dB/octave. The ripple in the modal register waveforms is an artifact due to the particular inverse filter setup used, which could cancel the influence from the two lowest formants only. This caused the "singer's formant" to appear as a ripple. Note that the amplitude difference between the first and second partial is much greater in falsetto than in modal register.

the Large experiments the vowel was [a:] and the fundamental frequency was 330 Hz. Then, the amplitudes of the four lowest partials will be rather dependent on the vibrato phase.

However, the main reason that the results differ between the spectral analyses of vowels and the analyses of the voice source probably is that acoustic intensity was not equated in the two types of studies. If the vowel is [a:] and the pitch is E4, the second partial will be close to the first formant. The amplitude of the partial underlying this formant is normally quite decisive to the overall acoustic intensity of the vowel. Thus, if two vowels are produced in different registers at the same acoustic intensity, the amplitude of the second source spectrum partial is presumably almost the same in both cases. How, then, should a singer phonate if he is required to produce an [a:] at this pitch at the same acoustic intensity in falsetto as in modal register? Probably by raising the amplitude of the second source spectrum partial in the case of falsetto. This can be achieved by increasing vocal effort. Thus, we arrive at the strange conclusion that equality in acoustic intensity may require a difference in vocal effort. If the above reasoning is correct, the difference in the results is a consequence of the fact that acoustic intensity was kept constant in one case while vocal effort was probably constant in the other case.

V. VIBRATO

A. Background

Vibrato occurs in most Western opera and concert singing and often in popular singing. Generally, it develops more or less automatically during voice training (Björklund, 1961). Acoustically, it corresponds to an undulation of the fundamental frequency. As the spectra of voiced sounds are harmonic, the frequencies of all partials vary in synchrony with the fundamental. The amplitude of a partial depends on how far it is from a formant, and the formant frequencies do not seem to vary appreciably with the vibrato. Therefore, each partial varies in amplitude synchronously with the vibrato.

As the vibrato is a rhythmic undulation (or modulation) of frequency it can be described by two parameters. One is the *rate* of vibrato (i.e., the number of undulations occurring during one second); the other is the *extent* of vibrato (the depth of the modulation expressed in a percentage of the average frequency). More often, however, the vibrato extent is given in number of cents. (One cent is the interval between two tones having the frequency ratio of $1 : 2^{1/1200}$.)

The physiological background of vibrato is unclear. In electromyographic measurements on laryngeal muscles, pulsations in synchrony with vibrato are generally observed (Vennard, Hirano, Ohala, & Frizell, 1970–1971). Moreover, the subglottic pressure and the transglottal air flow often undulate in synchrony with vibrato as can be seen in recordings published by Rubin, Le Cover, and Vennard (1967). An observation that may prove relevant has been reported by Weait and Shea (1977) who studied the glottal behavior in a bassoon player. They found that the glottal area varied in synchrony with vibrato. This can be interpreted as support for the hypothesis that vibrato originates in the laryngeal muscles while undulations in air-flow and subglottic pressure are secondary effects.

Several aspects of vibrato have been studied. As early as the 1930s Seashore (1938) summarized, among other things, a series of investigations that he and his co-workers had made on vibrato. He found the vibrato rate to be rather constant for any given singer but slightly different between singers. The mean for 29 singers was 6.6 undulations per second (extremes 7.8 and 5.9). The average extent was ±48 cents (extremes ±98 and ±31).

B. Perceptual Aspects

1. Vowel Intelligibility

As mentioned before, the identification of vowels is assumed to be related to the detection of peaks in the spectrum envelope. These peaks signal the frequencies of the formants, and the formant frequencies characterize the vowel. If the number of partials is low compared to the number of formants (i.e., if the fundamental frequency is very high), the peaks in the spectral envelope signaling the formant frequencies would be impossible to detect because there may not be a partial in the neighborhood of every formant frequency. It is not unreasonable to assume that vibrato plays a role here. If the frequency of a partial is slightly lower than that of a formant, an increase in fundamental frequency will *raise* the amplitude of that partial. If the partial is slightly higher in frequency than the formant, a *decrease* of the amplitude will result from the same situation, as is illustrated in Fig. 11. Thus, the phase relationship be-

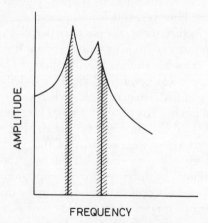

FREQUENCY

Fig. 11. Illustration of the fact that the amplitude and frequency of a partial in the spectrum of a vibrato tone vary in phase or in counter phase depending on whether the partial is slightly lower or higher than the closest formant. The hatched area represents the width of the frequency modulation. The frequency scale is linear.

tween the undulations in frequency and amplitude in a vibrato tone actually gives information about the frequency locations of the formants. The question, then, is whether the ear can detect and use this information. If so, vibrato would facilitate vowel identification for high-pitch vowels.

This question was studied in the experiment mentioned earlier concerning vowel identification in the soprano pitch range (Sundberg, 1977a). Each vowel in the test was presented both with and without vibrato. The interpretations made by phonetically trained subjects differed considerably. The degree of agreement between the interpretations was measured in the following manner. Each response vowel was ascribed a set of three formant frequencies. Then all responses obtained for a given stimulus vowel could be regarded as a cloud of points in a three-dimensional space, in which each dimension corresponds to a formant. The center of this cloud was determined. The mean distance between the individual points and the center was next computed using a formula for perceptual distance between vowels suggested by Plomp (1970). It was assumed that this average distance reflected the difficulty with which a vowel stimulus was identified as a specific vowel. The average distance between responses is shown in Fig. 12. As can be seen in the figure, there are no consistent differences between the values pertaining to vibrato tones and those obtained for vibrato-free tones. Therefore, it is reasonable to conclude that vibrato does not facilitate vowel identification. On the other hand, the results may have been rather different if the stimuli had been more like natural vowels sung by sopranos. It is often hard to predict how our ability to identify stimuli is affected when the stimuli do not resemble anything familiar.

2. Singleness in Pitch

It is a well-established fact that fundamental frequency generally determines pitch. In the case of vibrato tones, however, this is not quite true. While the fundamental frequency varies regularly in such tones, the pitch we perceive is perfectly constant as long as the vibrato rate and extent are kept within certain limits.

What are these limits? Ramsdell studied this question at Harvard University in a thesis work that unfortunately was never published. Ramsdell varied the vibrato rate and extent systematically and had listeners decide when the resulting tone possessed an optimum "singleness in pitch." His results for a 500 Hz tone are shown in Fig. 13. Later Gibian (1972) studied vibrato in synthetic vowels. He varied the vibrato rate and extent and had subjects assess the similarity of this vibrato with human voice vibrato. His results agree closely with Ramsdell's data as can be seen in the same figure. In addition to asking the listeners for the optimum singleness in pitch, Ramsdell also asked for an evaluation of the "richness" in the timbre. His data showed that the optimum in regard to singleness in pitch as well as timbral richness corresponds to the values of rate and extent typically observed in singers.

It is interesting that Ramsdell's curve approaches a straight line in the neighborhood of seven undulations per second. This implies that the extent is not very critical for singleness in pitch at this rate. In contrast to this, there is a strong opinion among

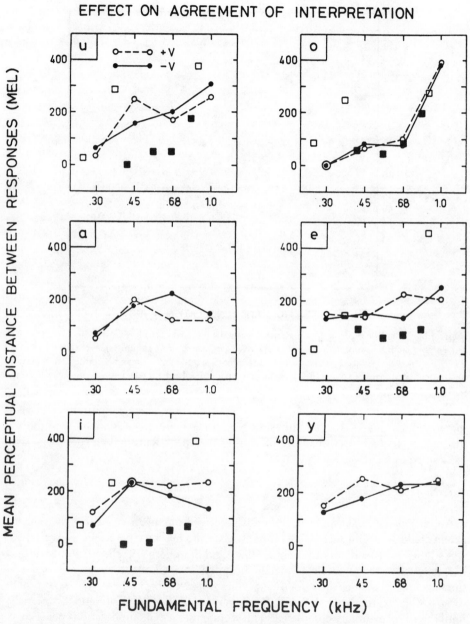

Fig. 12. Scatter of responses obtained when subjects attempted to identify synthetic vowels with high fundamental frequencies. The formant frequencies were those of the vowels given in the top left corner of each graph. Dashed lines pertain to vibrato vowels and solid lines to vibrato-free vowels. The squares give values reported by Stumpf (1926). They were observed when subjects identified vowels sung by two untrained singers (open squares) and one professional soprano (filled squares). The procedure for deriving the measure of the scatter is described in the text (reprinted from Sundberg (1977a).

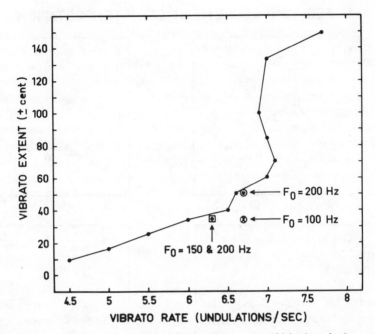

Fig. 13. Values of the vibrato extent at different vibrato rates which gives the impression of best singleness in pitch according to Ramsdell. The circled symbols show maximum values obtained by Gibian (1972) in a test where subjects judged the rate and extent closest to human singing. Ramsdell's data pertains to a frequency of 500 Hz while Gibian's data were obtained with the fundamental frequencies (F_0) indicated.

some singing teachers that not only slow but also fast vibrato rates are tolerable only if the extent is small. It would be interesting to repeat Ramsdell's experiment with modern equipment.

3. Pitch and Fundamental Frequency

Another perceptual aspect of vibrato is perceived pitch. Provided that the rate and extent are kept within acceptable limits, what is the pitch we perceive? This question was studied independently by Shonle (1975) and Sundberg (1972b, 1978b). Sundberg had musically trained subjects match the pitch of a vibrato tone by adjusting the fundamental frequency of a following vibrato-free tone. The two tones, synthetic sung vowels, were identical except for the vibrato. They were presented repeatedly until the adjustment was completed. The vibrato rate was 6.5 undulations per second, and the extent was ±30 cents. Figure 14 shows the results. The ear seems to compute the average of the undulating frequency, and perceived pitch corresponds closely to this average. Shonle worked with sinewave stimuli and arrived at practically the same conclusion. He was also able to show that it is the geometric mean, not the arithmetic mean that Sundberg worked with, that determines the pitch at least in the case of

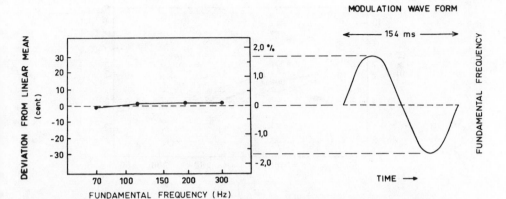

Fig. 14. Left graph: average for six musically trained subjects of the fundamental frequency of a vibrato-free synthetic vowel that gives the same pitch as a vibrato vowel according to Sundberg (1978b). The right graph shows the waveform, rate, and extent of vibrato used. The pitch of a vibrato vowel is seen to coincide almost perfectly with the frequency corresponding to the arithmetic mean of the undulating frequency.

sinewave signals. However, the difference between these two means is insignificant in musically acceptable vibratos.

It is frequently assumed that the vibrato is useful in musical practice because it reduces the demands on accuracy of fundamental frequency (see, e.g., Stevens & Davis, 1938; Winckel, 1967). One possible interpretation of this assumption is that the pitch of a vibrato tone is less accurately perceived than the pitch of a vibrato-free tone. Another interpretation is that the pitch interval between two tones that sound simultaneously can be determined with less accuracy when they have vibrato than when they are vibrato-free.

The first interpretation was tested by Sundberg (1972b, 1978b). The standard deviations obtained when subjects matched the pitch of a vibrato tone with that of a vibrato-free tone were compared with the standard deviations obtained from similar matchings in which both tones lacked vibrato. As can be seen in Fig. 15, the differences between the standard deviations were extremely small and dropped slightly with rising fundamental frequency. This implies that the vibrato reduces pitch-perception accuracy slightly for low frequencies. On the other hand, the effects are too small to explain any measurable effects in musical practice.

The second interpretation has not yet been tested, but it is tempting to speculate about it. If two simultaneous complex tones with harmonic spectra constitute a perfectly tuned consonant interval, some partials of one tone will coincide with some partials of the other tone. Let us consider two tones with fundamental frequencies of 200 and 300 Hz (i.e., producing an interval of a perfect fifth). In this case, every third partial of the lower tone (frequencies: 600, 1200, 1800...Hz) will coincide with every second partial of the upper tone. Let us now mistune the interval by raising the frequency of the upper tone to 300.5Hz. This frequency shift equals 2.9 cents, which

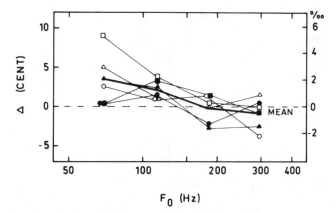

Fig. 15. Effect of a vibrato on pitch perception accuracy at different fundamental frequencies (F_0). Musically trained subjects first matched the pitch of a vibrato-free stimulus tone by adjusting the fundamental frequency of a subsequent response tone which also lacked vibrato. Then, the same experiment was repeated, except that a vibrato was added to the stimulus tone. Δ is the shift of standard deviation thereby obtained. The individual differences are given by the symbols whereas the heavy solid line shows the group average (reprinted from Sundberg, 1978b).

is impossible for almost any listener to detect under any experimental conditions. (The difference limen for frequency is at least 6 cents but may be considerably higher depending on the experimental method, see Rakowski, 1971.) On the other hand, the partials from the two tones will not coincide any longer. For instance, the fourth partial of the upper tone has a frequency of $4 \cdot 300.5 = 1202$ Hz. This partial will give two beats per second with the sixth partial of the lower tone, which has a frequency of 1200 Hz. There are no difficulties in detecting such beats, provided that both partials have similar and sufficiently high amplitudes. The point is that these beats will not occur if both tones have vibrato. Thus, if two voices sing perfectly "straight" (i.e., without vibrato), the demands on accuracy with respect to the fundamental frequency are higher than if they sing with vibrato. However, this advantage seems to be small. In an unpublished thesis work done at the Department of Speech Communication, Royal Institute of Technology in Stockholm, Ågren (1976) had musically trained subjects match different intervals formed by two simultaneous vibrato tones. The intervals were a major second, a major third, a pure fifth, and a pure octave. The tones were synthetic sung vowels. Some of the subjects managed to obtain a standard deviation as low as six cents in repeated matchings of a given interval. If we may believe that mistunings of this small magnitude can be detected even in musical practice, it would seem that the demands on pitch accuracy are extremely high even when the singers use vibrato. It is likely that the vibrato is accepted and used in singing for other reasons, as will be shown later.

Our conclusions are that the pitch of a vibrato tone is practically identical with the pitch of a vibrato-free tone with a fundamental frequency equal to the geometric mean of the fundamental frequency of the vibrato tone. Moreover, the accuracy with which the pitch of a vibrato tone is perceived is not affected to any appreciable extent by the vibrato.

VI. PITCH ACCURACY IN SINGING PRACTICE

A couple of investigations on the perceived pitch of vibrato tones were reviewed earlier. These investigations were made under well-controlled experimental conditions. Do the results obtained that way apply also to musical practice? A study of the accuracy of fundamental frequency in musical practice is likely to answer that question.

In a review of a number of investigations, Seashore (1938) included a wealthy documentation of fundamental frequency recordings of professional performances of various songs. The trend is that long notes are sung with an average fundamental frequency that coincides with the theoretically correct value. This is in agreement with the experimental findings reported previously. On the other hand, they often "begin slightly flat (about 90 cent on the average) and are gradually corrected during the initial 200 msec of the tone." Moreover, a great many of the long tones were observed to change their average frequency in various ways during the course of the tone. Bjørklund (1961) found that such deviations were typical for professional singers as opposed to nonprofessional singers. One possible interpretation of this is that pitch is used as a means of musical expression.

With regard to short tones, the relationship between fundamental frequency and pitch seems to be considerably more complicated. The case is illustrated in Fig. 16 showing the fundamental frequency during a coloratura passage as sung by a male singer. The singer judged this performance to be acceptable. The registration reveals a careful coordination of amplitude, vibrato, and fundamental. Each note takes exactly one vibrato period, and most of the vibrato periods seem to center around the target frequency. However, if we try to apply what has been shown about pitch perception for vibrato tones, we run into trouble. The average fundamental frequency in a coloratura passage does not change stepwise between the target frequencies corresponding to the pitches we perceive; rather the average rises and falls monotonically at an approximately constant rate. Thus, we cannot explain why the passage is perceived as a rapid sequence of discrete pitches. A possible explanation is that the average computation process is interrupted and started again each time there is a minimum in the amplitude and/or frequency curve. However, this is a clear case of an *ad hoc* hypothesis, and no experiments have been performed to support it.

An investigation of interest in this connection should be mentioned here. It has been shown that a glide is perceived as a pitch corresponding to the geometric mean of the extremes of the glide, provided that the product of the frequency change and the time for the change is not greater than five (Nábĕlek, Nábĕlek, & Hirsch, 1970). This case will certainly apply to some cases of short notes in singing, but it does not seem to apply to coloratura cases. For instance, the geometric mean of the upward glide does not agree with the geometric mean of the following downward glide in the same tone

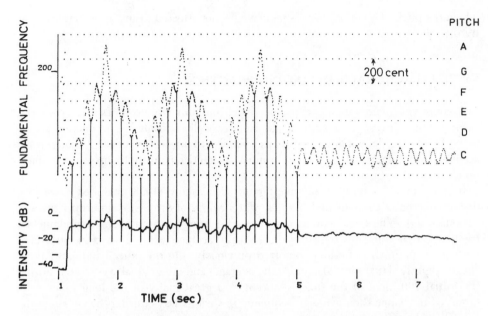

Fig. 16. Synchronous recording of fundamental frequency (upper graph) and overall intensity (lower graph) as measured in a professional singer performing a coloratura passage (C3, D3, E3, F3, G3, F3, E3, D3, C3, D3 . . .). The horizontal dotted lines in the upper graph show the frequencies midway between (i.e., on the geometrical mean of) the scale-tone frequencies calculated from the average frequency of the last note by means of the equally tempered scale.

(see Fig. 16). Moreover, difficulties seem to occur when the pitch is very high. In this case, the pitch changes between the scale tones are wide in terms of absolute frequency. Thus, at high pitches the condition of the product of the change and the time being less than five can hardly be fulfilled any longer. We have to conclude that at present we cannot explain how a coloratura passage can be perceived as a sequence of discrete pitches.

From what was just said, it seems that Seashore (1938) was right in saying that the musical ear is extremely generous and operates in the interpretive mood when it listens to singing. On the other hand, there are certainly limits for this generosity: There is generally an agreement among experts as to what is in tune and what is off pitch. This would lead us to assume that the analyzing properties of the ear are more important to the pitches we perceive from singing than Seashore assumed.

In a thesis work at the Department of Musicology, Stockholm University, Lindgren and Sundberg (1972) studied what musically experienced listeners considered to be off pitch. A tape was prepared including excerpts of phonograph recordings representing different degrees of singing off pitch along with several cases of apparently perfect intonation. A chart with the notation of the excerpts was given to the listeners, who were asked to circle each note they perceived to be off pitch. The fundamental frequency was analyzed by measuring the frequencies of the high overtones in sound spectrograms (sonagrams). The results showed that tones with an average frequency matching the theoretically correct value were mostly accepted as perfect intonation. However, several tones that did not meet this demand were also accepted as correct. Theoretically mistuned tones were accepted remarkably often (1) when they occurred on an unstressed position in the bar, (2) when they were a little sharp, and (3) when they occurred on emotionally prominent places in the text.

This last point again suggests that deviations from the theoretically perfect pitch is used as an expressive means in singing. Support for this assumption can be found in measurements of clarinet playing (Sirker, 1973). Also, it seems typical of music that the composer and the performer build up expectations in listener as to what might follow. Occasionally, minor deviations from what was expected are made. It is the author's belief that such deviations contribute to the excitement we can perceive when we listen to a good performance.

If it is true that deviations from theoretically correct frequencies are used as an expressive means in singing, an important conclusion regarding the benefit of the vibrato can be made. We have seen that vibrato-free representation of mistuned consonant intervals give rise to beats and beats seem to be avoided in most types of music. By adding a vibrato, the singer escapes the beats. Consequently, the vibrato allows him or her more freedom in using deviations from theoretically correct frequencies.

This point is illustrated in Fig. 17. It shows the distribution of fundamental frequencies averaged over approximately the duration of one vibrato cycle. The data pertain to a part of a song performed by a first-rate opera singer. For comparison, a registration of the same song performed by a singing synthesizer is shown (Sundberg, 1978b). The vibrato rate and extent were the same in the synthesis as in the real performance. The scale-tone frequencies are represented by peaks. These peaks are seen to be considerably wider in the case of the real singer than in the case of the synthesizer. This agrees with the assumption that deliberate deviations from expected pitches are used in singing. In the same figure a third distribution is shown. It pertains to the members of a distinguished barbershop quartet. The vibrato is not used in barbershop singing. Hence, the chords must be perfectly tuned to avoid beats, so the singers have very little freedom as regards fundamental frequency. The scale tones are seen to correspond to very narrow peaks. This means that the frequency value corresponding to a given scale tone varies extremely little in barbershop singing. It is likely that this is a consequence of the absence of vibrato. Although we need more measurements on vibrato-free singing, we may hypothesize that the vibrato offers the singer a freedom in the choice of fundamental frequencies and that this freedom is used for purposes of musical expression.

VII. PHRASING AND EMOTION

One of the most essential things about singing (and music in general) is the truly remarkable fact that a performer is able to use sound signals in such a way that phrases rather than sequences of unrelated tones are communicated to the listener. This

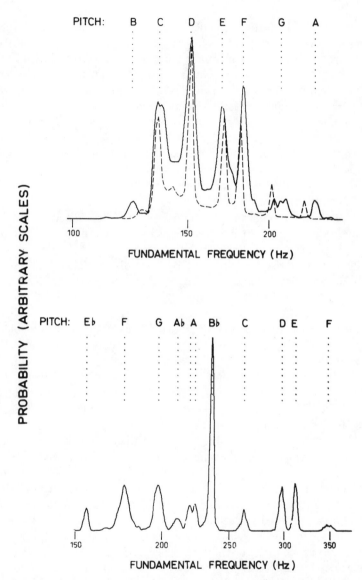

Fig. 17. Distribution of fundamental frequencies in singing. The upper graph pertain to a professional singer (solid curve) and a singing synthesizer (dashed curve) performing the same song. In both cases the fundamental frequency was averaged with a running time window corresponding to one vibrato cycle, approximately. Thus, the distributions should be identical if the singer was as accurate with respect to fundamental frequency as the synthesizer. The lower graph was obtained from a distinguished barbershop quartet (Happiness Emporium, Minneapolis) singing a chord progression. Note that the widths of the scale-tone peaks are generally much narrower in the barbershop singers who lack vibrato, than in the opera singer, who has vibrato. Note also that the pitch A is represented by two peaks in the case of the barbershop quartet presumably because it appeared several times in the song with different harmonic functions.

would be the perceptual effect of phrasing. Moreover, the performer can add something to these signals that evokes an emotional experience in the listener. Although this must be considered the essence of singing and music, we know little about how this effect is achieved. Two studies will be mentioned even though they merely touch on the problem.

Seashore (1938) regarded phrasing as a temporal phenomenon. He compared the durations of beats, bars, and phrases in a couple of performances of the same song. It turned out to be difficult to detect any consistent pattern in the deviations from the average durations of musical segments such as bars. Seashore's comment is "The singer's interpretation is accomplished by artistic deviations from this average.... In none of these singers is there the slightest approach to an even time for a measure." Thus, Seashore was convinced that these deviations are by no means random.

Sundberg (1978b) started from the hypothesis that the structure of the music is mirrored in a performance perceived as musically acceptable. Such a mirroring must be accomplished by means of a set of rules that operate on the structure. In other words, the application of the rules requires information about the structure, which means that the performer must be consciously or unconsciously aware of this structure. One question is how the singer announces that a particular sequence of notes belongs together and constitutes a structural unit, such as a phrase. A singer's performance of a song was analyzed, and certain regularities were observed. These regularities were formulated as tentative rules. The perceptual relevance of these rules was tested by implementing them one by one in a rule system used to control a singing synthesizer's performance of the same song. In sound examples, published with the investigation, one can experience how the different rules affect the performance. An apparent effect was that the tones sounded unrelated to each other as long as they did not form a long-term amplitude event. Thus, by introducing the same amplitude pattern that comprises an entire phrase, the tones in the phrase sound as if they belong together. This is a clear case in which systematic deviations from an average (namely the amplitude average) result in a specific musical effect. We can assume that systematic deviations from other averages, such as theoretically correct fundamental frequency or duration, are used analogously in singing and that the result is bringing the performance to an artistic agreement with the structure. However, a considerable amount of research is needed to corroborate this assumption.

The effects of the emotional content of the text on vocal performance has been formally investigated by Kotlyar and Morozov (1976). Eleven professional singers repeatedly performed 16 excerpts from various songs so as to represent different emotional atmospheres: joy, sorrow, fear, anger, and neutral. By means of a listening test, it was confirmed that the singers managed to convey the desired emotional information in performing these excerpts. A series of acoustic aspects of their performances were studied. It was found that each of the five emotions studied was manifested acoustically in different ways. For instance, the average syllable duration was shortest in fear and longest in sorrow. Fear and neutral were associated with the longest and the shortest unvoiced intersyllabic segments. Anger was performed with the loudest sound levels and fear with the lowest sound levels. Sorrow had slow-tone onsets, and anger and fear had rapid-tone onsets. Thus, each of the five emotions studied showed a specific pattern of acoustic characteristics.

The authors also tried to discover to what extent these characteristics were not only necessary but also sufficient to convey the emotional information. Thereby, they used an "artificial signal comprising a tone modulated by the amplitude of the envelope (observed in the performances), i.e. a signal deprived of such informative attributes as intonational and spectral characteristics." This amplitude-modulated signal was presented to 11 listeners who tried to identify the "possible emotional content." The results suggested that the amplitude-modulation characteristics of the voice are particularly efficient in communicating fear, sorrow, and anger (80, 66, and 60% correct identification) while neutral and joy seem to be signaled mainly along some other acoustic dimensions (24 and 8% correct identification).

It does not appear farfetched to assume that the acoustic characteristics used in singing in order to communicate an emotional atmosphere are the same as those which are used for the same purpose in speech. This assumption is supported by studies of emotional speech published by Fónagy (e.g., 1962, 1976). Moreover, it seems reasonable to hypothesize, as Fónagy does, that such characteristics are merely the acoustical reflections of general patterns of body movements. For instance, we expect no rapid body movements from a truly sad person, and, of course, we would not expect any rapid movements in those laryngeal structures that regulate voice fundamental frequency in that person. There seems to be reason to believe that vocal behavior under the influence of emotions is the mere translation into the acoustical domain of such general patterns of body movements. If this is correct, it seems to follow that our ability to appreciate singing should partly rely on our ability to infer the emotional state of another person from the person's way of speaking.

VIII. CONCLUDING REMARKS

In the present chapter two types of fact about singing have been considered. One is the choice of acoustic characteristics of vowel sounds that singers learn to adopt and that represent typical deviations from normal speech. Three examples of those characteristics have been discussed: (1) the pitch-dependent choice of formant frequencies that concerns high-pitched singing primarily in female voices, (2) the "singer's formant" that typically occurs in all voiced sounds in the male singing voice; and (3) the vibrato that occurs in both male and female singing. In all three examples we have strong reasons to assume that they serve a specific purpose. The pitch-dependent formant frequencies as well as the singer's formant are both resonatory phenomena that increase the audibility of the singer's voice when the orchestral accompaniment is loud. As resonatory phenomena occur independently of vocal effort, the increase in audibility is gained without expenses in terms of vocal effort; hence, a likely purpose in both these cases is vocal economy. The vibrato serves the purpose of allowing the singer a greater freedom in the choice of fundamental frequency as it eliminates beats with the sound of the accompaniment. Thus, in these three cases we see that *singing differs from speech in a highly adequate manner.* It is tempting to speculate that such characteristics have developed as a result of evolution; the singers who developed them became successful, and hence their technique was copied by other singers.

A second kind of fact about singing discussed in this chapter is the acoustic correlates of various voice classifications that can be assumed to be based on perception. Such classifications are not only tenor, baritone, and bass, etc., but also vocal effort (e.g., piano, mezzopiano, etc.) and register. We have seen that in most of these cases it was hard to find a common acoustic denominator, because the acoustic characteristics of the categories vary with vowel and fundamental frequency. Rather, the common denominator exists within the voice organ. In the case of the male voice classification—tenor, baritone, and bass—the characteristic differences in formant frequency could be assumed to result from morphological differences in the vocal tract. The same is true for vocal effort and register, because they reflect differences in the control and operation of the vocal folds. Therefore, we may say that these examples of voice classification seem to rely on the function of the voice organ rather than on the acoustic properties of voice sounds. This is probably revealing as to the way in which we perceive singing voices. We seem to interpret the sounds in terms of how the voice organ was used in producing the sounds.

With regard to artistic interpretation, it seems that it contains at least two different components. One is the marking of structural constituents of the music. This requirement on the performance of songs thus seems to be common to both speech and music, and probably, it has a perceptual background. The other component is the signaling of the emotional atmosphere underlying the text and the music. Even in this respect perception of singing seems closely related to perception of speech. The coding of emotions in speech and singing would be similar and probably founded on a "body language" for communication of emotions. If this is true, our acquaintance with human emotional behavior and particularly speech serves as a reference in our decoding of the emotional information in the sounds from a singer's voice.

ACKNOWLEDGMENTS

Si Felicetti of the Department of Speech Communication, KTH (Royal Institute of Technology) Stockholm, is acknowledged for her expert assistance in typing and editing this chapter. Its preparation was in part supported by the following funds: the Swedish Council for Planning and Coordination of Research, the Swedish Council for Research in the Humanities and Social Sciences, and the Swedish Natural Science Research Council.

REFERENCES

Ågren, K. Alt- och tenorröst och harmoniska intervall mellan dem. Thesis work in speech communication. Department of Speech Communication, KTH, Stockholm, 1976.

Ågren, K., & Sundberg, J. An acoustic comparison of alto and tenor voices. *Journal of Research in Singing*, 1978, *1* (3), 26–32.

Appelman, D. R. *The science of vocal pedagogy.* London: Indiana University Press, 1967.

Bartholomew, W. T. A physical definition of 'good voice quality' in the male voice. *Journal of the Acoustical Society of America*, 1934, *6*, 25–33.

Bjørklund, A. Analyses of soprano voices. *Journal of the Acoustical Society of America*, 1961, 33, 575–582.

Carlson, R., Fant, G., & Granström, B. Two-formant models, pitch, and vowel perception. In G. Fant & M. A. A. Tatham (Eds.), *Auditory analysis and perception of speech*. New York: Academic Press, 1975, pp. 55–82.

Cleveland, T. F. Acoustic properties of voice timbre types and their influence on voice classification. *Journal of the Acoustical Society of America*, 1977, *61*, 1622–1629.

Coleman, R. O. A comparison of the contributions of two voice quality characteristics to the perception of maleness and femaleness in the voice. *Journal of Speech and Hearing Research*, 1976, *19*, 168–180.

Colton, R. H. Spectral characteristics of the modal and falsetto registers, *Folia Phoniatrica*, 1972, *24*, 337–344.

Colton, R. H., & Hollien, H. Perceptual differentiation of the modal and falsetto registers. *Folia Phoniatrica*, 1973, *25*, 270–280.

Dmitriev, L., & Kiselev, A. Relationship between the formant structure of different types of singing voices and the dimensions of the supraglottal cavities. *Folia Phoniatrica*, 1979, *31*, 238–241.

Fant, G. *Acoustic theory of speech production*. The Hague: Mouton, 1960.

Fant, G. *Speech sounds and features*. Cambridge, Massachusetts: MIT Press, 1973.

Fant, G. Non-uniform vowel normalization. *Speech Transmission Laboratory, Quarterly Progress and Status Report*, 1975, No. 2–3, 1–19.

Flanagan, J. L. *Speech analysis, synthesis and perception*. Berlin and New York: Springer-Verlag, 1965.

Fónagy, I. Mimik auf glottaler Ebene. *Phonetica*, 1962, *8*, 209–219.

Fónagy, I. La mimique buccale. *Phonetica*, 1976, *33*, 31–44.

Gibian, G. L. Synthesis of sung vowels. *Quarterly Progress Report, Massachusetts Institute of Technology*, 1972, No. 104, 243–247.

Hollien, H. On vocal registers. *Journal of Phonetics*, 1974, *2*, 125–143.

Hollien, H., Keister, E., & Hollien, P. A. Experimental data on 'singer's formant.' *Journal of the Acoustical Society of America, Supplement 1*, 1978, *64*, S171 (Abstract).

Howie, J., & Delattre, P. An experimental study of the effect of pitch on the intelligibility of vowels. *The National Association of Teachers of Singing Bulletin*, 1962, *18:4*, 6–9.

Kotlyar, G. M., & Morozov, V. P. Acoustical correlates of the emotional content of vocalized speech. *Soviet Physics Acoustics*, 1976, *22*, 208–211.

Large, J. Towards an integrated physiologic-acoustic theory of vocal registers. *National Association of Teachers of Singing Bulletin*, February-March 1972, 18–36.

Large, J. Acoustic-perceptual evaluation of register equalization. *National Association of Teachers of Singing Bulletin*, October 1974, 20–41.

Large, J., Iwata, S., & von Leden, H. The primary register transition in singing. *Folia Phoniatrica*, 1970, *22*, 385–396.

Large, J., Iwata, S., & von Leden, H. The male operatic head register versus falsetto. *Folia Phoniatrica*, 1972, *24*, 19–29.

Large, J. & Shipp, T. The effect of certain parameters on the perception of vocal registers, *National Association of Teachers of Singing Bulletin*, October 1969, 12–15.

Lerman, J. W., & Duffy, R. J. Recognition of falsetto voice quality. *Folia Phoniatrica*, 1970, *22*, 21–27.

Lindblom, B., & Sundberg, J. Acoustical consequences of lip, tongue, jaw, and larynx movement. *Journal of the Acoustical Society of America*, 1971, *50*, 1166–1179.

Lindgren, H., & Sundberg, A., Grundfrekvensförlopp och falsksång. Thesis work, Department of Musicology, Stockholm University, 1972 (stencil).

Monsen, R. B., & Engebretson, A. M. Study of vibrations in the male and female glottal wave. *Journal of the Acoustical Society of America*, 1977, *62*, 981–993.

Morozov, V. P. Intelligibility in singing as a function of fundamental voice pitch. *Soviet Physics Acoustics*, 1965, *10*, 279–283.

Nábělek, I. V., Nábělek, A. K., & Hirsh, I. J. Pitch of tone bursts of changing frequency. *Journal of the Acoustical Society of America*, 1970, *48*, 536-553.

Nelson, H. D., & Tiffany, W. R. The intellegibility of song. *The National Association of Teachers of Singing Bulletin*, December 1968, 22-33.

Nordström, P-E. Female and infant vocal tracts simulated from male area functions. *Journal of Phonetics*, 1977, *5*, 81-92.

Plomp, R. Timbre as a multidimensional attribute of complex tones. In R. Plomp & G. F. Smoorenburg (Eds.), *Frequency analysis and periodicity detection in hearing*. Leiden: Sijthoff, 1970. Pp. 397-414.

Plomp, R. Continuity effects in the perception of sounds with interfering noise bursts. Paper given at the *Symposium sur la Psychoacoustique musicale, IRCAM, Paris*, July 1977.

Rakowski, A. Pitch discrimination at the threshold of hearing. *Proceedings of the 7th International Congress on Acoustics, Budapest*, 1971, *3*, 373-376.

Ramsdell, D. A. The psycho-physics of frequency modulation. Thesis, Harvard University (not seen, reported by F. Winckel, In *Music, sound, and sensation*. New York: Dover, 1967).

Rasch, R. A. The perception of simultaneous notes such as in polyphonic music. *Acustica*, 1978, *40*, 21-33.

Rothenberg, M. The glottal volume velocity waveform during loose and tight voiced glottal adjustments. In A. Rigault & R. Charbonneau (Eds.), *Proceedings of the 7th International Congress of Phonetic Sciences, Montreal, 1971*. The Hague: Mouton, 1972. Pp. 380-388.

Rubin, H. J., Le Cover, M., & Vennard, W. Vocal intensity, subglottic pressure and airflow relationship in singers, *Folia Phoniatrica*, 1967, *19*, 393-413.

Russo, V., & Large, J. Psychoacoustic study of the Bel Canto model for register equalization: male chest and falsetto. *Journal of Research in Singing*, 1978, *1* (3), 1-25.

Rzhevkin, S. N. Certain results of the analysis of a singer's voice. *Soviet Physics Acoustics*, 1956, *2*, 215-220.

Scotto di Carlo, N. Etude acoustique et auditive des facteurs d'intelligibilité de la voix chantée. In A. Rigault & R. Charbonneau (Eds.), *Proceedings of the 7th International Congress of Phonetic Sciences, Montreal, 1971*. The Hague, Paris: Mouton, 1972. Pp. 1017-1023.

Scotto di Carlo, N. Influence de l'articulation sur la musicalité de la phrase chantée. *Travaux de l'Institut de Phonétique d'Aix*, 1976, No. 3, 117-146.

Seashore, C. E. *Psychology of music*. New York: McGraw-Hill, 1938 & New York: Dover, 1967.

Shonle, J. I. Perceived pitch of vibrato tones. *Journal of the Acoustical Society of America*, 1975, *58*, S132 (Abstract).

Simon, P., Lips, H., & Brock, G. Etude sonagraphique et analyse acoustique en temps reel de la voix chantée a partir de differentes techniques vocales. *Travaux de l'Institut de Phonétique de Strasbourg*, 1972, No. 4, 219-276.

Sirker, U. Objektive Frequenzmessung und subjektive Tonhöhenempfinung bei Musikinstrumentklängen. *Swedish Journal of Musicology*, 1973, *55*, 47-58.

Slawson, A. W. Vowel quality and musical timbre as functions of spectrum envelope and fundamental frequency. *Journal of the Acoustical Society of America*, 1968, *43*, 87-101.

Smith, L. A., & Scott, B. L. Increasing the intelligibility of sung vowels. *Journal of the Acoustical Society of America*, 1980, *67*, 1795-1797.

Stevens, S. S., & Davis, H. *Hearing, its psychology and physiology*. New York: Wiley, 1938.

Stumpf, C. *Die Sprachlaute*. Berlin and New York: Springer-Verlag, 1926.

Sundberg, J. Formant structure and articulation of spoken and sung vowels. *Folia Phoniatrica*, 1970, *22*, 28-48.

Sundberg, J. Production and function of the 'singing formant'. In H. Glahn, S. Sørensen, & P. Ryom (Eds), *Report of the 11th Congress of the International Musicological Society*. Copenhagen: Editor Wilhelm Hansen, 1972, 679-686. (a)

Sundberg, J. Pitch of synthetic sung vowels. *Speech Transmission Laboratory, Quarterly Progress and Status Report*, 1972, No. 1, 34-44. (b) Later revised and published as Effects of the vibrato and the 'singing formant' on pitch. *Musicologica Slovaca* (in Memoriam M. Filip) 1978, *6*, 51-69. (b)

Sundberg, J. The source spectrum in professional singing. *Folia Phoniatrica*, 1973, *25*, 71-90.

Sundberg, J. Articulatory interpretation of the 'singing formant'. *Journal of the Acoustical Society of America*, 1974, *55*, 838–844.

Sundberg, J. Formant technique in a professional female singer. *Acustica*, 1975, *32*, 89–96.

Sundberg, J. Vibrato and vowel identification. *Archives of Acoustics (Polish Academy of Sciences)*, 1977, *2*, 257–266. (a)

Sundberg, J. Singing and timbre. In *Music room acoustics*. Stockholm: Royal Swedish Academy of Music Publications (Volume 17), 1977. Pp. 57–81. (b)

Sundberg, J. Studies of the soprano voice. *Journal of Research in Singing*, 1977, *1*, (1), 25–35. (c)

Sundberg, J. *Musikens ljudlära*. (2nd ed.) Stockholm: Proprius Förlag, 1978. (a)

Sundberg, J. Synthesis of singing. *Swedish Journal of Musicology*, 1978, *60*. (b)

Sundberg, J. & Gauffin, J. Waveform and spectrum of the glottal voice source. *Speech Transmission Laboratory, Quarterly Progress and Status Report*, 1978, No. 2–3, 35–50.

Terhardt, E., On the perception of periodic sound fluctuations (roughness). *Acustica*, 1974, *30*, 201–213.

Weait, C., & Shea, J. B. Vibrato: an audio-video-fluorographic investigation of a bassoonist. *Applied Radiology*, January–February 1977, *6:1*, 89–90, 148.

Vennard, W. *Singing, the mechanism and the technic*. (2nd ed.) New York: Fischer, 1967.

Vennard, W., Hirano, M., Ohala, J., & Fritzell, B. A series of four electromyographic studies. *National Association of Teachers of Singing Bulletin*, October 1970, 16–21; December 1970, 30–37; February–March 1971, 26–32; May–June 1971, 22–30.

Winckel, F. Physikalische Kriterien für objektive Stimmbeurteilung. *Folia Phoniatrica*, 1953, *5 Separatum*, 231–252.

Winckel, F. *Music, Sound and sensation. A modern exposition*. New York: Dover Publications, 1967.

Zwicker, F., & Feldtkeller, R. *Das Ohr als Nachrichtenempfänger*. (2nd ed.) Stuttgart: Hirzel Verlag, 1967.

4

Grouping Mechanisms in Music

Diana Deutsch

I. Introduction 99
II. Grouping Principles 100
III. Two-Channel Listening to Melodic Sequences 101
    A. The Scale Illusion 102
    B. Temporal Relationships as Determinants of Grouping 104
    C. The Octave Illusion 108
    D. Handedness Correlates 114
    E. Melody Perception from Phase-Shifted Tones 116
    F. Discussion 117
IV. Channeling of Rapid Sequences of Single Tones 118
    A. Grouping by Frequency Proximity 118
    B. Temporal Coherence as a Function of Frequency Proximity and Tempo 119
    C. Grouping by Frequency Proximity Builds with Repetition 120
    D. Grouping by Frequency Proximity and the Perception of Temporal Relationships 122
    E. Grouping by Good Continuation 124
    F. Grouping by Timbre 124
    G. Grouping by Amplitude 126
    H. Grouping by Temporal Proximity 126
    I. Perceptual Replacement of Missing Sounds 127
V. Voluntary Attention 127
VI. Conclusion 130
    References 130

I. INTRODUCTION

Music presents us with a complex, rapidly changing acoustic spectrum, often re-sulting from the superposition of sounds from many different sources. The primary task that our auditory system has to perform is to interpret this spectrum in terms of the behavior of external objects. This is analogous to the task performed by the visual system when it interprets the mosaic of light patterns impinging on the retina in terms of objects producing them (Gregory, 1970; Sutherland, 1973). Such a view of perception as a process of "unconscious inference" was proposed in the last century by Helmholtz (see Hemholtz, 1925), and we shall see that many phenomena of music perception are readily interpretable in this light.

Issues concerning organizational processes in music divide themselves basically into two. The first is the following. Given that we are presented with a set of first-order acoustic elements, how are these combined so as to form separate groupings? If all first-order elements were indiscriminately linked together, auditory shape-recognition operations could not be performed. There must, therefore, exist a set of mechanisms that permits the formation of simultaneous and sequential linkages between certain elements, and inhibits the formation of such linkages between others. Simple mechanisms underlying such linkages are explored in the present chapter. Second, we may enquire into the ways in which higher order abstractions are derived from combinations of first-order elements so as to lead to perceptual equivalences and similarities. This issue is explored in the next chapter, and it is assumed that such abstractions also form bases for grouping.

II. GROUPING PRINCIPLES

There are two basic questions involved in considering the mechanisms involved in grouping musical stimuli into configurations. The first concerns the stimulus *attributes* along which grouping principles operate. When presented with a complex sequence, our auditory system may group stimuli according to some rule based on the frequencies of its components, on their amplitudes, on the spatial locations from which they emanate, or on the basis of some complex attribute such as timbre. As we shall see, all these attributes can function as bases for organization and grouping in music. Furthermore, the principles determining what attribute is followed for any given sequence are both complex and rigid. We shall see, for example, that with one type of sequence, organization on the basis of frequency uniformly occurs; yet given a slight change in this sequence, organization on the basis of spatial location may occur instead. Such differences in organization can be interpreted in terms of strategies most likely to lead to the correct conclusions in interpreting our environment.

Second, we may pose the following question: Assuming that organization takes place on the basis of some dimension such as frequency, what are the *principles* governing grouping along this dimension? The Gestalt psychologists proposed that we group stimuli into configurations on the basis of various simple principles (Wertheimer, 1923). One of these is the principle of Proximity, which states that nearer elements are grouped together in preference to those that are spaced farther apart. An example of this principle is shown on Figure 1A, where the closer dots appear to be grouped together in pairs. Another is the principle of Similarity, which is illustrated on Figure 1B. Here, configurations are formed out of like elements, so that we perceive one set of vertical rows formed by the filled circles and another set formed by the unfilled circles. A third is the principle of Good Continuation, which states that elements that

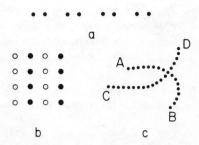

Fig. 1. Illustrations of the Gestalt principles of Proximity, Similarity, and Good Continuation.

follow each other in a given direction are perceived together. For instance, we perceptually group the dots in Figure 1C so as to form the two lines AB and CD. A fourth
principle, known as Common Fate, states that elements which move in the same
direction are perceived together.

It has been demonstrated that these principles are important determinants of grouping in visual arrays, and we shall see that this is true of music also. It seems reasonable
to suppose—as argued by Gregory (1970), Sutherland (1973), Hochberg (1974), and
Bregman (1978)—that grouping in conformity with such principles enables us to
interpret our environment most effectively. To give some examples, in the case of
vision, proximal elements are most likely to belong to the same object than elements
that are spaced farther apart. The same line of reasoning holds for similar elements
compared with those that are dissimilar. In the case of hearing, similar sounds are
likely to be emanating from the same source and different sounds from different
sources. A sound sequence that changes smoothly in frequency is likely to be emanating from a single source. Components of a complex sound spectrum that rise and fall
in synchrony are also likely to be emanating from the same source.

One more point should be made before reviewing the experimental evidence. When
we hear a tone, we attribute a fundamental pitch, a loudness, a timbre; and we hear
the tone at a given location. Each tonal percept may therefore be described as a bundle
of attribute values. If our perception is veridical, this bundle reflects the location and
characteristics of the sound emitted. We shall see, however, that in situations where
more than one tone is presented at a time, these bundles of attribute values may
fragment and recombine in other ways, so that illusory percepts result. Perceptual
grouping in music is therefore not simply a matter of linking different sets of stimuli
together; rather it involves a process whereby these stimuli are fragmented into their
separate attributes, followed by a process of perceptual synthesis in which the different
attribute values are recombined.

III. TWO-CHANNEL LISTENING TO MELODIC
SEQUENCES

The two-channel listening technique is particularly useful for studying organizational processes in music, since it enables different attributes to be set in opposition to

each other as bases for grouping. For example, grouping by spatial location may be set in opposition to grouping by frequency or by amplitude. Similarly, different principles governing grouping along a given dimension may be set in opposition to each other; for example, the principle of Proximity may be opposed to the principle of Good Continuation. The experiments to be described show that the nature of the stimulus configuration critically determines what grouping principle is adopted, and indicate that there are complex and rigid rules of precedence for these principles.

A. The Scale Illusion

The configuration that produced the scale illusion is shown in Fig. 2A. It can be seen that this consisted of a major scale, presented simultaneously in both ascending and descending form. When a tone from the ascending scale was delivered to one ear, a tone from the descending scale was simultaneously delivered to the other ear, and successive tones in each scale alternated from ear to ear (Deutsch, 1975b).

This sequence was found to give rise to various illusory percepts. The majority of listeners perceived two melodic lines, a higher one and a lower one, that moved in contrary motion. Further, the higher tones all appeared to be emanating from one earphone and the lower tones from the other (Fig. 2B). When the earphone positions were reversed, there was often no corresponding change in the percept. So, it appeared to the listener that the earphone that had been producing the higher tones was now producing the lower tones, and that the earphone that had been producing the lower tones was now producing the higher tones. A minority of listeners heard instead only a single stream of four tones, corresponding to the higher tones in the sequence, and little or nothing of the rest of the sequence was perceived.

So in considering what stimulus *attribute* was here used as a basic for grouping, we find that organization by spatial location never occurred; rather, organization was

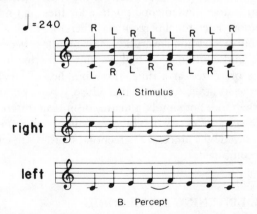

Fig. 2. (A) Representation of the configuration producing the scale illusion. This basic pattern was repetitively presented 10 times without pause. (B) Representation of the illusory percept most commonly obtained (from Deutsch, 1975b).

always on the basis of frequency. Second, in considering what grouping *principle* was adopted, we find that organization was always on the basis of frequency priximity. Listeners heard either two melodic lines, one corresponding to the higher tones and the other to the lower, or they heard the higher tones alone. No listener reported a full ascending or descending scale as a component of the sequence; so that grouping by Good Continuation never occurred.

Butler (1979a) has demonstrated that these findings may be extended to a broad range of musical situations. He presented the configuration shown in Fig. 2A to music students through spatially-separated loudspeakers, rather than earphones, in a free sound-field environment. The listeners notated separately the sequence that they heard as emanating from the speaker on their right and the sequence that they heard as emanating from the speaker on their left. In some conditions the stimuli were generated on a piano. Further, timbral and loudness differences were sometimes introduced between the stimuli presented through the different speakers. Butler found that despite these variations, virtually all responses reflected channeling by frequency proximity, so that higher and lower melodic lines were perceived, each apparently emanating from a different speaker. A further interesting finding was that when timbral differences were introduced between the tones presented through the two speakers, a new tone quality was perceived, but it seemed to be emanating simultaneously from both speakers. So, not only were the spatial locations of the tones perceptually rearranged in accordance with frequency proximity, but their timbres were rearranged also.

To determine whether these findings generalize to other melodic configurations, Butler presented listeners with the two-part contrapuntal patterns shown in Figs. 3a and 3b. Virtually all responses again reflected grouping by frequency range. For both configurations a perceptual reorganization occurred, so that a melody corresponding to the higher tones appeared to be emanating from one earphone or speaker and a melody corresponding to the lower tones from the other (Figs. 3c and 3d).

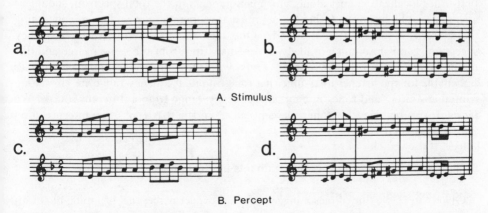

Fig. 3. (A) Two-part melodic patterns as presented to subjects through left and right earphones or speakers. (B) The patterns as most commonly notated by the subjects (from Butler, 1979a).

Fig. 4.   Passage from the final movement of Tschaikowsky's Sixth (*Pathetique*) Symphony. The combination of the Violin I and Violin II melodies produces the percept shown on the upper right. The combination of the viola and violincello melodies produces the percept shown on the lower right (from Butler, 1979b).

Butler (1979b) further drew attention to an interesting passage from the final movement of Tschaikowsky's Sixth (*Pathetique*) Symphony. As shown in Fig. 4, the theme and accompaniment are each distributed between the two violin parts. However, the theme is heard as coming from one set of instruments and the accompaniment as from the other. Whether it was Tschaikovsky's intention to produce a perceptual illusion here, or whether he expected the listener to hear the theme and accompaniment waft from one set of instruments to the other, we may never know!

How should such gross mislocalization effects be explained? Our acoustic environment is very complex, and the assignment of sounds to their sources is made difficult by the presence of echoes and reverberation (Benade, 1976). So, when a sound mixture is presented such that both ears are stimulated simultaneously, it is unclear from first-order localization cues alone which components of the total spectrum should be assigned to which source. Other factors must also operate to provide cues concerning the sources of these different sounds. One such factor is similarity of frequency spectrum. Similar sounds are likely to be emanating from the same source and different sounds from different sources. Thus, with these musical examples it becomes reasonable for the listener to assume that tones in one frequency range are emanating from one source, and tones in another frequency range from a different source. We therefore reorganize the tones perceptually on the basis of this interpretation (Deutsch, 1975a).

B. Temporal Relationships as Determinants of Grouping

Given the above line of reasoning, we should expect perceptual grouping of simultaneous sequences to be strongly influenced by the salience of first-order localization cues. Under the conditions we have been considering such localization cues were weak, since input was always to both ears simultaneously. However, under conditions where such cues are strong and unambiguous, organization by spatial location should be expected to take precedence over organization by frequency proximity. This should be the case, for instance, where the signals to the two ears are clearly separated in time.

An experiment was therefore performed to examine perceptual grouping as a function of the temporal relationships between the signals arriving at the two ears (Deutsch, 1978a, 1979). Listeners identified melodic patterns in which the component tones switched between the ears. Conditions were compared where input was to one ear at a time and where input was to the two ears simultaneously. Such simultaneity of input was achieved by presenting a drone to the ear opposite the ear receiving the component of the melody. In order to control for the effect of the drone apart from its providing a simultaneous input to the opposite ear, a further condition was included in which the drone and the melody component were presented to the same ear. In a fourth condition the melody was presented binaurally.

It was predicted that in the conditions in which input was to one ear at a time, identification of the melodic patterns should be difficult, reflecting perceptual grouping by spatial location. However, in the conditions where both ears received input simultaneously, identification of the melodic patterns should be much easier, and should reflect organization by frequency proximity in the presence of the contralateral drone.

The experiment employed the two melodic patterns shown in Fig. 5. On each trial, one of these patterns was presented ten times without pause, and listeners identified on forced choice which of these had been presented.

The four conditions of the experiment, together with the error rates in each, are shown in Fig. 6. It can be seen that when the melody was presented to both ears at the same time, identification performance was excellent. However, when the component tones of the melody switched from ear to ear with no accompanying drone, a severe performance decrement occurred. Yet when the drone was presented to the ear *opposite* the ear receiving the melody component, the performance level was again very high, even though the melody was still switching from ear to ear. This result cannot be attributed to processing the harmonic relationships between the drone and the melody

Fig. 5. Basic melodic patterns employed in experiment to study the effects on melody identification of rapid switching between ears. All tones were 30 msec in duration, and tones within a sequence were separated by 100-msec pauses (Deutsch, 1979).

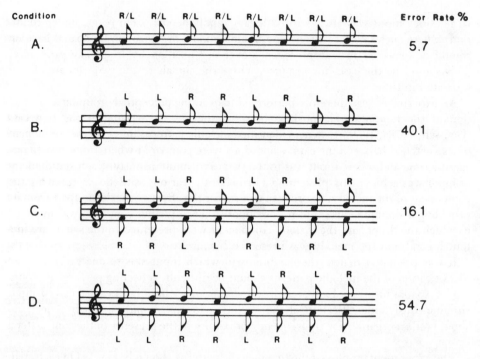

Fig. 6. Examples of distributions between ears of melodic pattern and drone in different conditions of the experiment. See text for details (from Deutsch, 1979).

components because when the drone was presented to the *same* ear as the one receiving the component of the melody, performance was below chance.

This experiment therefore demonstrates that with tones coming from different spatial locations, temporal relationships between them are important determinants of grouping. When signals are coming from two locations simultaneously, it is easy to integrate the information arriving at the two ears into a single perceptual stream. But when the signals coming from the two locations are clearly separated in time, subjective grouping by spatial location is so powerful as to prevent the listener from combining the signals to produce an integrated percept.

A related experiment comparing the effects of simultaneity with nonsimultaneity of input to the two ears was performed by Judd (1979). In this experiment listeners were presented with four-tone melodic patterns whose components alternated from ear to ear. Judd found that presenting noise to the ear contralateral to the ear receiving the melody component resulted in enhanced recognition performance. He also proposed an interpretation in terms of competing channeling mechanisms, reasoning that the strong localization cues present in the no-noise condition induced channeling by spatial location, and that the weaker localization cues due to the noise resulted in channeling by frequency proximity instead.

In the study by Deutsch (1979) the effects of onset–offset asynchrony between the tones arriving at the two ears were also examined. Such temporal overlaps between signals commonly occur in normal listening, and it was predicted that results here should be intermediate between those where the input to the two ears was strictly simultaneous and those where these inputs were clearly separated in time. Such findings were indeed obtained: performance levels under conditions of asynchrony were significantly worse than where the melody components and the contralateral drone were strictly simultaneous, yet significantly better than were the melody switched between ears without an accompanying drone. This is as expected from the present line of reasoning. Temporal similarities in the waveform envelopes of two simultaneous signals are important indicators that these signals are emanating from the same source (following the "principle of Common Fate"), and discrepancies would indicate that the signals are emanating from different sources (Tobias, 1972). We should therefore expect that asynchronies between the signals arriving at the two ears would increase the tendency to treat these signals as emanating from different sources, and so permit less integration of the pattern distributed between the two ears.

Two related experiments on the effects of asynchrony should here be cited. Rasch (1978) investigated the threshold for perception of a high tone when it was accompanied by a low tone. He found that delaying the onset of the low tone relative to the high tone produced a substantial lowering of threshold. Further, under conditions of asynchrony the subjective percept was strikingly altered, so that the two tones stood apart clearly rather than being fused into a single percept. Rasch advanced an interpretation of his findings along lines very similar to those presented here.

Rasch also noted that although temporal asynchrony had strong perceptual effects, it was not recognized as such by the listeners. The same observation was made in the present experiment. In the asynchronous conditions, one obtained the subjective impression of a "plopping" sound at the onset and offset of the tones, but it was difficult to describe this percept further. The strong effect found here due to temporal asynchrony was therefore not based on conscious inference.

Another related experiment is that of Bregman and Pinker (1978). These authors presented a simultaneous two-tone complex in alternation with a third tone, and introduced various conditions of onset–offset asynchrony between the simultaneous tones. They found that with increasing asynchrony there was an increased likelihood that one of the simultaneous tones would form a melodic stream with the third tone. Bregman and Pinker reasoned that asynchrony between the simultaneous tones resulted in a decreased tendency for these tones to be treated as emanating from the same source, and so facilitated a sequential organization by frequency proximity between one of these simultaneous tones and the alternating tone.

These various experiments on the effects of asynchrony bear on an issue that was raised a century ago by von Helmholtz. In his book *On the Sensations of Tone* (1885), he posed the question of how, given the complex, rapidly changing spectrum produced by several instruments playing simultaneously, we are able to reconstruct our musical environment so that some components fuse to produce a single sound impression, while others are heard as separate melodic lines which may be simultaneously perceived. For the latter instance, he posed the further question as to the basis on which such simultaneous melodic lines are constructed. Thus he wrote:

> Now there are many circumstances which assist us first in separating the musical tones arising from different sources, and secondly, in keeping together the partial tones of each separate source. Thus when one musical tone is heard for some time before being joined by the second, and then the second continues after the first has ceased, the separation in sound is facilitated by the succession of time. We have already heard the first musical tone by itself, and hence know immediately what we have to deduct from the compound effect for the effect of this first tone. Even when several parts proceed in the same rhythm in polyphonic music, the mode in which the tones of different instruments and voices commence, the nature of their increase in force, the certainty with which they are held, and the manner in which they die off, are generally slightly different for each . . . but besides all this, in good part music, especial care is taken to facilitate the separation of the parts by the ear. In polyphonic music proper, where each part has its own distinct melody, a principal means of clearly separating the progression of each part has always consisted in making them proceed in different rhythms and on different divisions of the bars (p. 59).

And later:

> All these helps fail in the resolution of musical tones into their constituent partials. When a compound tone commences to sound, all its partial tones commence with the same comparative strength; when it swells, all of them generally swell uniformly; when it ceases, all cease simultaneously. Hence no opportunity is generally given for hearing them separately and independently (p. 60).

C. The Octave Illusion

In the experiments so far described, channeling by frequency proximity was the rule when information was presented to both ears simultaneously. Channeling by spatial location occurred only with temporal separations between the stimuli presented to the two ears. We now examine conditions where channeling by spatial location occurred even though the input to the ears was strictly simultaneous. We shall see that this principle was adopted under special conditions of frequency relationship between the tones as they were presented in sequence at the two ears.

One stimulus configuration that induced melodic channeling by spatial location is shown in Fig. 7A. It can be seen that this consisted of two tones that were spaced an octave apart and repeatedly presented in alternation. The identical sequence was delivered to the two ears simultaneously; however, when the right ear received the high tone the left ear received the low tone, and vice versa. So, essentially the configuration was that of a two-tone chord, where the ear of input for each component switched repeatedly (Duetsch, 1974a,b, 1975a).

This sequence was found to produce various illusions, the most common of which is shown on Fig. 7B. It can be seen that this consisted of a single tone that alternated from ear to ear, and whose pitch also alternated from one octave to the other in synchrony with the localization shift. When the earphones were placed in reverse position, most listeners found that the apparent locations of the high and low tones remained fixed. So it seemed to these listeners that the earphone that had been

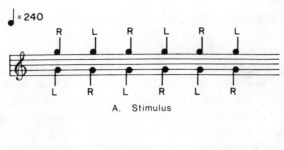

Fig. 7. (A) Representation of the configuration producing the octave illusion. (B) Representation of the illusory percept most commonly obtained (from Deutsch, 1974b).

producing the high tones was now producing the low tones, and that the earphone that had been producing the low tones was now producing the high tones.

It was hypothesized that this illusion results from the operation of two different selection mechanisms underlying the pitch and the localization percepts. To provide the perceived sequence of pitches (i.e., the melodic line) the frequencies arriving at one ear are followed, and those arriving at the other ear are suppressed. However, each tone is localized at the ear receiving the higher frequency signal, regardless of whether the higher or the lower frequency is in fact perceived (Deutsch, 1975a). This model was confirmed in later experiments (Deutsch, 1976, 1978b; Deutsch & Roll, 1976).

We can next ask whether the interactions giving rise to the octave illusion take place between pathways specific to information from the two ears, or whether instead pathways conveying information from different regions of auditory space are involved. In order to investigate this question, the stimuli were presented through spatially separated loudspeakers rather than earphones. It was found that the analogous illusion was obtained: A high tone apparently emanating from one speaker was perceived as alternating with a low tone apparently emanating from the other speaker (Deutsch, 1975a).

Setting aside the issue of where the tones appeared to be located in the octave illusion, and considering only what sequence of pitches was perceived, we note that here channeling was always on the basis of spatial location. This stands in sharp contrast to findings on the scale illusion, in which channeling was always on the basis of frequency proximity instead. Yet the stimuli producing these illusions were remarkably similar. In both cases listeners were presented with repeating sequences of sine wave tones at equal amplitudes and durations. In both cases the stimuli were continuous, and the frequencies presented to one ear always differed from the frequencies simultaneously presented to the other ear. Yet these two configurations gave rise to radically different channeling strategies. It is especially noteworthy that when two tones that were separated by an octave were simultaneously presented in the scale illusion, both tones were generally perceived (Fig. 2B). Yet when two tones that were separated by an octave were simultaneously presented in the octave illusion, only one of these was generally perceived (Fig. 7B). These differences in channeling strategy must therefore have resulted from differences in the patterns of frequency relationship between successive tones.

Considering the octave illusion further, we find that here the frequency emanating from one side of space was always identical to the frequency that had just emanated from the opposite side. It was therefore hypothesized that this factor was responsible for inducing melodic channeling by spatial location for this configuration. A further set of experiments was performed to test this hypothesis (Deutsch, 1980, 1981).

In the first experiment listeners were presented with sequences consisting of 20 dichotic chords. Two conditions were compared, which employed the basic configurations shown on Fig. 8A. The configuration in Condition 1 consisted of the repetitive presentation of a single chord, whose components stood in octave relation and alternated from ear to ear such that when the high tone was in the right ear the low tone was in the left ear, and vice versa. It can be noted that here the two ears received the same frequencies in succession. On half the trials the sequence presented to the right ear began with the high tone and ended with the low tone, and on the other half this order was reversed. On each trial, subjects judged whether the sequence began with the high tone and ended with the low tone, or whether it began with the low tone and ended with the high tone; and from these judgments it was inferred which ear was being followed for pitch.

The basic configuration in Condition 2 consisted of the repetitive presentation of two dichotic chords in alternation, the first forming an octave and the second a minor third, so that the entire four-tone combination constituted a major triad. It will be noted that here the two ears did not receive the same frequencies in succession. On half the trials the right ear received the upper component of the first chord and the lower component of the last chord, and on the other half this order was reversed.

The amplitude relationships between the tones presented to the two ears were systematically varied across trials, and the extent to which each location was followed was plotted as a function of these amplitude relationships. The results are shown on Fig. 8B. It can be seen that in Condition 1 the frequencies presented to one location were followed until a critical level of amplitude relationship was reached, and the other location was followed beyond this level. However, in Condition 2 there was no following on the basis of spatial location, even when the signals presented to the two locations differed substantially in amplitude. However, hypothesizing instead that the subjects were following this sequence on the basis of frequency proximity a very consistent result emerged: Three of the subjects consistently followed the low tones, and one consistently followed the high tones. This result is as expected if the critical factor responsible for channeling by spatial location here is that the same frequencies emanate in succession from different regions of auditory space.

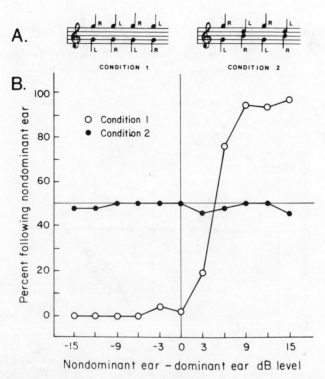

Fig. 8. (A) Configurations used in first experiment investigating the factors producing following on the basis of spatial location. (B) Percent following of nondominant ear in the two conditions of the experiment (from Deutsch, 1980a).

In a second experiment only two dichotic chords were presented on each trial. Two conditions were again compared, which employed the basic configurations shown on Fig. 9A. The configuration in Condition 1 consisted of two presentations of the identical chord, whose components formed an octave, such that one ear received first the high tone and then the low tone, while simultaneously the other ear received first the low tone and then the high tone. The identical frequencies were used throughout this condition. The basic configuration in Condition 2 consisted of two dichotic chords, each of which formed an octave, but which were composed of different frequencies. Trials employing chords composed of C and F♯ and of A and D♯ occurred in strict alternation, so that any given chord was repeated only after a substantial time period during which several other chords were interpolated.

Figure 9B shows the extent to which each location was followed in these two conditions, as a function of the amplitude relationships between the signals at the two ears. It can be seen that in Condition 1 following was clearly on the basis of spatial location. However, in Condition 2 such following did not occur, even when there were substantial amplitude differences between the signals at the two ears. Instead the subjects consistently followed these sequences on the basis of overall contour: Their

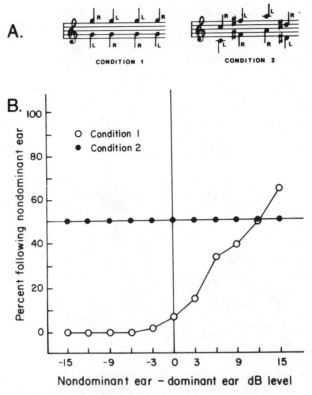

Fig. 9. (A) Configurations used in second experiment investigating the factors producing following by spatial location. (B) Percent following of nondominant ear in the two conditions of the experiment (from Deutsch, 1980a).

patterns of response indicated an ascending sequence when the second chord was higher than the first, and a descending sequence when the second chord was lower than the first. This was true even when the signals at the two ears differed substantially in amplitude.

It should be noted that following by contour here was consistent with following by frequency proximity, but that following the middle tones of the sequence (for example, the high C and the low F♯ in Fig. 9A) would have been equally consistent, since in either case the melodic interval formed by the two tones was a diminished fifth. So, in these sequences, overall contour was the factor that determined which tones were followed. Whether this served simply to "break a tie" or whether contour would win out in competition with frequency proximity in other configurations remains to be determined.

At all events, the second experiment showed, as did the first, that following by spatial location occurs in sequences where the same frequencies emanate in succession from two different regions of auditory space, and it occurs on other lines when this relationship does not hold. It is particularly interesting to note that relative amplitude was found not to be an important factor in either experiment. When following was by frequency proximity or by contour, this occurred in the face of substantial amplitude differences between the signals arriving at the two ears. When following was by spatial location, the switch from following one side of space to the other did not occur at the point where the amplitude balance shifted from one side of space to the other, but at a different level of amplitude relationship. Thus, amplitude here appeared to *set the scene* for following on the basis of spatial location rather than serving as a primary following principle. [It will be recalled that in the experiment by Butler (1979a) following by frequency proximity also occurred in the face of amplitude differences between signals emanating from different spatial locations.]

We can next ask whether the lack of following by spatial location in the second conditions of these two experiments was due to the delay between successive presentations of the same frequencies to the two locations or to the interpolation of tones of different frequencies. To examine the effect of interpolated information, we studied performance under two further conditions. As shown on Fig. 10A, the configuration

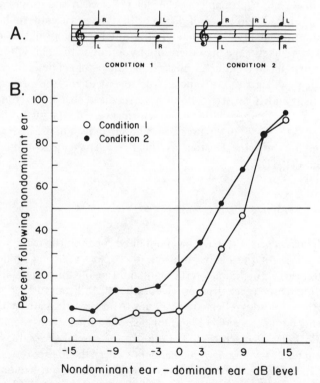

Fig. 10. (A) Configurations used in third experiment investigating the factors producing following by spatial location. (B) Percent following of nondominant ear in the two conditions of the experiment (from Deutsch, 1980a).

in these two conditions were identical, except that in Condition 2 a single tone was interpolated between the dichotic chords and the listeners were instructed to ignore this tone. As shown on Fig. 10B, there was a less pronounced following of the preferred spatial location in the condition in which the extra tone was interpolated. To investigate the effects of temporal dealy, we varied the time interval between the onsets of successive tones at the two ears. This was achieved either by changing the durations of the tones or by interpolating gaps between them. It was found that the strength of this effect decreased with increasing time between onsets of the identical frequencies at the two locations. It did not matter whether this increase was produced by lengthening the durations of the tones, or by interpolating gaps between them. Thus, both interpolated information and temporal delay were found to reduce channeling be preferred spatial location.

These experiments raise the question of why such a channeling mechanism should have developed. We may hypothesize that this mechanism enables us to follow new, ongoing auditory information with a minimum of interference from echoes or reverberation. In everyday listening, when the same frequency emanates successively from two different regions of auditory space, the second occurrence may well be due to an echo. This is made more probable as the delay between the onsets of these two occurrences is shortened. However, if different frequencies are interpolated between two occurrences of the identical frequency, other interpretations of the second occurrence are made more likely. We may therefore hypothesize that this falls into the class of mechanisms that act to counteract misleading effects of echoes and reverberation. Such an explanation has been advanced, for instance, for the precedence effect. Wallach, Newman and Rosenweig (1949) have reported that in listening to music a single image may be obtained with the waveform presented at two different spatial locations separated by 45–70 msec intervals. The second sound is, under these conditions, attributed to the same location as the first. Analogous findings have been reported by Haas (1951).

D. Handedness Correlates

Strong handedness correlates have been obtained for both the octave and the scale illusions. In the case of the octave illusion, there was a strong tendency among right-handers to hear the high tone on the right and the low tone on the left. This was not, however, found among left-handers (Deutsch, 1974). From further studies it was concluded that these findings reflected a tendency to perceive the pattern of frequencies presented to the dominant side of auditory space rather than the nondominant (Deutsch, 1975a, 1981; Deutsch & Roll, 1976). In the case of the scale illusion, there was also a strong tendency among right-handers to hear the higher tones on the right and the lower tones on the left; again this was not true of left-handers. Here the mislocalization of the higher tones to one spatial position and the lower tones to another cannot be interpreted in terms of a following of the input from one side of space rather than the other, since the higher and lower melodic lines were each composed of tones that emanated from both spatial locations. One may, however, interpret this handedness correlate as reflecting relatively more activity in the dominant hemisphere on the part of neural units underlying the higher tones, and relatively more activity in the nondominant hemisphere on the part of neural units underlying the lower tones. Justification for this view comes in part from neurological studies showing that patients who experience palinacousis tend to perceive the illusory sound as located on the side of auditory space contralateral to the lesion (Jacobs, Feldman, Diamond, & Bender, 1973). Further, when patients obtain auditory sensations upon stimulation of the temporal lobe, these sensations are also generally referred to contralateral auditory space (Penfield & Perot, 1963).

A prominence of dominant over nondominant pathways is therefore implicated in both the octave and the scale illusions. These findings may be related to those of other investigators who explored patterns of ear advantage in the processing of melodies or tonal sequences. Very mixed results have been obtained in these studies. Some have found left ear superiorities (Kimura, 1964, 1967; King & Kimura, 1972; Bartholomeus, 1974; Darwin, 1969; Zatorre, 1979; Spellacy, 1970; Spreen, Spellacy and Reid, 1970). Others have found no ear differences (Gordon, 1970; Bartholomeus, Doehring, & Freygood, 1973; Berlin, 1972; Doehring, 1971, 1972). Under yet other conditions right ear superiorities have been obtained instead (Halperin, Nachshon, & Carmon, 1973; Robinson & Solomon, 1974; Papcun, Krashen, Terbeek, Remington, & Harshmann, 1974; Natale, 1977). Bever and Chiarello (1974), and Johnson (1977) obtained a right ear superiority for musicians and a left ear superiority for nonmusicians in melody recognition.

Such inconsistencies are probably due to a variety of factors. With sequences generated by voice or by natural instruments, recognition may be achieved in part by spectral cues. Loudness and temporal cues may also serve as bases for judgment, and so on. It is not unreasonable to suppose that specific attributes of a melodic segment might be processed in different parts of the nervous system. For example, Gordon (1970) obtained a left ear advantage in processing dichotically presented chords that were generated by an electronic organ, yet in this same study he failed to find an ear difference in the processing of melodies. Gaede, Parsons and Bertera (1978), using monaural presentation, found a left ear advantage in processing chords, and yet a right ear advantage in melody recognition. Further, Charbonneau and Risset (1975) studied the processing of dichotic sound sequences that varied either in fundamental frequency or in spectral envelope. When fundamental frequency was varied, a right ear advantage was obtained. Yet when spectral envelope was varied, a left ear advantage was obtained instead. If the relative involvement of the two hemispheres differs, depending on the specific musical attribute being processed, this could explain such results. Furthermore, different categories of listener might utilize specific musical attributes to varying extents. This could explain the discrepancies in performance found between musicians and nonmusicians in sone studies.

Ear differences have been interpreted by some investigators in terms of a simple dichotomy in processing strategy: the left or dominant hemisphere is assumed to specialize in "analytic" processing; the right or nondominant hemisphere in "Gestalt" or "holistic" processing. However the meaning of such a dichotomy is far from clear. For instance, melody perception is held to be a "Gestalt" phenomenon. Indeed, Von Ehrenfels (1890) originally gave melody as an example of a Gestalt, because it retains its perceptual identity under transposition. However, in order to produce invariance under transposition, a set of specific intervals must be abstracted and their orders preserved. This requires a set of highly specific analyses. It would seem more useful, rather than invoking a nebulous "analytic–holistic" distinction, to attempt to pinpoint the types of processing responsible for different patterns of ear advantage.

There is a further factor that should be considered. This arises from findings on the scale illusion. When two melodies are simultaneously presented, one to each ear, the listener may not perceive these same melodies but may instead perceptually synthesize two different melodies, as shown in Figs. 2 and 3. When one of these melodies is later presented for recognition, accuracy may then be determined in part by the perceptual reorganization that had occurred during the dichotic presentation. For example, the typical right-handed listener, on perceiving the dichotic scale sequence, perceptually displaces the high tones from his left ear to his right, and perceptually displaces the low tones from his right ear to his left. A recent study has demonstrated that this phenomenon forms the basis of the apparent left ear advantage in dichotic listening to simultaneous sequences of tones (Deutsch, in preparation).[1]

E. Melody Perception from Phase-Shifted Tones

Another technique relating to melodic channeling on the basis of spatial location was employed by Kubovy and co-workers. Kubovy, Cutting and McGuire (1974) presented a set of simultaneous and continuous sine wave tones to both ears. One of these tones in one ear was phase shifted relative to its counterpart in the opposite ear. When these tones were phase shifted in sequence a melody that corresponded to the shifted tones was clearly heard. However, the melody was undetectable when the stimulus was presented to either ear alone. Subjectively, the dichotically presented melody was heard as occurring inside the head but displaced to one side of the midline, while a background noise was heard as localized to the opposite side. So, it was as though a source in one spatial position was producing the melody, and a different source in another spatial position was producing the noise.

Kubovy (1981) pointed out that there are two potential interpretations of this effect. First, the segregation of the melody from the noise could have been based on *concurrent difference cues;* i.e., the target tone may have been segregated because at that time its interaural disparity—or apparent spatial location—differed from that of the background tones. Alternatively, the effect could have been based on *successive difference cues,* i.e., the target tone may have been segregated because it had moved its apparent location. Two further configurations were therefore devised to determine which of

[1]For a review of the neurological substrates of music perception see Chapter 15.

these factors was responsible. In the first, the target tones moved while the locations of the background tones remained constant, producing a successive difference cue. In the second, the target tones themselves did not move, but the background tones did, so that the target tones were segregated from the others, producing a concurrent difference cue. Kubovy found that although both types of cue were effective in producing segregation, the successive difference cue was considerably more effective than the concurrent difference cue.

In another experiment, Kubovy and Howard (1976) presented six tones simultaneously, in such a way that each occupied a different apparent position in space. They then displaced each tone in turn to a new apparent position, and so produced a melody by successive difference cues. They studied the effect of interpolating temporal gaps of different durations between successive tone bursts, and found that the melody could still be heard through such gaps. Although there was considerable intersubject variability in sensitivity to the effect of the gaps, one subject performed perfectly with gaps of 9.7 seconds (the longest duration employed). Thus, this effect of a successive difference cue was found to be capable of acting over surprisingly long silent intervals.

It is interesting to note that in Kubovy's paradigm, configurations were formed from a fixed set of tonal frequencies that simply shifted their apparent positions in space. Melodic channeling resulted from these movements of spatial position. This is analogous to the situation in the octave illusion where two continuous tones interchange their positions in space, resulting in melodic channeling by spatial location. As we have seen, when successive configurations are formed from different frequencies, rather than identical frequencies, channeling on other lines occurs instead. The issue of how differences in the frequencies of successive chords would affect channeling in Kubovy's paradigm remains to be explored.

F. Discussion

We have found that the issue of how melodic channels are formed in two-channel listening situations is a complex one. Given certain stimulus configurations, channeling occurs on the basis of spatial location. Yet given other configurations, channeling occurs instead on the basis of frequency proximity or contour. In the conditions we have examined, amplitude plays a remarkably small role as a basis for channeling.

The radical differences in channeling strategy demonstrated here bear on certain apparent inconsistencies in the literature on divided attention. Certain investigators have found that the requirement to distribute attention across ears produced performance decrements on various tasks (e.g., Cherry & Taylor, 1954; Broadbent, 1954, 1958; Moray, 1959; Treisman, 1971). It was hypothesized that such decrements were due to an inability to switch attention between ears rapidly enough for the task demands. However, other investigators have found evidence against this view (e.g., Sorkin, Pastore, & Pohlman, 1972; Sorkin, Pohlman, & Gilliom, 1973; Moray, 1975;

Shiffrin, Pisoni, & Casteneda-Mendez, 1974; Pollack, 1978). It would appear from the work reviewed here that deficits in monitoring information simultaneously from two spatial locations should occur with certain types of stimulus configuration but not with others. It is probable that the configurations that give rise to such deficits are such as to induce the strong inference that the inputs to the two ears are emanating from separate sources rather than a single source. Integrating the information from such two sources would, in normal listening situations, lead to confusion in monitoring the environment. However, with configurations where there is an ambiguity of interpretation in terms of sources, integration of the information from the two ears could be the most useful strategy.

IV. CHANNELING OF RAPID SEQUENCES OF SINGLE TONES

A. Grouping by Frequency Proximity

Melodic channeling has also been studied with the use of rapid sequences of single tones. When these tones are in more than one frequency range, they tend to split apart perceptually, with the result that two or more melodic lines are heard in parallel. Composers often take advantage of this perceptual phenomenon with their use of pseudopolyphony, or compound melodic line. Here one instrument plays a rapid sequence of single tones which are drawn from different pitch ranges, so that two simultaneous melodic streams are clearly perceived. Figure 11a shows a segment of music that exploits this principle. Figure 11b shows the same segment with log frequency and time mapped into two dimensions of visual space. It can be seen that the principle of Proximity clearly emerges in the visual representation. At lower speeds, the tendency to group by pitch proximity still persists, but is subjectively less compelling.

One of the early experiments on this phenomenon was that of Miller and Heise (1950), who presented listeners with a sequence consisting of two tones that alternated at a rate of 10 per second. They found that when the frequencies of these tones differed by less than 15%, the sequence was heard as a trill (i.e., as a single string of related tones). However, when the frequency disparity between the alternating tones increased, the sequence was heard instead as two interrupted and unrelated tones. This phenomenon has been termed "fission" by several investigators (Van Noorden, 1975). Heise and Miller (1951) examined this phenomenon further, using sequences of tones that were composed of several different frequencies. They found that if one of the tones in a rapid repetitive sequence differed sufficiently in frequency from the others it was heard as in isolation from them.

Dowling (1967, 1973) has demonstrated the importance of this principle in a long term memory situation. He presented two well-known melodies with their component tones alternating at a rate of eight per second. Recognition of these melodies was

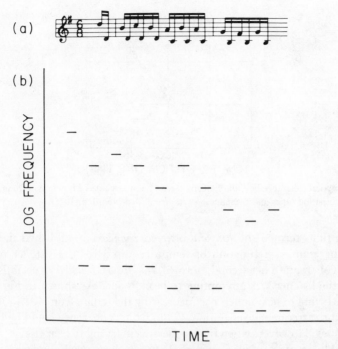

Fig. 11. Grouping of melodic stimuli on the basis of frequency proximity. Two parallel lines are perceived, each in a different frequency range (from Beethoven's *Six Variations on the Duet* "Nel cor piu non mi sento" from Paisiello's *La Molinara*).

found to be very difficult when they were in overlapping pitch ranges since their components were perceptually combined into a single stream. However, as one of the alternating melodies was gradually transposed so that their pitch ranges diverged, recognition became increasingly more easy.

B. Temporal Coherence as a Function of Frequency Proximity and Tempo

Temporal coherence is a term used to describe the subjective impression that a sequence of tones froms a connected series. Schouten (1962) studied the conditions giving rise to the perception of temporal coherence. He varied both the frequency relationships between successive tones in a sequence and also their presentation rate. As the frequency separation between successive tones increased, the tempo of the sequence had to be reduced in order to maintain the impression of temporal coherence between these tones.

Van Noorden (1975) investigated this phenomenon in detail. Listeners were presented with sequences of alternating tones, and were instructed either to try to hear temporal coherence or to try to hear fission. Two boundaries were determined by this

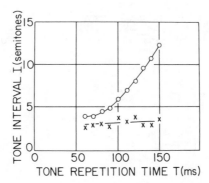

Fig. 12. Temporal coherence boundary (o) and fission boundary (x) as a function of frequency relationship between alternating tones and presentation rate (from Van Noorden, 1975).

method. The first, termed the *temporal coherence boundary*, established the threshold frequency separation as a function of tempo required for the listener to hear the sequence as coherent. The second, termed the *fission boundary*, established these values when the listener was attempting to hear fission. As shown in Fig. 12, when listeners were trying to hear coherence, decreasing the tempo from 50 to 150 msec per tone increased the frequency separation within which coherence could be heard from 4 to 13 semitones. However, when the listeners were trying to hear fission, decreasing the tempo had little effect on performance. Between these two boundaries there was a large region where the listener could alter his listening strategy at will, and so hear either fission or coherence. So within this region, attentional set was important in determining how the sequence was perceived; however outside this region, attentional set was not effective.

Bregman and Bernstein (quoted in Bregman, 1978) confirmed the finding of an interaction between frequency separation and tempo in judgments of coherence. They found that as two alternating tones converged in frequency, a higher rate of alternation was required for the sequence to split into two streams. This effect was found to hold throughout a substantial frequency range.

C. Grouping by Frequency Proximity Builds with Repetition

Several experiments have shown that the splitting of tonal sequences into streams on the basis of frequency proximity builds up with repetitive presentation. For instance, Van Noorden (1975) compared the temporal coherence boundary for two-tone, three-tone, and long repetitive sequences. With three-tone sequences the frequency change was either unidirectional or bidirectional. It was found that for unidirectional three-tone sequences, temporal coherence was observed at rates that were equal to or even higher than those for two-tone sequences. (This follows the principle of Good Continuation, as described below.) But with bidirectional three-tone sequences, the rate of frequency change had to be set much lower than for two-tone

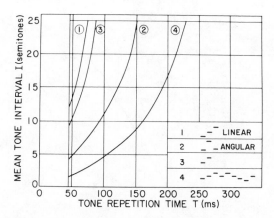

Fig. 13. Temporal coherence boundary for two-tone, three-tone undirectional, three-tone bidirectional, and continuous sequences (from Van Noorden, 1975).

sequences before coherence could be perceived. With long repetitive sequences the rate of frequency change had to be set lower still (Fig. 13).

In a related experiment, Bregman (1978) presented listeners with sequences consisting of two "high" tones (748 and 831 Hz) and one "low" tone (330 Hz). When this sequence split into two streams, the upper stream was perceived as an alternation of two high tones, and the lower stream as the steady repetition of a single tone. The experiment varied the number of tones packaged between four-second periods of silence. On each trial listeners adjusted the speed of the sequence until the point of splitting was determined. As shown on Fig. 14, as the package size increased, the speed required for segregation decreased.

Bregman interpreted these findings along the following lines. Stream segregation may be viewed as the product of a mechanism that acts to "parse" the auditory environment (i.e., to group together components of the acoustic spectrum in such a way as to recover the original sources). Such a mechanism would be expected to accumulate evidence over time, so that the segregation of acoustic components into groups should build up with repeated presentation.

Further evidence for the view that stream segregation results from a "parsing" mechanism was provided by Bregman and Rudnicky (1975). Listeners judged the order of two tones that were embedded in a four-tone pattern flanked by two "distractor" tones. The presence of the distractor tones made judgment of the order of the test tones difficult. However, when another stream of tones, called "captor" tones, was moved close to the "distractor" tones, this caused the "distractors" to combine with the "captors" to form a single stream, leaving the test tones in a stream of their own. This had the consequence that the order of the test tones was now easy to judge. Bregman and Rudnicky argue that this situation presents the listener with two simultaneously structured streams, of which the "distractor" tones can belong to either one, but not to both simultaneously. This is as expected on an interpretation in terms of an

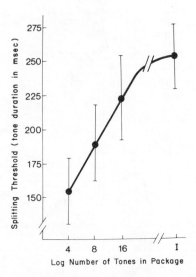

Fig. 14. Threshold for stream segregation as a function of number of tones per package. Two "high" tones were presented in alternation with a single "low" tone (from Bregman, 1978).

auditory parsing mechanism: any given tone is likely to be emanating from only one source; not from two sources simultaneously.

It should be noted that the cumulation of effect over time found by Bregman (1978) is analogous to cumulation effects found in the octave illusion, where the strength of tendency to follow the frequency presented to one side of auditory space rather than the other also builds up with repeated presentation, and builds up more rapidly as repetition rate increases. Analogous findings were obtained for the strength of tendency to localize toward the higher frequency signal in this illusion (Duetsch, 1976, 1978). Such a built-up of effect is also well interpreted in terms of evidence accumulation.

D. Grouping by Frequency Proximity and the Perception of Temporal Relationships

One striking consequence of the formation of separate streams out of rapidly presented sequences is that temporal relationships between the elements of different streams become difficult to process. This has been shown in several ways. Bregman and Campbell (1971) presented a repetitive sequence consisting of six tones: three from a high frequency range and three from a low frequency range. When these tones were presented at a rate of 10 per second, it was difficult for listeners to perceive a pattern of high and low tones that was embedded in the sequence.

Dannenbring and Bregman (1976) demonstrated a further perceptual consequence of this breakdown of temporal processing. They found that when two tones alternate at high speeds so that they produce separate perceptual streams, the tones in the two streams appear to be perceptually overlapping in time. A related study was performed by Fitzgibbon, Pollatsek, and Thomas (1974) who explored the perception of temporal gaps between tones occurring in rapid sequence. When a 20-msec gap was interpolated between tones in the same frequency range, detection of this gap was easy. However, when the gap was interpolated between tones in different frequency ranges, detection performance dropped considerably.

A further reflection of this breakdown of temporal processing was found by Van Noorden (1975). He studied detection of the temporal displacement of a tone that alternated continuously with another tone of different frequency and found that as the tempo of the sequence increased, the mean just noticeable displacement also increased. This increase was substantial for sequences where the tones were widely separated in frequency, but only slight for sequences where the frequencies were contiguous. These results paralleled those found for judgments of temporal coherence.

Such deterioration of temporal processing as a result of frequency disparity occurs with two-tone sequences also. Divenyi and Hirsh (1972) found that discrimination of the size of a temporal gap between a tone pair deteriorates with increasing frequency disparity between members of the pair. Further, Williams and Perrott (1972) measured the minimum detectable gap between tone pairs. They found that for tones of 100 and 30 msec duration, the threshold rose with increasing frequency disparity between members of the pair. However, Van Noorden (1975) showed that this deterioration of temporal processing is considerably greater for long repetitive sequences than for two-tone sequences; so that it develops as a consequence of stream formation (Fig. 15). This conclusion also follows from consideration of Bregman and Campbell's results (1971).

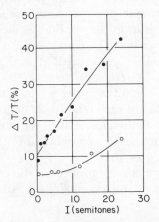

Fig. 15. ○ The just noticeable displacement ΔT/T of the second tone of a two-tone sequence as a function of tone interval I. ● The just noticeable displacement ΔT/T of one tone in a continuous sequence of alternating tones as a function of tone interval I (from Van Noorden, 1975).

E. Grouping by Good Continuation

Another principle found to be effective in producing grouping is that of Good Continuation. Bregman and Dannenbring (1973) found that when a repeating cycle consisting of a high tone alternating with a low tone tended to segregate into two streams, this splitting tendency was reduced when the high and low tones were connected by frequency glides. Similarly Nabelek, Nabelek, and Hirsh (1973) reported that for complex tone bursts, frequency glides between the initial and final tones resulted in more pitch fusion than when these tones were juxtaposed with no transitions.

Related experiments have involved the perception of rapid sequences of three or more tones. Divenyi and Hirsh (1974) studied order identification for three-tone sequences, and found that sequences with unidirectional frequency changes were easier to order than sequences with bidirectional frequency changes. Analogous results were obtained by Nickerson and Freeman (1974), Warren and Byrnes (1975), and McNally and Handel (1977) for four-tone sequences. Furthermore, Van Noorden (1975) found that a sequence of three tones was more likely to be judged as coherent if these tones formed a unidirectional rather than a bidirectional frequency change.[2]

F. Grouping by Timbre

The grouping of complex tones on the basis of sound type or timbre is an example of grouping by the principle of Similarity. (A visual example of such grouping is shown in Fig. 1b, where the open and closed circles each combine perceptually to form vertical rows.) Grouping on the basis of timbre is clearly apparent in natural musical situations (Erickson, 1975). Adjacent phrases are often played by different instruments to enhance their perceptual separation. Further, overlaps in pitch range are far more common where more than one instrument type is involved, reflecting the greater perceptual separation provided by the timbral difference.

A striking demonstration of grouping by timbre was produced by Warren, Obusek, Farmer and Warren (1969). They constructed repeating sequences consisting of four unrelated sounds, a high tone (1000 Hz), a hiss (2000 Hz octave band noise), a low tone (796 Hz), and a buzz (400 Hz square wave). Each sound was 200 msec in duration, and the sounds followed each other without pause. Listeners were quite unable to name the orders of the sounds in such repeating sequences. For correct naming to be achieved, the duration of each sound had to be increased to over half a second.

It appears that two separate factors are involved in this effect. The first factor is the organization of the elements of a sequence into separate streams on the basis of sound

[2]Further issues concerning the grouping of rapid sequences of tones involve the effect of average frequency difference between the tones. An extended discussion of these issues is beyond the scope of the present chapter, and the reader is referred to Warren and Byrnes (1975), Nickerson and Freeman (1974), and Divenyi and Hirsh (1978).

type, analogous to organization on the basis of frequency proximity. The second factor involves the lack of familiarity with such sound sequences. It has been shown that when verbal items are combined to form repeating sequences of this nature, correct ordering occurs at considerably faster rates (Warren & Warren, 1970; Thomas, Cetti, & Chase, 1971; Thomas, Hill, Carroll, & Garcia, 1970; Dorman, Cutting, & Raphael, 1975). It is likely that sequences composed of familiar musical sounds would also be more easily ordered. Although this has not been formally investigated, an observation by the author is of relevance here. It was found that a trained percussionist specializing in avant-garde music had little difficulty in discriminating sequences such as those created by Warren and his colleagues. This musician frequently produced such sequences in musical performance.

The question then arises as to the nature of the process that enables the rapid reconstruction of the order of components of complex yet familiar sound sequences such as in speech and music. Wickelgren (1969, 1976) has proposed that the correct ordering of speech components is based on an encoding of a set of context-sensitive elements that need not themselves be ordered. For instance, he proposed that the word "struck" is encoded not as the ordered set of phonemes /s/, /t/, /v/, /u/, /k/, but as the unordered set of context-sensitive allophones /♯^{s}t/, /s^{t}r/, /t^{r}u/, /r^{u}k/, /u^k♯/. Thus each of these context-sensitive elements contains some local information concerning how this element is ordered in relation to the other elements in the set. From such an unordered set of elements the information concerning their order can be derived.

This theory can readily be applied to auditory perception in general, and one may hypothesize that the easy identification of familiar sound sequences is mediated by an acquired set of such context-sensitive elements. For familiar sounds presented in unfamiliar order, these context-sensitive elements may not be encoded firmly enough to achieve correct identification.

An alternative proposal, suggested by Warren (1974), is that the ready identification of familiar sequences is mediated by a two-stage process. In the first stage the sequence is recognized in global fashion: as a "temporal compound" which can be distinguished from other compounds without being analyzed into its components. Other factors in addition to the perception of relationships between strictly adjacent items could be involved in such global processing. In the second stage there takes place an item-by-item analysis of the components of this compound and their orders.

Judgments of temporal order for only two disparate sounds are easier than for continuous repetitive sequences. Hirsh (1959) and Hirsh and Sherrick (1961) found that the threshold for ordering two disparate events was around 20 msec for highly trained listeners, though somewhat higher for untrained listeners (Hirsh, 1976). This superior performance is probably based on several factors. First, items that are preceded or followed by silence are more readily identified than those that are not (Warren, 1974). Second, there are fewer relationships to be judged between two events. And, third, an active process which organizes elements according to sound type probably acts to inhibit the perception of relationships between disparate elements, in a fashion analogous to the process that organizes elements by frequency proximity. This effect should be expected to cumulate with repetition.

G. Grouping by Amplitude

Amplitude has been shown to be an effective grouping principle in the perception of rapid sequences of single tones. Dowling (1973) in his experiment on perception of interleaved melodies found that loudness differences between the melodies resulted in an enhanced ability to hear them as separate. Van Noorden (1975) studied perception of sequences where the tones were of identical frequency but alternated in amplitude. He found that with amplitude differences of less than 5 dB a single coherent stream was heard, even though loudness differences were clear. However, with larger amplitude differences two separate streams of different loudnesses were heard instead. Under these conditions attention could be directed to the softer stream as well as to the louder one. With even larger amplitude differences between the alternating tones, the auditory continuity effect was produced, and the softer tone was heard as though continuing through the louder tone (see below).

H. Grouping by Temporal Proximity

When we attend to one melodic configuration rather than to another, we are forming figure-ground relationships analogous to those in vision (Gregory, 1970). Perception of sequences of tones that are interleaved in time may then be likened to visual perception of embedded figures. Divenyi and Hirsh (1978) drew this analogy, and argued that melodic configurations may be represented in two dimensions, with frequency providing one dimension and time the other (see also Julesz & Hirsh, 1972). Just as visual configurations can be more readily identified when these are spatially separated from background stimuli, so should melodic configurations be more readily identified when these are separated either in time or in frequency from background tonal stimuli.

As a test of this notion, Divenyi and Hirsh presented rapid three-tone patterns that could occur in any of six permutations and required subjects to identify on each trial which permutation had been presented. These three-tone patterns were embedded in sequences of seven or eight tones, but were not interleaved with them. Identification performance was superior when the irrelevant tones and the target tones were in different frequency ranges. Furthermore, performance levels varied considerably depending on the temporal position of the target pattern within the full sequence. Best performance was obtained when the target pattern occurred at the end of the sequence; performance was also relatively good when the target was located at the beginning, but it was close to chance when the target occurred in the middle of the sequence. Both temporal and frequency separation were therefore found to reduce interference from the background tones. Previously Ortmann (1926) had found that a single tone was more salient when it was the highest or lowest in a sequence, or when it was in the first or last position. Similar conclusions were drawn recently by Watson, Kelly, and Wroton (1975) and Watson, Wroton, Kelly, and Benbasset (1976). Divenyi and Hirsh's results, therefore, extended such findings to the case of melodic configurations. (Further issues involving grouping by temporal position are discussed in Chapter 9.)

I. Perceptual Replacement of Missing Sounds

So far we have examined several instances where our perceptual system reorganizes sound sequences in accordance with expectations derived from both the sequences themselves and our knowledge of the auditory environment. It has also been found that sounds which are not actually present in the stimulus may be perceptually synthesized in accordance with such expectations.

Various studies have shown that when two sounds are presented in alternation, the fainter sound may be heard as continuing through the louder one (Miller & Licklider, 1950; Thurlow, 1957; Vicario, 1960). More recently, Warren (1970) and Warren, Obusek, and Ackroff (1972) showed that if a phoneme in a sentence is replaced by a louder noise, the missing phoneme may be perceptually synthesized. Analogous results were obtained with nonverbal sounds. In a set of parametric studies, Warren and his colleagues have demonstrated that this "auditory induction effect" occurs only under stimulus conditions where it would be reasonable to assume that the substituted sound had masked the missing one.

Dannenbring (1976) produced another version of this effect. He presented a sine wave tone that repeatedly glided up and down in frequency. When a loud noise burst was substituted for a portion of this sound, it still appeared to glide through the noise. However, if the tone changed in amplitude just before the noise burst, producing evidence that something had happened to the tone itself, rather than its simply being masked, the tendency to hear the tone as continuing through the noise was reduced (Bregman & Dannenbring, 1977).

V. VOLUNTARY ATTENTION

We now turn to a consideration of the effects of voluntary attention on channeling phenomena. In listening to music outside the laboratory, we have the impression that we can direct our attention at will; listening now to a melodic line, now to its accompaniment, now to a chosen instrument, and so on. Yet the conditions under which such attention focusing is indeed under voluntary control remain to be determined. We are dealing with two issues here. First, we may examine the role of voluntary attention in the initial division of the configuration into groupings. Second, we may examine the role of voluntary factors in determining which grouping is attended to, once such a division is established. Concerning the first issue, we have described several configurations where a particular grouping principle is so strong that listeners are generally unaware of alternative organizations. For example, most people on hearing the scale illusion form groupings so strongly on the basis of frequency proximity that they hear tones in one frequency range as emanating from one source, and tones in another frequency range as emanating from a different source. They there-fore believe that they are attending to one spatial location rather than to another; yet in reality they are synthesizing information from two different locations (Deutsch, 1975b). The same is true for the two-part contrapuntal patterns devised by Butler (1979a). Similarly, on listening to the octave illusion, many people believe that a single high tone is being delivered intermittently to one ear, and a single low tone intermittently to the other ear. Yet in fact they are being presented with a continuous two-tone chord. So, here again involuntary organizational mechanisms are so strong that the listener is una-ware of the nature of the stimulus configuration. The sequence of Kubovy *et al.* (1974) provides another example. Here one hears a melody as in one spatial location and a background noise as in another, yet in reality a continuous chord is being delivered to both ears.

However, when we consider the role of voluntary attention in determining which of two channels is attended to, once these have been formed, we find that in all these examples voluntary attention plays a prominent role. For example, in the scale illu-sion listeners who hear two melodic lines in parallel can choose at will to attend to either the higher or the lower one. Even those listeners who initially hear only the higher melodic line may after repeated presentations focus their attention on the lower one. Again in Butler's contrapuntal patterns we can choose at will to listen to the higher or the lower of the two melodies that we have perceptually synthesized. In the case of the octave illusion, those listeners who unambiguously hear a high tone in one ear alternating with a low tone in the other ear can focus their attention on either the high tone or the low one. Similarly, with the configuration of Kubovy *et al.* (1974), listeners can direct their attention to either the melody or to the noise.

When we consider channeling of rapid sequences of tones, we also find that strong involuntary factors are involved in the formation of initial groupings. Thus, the inability to form order relationships across streams based on frequency proximity (Bregman & Campbell, 1971), sound type (Warren *et al.*, 1969), or spatial location (Deutsch, 1979) cannot readily be overcome by voluntary attention focusing.

However, other examples have been given where voluntary attention does play a role. In exploring the temporal coherence boundary, Van Noorden (1975) found that within a given range of tempos and of frequency relationships, listeners may direct their attention at will, hearing either fission or temporal coherence (Fig. 12). An ambiguous situation where channeling by timbre was set in competition with channel-ing by pitch was created by Erickson (1974) in a compositon called *LOOPS*. Here, a repeating melodic pattern was performed by five instruments, with each instrument playing a different note in the manner of a hockett, so that each pitch was eventually played by every instrument. Under these conditions listeners can often choose to follow the sequence on the basis of either timbre or pitch. It therefore appears that although there are strong involuntary components in the formation of groupings, ambiguous stimulus situations may be set up where voluntary attention can be the determining factor.

Considering the issue of voluntary factors in determining which stream is attended to, once a set of alternatives have been formed, we find that voluntary attention focusing is easily achieved with rapid sequences also. For instance, Van Noorden (1975) reports that in cases where two streams were formed on the basis of frequency proximity, the listener was able to direct his attention at will and concentrate on either the upper stream or the lower one. However, he noted that an involuntary component was also present: The listener's percept would sometimes switch spontaneously to the stream he was attempting to ignore. This was true even when the unattended stream was less salient. Similar observations were made by present author using streaming by spatial location in patterns such as on Fig. 6.

In summary, it appears that the initial division of the stimulus configuration into groupings is often outside the listener's voluntary control, though ambiguous situations may be generated where attention focusing can be effective. In contrast, once a set of groupings is established, voluntary attention focusing plays a prominent role in determining which of these is attended to. This division of the attentional process into two stages corresponds in many respects to the stages identified as preattentive and postattentive by Neisser (1967) and Kahneman (1973) among others. These terms, however, have often been taken to imply different depths of analysis at these two stages, yet the issue of depth of analysis remains unsettled (Deutsch & Deutsch, 1963; Keele and Neill, 1979).

We may next consider the consequences of the selective attention process for the unattended material (i.e., for the component of music that serves as "ground" when attention is focused on another component which serves as "figure".[3] Considering the analogous issue for streams of speech, Cherry (1953) and Cherry and Taylor (1954) presented subjects with two messages, one to each ear, and required them to shadow one of these. They found that the subjects were able to report virtually nothing about the message presented to the nonattended ear, not even what language it was in. Other studies have produced similar findings (Kahneman, 1973). Recently, the present author set up an analogous situation for musical stimuli. Two familiar folk songs were recorded by piano, and were simultaneously presented, one to each ear. Listeners were required to shadow one of the melodies by singing, and were later asked to describe what had been presented to the other ear. Analogous to Cherry's finding, no listener was able to name the unattended melody, and none was able to describe much about the stimulus. Thus, voluntary attention focusing on one channel of a musical configuration can have the effect of suppressing the other channel from conscious perception.[4]

The question then arises as to what extent the unattended signal is processed under these conditions. This is a controversial issue in the literature on speech materials. Broadbent (1958) proposed that in selective listening a filter sorts out simultaneously presented stimuli on the basis of gross physical characteristics, such as spatial location or frequency range. Stimuli that share a characteristic that defines the relevant "chan-

---

[3]The author is indebted to R. Erickson for raising this question.

[4]Channeling by spatial location was here facilitated by the fact that the messages delivered to the two ears were asynchronous. Had they been synchronous, as with the stimuli used by Deutsch (1975b) and Butler (1979a), it would not have been possible for the listener to focus attention on one ear rather than the other.

nel" are then perceptually analyzed further, whereas the other stimuli are simply filtered out. This theory was found to be unable to account for certain findings—for instance, that the meaning of words may be important determinants of selective attention (Grey & Wedderburn, 1960; Treisman, 1960). Consequently, Treisman (1960, 1964) suggested a modification of filter theory to accommodate these findings. She proposed that the unattended message is not totally rejected, as Broadbent had suggested, but rather attenuated. An alternative view was taken by Deutsch and Deutsch (1963) who proposed that all input, whether attended to or not, is completely analyzed by the nervous system. The information thus analyzed is then weighted for importance or pertinence. Such weightings are determined both by long-term factors (for instance, there is a long-term predisposition to attend to one's own name) and by factors determined by the current situation. The information with the highest weighting of importance then controls awareness. Recent studies (e.g., Lewis, 1970; Corteen & Wood, 1972; Shiffrin & Schneider, 1977) have provided strong evidence for this view, but the issue remains controversial. In the case of music, this has not yet been the subject of experimental investigation.

VI. CONCLUSION

In this chapter we have focused on musical channeling phenomena in two types of situation. First, we have explored the perceptual consequences of presenting two simultaneous sequences of tones in different spatial locations. Second, we have investigated channeling when rapid sequences of single tones were presented. In general, relatively simple stimulus configurations were examined, and grouping or channeling on the basis of higher order abstractions was not considered. The formation of such abstractions is the subject of Chapter 9 and we shall assume that these can also serve as bases for grouping.[5]

REFERENCES

Bartholomeus, B. Effects of task requirements on ear superiority for sung speech. *Cortex*, 1974, *10*, 215–223.
Bartholomeus, B. N., Doehring, D. G., & Freygood, S. D. Absence of stimulus effects in dichotic singing. *Bulletin of the Psychonomic Society*, 1973, *1*, 171–172.
Benade, A. H. *Fundamentals of musical acoustics*. London and New York: Oxford University Press, 1976.
Berlin, C. I. Critical review of the literature on dichotic effects—1970. In 1971 reviews of scientific literature on hearing. *American Academy Ophtology Otology* 1972, 80–90.
Bever, T. G., & Chiarello, R. J. Cerebral dominance in musicians and nonmusicians. *Science*, 1974, *185*, 537–539.
Bregman, A. S. The formation of auditory streams. In J. Requin (Ed.), *Attention and Performance*. (Volume VII) Hillsdale, New Jersey: Erlbaum, 1978. Pp. 63–76.
Bregman, A. S., & Campbell, J. Primary auditory stream segregation and perception of order in rapid sequences of tones. *Journal of Experimental Psychology*, 1971, *89*, 244–249.

[5]This work was supported by United States Public Health Service Grant MH-21001.

Bregman, A. S., & Dannenbring, G. L. The effect of continuity on auditory stream segregation. *Perception & Psychophysics*, 1973, *13*, 308–312.

Bregman, A. S., & Dannenbring, G. L. Auditory continuity and amplitude edges. *Canadian Journal of Psychology*, 1977, *31*, 151–159.

Bregman, A. S., & Pinker, S. Auditory streaming and the building of timbre. *Canadian Journal of Psychology*, 1978, *32*, 20–31.

Bregman, A. S., & Rudnicky, A. I. Auditory segregation: Stream or streams? *Journal of Experimental Psychology: Human Perception and Performance*, 1975, *1*, 263–267.

Broadbent, D. E. The role of auditory localization in attention and memory span. *Journal of Experimental Psychology*, 1954, *47*, 191–196.

Broadbent, D. *Perception and communication*. Oxford: Pergamon, 1958.

Butler, D. A further study of melodic channeling. *Perception & Psychophysics*, 1979, *25*, 264–268. (a)

Butler, D. Melodic channeling in a musical environment. *Research Symposium on the Psychology and Acoustics of Music, Kansas*, 1979. (b)

Charbonneau, G., and Risset, J-C. Differences entre oreille droite et oreille gauche pour la perception de la hauteur des sons. *Comptes Rendus, Académie des Sciences, Paris*, 1975, *281*, 163–166.

Cherry, E. C. Some experiments on the recognition of speech, with one and two ears. *Journal of the Acoustical Society of America*, 1953, *25*, 975–979.

Cherry, E. C., & Taylor, W. K. Some further experiments upon the recognition of speech, with one and with two ears. *Journal of the Acoustical Society of America*, 1954, *26*, 554–559.

Corteen, R. S., & Wood, B. Autonomic responses to shock-associated words in an unattended channel. *Journal of Experimental Psychology*, 1972, *94*, 308–313.

Dannenbring, G. L. Perceived auditory continuity with alternately rising and falling frequency transitions. *Canadian Journal of Psychology*, 1976, *30*, 99–114.

Danndenbring, G. L., & Bregman, A. S. Stream segregation and the illusion of overlap. *Journal of Experimental Psychology: Human Perception and Performance*, 1976, 2, 544–555.

Darwin, C. J. Auditory Perception and Cerebral Dominance. Doctoral dissertation, University of Cambridge, 1969.

Deutsch, D. An auditory illusion. *Journal of the Acoustical Society of America*, 1974, *55*, S18–S19. (a)

Deutsch, D. An auditory illusion. *Nature (London)*, 1974, *251*, 307–309. (b)

Deutsch, D. Musical illusions. *Scientific American*, 1975, *233*, 92–104. (a)

Deutsch, D. Two-channel listening to musical scales. *Journal of the Acoustical Society of America*, 1975, *57*, 1156–1160 (b)

Deutsch, D. Lateralization by frequency in dichotic tonal sequences as a function of interaural amplitude and time differences. *Journal of the Acoustical Society of America*, 1976, *60*, S50.

Deutsch, D. Binaural integration of tonal patterns. *Journal of the Acoustical Society of America*, 1978, *64*, S146. (a)

Deutsch, D. Lateralization by frequency for repeating sequences of dichotic 400-Hz and 800-Hz tones. *Journal of the Acoustical Society of America*, 1978, *63*, 184–186 (b)

Deutsch, D. Binaural integration of melodic patterns. *Perception & Psychophysics*, 1979, *25*, 399–405.

Deutsch, D. Two-channel listening to tonal sequences. In R. S. Nickerson and R. W. Pew (Eds.), *Attention and performance*. (Volume VIII) Hillsdale, New Jersey: Erlbaum, 1980.

Deutsch, D. The octave illusion and auditory perceptual integration. In J. V. Tobias and E. D. Schubert (Eds.), *Hearing research and theory*. (Volume I). Academic Press: New York, 1981.

Deutsch, D., *Left ear advantage for dichotic tonal sequences: an artifact of the scale illusion*. In preparation.

Deutsch, D., & Roll, P. L. Separate 'what' and 'where' decision mechanisms in processing a dichotic tonal sequence. *Journal of Experimental Psychology: Human Perception and Performance*, 1976, 2, 23–29.

Deutsch, J. A., & Deutsch, D. Attention: Some theoretical considerations. *Psychological Review*, 1963, 70, 80–90.

Divenyi, P. L., & Hirsh, I. J. Discrimination of the silent gap in two-tone sequences of different frequencies. *Journal of the Acoustical Society of America*, 1972, *52*, 166S.

Divenyi, P. L., & Hirsh, I. J. Identification of temporal order in three-tone sequences. *Journal of the Acoustical Society of America*, 1974, *56*, 144–151.

Divenyi, P. L., & Hirsh, I. J. Some figural properties of auditory patterns. *Journal of the Acoustical Society of America*, 1978, *64*, 1369-1386.

Doehring, D. G. Discrimination of simultaneous and successive pure tones by musical and nonmusical subjects. *Psychonomic Science*, 1971, *22*, 209-210.

Doehring, D. G. Ear asymmetry in the discrimination of monaural tonal sequences. *Canadian Journal of Psychology*, 1972, *26*, 106-110.

Dorman, M. F., Cutting, J. E., & Raphael, L. J. Perception of temporal order in vowel sequences with and without formant transitions. *Journal of Experimental Psychology: Human Perception and Performance*, 1975, *104*, 121-129.

Dowling, W. J. Rhythmic Fission and the Perceptual Organization of Tone Sequences. Unpublished doctoral dissertation. Harvard University, Cambridge, Massachusetts, 1967.

Dowling, W. J. The perception of interleaved melodies. *Cognitive Psychology*, 1973, *5*, 322-337.

Ehrenfels, C. Von. *Uber Gestaltqualitäten Vierteljahrschrift fur Wissenschaftliche Philosophie*, 1890, *14*, 249-292.

Erickson, R. *Sound structure in music*. Berkeley, California: University of California Press, 1975.

Erickson, R. LOOPS, an informal timbre experiment, Center for Music Experiment, University of California, San Diego, 1974.

Fitzgibbon, P. J., Pollatsek, A., & Thomas, I. B. Detection of temporal gaps within and between perceptual tonal groups. *Perception & Psychophysics*, 1974, *16*, 522-528.

Gaede, S. E., Parsons, O. A., and Bertera, J. H. Hemispheric differences in music preparation: aptitude vs. experience. *Neurophychologia*, 1978, *16*, 369-373.

Gordon, H. W. Hemispheric asymmetries in the perception of musical chords. *Cortex*, 1970, *6*, 387-398.

Gray, J. A., & Wedderburn, A.A.I. Grouping strategies with simultaneous stimuli. *Quarterly Journal of Experimental Psychology*, 1960, *12*, 180-184.

Gregory, R. L. *The intelligent eye*. New York: McGraw-Hill, 1970.

Hass, H. Über den einfluss eines Einfachechos auf die Hörsamkeit von Sprache. *Acustica*, 1951, *1*, 49-52.

Halperin, Y., Nachshon, I., & Carmon, A. Shift of ear superiority in dichotic listening to temporally patterned nonverbal stimuli. *Journal of the Acoustical Society of America*, 1973, *53*, 46-50.

Heise, G. A., & Miller, G. A. An experimental study of auditory patterns. *American Journal of Psychology*, 1951, *64*, 68-77.

Hirsh, I. J. Auditory perception of temporal order. *Journal of the Acoustical Society of America*, 1959, *31*, 759-767.

Hirsh, I. J. Order of events in three sensory modalities. In S. K. Hirsh, D. H. Eldridge, I. J. Hirsh, & S. R. Silverman (Eds.), *Essays honoring Hallowell Davis*, St. Louis, Missouri: Washington University Press, 1976.

Hirsh, I. J., & Sherrick, C. E. Perceived order in different sense modalities. *Journal of Experimental Psychology*, 1961, *62*, 423-432.

Hochberg, J. Organization and the Gestalt Tradition. In E. C. Carterette & M. P. Friedman (Eds.), *Handbook of perception*. (Volume 1) New York: Academic Press. Pp. 180-211.

Jacobs, L., Feldman, M., Diamond, S. P., & Bender, M. B. Palinacousis: Persistent or recurring auditory sensations. *Cortex*, 1973, *9*, 275-287.

Johnson, P. R. Dichotically-stimulated ear differences in musicians and nonmusicians. *Cortex*, 1977, *13*, 385-389.

Judd, T. Comments on Deutsch's musical scale illusion. *Perception and Psychophysics*, 1979. *26*, 85-92.

Julesz, B., & Hirsh, I. J. Visual and auditory perception—An essay of comparison. In E. E. David and P. B. Denes (Eds.), *Human communication: A unified view*. New York: McGraw-Hill, 1972. Pp. 283-340.

Kahneman, D. *Attention and effort*. Englewood Cliffs, New Jersey: Prentice-Hall, 1973.

Keele, S. W., and Neill, W. T. Mechanisms of attention. In E. C. Carterette and M. P. Friedman (Eds.), *Handbook of Perception* (Vol. 9) New York: Academic Press, 1979.

Kimura, D. Left-right differences in the perception of melodies. *Quarterly Journal of Experimental Psychology*, 1964, *16*, 355-358.

Kimura, D. Functional asymmetry of the brain in dichotic listening. *Cortex*, 1967, *3*, 163-178.

King, F. D., & Kimura, D. Left-ear superiority in dichotic perception of vocal nonverbal sounds. *Canadian Journal of Psychology*, 1972, *26*, 111-116.

Kubovy, M. Concurrent pitch-segregation and the theory of indispensable attributes. In M. Kubovy and J. Pomerantz (Eds.), *Perceptual organization*. Hillsdale: Erlbaum, New Jersey, 1981.

Kubovy, M., Cutting, J. E., & McGuire, R. M. Hearing with the third ear: Dichotic perception of a melody without monaural familiarity cues. *Science*, 1974, *186*, 272–274.

Kubovy, M., & Howard, F. P. Persistence of a pitch-segregating echoic memory. *Journal of Experimental Psychology: Human Perception and Performance*, 1976, *2*, 531–537.

Lewis, J. L. Semantic processing of unattended messages using dichotic listening. *Journal of Experimental Psychology*, 1970, *85*, 225–228.

McNally, K. A., & Handel, S. Effect of element composition on streaming and the ordering of repeating sequences. *Journal of Experimental Psychology: Human Perception and Performance*, 1977, *3*, 451–460.

Miller, G. A., & Heise, G. A. The trill threshold. *Journal of the Acoustical Society of America*, 1950, *22*, 637–638.

Miller, G. A., & Licklider, J.C.R. The intelligibility of interrupted speech. *Journal of the Acoustical Society of America*, 1950, *22*, 167–173.

Moray, N. Attention in dichotic listening; Affective cues and the influence of instructions. *Quarterly Journal of Experimental Psychology*, 1959, *11*, 56–60.

Moray, N. A date base for theories of selective listening. In P.M.A. Rabbitt and S. Dornic (Eds.), *Attention and performance*. (Volumn V) New York: Academic Press, 1975.

Nabelek, I. V., Nabelek, A. K., & Hirsh, I. J. Pitch of sound bursts with continuous or discontinuous change of frequency. *Journal of the Acoustical Society of America*, 1973, *53*, 1305–1312.

Natale, M. Perception of neurolinguistic auditory rhythms by the speech hemisphere. *Brain and Language*, 1977, *4*, 32–44.

Neisser, U. *Cognitive Psychology*. New York: Appleton, 1967.

Nickerson, R. S., & Freeman, B. Discrimination of the order of the components of repeating tone sequences: Effects of frequency separation and extensive practice. *Perception & Psychophysics*, 1974, *16*, 471–477.

Ortmann, O. On the melodic relatively of tones. *Psychological Monographs*, 1926, *35* (whole No. 162).

Papcun, G., Krashen, S., Terbeek, D., Remington, R., & Harshman, R. Is the left hemisphere specialized for speech, language and/or something else? *Journal of the Acoustical Society of America*, 1974, *55*, 319–327.

Penfield, W., & Perot, P. The brain's record of auditory and visual experience. *Brain*, 1963, *86*, 595–696.

Pollack, I. Temporal switching between binaural information sources. *Journal of the Acoustical Society of America*, 1978, *63*, 550–558.

Rasch, R. A. The perception of simultaneous notes such as in polyphonic music. *Acustica*, 1978, *40*, 1–72.

Robinson, G. M., & Solomon, D. J. Rhythm is processed by the speech hemisphere. *Journal of Experimental Psychology*, 1974, *102*, 508–511.

Schouten, J. F. On the perception of sound and speech; Subjective time analysis. *Fourth International Congress on Acoustics, Copenhagen Congress Report II*, 1962, 201–203.

Shiffrin, R. M., Pisoni, D. B., & Castaneda-Mendez, K. Is attention shared between the ears? *Cognitive Psychology*, 1974, *6*, 190–215.

Shiffrin, R. M., & Schneider, W. Toward a unitary model for selective attention, memory scanning and visual search. In S. Dornic (Ed.), *Attention and performance*. (Volume VI) Hillsdale: Earlbaum, 1977. Pp. 413–440.

Sorkin, R. D., Pastore, R. E., & Pohlmann, L. D. Simultaneous two-channel signal detection. II. Correlated and uncorrelated signals. *Journal of the Acoustical Society of America*, 1972, *51*, 1960–1965.

Sorkin, R. D., Pohlmann, L. D., & Gilliom, J. D. Simultaneous two-channel signal detection. III. 630- and 1400-Hz signals. *Journal of the Acoustical Society of America*, 1973, *14*, 101–109.

Spellacy, F. Lateral preferences in the identification of patterned stimuli. *Journal of the Acoustical Society of America*, 1970, *47*, 574–578.

Spreen, O., Spellacy, F., and Reid, J. R. The effect of interstimulus interval and intensity on ear asymmetry for nonverbal stimuli in dichotic listening. *Neurophychologia*, 1970, *8*, 245–250.

Sutherland, N. S. Object recognition. In E. C. Carterette & M. P. Friedman (Eds.), *Handbook of Perception*. (Volume III) New York: Academic Press, 1973. Pp. 157–186.

Thomas, I. B., Cetti, R. P., & Chase, P. W. Effect of silent intervals on the perception of temporal order for vowels. *Journal of the Acoustical Society of America*, 1971, *49*, 584.

Thomas, I. B., Hill, P. B., Carroll, F. S., & Garcia, B. Temporal order in the perception of vowels. *Journal of the Acoustical Society of America*, 1970, *48*, 1010–1013.

Thurlow, W. An auditory figure-ground effect. *American Journal of Psychology*, 1957, *70*, 653–654.

Tobias, J. V. Curious binaural phenomena. In J. V. Tobias (Ed.), *Foundations of modern auditory theory*. (Volume II) New York: Academic Press, 1972.

Treisman, A. M. Contextual cues in selective listening. *Quarterly Journal of Experimental Psychology*, 1960, *12*, 242–248.

Treisman, A. M. Selective attention in man. *British Medical Bulletin*, 1964, *20*, 12–16.

Treisman, A. M. Shifting attention between the ears. *Quarterly Journal of Experimental Psychology*, 1971, *23*, 157–167.

Van Noorden, L.P.A.S. Temporal Coherence in the Perception of Tone Sequences. Unpublished doctoral dissertation. Technische Hogeschoel Eindhoven, The Netherlands, 1975.

Vicario, G. L'effetto tunnel acustico. *Revista di Psyicologia*, 1960, *54*, 41–52.

Von Helmholtz, H. *On the sensations of tone as a physiological basis for the theory of music*. (2nd English ed.) New York: Dover, 1954. (Originally published 1859)

Von Helmholtz, H. *Helmholtz's physiological optics*. (Translated from the 3rd German ed.) (1909–1911 by J.P.C. Southall, ed.) Rochester, New York: Optical Society of America, 1925.

Wallach, H., Newman, E. B., & Rosenzweig, M. R. The precedence effect in sound localization. *American Journal of Psychology*, 1949, *62*, 315–336.

Warren, R. M. Perceptual restoration of missing speech sounds. *Science*, 1970, *167*, 392–393.

Warren, R. M. Auditory temporal discrimination by trained listeners. *Cognitive Psychology*, 1974, *6*, 237–256.

Warren, R. M., & Byrnes, D. L. Temporal discrimination of recycled tonal sequences: Pattern matching and naming of order by untrained listeners. *Journal of the Acoustical Society of America*, 1975, *18*, 273–280.

Warren, R. M., Obusek, C. J., & Ackroff, J. M. Auditory induction: Perceptual synthesis of absent sounds. *Science*, 1972, *176*, 1149–1151.

Warren, R. M., Obusek, C. J., Farmer, R. M., & Warren, R. P. Auditory sequence: Confusions of patterns other than speech or music. *Science*, 1969, *164*, 586–587.

Warren, R. M., & Warren, R. P. Auditory illusions and confusions. *Scientific American*, 1970, *223*, 30–36.

Watson, C. S., Kelly, W. J., & Wroton, H. W. Factors in the discrimination of tonal patterns. II. Selective attention and learning under various levels of uncertainty. *Journal of the Acoustical Society of America*, 1976, *60*, 1176–1186.

Watson, C. S., Wroton, H. W., Kelly, W. J., & Benbasset, C. A. Factors in the discrimination of tonal patterns. I. Component frequency, temporal position and silent intervals. *Journal of the Acoustical Society of America*, 1975, *75*, 1175–1185.

Wertheimer, M. Untersuchung zur Lehre von der Gestalt II. *Psychologische Forschung*, 1923, *4*, 301–350.

Wickelgren, W. A. Context-sensitive coding, associative memory and serial order in (speech) behavior. *Psychological Review*, 1969, *76*, 1–15.

Wickelgren, W. A. Phonetic coding and serial order. In E. C. Carterette and M. P. Friedman (Eds.), *Handbook of Perception*. (Volume VII) New York: Academic Press, 1976. Pp. 227–264.

Williams, K. N., and Perrott, D. R. Temporal resolution of tonal pulses. *Journal of the Acoustical Society of America*, 1972, *51*, 644–647.

Zatorre, R. J. Recognition of dichotic melodies by musicians and nonmusicians. *Neurophychologia*, 1979, *17*, 607–617.

5

The Listener and the Acoustic Environment

R. A. Rasch and R. Plomp

I.	Introduction	135
II.	Methodology	137
III.	Level Effects of Indirect Sound: Loudness	140
IV.	Temporal Effects of Indirect Sound: Definition	141
V.	Spatial Effects of Indirect Sound: Spaciousness	142
VI.	The Compromise between Definition and Spaciousness	145
VII.	Conclusion	146
	References	146

I. INTRODUCTION

If a sound source and a listener are situated in an open field without any sound-reflecting surfaces in the neighborhood, the emitted sound will reach the ears of the listener only via the straight line that connects source and listener. The sound image that the listener receives will roughly correspond to the sound emitted by the source. However, that is not the usual situation in listening to music. Producing musical sounds and listening to them is almost always done in rooms or halls—technically speaking, in enclosed spaces. These enclosed spaces have bounding surfaces (walls, floor, ceiling) that reflect the incident sound. Because of these reflections the emitted sound does not only reach the ears of the listener via the straight line from source to listener, but also via numerous other paths. The sound that reaches the listener without any reflection is called the *direct sound;* the sound that arrives after one or more reflections is called the *indirect sound* or *reverberation* (see Fig. 1). The presence of an indirect sound field has a profound influence on the sound image that the

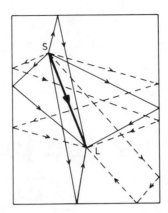

Fig. 1. Some sound paths from a sound source S to a listener L. The direct sound has been indicated with a heavy solid line. The four sound paths, including single reflections, have been drawn as thin solid lines. Slashed lines indicate sound paths with multiple reflections of which only a small selection has been included. As a matter of fact, the radiated sound is attenuated proportional to the square of the length of the path and by every reflection.

listener receives. The subjective effects of the indirect sound field make up what is loosely called the *acoustics* of a room or hall.

Whereas the physical aspects of sound in an enclosed space have been studied for almost a century (see Beranek, 1954; Kuttruff, 1973; Meyer, 1970), the subjective effects cannot claim a long history of research. Research in subjective room acoustics begins after World War II, and its results up to now are mainly tentative. This chapter gives a summary of empirical evidence from the experimental literature on subjective musical room acoustics, which centers in the United States, Great Britain, Germany (West and East), and Japan (Rasch 1977).

We will first briefly examine the physical aspects of indirect sound. Fig. 1 shows several paths by which the sound of a source can reach a listener. Since all sound paths work equally well in both directions, source and listener can always be interchanged. The differences between a situation with and one without indirect sound may be summarized in three points:

1. The indirect sound *adds sound energy* at the position of the listener, resulting in a higher intensity than there would be without indirect sound. The gain can be substantial and depends, of course, on the sound absorption (and reflection) of the boundaries. It can be up to 10 or 15 dB.

2. The indirect sound *arrives later* than the direct sound because its path is always longer. If the velocity of sound is approximately 340 m/sec, it can be stated that every additional meter in a sound path causes a delay of 3.4 msec. Roughly, the time delays of indirect sound can be up to 100 msec per reflection. If the indirect sound includes some strong single late reflections with delays of more than 50 msec, these are called *echoes*.

3. The indirect sound *arrives from other directions* than the direct sound. Usually, it

is possible to distinguish some discretely traceable reflections from the walls and ceiling that arrive first after the direct sound and a mass of diffuse later reflections coming from all directions.

The corresponding subjective effects may be described as follows:

1. The increase in sound intensity is perceived as an increase in *loudness*.
2. The later arrival of indirect sound has the effect that the source seems to sound a little longer than it really does. The direct sound is followed by a "cloud" of indirect sound. This gives continuity to a stream of notes that may have small discontinuities, such as staccato notes. But the indirect sound may also coincide with or even mask the direct sound of the succeeding notes, which may confuse the sound image to a lesser or greater extent. The temporal aspects of indirect sound correspond to the subjective attribute *definition*, the ability to distinguish and to recognize sounds.
3. The incidence of sound from all directions results in an impression of *spaciousness*. This is usually considered a positive quality, although it seems necessary that the position of the sound source should be recognizable in the sound field.

These three effects of indirect sound, both physical and subjective, can be quantified in scales, as will be shown later in this chapter. One of the aims of subjective musical acoustics is to relate subjective to objective scales. The objective and subjective effects are both based on one physical phenomenon (the indirect sound), and, therefore, the scales are not independent. Very often the values on different scales can be predicted from each other. Some scales have a positive extreme corresponding to a condition with a lot of indirect sound; some other scales have a positive extreme corresponding to a condition with no indirect sound.

II. METHODOLOGY

The subjective effects of a room on the perceived sound can be separated in theoretical description. However, in practical situations and even under laboratory conditions, they can never be separated because they are all dependent on one physical source, the indirect sound. For this reason, and some other ones, the methodology of subjective acoustics research is a rather complicated affair. There are some methodological problems that are specific to subjective room acoustics. They give good insight into what kinds of research and results may be expected in this field. We will deal with three such problems.

First, there is the problem of subjective response. The most direct way to measure this response is to ask the listener to report verbally his or her subjective impression of the acoustics of a room or hall. This method was used by Beranek (1962), who based his work on interviews with musicians (mainly conductors and soloists) and music critics. Hawkes and Douglas (1971) and Wilkens (1977) made extensive use of semantic differentials. They opened the way for statistical analyses, including correlation and factor analyses. The subjective factors found can be, more or less successfully, related to measured physical factors (Yoshida, 1965). An objection to this method is that one cannot be sure how the subjects interpret the verbal scales, especially with terms that are not applied to acoustical aspects in normal use. Better in this respect are nonverbal multidimentional scaling techniques, in which the similarity or dissimilarity between various acoustical conditions has be to compared (Yamaguchi, 1972; Edwards, 1974), or only a preference has to be reported (Schroeder et al., 1974). These methods lead to unlabeled factors that can be filled in by comparing them with physical factors. Some researchers, such as Reichardt and co-workers in Dresden, made use of methods borrowed from psychophysics, such as detectability thresholds and difference limens. These methods permit only indirect conclusions concerning subjective aspects, but they are more reliable and more reproducible, both intra- and inter-individually, than subjective methods, such as interviews and semantic differentials.

A second problem lies in the method of presentation of the acoustical situation for subjective evaluation. In a number of studies audiences at live performances have been interviewed. An advantage of this method is its directness. However, it is difficult to compare performances in different halls or different performances in the same hall. In order to cope with these difficulties, researchers have performed experiments with synthetic sound fields, with the aid of which the acoustics of a hall are simulated in the laboratory (see also Wilkens & Kotterba, 1978).

These synthetic sound fields are constructed with loudspeakers in an anechoic chamber. The positions of the loudspeakers determine the angles of incident sound, thus simulating direct sound and indirect sound coming from several directions. All loudspeakers, except for the one for direct sound, are connected to time-delay and attenuation circuits. The music reproduced in such a synthetic sound field must have been recorded without reverberation. A typical setup for a synthetic sound field is illustrated in Fig. 2. It contains the following elements:

1. A loudspeaker in front of the subject, simulating the direct sound. Sometimes two loudspeakers at short distances are used.

2. Two loudspeakers, obliquely placed to the right and to the left. They simulate the first reflections from the walls. These reflection arrive 10 to 50 msec after the direct sound.

3. A loudspeaker mounted above the subject, simulating a ceiling reflection.

4. Several loudspeakers placed on all sides, simulating the later diffuse reverberation (see Fig. 2).

The time and intensity patterns of a sound field can be represented by a echogram or reflectogram. This is a diagram indicating the time delay and intensity of the various components of a sound field, determined relative to the direct sound. The reflectogram of a room or hall can be measured, for instance, by recording the acoustic response to an impulse (Fig. 3); the reflectogram of a synthetic sound field can be derived from its construction, as a matter of fact (Fig. 4). The reflection patterns used in synthetic sound fields are inspired by possible live reflectograms. A recent development in synthetic sound fields is to use headphones and to add the

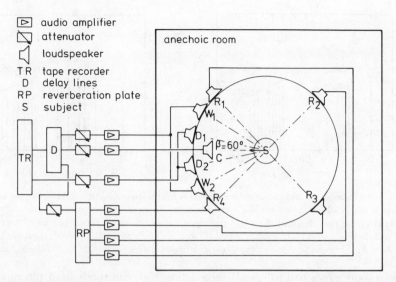

Fig. 2. Example of a synthetic sound field in an anechoic room. The depicted loudspeakers simulate the direct sound (D_1 and D_2), two wall reflections (W_1 and W_2), one ceiling reflection (C, with angle of incidence 60°), and diffuse reverberation (with four loudspeakers R_1, R_2, R_3, and R_4). The arrow indicates the viewing direction of the subject.

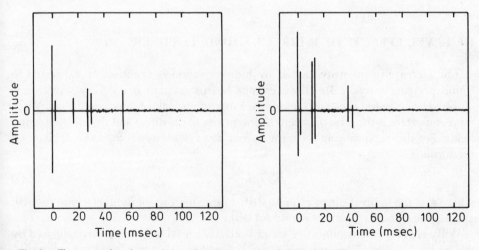

Fig. 3. Two examples of acoustic impulse responses recorded in rooms. The single peaks correspond to the direct sound and the early discrete reflections from walls and ceiling. These early reflections are followed by much weaker diffuse reverberation (based on Thiele, 1953, Figs. 15k and 16c.

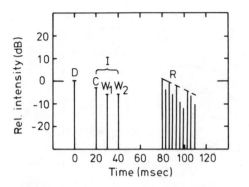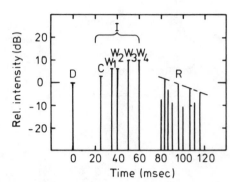

Fig. 4. Two examples of acoustic impulse responses of synthetic sound fields. Actually, the synthetic sound field is the result of the choice of a certain impulse response. The impulse response dictates the attenuation and the time delay of the various components of the sound field. The impulse responses depicted include direct sound (*D*), indirect sound (*I*) with wall reflections (*W*), ceiling reflections (*C*), and reverberation (*R*). The vertical scale is a logarithmic scale (based on Reichardt *et al.*, 1975, Figs. 3–2 and 4a).

acoustic response of a hall to "dead" recorded music with the help of filtering techniques (Schroeder, 1975, 1979).

A third problem lies in the choice of subjects. Who gives the best judgment? Average concert goers are often not aware of the acoustical properties of the hall in which they listen to musical performances. Acousticians and sound technicians do have such an awareness, but they may be less sensitive to the relevant musical criteria. Musicians have their own place in this respect, both literally and metaphorically. As a rule, the investigator tries to find subjects belonging to several of these categories mentioned, such as music critics, acousticians and technicians with a musical background or interest, composers, conductors, and so on.

III. LEVEL EFFECTS OF INDIRECT SOUND: LOUDNESS

The increase in intensity caused by indirect sound is traditionally expressed in sound pressure levels (dB). However, our hearing system is not very sensitive to absolute levels unless these are outside the range of normal listening conditions. Much more important is the ratio between the intensities of the direct and the indirect sound fields. For this ratio we coin the term *indirect/direct ratio* (abbreviated as *i/d*) given by the formula

$$R = L_i - L_d \tag{1}$$

where R is the indirect/direct ratio (in dB), L_i the intensity of indirect sound (in dB), and L_d the intensity of direct sound (in dB).

Wilkens's (1977) first subjective factor is clearly a level factor. It is characterized by the variables "large," "sounding," "loud," "brilliant," "strong," and "penetrating." Typical sound pressure levels of classical music performed in concert halls are within the range of 60 to 90 dB (Winckel, 1962).

IV. TEMPORAL EFFECTS OF INDIRECT SOUND: DEFINITION

The subjective aspects of the temporal effects of indirect sound will be called *definition*. It is a negative scale in the sense that good definition implies little or no indirect sound. Other terms found in the literature are "clarity" (Beranek, 1962, pp. 36–40) and "clearness" (Mafune & Yoshida, 1968). The German term is *Durchsichtigkeit* (Reichardt, Abdel Alim, & Schmidt, 1975; Reichardt & Lehmann, 1976). Definition may be described subjectively as that which enables the listener to distinguish temporal details in the musical sound, and, as such, it is a necessary condition for listening to music. Beranek (1962) distinguishes between horizontal definition (holding for successive sounds) and vertical definition (holding for simultaneous sounds). The same distinction is made by Reichardt (1975) when he refers to temporal and register definition. The physical counterpart of vertical or register definition is not very clear, however. Hawkes and Douglas (1971) do not make this distinction. Their definition factor correlates with the variables "good definition," "clear," and "brilliant." Wilkens's (1977) second factor is a definition factor. Variables strongly loading this factor are "clear," "concentrated," and "definite." It is remarkable that some evaluative variables like "pleasant," "liked," and "nice" had their highest loadings on this factor.

Mafune and Yoshida (1968) found a high correlation between definition and the intelligibility score for speech. There was also a high correlation with a subjective measure for listening comfort. Yamaguchi (1972) found two subjective definition factors, both correlated with intelligibility: speech definition (a d/i ratio taking the indirect sound within 50 msec after the direct sound as direct sound) and sound pressure level. The physical factors supporting a good musical definition are evidently closely related to the factors ensuring a good understanding of speech.

Several physical scales can be given that quantify the temporal effects of indirect sound. It must be mentioned, however, that the relationship between the physical and subjective aspects have not yet been worked out in detail for all scales. The classical scale is the *reverberation time* T, the time required for the sound intensity to decay by 60 dB after abruptly stopping the sound source. This can be extimated from the physical characteristics of a room or hall by the following formula:

$$T = \frac{V}{6\alpha S} \tag{2}$$

where T is the reverberation time in sec, V, the volume in m^3, S the surface of bounding areas in m^2, and α the mean absorption coefficient of the boundaries (fraction of sound energy not reflected).

Optimal reverberation times have been reported in the literature. Kuhl (1954) mentions: 1.5 sec for classical and contemporary music and 2.1 sec for romantic music. Beranek's figures (1962, pp. 425–431) differ only slightly: 1.5 sec for baroque music and Italian opera, 1.7 sec for classical music and Wagnerian opera, and 2.1 sec for romantic music. Optimal reverberation times for music are higher than for speech.

A second physical measure of definition is the *modulation transfer function* or MTF

(Houtgast & Steeneken, 1973; Steeneken & Houtgast, 1980). If the intensity of a sound source is modulated, the modulation depth at a distance decreases to a greater or lesser extent because of the indirect sound. With a lot of indirect sound the valleys in the temporal envelope will be filled, the more so for higher modulation frequencies. The degree of modulation retained at the listener's position may be used as a measure of the influence of the indirect sound. The modulation transfer depends on the modulation frequency so that the actual measure is a curve, the modulation transfer function. For speech the relevant modulation frequency range is from 0.4 to 20 Hz. By weighting the modulation frequencies, the information in the curve can be condensed to a single measure. Up to now, the modulation transfer approach has only been applied to speech communication problems, but application to musical acoustics, both objective and subjective, seems worthwhile. Macfadyen's (1970) confusion index, the minimum perceivable modulation depth expressed in dB of an amplitude-modulated white noise (modulation frequency 10 Hz), is related to the modulation-transfer approach. Macfadyen used his measure to assess the subjective definition of different seating positions in a hall under various acoustical conditions.

A third physical measure for definition is an adaptation of the i/d ratio, called *clarity* by Reichardt *et al*. (1975). It is actually a d/i ratio, in which the direct sound has been expended to include in addition the indirect sound coming within 80 msec after the direct sound:

$$C = L'_d - L'_i \tag{3}$$

where C is the clarity (physical definition) (in dB), L'_d is the intensity of direct sound plus indirect sound within 80 msec in (dB), L'_i is the intensity of indirect sound, arriving more than 80 msec after the direct sound (in dB). With this measure a good prediction of subjective definition is possible. Definition seems to be optimal when there is no indirect sound. This is not realistic in practical situations because another indispensable, positive aspect, spaciousness, depends on indirect sound. Reichardt *et al*. (1975) state that clarity should be at least 1.6 dB.

V. SPATIAL EFFECTS OF INDIRECT SOUND: SPACIOUSNESS

The subjective aspects of the spatial effects of indirect sound are indicated here by the term *spaciousness*. In the literature no prevailing term has come up yet. One finds terms such as "liveness" (Maxfield & Albersheim, 1947; Beranek, 1962), "richness" (Mafune & Yoshida, 1968; Yoshida, 1965), "ambience" (Lochner & DeVilliers Keet, 1960), "fullness of tone" (Beranek, 1962), "spatial responsiveness" (Marshall, 1967), "spatial impression" (Barron, 1971), "resonance" (Hawkes & Douglas, 1971), and "reverberance" (Hawkes & Douglas, 1971). In the German literature the list of terms is restricted to *Raumeindruck*, *Räumlichkeit* and *Halligkeit* (room impression, spaciousness, and reverberance, respectively) in papers by Reichardt and co-workers; and Kuhl 1977, 1978). The German authors treat *Raumeindruck* as a generic term, with *Räumlichkeit* and *Halligheit* as special aspects.

The subjective aspects of spaciousness have been described by Maxfield and Albersheim (1947) as follows: (1) a change in the general tone quality, stated by musicians to be improved "resonance" or "roundness;" (2) the blending of the sound from the various instruments of an orchestra into a single coordinated sound; (3) the sense of acoustic perspective; and (4) the realization on the part of the listener of the approximate size of the auditorium. Beranek (1962, pp. 22–24) mentions the following aspects of "liveness" or a "live room": more uniform loudness, enhancement of bass and treble, fullness of tone, range of crescendo, sound diffusion, intimacy and texture. In this list level and temporal effects are also included. Reichardt *et al.* (1974), Kuhl (1977), and Reichardt and Lehmann (1978a) give lists that do not differ essentially from the items mentioned. Hawkes and Douglas (1971) describe a factor resonance/reverberance, characterized by the variables "resonant," "reverberant," "responsive," and "large dynamic range." Wilkens' (1977) third factor may be regarded as spaciousness factor, with the corresponding variables "weak," "round," "blunt," "dark," and "not-treble."

Maxfield and Albersheim (1947) first connected "liveness" with the *i/d ratio*. This approach has in particular been elaborated by Reichardt and co-workers at the Technological University of Dresden. They used the *d/i* ratio, referred to as *Hallabstand* (Schmidt & Lehmann, 1974). Their first publication (Reichardt & Schmidt, 1966) describes a spaciousness scale with 15 subjectively just-distinguishable points. The relation between the *i/d* ratio and subjective spaciousness is represented in Fig. 5. This scale was based on measurements with synthetic sound fields consisting of direct sound and diffuse reverberation with $T = 2$ sec.

In later research it became evident that not only the amount of indirect sound but

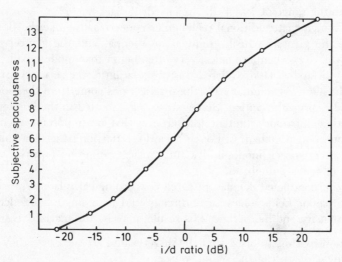

Fig. 5. Subjective spaciousness as a function of the *i/d* ratio (based on Reichardt & Schmidt, 1966, Fig. 5).

also its temporal spread affects spaciousness. Sound fields with equal i/d ratios but different reverberation times may have slightly different spaciousnesses. Actually, the early discrete reflections that come before the diffuse reverberation act subjectively as direct sound, not as indirect sound. Also, the angle of incidence influences the subjective spaciousness. Indirect sound that comes from the frontal direction strengthens the direct sound subjectively.

Reichardt *et al.* (1974, 1978) and Reichardt and Lehmann (1978a,b) summarize the spaciousness effects of the various indirect components of a sound field as follows:

1. Indirect sound arriving within 25 msec after the direct sound counts as direct sound.

2. Sound arriving between 25 to 80 msec after the direct sound must be divided into two components: (2a) the sound arriving with an angle up to 40° relative to the direct sound must be counted as direct sound, and (2b) the sound arriving from side and rear directions must be counted as indirect sound.

3. Sound arriving later than 80 msec after the direct sound must be counted as indirect sound.

With these rules a corrected i/d ratio can be constructed to predict spaciousness:

$$iR = L''_i - L''_d \qquad (4)$$

where R equals spaciousness, L''_d the intensity of direct sound, plus indirect sound, within 25 msec from all directions and within 80 msec from front directions (in dB), and L''_i the intensity of all other components of indirect sound (in dB).

Reichard and Lehmann (1978b) found the correlation between their i/d ratio and the subjectively judged spaciousness as determined in two concert halls to be 0.64 and 0.65, respectively. I/d ratios in these concert halls differed with seat position but were mostly within the range of 2 to 4 dB (Reichardt & Sarkov, 1972).

It is well known that traditional rectangular concert halls—like the Boston Symphony Hall, the Grosser Musikvereinsaal in Vienna, and the Concertgebouw in Amsterdam—have excellent acoustics, very often better than modern halls, which are wide and low. Marshall (1967) related this observation to the relatively strong early reflections. In high, rectangular halls these reflections come from the side walls; in wide, low halls, from the ceiling. Since our ears are located in the horizontal plane, lateral reflections introduce interaural differences that are important in contributing to the perception of spaciousness. For this reason, reflection panels hanging from the ceiling may affect speech intelligibility and musical definition positively, but their spaciousness effects are doubtful.

Barron (1971) conducted detailed research concerning early lateral reflections. He used synthetic sound fields consisting of direct sound and a single side reflection at 40° of varying intensity and delay time. His results may be summarized as follows:

1. Reflections within 10 msec after the direct sound are too early; they result in a subjective sideward shift of the sound source.

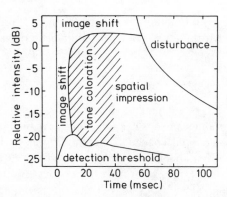

Fig. 6. Subjective effects of a sound field, consisting of direct sound and a lateral reflection with an angle of incidence of 40° with variable attenuation and time delay. The "tone coloration" is caused by the addition of a sound signal and its delayed repetition. The disturbances are usually called echoes (from Barron, 1971, Fig. 5).

2. Relatively strong reflections later than 50 msec after the direct sound disturb the sound image. They are perceived as echoes, distinct from the direct and early indirect sound.

3. Reflections of 20 to 25 dB weaker than the direct sound are below threshold.

4. In between the aforementioned effects there is a region of *spatial impression*. Most important for this are the reflections arriving between 40 and 100 msec after the direct sound. Reflections between 10 and 40 msec can give rise to a distortion of the timbre as an effect of the addition of the direct sound with its delayed repetition (see also Lochner & DeVilliers Keet, 1960 and Bilsen, 1968). Barron's results are illustrated in Fig. 6. The importance of lateral reflections was confirmed by Kuhl's (1978) experiments.

VI. THE COMPROMISE BETWEEN DEFINITION AND SPACIOUSNESS

The right amount of definition and spaciousness are decisive for good subjective room acoustics. However, definition is negatively correlated with indirect sound while spaciousness is positively correlated. So, it will not come as a surprise that definition and spaciousness have a high negative intercorrelation. This means that in practice a compromise between requirements for definition and spaciousness is always necessary.

However, comparing the formulas for clarity (objective definition) and objective spaciousness, one will notice that one component of the sound field affects both definition and spaciousness positively. It is the sound coming from the sides and from the rear later than 40 msec and earlier than 80 msec after the direct sound. Coming earlier than 80 msec, it functions as direct sound with respect to definition. Coming from nonfront directions, it functions as indirect sound with respect to spaciousness. It may be concluded that these reflections are of great importance for good acoustics of a room or hall.

VII. CONCLUSION

Subjective musical room acoustics is a relatively new field of scientific enquiry. It does not possess time-honored concepts, methods, or basic results. It is not yet a standard component of handbooks, textbooks, university curricula, or scientific institutions. Its nature is to a large extent interdisciplinary. Methods and concepts have been derived from physical acoustics as well as from psychology and from musicology. However, the rapid growth of the literature concerning its problem areas during the last decade shows that it will soon become an undispensable part of both room acoustics and psychophysics.

Out of the recent literature two important subjective features of room acoustics have emerged: definition and spaciousness. A number of definitions and measurement procedures for both the subjective attributes and its objective counterparts have been proposed, which include a wide range of ways of thinking. Much research will still be needed before the interrelation between the two basic concepts as well as their connection with physical–acoustical properties are fully understood. However, there are several methods available that promise good progress, such as simulation techniques for room acoustics, the indirect/direct ratio, and the modulation-transfer function. These methods have a mainly physical background. They should be applied along with methods such as factor analysis and multidimensional scaling, which have a predominantly psychological origin. The recognition of the hybrid nature of subjective musical room acoustics is essential for the solving of its questions and problems.

REFERENCES

Barron, M. The subjective effects of first reflections in concert halls—the need for lateral reflections. *Journal of Sound & Vibration*, 1971, *15*, 475–494.
Beranek, L. L. *Acoustics*. New York: McGraw-Hill, 1954.
Beranek, L. L. *Music, acoustics and architecture*. New York: Wiley, 1962.
Bilsen, F. A. On the Interaction of Sound With its Repetitions. Dissertation, Technological University Delft, 1968.
Edwards, R. M. A subjective assessment of concert hall acoustics. *Acustica*, 1974, *39*, 183–195.
Hawkes, R. J., & Douglas, H. Subjective acoustic experience in concert auditoria. *Acustica*, 1971, *24*, 135–150.
Houtgast, T., & Steenken, H.J.M. The modulation transfer function in room acoustics as a predictor of speech intelligibility. *Acustica*, 1973, *28*, 66–73.
Kuhl, W. Über Versuche zur Ermittlung der günstigsten Nachhallzeit grosser Musikstudios. *Acustica*, 1954, *4*, 618–634.
Kuhl, W. In der Raumakustik benützte hörakustische Termini. *Acustica*, 1977, *39*, 57–58.
Kuhl, W. Räumlichkeit als Komponente des Raumeindrucks. *Acustica*, 1978, *40*, 167–181.
Kuttruff, H. *Room acoustics*. London: Applied Science Publishers, 1973.

Lochner, J. P., & De Villiers Keet, W. Stereophonic and quasi-stereophonic reproduction. *Journal of the Acoustical Society of America*, 1960, *32*, 393–401.

Macfadyen, K. A. A method of assessing musical definition in an auditorium. *Applied Acoustics*, 1970, *3*, 181–190.

Mafune, Y., & Yoshida, T. Psychometric approach to the room acoustics, Report II: Distribution of subjective evaluations in five auditoriums and discussion. *Sixth International Congress on Acoustics, Tokyo*, Paper E-2-9, 1968.

Marshall, A. H. A note on the importance of room cross-section in concert halls. *Journal of Sound and Vibration*, 1967, *5*, 100–112.

Maxfield, J. P., & Albersheim, W. J. An acoustic constant of enclosed spaces with their apparent liveness. *Journal of the Acoustical Society of America*, 1947, *19*, 71–79.

Meyer, J. *Acoustics and performance of music*. Frankfurt am Main: Das Musikinstrument, 1978.

Rasch, R. A. Subjective muzikale zaalakoestiek: Een overzicht. *Mens en Melodie*, 1977, *32*, 70–81.

Reichardt, W. Vergleich der objectiven raumakustischen Kriterien für Musik. *Hochfrequenztechnik und Elektroakustik*, 1970, *79*, 121–128.

Reichardt, W., Abdel Alim, O., & Schmidt, W. Definition und Messgrundlage eines objektiven Masses zur Ermittlung der Grenze zwischen brauchbarer und unbrauchbarer Durchsichtigkeit bei Musikdarbietung. *Acustica*, 1975, *32*, 126–137.

Reichardt, W., & Lehmann, U. Sind Raumeindruck und Durchsichtigkeit des Hörerlebnisses im Konzertsaal Gegensätze? *Applied Acoustics*, 1976, *9*, 139–150.

Reichardt, W., & Lehmann, U. Raumeindruck als Oberbegriff von Räumlichkeit und Halligkeit, Erläuterungen des Raumeindrucksmasses R. *Acustica*, 1978, *40*, 277–290. (a)

Reichardt, W., & Lehmann, U. Definition eines Raumeindrucksmasses R zur Bestimmung des Raumeindrucks bei Musikdarbietungen auf der Grundlage subjektiver Untersuchungen. *Applied Acoustics*, 1978, 99–127. (b)

Reichardt, W., & Sarkov, N. Bestimmung der optimalen Räumlichkeit für eine Musikprobe im Bezugsschallfeld. *Zeitschrift für elektronische Informations- und Energietechnik*, 1972, *2*, 49–52.

Reichardt, W., & Schmidt, W. Die hörbaren Stufen des Raumeindrucks bei Musik. *Acustica*, 1966, *17*, 175–179.

Reichardt, W., Schmidt, W., Lehmann, U., & Ahnert, W. Definition und Messgrundlagen eines "wirksamen Hallabstand" als Mass für den Raumeindruck bei Musikdarbietungen. *Zeitschrift für elektronische Informations- und Energietechnik*, 1974, *4*, 225–233.

Schmidt, W., & Lehmann, U. Eignung von Hallabstand oder Hallmass zur objektiven Bestimmung des Raumeindrucks. *Zeitschrift für elektronische Informations- und Energietechnik*, 1974, *4*, 161–168.

Schroeder, M. F. Models of hearing. *Proceedings of the IEEE*, 1975, *63*, 1332–1350.

Schroeder, M. F. *Music perception in concert halls*. Stockholm: Royal Swedish Academy of Music, 1979.

Schroeder, M. F., Gottlob, D., & Siebrasse, K. F. Comparative study of European concert halls: correlation of subjective preference with geometric and acoustic parameters. *Journal of the Acoustical Society of America*, 1974, *56*, 1195–1201.

Steeneken, H.J.M., & Houtgast, T. A physical method for measuring speech-transmission quality. *Journal of the Acoustical Society of America*, 1980, *67*, 318–326.

Thiele, R. Richtungsverteilung und Zeitfolge der Schallrückwürfe in Räumen. *Acustica*, 1953, *3*, 291–302.

Wilkens, H. Mehrdimensionale Beschreibung subjektiver Beurteilungen der Akustik von Konzertsälen. *Acustica*, 1977, *38*, 10–23.

Wilkens, H., & Kotterba, B. Vergleich der Beurteilung verschiedener raumakustischer Situationen bei Anregung eines Raumes mit einem Orchester oder Lautsprechern. *Acustica*, 1978, *40*, 291–297.

Winkel, F. Optimum acoustic criteria of concert halls for the performance of classical music. *Journal of the Acoustical Society of America*, 1962, *34*, 81–86.

Yamaguchi, K. Multivariate analyses of subjective and physical measures of hall acoustics. *Journal of the Acoustical Society of America*, 1972, *52*, 1271–1279.

Yoshida, T. Psychometric approach to the room acoustics. *Fifth Internation Congress on Acoustics, Liège*, Paper B 18 (1965).

Rhythm and Tempo

Paul Fraisse

I.	Definitions	149
II.	Rhythm and Spontaneous Tempo	151
	A. Spontaneous Rhythmic Movements	151
	B. Spontaneous Tempo	153
	C. Motor Induction and Synchronization	154
	D. Subjective Rhythmization	155
III.	Rhythmic Forms	157
	A. Regular Groupings	157
	B. Patterns in Time	162
	C. Patterns of Time	165
IV.	The Perception of Musical Rhythms	170
V.	Conclusion	175
	References	177

I. DEFINITIONS

The task of those who study rhythm is a difficult one, because a precise, generally accepted definition of rhythm does not exist. This difficulty derives from the fact that rhythm refers to a complex reality in which several variables are fused. Our aim will be to distinguish these variables successively. However, since this work is devoted to music, it is necessary to emphasize that the problem has been complicated by music theorists who have often chosen, due to their personal aesthetic preferences, to recognize only one of the several aspects of rhythm.

Can etymology help us? Rhythm comes from the Greek words ρυθμος (rhythm) and ρέω (to flow). However, as Benveniste (1951) has shown, the semantic connection between rhythm and flow does not occur through the intervention of the regular movement of waves, as was often believed. In Greek one never uses *rheo* and *rhythmos* when referring to the sea. *Rhythmos* appears as one of the key words in Ionian philosophy, generally meaning "form," but an improvised, momentary, and modifiable form. *Rhythmos* literally signifies a "particular way of flowing." Plato essentially applied this term to bodily movements, which, like musical sounds, may be described in terms of numbers. He wrote in *The Banquet* "The system is the result of rapidity and of slowness, at first opposed, then harmonized." In *The Laws* he arrived at the fundamental definition that rhythm is "the order in the movement." We will adopt this definition, which, even in its generality, conveys different aspects of rhythm.

However, an essential distinction asserts itself. Rhythm is the ordered characteristic of succession. This order may be conceived or perceived. We speak of the rhythm of the days and of the nights, of the seasons, and of rapid or of very slow physical phenomena (such as that of light frequencies or of the planets, respectively). If by direct or by indirect observation, we ascertain the successive phases of these phenomena, in none of these cases do we directly perceive the order—that is to say, the succession of the phases itself. The rhythm is thereby inferred from a mental construction.

However, there exist cases in which there is, properly speaking, the perception of rhythm, such as in dance, song, music, and poetry. We then find precisely the connection that Plato made between order and human movement: All of the rhythms that we perceive are rhythms which originally resulted from human activity. The first psychologists of the nineteenth century felt this relationship. Mach (1865) placed motor activity at the center of our experience of rhythm, and Vierordt (1868), several years later, began to record rhythmic movements.

Let us, nevertheless, insist on the fact that rhythm is a perceptual quality specifically linked to certain successions, a *Gestaltqualität*, according to Von Ehrenfel's definition. At this point, in order to clarify the rest of our discussion, it is necessary to specify the characteristic traits of this rhythmic perception.

Most generally, we say that there is rhythm when we can predict on the basis of what is perceived, or, in other words, when we can anticipate what will follow. In this guise, we return to the idea of order found in Plato and in the most modern definitions, such as Martin's (1972): "Inherent in the rhythmic concept is that the perception of early events in a sequence generates expectancies concerning later events in real time (p. 503)."

This characteristic appears in its true form if we compare rhythm with arrhythmia. All sequences of random stimulations will be considered arrhythmic (see Section III,C,1). Nevertheless, one can more or less anticipate what is to follow, and from this the difficulties arise. At one extreme, we have the isochronous repetition of the same stimulus: the pulse, the march, the tick-tock of a clock. This repetition can be that of a pattern of stimuli having analogous structures, as in a waltz or an alexandrine. At the other extreme, we have a succession of relatively different patterns, as in free verse or in certain modern music.

The anticipation can only be temporal; that is to say, linked to the organization within the duration. But what is organized in this way? At this point, there is often a misunderstanding. Is rhythm born out of a series of stimuli, whose temporal characteristics are fundamental, as one could be led to believe by a description of a poetic sequence, in terms of breves and longs, or by the reading of a musical score where each note is of a precise length? Or is rhythm born out of the ordering of the temporal intervals among the elements marked by a difference in intensity, of pitch or of the timbre? These two propositions are opposed by all theorists of rhythm. The problem is, without doubt, as old as is music. Plato in *The Republic* already made fun of a critic of his era: "I vaguely remember" he wrote, "that he spoke of anapaestic verse. . . ; I don't know how he arranged them and established the equality of the up beat and of the fall by a combination of long and breve. . . ." The problem remains: Is rhythm the arrangement of durable elements, or is it the succession of more or less intense elements, the upbeat and the fall, the *arsis* and the *thesis* of the Greeks being the most simple example? We will see that both forms of organization exist, one type of relation prevailing over the other. Moreover, they are most often linked and interdependent. Rhythm is the perception of an order.

One of the perceptual aspects of rhythmic organization is *tempo*. It can be lively or slow. It corresponds to the number of perceived elements per unit time, or to the absolute duration of the different values of the durations. Evidently, one passed from a definition based on frequency to a definition based on duration. We will use both of them. The possibility of rhythmic perception depends on tempo, because the organization of succession into perceptible patterns is largely determined by the law of proximity. When the tempo slows down too much, the rhythm and also the melody disappear.

We have chosen to begin this chapter with the most simple perceptions and to end up with the most complex ones, which are evidently those of artistic rhythms. The reason is not because the simple explains the complex, but because simple configurations can be more easily analyzed (see also Fraisse, 1956, 1974).

II. RHYTHM AND SPONTANEOUS TEMPO

A. Spontaneous Rhythmic Movements

The most easily perceived rhythm is one that is produced by the simple repetition of the same stimulus at a constant frequency. In the rest of this article, we will call this a *cadence*. The simplest examples are the beating of a clock or of a metronome. But the most important fact is that these rhythms are characteristic of some very fundamental activities such as walking, swimming, and flying. Both animals and people move about with rhythmic movements characteristic of their species. The first rhythmic movement found in the human new-born is sucking, with periods that follow at intervals of from 600 to 1200 msec. This regularity is interrupted by spontaneous pauses, but sucking movements occur at a cadence that seems to be characteristic for each infant. Later on, walking appears. While one of the limbs supports the body weight, the other swings forward, before serving, in turn, as support. In the adult there is also a brief period (100 msec) of double support. The duration of the step is about 550 msec, and corresponds to a frequency of 110–112 per minute (Mishima,

1965). This frequency depends a little on anthropometric differences between individuals, age, and environmental conditions. This spontaneous activity, which is similar to a reflex, is a fundamental element of human motor activity. It plays an important role in all of the rhythmic arts.

Spontaneous activities reveal that physiological settings exist in the human organism, and, more generally, in all living things, which are regulated by peripheral afferents and, above all, by nervous centers situated at different levels. The tempo of walking, for example, seems to be determined by the medulla. From these centers and from their activity, we have other manifestations, among which it is necessary to cite the heartbeat (with an average of 72 beats per minute) and the electrical oscillations of the cerebral cortex with frequencies varying from 1 to 3 per second for delta waves, from 14 to 30 for beta waves, and most characteristically, from 8 to 13 for alpha waves.

We still do not know where the different biological clocks that assure the regularity of these phenomena are located. However, one can think that an autorhythmicity is characteristic of certain nervous tissues. Even though Sherrington has shown that a nerve follows the rhythm of an excitation whatever its frequency, it is not the same when the excitation crosses a nervous center. The frequency of the response is then different from that of the excitation. Also, the myotatic reflex follows the cadence of a mechanical excitation up to a frequency of 4 to 5 per second. For values higher than this, a halving of the frequency of the response occurs every second shock, and for even higher values, every third shock is effective (Paillard, 1955). This fact, reminiscent of the general properties of oscillating circuits, is suggestive.

Among spontaneous movements, it is necessary to cite rocking, which clearly intervenes in games or in dances, but which is manifested from the most tender age on by the beating of the foot of the newborn lying on his back (average age of appearance 2.7 months). As soon as the child can remain seated, the rocking of the trunk appears (toward 6 months). This rocking of the trunk can be considered essentially as a movement of the head, of which one observes different modalities: rocking while on all fours (forward–backward), standing, or on the knees. In most children these movements are transitory, but in others they can last for months, sometimes until 2–3 years and even until 5 years of age. One encounters, moreover, other forms of rocking in the older child (movement of the legs, for example, while seated). Also, the use of the rocking-chair is not without a relation to this type of behavior. There is little precise information regarding the frequency of these rockings. They occur within the range of spontaneous tempos (.5–2 per second), and this frequency depends on the muscular mass concerned.

It is necessary to note that rocking is related neither to vegetative functions (as is the heart) or to relational functions (sucking, walking); it appears when the child is idle or at the moment of falling asleep. In the adult it also translates into an absence of voluntary control or a state of distraction. These movements seem to correspond to a regulation of nervous tension. The postural activity with its tonic effects then takes preponderance over the relational activity (Wallon, 1949). It above all appears when the possibility of communicating with the environment is reduced, as when the movements of the child are restricted by the intervention of an adult or by illness. It is frequent in mental deficiency, neurosis or dementia. In all of these cases, rocking seems to aim at the maintenance of a state of excitation, and it has a heavy affective connotation.

B. Spontaneous Tempo

The periodic activities that we have just mentioned have their own spontaneous tempo. Stern (1900) thus thought that a psychic tempo characteristic of voluntary activity exists. In order to determine this tempo, he proposed a simple motor activity: tapping a spontaneous tempo on a table. History has shown the fecundity of this proposed test, but has not confirmed the existence of a psychic tempo characteristic of all an individual's activities. There are only weak correlations between the different repetitive tests executed at a spontaneous tempo. Factorial analysis always reveals a plurality of factors (Allport and Vernon, 1933; Rimoldi, 1951).

Spontaneous tempo, also called *personal tempo* (Frischeisen-Köhler, 1933a) or *mental tempo* (Mishima, 1951–1952) and measured by the natural speed of tapping, is of great interest. The length of the interval between two taps varies, according to the authors, from 380 to 880 msec. One can assert that a duration of 600 msec is the most representative. All of the research underscores the great interindividual variability of this tempo (from 200 to 1400 msec, Fraisse, Pichot, & Clairouin, 1949). By contrast, individual variability is slight. One can verify this within a trial: the variability of intervals is from 3 to 5%, which is in the range of the differential threshold for durations of this type. Also, there is great reliability from one trial to another: the correlations are of the order of .75 to .95 (Harrel, 1937; Rimoldi, 1951). This reliability indicates that spontaneous tempo is characteristic of the individual, a statement reinforced by twin reserach. Differences in tempo between two identical twins (homozygous) are no larger than between two executions of spontaneous tempo by the same subject; however, the differences between two heterozygous twins are as great as between two individuals chosen at random (Frischeisen-Köhler, 1933a; Lehtovaara, Saarinen, & Järvinen, 1966).

Spontaneous tempo of the forefinger has a good correlation with that of the palm of the hand, with the swinging of the leg of a seated subject, and with the swinging of the arm when the subject is standing (Mishima, 1965).

It is necessary to distinguish between spontaneous tempo and *preferred tempo*. The latter corresponds to the speed of a succession of sounds or of lights that appears to be the most natural—that is to say, to a regular succession judged as being neither too slow nor too fast. Since the nineteenth century a number of German scientists have sought the interval which appeard to be neither too short nor too long. The most frequent determination has been about 600 msec. In this regard, Wundt examined the natural duration of associations between two perceptions, and he proposed a value of 720 msec.

Since Wallin (1911), the preferred tempo has most frequently been measured using a metronome. The results found are fairly close to 500 msec (Wallin, 1911;

Frischeisen-Köhler, 1933b; Mishima, 1956). Possibly, this value is in part determined by the scale of tempos which the metronome offers. The preferred tempo of an individual is an constant as is spontaneous tempo, but the correlations between the two tests are not higher than .40 (Mishima, 1965).

It is striking that the rhythm of the heart, of walking, of spontaneous and of preferred tempo are of the same order of magnitude (intervals of from 500 to 700 msec). It has been tempting to study whether one of these rhythms serves in some way as a sort of *pacemaker* for the others. The rhythm of the heart, the most often invoked, is not correlated with spontaneous tempo (Tisserand & Guillot, 1949–1950). Moreover, it has been verified several times that an acceleration of the hearbeat does not correspond to an acceleration of spontaneous tempo. By contrast, one finds a noteworthy correlation between the rhythm of walking and of spontaneous tempo (.28, Harrison, 1941; .68, Mishima, 1965). However, we cannot assume that one phenomenon can be explained by the other. There is only a narrow range of frequencies of natural or voluntary rhythms and of preferred tempo.

C. Motor Induction and Synchronization

Spontaneous motor tempo and preferred tempo do not only have comparable frequencies, but observations and experiments show that they are also often associated. People fairly easily accompany with a motor act a regular series of sounds. This phenomenon spontaneously appears in certain children toward one year of age, sometimes even earlier. Parents are surprised to see their child sitting or standing, rocking in one way or another while listening to rhythmic music. From the age of 3–4 years on, the child is capable of accompanying, when requested, the beating of a metronome (Fraisse et al., 1949). This accompaniment tends to be a synchronization between the sound and a tap—that is to say, that the stimulus and the response occur simultaneously.

This behavior is all the more remarkable, as it constitutes an exception in the field of our behaviors. As a general rule, our reactions succeed the stimuli. In synchronization the response is produced at the same time as the appearance of the stimulus. A similar behavior is possible only if the motor command is anticipated in regard to the moment when the stimulus is produced. More precisely, the signal for the response is not the sound stimulus but the temporal interval between successive signals. Synchronization is only possible when there is anticipation—that is, when the succession of signals is periodic. Thus, the most simple rhythm is evidently the isochronal production of identical stimuli. However, synchronization is also possible in cases of more complex rhythms. What is important is not the regularity but the anticipation. The subjects can, for example, synchronize their tapping with some series of accelerated or decelerated sounds, the interval between the successive sounds being modified by a fixed duration (10, 20, 50, 80, or 100 msec). Synchronization, in these cases, remains possible, but its precision diminishes with the gradient of acceleration or of deceleration (Ehrlich, 1958).

The spontaneity of this behavior is attested to by its appearance early in life and also by the fact that the so-called evolved adult has to learn how to inhibit his involuntary movements of accompaniment to music. Experiments confirm these observations. When subjects were presented with a regular series of sounds and asked to tap for each sound, they spontaneously synchronized sound and tap. When asked not to synchronize but to respond *after* each sound, as in a reaction-time experiment, all of the subjects found this task difficult, the more so the higher the frequency of sounds (Fraisse, 1966). The same difficulty arose when the subjects were asked to syncopate—that is, to interpolate the series of taps between the series of sounds. The subjects habitually succeeded only when the intervals between the sounds were longer than one second (Fraisse & Ehrlich, 1955). Conversely, it has been shown (Fraisse, 1966) that synchronization is established very rapidly, and that it is acquired from the third sound on. Let us add, in anticipation of what is to follow, that the synchronization of repetitive patterns is also realized from the third pattern on.

Not only is synchronization possible at the frequency of preferred tempo, but it is also possible in the whole range of frequencies of spontaneous tempos. More precisely, one observes that synchronization is most regular for intervals of 400 to 800 msec. If the frequencies are faster or slower, the separation between taps and sounds is more variable. For rapid cadences it is, above all, a perceptual problem: the interval between two sounds is not perceived exactly enough to permit precise synchronization (Michon, 1964). The subject oscillates between exaggerated anticipations and delays when the tap follows the sound as in a reaction time situation (Fraisse, 1966). In conclusion, the range in which synchronization is possible is at sound intervals of 200 to 1800 msec between the sounds.[1]

The synchronization that we have considered in its most elementary forms plays a fundamental role in music, not only in dance but also in all instances in which several musicians play together. The unity of their playing is possible only when they are capable of anticipation. One of the roles of the conductor of an orchestra is to furnish the signals that will result in synchronization between musicians.

D. Subjective Rhythmization

If one listens to identical sounds that follow each other at equal intervals, that is to say, a cadence, these sounds seem to be grouped by twos or by threes. Since nothing

---

[1]In speaking of synchronization, it is necessary to specify what is synchronized with what. In effect, if one measures the temporal separation between a tap of the forefinger and the sound, one finds that the tap slightly anticipates the sound by about 30 msec. The subject does not perceive this error systematically. This was pointed out as early as 1902 by Miyake. Moreover, this error is greater if the sound is synchronized with the foot. The difference between hand and foot permits us to think that the subject's criterion for synchronization is the coincidence of the auditory and of the tactile-kinesthetic information at the cortical level. For this coincidence to be as precise as possible, the movement of tapping should slightly precede the sound in order to make allowance for the length of the transmission of peripheral information. This length is all the greater when the distance is longer (Fraisse, 1980, pp. 252–257).

objectively suggests this grouping, this phenomenon has been termed *subjective rhyth-mization*. This expression, which appeared at the end of the nineteenth century (Meumann, 1894; Bolton, 1894), must today be considered inadequate, because all perceived rhythm is the result of an activity by the subject since, physically, there are only successions. The observations made using sound series were later confirmed by using visual series (Koffka, 1909). When one thus listens to a cadence, introspection reveals that grouping seems to correspond to the lengthening of one of the intervals. If one continues to be attentive, it seems that one of the elements of the group, the first in general, also appears to be more intense than the others.

These introspective notions were confirmed by authors who asked their subjects to accompany each of the sounds by a tap (Miyake, 1902; Miner, 1903; MacDougall, 1903; Temperley, 1963). The recording of the taps corresponded to introspective observation. There were temporal differentiations and corresponding accentuations. This phenomenon, today seemingly banal, which preceded the work of the Gestalts, was considered extraordinary. Its significance remains important at the present time since it underscores the perceptual and spontaneous character of rhythmic grouping.

In his pioneering study, Bolton (1894) worked on the problem of the limits of the frequencies at which subjective rhythmization could appear. He gave as the lower limit an interval of 115 msec, and as the upper limit, 1580 msec. These limits should command our attention, since they are approximately those of the durations on which all of our perceptions of rhythm are based. The lower limit (about 120 msec) corresponds to the psychophysiological conditions of the distinction between two successive stimuli. It corresponds to the minimal interval between two rapid motor taps. The upper limit has a very important perceptual significance, revealed at the phenomenological level. It corresponds to the value at which two stimuli (or two groups of stimuli) are no longer perceptually linked.

In order to understand this, let us take the example of the tick-tock of a clock. The sounds are linked together in groups of two. Let us suppose that one can slow down this tick-tock indefinitely. There comes a moment when the tick and the tock are no longer linked perceptually. They appear as independent events. This upper limit is also that where all melody disappears, and is substituted by isolated notes. The limit proposed by Bolton (1580 msec) is without doubt too precise. MacDougall rightly situated it between 1500 and 2000 msec. We propose retaining a value of about 1800 msec. Beyond this duration subjective rhythmization becomes impossible. If one asks the subjects to continue isochronous sequences by tapping, one finds (Fraisse, 1956, pp. 13–14) that the variability of these sequences is minimal around an interval of 600 msec, that it increases a little for shorter intervals, and increases substantially beyond 1200 msec. The linkage is no longer susceptible to precise perceptual control.

On the motor level, we also find an optimum of about 600 msec for perceptual organization. This length is also that which is perceived with the greatest precision (Fraisse, 1963, p. 119; Michon, 1964).

The importance of all of these parameters will appear when we discuss more complex rhythms.

III. RHYTHMIC FORMS

A. Regular Groupings

As soon as a difference is introduced into an isochronous sequence of elements, this difference produces a grouping of the elements included between two repetitions of the difference. One then speaks of objective rhythmization. This difference can be a lengthening of a sound, an increase in its intensity, a change in pitch or in timbre, or simply a lengthening of an interval between two elements. This fact suggests two types of question: (a) the possible durations of rhythmic groups and (b) the nature of the effects principally produced by modifications in intensity or in duration.

1. The Duration of Groups

If one accentuates or lengthens one sound out of two, three, or four, this produces the perception of a repetitive group of two, three, or four elements. We already know that the interval between the elements is important and that the perception of the rhythm, objective or subjective, disappears if the intervals are either too short or too long. By asking subjects to produce groups of three or four taps, we found that there was, on the average, an interval of 420 msec between the taps of groups of three, and of 370 msec between groups of four (Fraisse, 1956, p. 15).

Within these limits of succession one can perceive groups of from two to six sounds that correspond to the boundaries of our immediate memory or of our capacity of apprehension. In order to obtain a good rhythmization, it is necessary when the number of elements increases to increase the frequency of the successive sounds. MacDougall (1903), while employing a method of production, found that the longer the groups were the faster the frequencies of the sounds. Thus, a group of four is only 1.8 times as long as a group of two, while a group of six is 2.2 times as long. Everything happens as if the subject was trying to strengthen the unity of the group when the number of elements to be perceived is larger.

By employing the method of reproduction of auditory series (while preventing the subject from counting by a concomitant verbalization), we found that for an interval of 17 msec, 5.7 elements were accurately perceived (total duration 800 msec); for an interval of 630 msec, 5.4 elements (total duration 2770 msec); and for an interval of 1800 msec, 3.3 elements (total duration 4140 msec). Thus, there is an interaction between the number of elements and their frequency. The total length of possible groupings depends on both. However, more complex groupings of sounds can be perceived (such as those that we will study in Section III), if subunits analogous to those that are called "chunks" can be created. Thus, one can come to perceive about 25 sounds as a unity (Dietze, 1885; Fraisse and Fraisse, 1937) if they form five subgroups of five sounds following each other at a rapid frequency (180 msec). However, the total length of the groups, in this extreme case, cannot be more than 5 sec.

This limit is found in the rhythmic arts. The slowest adagio in a 9/4 bar is no longer than 5 sec, and the longest lines of poetry have from 13 to 17 syllables, the time necessary to recite them being no longer than from 4 to 5 sec (Wallin, 1901). This length of from 4 to 5 sec is, however, an extreme limit that allows only unstable groupings. For the groups of sounds produced by subjects, MacDougall (1903) gives 3 sec as a practical limit. According to Sears (1902), the average length of a musical bar in religious hymns is 3.4 sec. According to Wallin (1901), the average duration of lines of poetry is 2.7 sec.

This duration limit corresponds to what has been called the *psychological present*. We know that we can perceive, relatively simultaneously, a series of successive events (for example, a telephone number or the elements of a sentence). This phenomenon is also called *short-term storage* or even *precategorical acoustic storage* (Crowder & Morton, 1969). We prefer, however, in the case of rhythm to speak of the psychological present. This term expresses well the organization of a sequence of events into a perceptual unity. It corresponds to our limit in organizing a succession. A similar unity introduces a perceptual discontinuity in the physical continuum into the psychological present. One should not repeat the mistake that James (1891) made when he thought that there was a continuous sliding of the present into the past. He cited as an example the recitation of the alphabet. If one's present is at moment t: C D E F G, at moment $t + 1$ it will be D E F G H, C having disappeared and having been replaced by H. This analysis is inexact. Language, as well as rhythm, shows that one group of stimuli succeeds another group.

Today, it is easier to accept as true the principle of the temporal *Gestalt*. At the beginning of the twentieth century, psychologists were very much preoccupied with associative links as the basis of the unification of rhythmic groups. Two hypotheses were dominant about 1900. One, introduced for the first time by Bolton (1894), referred to the pulse acts of attention; these acts follow each other. This is only a description of the same sort as that of the psychological present, although perhaps, it is less subtle. The other hypothesis looked for the unification of successive sensations through the unity of a kinesthetic response. Miner (1903) wrote: "In feeling the groups to be units is an illusion due to the presence of movement or strain sensations along with the sensations that are grouped." In this form this hypothesis goes beyond associationism. However, it is true that the perception of successive groups is facilitated if there is an accompaniment of sounds by synchronized movements that can, according to their frequency, correspond either to each of the sounds or to a single sound per group. This fact is observed in objective and subjective rhythmization. Temperley (1963) observed a negative correlation between the frequency of motor responses and the frequency of a cadence, the subject tapping only once for every two or three sounds. Miner (1903) had previously observed the same phenomenon when a person taps his or her foot to a piece of music. Movement does not create the grouping; however, the more the rhythmic experience is sensory-motor, the more it is complete (see Section III).

2. Factors in Grouping

Any differentiation in an isochronous series of identical elements serves as a basis for grouping. However, they do not all have the same effects as far as the organization of a temporal series is concerned. In general, a noteworthy lengthening of the duration of a sound or of the interval between two sounds determines the end of a group; this longer duration allows one to distinguish between two successive patterns. It imposes itself in subjective rhythmization. This lengthening creates a rupture between two groups. We call it *pause*. Its duration is not random and cannot be assimilated to a gap or to a ground according to Rubin's terminology. In effect, the perception of rhythm is not only that of a grouping but also that of a linking of groups called *Gestaltverkettung* by Werner (1919) and *Fugengestalten* by Sander (1928). In his 1909 dissertation, Koffka noted the following striking behavior: If a subject was given three lights—a, b, c—and if he was asked to continue the rhythm, he not only reproduced the intervals between a and b and c but also linked the groups of lights as though the interval between the final c of the first group and the initial a of a second one had been proposed to him. Out of seven subjects five did not even see that there was a problem.

When asked to tap regularly in groups of three or of four, subjects spontaneously separated the groups by a pause that was from about 600 to 700 msec. With more complex patterns the duration of the pause was at least equal to that of the duration of the longest interval inside the pattern. Otherwise, there was a reorganization of the pattern, so that the longest interval played the role of the pause. However, the pause was never longer than 1800 msec; since, if such were the case, there would no longer be the perception of a chain of patterns but only the perception of isolated patterns. Wallin (1901) found that the pause at the end of a line of poetry was, on the average, 680 msec. Evidently, pauses in the strict sense of the word do not exist in a musical sequence; still, one exists at the end of each pattern in the form of a slight interval.

Most often, it has been assumed that the structuring of patterns was based on the accentuation of one or of several elements. This accentuation already appears, as we have seen, in subjective rhythmization. It is important in music where the pause—*stricto sensu*—does not play a role. The accented element, when it determines the length of a group, also determines the nature of the grouping. The objective accent is situated most spontaneously at the beginning of the pattern. This fact has already appeared in subjective rhythmization.

A regular succession of a strong and of a weak sound of equal duration is perceived in 60% of the cases as a succession of trochees (strong–weak) and in 40% of the cases as a series of iambuses (weak–strong) (Fraisse, 1956, p. 95). Other discussions continued—and are continuing—concerning the relative role of accents and of pauses. In reality, there is an interaction between the two factors producing segregation. An important lengthening of a sound leads it to play the role of a pause. A slight lengthening of the duration of a sound makes it appear more intense and confers upon it the role of an accent. It then, most often, becomes the first element of a pattern. Reciprocally, the accenting of an element slightly modifies its duration or, if one prefers, the interval that follows it. Thus, while synchronizing the taps with a regular series of strong and weak sounds, we found, as did initially Miyake (1902), that the intervals between the taps depended on the perceived structure (Fraisse, 1956, pp. 95–96).

trochee	484–452 msec
iambus	432–520 msec

A general fact is observed: the most intense element is lengthened. But it is lengthened more when it terminates the pattern, as the effect of the properly so-called accent adds itself to the effect of the pause.

The most intense sound is spontaneously lengthened even by musicians (Stetson, 1905; Vos, 1973). In prosody when the structure is fundamentally in breves and longs, the accent is always placed on the long element. There is between the lengthening of the duration and the accent, a certain functional and perceptual equivalence. If the more intense sounds are perceived as being longer, the longer sounds are perceived as being more intense.

Evidently, by modifying the intervals between sounds of different intensities, one can make the trochees or the iambuses, for example, more frequent. This experiment was performed by Woodrow (1909) who was able to establish a point of indifference where the iambus had as many chances of being perceived as the trochee, the dactyl as the anapaest. It suffices to lengthen relatively the interval that follows the weak sound or that precedes the strong sound. Since grouping can be obtained by modifying durations or accents, and since there is an interaction between these two factors, simplistic conclusions can be discounted such as those which affirm that the perception of rhythm is based only on the perception of durations or of accents. But the roles of durations and of accents are not the same. The duration of the elements or of the intervals which separate them (in the rhythmic arts these are barely distinguishable) is always a precise quantity. Experiments show that in performances durations are less variable than are accents. By making subjects tap repetitive forms, Brown (1911) found that the relative variability of accents was of the order of 10 to 12% and those of durations of 3 to 5%. This result was confirmed by Schmidt (1939). One finds the same results in vocal performances.

One can then modify in the repetition of patterns the strength—but not the place—of some accents without modifying the nature of the perceived rhythm. One can also modify the duration of the elements, but to a lesser degree. Variations of about 6% do not in any way alter the nature of the rhythm. They are still acceptable at 12% but not beyond (Wallin, 1911). Modifications of accents can be very much more important, and artists use them a great deal.

We have reasoned until now as though accentuation signified an increase in intensity. However accents, as we said, can be produced by a slight increase in duration. They can also be obtained by changes in pitch or in timbre. A change in pitch brings with it rhythmic segregation. However, according to the best study (Woodrow, 1911), the highest sound can be spontaneously placed at the beginning as well as at the end of a group. There is also an interaction of some sort between the intensities and the pitches of sounds. In a series of sounds the highest appears subjectively as the most intense, and vice versa.

If differences in duration, in intensity, and in pitch can organize rhythmic groups, the intensity of the accent has a specific role that we have already noticed in subjective rhythmization. The periodic repetition of accents more or less induces motor reactions that repeat themselves regularly and reinforce the salience of the perceived patterns.

We have described the modifications, which in a series of isochronous sounds, produce rhythmic structures (Fraisse, 1975). We have not explained them. We can state that these perceptual laws are identical to those pointed out by the Gestaltists, and in particular by Wertheimer (1922, 1923). The pause underscores the importance of proximity, the accent, that of repetition of identical elements, or of good continuation.

This comparison still does not explain anything, as Gestalt laws are themselves unexplained. However, current research on the perceptions of the new-born have at least shown the great precocity of these perceptual laws in the spatial domain (Vurpillot, Ruel, & Castrec, 1977). It has recently been demonstrated that the very young child is also sensitive to differences in rhythms. Demany, McKenzie, & Vurpillot (1977), by using a habituation paradigm with an operant response consisting of the fixation of a visual target, showed that the new-born child (71 ± 12 days) discriminates a series of isochronous sounds (duration 40 msec with intervals of 194 msec) from a series of patterns of four sounds separated by intervals of 194, 97, 194, 297 msec. They can also discriminate a pattern of the type 97, 291, 582 msec from another pattern 291, 97, 582 msec. These sequences are here described in an arbitrary manner, as we remain ignorant as to how the child groups sounds.

However, a child of this age does not perceive a difference in tempo between a series composed of sounds of 500 msec followed by intervals of 500 msec and another series composed of sounds of 1000 msec followed by intervals of 1000 msec (Clifton & Meyers, 1969). Does the technique of this experiment have any flaws? Were the chosen tempos too slow? One does not know at present, but Berg (1974) and then Leavitt, Brown, Morse, & Graham (1976) found that a simple change of tempo between two simple structures (series of sounds of 400 msec followed by an interval of 600 msec compared with a series of sounds of 800 msec followed by an interval of 1200 msec) was discriminated. According to Chang and Trehib (1977), children at 5 months are capable of discriminating groups of two from groups of four sounds (children of this age are also capable of discriminating between identical groups composed of different sounds). Allen, Walker, Symonds, and Marcell (1977) also found that children can at 7 months distinguish an isochronous succession from an iambic type of grouping.

Rhythmic grouping thus appears very early in life. In consequence, hypotheses that consider it as a voluntary activity, such as the pulse of attention or a motor accompaniment, are invalid. Furthermore, the law of proximity seems to be very primitive in time, as it is in space [Brunswick (1956) to the contrary]. Beyond early childhood the child becomes capable of perceiving or of reproducing more and more complex forms and, in particular, rhythmic structures that are not repetitive (Fraisse et al., 1949; Zenatti, 1976).

In order to summarize the effects of pause and of accent, we can say

1. Any noteworthy lengthening of a sound or of an interval between sounds plays the role of a pause between two successive groups.

2. Any sound, qualitatively different from the others, especially as to its intensity, plays the role of an accent that begins the group. When these two principles act simultaneously, one can as well say that the pause preceded the accent (Vos, 1977) as the converse.

3. More intense sounds are perceived as relatively lengthened and longer sounds as relatively more intense.

B. Patterns in Time

We will now attempt to understand the laws underlying the organization of groups when several elements are different from each other. In other words, we are going to study patterns in time (Handel, 1974). One preliminary remark is important. In a complete series of sounds the first perceived pattern tends to impose its structure on the later patterns. It becomes a privileged form of grouping (Preusser, Garner, & Gottwald, 1970a), and this fact confirms the importance of predictability as the basis of rhythmic perception. In order to avoid this effect, it is necessary to use artifices so that no pattern imposes itself due to its initial position. One can, for example, increase the intensity or the frequency of the sounds little by little, use long presentations in order to allow reorganizations, present random series before ordered ones, etc.

1. What happens if in a potential pattern there are several intense sounds? We mixed loud sounds (L) of 100 dB with softer sounds (S) of 75 dB (Fraisse & Oléron, 1954) in patterns of four or five sounds. The sounds were brief and between them the intervals were equal (475 msec for four sounds, 380 msec for five sounds). The subjects had to listen to a long series and then consecutively reproduce three times the perceived patterns by tapping on a key which thereby enabled the measurement of the force of the tap. The subjects grouped, as much as possible, sounds of the same intensity, all of which resulted in the construction of runs. Thus, beginning with a sequence L S S L L S S L S S, etc., one does not perceive the pattern L S S L but the pattern L L S S and, less often, S S L L. The pattern includes the smallest possible number of runs and is at the same time the simplest.

2. What happens if the number of loud sounds is greater than that of soft sounds? The subjects in their reproduction can invert the relative force of the elements and reproduce, for example, the series L L L S in the form S S S L or L S S S. These inversions are reminiscent of those which one can perceive in figure-ground reversals of spatial forms and allow us to think that, in these cases, the differentiating element is the least frequent one.

We have found the same phenomena by using sounds of different pitches (for example, sounds of 1040 Hz in combination with sounds of 760 or 520 Hz) (Ehrlich, Oléron, & Fraisse, 1956). The subjects tend to regroup so that the sharpest sounds tend to begin the group. With the same technique of reproduction, we have also found that the least numerous elements, high or low, were accented.

This type of research was developed by Garner and his colleagues using longer series. The first study was by Royer and Garner (1966). The patterns had eight sounds of two different types (two buzzers) and were repeated until the subject was capable of finding a pattern and of tapping it on two different keys. The authors of this research were, above all, concerned with estimating the effect of response uncertainty, evaluated in bits, on the identification of a pattern in a series. The first observation they made was that the subjects did not proceed by trial and error; they only began to respond when they had identified a pattern, and at that moment, the pattern would be responded to in complete synchrony and with little difficulty. Thus, construction does not proceed element by element, but wholistically. As for the rest, their hypothesis was partially confirmed. The simple patterns were organized quickly and the complex ones more slowly, which confirms Garner's (1962) thesis according to which perceptually good patterns should have few alternatives. This research showed that the most often chosen organizations were those in which the number of changes was minimal—that is, where the sounds of the same quality grouped themselves to the maximum extent. Thus, the pattern X X X O X X O O was the most often perceived (61 times out of 128), and from the same elements, the pattern next most often perceived was O X X O O X X X (31 times out of 128); however, the pattern X O X X O O X X was practically never perceived (once out of 128). As one also notices by this example, the longest run tended to begin the pattern. It could sometimes end the pattern, but it was practically never in the middle.

Later research (Royer & Garner, 1970; Preusser, Garner, & Gottwald, 1970a), most often using sounds presenting little difference in pitch, have confirmed this result. The longest run was placed at the beginning or, more frequently, at the end of the pattern. The solution evidently depended on the structure of the whole and on the relative length of the longest run. Thus, in the example mentioned above, the longest run more often began the pattern than finished it; another pattern X X X X O O O I O was perceived only in 36 cases out of 128 whereas the pattern O O I O X X X X was perceived 61 times out of 128.

The place and the role of the run were the main determinants of grouping. Others could also play a role, all of which corresponded to making simplifications prevail. Thus, when possible, the subject chose a directional simplicity with run lengths either increasing or decreasing in regular order (Preusser, Garner, & Gottwald, 1970b). The most redundant and/or symmetric forms (for example, X O X O, or still, X X O O X O O O—where the first, third, and fifth elements were conspicuous) were more easily perceived than the pattern X X O X O X O O that did not have a simple structure nor a longer run than the others (Sturger & Martin, 1974).

Preusser et al. (1970b) and also Handel (1974) have analyzed these results in terms of figure-ground relations by claiming that one of the elements plays the role of figure, and the other that of ground. In particular, they rely on the fact that if one of the elements is replaced by an empty interval, the laws of organization are the same. In the case in which the longest run is at the beginning of a pattern, it plays the role of figure and the pattern obeys the *run principle*. When it is at the end, it plays the role of ground, and the authors then speak of the *gap principle*.

The distinction between figure and ground, however, does not appear to be relevant. In a rhythmic structure there is no ground. Even the empty intrapattern intervals are part of the structure. As for the interpattern intervals, even though they have a different status, they nevertheless form links between the successive subpatterns. In the types of structures used in this research, there is no pause, *stricto sensu*, between the patterns. We also think that when the longest run is at the end of a pattern, it plays the role of accent more than that of a gap. Reference to poetry or to music, moreover, helps us to understand that all of the elements that structure a succession play a role. There is, between all of them, a relation that is not that of all-or-none (figure-ground) but of a hierarchy of salience.

What is the influence of tempo on patterns in time? All of the presented results were obtained using frequencies of two to three per second. What is the result when one increases or decreases this frequency? A frequency of two to three per second appears as an optimum. For more rapid frequencies (eight per second), more time is needed in order to discover the pattern in the presented sequence. However, the structuring phenomenon still occurs as an "integrated, immediate, compelling, and passive" process. In contrast, at the lowest frequency, .8 (which still is not very low), the subject constructs the pattern that is learned little by little according to an "integrated, derived, intellectualized and active" process (Garner & Gottwald, 1968).

Garner and Gottwald have also found that, at the lowest frequency, the structuring of patterns was all the more difficult if they deviated more from patterns constructed according to the run principle. Preusser (1972) systematically stated the problem of the interaction between the frequency of the elements and the structuring of the patterns. With two sounds of 238 and 275 Hz, the frequency being rapid (four per second), the subjects tended to place the longer run at the end of the pattern, making it play the role of a gap according to Preusser, of an accent plus pause according to us. At the slowest frequency (one per second), the longest run tended to begin the pattern. Why, at the most rapid frequency, was the run at the end? This solution seems to be characteristic of *perceived* rhythm whereas the initial run would be more characteristic of *constructed* rhythm, if we use Garner and Gottwald's distinction. Moreover, Preusser used two criteria in order to detect a pattern. One was to reproduce the pattern on one or two keys. The other consisted of asking the subject to describe the perceived rhythm by means of symbols. The delay necessary to describe the pattern is at least twice that which is necessary to reproduce it. This fact, previously found by Oléron (1959), confirms the wholistic character of rhythmic perception and also the compatibility between perceived patterns and motor patterns. In order to describe rhythms, it is necessary to analyze their structure, but this analysis is not necessary in order to reproduce them.

C. Patterns of Time

Rhythm, understood as "order of movement" is evidently based on an order which is primarily temporal. Until now we have envisaged only the most simple temporal situation: the isochronous repetition of sounds. What are the more complex temporal situations that permit perception of rhythm, and following Handel's expression (1974), what are the characteristic patterns of time?

1. Rhythm and Arrhythmia

If rhythm is order, arrhythmia is disorder (i.e., it is *a priori*, a sequence of continuous sounds where no temporal organization is perceptible). A computer can create this type of sequence. Can man? We asked subjects to produce an uninterrupted series of taps as irregularly as possible. We also asked them, in contrast, to produce patterns of five or six sounds having an internal structure of their choice, while trying to avoid reproducing known tunes (Fraisse, 1946–1947). While subjects found the task of producing a series of patterns easy, they nevertheless found it difficult to produce an irregular sequence. In order to study temporal structure, we have calculated the successive ratios between durations by computing the ratio of the shorter of the two intervals to the longer.

The first characteristic fact, in rhythm as well as in arrhythmia, is that a ratio of near-equality between two successive intervals predominates (40% of the ratios are less than 1.2). It is as though every sequence were based on a tendency to produce an interval equal to the preceding one, which is evidently the easiest and the most economical activity.

Rhythmic and arrhythmic sequences are constructed on the basis of this regularity. However, the way of breaking regularity is different in the two cases. In arrhythmia, the higher the ratio the less frequent it is. The rupture with equality then happens by a lengthening (or by a decrease) of the preceding interval: small differences become numerous, large ones become rare. In rhythm, on the contrary, small differences are rare. When the subject has broken the regularity, he or she produces a new interval of a noticeable duration. The difference forms about a ratio of one to two.

If one considers the absolute durations of the intervals, one finds the following results:

Intervals less than (msec)	Rhythm (%)	Arrhythmia (%)
400	56.2	35.2
1000	92	75.8
1800	98	93.8

First, these numbers indicate that in order to *perceive* regularities or irregularities, we use few intervals larger than 1800 msec. These would break the succession of sounds into independent sequences. It is also necessary to note the high proportion of short intervals in the rhythmic patterns. Moreover, ratios of the order of one to two inter-

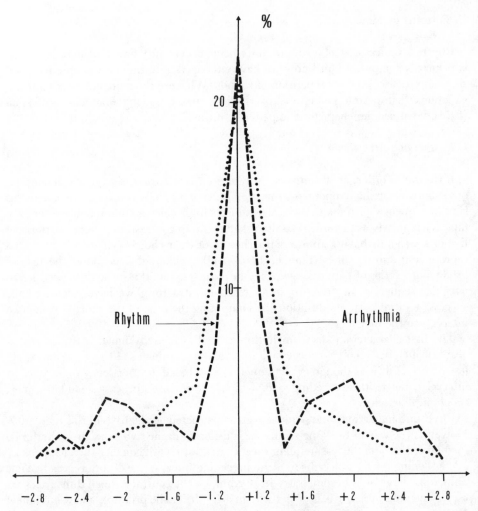

Fig. 1. Frequency of the ratios between successive intervals for rhythmic and arrhythmic sequences. 1 indicates equality of the intervals. Negative values indicate that the second interval is shorter than the first; positive values indicate that the second interval is longer than the first. Class interval equals .2 (i.e. class 1.2 includes ratios between −1.09 and +1.09). Only ratios inferior to 2.9 are represented here; they correspond to 85% of the ratios with rhythmic sequences and 86.19% with arrhythmic sequences (from Fraisse, 1946–47, *47–48*, 11–21 by courtesy of *Année Psychologique*).

vene most often only when the time that we call short (less than 400 msec) follows or precedes the time that we call long.[2]

A more complete analysis reveals that the relative equalization of durations in rhythmic patterns is not only produced between adjacent intervals. One thus finds patterns 680-260-630-280 (in msec) and patterns 280-300-850-290-850 (in msec) with

[2]Here the word "time" is used as synonymous with duration or with interval until Section IV, where we use time according to common usage.

equalization of the short times on the one hand and of the long times on the other hand. This phenomenon is found in patterns of three or four taps. Here are some examples (average of 10 subjects): 210-480-490 msec; 470-190-430 msec; etc. (Fraisse, 1956). The hypothesis that we formulated above—that is, of a simple tendency to repeat equal intervals—is only partially exact since we find the phenomenon of equalization between nonadjacent intervals. Briefly, patterns are characterized by a composition of basically two sorts and only two sorts of time: *short times* of 200 to 300 msec and *long times* of 450 to 900 msec. If one looks not only at the averages but at the individual performances, one finds that between short times, adjacent or not, 84% of the ratios are less than 1.15 and 97% are less than 1.55. Between long times, 54% of the ratios are less than 1.15 and 94% are less than 1.55. The modal value of the ratios' long times—short times is 2.4 of which 95% are less than 1.55. This ratio 1.55 seems to be the dividing point between two sorts of time.

If two durations belong to the same category, there is a tendency to equalize these durations. We prefer to say that there is assimilation since this equalization is not absolute. Among durations of differing categories, there is a sharp distinction. Assimilation and distinction bring us back to the classical perceptual laws which correspond to a principle of economy in perceptual organization (Fraisse, 1947).

2. Temporal Rhythms as Structure

Our previous analyses already confirm that temporal intervals in rhythmic structures are interdependent. However, one can go further and show that the basic pattern described previously corresponds to "good form." Are we capable of producing or of reproducing any other patterns? One can demonstrate, in several ways, the salience of good form.

First, by a conflict between space and time: if one lays out before the subject 4, 5, or 6 targets at different distances while asking him to tap them successively as quickly as possible without stopping, he establishes a veritable rhythmic pattern of taps. This temporal pattern is simpler than the spatial pattern. Unequal spaces are gone through either in equal times or in very distinct times (ratios of two to three) (Montpellier, 1935). When the subject is auditorily presented with temporal patterns that differ from a basic temporal model and asked to reproduce these patterns, one observes deformations of the model by a systematic reorganization that simplifies it. If there are, for example, in the model three unequal intervals, the subject tends toward a reproduction of two intervals. Let us take the very simple case of a structure with a first interval of 190 msec, a third interval of 450 msec, and a second interval which has, depending on the model, a duration of 210 to 690 msec. At first there is assimilation of the first to the second duration and then there is assimilation of the second to the third duration.

Good form then, is not only a spontaneous form but a dynamic organization that imposes itself in production or reproduction.

We can find, in very different contexts, examples of this type of structure based on ratios of two durations only. When Samuel Morse attempted to create an alphabet based on the play of durations, the Morse code, composed of two durations called dots and dashes, was invented. Greco–Latin prosody was based on the opposition of two durations: breves and longs. In music, there is, at any given moment, a play of two notes that are in a ratio of one to two or one to three (double quaver and quaver, quaver and crotchet, quaver and pointed crotchet). These two notes represent 85 to 95% of the movement (Fraisse, 1956, p. 107). The first theorist of rhythm, Aristoxenus of Tarentum, distinguished two sorts of beats corresponding to the upbeat and the fall. One was the first beat upon which only one syllable or one note could fall; the other was worth two or three first beats. Aristoxenus claimed that only ratios corresponding to whole numbers are rational.

This generality, regarding the use of only two durations, corresponds, according to us, to a perceptual requirement revealed by psychophysics. Research done on information theory in order to measure channel capacity has shown that the channel is always limited by our ability to distinguish in an absolute way, several levels of stimulation. This capacity, which is about five, varies with the nature of the sensation. In the case of duration, the studies by Hawkes (1961), Murphy (1966), and Bovet (1974) have shown that even trained subjects could differentiate only two or, at the most, three durations in the range of perceived durations (below 2 sec). If the durations were more numerous, confusion arose.

However, these laws do not apply to the time interval between two patterns that we have called pause. Phenomenally, a pattern ends with the last element. But between one pattern and the next there is, as was revealed by subjective rhythmization, a pause that corresponds to the length of the last note in the case of music and that is an empty time in the case of taps.

Let us take one more step in the analysis of temporal patterns. When they are quite long, they often split up into several subunits. A pattern of six sound-taps is often decomposed into two subunits of 3 + 3, of 4 + 2, or of 2 + 2 + 2 as the case may be. In this case, the interval between two subunits has the characteristic of a pause: it is at least equal to the longest duration but it is not necessarily equal to it, while being more integrated with the pattern than with the pause, *stricto sensu*, between two patterns. This type of analysis explains, we think, certain groupings that intervene when models have eight or ten sounds, as in research such as Garner's

If a subject taps a pattern at his spontaneous tempo and if he is asked to continue to tap the same pattern more quickly or more slowly, it is seen that the ratio long time—short time is maximal at the spontaneous tempo. When the tempo slows down a great deal, there is no longer a sharp distinction between long time and short time. At the limit the durations are almost equal. We have seen rhythm born from a rupture with regular movement; we see it disappear by a return to this movement.

The previous analyses were based on methods of production and of reproduction of fairly short patterns. Preusser (1972) has produced new data. He not only had patterns reproduced with two types of elements (see Section III,B), but he also constructed similar patterns that presented only one type of element by replacing the other by an empty temporal interval. Two organizational principles were obvious from this work (1) the run principle: the longest run begins the pattern (for example, $3''1'$)[3] and (2) the gap principle: the longest interval terminates the pattern (for example, $1'3''$).

If these two principles are compatible, as in $3'1''$, the pattern is correctly identified in 90% of the cases. If they are incompatible, as in the first two examples cited the gap principle is, on the average, the decisive factor in 68% of the cases and the run principle in 32% of the cases. When there are three runs, which we consider as three subunits, a third principle, which we have already detected in spontaneous rhythms, is added to the two earlier principles: The sequence of run lengths produces an upward progression (for example, $1'2'3'$). This principle evidently gives rise to an organization differing from one starting with the longest run. Preusser has compared these results with those found in the case of sequences of eight elements composed of two sounds of a different nature. By comparing the results of the two studies he concludes that the gap principle plays a more important role when there is only one element. This confirms our previous conclusions. Of two elements, one is not figure and the other ground since the empty intervals have a stronger structuring effect than the element considered as the ground in their analyses.

Handel's research (1974) brought along a supplementary piece of information. He had the duration of sounds varied (ratio of 1 to 5), and he found that, most often, the short durations began the pattern and that the long durations ended it. This effect is all the more marked when the run of the short and/or of the long durations is longer.

More recent research by Vos (1977) produced comparable results obtained by another method. The subjects had to judge, for a sequence of two durations which were in a ratio of 1 to 4, whether it was an iambus or a trochee; for a series of three durations, whether it was a dactyl, an anapaest, or an amphibrach. He used three principles in order to explain the obtained results: (1) Tones that are separated by short intervals are perceptually grouped together; (2) the first tone of a perceptual group is a tone that is immediately preceded by a long interval (which is another example of the role of the pause, or of the gap principle); and (3) long tones are perceived as accented and short tones as nonaccented.

All authors are in agreement that complexity is important among the factors which intervene to produce greater or lesser salience of rhythmic patterns. This is difficult to evaluate. It seems that one can draw several conclusions from research done on Morse code signals: the relative difficulty in learning each signal can be considered to be an index of its complexity. If using Plotkin's (1943) results, we divide the signals into three categories of 12—easy, average, and difficult to learn—we can calculate three indices, keeping in mind that the number of dots and dashes varies from three to five elements: (a) the number of elements in a signal (N), (b) the number of signals having only one category of elements, dots or dashes (E), and (c) the number of signals in which there is an interleaving of elements (for example: - - . . -) in contrast to those in

---

[3]The digits represent the number of elements which follow each other, the hyphens, the intervals which are equal in duration to the elements.

which there are only two runs (for example: - - -..) (R). One finds the following results:

	N	E	R
Easy signals	2.9	8	0
Average signals	4.2	1	3
Difficult signals	3.9	0	6

Complexity increases a little with the length of the signals and, above all, with the multiplication of runs, as was stated by Preusser (1970; Preusser et al., 1972). Signals with only one type of element are always easy.

Generally, one can say that, the more a temporal form is brief and simple, the easier it is to perceive. Vos (1973) attempted to calculate the indices of complexity by taking into account the indices mentioned above as well as the ratio between the length of subunits.

One can, moreover, more closely approach music by studying how syncopated auditory rhythms are perceived. Polyrhythms are defined as the simultaneous presentation of two pulse trains such that the rates are not integral multiples of each other (for example, three against four). Each pulse train is a series of regularly recurrent stimuli (Oshinsky & Handel, 1978). How will this ambiguous pattern be perceived, the criterion being the choice made by the subject asked to tap in synchrony with the pattern in question? Will he follow the pattern of three or that of four elements? The most remarkable result was that the subjects most often preferred to accompany the pattern of three rather than that of four elements but that this tendency was not the same for all tempos. In this research the pattern had a duration that varied from .96 to 2.4 sec. There was a reversal of the tendency for durations of 1.2 or of 1.6 sec depending on the pitch of the sounds. These tendencies were about the same when the two patterns of three and of four consisted of identical sounds or when they consisted of sounds of differing pitch.

Is it also necessary to underscore the fact that synchronizations are very rapidly established? The subjects began to tap in a stable way after about 3 sec, which proves that the two trains of stimuli were not analyzed. The majority of subjects, moreover, did not detect that there was an ambiguity in the polyrhythms.

IV. THE PERCEPTION OF MUSICAL RHYTHMS

The above analyses have permitted us to extract the laws characteristic of rhythm perception. However, the stimuli used were far from musical, since these researches used only taps, identical sounds, or at best, two types of sound of different duration, intensity, or pitch. Musical rules, however, do not escape the fundamental laws that we have demonstrated. Without doubt, these laws do not explain music any more than gravity explains the art of architecture. But there is not an architect who ignores gravity any more than there is a musical rhythm that does not respect perceptual laws.

First, it is necessary to underscore the difficult problem of vocabulary that we have evoked by distinguishing rhythm, which is the perception of a pattern, and meter, which allows the description of a musical composition. We will use this distinction as we consider the perceived rhythm and meter used by the composer.

A musical composition is a synthesis of very different stimuli that are perceptually unified much as forms and colors are unified in a painting. We distinguish melody, harmony, timbre, and a rhythmic organization consisting of the succession of rhythmic patterns, at the same time identical to themselves and also varying continuously. The unity assures the characteristic of anticipation, which seems to us to be fundamental, and that Steedman (1977) finds, for example, when he tries to discover in a fugue by Bach the algorithms that allow one to give an account, if not of the rhythm, at least of its meter. What appears fundamental to him is the "principle of consistency" that corresponds to the fact that there is, with the passage of time, a constancy of predictable forms from the first bars on.

These patterns are composed of subunits that metrically correspond to times and, in performance and in perception, to a succession of beats. The metrics tell us that there are bars at two, three, four, and even nine times, but perceptually the bars at four times are often reduced to binary rhythm and the others to combinations of substructures. The longest bars have hardly more than nine times and are generally understood as a triple ternary rhythm. Reciprocally, the simplest bars can group themselves into periods as do the lines of poetry into stanzas. A famous example is that of the scherzo of Beethoven's Ninth Symphony, written in 3/4 bars, in which Beethoven indicated *ritmo a tre battute* in order to indicate that it is necessary to regroup three bars into one rhythmic unity.

Musical rhythm is based on a precise temporal organization of bars and the play of accents. Let us summarize two points. Rhythmic pattern has a duration of from 2 to 5 sec. In recent research Vos (1976) measured the duration of different bars in the *Well-Tempered Clavier* by Bach using a recorded performance. Their duration was 1.75 sec for a 2/4 bar, 3.0 sec for a 3/4 bar, and 4.8 sec for a 6/4 bar. These are only examples that permit us to say that the durations of the longest bars correspond to the possibilities of unifying successive elements into a pattern.

The bars repeated themselves and were metrically identical in their structure but varied in particular by syncopations. Sears (1902) found a variability in the duration of 3% between successive patterns of religious chants. Weaver (1939) studied the variability of a piece of music where there was a succession of normal bars and syncopated bars. The subjects, conservatory students, tapped rhythms with their right hand while they kept the tempo by moving a foot. The presence of syncopated bars does not prevent the very great temporal regularity of the executed rhythms (variability from 2% to 4% between successive patterns). The bars are composed of notes whose duration is specified by the composer who indicates the tempo. We have already mentioned the important statistical result that we found by studying the notes used in pieces having a metric unity.

Table I gives the proportion of each note in each piece studied. It is immediately evident that the compositions are based on two notes that represent more than 80% of the notes used. They are in a ratio of 1:2, sometimes 1:3. The briefest among them is

TABLE I

Frequency of Notes

Composer and tempo	o	𝅗𝅥.	𝅗𝅥	♩.	♩	♪.	♪	♬	Frequency of the two main notes
Chopin I ♩ = 132			1	29	3	52	15		81
Chopin II Tempo Giusto		1	6	10		83			93
Beethoven I Adagio				14	5	23	56	2	79
Beethoven II Allegro Vivace	13	1		54		32			86
Beethoven III Adagio			8		29	31	32		63
Debussy I ♩ = 66	1	4	1	10		29	55		84
Debussy II ♪ = 184			1			44	55		99
Fauré I ♩ = 52				4	22	74			96
Fauré II ♩ = 96		1	1	23		61	14		84
Stravinsky I ♩ = 112			5	21		74			95
Stravinsky II ♩ = 112				4		43	45	8	88
Bela Bartok I ♩ = 100			8	24		68			92
Bela Bartok II ♩ = 72		3	9	11	12	65			77
Bela Bartok III ♩ = 60	1			15		13	71		84
Weill K. ♩ = 84			2	29		61	8		90

also the most frequent. The duration of notes in our examples varies—taking into account the tempos—from 150 to 290 msec. These values are again found in performances recorded by Gabrielsson (1973). We found, in spontaneous rhythms, durations going from 180 to 280 msec, and we have already stated that the shortest time was also the most frequent. These comparisons are striking. The massive use of two different notes is explained, we said, by the difficulty in identifying more than two durations. (However, let us not forget that composers use other, longer durations that have an important aesthetic role and which permit syncopations and pauses.)

The two basic notes, moreover, do not have the same perceptual status (Table I). The brief note, or the interval that we have called *short time*, does not last. One was able to speak of point in time and, for the rapid succession of two sounds, of a collective perception (Schultze, 1908). The other note on the contrary, which is double or triple the first one, corresponds to the perception of a *duration*. These notes vary between 300 and 900 msec—that is, the range of durations which appear as neither too brief nor too long and which are centered around an optimal duration of 600 msec, which is also that of spontaneous tempo.

Comparisons with the results of our analysis also lead us to consider the ratio of 1.5 between two successive notes (or two intervals) that appeared to us as ambiguous from the perceptual viewpoint. It corresponds to the case of the pointed note. In partitions, one rarely finds a succession of two notes in a ratio of 1.5, and musicians are acquainted with the difficulty of realizing such a succession. The pointed note is most often differentiated from another note, in a ratio of 1 to 3, as between a ♪ and a ♩.

Even in the case where a pointed quaver follows a double quaver (ratio of 1:3), the ratio is distorted in the performances recorded by Gabrielsson (1973a); it is closer to 1:4 than 1:3. The ratio of 1:2 between the quavers and the double quavers is often slightly increased, especially when there is syncopation. The ratio of equality between two ♪ or two ♩ is not strictly respected but the difference does not attain 1.2, which remains within the limits found in the spontaneous production of tapped rhythms.

However, it is equally necessary to remember that, at the level of composition, and also of perception, notes are grouped into what in metric one calls a *time*. Two ideas are fundamental in order to define a bar, the number and duration of each time. The bar, in principle, has a unity that provides the relative accentuations of each of the times, the first being, in classical music, the most accentuated. Two questions are important: What do musicians do? And what does the audience perceive?

The accentuation of a note slightly lengthens its duration, a fact that we have already found in nonmusical rhythms. The difference in accentuation of diverse notes, in a dance rhythm, can vary from 10 dB in piano performances to 20 dB in percussion performances (Gabrielsson, 1973).

In general, the first time is accentuated. But how does the subject perceive succession and grouping of times? Recent research by Vos (1978) brings along a first answer. On commercial versions of Bach's preludes, subjects familiar with classical music but not particularly acquainted with the pieces chosen were asked to tap in synchrony with the beginning of each bar—that is, with the beginning of the perceived rhythmic pattern. The subject did not tap in all cases on the first beat of the bar. Let us take the example of a 2/4 bar that lasted 1.75 sec. Forty percent of the subjects tapped in synchrony with the first beat | 1̌ 2 |;[4] 45% tapped on the second beat of the measure thus linked in a rhythmic pattern with the first beat of the following measure | 1 2̌ | 1 2̌ |; 10% tapped each beat. For a 3/4 bar, 20% tapped each beat. Eighty percent tapped as if it were a bar with two beats, grouping two of the three beats, the last beat of a bar being grouped one time out of two with the first beat of the following bar | 1̌ 2 3̌ | 1 2 3 |. This result shows that arguments regarding the place of accent are irrelevant since for the same musical performance, some perceive, as one can predict, the accent on the first beat, whereas others do so on the last. In the same ternary sequence, a binary perception corresponds to an accent successively placed on the first and last beats. As a general rule, the intervals between the subjects' taps were shorter than the length of the bars. These varied between 1.75 sec and 4.8 sec in the examples studied and the intervals between the taps varied from .8 sec to 2.4 sec. Vos wondered, without being able to answer, whether it was the melodic saliency that led to these cuts or whether it was the difficulty of storing too long a series in short-term memory? Without ignoring the importance of melodic structure, we think that the generality of the observed phenomenon is particularly explained by limits in storage capacity and by the necessity of maintaining a perceived succession between successive taps. From this point of view, tempo plays a decisive role.

[4]The sign ">" indicates the place of the tap.

The ease of the task of motor accompaniment to musical rhythm brings us back to the perceptual and motor aspects of rhythm that we have found in the most simple rhythmic forms. Musical time, like the foot in poetry, recalls the origins of rhythm or chant, dance and music linked by the beat of the foot made by a succession of *arsis* and of *thesis*. In the time of the Greeks, theorists already debated whether the accent corresponded to *arsis* or to *thesis*. Aristoxenus of Tarentum, moreover, did not speak of upbeat and of fall but of high times and of low times.

This link between rhythmic perception and movement also appeared in research requiring judgments and not performances. Gatewood (1927) asked subjects to listen to diverse pieces of music and report which of the four following qualities: rhythm, melody, harmony, or pitch appeared to be dominant. For each of the pieces, the subjects had to indicate impressions as evoked by these pieces. Impression of movement was perceived in 64% of the pieces in which rhythm was dominant, 25% of the pieces in which melody was dominant, 15% of the pieces in which harmony was dominant, and 12% of the pieces in which pitch was dominant. The movement thus appeared associated with rhythm and was, moreover, also present in the pieces where melody, harmony, or pitch were judged to be predominant.

More recent work has dealt with the problem of the dimensions of the rhythmic experience. Gabrielsson (1973a) set out from three sorts of musical samples: (a) monophonic structures played on a piano or on a drum, (b) polyphonic structures of diverse dances, in which the rhythm arises from the play of the pitch of percussion instruments and of their duration without melodic intervention, and (c) real music (most often dances).

By using diverse methods (judgments of similarity of two sequences, estimates from adjectives recalling the semantic differential, performance with monophonic rhythms, free verbal descriptions) and by using the methods of factorial analysis and of multidimensional analysis, Gabrielsson (1973b) could sum up his results by distinguishing three groups of dimensions:

1. *Structural properties of rhythm.* One distinguishes here what we call the relationship between perceived rhythms and the bar: coincidence or not, place of accent(s), degrees of perceptual prominence of a basic pattern—accentuation versus clearness, simplicity versus complexity, or uniformity versus variation in the pattern. "The more different note values used, the more duration of duration patterns, the more syncopation, the more variation in instrumentation, the more leaps in a melody, the more changes in harmonic functions, etc. the more varied and in most cases, the more complex the rhythm will be judged to be (Gabrielsson, 1973b p. 10)."

2. *Movement properties.* This defines rapidity and tempo forward movement (depending on the fact that in a pattern the movement seems to accelerate or decelerate) and movement characteristics (i.e., different aspects of experienced movements in relation to rhythmic experience: dancing–walking; floating–stuttering; solemn–swinging, and others).

3. *Emotional aspects.* Gabrielsson thinks that these are characterized by the dimensions of vital–dull, excited–calm, rigid–flexible, and solemn–playful.

V. CONCLUSION

All the above approaches attest to some links that exist between rhythmic perception and movement. This has led us several times to speak, as did Ruckmick (1927), of rhythmic experience, thereby enlarging the perceptual aspect as it is most often accompanied by motor stimuli and by emotional reactions.

Perception is first of a temporal order—that is, of a regularity. It is, moreover, striking that in music the temporal data—at least that of the notes—are always explicit. This necessary condition is not always sufficient. The ordered elements can, in effect, be varied as to duration, intensity, pitch, and contain silences. The rhythmic structures are always perceptually complex.

However, rhythm, differing from melody, is made up, above all, of temporal and intensive patterns. One aspect can predominate over the other. The Gregorian chant is the best example of a temporal structuring without intensity and without periodicity. The march and most dances represent the other extreme where the pattern of accents imposes itself with its regularity and where isochronous patterns repeat each other.

All classical music falls between these two extremes. In order to understand the play of regularity and variety, it is perhaps necessary to mention the most simple studies. Brown (1911) has shown that while tapping successions of rhythmic patterns, the variability of the durations is half as strong as that of the intensities. Let us complete what we said above. If in music the durations are always explicit, the indications of accents are much more vague. The rule that states that the first beat of the bar is always accented is only a convention. We have seen that bars, even those of a classical musician such as Bach, and even when played by the same orchestra, can be perceived in multiple ways.

In all polyphonic musical performances, it is necessary however, that there be a regularity in order to permit the anticipation of playing and the synchrony of the artists. In reality, all musical performances consist of isochronous repetition and, simultaneously, of more varied patterns, but which, in a complex way, fit into the play of isochronous repetitions. Perhaps Chopin's remark can be generalized: "Let your left hand be an intransigent and rigorous orchestra conductor and your right hand do what it wants." In the same spirit one can cite this passage from a letter written by Wagner to Liszt (Dumesnil, 1949) that singers respect the duration of notes "by staying within the indicated bar . . . if they leave it, in order to go further, let them do so with an intelligent liberty and instil fire rather than caution, thereby entirely making the continuity which the bar imposes disappear. If only they produce the impression of an animated and poetic style, we will have won everything."

It is necessary not to dissociate the motor *behaviors* linked to rhythms from these complex perceptions. Still, two aspects are to be considered here. The play of music is always based on movements. Some are very voluntary and lengthily learned in order to go beyond simple determinisms. Others, on the contrary, give way to these determinisms. They appear when the repetitions of accented patterns impose themselves on the player and on the listener. This subtle or rough motor component has the effect that rhythmic perception is plurisensorial. This is why we speak of rhythmic experience. The movement brings along more particularly affective reactions which are also a component of this experience. The affective aspect is all the more important, in part, because the anticipation of successive patterns facilitates synchrony between individuals. They are spontaneously realized in marches and in dances. All socialization of behavior, as is well known, reinforces their affective impact.

This said, in spite of the plurality of rhythmic components and of artistic realizations, is there a general sense of rhythm? We have explored this aspect (Hiriarborde & Fraisse, 1968) by using factorial analysis on a series of tests—some predominantly perceptual (discrimination, reproduction, transcription of temporal or intensive structures), others predominantly motor (adaptation to a change in pattern, polyrhythmic hand-foot, synchronization with good or with ambiguous forms)—and by using the batteries of musical aptitude tests developed by Seashore and Wing. All of these tests were in positive correlation with each other, except for the tests of intensity discrimination and pitch discrimination from the battery by Seashore, and the tests of choice of the best harmonization and judgment of rhythmic accent by Wing.

Using a centroid analysis and by looking for the orthogonal factors, we found three main factors:

1. *Perceptual structuration*. The tests that are the most saturated in this factor are based on the discrimination of temporal structures.

2. *Rhythmic anticipation*. The tests that are the most saturated in this factor are those of synchronization and several of those by Seashore and by Wing that imply the memorization of a pattern in order to compare it with a following one.

3. *Practo-rhythmic*. The tests that are the most saturated in this factor are those of coordination with alternate movements of the hand and foot and those of adaptation to changes in rhythm, both of which require a voluntary control of rhythmic movement. Moreover, we found a musical factor and a factor of discrimination.

Thackray (1969) carried out a similar study based on his experience as a music teacher. He started from a battery of tests which he classified into three categories:

1. *Rhythmic perception:* Perceiving the number of sounds in a pattern, distinguishing two cadences, comparing durations, identifying the place of an accent in a pattern.

2. *Rhythmic performance:* reproducing temporal and intensive patterns of sounds and of a short melody, conserving a tempo.

3. *Rhythmic movement:* rhythmic quality of movements that put the whole body to play—sequences of (rhythmic) movements, following music in which the tempo, the bar, and so on are varied.

The correlations between all these tests are quite high, especially within the same group of tests. Using these results and applying the method of Spearman-Burt, Thackray, in effect, extracted a general factor. We also could have extracted one had we chosen this method of analysis. We think, however, that a plurality of factors better accounts for the plurality of rhythmic aptitudes that correspond, moreover, to the plurality of the aspects of rhythm, as Thackray hypothesized himself when constructing his tests.

REFERENCES

Allen, T. W., Walker, K., Symonds, L., & Marcell, M. Intrasensory and intersensory perception of temporal sequences during infancy. *Developmental Psychology*, 1977, *13*, 225-229.

Allport, G. W., & Vernon, P. E. *Studies in expressive movement.* New York: Macmillan, 1933.

Benveniste, E. La notion de "rythme" dans son expression linguistique. *Journal de Psychologie Normale et Pathologique*, 1951, *44*, 401-411.

Berg, W. K. Cardiac orienting responses of 6- and 16-weeks-old infants. *Journal of Experimental Child Psychology*, 1974, *17*, 303-312.

Bolton, T. L. Rhythm. *American Journal of Psychology*, 1894, *6*, 145-238.

Bovet, P. *Quantité d'information transmise dans la perception des durées brèves.* Thèse de 3e cycle, Université René Descartes, Paris, 1974 (unpublished).

Brown, W. Temporal and accentual rhythm. *Psychological Review*, 1911, *18*, 336-346.

Brunswik, E. *Perception and the representative design of psychological experiments.* Berkeley and Los Angeles, California: University of California Press, 1956.

Chang, M. W., & Trehib, S. E. Infant's perception of temporal grouping in auditory patterns. *Child Development*, 1977, *48*, 1666-1670.

Clifton, R. K., & Meyers, W. J. The heart rate response of fourth-month-old infants to auditory stimuli, *Journal of Experimental Child Psychology*, 1969, *7*, 122-135.

Crowder, R. G., & Morton, J. Precategorical acoustic storage (P A S). *Perception & Psychophysics*, 1969, *5*, 365-373.

Demany, L., Mc Kenzie, B., & Vurpillot, E. Rhythm perception in early infancy, *Nature (London)*, 1977, *266*, 718-719.

Dietze, G. Untersuchungen über den Umfang des Bewusstseins bei regelmässig auf einander folgenden Schalleindrücken. *Philosophische Studien*, 1885, *2*, 362-393.

Dumesnil, R. *Le rythme musical.* Paris: La Colombe, 1949.

Ehrlich, S. Le mécanisme de la synchronisation sensori-motrice. *L'Année Psychologique*, 1958, *58*, 7-23.

Ehrlich, S., Oléron, G., & Fraisse, P. La structuration tonale des rythmes. *L'Année Psychologique*, 1956, *56*, 27-45.

Fraisse, P. Mouvements rythmiques et arythmiques. *L'Année Psychologique*, 1946-1947, *47-48*, 11-21.

Fraisse, P. De l'assimilation et de la distinction comme processus fondamentaux de la connaissance. In *Miscellanea Psychologica Albert Michotte.* Louvain: Institut Supérieur de Philosophie, 1947. Pp. 181-195.

Fraisse, P. *Les structures rythmiques.* Louvain: Editions Universitaires, 1956.

Fraisse, P. *Psychology of time.* New York: Harper, 1963.

Fraisse, P. L'anticipation de stimulus rythmiques. Vitesse d'établissement et précision de la synchronisation. *L'Année Psychologique*, 1966, *66*, 15-36.

Fraisse, P. *Psychologie du rythme.* Paris: Presses Universitaires de France, 1974.

Fraisse, P. Is rhythm a gestalt? In S. Ertel, L. Kemmler, & Stadler (Eds.), *Gestalttheorie in der modernen Psychologie.* Darmstadt: Steinkopff, 1975. Pp. 227-232.

Fraisse, P. Les synchronisations sensori-motrices aux rythmes. In J. Requin (Ed.), *Anticipation et comportement.* Paris: Editions C.N.R.S. 1980.

Fraisse, P., & Ehrlich, S. Note sur la possibilité de syncoper en fonction du tempo d'une cadence. *L'Année Psychologique*, 1955, *55*, 61-65.

Fraisse, P., & Fraisse, R. Etudes sur la mémoire immédiate. I. L'appréhension des sons. *L'Année Psychologique*, 1937, *38*, 415-423.

Fraisse, P., & Oléron, G. La structuration intensive des rythmes. *L'Année Psychologique*, 1954, *54*, 35-52.

Fraisse, P., Pichot, P., & Clairouin, G. Les aptitudes rythmiques. Etude comparée des oligophrènes et des enfants normaux. *Journal de Psychologie Normale et Pathologique*, 1949, *42*, 309-330.

Frischeisen-Köhler, I. *Das Persönliche Tempo. Eine erbliologische Untersuchung*. Leipzig: Thieme, 1933. (a)

Frischeisen-Köhler, I. Festsellung des weder langsamen noch schnellen (mittelmässigen) Tempos. *Psychologische Forschung*, 1933, *18*, 291-298. (b)

Gabrielsson, A. Similarity ratings and dimension analyses of auditory rhythm patterns. I. *Scandinavian Journal of Psychology*, 1973, *14*, 138-160. (a)

Gabrielsson, A. Studies in rhythm. Acta Universitatis Upsaliensis 7, Uppsala 1973. (b)

Garner, W. R. *Uncertainty and structure as psychological concepts*. New York: Wiley, 1962.

Garner, W. R., & Gottwald, R. L. The perception and learning of temporal pattenrs. *Quarterly Journal of Experimental Psychology*, 1968, *20*, 97-109.

Gatewood, L. L. An experimental study of the nature of musical enjoyment. In M. Shoen (Ed.). *The effects of music*. New York: Harcourt, 1927.

Handel, S. Perceiving melodic and rhythmic auditory patterns. *Journal of Experimental Psychology*, 1974, *103*, 922-933.

Harrel, T. W. Factors influencing preference and memory for auditory rhythm. *Journal of General Psychology*, 1937, *17*, 63-104.

Harrison, R. Personal tempo and the interrelationships of voluntary and maximal rates of movement. *Journal of General Psychology*, 1941, *24-25*, 343-379.

Hawkes, G. R. Information transmitted via electrical cutaneous stimulus duration. *Journal of Psychology*, 1961, *51*, 293-298.

Hiriartborde, E., & Fraisse, P. *Les aptitudes rythmiques*, Monographies françaises de Psychologie, Paris. CNRS, 1968.

James, W. *The principles of psychology*. London: Macmillan, 1891. (2 Vols.)

Koffka, K. Experimentelle Untersuchungen zur Lehre von Rhythmus. *Zeitschrift für Psychologie*, 1909, *52*, 1-109.

Leavitt, L. A., Brown, J. W., Morse, P. A., & Graham, F. K. Cardiac orienting and auditory discrimination in 6 week-old-infants. *Developmental Psychology*, 1976, *12*, 514-523.

Lehtovaara, A., Saarinen, P., & Järvinen, J. Psychological studies on twins. II. The psychomotor rhythm: environmental versus hereditary determination. *Reports from the Psychological Institute, University of Helsinki*, 1966, No. 3.

Mac Dougall, R. The structure of simple rhythm forms. *Psychological Review, Monograph Supplements*, 1903, *4*, 309-416.

Mach, E. Untersuchungen über den Zeitsinn des Ohres. *Sitzungeberichte der Wiener Akademie der Wissenschaften*, 1865, K*ℓ*, 51.

Martin, J. G. Rhytmic (hierarchical) versus serial structure in speech and other behavior. *Psychological Review*, 1972, *79*, 487-509.

Meumann, E. Untersuchungen zur Psychologie und Aesthetik des Rhythmus, *Philosophische Studien*, 1894, *10*, 249-322, 393-430.

Michon, J. A. Studies on subjective duration. I. Differential sensitivity in the perception of repeated temporal intervals. *Acta Psychologica*, 1964, *22*, 441-450.

Miner, J. B. Motor, visual and applied rhythms. *Psychological Review, Monograph Supplements*, 1903, *5*, 1-106.

Mishima, J. Fundamental research on the constancy of "mental tempo". *Japanese Journal of Psychology*, 1951-1952, *22*, 27-28.

Mishima, J. On the factors of the mental tempo. *Japanese Psychological Research*, 1956, *4*, 27-38.

Mishima, J. *Introduction to the morphology of human behavior. The experimental study of mental tempo*. Tokyo: Tokyo Publishing, 1965.

Miyake, I. Researches on rhythmic activity. *Studies from the Yale Psychological Laboratory*, 1902, *10*, 1-48.

Montpellier, G. de. *Les altérations morphologiques des mouvements rapides*. Louvain: Institut Supérieur de Philosophie, 1935.

Murphy, L. E. Absolute judgments of duration. *Journal of Experimental Psychology*, 1966, *71*, 260-263.

Oléron, G. Etude de la "perception" des structures rythmiques, *Psychologie Française*, 1959, No. 4, 176-189.

Oshinsky, J. S., & Handel, S. Syncopated auditory polyrhythms: Discontinuous reversals in meter interpretation. *Journal of the Acoustical Society of America*, 1978, *63*, 936-939.

Paillard, J. *Réflexes et régulations d'origine proprioceptive chez l'homme*. Paris: Arnette, 1955.

Preusser, D. The effect of structure and rate on the recognition and description of auditory temporal patterns. *Perception & Psychophysics*, 1972, *11*, 233-240.

Preusser, D., Garner, W. R., & Gottwald, R. L. The effect of starting pattern on descriptions of perceived temporal patterns. *Psychonomic Science*, 1970, *21*, 219-220. (a)

Preusser, D., Garner, W. R., & Gottwald, R. L. Perceptual organization of two-element temporal patterns as a function of their component one-element patterns. *American Journal of Psychology*, 1970, *83*, 151-170. (b)

Plotkin, L. Stimulus generalization in Morse code learning. *Archives of Psychology*, 1943, No. 287.

Rimoldi, H.J.A. Personal tempo. *Journal of Abnormal and Social Psychology*, 1951, *46*, 283-303.

Royer, F. L., & Garner, W. R. Response uncertainty and perceptual difficulty of auditory temporal patterns. *Perception & Psychophysics*, 1966, *1*, 41-47.

Royer, F. L., & Garner, W. R. Perceptual organization of nine element auditory temporal patterns, *Perception & Psychophysics*, 1970, 7, 115-120.

Ruckmick, C. A. The rhythmical experience from the systematic point of view. *American Journal of Psychology*, 1927, *39*, 355-366.

Sander, F. Experimentelle Ergebnisse der Gestaltpsychologie. *10 Kongres für Experimentelle Psychologie, Iena*, 1928, p. 23.

Schmidt, E. M. Uber den Aufbau rhythmischer Gestalten. *Neue Psychologische Studien*, 1939, *14*, 1-98.

Schultze, F. E. Beiträg zur Psychologie des Zeitbewusstseins. *Archiv für die Gesamte Psychologie*, 1908, *13*, 275-351.

Sears, G. H. A contribution to the psychology of rhythm. *American Journal of Psychology*, 1902, *13*, 28-61.

Steedman, M. J. The perception of musical rhythm and metre. *Perception*, 1977, *6*, 555-569.

Stern, W. Das psychisch Tempo. In *Uber psychologie der individuellen differenzen*. Leipzig: Barth, 1900.

Stetson, R. H. A motor theory of rhythm and discrete succession. *Psychological Review*, 1905, *12*, 250-270, 292-350.

Sturger, P. T., & Martin, J. G. Rhythmic structure in auditory temporal pattern perception and immediate memory. *Journal of Experimental Psychology*, 1974, *102*, 377-383.

Temperley, N. M. Personal tempo and subjective accentuation. *Journal of General Psychology*, 1963, *68*, 267-287.

Thackray, R. *An investigation into rhythmic abilities*. Londres: Noveleo, 1969.

Tisserand, M., & Guilhot, J. Etude du tempo de 335 sujets masculins dans la région parisienne. *Biotypologie*, 1949-1950, *10,11*, 89-94.

Vierordt, K. *Der Zeitsinn nach Versuchen*. Tübingen: Laupp, 1868.

Vos, P. G. Pattern perception in metrical tone sequences. Unpublished thesis, University of Nijmegen, 1973.

Vos, P. G. Identification of metre in music. Report 76 ON 06. University of Nijmegen, 1976.

Vos, P. G. Temporal duration factors in the perception of auditory rhythmic patterns. *Scientific Aesthetics*, 1977, *1*, 183-199.

Vos, P. G., Leeuwenberg, E. L., & Collard, R. F. What melody tells about meter in music. Report 78 FU 03. University of Nijmegen, 1978.

Vurpillot, E., Ruel, J., & Castrec, A. Y. L'organisation perceptive chez le nourrisson: réponse au tout et à ses éléments. *Bulletin de Psychologie*, 1977, *30*, 396-405.

Wallin, J.E.W. Researches on the rhythm of speech. *Studies from the Yale Psychological Laboratory*, 1901, *9*, 1-142.

Wallin, J.E.W. Experimental studies of rhythm and time. *Psychological Review*, 1911, *18*, 100-131, 202-222.

Wallon, H. *Les origines du caractère chez l'enfant*. Paris: Presses Universitaires de France, 1949.

Weaver, H. E. Syncopation: a study of musical rhythms. *Journal of General Psychology*, 1939, *20*, 409-429.

Werner, H. Rhythmik, eine mehrwertige Gestaltenverkettung. *Zeitschrift für Psychologie*, 1919, *82*, 198-218.

Wertheimer, M. Untersuchungen zur Lehre von der Gestalt. *Psychologische Forschung*, 1922, *1*, 47-58.

Wertheimer, M. *Psychologische Forschung*, 1923, *4*, 301–350.

Woodrow, H. A quantitative study of rhythm. *Archives of Psychology*, 1909, *18*, No. 1.

Woodrow, H. The role of pitch in rhythm. *Psychological Review*, 1911, *18*, 54–71.

Zenatti, A. Jugement esthétique et perception de l'enfant entre 4 et 10 ans dans des épreuves rythmiques. *L'Année Psychologique*, 1976, *76*, 93–115.

7

Timing by Skilled Musicians
Saul Sternberg, Ronald L. Knoll,
and Paul Zukofsky

I.	Introduction: Perception, Production, and Imitation of Fractions of the Beat	182
	A. Previous Studies of the Psychophysics of Time	183
	B. Procedures and Notation	184
	C. Subjects	185
	D. Caveats	186
	E. Principal Findings	186
II.	Perceptual Judgment of Beat Fractions	187
	A. Single-Fraction Perceptual Judgment (Experiment 1)	188
	B. Multiple-Fraction Perceptual Judgment (Experiment 2)	194
	C. Judgment Precision	196
III.	Production of Beat Fractions	198
	A. Use of Tap-Click Synchronization to Correct for Differential Subjective Delays	198
	B. Expectations from a Feedback Model of Production	200
	C. One-Response Production (Experiment 3)	200
	D. Rejection of the Feedback Model	201
	E. Repeated-Response Production (Experiment 4)	202
	F. Production Precision: Evidence Against a Reaction-Time Explanation of the Production Error	203
	G. Implications of Other Analyses of Psychophysical Scaling for the Production–Perception Disparity	205
IV.	Imitation of Beat Fractions	207
	A. Four Simple Alternatives for Imitation	207
	B. One-Response Imitation (Experiment 5)	209
	C. Choice Among Alternative Imitation Functions: Rejection of Accuracy and Full-Concatenation Models	209
	D. Implicit Scaling of Beat Fractions from Imitation and Production Data	211

[1]The research described in this chapter was conducted in the Human Information-Processing Research Department of Bell Laboratories, Murray Hill, N.J. Much of it was described in a doctoral dissertation in psychology submitted by R. L. Knoll to Princeton University.

 V. A Shared-Process Model of the Perception, Production, and Imitation of Beat Fractions ..   212
     A. Definition of the Model   212
     B. Restrictions on the Four Processes   214
 VI. Further Analysis of Perceptual Judgment   215
     A. Attention Shifts and Delays: Effect of Marker-Click Pitch (Experiment 6)   215
     B. Time Marking by Onset versus Offset: Invariance of Judgment with Prolonged Markers
        (Experiment 7)   216
     C. A Test of the Rate Constancy of Subjective Time Between Beats: Effect on Fraction
        Perception of Fraction Location Relative to the Beat (Experiment 8)   217
     D. A Constraint on the Precision of Dual Time Judgments and Its Implications for Timing
        Models and the Use of Feedback   218
     E. The Dependence of Perceptual Judgment on Duration versus Fraction: Effects of the Beat
        Interval (Experiment 9)   220
 VII. Further Analysis of Production   224
     A. Production Errors with Musical Instruments (Experiment 10)   224
     B. Production with Marker-Click Feedback (Experiment 11)   225
     C. Production of Single versus Multiple Subdivisions of the Beat (Experiment 12)   226
 VIII. Summary   229
     Glossary   231
     Appendices   231
     A. Staircase and Constant Stimulus Methods   231
     B. Additional Details of Design and Procedure   233
     C. Measures of Location of the Psychometric Function   234
     D. Measures of Spread of the Psychometric Function   236
     E. Stimulus-Averaging versus Response-Averaging Methods for Deriving a Psychophysical
        Scale   236
     References   237

I. INTRODUCTION: PERCEPTION, PRODUCTION, AND IMITATION OF FRACTIONS OF THE BEAT

In this chapter we report 12 experiments that explore how skilled musicians perceive time and time performance in contexts similar to those in music. We discuss some of the perception and performance constraints we found and their implications for underlying timing mechanisms. Our emphasis is on the short time intervals—fractions of a second—that are among the shortest durations specified by musical notation. In our experiments, as in Western music, these intervals occur in the context of a train of periodic beats and are defined as fractions of the beat interval, or duration ratios. Because the beats are provided externally, our experimental tasks are probably most directly analogous to aspects of ensemble playing or of solo playing with a metronome or conductor. Musician subjects are among the best for answering questions about the relation between notation and performance, the constraints on the precision of ensemble playing, and temporal illusions in listening. We hope, however, that the constraints and mechanisms we uncover are relevant to human timing in general; our choice of musicians as subjects in timing experiments is based on our belief that a fruitful approach to the understanding of any human function is the study of skilled practitioners of that function.

We have examined the performance of skilled musicians in three laboratory tasks designed to capture aspects of musical practice: perception, production, and imitation of fractions of the beat interval. All three functions are required of musicians during ensemble rehearsal and performance, for example. It is plausible that because of the requirement that players "keep together," performing experience would cause the three functions to become at least consistent with each other and probably "correct" (consistent with the notation) as well. Neither of these expectations was borne out by our experiments; instead, we observed surprisingly large systematic errors and inconsistencies across these laboratory tasks. In agreement with our observations, the one study of the temporal coordination of ensemble playing of which we know (Rasch, 1979) reveals considerable inaccuracy even in unison attacks.[2] Our findings suggest that other studies of timing in actual musical performance would be of great interest, but unfortunately too little is known at present for us to comment on the extent to which our findings apply outside the laboratory.

The study of performance in our three different but related tasks, together with the analysis of relations among performances, permits some surprisingly strong inferences about these timing mechanisms. Some of our experiments may also be regarded as first steps in establishing a relation (a psychophysical function) between traditional Western musical notation—a notation that specifies time ratios—and the corresponding perceived and produced time ratios among people highly trained in use of the notation.

A. Previous Studies of the Psychophysics of Time

There is a vast, conflicting literature on the psychology of time that we shall only touch on here; we refer the interested reader to Fraisse (1963, 1978), Poppel (1978), Sternberg & Knoll (1973), Woodrow (1951), and Zelkind & Sprug (1974) for reviews and references.

For time intervals greater than a second, there is a long history of experiments focused on determining the psychophysical function relating subjective to actual duration. Most investigators have assumed that estimation and production are consistent, in the sense that they reflect the same psychophysical function. (We shall see this assumption fail dramatically in our experiments.) Investigators have agreed less well on how to account for reproduction (imitation) performance.[3] Based on his review of the data from over 100 studies of the reproduction, production, and estimation of

---

[2]The limitation in Rasch's analysis of trio playing to measurement of unison attacks probably implies that note sequences representing small fractions of a beat—where we found the largest errors and inconsistencies—were underrepresented.

[3]For example, according to Eisler's (1976) analysis, the subject in a reproduction task produces an interval whose subjective duration is half of the subjective duration of the sum of itself and the presented interval. This leads to a nonlinear relation between the presented and reproduced intervals. According to other models (e.g., Carlson & Feinberg, 1968), the subject produces an interval that is subjectively equal to the presented interval; this implies a linear reproduction function of unit slope, regardless of the underlying psychophysical function.

time intervals, Eisler (1976) concluded that subjective duration D is a power function of objective duration d with an exponent of about .9: $D = ad^{.9}$. (An exponent less than unity implies that the subjective ratio of two time intervals is smaller than the corresponding objective ratio; for example, 2 sec would appear less than twice as long as 1 sec.)

For intervals smaller than one second, the data are both more sparse and less consistent. Both Michon (1967) and Svenson (1973) report magnitude-estimation data supporting a change in the exponent of the power function at about .5 sec; whereas the exponent is approximately 1.0 for intervals greater than .5 sec, its value decreases to about .5 for smaller intervals. However, other investigators report either no such change in the function (e.g., Steiner, 1968) or changes at different points (Nakajima, Shimojo, & Sugita, 1980; see also Zwicker, 1969, and Fastl, 1977).[4] According to one view of human timing that has attracted interest, there exists a central timing process (or "clock") that functions similarly in the judgment, production, and reproduction of duration; results from experiments with time intervals greater than a second provide some evidence favoring such a common central process.[5] The discontinuities in judgment revealed in the experiments of Michon and Svenson suggest that a more sensitive test of a common central timing process might be obtained with time intervals less than a second; this suggestion provides one framework for the present investigation.

Despite the importance of time ratios in music, we know of no substantial studies in which judgments or productions of a range of *ratios* have been systematically examined.[6]

B. Procedures and Notation

We have examined performance in three basic tasks (illustrated on the left side of Fig. 1) and variations thereof. All three involve a train of beats specified by *beat clicks;* in most experiments the time from one beat click to the next (*beat interval b*) was 1.0 sec. In describing these tasks we denote stimuli by lower-case letters and responses by upper-case letters.

In the *perceptual judgment* task, one (or more) of the beat clicks was followed by a *marker click*, to form a *time-pattern stimulus* (see Fig. 1A). The time interval between beat and marker clicks (called the *fractional interval*) was to be judged in relation to the beat interval. (For example, if the *stimulus fraction* is $f = 1/8$ and the beat interval is $b = 1000$ msec, the fractional interval is $bf = 125$ msec.) In musical terms our fractions corresponded to note values between a 32nd note ($\flat$) and a quarter note ($\quarternote$), in which the quarter note equals one beat and the rate (in most experiments) was 60 beats

---

[4]Data from the three subjects in the study by Nakajima *et al.* (1980) are too inconsistent to justify firm conclusions.

[5]See Treisman (1963), .25–6 sec; Carlson & Feinberg (1968, 1970), 1–10; and Adam, Castro, & Clark (1974), 3–40 sec.

[6]Except in one small study (Richards, 1964), the only ratios studied in production or perception tasks have been 1:2 (halving) and 2:1 (doubling). Povel (1981) has studied a range of ratios, but only in an imitation task.

per minute. The subject's response in this task was made in terms of *fraction names*, N. (For example, he or she might be asked to decide whether the stimulus fraction appeared to be less than or greater than $N = 1/8$th of a beat.) The fraction name was specified both in musical notation and as a numerical fraction; for example, the subject in this case would be asked whether the marker click was early or late relative to the pattern ♩ ♪♩.. . (The *correct* or *target* fractional interval for $N = 1/8$, given b $= 1000$ msec is, of course, $bN = 125$ msec.) The outcome of this procedure is the determination, for each of a set of fraction names, which stimulus fraction f corresponds to it. The relation between f and N defines a *judgment function*, $f = \mathbf{J}(N)$.[7]

In the *production* task a train of beat clicks was presented, but no marker click (see Fig. 1C). The "stimulus" here was a *fraction name n*. The subject made a *timed response* by tapping his or her finger after a beat click, with the aim of producing a fractional interval between click and tap whose duration was appropriate for the specified fraction name. The ratio of fractional interval to beat interval gives the *produced fraction F*; the fractional interval is bF. The outcome of this procedure is the determination, for each of a set of fraction names n the average value of the fraction F produced to correspond to it. The relation between F and n determines a *production function $F = \mathbf{P}(n)$*.

In the *imitation* task the stimulus was a *time-pattern stimulus*, as in the judgment task (defined by the beat interval b and the fractional interval bF) and the response was a timed response F, as in the production task (see Fig. 1E). The subject attempted to equate the produced fraction F to the stimulus fraction f. The outcome of this procedure is the determination—for each of a set of stimulus fractions f—the average value of the fraction F produced to correspond to it. The relation between F and f determines an *imitation function, $F = \mathbf{I}(f)$*.[8]

Note that the marker click and the timed response of our basic procedures were single offbeat events. Although not frequent in earlier music, the playing of a note after the beat without playing a note on the beat is not unusual in the music of the past 60 years.

C. Subjects

Our principal subjects were three professional musicians: Susan Bush, flutist (SB); Pamela Frame, 'cellist (PF); and Paul Zukofsky, violinist and conductor (PZ). PZ, who had substantially more musical experience than SB or PF, produced data that were more consistent, both within and across experiments. For this reason (and because results from other subjects usually agreed with his), we tend to weight his data more heavily. We obtained a small amount of corroborative data from Pierre Boulez (PB),

[7] Note that we have expressed the stimulus f as a function $\mathbf{J}$ of the response N for convenience in later discussion. We shall use the opposite convention for production and imitation.

[8] In some instances in which there is no ambiguity and the beat interval is 1 sec, we shall use the fraction symbols (n, N, f, and F) also to denote fractional intervals (bn, bN, bf, and bF). Note also that we do not distinguish notationally between quantities such as n, N, f, and F, and their means.

composer and conductor. In Experiment 12 we used two experienced amateur players (JM and SS) as well as PZ.

We carefully avoided informing subjects (including PZ and SS, coauthors) in any way about their performance until after the series of experiments in which they participated was complete, and deliberately provided no trial-to-trial feedback.

D. Caveats

Most of our 12 experiments made use of three subjects, a relatively small number, expecially given instances of inconsistency. We are confident of our major conclusions, however, especially because we found the same trends in more than one experiment. Nonetheless, we suggest caution in generalizing from our findings. We used only two subjects in Experiments 6 and 8, and only one subject in Experiments 7 and 11; results from these experiments should therefore be treated with special caution. Our most stable subject (PZ) served in all 12 experiments, permitting useful comparisons. Some of our findings are clear as well as surprising; nonetheless, they should be regarded as starting points to be confirmed and extended.

E. Principal Findings

In Experiments 1–5 we employed two variants each of the judgment and production tasks, and one variant of the imitation task. All three procedures resulted in proportional errors that are large (20–50%) for small fractions.

As described above, we define beat fractions (and values of N, n, F, and f) in terms of the interval between a tap or marker click and the *previous* beat click: we call these *forward fractions*. It should be noted, however, that a large forward fraction (such as 7/8) corresponds to a small *reverse fraction* (1/8) measured from tap or marker click to the *next* beat. Data from all three procedures hint at systematic errors associated with small reverse fractions that are qualitatively similar to the errors we observe for small (forward) fractions. In this report we emphasize performance for small values of n and f, however, because it is more reliable in all three tasks, and we have more data in that region.

Subjects tend to "overestimate" small fractions (Section II). The fraction names N associated with stimulus fractions f are too large: $f = \mathbf{J}(N) < N$. From this result one might expect that the fraction $F = \mathbf{P}(n)$ produced in response to a stimulus name n would be too small. Instead, produced fractions are too large: $F = \mathbf{P}(n) > n$ (Section III). For example, though a stimulus fraction had to be shorter than 1/8 to be called "1/8," when subjects tried to produce a fraction of "1/8" they produced an interval greater than 1/8.

This inconsistency between judgment and production performance for small fractions requires us to reject feedback models of production (Sections III,B and III,D), in which produced fractions are adjusted by judging them.

Imitation performance (Section IV) is very similar to production performance: for small fractions, $F = \mathbf{I}(f) > f$. The existence of systematic errors in imitation argues against models in which the same transformations (psychophysical functions) relate stimulus fractions and produced fractions to their internal representations. Quantitative comparison of the imitation error to the judgment and production errors argues against a concatenation model of imitation, in which a fraction name produced by a covert judgment then serves as input to the production process.

Taken together, results from the three tasks suggest an information-flow model containing four processes (Section V) with an input process shared by judgment and imitation, and an output process shared by production and imitation. Nothing quantitative is assumed about the four processes, yet properties of the data permit some surprisingly strong inferences about them. The model is outlined in Fig. 7; readers may find it helpful to examine this figure before reading further.

In Section VI we explore and dismiss three potential sources of errors in judgment: the time to shift attention from beat to marker (Section VI,A), the possible importance of stimulus offsets ("releases") as well as onsets ("attacks") (Section VI,B), and the possibility that the rate at which subjective time elapses varies with location within the beat interval (Section VI,C).

We report evidence of a special difficulty associated with concurrent time judgments (Section VI,D), and by varying the beat interval we demonstrate that the judgment error can be described neither in terms of the fraction f alone or the fractional interval bf alone (Section VI,E).

In Section VII we explore and dismiss five potential sources of the errors in production: the use of finger-tap responses rather than notes played on musical instruments (Section VII,A), the absence of adequate response feedback (Section VII,B), the possibility of a distortion of subjective time near the beat (Section VII,C), and the use of single isolated responses that do not fill the beat interval and of off-beat responses not accompanied by any on-beat response (Section VII,C). We also note a tendency for errors in production to be accompanied by displacement (phase shift) of the subjective beat.

Details of experimental method and analysis are given in five appendices. We recommend that readers not interested in technical details omit these appendices, as well as the footnotes and Sections II,C, III,F, III,G, and IV,D.

II. PERCEPTUAL JUDGMENT OF BEAT FRACTIONS

Our principal aim in Experiments 1 and 2 was to determine the stimulus fractions f that were judged to be equivalent to various fraction names N; we would thereby have a psychophysical scale $f = \mathbf{J}(N)$ for fractions of a beat. (Note that in this chapter the term "scale" never denotes a musical scale.) A secondary aim was to measure the *precision* of expert judgments of beat fractions—the sensitivity of judgment probabilities to changes in f. We explored two different methods that permitted us to determine, for each of a set of fraction names, the stimulus fraction f that was subjectively equivalent to it; values of N ranged from 1/8 of a beat to 1 (a full beat). In

Experiment 1 (single-fraction judgment), a fraction name N was specified and the subject then judged, for each of a set of stimulus fractions, whether it was larger or smaller than N. In Experiment 2 (multiple-fraction judgment), the subject selected a response from a set of eight categories (such as "between 1/8 and 1/7 of a beat") whose boundaries were defined by fraction names. Our use of both single- and multiple-fraction procedures was motivated partly by a desire to assess the invariance over experimental methods of the systematic perceptual errors we discovered. Other differences between the procedures are discussed below.

A. Single-Fraction Perceptual Judgment (Experiment 1)

The stimulus patterns in Experiments 1, 3, and 5 are represented on the left side of Fig. 1; the pattern of beat clicks was held constant across these experiments to minimize stimulus differences among the three procedures. Two preliminary beat clicks were followed by a pause ("rest") of one beat (symbolized by a broken line) and then by two more beat clicks. (We used the pause so as to separate the stimulus and response components of each trial in the imitation task.) On each trial in Experiment 1 (Fig. 1A) the final beat click was followed by a marker click. Subjects judged whether the beat fraction appeared too large or too small relative to a specified fraction name N.[9]

Subjects judged fractions in relation to the fraction names 1/8, 1/6, 1/4, 1/2, 3/4, 5/6, 7/8, and 1. The name stayed the same for 75 consecutive trials as the stimulus fraction was varied by an "up-and-down" or "staircase" procedure. (The effect of the staircase procedure is to concentrate the stimuli close to the fraction that is judged to be neither too large nor too small relative to the specified name—i.e., subjectively equivalent to it. See Appendix A for more information about our use of this procedure.)

For each fraction name the resulting data permitted us to estimate the stimulus fraction f subjectively equal to it, which we call the "PMF mean". They also provided a measure of judgment variability discussed in Section II,C, which we call the "SD (standard deviation) of the PMF." Readers not interested in details of method need not understand how these estimates are determined. For each fraction name the method starts with the estimated psychometric function (PMF) provided by our data: a function, usually S-shaped, that associates with the value of each stimulus fraction the proportion of trials on which that fraction appeared "too large." The *location* of the PMF on the f-axis for a specified fraction name is, roughly, the stimulus value where judgment probabilities change most rapidly as the stimulus fraction is changed. This location separates two intervals on the f-axis: a "small-f" region where f tends to be judged too small relative to the name N and a "large-f" region where f tends to be judged too large. The location therefore corresponds to a fraction f that appears

---

[9]Subjects actually selected responses from six alternatives, representing three degrees of confidence for "larger" and three for "smaller." For the present report, however, we have pooled responses from each of the two sets of three to produce two response classes.

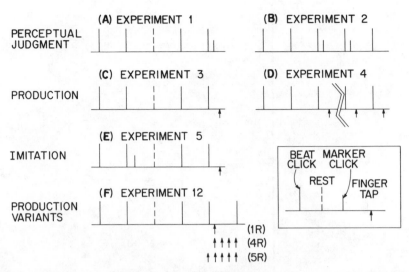

Fig. 1. Time-pattern stimuli and finger responses in six experiments. Beat and marker clicks were 5-msec tone bursts of 3000 and 2500 Hz, respectively, presented over headphones at approximately 30 dB above threshold. The tone bursts started at a zero-crossing and were gated by a voltage controlled amplifier so as to have a 1-msec rise time, a 3-msec steady level, and a 1-msec fall time. Judgment responses were made with a multiple response keyboard. Finger-tap responses were made by tapping on a plate and thereby completing an electric circuit. The interval between successive beat clicks was 1 sec in Experiments 1–5 and .5 sec in Experiment 12. Presented fractions were defined by the time interval between beat click and marker click. Produced fractions were defined by the time interval between beat click and tap, corrected for differential delays (see Section III,A). The train of events on each trial in Experiment 4 included ten finger-tap responses.

subjectively equal to N. A conventional measure of location is the estimated 50% point, or median, of the PMF (i.e., the f-value for which the judgments are equally divided between "smaller than N" and "larger than N"). Instead we report the estimated *means* of PMFs as location measures; our preference for the mean over the median—which differ little in these experiments—is explained in Appendix C, together with our estimation method.

A set of such PMF means establishes a *judgment function*, $f = \mathbf{J}(N)$, a psychophysical scale that associates with each fraction name N, its subjectively equal fraction.[10] (The inverse function, $N = \mathbf{J}^{-1}(f)$, to be used in Section IV,A, therefore gives the value on the name scale associated with a specified stimulus fraction.)

The results are shown in Table I; column labels give the fraction name and its equivalent fractional interval in msec, and row 1 shows the mean stimulus fraction for the three subjects (SB, PF, and PZ). If judgments were free of systematic error, entries in this row would equal the column headings. Instead, as shown by the

[10]Note that this procedure for establishing a psychophysical function, in which averaging is performed in the *stimulus* domain, differs from more common procedures in magnitude and category scaling in which *responses* are averaged. In Appendix E we discuss a comparison of the two methods applied to data from Experiment 2 (multiple-fraction judgment) in which, unlike Experiment 1, both methods can be applied.

TABLE I

Results from Experiments 1–5 and Six Critical Contrasts[a,b]

Experiment or contrast		Fraction name N, n (in judgment, production, or fraction f (in imitation) (and corresponding fractional interval)										SE (df)
	1/8 (125)	1/7 (143)	1/6 (167)	1/5 (200)	1/4 (250)	1/3 (333)	1/2 (500)	3/4 (750)	5/6 (833)	7/8 (875)	1 (1000)	
1. Single-fraction judgment, J_1	85.3 (z)	—	125.5 (fz)	—	265.2	—	455.3 (z)	787.3	835.4 (b)	883.9 (b)	977.8	23.9 (14)
2. Multiple-fraction judgment, J_2	59.3 (*bfz)	79.7 (*bfz)	105.4 (*bfz)	154.4 (*bfz)	207.3 (*bf)	303.6	451.7 (*bz)	—	—	—	—	10.1 (12)
3. One-response production, P_3	139.1	—	197.8 (*b)	—	259.3	—	486.3	759.5	812.3	865.7 (z)	1023.3	11.7 (14)
4. Repeated-response production, P_4	156.8 (bz)	181.4 (bz)	190.4 (bfz)	—	256.7 (z)	—	500.1	743.9	814.2 (b)	853.7 (b)	—	18.3 (14)
5. Imitation, I_5	158.2 (*z)	—	185.2 (z)	—	254.5	—	491.0	773.0	800.8 (*f)	853.3	986.6	14.6 (14)
6. $P_3 - J_1$ (Alternative 2)[c]	53.8 (z)	—	72.3 (*fz)	—	−5.9	—	31.0 (z)	−27.8	−23.1 (z)	−18.2 (bz)	45.5 (z)	28.2 (14)
7. $P_4 - J_2$ (Alternative 3)	97.5 (*bfz)	101.7 (*bfz)	85.0 (*bfz)	—	49.4 (*b)	—	48.4 (*bz)	—	—	—	—	10.0 (8)
8. $P - J$ (mean)	75.7 (*bz)	—	78.7 (*bz)	—	21.8 (bz)	—	39.7 (*bz)	—	—	—	—	10.0 (6)
9. $J_1^{-1} - I_5$ (Alternative 2)[c]	34.2 (f)	—	17.0	—	11.0 (z)	—	43.2 (z)	−57.3 (fz)	7.3 (fz)	−4.4 (z)	—	26.0 (6)
10. $P_3 - I_5$ (Alternative 3)	−19.1	—	12.6	—	4.8	—	−4.7	−13.5	11.5 (z)	12.4 (z)	33.7 (b)	17.2 (14)
11. $P_3 J_1^{-1} - I_5$ (Alternative 4)[c]	52.5 (f)	—	29.6	—	10.8	—	36.0 (z)	−62.0 (fz)	−1.7 (fz)	35.9 (z)	—	29.3 (6)

190

[a] Entries in rows 1 and 2 (3 and 4) are mean presented (produced) fractional intervals associated with the fraction names specified by column headings. Entries in row 5 are mean produced fractional intervals associated with presented fractions specified by column headings. Entries in rows 6–11 are the mean differences indicated. All entries are in msec.

[b] The letters b, f, z are the last initials of our three principal subjects SB, PF, and PZ. A letter is placed next to an entry if the corresponding subject's value of that entry differs significantly ($p < .05$) from the column heading (rows 1–5) or from zero (rows 6–11); the tests for individual subjects were based on the between-replications variance pooled over fractions. The asterisk indicates that the mean over subjects is significantly ($p < .05$) different from the column heading (rows 1–5) or from zero (rows 6–11). Each condition in Experiments 1, 3, and 5 had two replications of the procedure; each condition in Experiments 2 and 4 had from one to three replications. Questions about characteristics of the "population" of subjects from which our "sample" of three was drawn depend on tests of the mean cell entries over subjects. For Experiments 1, 3, and 5 such tests were based on fractions × subjects × replications analyses of variance in which replications was regarded as a fixed effect. For Experiments 2 and 4, results from different replications were averaged and subjected to fractions × subjects analyses of variance. SE estimates used for t-tests of cell entries are based on subjects × fractions interaction mean squares, whose dfs are also indicated.

[c] Data from subject SB were excluded from the means in rows 9 and 11 because the between-replications variances for these contrasts are greater than those of PF and PZ by a factor of about 19. (This exclusion has the effect of producing means that are heavily weighted by degree of precision.) None of SBs values of the contrasts associated with alternatives 2 and 4 differed significantly from zero.

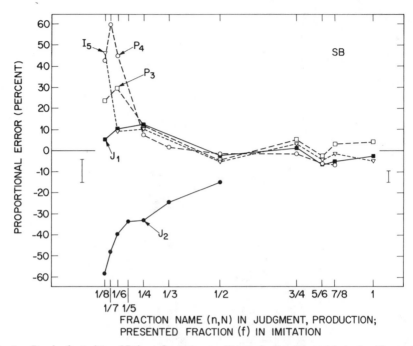

Fig. 2. Results for subject SB from five judgment (**J**), production (**P**), and imitation (**I**) experiments, Ordinate values denote signed proportional error: $(f-N)/N$ for judgment, $(F-n)/n$ for production, and $(F-f)/f$ for imitation, in percentage units. Corresponding abscissa values are N, n, and f, respectively, expressed as fractions. Subscripts are experiment numbers.

accompanying letters, six of the 24 tests of individual data indicated significant departures from equality. Judgment variability tends to increase with fraction size. (See Section II,C, and Getty, 1975, for examples.) This is one reason for our representing the data for individual subjects in Figs. 2, 3, and 4 as signed proportional error (in percent) versus N-value. Our second reason is the importance in music of time ratios and of the rates at which notes occur. The value of $J(1/8)$ from a brief session with our fourth subject, PB, is included in Fig. 4.[11]

A numerical example of the proportional error measure for $N = 1/8$ may be helpful.

---

[11] As noted in Section I,E, a large fraction (such as 7/8) defined from the *previous* beat (as described by the instructions to subjects) corresponds to a small fraction (1/8) measured relative to the *next* beat. If such small reverse fractions were overestimated we would expect that just as we tend to find $J(N) < N$ for $N < 1/2$, so we would find the symmetric relation $[1 - J(N)] < 1 - N$, equivalent to $J(N) > N$, for $N > 1/2$. For PZ and PF both relations tend to obtain, indicating symmetry, although the effect for large fractions is not significant; for SB both relations tend to be reversed, also indicating symmetry. Since the beat following the response was not represented by a click in this procedure, as was the previous beat, any such symmetry suggests that the beat click itself may not be an important determinant of performance and that there is indeed an internal event associated with the final beat. One deficiency of our proportional error plots, of course, is that they obscure systematic irregularities associated with large fractions.

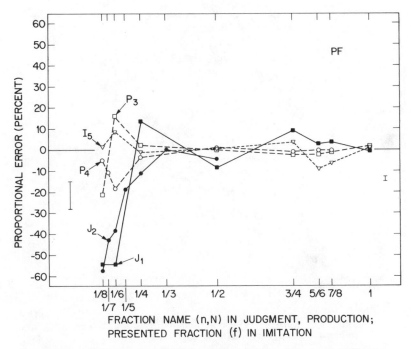

FRACTION NAME (n,N) IN JUDGMENT, PRODUCTION;
PRESENTED FRACTION (f) IN IMITATION

Fig. 3.   Results for subject PF from five experiments. See caption of Fig. 2.

PB's judgment data implied that relative to a beat interval of 1 sec, 62 msec was subjectively equal to 1/8 of a beat (125 msec): $J(1/8) = 62$. Since $[J(1/8) - 125]/125 = (62 - 125)/125 = -.50$, there was a -50% error: the fraction that was judged subjectively equal to 1/8 of a beat was 50% too small. Put another way, the name (1/8) assigned to $f = 62$ was 100% too large: an instance of surprisingly radical overestimation.

Figure 5 shows a different representation of the data from PZ, the most stable of our three principal subjects. Here, $\ln(bf)$ is plotted against $\ln(N)$. If $f = J(N)$ were a power function, the judgment data in this figure could be well fitted by a straight line. (The slope of such a line is the exponent of the corresponding power function.) Clearly, no one power function can describe these data; if separate linear segments were fitted to small-N and large-N ranges, exponents would be about 1.81 for small fractions ($N \leq 1/4$), and close to unity for larger fractions.[12] We defer further discussion of the judgment data to the next section.

---

[12]Note that the more conventional judgment function derived from "magnitude estimation" procedures, in which the experimenter specifies f and the subject provides N, would give an average N as a function of f; $N = M(f)$. M can be regarded as the inverse of J; if they were power functions, their exponents would be reciprocals. (The exponent of M for small fractions is about .55 for the data in Fig. 5.) The change in the exponent of J as n is increased therefore conforms approximately to the findings for magnitude scaling of subjective duration reported by Michon (1967) and Svenson (1973), mentioned in Section I.

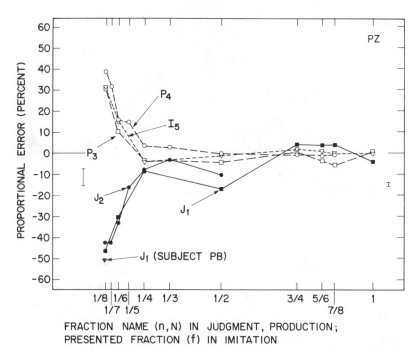

FRACTION NAME (n, N) IN JUDGMENT, PRODUCTION;
PRESENTED FRACTION (f) IN IMITATION

Fig. 4. Results for subject PZ from five experiments and one datum from subject PB. See caption of Fig. 2.

B. Multiple-Fraction Perceptual Judgment (Experiment 2)

The stimulus pattern used in Experiment 2 is represented in Fig. 1B. On each trial the subject heard five beat clicks, with marker clicks following the third and fourth; subjects therefore had two opportunities to observe the beat-marker interval before each judgment. This interval was varied from trial to trial over a wide range (from a minimum of 43 msec to a maximum of 891 msec) by a constant-stimulus method (see Appendix A). The subject selected a response from a set of eight categories, each denoting a range of fraction names and bounded by "simple" fractions (involving small integers): "less than 1/8 of a beat," "between 1/8 and 1/7," "between 1/7 and 1/6,"..., "between 1/3 and 1/2," and "greater than 1/2." The eight ordered categories define seven between-category boundaries on a hypothetical response continuum. For each boundary and each stimulus fraction f we determined the proportion of responses in all categories above that boundary. Regarded as a function of f, this proportion for a specified boundary defines an estimated PMF; this procedure produces seven such PMFs. (Consider, for example, the boundary $N = 1/7$ between the second and third category. Responses to a fraction f in categories above that boundary—categories 3 through 8—are all associated with judgments that f appears

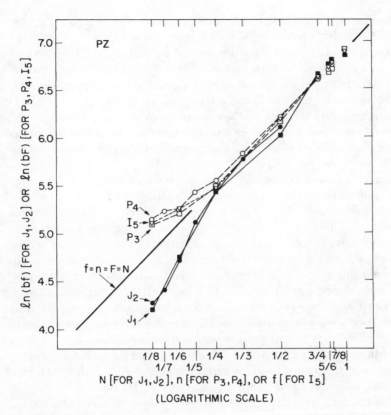

Fig. 5. Results for subject PZ from five judgment (**J**), production (**P**), and imitation (**I**) experiments. Ordinate values are natural logarithms of the fractional intervals *bf* (for judgment) and *bF* (for production and imitation) in msec. Abscissa values represent *N* (for judgment), *n* (for production), and *f* (for imitation), also on a logarithmic scale. Subscripts are experiment numbers. To make units the same on abscissa and ordinate, multiply abscissa values by the beat interval (1000 msec). Power functions are represented as straight lines on this kind of graph.

greater than 1/7 of a beat. As *f* is increased, the proportion of judgments in this "supercategory" increases, defining an estimated PMF associated with *N* = 1/7.)

As in Experiment 1, means of the resulting set of PMFs were used to establish a judgment function, *f* = **J**(*N*), for each subject.[13] The mean function for three subjects

---

[13]This judgment function can be regarded as associating an average stimulus value with each of a set of values (category boundaries) on the response continuum. For each partitioning of the eight categories into the pair of "supercategories" defined by a particular boundary, we treated the data in the same way as in Experiment 1 (see Appendix C). Experiment 2 can also be treated by the more conventional procedure in which an average *response* value is associated with each of a set of *stimuli*. To permit such averaging in the present data, the value of a category response could be taken to be the geometric mean of the values of its two boundaries, for example. That the judgment functions from the two procedures are similar is shown in Appendix E, which also explains our preference for the PMF method.

is presented in row 2 of Table I, individual proportional error data are shown in Figs. 2, 3, and 4, and $\ln(f)$ versus $\ln(N)$ for PZ is shown in Fig. 5.

In Experiment 1, PF and PZ (corroborated by PB) showed large and systematic overestimation of small stimulus fractions, while SB did not. In Experiment 2, however, all three principal subjects showed this effect; quantitative agreement between Experiments 1 and 2 was excellent for PZ, good for PF, but poor for SB. Of the 21 tests based on individual data in Experiment 2, 16 indicated significant departures from equality of N and $J(N)$, and each of the mean differences also proved significant. Taken together, our data show that musicians radically overestimate small fractions of a beat: $N > f = J(N)$.

Although we cannot explain the anomalous results from SB in Experiment 1, we are more impressed by the consistency of PZs mean data between experiments than by the inconsistency of SBs: PZ is the most experienced musician among our principal subjects, and his data *wthin* experiments are by far the most consistent. In Experiment 1 each trial included only one presentation of the fraction to be judged; the fraction size was varied by a staircase procedure over a narrow range of equally spaced values, and subjects had to judge stimulus fractions relative to only a single "target" fraction name during a group of trials. In Experiment 2, on the other hand, each trial included two successive presentations of the fraction to be judged; the fraction size was varied over a wide range and over unequally spaced values by a constant stimulus method; and subjects had to judge stimulus fractions relative to an array of seven fraction names (category boundaries). We conclude that the mean values of the criteria that subjects employ in making these perceptual judgments are affected little by either the number of observations per trial, the range of fractions to be judged, or the number of fractions with respect to which each judgment was made. We shall see in the next section, however, that the choice of procedure does influence the precision of these judgments. [14]

C. Judgment Precision

Insofar as a subject is more sensitive to the stimulus fraction, his judgment probabilities will change more rapidly as the fraction is changed, and the PMF will rise more steeply, or have less *spread*. It is convenient to regard the PMF as a (cumulative) distribution function characterized by a standard deviation (SD) as well as a mean. The SD of the PMF is one measure of its spread, and therefore of the imprecision or variability of judgments. [15]

---

[14]On each trial in Experiment 1, both N and f were provided to the subject; there is some question whether the value of N associated with the stimulus f by the function $f = J(N)$ should be regarded as a response to f. In Experiment 2, where the subject explicitly selected an interval on a continuum of N-values, there is less uncertainty in identifying N as the response. Because of this, together with similarity of the two judgment functions for each of two subjects, we shall regard f as "input" and N as "output" for both experiments.

[15]An alternative and more traditional measure of precision is the difference threshold (DL), which is defined as half of the interquartile range or, roughly, the change in the stimulus fraction required to change

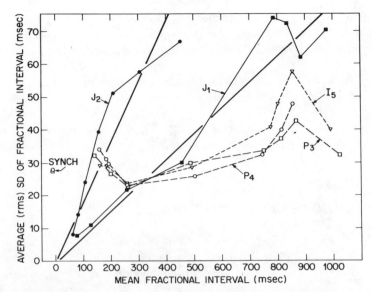

Fig. 6. Performance variability in five experiments. Root mean squared SDs (in msec) over replications and subjects. For judgment experiments J_1 and J_2, SDs were estimated from PMFs regarded as cumulative distributions of the fractional interval *bf*. (See Appendix D.) For production (P_3 and P_4) and imitation (I_5) experiments, SDs were calculated from the distributions of the fractional interval *bF*. Also shown is the rms SD from the synchronization condition (Section III,A). In all cases, the SD(*x*) of a quantity *x* is plotted as a function of the mean M(*x*) of that quantity. Linear functions passing through the origin—which represent Weber laws SD(*bf*) = *k*M(*bf*) with *k*=.08 and *k*=.19 for judgment Experiments 1 and 2, respectively—were fitted by eye.

Fig. 6 includes average SDs of the PMFs in Experiments 1 and 2.[16] In both experiments the SD increases approximately in proportion to *f*, consistent with a Weber law; proportionality constants are about .08 and .19 for Experiments 1 and 2, respectively. (Sampling error in these data preclude a powerful test of the Weber law, however.) Getty (1975) discusses related data and some of the implications of Weber's law for timing models. Insofar as a fraction has been better learned than others or is easier to "compute" given a beat interval, one might expect it to show greater precision (smaller SD) and therefore fall below the Weber law line; there is no dramatic evidence supporting this conjecture, however. Judgment precision is systematically greater (smaller SDs) in the one-fraction than the multiple-fraction procedure, despite

the proportion of "larger than" judgments from .50 to .75. See Appendix D for a discussion of our preference for the SD and our method of estimating it.

[16]The figure actually shows square roots of mean variances (root mean square SDs). Throughout this paper we have chosen to average variances rather than SDs because different sources of variability (such as fraction and subject, in perceptual judgments, or timing and response mechanisms, in production) are more likely to be additive in variance units. We have shown SD rather than SD² in the figure, however, because the expression of Weber's law, SD = *kf*, where *k* is a constant, is then simply a straight line through the origin.

the similarity of judgment means discussed above. (This finding suggests that the range of stimuli f or of fractions N with respect to which judgments are made has a large effect on the variability of subjects' criteria, but only a small effect on their means.)

Despite the systematic errors shown by the judgment function, Fig. 6 reveals the precision of the judgments to be high. For example, in Experiment 2, the f-value that was subjectively equal to $N = 1/8$ (125 msec) was 59.3 msec, and the SD was 7.9 msec. This implies that an f-value of only 72 msec would be judged "larger than 1/8" on 95% of the trials, even though this f-value is 53 msec (or 42%) smaller than the "correct" value.

III. PRODUCTION OF BEAT FRACTIONS

The systematic errors in perceptual judgment discussed above, which are proportionately very large for small fractions of a beat, make it particularly interesting to examine musicians' accuracy in *producing* brief time intervals defined as beat fractions. We used a method of *timed response*. The subjects' task in Experiments 3 and 4 was to use a finger tap to terminate a time interval that started with a beat click and thereby produce a beat fraction F that corresponded to a specified fraction name n. (Subjects could hear as well as feel themselves tapping, since the earphones that delivered the clicks provided negligible attenuation of other sounds. A reader who taps the hard surface of a desk top will hear a "thump" similar to what our subjects heard.)

Our aim was to determine the relation between a set of fraction names and the set of corresponding fractions, and thereby establish a production function, $F = P(n)$. A secondary aim was to measure the precision of such expert timed responses—the variability of the time intervals they defined. Again we used two methods, to assess the invariance of the systematic timing errors we discovered. One method required a single timed response on each trial; the other required a repeated series of responses corresponding to a fixed-beat fraction, thereby permitting more immediate adjustment to perceptual feedback.

A. Use of Tap-Click Synchronization to Correct for Differential Subjective Delays

We wished to compare the timing mechanisms used in perceptual judgment with those used in production and imitation, partly to test the idea that they are the same. It is possible, however, that the subjective delays associated with events that mark the ends of the relevant intervals—beat click, marker click, or finger tap—are different. By correcting for any such differences we can examine the timing mechanisms more directly.

This need for correction seems especially acute for finger taps. Even abrupt taps are extended in time, which makes it unclear how to associate a single time point with a response. Our equipment measured the time at which the finger first contacted a metal plate, but the subjective time of the response might be equally well described by the time when the "command" to make the response is issued, the time when maximum pressure is achieved, the time when the finger breaks contact with the plate, or some other feature of the response, possibly adjusted by perceptual delays.

Suppose that the beginning and end of an interval are marked by events b and e, respectively, T_b and T_e are their physical occurrence times, and D_b and D_e are the delays in registering the events internally. (For a tap, the mean "delay" may be negative.) Then the registration times are $T_b + D_b$ and $T_e + D_e$; and whereas the objective interval between events is $T_e - T_b$, the interval between registration times is $(T_e - T_b) + (D_e - D_b)$. Thus, to correct the measured interval for internal delays, we must estimate the delay difference, $D_e - D_b$.

If the two delays are equal, the difference is zero, and no correction is needed. For the perceptual judgment experiments, in which both ends of the relevant interval were marked by the same class of events (clicks), we felt that equality of delays was a plausible starting assumption. (In Section VI we report some findings favorable to this assumption.)

Our solution to this problem in the production experiments, where the critical interval begins with a beat click and ends with a finger tap, was to measure the difference between the two subjective delays by using a special condition in which subjects were asked to synchronize their responses with beat clicks. This synchronization task can be thought of as a production task with $n = 0$, except for the occurrence of a beat click at the time when the response should occur. Since we shall be using $\mathbf{P}'(n)$ to denote the raw (uncorrected) mean production time for fraction n, we use $\mathbf{S}'(0)$ to denote the mean measured response "delay," $\mathbf{S}'(0) = T_t - T_c$, where t and c denote tap and click, respectively. Suppose that the subjects succeed in locating the mean of their distributions of subjective occurrence times of responses coincident with the mean of the subjective beat times. The registration-time difference defined above is then zero: $(T_t - T_c) + (D_t - D_c) = 0$. It follows that $-\mathbf{S}'(0) = D_t - D_c = T_c - T_t$ provides the desired estimator of the delay difference.

The raw (uncorrected) mean production times $\mathbf{P}'(n)$ were corrected by subtraction: $\mathbf{P}(n) = \mathbf{P}'(n) - \mathbf{S}'(0)$. In the synchronization conditions, subjects responded slightly before the beat click [$\mathbf{S}'(0) < 0$], implying that the subjective delay associated with the tap response was greater than the perceptual delay associated with the beat click. The corrections, then, slightly increase the measured values of $\mathbf{P}(n)$. Application of the synchronization correction depends on the assumption that the difference between these beat-click and tap delays in the production task is the same as in the synchronization task and is independent of the interval between beat click and tap (which in turn depends, in production, on the specified fraction name).[17]

---

[17] One objection to the use of the synchronization correction is based on the possibility that this assumption will be violated. For example, constraints on attending simultaneously or in close succession to click and tap might produce special differential delays ("prior-entry" effects). See Sternberg and Knoll (1973), Section VI.

B. Expectations from a Feedback Model of Production

What relation might we expect between performances in the judgment and production tasks? One appealing hypothesis is a simple feedback process in which a subject (1) judges the size of each produced fraction F with respect to the target-fraction name n using the same perceptual mechanisms in this judgment as in the judgment task itself, and (2) adjusts subsequent productions accordingly.[18] One would then expect systematic errors in judgment and production tasks to be equal to that $P(n) = J(N)$ when $n = N$. For example, if an interval of 62 msec is *judged* to correspond to 1/8 of a 1-sec beat [$J(1/8) = 62$], the same interval (after correction for differential subjective delays) should be *produced* for 1/8 of a beat [$P(1/8) = 62$].

C. One-Response Production (Experiment 3)

On each trial in Experiment 3 (Fig. 1C), the subject attempted to respond with a single finger tap following the last beat click so as to produce a fraction F that corresponded to a specified fraction name n. The name remained the same for 25 consecutive trials. We used the same fraction names as used in Experiment 1 to define a set of experimental conditions. For each condition we calculated a mean raw response time, $P'(n)$.

In a synchronization condition, the subject attempted to synchronize the finger tap with a beat click added at the end of the normal stimulus pattern. The resulting values of $S'(0)$ were -13.8 msec, -16.3 msec, and -9.0 msec, for subjects SB, PF, and PZ, respectively.

The mean production function, $P(n) = P'(n) - S'(0)$ for the three subjects is presented in row 3 of Table I, individual proportional error data are shown in Figs. 2, 3, and 4, and $\ln(F)$ versus $\ln(n)$ for PZ is shown in Fig. 5. PZ and SB show large positive proportional errors (overproduction) for fractions 1/8 and 1/6. Because PF does not show this effect, the error shown by the mean production time for small fractions is somewhat smaller; for only one of the eight means (for $n = 1/6$) is the inaccuracy significant. Proportional errors for larger fractions are small and of varying sign, with a slight tendency for produced intervals associated with the largest fractions (5/6, 7/8) to be too small (underproduction).[19]

---

[18]Carlson and Feinberg (1968) and Adam, Castro, and Clark (1974) present data that favor an "internal clock" or counter model that applies to both judgment and production of time intervals in a range from 1 to 40 seconds. According to Carlson and Feinberg's model, systematic errors in production and judgment result from changes in the counter's rate between learning the count to be associated with a time interval specified by name and performing the experimental tasks. The resulting relation between errors in production and judgment is consistent with a feedback model. Furthermore, because the counter rate is assumed not to change systematically between stimulus and response in an imitation (reproduction) task (Section IV), this kind of model requires imitation to be accurate. Given that fractions are being judged in our experiments, however, and the beat interval (which can "calibrate" the counting rate) is presented on each trial, the counter mechanism does not easily lend itself to explaining any systematic errors in our tasks.

[19]This tendency can also be described as overproduction of the small "reverse fractions" 1/6 and 1/8 that are defined by the intervals between tap and subsequent beat. A tendency toward such symmetry in

D. Rejection of the Feedback Model

All three subjects show large discrepancies between $P(n)$ and $J(N)$ for the two smallest fractions. In row 6 of Table I are shown values of the difference $P(n) - J(N)$ for the matched procedures of Experiments 1 and 3. The feedback model requires this difference to be zero for all values of $n=N$; for the two smallest fractions it is substantially greater than zero, especially in relation to the precision (Fig. 6) of perceptual judgments. The two largest fractions show smaller but directionally symmetric discrepancies.[20]

A numerical example based on mean data from Experiments 1 and 3 (rows 1 and 3 of Table I) may help to clarify the failure of the feedback model. The mean interval *produced* to correspond to $n = 1/8$ was $P(1/8) = 139.1$ msec. To what fraction name N would this interval correspond if the same perceptual judgment mechanisms were used as in Experiment 1? Since $J(1/8) = 85.3$ msec and $J(1/6) = 125.5$ msec, N is clearly greater than 1/6; since $J(1/4) = 265.2$ msec, it is clearly less than 1/4. To determine N exactly, we must solve $J(N) = 139.1$ msec for N. If we regard fraction names as lying on a continuum, and use linear interpolation, we find the corresponding fractional interval to be 174.8 msec or slightly greater than 1/6 of a beat. Thus, if subjects perceived intervals between click and tap in the same way as intervals between two clicks, the average subject would *perceive* the interval he or she *produced* for 1/8 as larger than 1/6.

Differences between judgment and production procedures could, in principle, result from "constant errors" based on differential subjective delays for which we have not corrected. (We have not attempted to estimate or correct for any delay difference between beat click and marker click in the judgment task, partly because of findings discussed in Section VI. The synchronization-based correction that we did apply to the production data might be inappropriate.) But on the most straightforward view, the absolute effects of differential delays should be of the same size for all fraction values. Hence, insofar as the inconsistency between perception and production depends on fraction size (which it does reliably, as shown below), we have to search elsewhere for an explanation.

One possibility is that although discrepant feedback was available, the time interval between successive trials and the number of stimulus events between one response and the next prevented subjects from making appropriate corrections. Because our subjects said neither that they were dissatisfied with their productions nor that they "came in late," this possibility seems unlikely. Nonetheless, it was tested in Experiment 4, which called for timed responses to 10 successive beat clicks on each trial.

---

judgment performance was noted in footnote 10. Note, however, that when the *precision* of performance (Fig. 6) is considered, rather than its *mean*, performance at the two ends of the beat interval appears far from symmetric.

[20]$J(1)$ and $P(1)$ can be regarded as alternative measures of the *subjective* beat interval. That they differ (significantly for PZ) suggests that this interval might be task dependent (also suggested by findings in Experiment 12). Deviations of $P(1)$ and $J(1)$ from 1000 msec are sufficiently small, however, so that our use of the actual rather than subjective beat interval to define beat fractions makes little difference, especially for small fractions.

E. Repeated-Response Production (Experiment 4)

On each trial in Experiment 4, we presented 12 beat clicks. As shown in Fig. 1D, subjects attempted to make 10 consecutive finger-tap productions so as to produce a fraction that had been specified by name. The first response was produced after the third beat click. We used the fraction names 1/8, 1/7, 1/6, 1/4, 1/2, 3/4, 5/6, and 7/8; the name remained the same for 25 consecutive trials. For each fraction name n and each position k in the sequence of 10 responses, we determined the mean raw response time, $\mathbf{P}'_k(n)$.

In a synchronization condition, subjects attempted to make tap responses that coincided with each of the last 10 beat clicks, thereby generating values of $\mathbf{S}'_k(0)$ for $k = 1,\ldots, 10$. The corrected response time was obtained by subtraction: $\mathbf{P}_k(n) = \mathbf{P}'_k(n) - \mathbf{S}'_k(0)$.

Trend over Repeated Responses

Subjects produced large positive errors ("too late") for the smallest three fractions (1/8, 1/7, 1/6). Values of $\mathbf{P}_k(n)$ averaged over these fractions and the three subjects, for $k = 1,\ldots, 10$, were 168.4, 172.9, 176.9, 180.0, 175.4, 181.4, 176.3, 184.5, 176.6, and 169.8 msec, respectively. There is no evidence of a decrease in the size of the error over repetitions. (The slope of a line fitted to these values is .43 msec/repetition.) It is also instructive to compare the time of the first response $\mathbf{P}_1(n)$ (with synchronization correction $\mathbf{S}'_1(0) = -13.4$ msec) with the time of the mean response $\mathbf{P}(n)$ (with $\mathbf{S}'(0) = -24.9$ msec), separately for the three fractions. For 1/8, 1/7, and 1/6, values for the first response (mean response) are, respectively, 151.9 (156.8), 169.5 (181.4), and 183.9 (190.4) msec.

There is no evidence that subjects used feedback from one response to the next in the repeated response procedure to reduce the size of their production errors.

Means over Repeated Responses

Further analyses were based on mean response times over the 10 positions. These were adjusted by the mean synchronization corrections; $\mathbf{S}'(0)$ was -22.6, -35.2, and -16.9 msec for SB, PF, and PZ, respectively.

The mean of the production functions, $F = \mathbf{P}(n)$, for the three subjects is presented in row 4 of Table I, individual proportional error data are shown in Figs. 2, 3, and 4, and ln (F) versus ln(n) for PZ is shown in Fig. 5.[21] As in Experiment 3, PZ and SB show large positive proportional errors for small fractions, whereas PF does not; in addition, PZ and SB show negative errors for large fractions, whereas PF does not, providing further evidence for the symmetry in performance at the two ends of the

---

[21]Like the judgment function, ln(F) versus ln(n) cannot be fitted by a single power function (straight line). A two-limb fit gives an exponent of about .57 for the range $1/8 \leq n \leq 1/4$ and about 1.0 for $n > 1/4$.

beat interval mentioned in Sections II,A and III,C. Agreement between Experiments 3 and 4 is best for PZ. Again, performance for large fractions is relatively accurate.

Values of the difference $P(n) - J(N)$ appropriate for another test of the feedback model are provided in row 7 of Table I. We used judgment data from Experiment 2 because it provides values that are independent of Experiment 1, because it was run in close temporal proximity to Experiment 4, and because the stimulus conditions (Figs. 1B and 1D) were similar. All three subjects show large discrepancies between judgment and production of small fractions. Each of the five mean values of the difference in row 7 of Table I (values for all the fractions $n = N$ that were common to the two experiments) is significantly and substantially greater than zero; the difference diminishes reliably as fraction size increases. (This implies, of course, that the proportional difference decreases to an even greater extent.) The failure of the feedback model is even more dramatic for these data than for the initial test (row 6 of Table I).[22]

Our best estimates of production-perception discrepancies are obtained by combining the two tests; means for the fraction values that are common to the four experiments are given in row 8 of Table I. The mean contrast is significantly greater than zero ($t_7 = 4.41$; $p < .005$), and the difference depends significantly on fraction size ($F_{3,6} = 7.56$; $p < .025$).

F. Production Precision: Evidence against a Reaction-Time Explanation of the Production Error

Average SDs of production and synchronization times are included in Fig. 6 for Experiments 3 and 4. Data from the two experiments are in good agreement; data from each of the three subjects averaged over the two experiments produced a U-shaped function with a minimum SD (maximum precision) between $n = 1/4$ and $n = 1/2$.[23] The precision of synchronization performance, with mean $S'(0)$, is slightly but not reliably greater than the precision of production of a whole beat, with mean $P'(1)$.

For fractions $n \geq 1/4$, production precision exceeds judgment precision, but this

[22]It remains a puzzle how production performance might be calibrated (or learned) by players without feedback about the timing of individual responses. One possibility is that the association of produced fractions with fraction names is learned through attempts to produce extended sequences of temporally regular notes that fully occupy the interval between one beat and the next. Counting, rather than the timing of individual responses, could then provide a measure by which to adjust the rate. Given this possibility (and also to assess the generality of our findings), it is interesting to ask whether the first response by a subject attempting to produce a temporally regular sequence displays the same pattern of errors as that obtained with a single response. This question is considered in Section VII,C, in a study of multiple divisions of the beat.

[23]A U-shaped function with a minimum in this range has also been obtained from one subject in a time production task by A. B. Kristofferson (1976; Experiment II). Experimental conditions differed considerably from ours, with feedback provided on each trial, and the one subject had about 10 times as much practice in the experimental task as ours did. Nonetheless, his minimum SD (about 12.7 msec) did not differ significantly from the minimum (22.2 msec) of the mean SD produced by our subjects.

relation is reversed for small fractions. Insofar as subjects do not experience their productions of small fractions as highly variable, we therefore have further evidence against the feedback model.

One explanation of the production errors for small fractions (but not the similar errors for small "reverse fractions") attributes them to a combination of musical training and the existence of a minimum reaction time (RT). The minimum voluntary RT to auditory stimuli is between 100 and 150 msec. Furthermore, there are delays (which differ across instruments) between excitation and acoustic response. The combination of these two effects makes it virtually impossible to produce a note 125 msec after a signal to respond such as a beat, when the event that triggers the response is the beat itself. Players could try to "anticipate" the beat (by timing their responses from the penultimate beat), but since the occurrence of the beat in musical performance is variable, this might be risky. Players therefore appear to be in a situation in which they are musically required to produce discriminably different response delays, some of which are less than the minimum RT.

One possible solution would be to time responses from the final beat, but bias the productions so that the intervals for small fractions are both greater than the minimum RT and distinctive. For example, if to respond later than the minimum reaction time a subject produces an interval of 150 msec (rather than 125 msec) for 1/8 of a beat, then an interval greater than 150 msec must be produced for 1/7 of a beat, etc.

However, the variability of the production-time distributions suggests that responses associated with small fractions may be timed from the penultimate beat. (Synchronization responses presumably *must* be timed from this beat.) Hence, the production errors may *not* be due to a constraint imposed by a minimum RT. The argument (whose impetus and conceptual framework is provided by Snodgrass, Luce, and Galanter, 1967) is as follows.

We start by assuming that the variance of a distribution of response delays increases monotonically (or at least does not decrease) as the mean of the distribution increases, where the mean is measured relative to the reference signal from which subjects time their responses.[24] Therefore, if all responses were timed from the final beat click, we would expect the variance to increase monotonically with fraction size. As we have seen, this expectation is violated by our data. One interpretation of the increased variability for small fractions is that subjects were timing their responses from the penultimate beat click in these conditions. The most salient errors in production are then not the result of a constraint imposed by the minimum RT.

If subjects timed small fractions from the penultimate beat click but large fractions from the final beat click, the argument above, in its simplest form, implies that no large-n productions should have variances greater than the small-n productions. One difficulty is the suggestion in the data (Fig. 6) of a peak in the SD-function when $n = 7/8$. (Because this difference between the SD at $n = 7/8$ and $n = 1/8$ is shown only by

[24] See, e.g., Snodgrass, Luce, and Galanter (1967) for intervals $\geq .6$ sec, Treisman (1963) for intervals $\geq .25$ sec, and references cited therein.

SB and PZ, the mean difference is not reliable, however.) A slight elaboration of our account can deal with this difficulty. Suppose that the response for small fractions can be triggered either by perception of the final beat click *or* by a timing process initiated by the penultimate beat click, whichever occurs first. This could shorten production delays that would otherwise be exceptionally long, thereby reducing the variance. (See Kornblum, 1973.) Evidence favorable to such a facilitation effect of the final beat click is provided by a comparison we made with PZ between one-response production of $n = 1/8$ and the same procedure with the final beat click replaced by a "rest" (or an "imaginary beat"). Omission of the click increased the mean response delay by about 17% (from 149.5 to 175.5 msec), thereby increasing the mean error, but more than doubled the SD (from 26.0 to 70.2 msec).[25]

However, our argument for the idea that subjects timed their productions of small fractions from the penultimate beat click depends on the assumption, introduced above, that the variance of a produced time interval cannot decrease as its mean increases. Even if true for time intervals defined in isolation, this assumption may be false for intervals that are defined as different fractions (or multiples) of a standard interval, as in our production task. Perhaps fractions that are "simpler," or more practiced, or that require less "computation" (such as $n = 1$) are produced more reliably. In models in which timing is accomplished by counting a stream of internal events until a criterion is reached, the reliability with which the criterion count is *set* may have to be considered as well as the variability of the inter-event intervals. This possibility is supported in our data by the (statistically significant) reduction in variability from $P(7/8)$ to $P(1)$.

G. Implications of Other Analyses of Psychophysical Scaling for the Production–Perception Disparity

Readers with a special interest in psychophysical scaling may find it interesting to consider our perception and production experiments in relation to the "magnitude estimation" and "magnitude production" methods used to investigate many perceptual domains. These methods often produce power-function relations between stimulus and response values; such psychophysical scales are often summarized by power-function exponents. The exponent β determines how ratios of stimuli ($\phi_1 < \phi_2$) are mapped onto ratios of the numerical magnitudes or names ($\psi_1 < \psi_2$) associated with them: $\psi_2/\psi_1 = (\phi_2/\phi_1)^\beta$. An exponent larger (smaller) than 1.0 implies that the name ratio is larger (smaller) than the stimulus ratio.

Partly because there is a "correct" relation between n and F that musicians are presumably trained to achieve, we are interested in the relation between n-values and F-values and not merely in the relation between *ratios* of pairs of n-values and pairs of F-values. (The latter relation, but not the former, is captured by the exponent of a fitted power function.) Sizes of the exponents are nonetheless useful to consider. We

---

[25]This comparison also suggests that the existence of a positive production error for small fractions does not depend on the presence of an actual beat click.

have already noted that both $\mathbf{J}(N)$ and $\mathbf{P}(n)$ deviate dramatically from power functions if the full range of fractions is considered. However, power functions fitted only to the data for small fractions fit reasonably well and do capture one aspect of the discrepancy between perception and production. A power function fitted to the data for small fractions in our experiments has an exponent greater than 1.0 for production but less than 1.0 for perception.

Under some conditions with other perceptual continua, magnitude production exponents are larger than those obtained in magnitude estimation. There are at least three reasons why our finding may not be an instance of the same phenomenon. First, Teghtsoonian and Teghtsoonian (1978) have shown that the difference between exponents depends on the stimulus range and, indeed, is reversed for narrow ranges. Stimulus ranges in our two perception experiments differed greatly; their endpoints were about 50 and 850 msec in Experiment 2, but only about 90 and 140 msec (for PZ and $n = 1/6$, for example, in Experiment 1. Nonetheless, we obtained good agreement between experiments for PZ and PF. In both production experiments, the stimulus (fraction name) was fixed for a long series of responses (25 and 250 responses in Experiments 3 and 4, respectively). The best description to assign to the stimulus range in this case would therefore appear to be "narrow."

Second, the Teghtsoonians argued that the effect depends on the avoidance by subjects of extreme response ratios (i.e., either much larger or much smaller than unity). This analysis seems inapplicable in a straightforward way to Experiment 1, where the overt responses were "larger than N" and "smaller than N." (To make it applicable, one could assume that subjects produce covert responses of particular N-values that they then categorize in terms of the specified target N-value to determine the overt response.)

Third, if mechanisms of the kind discussed by the Teghtsoonians were responsible for the difference we observed between $\mathbf{J}(N)$ and $\mathbf{P}(n)$ for small fractions, we would expect a difference in the same direction for large fractions, contrary to what we observed.

In the discussion above we have assumed that time *ratios* F or f (between produced or stimulus intervals and the beat interval) are the objects to be produced or judged. A less obvious alternative is to consider these objects to be time *intervals* bF or bf. In that case, a procedural difference between our experiments and many others becomes important. The Teghtsoonians argue persuasively that in choosing a response on one continuum to associate with a stimulus on another, subjects refer to the prior stimulus and prior response and choose a response that generates a response ratio equal to the subjective stimulus ratio. With traditional methods the prior stimulus and response are those from the previous trial and usually vary from one trial to the next. In contrast, with our methods the (large) beat interval b—corresponding to fixed prior values ("standards") $f = 1$ and $N = 1$ on the two continua—is presented on each trial, becomes a prior stimulus, and can perhaps be regarded as generating a prior response. Suppose that we accept this alternative analysis (together with the idea that subjects produce covert N-responses in Experiment 1). Then, if subjects tend to avoid extreme response ratios, they would both overproduce and overestimate small fractions but not large ones, as observed. The Teghtsoonians' analysis can therefore provide one viable account of the perception-production difference, if we combine it with rejection of the feedback model.[26] [27]

Two findings incline us against the interval alternative. The first, by Michon (1967), is the absence of effects of stimulus range in an experiment on magnitude estimation of time intervals. Given this finding, one would have to argue that the psychophysics of beat fractions and of time intervals differ, with the former more like other sensory domains, or that although the standard interval (like a beat interval) was not presented on each trial in Michon's experiment, subjects presented a fixed standard to themselves.

The second finding is our own, emerging from a comparison of perceptual judgments of beat fractions across different beat intervals (described in Section VI,E). This experiment permitted us to remove the confounding of the duration of the interval being judged with its fraction value. A straightforward application of the interval alternative, based on avoidance of extreme response ratios, implies that the judgment error depends only on the response (the N value) and therefore on the fraction f rather than the interval bf; in contrast, we found that the error depends on both fraction value and interval duration.

IV. IMITATION OF BEAT FRACTIONS

In both the judgment and production tasks, subjects must associate beat fractions and their names. In the imitation task (sometimes called the method of reproduction), this association is not called for, at least not explicitly: the "input" is the same stimulus f, as in the judgment task, and the "output" is a timed response F, as in the production task. The relation, $F = \mathbf{I}(f)$, between f and F in the imitation task may therefore tell us whether the systematic errors found in the other tasks depend on the requirement to associate names with beat fractions. More generally, by exploring the imitation task and its relation to the judgment and production tasks, we hoped to explain or describe the production-perception disparity in terms of characteristics of internal transformations, some of which may be shared by pairs of the three tasks and some of which may be task-specific.

A. Four Simple Alternatives for Imitation

There are four simple and interesting possible outcomes of the imitation experiment, two of which have been explicitly considered in studies of time-interval perception.

[26]The possible inconsistency in conventional procedures between magnitude estimates (of stimuli controlled by the experimenter) and feedback from magnitude productions (controlled by the subject) is also a puzzle, of course.

[27]Insofar as symmetric errors are found for large fractions—as discussed in Sections II,A; III,C; and III,E—this account would, of course, have to be elaborated.

Alternative 1: Accurate Imitation

The first possibility is that despite errors in the other tasks, imitation (after the synchronization correction) will be accurate: $F = \mathbf{I}(f) = f$. The imitation function is thus the identity transformation for which output equals input and which we denote "**E**", and we have $\mathbf{I} = \mathbf{E}$. This outcome would follow from any model in which the errors found in the judgment and production tasks result from the processing of fraction names: Carlson and Feinberg discuss an example of such a model based on a "clock" or event-counting process.[28]

Alternative 2: Imitation Consistent with Perceptual Judgment

A second possibility is that the relation between f and F in imitation is the same as the relation between f and N in the perceptual judgment task so that $\mathbf{I}(f) = \mathbf{J}^{-1}(f)$, or $\mathbf{I} = \mathbf{J}^{-1}$. This consistency could arise if the stimulus pattern, which is common to the two tasks, is processed in the same way, leading to the same internal representation, and if the further transformations of this representation (that lead to F in imitation and N in judgment) are equivalent.

Alternative 3: Imitation Consistent with Production

A third possibility is that the relation between f and F in imitation is the same as the relation between n and F in production so that $\mathbf{I}(f) = \mathbf{P}(n)$ when $f = n$. The relation $\mathbf{I} = \mathbf{P}$ could arise, for example, if f and n generate a common internal representation when $f = n$, which is then transformed by the same processes in the two tasks to produce F.

Alternative 4: Imitation Combines the Errors of Judgment and Production

The fourth possibility is easiest to motivate by considering a model of imitation performance that would generate it. We describe this as a *full-concatenation* model because it calls for the application of all of the internal transformations used in the other two tasks. According to this model, the subject covertly assigns to f a value on a continuum containing fraction names $N = \mathbf{J}^{-1}(f)$ (just as in the judgment task) and then produces the timed response $F = \mathbf{P}(N)$ that corresponds to that N-value (just as in the production task). We ignore, for the present, the possibility that special difficulties would be introduced by N-values that did not correspond to simple fractions. The result is $F = \mathbf{I}(f) = \mathbf{P}[\mathbf{J}^{-1}(f)]$. (We represent this by $\mathbf{I}(f) = \mathbf{P}\mathbf{J}^{-1}(f)$ or $\mathbf{I} = \mathbf{P}\mathbf{J}^{-1}$.) Note that since $\mathbf{J}^{-1}(x) > x$ and $\mathbf{P}(x) > x$ for small x (on average), the two combined errors are in the same direction. Thomas and Brown (1974, Section V)

---

[28]See footnote 18 for a description of the model.

assumed a full-concatenation model in their study of the filled-duration illusion in the perception of time intervals.[29,30]

B. One-Response Imitation (Experiment 5)

In Experiment 5 (Fig. 1E) the first pair of beat clicks was followed by a marker click. (In the corresponding judgment task of Experiment 1, the marker followed the second pair of beat clicks, so the contexts for the time-pattern stimuli in the two experiments were not precisely the same.) The subject attempted to respond with a single finger tap after the final beat click (as in the corresponding production task of Experiment 3) to imitate the presented fraction defined by the marker click. The fractions to be reproduced were the objectively correct fractions that correspond to the fraction names used in Experiments 1 and 3.[31] In the imitation task, however, no name was specified to the subjects. The fraction to be imitated remained the same for 25 consecutive trials. We determined the raw mean response time, $I'(f)$ for each fraction; we then corrected this value by subtraction: $I(f) = I'(f) - S'(0)$, with the same synchronization correction used in Experiment 3.

Mean values of $I(f)$ are given in row 5 of Table I, proportional error curves for individual subjects are shown in Figs. 2, 3, and 4, $\ln(F)$ versus $\ln(f)$ is plotted for PZ in Fig. 5, and mean SDs are shown in Fig. 6. As in the production task, imitations of the small fractions 1/8 and 1/6 tend to be too large, and imitations of the complementary large fractions 7/8 and 5/6 tend to be too small. Symmetric distortion in the direction of 1/2 has also been described by Fraisse (1956, Chapter IV) and Povel (1981). Note, however, that the effect is absent in our data for the fractions (1/4, 3/4) closest to 1/2.

C. Choice among Alternative Imitation Functions: Rejection of Accuracy and Full-Concatenation Models

To test the four alternative possibilities for imitation performance outlined in Section IV,A, we calculated deviations between the observed imitation function and the function expected from that alternative for each replication within each subject's

[29]If we add to this model the assumption that the component operations are stochastically independent, it follows that the variance of F in imitation must be at least as great as the variance of F in production. It must also be at least as great as the variance that would be induced in the production of F by virtue of variability in the N-values on which responses are based in the judgment task. Given plausible assumptions, the SD that measures this induced variability can be estimated by multiplying the SD of the appropriate PMF from the judgment task by the derivative of the production function $P(n)$ at the appropriate n-value. [Since $P(n) \cong n$ for n $\geq$ 1/4, this derivative is close to 1.0 for $n \geq 1/4$.]

[30]Imitation would also combine the errors of judgment and production if, for example, it shared just an input process with the former and just an output process with the latter *and* if these two processes were fully responsible for the errors in their respective tasks.

[31]It is a limitation of the experiment that other fraction values, such as those *judged* to be equivalent to simple fraction names, were not used as stimuli for imitation.

data, based on results from the matched procedures of Experiments 1, 3, and 5. For example, for Alternative 2 we calculated the contrast $J_1^{-1} - I_5$ for each fraction; insofar as this alternative is valid, these contrasts (whose means over subjects are displayed in row 9 of Table I) should be close to zero.[32]

Numerical examples for Alternatives 2 and 4 may be helpful; we shall base them on second replication data from PZ, for $f = 1/8$ ($bf = 125$). These examples are clearer when the argument of J is expressed in fractional intervals (in msec) rather than fractions. Thus, for Alternative 2, $J(1/6) = J(166.7) = 96.6$, and $J(1/4) = J(250) = 206.2$. Linear interpolation gives $J(188.6) = 125$, or $J^{-1}(1/8) = J^{-1}(125) = 188.6$. According to Alternative 2, this value should be equal to $I(1/8) = 161.1$. The contrast is $J^{-1}(1/8) - I(1/8) = 27.5$ msec.

For Alternative 4 we need $P[J^{-1}(1/8)]$, and from above we have $J^{-1}(1/8) = 188.6$. We therefore need $P(188.6)$. Second replication data from PZ give $P(1/6) = P(166.7) = 170.3$ and $P(1/4) = P(250) = 242.0$. Linear interpolation gives $P(188.6) = 189.2$. According to Alternative 4, this value should be equal to $I(1/8) = 161.1$. The contrast is $P[J^{-1}(1/8)] - I(1/8) = 28.1$ msec.

We have used three methods to compare the relative goodness of fit of the four alternatives to our data. Since none of these methods is ideal, but taken together they point clearly in one direction, we mention results from all three. We restrict our attention to the seven fractions $1/8 \leq f \leq 7/8$ for which we were able to calculate contrasts for all four alternatives. For Alternatives 1 through 4, respectively, the numbers of individual subject contrasts (of 21 possible) that reach significance are 3, 8, 2, and 7, respectively, favoring Alternatives 1 and 3. The numbers of tests of means over subjects that reach significance are 2, 0, 0, and 0, however, indicating more consistency over subjects in the failures of Alternative 1 and thereby favoring Alternative 3. The mean squared deviations (contrasts) for the four alternatives are 514, 972, 148, and 1454, respectively, clearly favoring Alternative 3; the same ordering is observed for the mean squared deviations associated with the three smallest fractions, which fall within the range of our most interesting and surprising findings.

Taken together then, our results favor Alternative 3 (imitation consistent with production) for the range of fractions we examined and permit us to reject the two alternatives considered in Section IV,A (accurate imitation, and the full-concatenation model) that have been previously considered for longer durations.

Further evidence bearing on the choice among the four alternatives can be found in relations among the variabilities of performance in the three tasks (Fig. 6). First, the SD functions for I_5 and P_3 are strikingly similar in form, again favoring Alternative 3. The increasing divergence of the two functions with size of the produced fraction is statistically significant, however ($t_2 = 8.4$; $p < .02$). In the context of the mechanism proposed in Section IV,A, for Alternative 3, this divergence could arise if the value of the common internal representation is more variable when it is derived from f than from n

---

[32]Note that nonlinearities in the computation for Alternatives 2 and 4 result in discrepancies between the *mean contrasts* displayed in rows 9 and 11 of Table I and *contrasts of the means* of the components in rows 1, 3, and 5.

and if this variability difference grows with f. Second, although the SD of imitation is no smaller than the SD of production (as required by the full-concatenation model together with a stochastic independence assumption; see footnote 29), the SD of imitation *is* smaller than the corresponding variability measure associated with the judgment task, which violates an additional requirement of that model. This observation argues further against Alternative 4.

D. Implicit Scaling of Beat Fractions from Imitation and Production Data

Performances in the judgment, production, and imitation tasks interest us primarily because of the light they and the relations among them can shed on underlying timing mechanisms. As already discussed, however, the judgment and production tasks can also be regarded as two different methods for establishing a psychophysical scale—a function that relates the beat fraction f and its subjective magnitude. In each method the scale is established by identifying the subjective magnitude with an n-value. Both methods are explicit in that the subject's response is identified directly with one of the terms in the function. If we believe there is one "true" scale, then the fact that the two methods disagree implies that the scale derived from at least one of them is incorrect. As discussed in Section III,G, this difficulty also arises in other perceptual domains and has been attributed to effects on response-generation processes that distort the inferred association between stimuli and their internal representations. In Section III,F, we considered one such explanation (the existence of a minimum RT) for the systematic error we found in production.

The assumption required to use judgment and production tasks as explicit scaling methods—that responses accurately reflect magnitudes of the internal representations that are the objects of interest in psychophysics—is therefore subject to question. We can replace this assumption by a much weaker one if we use an *implicit scaling procedure* in which the scale is derived by combining data from production and imitation. The weaker assumption permits response biases or other distorting effects associated with responses to exist and requires only that those that operate in the generation of the timed response (F) in production also operate in the generation of the timed response in imitation. Under this assumption (which we use in developing the model described in Fig. 7) if a stimulus n_0 in production leads to the same timed response as does a stimulus f_0 in imitation so that $\mathbf{P}(n_0) = \mathbf{I}(f_0)$, then the internal representations of n_0 and f_0 that are used by the (common) response generation processes must have equal magnitude. The equation $\mathbf{P}(n) = \mathbf{I}(f)$ therefore establishes a scale relating n and f that is free of response effects; it may be written $n = \mathbf{P}^{-1}\mathbf{I}(f)$.

Let us consider what the four simple alternatives for imitation (Section IV,A) imply about the resulting implicit scale:

1. *Accurate imitation.* Since $\mathbf{I}$ is the identity transformation in this case, $n = \mathbf{P}^{-1}\mathbf{I}(f) = \mathbf{P}^{-1}(f)$ or $f = \mathbf{P}(n)$, so that the implicit scale is the same as the scale based on production.

2. *Imitation consistent with judgment.* Here $I = J^{-1}$. Hence $n = P^{-1}I(f) = P^{-1}J^{-1}(f)$; or $f = JP(n)$. Since $P(x) > x$ and $J(x) < x$ for small x, the relation between f and n specified by the implicit scale depends on relative magnitudes of the errors in J and P.

3. *Imitation consistent with production.* Here $I = P$. Hence $n = P^{-1}I(f) = I^{-1}I(f) = f$, so the implicit scale is free of systematic error (veridical).

4. *Imitation combines errors.* Here $I = PJ^{-1}$. Hence, $n = P^{-1}I(f) = P^{-1}PJ^{-1}(f) = J^{-1}(f)$, so that the implicit scale is the same as the scale based on perceptual judgment.

We have seen above that results of the imitation experiment favor Alternative 3. One implication is that despite the inaccuracy (and inconsistency) of the explicit scales based on judgment and production data, the implicit scale based on combining results from the two tasks with a common response (imitation and production) is free of systematic error.

V. A SHARED-PROCESS MODEL OF THE PERCEPTION, PRODUCTION, AND IMITATION OF BEAT FRACTIONS

In this section we present an information-flow model of performance in our three tasks. It is a minimal model in that we make as few assumptions as we can and limit ourselves to accounting for major features of the data. We think of each task as involving processes that perform input, translation, and output functions, and a principle of parsimony leads us to assume that different tasks share whatever processes they can. Given this starting point, the model incorporates the minimum possible number of constituent processes.

A. Definition of the Model

The processes in the model responsible for judgment performance are represented by the two upper boxes in Fig. 7. A time-pattern stimulus f generates an internal uncategorized or "analog" representation by a transformation T_{fa}. (We call the representation "analog" only to indicate that it does not reflect a categorization of the stimulus that maps 1-1 onto fraction names.)[33] This representation must then be converted by a transformation T_{aN} into an internal "name" representation to generate the required fraction-name response N. The resulting compound transformation is denoted $T_{aN} T_{fa}$.

The processes in the model responsible for production performance are represented by the two lower boxes in the figure. A fraction-name stimulus n is converted into an internal analog representation by a transformation T_{na}, which is then used to generate

---

[33]One possibility is that this representation encodes both fraction (normalized marker interval) and beat interval. An alternative is that the beat interval is reflected by the rate of an internal clock or accumulator so that the analog representation has to encode only the marker interval in terms of the count or value accumulated.

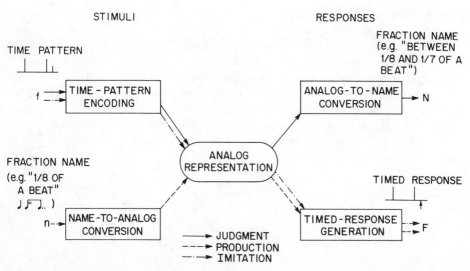

Fig. 7. A shared-process information-flow model of the perception, production, and imitation of beat fractions. The model incorporates four processes that convert time-pattern (*f*) or fraction-name (*n*) stimuli into time-pattern (*F*) or fraction-name (*N*) responses and that make use of a common intervening representation. Transformations carried out by the four processes are symbolized by $T_{input,output}$. Paths of information flow for the three tasks are represented by unbroken, broken, and dotted arrows, respectively.

the required timed response by a transformation T_{aF}.[34] Since no feedback process has been incorporated in this account and judgment and production share no common processes, the inconsistency between perception and production is not paradoxical.

A full-concatenation model of imitation (Alternative 4) would most naturally be represented by a system in which the upper and lower pair of processes had separate intervening representations, instead of the common analog representation shown in Fig. 7. Information could then not flow directly from time-pattern encoding to timed-response generation. Instead, a covert response output of the pair of processes used in judgment would become the input for the pair of processes used in production; the resulting compound transformation converting *f* to *F* would be $T_{aF} T_{na} T_{aN} T_{fa}$. Because such a model can be rejected, we adopt a *partial-concatenation model* of imitation, which shares only the encoding process of the judgment task and the response-generation process of the production task and makes use of an internal representation that is common to the two tasks. The resulting compound transformation converting *f* to *F* is $T_{aF} T_{fa}$.[35,36]

---

[34]Again there are several ways in which the (subjective) beat interval might be represented to provide the information that must be incorporated with the fraction name to define the response.

[35]Note that it is only because production and perception errors are not compensatory (i.e., do not conform to the feedback model) that we can discriminate a partial- from a full-concatenation model of imitation.

[36]An alternative two-process model of imitation in the same spirit would separate the information flow in judgment and production into phases that precede and follow the establishment of internal *name* repre-

B. Restrictions on the Four Processes

Experiments to be described in Sections VI and VII help further to elucidate performance in the judgment and production tasks, and will eventually help to flesh out the skeleton shown in Fig. 7. Even with the results presented thus far, however, if we assume the structure of the model some interesting and surprising inferences can be made about the relations among the transformations T_{fa}, T_{aN}, T_{na}, and T_{aF} carried out by its four component processes. Given these four transformations, there are six transformation pairs; our data permit an inference about the relation between the members of each pair.

The starting points for these inferences are idealizations of four of the properties that appear to characterize performance in the three tasks. The four properties are as follows:

a. $J \neq E$. (There are systematic errors in judgment.)
b. $P \neq E$. (There are systematic errors in production.)
c. $P = I$ (When $n = f$, response times in imitation and production are the same.)
d. $I \neq J^{-1}$. (The response fraction F in imitation is not equal to the name N associated with the same f in judgment.)

To make the inferences, we start by using the model to write each of the functions J, P, and I in terms of the pair of transformations they reflect: $J^{-1} = T_{aN}T_{fa}$, $P = T_{aF}T_{na}$, and $I = T_{aF}T_{fa}$. The inferences are as follows:

1. From property (c) we have $T_{aF}T_{na} = T_{aF}T_{fa}$, or $T_{na} = T_{fa}$. The two input transformations are therefore the same, and hence the internal (analog) representations of stimuli n and f have the same magnitude when $n = f$. This corresponds to the observation that the implicit scale relating f to n (Section IV,D) is free of error. Identity of the input transformations of n and f suggest that performance is not an accidental property of input processes; changes in details of the time-pattern stimulus should therefore not have major effects on performance. Evidence favoring this suggestion is presented in Sections VI,A, and VI,B.

2. From property (a) we have $J^{-1} \neq E$ or $T_{aN}T_{fa} \neq E$ and hence $T_{aN} \neq T_{fa}^{-1}$. (Not surprisingly, given errors in judgment, its input and output transformations are not inverses.)

3. Combining (1) and (2), we find $T_{aN} \neq T_{na}^{-1}$. Thus, the transformations analog to name (in judgment) and name to analog (in production) are not inverses.

4. From property (b) we have $T_{aF}T_{na} \neq E$, or $T_{aF} \neq T_{na}^{-1}$. (Not surprisingly, given errors in production, its input and output transformations are not inverses.)

5. Combining (1) and (4), we find $T_{fa} \neq T_{aF}^{-1}$. Thus, the transformations time-pattern stimulus to analog (in judgment and imitation) and analog to timed response

---

sentations rather than (the earlier) internal *analog* representations. We prefer our alternative because it seems less likely to us that an interesting or plausible transformation (other than the identity transformation) would relate stimulus or response *names* to their internal representations than that such a transformation would relate stimulus or response *times* to their internal representations.

(in production and imitation) are not inverses. This could also have been inferred from $I \neq E$.

6. From property (d) we have $T_{aF}T_{fa} \neq T_{aN}T_{fa}$, or $T_{aF} \neq T_{aN}$. In other words, the two output transformations are distinct (unlike the two input transformations): values of the N and F derived from the same internal (analog) representation are distinct. A difference between the output transformations for N and F makes it plausible that changes in response details might influence performance in production and imitation; some tests of this possibility are presented in Section VII.

VI. FURTHER ANALYSIS OF PERCEPTUAL JUDGMENT

In Sections VI and VII we report results of our search for explanations of the errors associated with small fractions in the judgment and production tasks; we describe four variations of the judgment task and three variations of the production procedure. Our aim in most of these experiments was to determine not whether there was *any* effect of changes in experimental conditions, but whether there were any effects large enough to suggest major sources of the performance errors.

A. Attention Shifts and Delays: Effect of Marker-Click Pitch (Experiment 6)

The presented fraction is defined by the difference between the onset times of the beat and marker clicks. The *subjective* occurrence time of a click, however, may differ from its objective time by an amount that depends on perceptual delay (possibly influenced by the amount of processing required to mark its occurrence). To the extent that the perceptual delays of the beat and marker clicks differ, the presented fraction that is judged subjectively equal to a fraction name will differ from the objective fraction that corresponds to that name, even in the absence of other perceptual distortions. As mentioned in Section III,D, we felt that equality of perceptual delays was a plausible starting assumption for beat and marker clicks. In this section and the next we report results that bear on its validity.

For the perceptual judgment data described thus far, the beat and marker clicks had different pitches. In one possible explanation of the judgment errors, perception of the marker click is assumed to be delayed by the shift of attention from the pitch of the beat clicks to the pitch of the marker click. (For example, findings by Van Noorden, 1975, suggest that the delay might increase with the pitch difference by about 100 msec/octave.) Suppose that this attention shift can be initiated, and possibly completed, after the beat click but before the marker click, if there is enough time between them. (The marker pitch could be learned from earlier trials.) Suppose further that if the shift has not been completed before the marker click, a time interval is required for the marker to attract attention, whose duration decreases with time after the beat click; perception of the marker is delayed until the attention shifts. This would explain both the judgment error for small fractions and its decrease in magnitude for larger fractions.

This hypothesis implies that the errors associated with small fractions should be influenced by any manipulation that alters the time to shift attention, such as variation of the pitch difference between the beat and marker clicks.

A second reason to suspect that the pitch difference may be implicated in the judgment errors is based on its possible influence on perceptual organization of the series of clicks into sequential groups (Woodrow, 1909, 1951) or simultaneous streams (Bregman, 1978).

To investigate the effect of pitch differences, we had two subjects (PZ and SB) perform in the procedure of Experiment 1 with $N = 1/8$, one second beat intervals, and marker clicks of 1700, 2500, and 3000 Hz; the beat-click frequency was always 3000 Hz. The frequency of the marker click remained the same for 75 consecutive trials, and $J(1/8)$ was derived from the last 50 trials of the staircase procedure. According to the attention-shift hypothesis, $J(1/8)$, the f-value associated with $N = 1/8$ should be greater (and closer to 1/8) when marker and beat clicks are closer in pitch.

An analysis of variance failed to show a significant effect on $J(1/8)$ due to the frequency variation: for marker-click frequencies of 1700, 2500, and 3000 Hz, $J(1/8)$ had mean values of $f = 79.2$, 69.6, and 69.9 msec, respectively, with a standard error (based on 2 df) of 2.1 msec (a nonsignificant effect in the wrong direction). These results make unlikely an explanation of the estimation errors in terms of the time to shift attention along the pitch continuum.

B. Time Marking by Onset versus Offset: Invariance of Judgment with Prolonged Markers (Experiment 7)

In general, one might expect the internal response to any brief stimulus to differ from the stimulus itself in both shape and duration (see Sternberg & Knoll, 1973, Sec. IV; Fastl, 1977). Furthermore, the subjective occurrence time of a stimulus should depend on the particular feature of the internal response used to mark it. If the internal responses produced by the beat and marker clicks were different or if different features were used to mark their occurrence times, these differences by themselves could produce the observed judgment errors. For example, if the subjective duration of a time interval delimited by a pair of clicks corresponded to an interval delimited by the *onset* of the internal response produced by the first and the *offset* of the internal response produced by the second, the subjective duration would be greater than the objective duration, defined as the difference between click onset times.[37]

To test this possibility we conducted a small perceptual judgment experiment

---

[37]If auditory signals are presented in close temporal proximity, the internal representation of one (especially the second) is probably affected by the presence of the other (e.g., Duifhuis, 1973; Fastl, 1977; Penner, 1974). Thus, forward masking causes the first of two clicks to elevate the detection threshold of the second. Such effects become negligible with delays of at most 100 msec, however, and are therefore unlikely to be important in determining the judgment error.

(with PZ as the only subject). We used the procedure and stimulus values of Experiment 2 and compared the normal time-pattern stimuli (with all clicks 5 msec in duration) with stimuli in which the marker duration was 62 msec. Let us assume that relative to its onset, the perceived offset time of a tone burst is delayed by about the same amount as its duration is increased. Given the hypothesis, then, we are led to expect an increase in $f = J(N)$ of about 57 msec in the prolonged marker condition. Instead, we obtained no change: over six fraction names the measured mean increase was a negligible .6 $\pm$ 1.9 msec. (The SE is based on variability among the effects on PMF means for N = 1/7, 1/6, 1/5, 1/4, 1/3 and 1/2. For N = 1/8 there were insufficient data to generate a PMF.) There was neither a main effect of marker duration nor an interaction of marker duration with fraction size.

It is reasonable to suppose that any feature of an internal response whose occurrence time is invariant with changes in stimulus duration is located at or near the beginning of that response. The absence of an effect of marker duration therefore argues that the onset rather than the offset of the marker response is the critical feature that determines its subjective occurrence time, and suggests that the systematic judgment errors cannot be attributed to different features of the internal response being used to define the occurrence times of beat click and marker click. (If the offset rather than onset of the *beat* click were used by subjects, the resulting judgment error would be in the wrong direction.)[38]

C. A Test of the Rate Constancy of Subjective Time between Beats: Effect on Fraction Perception of Fraction Location Relative to the Beat (Experiment 8)

In the perceptual judgment experiments reported thus far, the conditions for which systematic errors are largest have two features in common: first, the interval to be judged is small, and, second, it occurs in close temporal proximity to (indeed, is bounded by) the beat click. Suppose that subjective time during the beat interval was inhomogenous in the sense that relative to physical time it elapsed faster near the beat and more slowly elsewhere in the beat interval. Then small fractions defined by intervals near the beat would be overestimated, as observed, but the same small fractions elsewhere in the beat interval, and large fractions initiated by the beat, might not be. To determine how proximity to the beat of the interval being judged affects perceptual judgment, we instructed subjects PZ and PF to judge whether the interval between a pair of marker clicks was larger or smaller than 1/8 of a beat for marker pairs at six different locations within the beat interval.

The beat and marker clicks were 5-msec tone bursts of 3000 and 2500 Hz, respectively. We used four intervals between markers (50, 60, 70, and 80 msec) chosen based on earlier results to permit us to estimate PMFs for judgments relative to 1/8 of

---

[38]We conjecture that this finding reflects a general property of the perception of musical timing and rhythm: the dominance of the sequence of time intervals between the *onsets* of successive notes (attacks) and the relative unimportance of offset times, which probably serve articulative rather than timing functions.

a 1-sec beat interval. (If effects of proximity to the beat in this initial experiment had been large, of course, this set of intervals might not have provided sufficiently complete functions at all proximities.) On each trial we presented clicks for three beats— B_1, B_2, and B_3; subjects were asked to imagine the next two beats, B_4 and B_5. A marker-click pair, M_1 followed by M_2, defined one of the four intervals, and was located at one of six positions within the sequence of beats, as follows: (1) symmetric about the midpoint of B_3 and B_4, (2) such that M_2 preceded B_4 by 100 msec, (3) such that M_2 was simultaneous with B_4, (4) such that M_1 was simultaneous with B_4, (5) such that M_1 followed B_4 by 100 msec, (6) symmetric about the midpoint of B_4 and B_5.

Position 4 is, of course, the arrangement that had been used in our previous experiments in which the interval to be judged is initiated by the beat, except that the event that marks the beat is a marker click rather than a beat click. (For this position, then, beat B_4 is signaled by a click and is not imaginary, unlike the other positions.) At position 3 the interval to be judged is terminated by the beat. At positions 1 and 6 the interval to be judged is as far as possible from any beat. The six positions combined with four marker intervals defined 24 stimuli that were presented in random sequence (method of constant stimuli).

We found no systematic effects of proximity to the beat on either PMF means [values of J(1/8)] or SDs. Over the two subjects, average PMF means for the six positions are 57.5, 61.7, 55.9, 60.0, 58.3, and 56.7 msec, respectively; (rms) average PMF SDs are 9.4, 10.9, 7.0, 5.5, 12.5, and 4.4 msec, respectively. Over the six positions the average PMF mean is 58.3 msec, and the (rms) average SD is 8.8 msec.[39] Again, the judgment error is surprisingly large: 58.3 msec is about 53% smaller than the correct value of 125 msec.[40] These results show that the judgment error depends neither on the judged interval being bounded by a beat click nor on the proximity of the judged interval to the beat. The rate at which subjective time elapses during the beat interval appears to be constant.

D. A Constraint on the Precision of Dual Time Judgments and Its Implications for Timing Models and the Use of Feedback

A further variation of the perception task revealed an interesting and unexpected limitation in the judgment of time intervals. In an extension of Experiment 8, we

---

[39]It is instructive to compare these results to findings for the same two subjects in Experiments 1 and 2. Like Experiment 2 the present experiment involved a method of constant stimuli rather than a staircase procedure; like Experiment 1 the present experiment called for a narrow range of f-values. Since results of Experiments 1 and 2 at $N = 1/8$ for PZ and PF were similar, we have combined them to obtain a PMF mean of 62.5 msec and an SD of 7.7 msec. The present experiment produced almost identical values, suggesting that uncertainty from trial to trial about the position of the interval to be judged (which was much greater in the present experiment) is an unimportant factor in judgment performance.

[40]Because the two marker clicks had the same frequency (2500 Hz), these results also provide further evidence against the notion that the estimation errors result from a pitch difference between the clicks bounding the interval to be judged.

instructed one subject (PZ) first to estimate the duration of the brief interval bounded by the marker clicks (relative to 1/8 of a beat), as in the main experiment, and then also to judge whether the longer interval between the last beat click and the marker pair was less than or greater than one beat interval (i.e., marker clicks before or after B_4). The subject was instructed to perform accurately in judging the brief interval (primary task) and, having done so, to judge the long interval (secondary task) as accurately as he could.

The need to make the long-interval judgment did not substantially alter either the mean or the SD of the duration PMF: without the secondary task these parameters were 54.4 and 6.0 msec, respectively; with the added task they were 58.1 and 7.9 msec, respectively. On the other hand, the subject's precision in judging the long interval appears to have been greatly impaired by having also to judge the brief interval. One measure of the loss in precision is obtained by comparing performance in the secondary task to earlier performance (Experiment 1, $N = 1$), judging only the position of a single marker click relative to the beat; this comparison reveals that the SD of the PMF from the secondary task is more than *10 times* the SD obtained in the single-judgment, single marker-click procedure.[41] (In Experiment 1 the mean and SD of the PMF were 962.5 and 48.8 msec, respectively, versus 1114.5 and 502.6 msec, respectively, in the secondary task.)[42]

It is helpful to consider this observation in relation to a particular class of mechanisms that may underlie the timing process. One candidate for the analog representation in the information-flow model of Section V is the value attained by an internal clock or accumulator. (See Creelman, 1962; Treisman, 1963; Wing, 1973; Eisler, 1975; and Getty, 1976, for particular realizations of this idea.) In the judgment task, for example, the hypothesized clock starts with the initial event defining the interval and stops with the terminal event. (Alternatively, the current value of the clock is "saved" when the terminal event is detected.) Results of the dual-task variation of Experiment 8 require elaboration of such clock models to explain why the two successive intervals (the long interval from the beat to the first marker and the short interval from the first to the second marker) could not both be accurately judged.

One possibility is that the timing process permits only intervals that are similar in duration to be accurately classified in quick succession or concurrently. For example, the clock might have an adjustable rate: a slow rate for accurately judging large intervals and a fast rate for accurately judging small intervals.[43]

[41]Strictly speaking, to control for the possibility that the poor performance in the secondary task might be due to the physical nature of the stimuli (the end of the long interval was defined by two marker clicks rather than one), performance in the secondary task should be compared for conditions that have identical physical stimuli and that differ only by the presence or absence of the primary duration judgment. Although this control is logically necessary, and therefore should be used in further investigation of the phenomenon, it would surprise us if such enormous changes in performance could be explained by such minor variation of the physical stimuli.

[42]Thus, a marker pair in position 1 (500 msec before B_4) was judged to have occurred *after* B_4 with probability about .11; a pair in position 6 (500 msec after B_4) was judged to have occurred *before* B_4 with probability about .22.

[43]This limitation could explain our finding that the multiple-fraction procedure (Experiment 2) elicited

According to a second possibility, the clock cannot be started and stopped rapidly, permitting precise timing of only one of two adjacent intervals and requiring use of an alternative, less precise mechanism for timing the interval from the beat click to the first marker click.[44]

Either of the above possibilities could also account for failure of the feedback model of production (Section III,D), if we assume that the same timer is used for production as for perception. To produce a fraction appropriate for a specified name, subjects must time an interval from the beat click to the *initiation* of the response. Since there is a delay between the start of a response and its actual occurrence, it is possible that having accurately timed when to initiate the response, subjects cannot also accurately judge when the response occurs. Alternatively, suppose that timing for the production of small fractions is initiated by the penultimate beat (Section III,F) but that judgment of fractions of all sizes depends on timing from the final beat. Again, the constraints on timing discussed above would prevent the perceptual mechanisms used in the judgment task from being used to evaluate feedback for small fractions in the production task.

E. The Dependence of Perceptual Judgment on Duration versus Fraction: Effects of the Beat Interval (Experiment 9)

In this section we examine two simple alternative ways to characterize perceptual judgment performance and the mechanisms responsible for judgment errors. One is a *duration model*, according to which the fundamental variable is the duration of the fractional interval. For a specified fraction name N the correct value of this interval can be represented as bN, where b is the beat interval and N is the fraction name; the obtained (matched) value is then bf, the absolute error is $bf - bN$, and the relative error is $(bf - bN)/bN$. According to the duration model, judgment error depends only on the correct duration bN; once that is specified there is no further effect of beat interval on either the absolute or relative error. For example, the mean judgment error for $N = 1/8$ at $b = 1000$ msec should be the same as the mean error for $N = 1/6$ at $b = 750$ msec, since in both cases the correct duration is $bN = 125$ msec. The attention-shifting mechanism considered in Section VI,A exemplifies such a model.

The second alternative is a *fraction model*, according to which the fundamental variable is the fraction, or duration *ratio*. For a specified fraction name N the correct fraction is N itself, the obtained value is f, the absolute error is $f - N$, and the relative error is $(f - N)/N$. According to the fraction model, judgment error depends only on the correct fraction; once that is specified, there is no further effect of beat interval on either the absolute or relative error. For example, the mean judgment error (expressed

---

lower judgment precision than the single-fraction procedure (Experiment 1). It could also explain the finding by Vorberg and Hambuch (1978) that subjects attempting to produce precisely timed rhythmic patterns control the timing with a set of *chained* "timers" that produce approximately equal durations rather than hierarchically *nested* (concurrent) "timers" that produce highly disparate durations.

[44]In developing this possibility, the accuracy with which subjects judge the regularity (equality) of trains of successive intervals (Schulze, 1978) would have to be considered.

TABLE II
Experiment 9: Design and Mean Data[a]

Beat interval (b) (msec)	Fraction name (N)							
	1/8		1/6		1/4		1/2	
750	.078 (.125)	58 (94)	α .108 (.167)	81 (125)	β .203 (.250)	152 (188)	δ .475 (.500)	356 (375)
1000	α .075 (.125)	75 (125)	.098 (.167)	98 (167)	γ .238 (.250)	238 (250)	.450 (.500)	450 (500)
1500	β .102 (.125)	153 (188)	γ .158 (.167)	236 (250)	δ .250 (.250)	374 (375)	.456 (.500)	683 (750)

[a]Left-hand cell entries are relevant to the fraction model. Upper left entry is the obtained mean fraction f; lower left entry (in parentheses) is the target fraction N (equal within each column). Right-hand cell entries are relevant to the duration model. Upper right entry gives the mean obtained duration bf in msec. Lower right entry (in parentheses) gives target duration bN. Pairs of cells marked with the same Greek letter have equal target durations.

as a fraction) for $N = 1/8$ should be the same for all beat intervals. A mechanism in which the beat interval has its effect by controlling the rate of an internal clock exemplifies such a model.

On the basis of the judgment experiments considered above, the two models cannot be distinguished because the beat interval was constant (1 sec). In Experiment 9 we used the procedure of Experiment 1 to compare judgment performance by SB, PF, and PZ for each of four fractions ($N = 1/8, 1/6, 1/4,$ and $1/2$) at three different beat intervals ($b = 750, 1000,$ and 1500 msec). The fractions were chosen so that we could examine performance with the same target *fraction* N at each of three beat rates (permitting a test of the fraction model) and also with the same target *duration* bN at two beat rates each (permitting a test of the duration model). These two possibilities are most easily seen by examining cell entries in Table II. The design is orthogonal with respect to N and b; each of the four columns represents the same target *fraction* (left value in parentheses) for different beat intervals. Greek letters indicate those cells that represent the same target *duration* (right value in parentheses) at different beat intervals. For example, for both of the cells marked β ($N = 1/4, b = 750,$ and $N = 1/8, b = 1500$) the target duration is 188 msec.

Tests of both models involved the examination of row (beat-interval) effects in an appropriate two-way table. Let us consider the fraction model first. Here the two-way table has three rows (beat interval) and four columns (fraction name). If the fraction model is correct there should be neither a row effect nor an interaction of rows with columns: error measures associated with the three cells in each column should be equal. (Means over subjects of the obtained fraction values, shown at the upper left to each cell in Table II, appear, in contrast, to change systematically with beat interval.)

For the duration model the full design is not orthogonal; tests are made possible by reducing the design. Four fractional intervals—with durations 125, 188, 250, and 375 msec—each appear at a "smaller" and "larger" beat interval in Table II in cells designated by Greek letters. The reduced two-way table therefore has two rows ("smaller" and "larger" beat interval) and four columns (one per fractional interval). If the duration model is correct there should be neither a row effect nor an interaction of rows with columns in the reduced table: Error measures associated with the two cells in each "column" (marked by the same Greek letters in Table II) should be equal. (That pairs of beat intervals differ from column to column does not invalidate the test of this null hypothesis.) The pairs of mean obtained interval values for the same target interval, shown in Table II, do appear to depend little on beat interval. For example, for the two cells marked α, for which the correct duration is 125 msec, we obtained 81 msec at the smaller (750 msec) beat interval and a similar 75 msec at the larger (1000 msec) beat interval. (The analysis will show this independence of beat interval to be an artifact due to averaging over subjects, however.)

We were able to use the same error measure in tests of both models, based on analysis of variance. This was possible, first, because for each model absence of row effects and interactions for its absolute error would imply their absence for its relative error[45] and, second, because the two relative error measures [$(bf - bN)/bN$ for duration and $(f - N)/N$ for fraction] are equal.

Results of the analyses of variance for the two models are shown in the upper and lower halves of Table III. For the group analyses neither test shows a significant main effect of rows (b) nor a significant row-column interaction. Both analyses, however, reveal significant interactions of beat interval and subjects, indicating that there are row effects for individual subjects and thereby violating the models; differences among these effects for individuals are apparently large enough so that they cancel each other or otherwise render the main effects insignificant.

Results of the group analyses are consistent with the possibility that each subject's behavior conforms with one of the two models but that the same model does not apply to all three subjects. We tested this possibility by performing the same analyses for each subject separately; results are shown in the right-hand section of Table III. Both models are rejected by these individual analyses, with all three subjects providing evidence against the fraction model and two subjects providing (somewhat weaker) evidence against the duration model. For PZ, duration accounted for a larger percentage of variance than did fraction (76 versus 27%, respectively). For PF, the ordering was the same but the difference was small (80 versus 75%, respectively). Thus,

---

[45]Relative error can be obtained from absolute error in each case by dividing by the value of the column factor (correct duration or correct fraction). Suppose a two-way table of absolute errors has no row effects or row-column interactions. Then transforming its cell entries in a way that depends only on the column factor produces a new two-way table that also can have no row effects or row-column interactions. (If there is no row effect within any column before the transformation then there can be none after the transformation.)

TABLE III

Results of Analyses of Variance for Duration and Fraction Models

Model	Factor	p-value from group analysis	p-values from individual analyses PZ	SB	PF
Fraction	Beat interval (b)	n.s.[a]	<.001	<.005	<.01
	Fraction (N)	n.s.	<.001	n.s.	<.001
	Subjects (s)	<.001	—	—	—
	$b \times s$	<.001	—	—	—
	$N \times s$	<.001	—	—	—
	$b \times N$	n.s.	<.001	n.s.	<.025
	$b \times N \times s$	<.005	—	—	—
Duration	Beat interval (b)	n.s.	<.005	n.s.	<.05
	Duration (bN)	n.s.	<.001	n.s.	<.001
	Subjects (s)	<.001	—	—	—
	$b \times s$	<.001	—	—	—
	$bN \times s$	<.001	—	—	—
	$b \times bN$	n.s.	n.s.	n.s.	n.s.
	$b \times bN \times s$	<.01	—	—	—

[a] n.s. = not statistically significant ($p > .05$).

although both simple models can be rejected convincingly, the data favor the duration over the fraction model.

Experiments 1 and 2 had a fixed beat interval of 1 sec and are therefore insensitive to the distinction between fraction and duration. To generalize from the results of Experiment 9, we must demonstrate that the findings do not depend on its special conditions, in which the beat interval was changed within sessions. One test of the invariance of performance is to compare the results of Experiments 1, 2, and 9 for those conditions common to all of them (i.e., a beat interval of 1 sec and fraction names of 1/8, 1/6, 1/4, and 1/2). An analysis of variance with the factors experiment, fraction name, and subject resulted in a significant effect of fraction name $F_{3,5} = 7.64$, $p < .025$, but a nonsignificant effect of experiment $F_{2,4} = .73$. Thus, performance (the size of mean judgment errors) at one beat interval appears not to be influenced by the subject having recently worked with other beat intervals. (This finding is consistent with a common belief about musical performance.)

In summary, although performance is better described in terms of the duration being judged than the fraction, the consistent effects of beat interval require us to reject a model in which duration is the sole determinant: beat interval as well as fractional interval influences the size of the judgment error.[46]

[46]If one considers the beat interval to be a standard against which each fractional interval is compared, this conclusion bears on the typical magnitude estimation paradigm in research on time perception. The

VII. FURTHER ANALYSIS OF PRODUCTION

In this section we describe results from three variations of the production task, aimed at testing hypotheses about major sources of the systematic error for small fractions.

A. Production Errors with Musical Instruments (Experiment 10)

One potential source of the production errors we observed is our choice of finger tapping as a response; our subjects are skilled players but not necessarily skilled finger tappers. It was possible that the errors would disappear if subjects used their instruments instead. We tested them in the one-response production task of Experiment 3 (Fig. 1C) using their instruments: flute (SB), cello (PF), and violin (PZ). On each trial a subject played a single note after the final beat click, attempting to produce an interval that corresponded to a specified fraction between the click and the beginning of the note. We measured the occurrence time of the note with an acoustic energy detector; its threshold was adjusted to be relatively low so that it would be exceeded near the start of the acoustic signal. The fraction name (n = 1/8, 1/2, or 1) remained the same for 25 consecutive trials. In Experiment 3 mean response times (corrected by synchronization) for these three fractions were 139.1, 486.3, and 1023.3 msec, respectively. Corresponding response times in Experiment 10 were 195.0, 480.0, and 1018.3 msec, respectively.[47] One reason the mean difference between experiments is so large at n = 1/8 is that whereas PF differed from the other two subjects in Experiments 3 and 4 in not showing a positive production error at n = 1/8, she did produce a substantial positive error in Experiment 10, bringing her into conformity with the other subjects. SDs of the response delays did not differ systematically between experiments; (rms) average SDs over fractions and subjects were 31.5 msec for finger taps and 34.0 msec for instrument notes. Mean values of $P(1/2)$ and $P(1)$ were almost identical between experiments, but $P(1/8)$ was substantially larger in Experiment 10. Each of the three subjects shows this interaction between n-value and response mode, and an analysis of variance shows it to be significant.[48] That the mean response delay at n = 1/8

---

existence of a beat-interval effect suggests that results of magnitude estimation tasks that employ an explicit standard interval may depend on the size of the standard. In the absence of an explicit standard, subjects may use an implicit standard. This could increase variability within or between experiments if, for example, the implicit standard varied between subjects or depended on experimental manipulations such as the distribution or range of intervals to be judged.

[47]Values from Experiment 10 are raw response times with no synchronization correction applied. Unfortunately, we collected synchronization data with musical instruments only for PZ; for him, $S'(0)$ was 4.2 msec (as compared to −9.0 msec for one-response finger taps). Results from the present experiment are sufficiently clearcut so that the absence of these small corrections is unlikely to affect our conclusions. Note that a synchronization correction would change all three response times by the same amount and would therefore have no effect on differences among $P(n)$ values.

[48]The differences between absolute errors at n = 1/8 and n = 1, $[P(1/8)-1/8]-[P(1)-1]$, for SB, PF, and PZ are 47.6, 49.8, and 57.8 msec, respectively.

associated with the musical instrument production was much larger than that of the tap response suggests that the errors measured with the tap response may *underestimate* the size of errors that occur in a more natural context.

B. Production with Marker-Click Feedback (Experiment 11)

The disparity between performances for small fractions in the perceptual judgment and production tasks led us to reject the feedback model of production, but we did not scrutinize the feedback itself. The feedback available from tapping the finger in the production task probably includes tactile, proprioceptive, and auditory cues, but did not include the marker click we used in the judgment task.[49] Could this difference between the events that terminated the critical intervals in the two tasks explain the perception-production disparity?

We asked this question in a small production experiment with one subject (PZ), in which each finger tap produced a marker click identical to the markers in Experiments 3 and 4, thereby providing augmented feedback.[50] With this procedural change the sequences of clicks in the judgment and production tasks (but not necessarily their timing) become identical. The critical difference between tasks is limited to how the timing of the final (marker) click is controlled: in one case the subject controls it directly by choosing when to tap his finger, attempting to make the click time correspond to a specified fraction; in the other case the experimenter controls the click time, and the subject judges it relative to that fraction. We used both one-response and repeated-response procedures.

For this subject, the mean value of $J(1/8)$ over perceptual judgment Experiments 1 and 2 together with the corresponding conditions in Experiments 6 and 9 is 64.3 ± 3.5 msec (SE based on between-experiment variation). For production without marker-click feedback, the mean value of $P'(1/8)$ over Experiments 3 and 4 is 158.5 ± 2.9 msec. For production under the new condition with augmented feedback, the mean $P'(1/8)$ was 149.0 ± 2.9 msec.[51] (With click feedback the one-response and repeated-response procedures produced values that differed by only 4 msec.) Thus, the effect on $P'(1/8)$ of adding marker-click feedback is small and not statistically significant, whereas $P'(1/8)$ values from experiments both with and without augmented feedback differ reliably from $J(1/8)$. Again, despite the large disparity between production and judgment, the subject appeared satisfied with his performance.

That the disparity was maintained—even when the cues in production that were

---

[49]The cues comprising finger-tap feedback may have been less salient and punctate than marker clicks, and might therefore have limited the precision of subjects' knowledge of the occurrence times of their responses. That the production error generalizes to played notes (Section VII,A) seems to argue against this as a major basis for the error, however.

[50]We actually ran SB as well, but her data were too few and too variable to be conclusive.

[51]We report uncorrected response times because the validity of any correction based on the tap-click synchronization procedure is suspect under these conditions; with an additional tap-produced click, special perceptual mechanisms may be available on which to base simultaneity judgments of marker click and beat click – mechanisms not available for judgments of the timing of taps versus clicks.

available for use as feedback included the same marker click as in perceptual judgment—supports our suggestion (Section VI,D) that subjects process stimulus information differently in the judgment task from the way they process feedback in the production task.

C. Production of Single versus Multiple Subdivisions of the Beat (Experiment 12)

The existence of large production errors for small fractions suggests a paradox: How can this finding be reconciled with our belief that musicians are able to produce response sequences that fill the beat interval accurately and evenly? Could the production error depend on our use of a single, isolated response? Suppose that beats are salient and relatively precise periodic time references. Then the task of accurately producing a sequence of evenly spaced responses, one or more of which are coincident with beats (certainly a more frequent pattern in music than the production of an isolated offbeat response) might be easier because better information might be available for error correction.

Experiment 12 was designed partly to explore this possibility. The three conditions are shown in Fig. 1F and are designated 1R, 4R, and 5R in accordance with the number of tap responses required. For descriptive purposes it is convenient to define potential responses in five positions, R_1, R_2,...,R_5. Accurate performance would require R_1 and R_5 to be coincident with beat clicks and would require the five tap times to be evenly spaced, dividing the beat interval into quarters. In Condition 1R only one of the responses (R_2) was executed; this is the condition studied in our other production experiments. In Condition 4R the first executed response is R_2, as in 1R, but the three following responses are executed as well; accurate performance would require the last response to be coincident with the beat. In Condition 5R all five responses are executed.

We used a beat interval of .5 sec instead of the 1.0 sec interval used in our other production experiments. The fractional interval associated with $n = 1/4$ therefore corresponds to 1/8 in previous experiments. Pilot work had demonstrated the existence of a production error in the 1R condition with the shorter beat interval; the experiment incidentally tests the generality of the production error at a different beat interval.

If the production error depends on planning and performing an isolated response shortly after the beat, then R_2 should be delayed only in Condition 1R. An alternative explanation of the error is similar to one we considered (and rejected) for the judgment error in Section VI,C: the possible inhomogeneity of subjective time during the beat interval. Because judgment and production appear to depend on timing mechanisms that are at least partially distinct, our rejection of such a possibility for the judgment task does not preclude it as an explanation of the production error. If subjective time elapsed relatively slowly near the beat, then R_2 would be delayed in all three conditions of Experiment 12.

The subjects were PZ and two experienced amateur players, JM and SS. Conditions were held constant for sequences of 25 trials, providing opportunities for detected errors to be corrected on later trials. Subjects tapped with alternate index fingers, chosen so that they used the same finger to produce R_2 in all conditions. We treated R_1 (in Condition 5R) as synchronization data and adjusted all response times by subtraction (as discussed in Section III,A). R_1 occurred early, on average, with the mean $S'(0) = -29.5$ msec.[52] Results are displayed in Fig. 8.

Condition 1R produced a large and reliable positive mean error of 59.1 ± 16.6 msec, or 47%, thereby generalizing our finding to additional subjects and a shorter beat interval.[53] When R_2 was the initial response in the 4R condition, it was produced with as much delay as in the 1R condition. This result shows clearly that the production error is not a consequence of our requiring an isolated response. The mean occurrence time of R_2 in the 5R condition was 119.7 msec, which corresponds to a negligible negative error. Thus, it is the withholding of R_1 that causes the error in R_2. The accuracy of the interval between R_1 and R_2 in Condition 5R argues against any explanation that depends on a distortion of subjective time near the beat during the production task. Rather than being associated with the first subdivision *after* the beat, the production error for small forward fractions is associated with the absence of a response *on* the beat (i.e., with "coming in" shortly after the beat).[54]

Let us consider the occurrence times of the remaining responses in Conditions 4R and 5R. The displaced parallel lines in Fig. 8 fit well, indicating that the mean times

---

[52]The use of this correction is supported, for the average data, by the fact that it places the mean time of R_5 in Condition 5R within 3 msec of the final beat click. (Indeed, the time between R_1 and R_5 can be regarded as a measure of the subjective beat interval.) As we shall see, however, the remarkable accuracy of the mean response rate (or subjective beat interval) implied by this result is an artifact of averaging and does not apply to the data from individual subjects. Using the notation $P(n;b)$, for PZ we have $P(1;500) = 437 ±$ 20 msec, indicating a subjective beat interval that is too short. In contrast, from Experiment 3 for PZ we have $[P(1;1000)]/2 = 506 ± 2$ msec. Since the new condition is distinguished by "filling" the interval with repeated taps, the reliable difference may be an instance in production of a "filled-duration illusion" (Michon, 1965; Ornstein, 1969) that has frequently been observed in judgment tasks. Since the synchronization correction depends on a different finger from the finger used for R_2, in evaluating the timing of R_2 we must consider the possibility of a timing difference between fingers that would produce a sawtooth pattern of production times. Figure 8 shows that any such difference is small.

[53]It is important to determine whether the production error depends exclusively on either the target interval bn (duration model) or the target fraction n (fraction model). (We asked this question about perception in Section VI,E.) Comparison of these results to production performance in Experiment 3, in which the beat interval was twice as long, provides a small amount of evidence (from PZ only) bearing on this question. Using the notation $P(n;b)$, we have for PZ, $P(1/4;500) = 151 ± 8$ msec, $P(1/8;1000) = 164 ± 6$ msec, and $P(1/4;1000) = 242 ± 6$ msec. Whereas the interval error difference between the first two (equal bn) is small and not significant, the fraction-error difference between the first and third (equal n) is large and significant. These results argue against a fraction model for the production error and provide (weak) evidence favoring a duration model.

[54]One possibility is that withholding a response on the beat (R_1) requires the establishment of an inhibitory state that takes time to dissipate and thereby delays R_2. This mechanism could not also lead to the enlargement of short intervals *initiated* by finger taps before the beat, however, that we observed in Experiments 3 and 4. (See Sections III,C and E.)

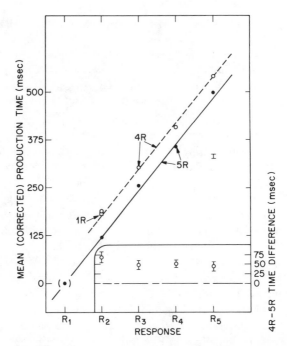

Fig. 8. Mean production times and production-time differences in Experiment 12 (multiple divisions of the beat). The main panel (left-hand ordinate) shows mean production time for each response in the three conditions, after a synchronization correction (-29.5 msec) based on R_1 is applied. (This forces production time for R_1 to be zero.) Parallel lines were fitted by least squares and then adjusted such that the 5R line passes through the R_1 point. The displayed ± 1 SE bar is appropriate for assessing adequacy of the fitted lines. The inset (right-hand ordinate) shows differences between production times of corresponding responses in 4R and 5R conditions together with SEs appropriate for assessing deviations from zero.

between successive responses are close to being equal, both within and between conditions.[55] The remarkable implication for Condition 4R is that the production error in R_2 is propagated through the three succeeding responses. This phenomenon seems best described as *displacement of the subjective beat*. Having produced R_2 with a delay, subjects do not "catch up" because their perception of the train of beats has also been shifted.[56] The lower panel of Fig. 8 displays the occurrence-time differences

[55]If subjects' response rates were accurate, the slope of the fitted lines (mean interresponse time) would be 125 msec/response. The actual mean interresponse time for Condition 5R alone is remarkably close to this value: 123.0 msec. This is an accident of averaging three very different values, however: for JM, SS, and PZ, the mean interresponse times in Condition 5R were 142.6, 117.2, and 109.3 msec, respectively. Such rate inaccuracies imply that even in Condition 5R the final response is far from coincident with the final beat click, again suggesting a surprising insensitivity to the time relation between a response and an external stimulus. (For example, in Condition 5R, PZ's mean R_1 occurred 34.7 msec before its beat click, and his mean R_5 occurred 88.3 msec before its beat click. If R_1 was subjectively coincident with its beat click, then R_5 should have subjectively anticipated the next beat by 53.6 msec, on average.)

[56]That there is a final *actual* beat click that is *not* shifted (and that should be coincident with the final response) raises the same question about beat displacement in 4R as it does about the incorrect response rate in 5R.

of corresponding responses in Conditions 4R and 5R; they range from 67.8 ± 13.9 msec for R_2 to 44.1 ± 12.3 msec for R_5. All three subjects show a decline in this difference with response number, suggesting that the amount of beat displacement is smaller than the full production error. The decline is not statistically significant, however; it remains for another experiment to determine whether all or only some of the production error is transformed into displacement of the beat. In either case, if subjects judge their response delays relative to the subjective beat, then the beat-displacement effect may help to explain why subjects seem satisfied with their delayed responses in the production task, and why the feedback model fails.

VIII. SUMMARY

In a series of experiments we have explored the judgment, production, and imitation (reproduction) of time ratios by three professional musicians. In five initial experiments we found that for small fractions in all three procedures our subjects exhibited systematic and substantial errors. In the judgment task they associated small stimulus fractions with names that were too large (*overestimation*). In both the production task (targets specified by fraction name) and the imitation task (targets specified by fractional interval) our subjects produced intervals that were too large (*overproduction*).

The relation between judgment and production errors requires us to reject feedback models of production, in which a subject uses judgment of the time interval from perceived beat click to perceived response (response feedback) to adjust produced fractions. The approximate equality of production and imitation errors, together with the existence of systematic errors in judgment, argues that imitation is not accomplished simply by concatenating the processes used in judgment and production. Instead, we propose a model containing four internal transformations, in which judgment and production share no transformations and imitation shares one transformation with judgment and another with production. Our data permit us to infer relations among the four transformations. Since production and imitation share the same response, data from these two tasks implicitly define a psychophysical scale for fractions of a beat (a function that relates stimulus fractions to their names) that is independent of potential distortions due to response generation; our results indicate that this implicit scale is free of systematic error, unlike the scales for fractions of a beat that are defined (explicitly) by our judgment and production data.

Results from seven additional experiments increase the generality of our findings and help discriminate among alternative explanations of the judgment and production errors. (1) In the judgment task, changing the pitch of the marker click had little effect, indicating that the overestimation we observed is not a consequence of delays in shifting attention from beat click to marker click. (2) Because performance remained approximately invariant as we altered marker duration, we conclude that subjective onsets rather than offsets of marker and beat clicks were used to mark their occurrence times, discrediting an explanation based on the use of marker offsets. (3) When we varied proximity to the beat of the fractional interval being judged and found no effect on the judgment error, we rejected the possibility of a distortion of subjective time near the beat. (4) The judgment error depends more on the absolute size (duration) of the judged interval than on its size relative to the beat interval (fraction), but both factors have systematic effects; this finding argues against any model in which either interval alone or fraction alone determines the error. (5) The unexpectedly poor judgment precision we encountered when a subject had to judge two disparate intervals within the same stimulus pattern suggests reasons for failure of the feedback model of production; they are based on the possibility that the timing of two such intervals may be required in the production task if a subject attempts both to time the initiation of a response and to judge when it actually occurs.

In the production task, we found that (a) enriching the potential perceptual cues (feedback) that mark responses had little effect on performance, and that (b) when subjects used their musical instruments to perform the task they produced even larger mean errors for small fractions than in productions with finger taps. (c) Evidence from production variability suggests that the overproduction we observed is not a consequence of the existence of a minimum reaction time. In an experiment requiring multiple subdivisions of the beat interval, we found that (d) the production delay did not depend on the number of responses produced within a beat interval, but did depend on withholding a response on the beat that initiates that interval (so the first response is required to occur after the beat). (e) Responses that followed such an initial production, including one that was supposed to be coincident with the following beat, were delayed almost as much as the initial response, suggesting that displacement of the subjective beat accompanies the production error. If subjects judged their response delays relative to the subjective beat, this would provide another explanation for failure of the feedback model of production.

Among the issues that should be addressed in future research is the effect of musical training on performance in these tasks, and the basis of the inconsistencies we observed within and among skilled performers. To help understand the extent to which our results reflect properties of human timing in general rather than musical training it would be desirable to modify our paradigms to examine the performance of subjects unskilled in the use of musical notation. Studies of additional musicians would perhaps illuminate the differences we observed among our three subjects. More measurements are needed that would permit comparison of production and perception of small fractions versus large fractions (small "reverse fractions"). Our results raise the question whether similar errors are manifested in contexts that are more musical and in performance of actual music. If they are, we need to know how musicians reconcile the perception-production conflict suggested by our experiments, and exactly what role is played by response feedback in human performance requiring precise timing.

ACKNOWLEDGMENTS

We are especially indebted to Max V. Mathews for encouraging our collaboration, to Stephen Monsell, Marilyn L. Shaw, and Robert Teghtsoonian for helpful discussions and advice, and to A.S. Coriell for technical support. We also thank R.D. Luce, D.L. Noreen, R.T. Ollman, S. Roberts, D.A. Rosenbaum, D.L. Scarborough, M.S. Schoeffler, and J. Sloboda for useful comments on earlier drafts, and W.J. Kropfl and M.J. Melchner for technical help.

GLOSSARY

Here we provide a list of the main symbols used in order of appearance in the text, with brief definitions and numbers of the sections in which they are introduced.

b Beat interval: time interval between one beat and the next. I,B

f Stimulus fraction: ratio of stimulus interval duration to beat interval duration. I,B

n Fraction name specified in numerical and musical notation. I,B

N Fraction-name response in the judgment task. I,B.

$J(N)$ Judgment function: defines relation between stimulus fraction and fraction-name response, $f = J(N)$. I,B

F Produced fraction in production and imitation tasks: ratio of delay of timed response to beat interval. I,B

$P(n)$ Production function: defines relation between fraction-name stimulus and produced fraction, $F = P(n)$. I,B

$I(f)$ Imitation function: defines relation between stimulus fraction and produced fraction, $F = I(f)$. I,B

PMF   Abbreviation of the term "psychometric function," a function that associates with each stimulus fraction the proportion of "too large" judgment. II,A

G^{-1} If $y = G(x)$ denotes an operation that converts x to y, the operation that converts y to x is denoted G^{-1}: $x = G^{-1}(y)$. (Requires that there is only one value of x for each y.) II,A

$\ln(x)$ Natural logarithm of x. II,A

SD   Standard deviation. II,C

DL   Difference threshold: half the change in stimulus fraction required to change the proportion of "larger than" responses from .25 to .75. II,C

$S'(0)$ Produced fraction in synchronization task. III,A

$P'(n)$ Production function uncorrected for response delays: $P(n) = P'(n) - S'(0)$. III,A

$I'(f)$ Imitation function uncorrected for response delays: $I(f) = I'(f) - S'(0)$. IV,C

RT   Reaction time. III,F

T_{fa} Transformation of stimulus fraction to analog representation. IV,B

T_{aN} Transformation of analog representation to fraction-name response. IV,B

T_{na} Transformation of fraction-name stimulus to analog representation. IV,B

T_{aF} Transformation of analog representation to produced fraction. IV,B

E Identity (or equality) transformation, $E(x) = x$. IV,B

APPENDICES

A. Staircase and Constant Stimulus Methods

1. Collection of Staircase Data

The "staircase" or "up-and-down" procedure used in Experiments 1, 6, and 9 can be regarded as a method of collecting observations in which the stimulus presented on each trial depends on both the stimulus and the response of the immediately previous trial. On the first trial in this procedure a fractional interval (bf) either longer or shorter than the "correct" or "target" interval (bN) is presented. If the subject presses the key indicating that he or she judged the presented fraction to be "too small" relative to the fraction-name target, a longer interval is presented on the next trial. If the subject presses the "too large" key, a shorter interval is presented on the next trial. The subject is required to make one of these two responses; no "equal" response is available. The amount by which the interval is changed is called the *step size*. Use of the procedure depends on the assumption that the probability of a "too large" response increases monotonically with interval duration.

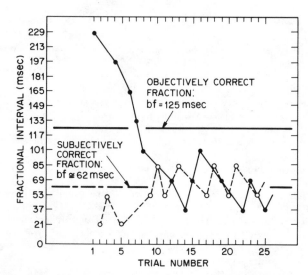

Fig. 9. Example of staircase procedure used in Experiment 1. The subject was PB. The fractional interval presented on a trial is shown versus trial number. Two staircases with regularly interleaved stimulus values were randomly interleaved across trials. Value of the stimulus presented on each trial depended on the history of the staircase selected on that trial. The line leaving a point rises if the response was "too small" and falls otherwise.

The immediate result of applying this stimulus selection rule is to choose an interval for each trial so as to reduce the likelihood of the previous response; the long-term result is to increase the number of presented intervals in the region where the subject is maximally uncertain (proportions of the two judgments approximately equal to each other and to .50), and where the proportion of "too large" judgments increases from being less than .50 to more than .50. We assume that in this region the presented fraction is *subjectively* close in value to the target fraction. In practice more reliable data are obtained if two or more independent staircases are randomly interleaved over trials and contain interleaved arrays of stimulus values. Under these conditions a large step size (e.g., 2.5σ, where σ is the SD of the PMF) has the virtue of producing rapid convergence with minimal bias. (See Kappauf 1967, 1969; Levitt, 1971; and references therein.)

Figure 9 illustrates 25 trials of the initial staircase procedure of Experiment 1 with data collected from PB when he was judging fractions relative to $N = 1/8$. On each trial the subject had to judge whether the presented fraction was too small or too large relative to 1/8 of a beat. The fractional interval (bf) is represented on the ordinate; a horizontal line marks the correct value ($bf = 125$ msec) for $N = 1/8$ and $b = 1000$. Trials are represented on the abscissa. Two staircases started at intervals much smaller and larger than 125 msec. Staircase 1 (broken line) started at 21 msec, and staircase 2 (solid line) started at 229 msec. For each staircase the step size was 32 msec, and the arrays of stimulus values were interleaved, giving a pooled array of stimulus values with 16-msec spacing. The selection of which staircase to use on a trial was random. If an interval was judged too small (large) relative to the target fraction, the next time that staircase was selected a larger (smaller) fraction was presented. In this manner, the staircases converged to a region where the subject was maximally uncertain. In the case shown in Fig. 9, the interval subjectively equivalent to $N = 1/8$, estimated by the mean of the PMF, was 62 msec.

We used two successive staircase procedures in Experiments 1, 6, and 9. First we ran 25 trials with only two interleaved staircases (as exemplified in Fig. 9) to obtain rapid convergence. The starting values (one smaller and one larger) were chosen to be symmetric about bN; 50 additional trials were then run with four interleaved staircases to provide the data we used to estimate the PMF. The new array of stimulus values and the four starting points were determined from the estimated mean and standard deviation ($\hat{\sigma}$) of the PMF for that fraction, based on the first 25 trials. The step size of each staircase was adjusted to be $2.5\hat{\sigma}$, the pooled array of stimulus values had a spacing of $2.5\hat{\sigma}/4$, and the four starting points were separated from the mean by -9, -2, $+4$, and $+9$ step values. By widely distributing the starting points of the 50-trial series about the mean based on the initial 25-trial series we hoped to minimize bias. The proportion of "too large" responses was calculated for each fractional interval that had been presented, to obtain an empirical PMF.[57]

2. Psychometric Function

The plotted points at each stimulus (ordinate) value in Fig. 9 can be used to estimate a PMF. Thus, the fractional interval $bf = 69$ msec was presented on four occasions (trials 12, 15, 19, and 23). The response was "too large" on all but one (trial 15). (Only on that trial is the next bf value in that staircase increased.) The estimated PMF value at $bf = 69$ msec is therefore the proportion .25.

Although the sample based only on the illustrative data shown in Fig. 9 is very small (with only 21 judgments in the range from $21 \leq bf \leq 101$ msec) the estimated PMF shows no reversals: stimulus values bf (in msec), together with their associated sample sizes k and proportions p of "too large" responses, in the form (bf, k, p), are (21, 2, .00), (37, 3, .00), (53, 6, .17), (69, 4, .75), (85, 4, 1.00), and (101, 2, 1.00).

3. Constant-Stimulus Method

In the method of constant stimuli of Experiments 2, 7, and 8, the fractional interval on each trial was selected randomly without regard to the subject's prior responses from a set of intervals chosen in advance. In Experiments 2 and 7, for example, each set contained 24 different intervals, covering a wide range and with a spacing that increased with interval size.

B. Additional Details of Design and Procedure

In this section we mention some details of design and procedure of our 12 experiments not discussed elsewhere.

Experiment 1. The order of the judgment, production, and imitation procedures in Experiments 1, 3, and 5 was balanced in a 3×3 Latin square design within each of the two replications: each procedure was studied first, second, and third for some subject. For each subject the order of the three procedures was reversed between the first and second replications. (The Latin squares in the two replications were therefore mirror images.) Three distinct orders of fraction names were paired with the procedures so that the complete design for each replication was a Graeco–Latin square. In each replication for each fraction name, an initial 25 practice trials with only two interleaved staircases provided approximate estimates for the mean and variance of the PMF. Following a brief pause, 50 additional trials were run with four interleaved staircases.

Experiment 2. Fractional intervals were varied by the method of constant stimuli. On each trial the interval between beat click and marker click was determined by random selection without replacement from a set of 24 intervals. The subject was given a brief rest after each cycle through the 24 intervals; 7 such cycles defined a session. To reduce the impact of any effects associated with specific intervals, four different sets of 24 intervals were used in the course of the experiment. (The smallest and largest interval differed from set to set; over all sets intervals ranged from 43 to 891 msec.) The spacing between successively larger intervals increased approximately in the same way (harmonically) as the spacing between successively larger fraction names (1/8, 1/7, ..., 1/2). The first cycle of each session was considered

---

[57]A staircase procedure is typically designed to produce data that estimate a particular quantile of the PMF, such as the 50% point (the median), rather than the entire PMF. However, results from a Monte Carlo study (Sternberg & Knoll, unpublished) show that the empirical PMF, derived from the application of the staircase procedure to a known PMF, shows little distortion when independent staircases contain interleaved grids of step values, the step size of individual staircases is large, and the underlying PMF is symmetric.

practice and was excluded from the analysis; a session therefore contributed 6 test trials for each of 24 intervals to the analysis. The number of sessions run for SB, PF, and PZ was 4, 3, and 5, respectively.

Experiment 3. Each of two replications of each of the eight production conditions involved 25 trials and was run as part of the balanced Latin square design described for Experiment 1. Eight replications of the synchronization condition and four additional replications of the production condition with $n = 1$ were run after the main experiment; performance in the production condition indicated no systematic change relative to the main experiment.

Experiment 4. Principal conditions included synchronization and eight n-values. Each replication of a condition included 25 trials, or 250 responses. Number of replications per condition per subject varied from 1 to 4 and averaged approximately 2; conditions were run in an irregular order. Plots of results for individual subjects (Figs. 2–4) also show results for conditions ($n = 1/5, 1/3$) run on only a subset of the subjects.

Experiment 5. Each of two replications of each of the eight imitation conditions involved 25 trials and was run as part of the balanced Latin square design described for Experiment 1.

Experiment 6. The staircase procedure was run as in Experiment 1. Either one or two replications were run per condition; the order of conditions differed across subjects.

Experiment 7. The constant stimulus method of Experiment 2 was used with one session run for each of the two conditions. Intensity of the prolonged marker was reduced from 30 dB above threshold to about 21 dB to make the loudness of brief and prolonged markers more similar.

Experiment 8. In each cycle of 24 trials each stimulus was presented once. Seven cycles defined a session; one session was run per subject. The first cycle of a session was considered practice; each stimulus is therefore represented six times in the data for an individual subject.

Experiment 9. The order of the three beat intervals was balanced across subjects in a 3×3 Latin square design. In the first replication the order of the four N-values differed across subjects, but for an individual subject the order was the same for all three beat intervals. The four N-values within each beat interval were run consecutively before the beat interval changed. In the second replication the order of the 12 conditions was reversed for each subject. Use of the staircase procedure was similar to that in Experiment 1 except that in the second replication the initial 25-trial series was omitted and starting points were based on performance in the first replication.

Experiment 10. We asked subjects to choose a note that they felt they could produce consistently: PZ bowed an open A string on the violin, SB played C above middle C on the flute, and PF bowed D below middle C on the cello. All subjects started with a single replication of 25 trials with $n = 1/4$ for practice and then completed two replications each for $n = 1/8, 1/2$, and 1; the order of fraction names was varied between subjects and was reversed from the first to second replication within each subject.

Experiment 11. Two replications (of 25 trials) were run, first in the repeated-response procedure and then in the one-response procedure.

Experiment 12. Each condition was studied in three replications (of 25 trials). Within each subject the order of conditions was balanced. All three subjects are right-handed; SS and PZ performed response R_2 with their right index fingers, and JM performed R_2 with her left index finger.

C. Measures of Location of the Psychometric Function

Both staircase and constant-stimulus methods in our perceptual judgment experiments gave rise to PMFs. Among our considerations in choosing a location measure were (1) our desire to reduce nonadditive distortions in estimates of the effects of interest on underlying processes, (2) our desire to compare the location measure to corresponding measures in production and imitation with the idea that a common underlying process might contribute to all three, (3) our reluctance to assume a functional form for the PMF (such as cumulative Gaussian), (4) the smallness of sample sizes at each stimulus value for individual subjects, and (5) our interest in a spread measure as well.

It is convenient to regard the "true" PMF as a cumulative distribution function and the observed PMF as an estimate of this function. The most common location measure used in psychophysics is the *median* (the 50% point) of the PMF. Instead, we used an estimate of the *mean;* comparisons of the two revealed extremely good agreement.

It may be helpful first to consider why we favor the mean over the median for the production and imitation experiments. For production, suppose that the time between beat click and timed response is the sum of a timing component $X_t(n)$ that interests us and that varies with fraction name n and other components such as input and output delays, X_s and X_r, that vary from trial to trial but do not depend on target fraction: $X(n) = X_t(n) + X_s + X_r$; $\mathrm{Var}\,(X_s + X_r) > 0$. Then changes with n in the *mean* of $X(n)$ accurately reflect changes in the mean of the process of primary interest X_t, whatever the distributions of X_t and $X_s + X_r$. (The mean of a sum of random variables equals the sum of the means.) This property does not characterize the median, however. It follows, for example, that if an estimate of the mean of $X_s + X_r$ is available, it can be used to "correct" the observed $X(n)$; this is not possible, in general, for the median. The same argument, with f substituted for n, applies to imitation. Similarly, the PMF may reflect processes such as X_s and X_r as well as a timing process that interests us; given plausible assumptions the mean is preferable there also. Furthermore, if we use the mean for production and imitation experiments and wish to compare results across experiments, the mean becomes the favored statistic for judgment experiments.

We used the Spearman-Kärber (S-K) method to estimate PMF means (Spearman, 1908; Epstein & Churchman, 1944; Church & Cobb, 1973). Let stimulus fractions be f_i, $i = u, u+1, \ldots, v$, and let p_i be the proportion of "too large" responses for stimulus f_i, which estimates a corresponding response probability $Pr\,\{L; f_i\}$. Let f_u be a stimulus such that we can assume $Pr\,\{L; f\} = 0$ for $f < f_u$, and let f_v be a stimulus such that we can assume $Pr\{L; f\} = 1.0$ for $f \geq f_v$. Then the S-K estimate of the rth raw moment of the PMF is

$$ m_r' = \sum_{i=u}^{v} (p_i - p_{i-1}) \left(\frac{f_i^{r+1} = f_{i-1}^{r+1}}{(r+1)\,(f_i - f_{i-1})} \right) ; $$

the estimated mean m_1' is obtained by setting $r = 1$.[58,59] The PMF mean can be regarded as a weighted stimulus average, where the weighting function is the derivative of the PMF, a measure of the sensitivity of the response probability to changes in the stimulus. Stimulus values in a region where the PMF rises more steeply contribute more to its mean.

We prefer to avoid strong assumptions about the form of the true PMF, or even about its symmetry. (If the PMF were symmetric then the sample mean and median would estimate the same quantity, of course.) We do feel justified in assuming that the true PMF is nondecreasing. Because our sample sizes are small, however, the *empirical* PMFs are occasionally nonmonotone. In such instances, we have used monotone regression to estimate the best-fitting (least squares) set of nondecreasing proportions $\{p_i^*\}$ from the empirical PMF $\{p_i\}$ before estimating parameters. (See Ayer, Brunk, Ewing, Reid, & Silverman, 1955; Kruskal, 1964; and de Leeuw, 1977.)[60,61]

For the data from Experiment 1, we compared and found excellent agreement between conventional median estimates obtained by applying linear interpolation to the $\{p_i^*\}$, and S-K mean estimates. The two replications for each of three subjects provided six sets of PMFs, with 8 PMFs per set. For the six sets of data, linear correlations of means versus medians ranged from .9995 to .9998, and slopes of the linear regression of means on medians ranged from .999 to 1.018.

---

[58]This is actually a modified S-K estimator, appropriate for a continuous distribution function (a piecewise linear integrated histogram) rather than a discrete distribution function.

[59]In our application of this method, as shown by the estimation equation, the proportions p_i enter with equal weights. An alternative would be to weight them by considering differences in sample size and binomial variability. Fortunately, for PMFs derived from staircase data, the distribution of observations is approximately triangular and is centered where $p_i \cong .5$; this compensates approximately for differences in binomial variability and justifies the use of equal weights.

[60]This "monotonizing" procedure can probably be improved upon by regarding the $\{p_i\}$ as estimates of values of an underlying continuous rather than a discrete distribution function.

[61]Note that at least one advantage of applying monotone regression is that without it the more conventional quantile measures of location and spread may not be uniquely defined. If only the S-K estimate of location is desired, the monotonizing transformation is not necessary, since it does not alter the estimated mean. We have used it because it influences the spread measure (SD estimate) based on the S-K method and is necessary to permit comparison of quantile with moment estimators.

D. Measures of Spread of the Psychometric Function

The conventional measure of spread (or precision) of the PMF is the DL, defined as half of the interquartile range. We obtained DLs for the PMFs in Experiments 1 and 2 by applying linear interpolation to the $\{p_i^*\}$. We compared these quantile measures to a set of corresponding SD estimates; these were based on m_1' and m_2' values obtained by applying the S-K method to the same $\{p_i^*\}$. (See Epstein & Churchman, 1944; Chmiel, 1976.)

Six sets of PMFs were used for the comparison, obtained from the three subjects in each of the two experiments. For each set of PMFs we determined a constant k such that $\overline{SD} = k\overline{DL}$, where $\overline{SD}$ and $\overline{DL}$ are means over the set of PMFs. (The relation between SD and DL depends on the shape of the PMF. For a Gaussian PMF, for example, $k = 1.48$. The mean of the six k-values we obtained is 1.53, suggesting that our PMFs are approximately Gaussian.) Our aim was to compare the variabilities of the two spread measures. This requires first adjusting them to have the same mean; we did so by multiplying the DLs in each set by the k-value obtained for that set. For each set of PMFs, we determined the variance of each spread measure SD and kDL across replications of the same condition (fraction name) and pooled these variances over fractions. The ratios of Var(kDL) to Var(SD) ranged from 1.5 to 11.0 over the six sets of PMFs, with a mean of 5.7 ± 1.7. This surprising finding indicates convincingly that, at least for our small-sample PMFs, the conventional quantile measure of spread (the DL) is far less reliable than the S-K estimator of the SD, and supports our use of the SD in the present report.

E. Stimulus-Averaging versus Response-Averaging Methods for Deriving a Psychophysical Scale

Our method of determining the judgment function, $f = J(N)$, was to associate with each value of N the mean of the corresponding PMF. For each of a set of response (N) values this method can be regarded as providing a weighted mean stimulus, where the weighting function is given by the steepness (derivative) of the PMF. Stimulus averaging has at least three virtues relative to the more conventional response-averaging method (to be discussed below): (1) it can be applied to data from single-fraction as well as multiple-fraction experiments; (2) it does not require us to treat response values as being defined on an interval scale, as do response-averaging methods; and (3) each PMF mean presumably reflects only one subjective criterion because it is associated with only one N-category boundary. A response-averaging method depends, in general, on associating a set of more than two N-values with each f-value; the response average therefore reflects more than one criterion on the subjective N-scale. Such a method seems less comparable with the straightforward analysis of production and imitation, in which performance in any condition presumably depends on only one criterion, as in the single-fraction judgment experiment. Oyama (1969) described a similar stimulus-averaging method applied to magnitude estimates of loudness, and argued in its favor by noting virtue (2) above.

Despite these advantages it seemed important to check whether the results we obtained in the judgment experiment could be attributed to the unorthodox method we used to construct the judgment function. Data from the multiple-fraction judgment procedure of Experiment 2 permitted comparison of the two methods. Each of the six central response alternatives in that experiment were defined in terms of two category boundaries, such as "between 1/8 and 1/7." To average responses, we defined the value of each response to be the geometric mean of its two boundaries; the set of such response values associated with each stimulus fraction f was then averaged, again using the geometric mean.[62]

Seven stimulus intervals were defined, containing approximately equal numbers of fractions; the set of average responses within each interval were themselves averaged (using geometric means) and associated with the geometric mean stimulus fraction. The $J(N)$ functions are truncated in the response-averaging

---

[62]Use of the geometric mean is common in response-averaging methods; it is equivalent to applying the arithmetic mean to logarithms of response values and is thought to be appropriate when the psychophysical scale is linear on logarithmic coordinates, as in the case of a power function.

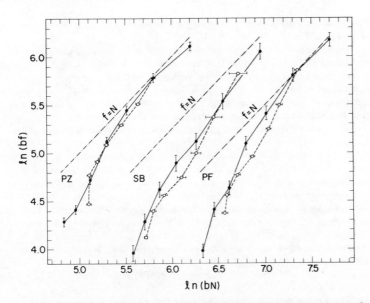

Fig. 10. Comparison of psychophysical scales derived by two different averaging methods from the multiple-fraction judgment experiment. The scale relates fractional intervals (*bf*) specified by time-pattern stimuli to fraction names expressed as intervals (*bN*). Data for SB (PF) are displaced .75 (1.5) log units to the right. Values derived from PMFs (weighted stimulus averaging for specified *N*) are shown by filled circles and unbroken lines. Values derived by response averaging (for specified *f*) are shown by open circles and broken lines. Lines representing *f = N* are included for reference. Bars represent ±1 SE; SEs are based on variability across replications in the quantity averaged.

method because a stimulus must be excluded if any response to that stimulus falls in one of the end categories ("less than 1/8" or "greater than 1/2"), for which an acceptable response value cannot be defined.

Results from this procedure are shown in Fig. 10, together with results from the stimulus-averaging (PMF) method. For the PMF method, the eight response categories provide seven category boundaries and thus seven values of **J**(*N*).

Estimates shown of ±SE are based on between-replications SDs. These were pooled over fractions for the PMF method. For the response-averaging method, the SDs were smoothed by linear regression of SDs on means. The difference in SE estimates between the two methods can be regarded primarily as a result of the **J**(*N*) slopes being considerably greater than unity.

The scale based on the PMF method for each subject can be seen to be very similar to the scale based on response averaging. Oyama (1968) drew the same conclusion when he compared stimulus- and response-averaging methods for deriving a scale of loudness.

REFERENCES

Adam, N., Castro, A., & Clark, D. Production, estimation, and reproduction of time intervals during inhalation of a general anesthetic in man. *Journal of Experimental Psychology*, 1974, *102*, 609–614.

Ayer, M., Brunk, H. D., Ewing, G. M., Reid, W. T., & Silverman, E. An empirical distribution function for sampling with incomplete information. *Annals of Mathematical Statistics*, 1955, *26*, 641–647.

Bregman, A. S. The formation of auditory streams. In J. Requin (Ed.), *Attention and performance VII*. Hillsdale, N.J.: L. Erlbaum Associates, 1978. pp. 63–75.

Carlson, V. R., & Feinberg, I. Individual variations in time judgments and the concept of an internal clock. *Journal of Experimental Psychology*, 1968, 77, 631–640.

Carlson, V. R., & Feinberg, I. Time judgment as a function of method, practice, and sex. *Journal of Experimental Psychology*, 1970, 85, 171–180.

Chmiel, J. J. Some properties of Spearman-type estimators of the variance and percentiles in bioassay. *Biometrika*, 1976, 63, 621–626.

Church, J. D., & Cobb, E. B. On the equivalence of Spearman-Kärber and maximum likelihood estimates of the mean. *Journal of the American Statistical Association*, 1973, 68, 201–202.

Creelman, C. Human discrimination of auditory duration. *Journal of the Acoustical Society of America*, 1962, 34, 582–593.

de Leeuw, J. Correctness of Kruskal's algorithms for monotone regression with ties. *Psychometrika*, 1977 42, 141–144.

Duifhuis, H. Consequences of peripheral frequency selectivity for nonsimultaneous masking. *Journal of the Acoustical Society of America*, 1973, 54, 1471–1489.

Eisler, H. Subjective duration and psychophysics. *Psychological Review*, 1975, 82, 429–450.

Eisler, H. Experiments on subjective duration 1868–1975: A collection of power function exponents. *Psychological Bulletin*, 1976, 83, 1154–1171.

Epstein, B., & Churchman, C. W. On the statistics of sensitivity data. *Annals of Mathematical Statistics*, 1944, 15, 90–96.

Fastl, H. Subjective duration and temporal masking patterns of broadband noise impulses. *Journal of the Acoustical Society of America*, 1977, 61, 162–168.

Fraisse, P. *Les structures rythmiques*. Louvain: Publications Universitaires de Louvain, 1956.

Fraisse, P. *The psychology of time*. New York: Harper & Row, 1963.

Fraisse, P. Time and rhythm perception. In E. C. Carterette & M. P. Friedman (Eds.), *Handbook of perception, vol. VIII: Perceptual coding*. New York: Academic Press, 1978. pp. 203–254.

Getty, D. Discrimination of short temporal intervals: A comparison of two models. *Perception & Psychophysics*, 1975, 18, 1–8.

Getty, D. Counting processes in human timing. *Perception & Psychophysics*, 1976, 20, 191–197.

Kappauf, W. E. *Empirical modifications in the up-and-down method and its estimates of μ and σ*. Report No. 2, National Institutes of Health Research Grant NB-105576-01, University of Illinois, 1967.

Kappauf, W. E. An empirical sampling study of the Dixon and Mood Statistics for the up-and-down method of sensitivity testing. *American Journal of Psychology*, 1969, 82, 40–55.

Kornblum, S. Simple reaction time as a race between signal detection and time estimation: A paradigm and model. *Perception & Psychophysics*, 1973, 13, 108–112.

Kristofferson, A. B. Low-variance stimulus-response latencies: Deterministic internal delays? *Perception & Psychophysics*, 1976, 20, 89–100.

Kruskal, J. B. Nonmetric multidimensional scaling: A numerical method. *Psychometrika*, 1964, 29, 115–129.

Levitt, H. Transformed up-down methods in psychoacoustics. *Journal of the Acoustical Society of America*, 1971, 49, 467–477.

Michon, J. A. Studies on subjective duration II: Subjective time measurement during tasks with different information content. *Acta Psychologica*, 1965, 24, 205–212.

Michon, J. A. Magnitude scaling of short durations with closely spaced stimuli. *Psychonomic Science*, 1967, 9, 359–360.

Miller, R. G., & Halpern, J. W. Robust estimators for quantal bioassay. *Biometrika*, 1980, 67, 103–110.

Nakajima, Y., Shimojo, S., & Sugita, Y. On the perception of two successive sound bursts. *Psychological Research*, 1980, 41, 335–344.

Ornstein, R. E. *On the experience of time*. Harmondsworth: Penguin Books, 1969.

Oyama, T. A behavioristic analysis of Stevens' magnitude estimation method. *Perception & Psychophysics*, 1968, 3, 317–320.

Penner, M. J. Effect of masker duration and masker level on forward and backward masking. *Journal of the Acoustical Society of America*, 1974, 56, 179–182.

Pöppel, E. Time Perception. In R. Held, H. Leibowitz, & H. Teuber (Eds.), *Handbook of sensory physiology*, *volume VIII: Perception*. Berlin: Springer-Verlag, 1978. pp. 713-729.

Povel, D. J. Internal representation of simple temporal patterns. *Journal of Experimental Psychology: Human Perception and Performance*, 1981, 7, 3-18.

Rasch, R. A. Synchronization in performed ensemble music. *Acustica*, 1979, 43, 121-131.

Richards, W. Time estimates measured by reproduction. *Perceptual and Motor Skills*, 1964, 18, 929-943.

Schulze, H. The detectability of local and global displacements in regular rhythmic patterns. *Psychological Research*, 1978, 40, 173-181.

Snodgrass, J., Luce, R. & Galanter, E. Some experiments on simple and choice reaction time. *Journal of Experimental Psychology*, 1967, 75, 1-17.

Spearman, C. The method of 'right and wrong cases' ('constant stimuli') without Gauss's formulae. *British Journal of Psychology*, 1908, 2, 227-242.

Steiner, S. Apparent duration of auditory stimuli. *Journal of Auditory Research*, 1968, 8, 195-205.

Sternberg, S., & Knoll, R. L. The perception of temporal order: Fundamental issues and a general model. In S. Kornblum (Ed.), *Attention and performance IV*. New York: Academic Press, 1973. pp. 629-685.

Svenson, O. Magnitude estimation of time intervals delimited by light flashes of different spatial separation. *Reports from the Psychological Laboratories* (*Report No. 394*). Stockholm: University of Stockholm, 1973.

Teghtsoonian, R., & Teghtsoonian, M. Range and regression effects in magnitude scaling. *Perception & Psychophysics*, 1978, 24, 305-314.

Thomas, E., & Brown, Jr., I. Time perception and the filled-duration illusion *Perception & Psychophysics*, 1974, 16, 449-458.

Treisman, M. Temporal discrimination and the indifference interval: Implications for a model of the "internal clock." *Psychological Monographs: General and Applied*, 1963, 77 (Whole No. 576).

Van Noorden, L.P.A.S. *Temporal coherence in the perception of tone sequences*. Doctoral thesis, Eindhoven University of Technology, The Netherlands, 1975.

Vorberg, D., & Hambuch, R. On the temporal control of rhythmic performance. In J. Requin (Ed.), *Attention and performance VII*. New Jersey: Lawrence Erlbaum Associates, 1978. pp. 535-555.

Wing, A., & Kristofferson, A. B. The timing of interresponse intervals. *Perception & Psychophysics*, 1973, 13, 455-460.

Woodrow, H. A quantitative study of rhythm: The effect of variations in intensity, rate and duration. *Archives of Psychology*, 1909, 14, 1-66.

Woodrow, H. Time perception. In S. S. Stevens (Ed.), *Handbook of experimental psychology*. New York: Wiley, 1951. pp. 1224-1236.

Zelkind, I., & Sprug, J. (Eds.) *Time research: 1172 studies*. Metuchen, N.J.: The Scarecrow Press, Inc., 1974.

Zwicker, E. Subjektive und objektive Dauer von Schallimpulsen und Schallpausen. *Acustica*, 1969, 22, 214-218.

8

Intervals, Scales, and Tuning

Edward M. Burns and W. Dixon Ward

I.	Introduction	241
II.	Are Scales Necessary?	243
III.	Musical Interval Perception	246
	A. Identification of Isolated Musical Intervals	246
	B. Adjustment of Isolated Musical Intervals	249
	C. Musical Interval Discrimination and Categorical Perception	250
IV.	Natural Intervals and Scales	255
	A. Natural Intervals and Their Possible Basis	255
	B. Natural Scales and Temperament	256
	C. Experimental Evidence Relevant to Natural Intervals and Scales	257
	D. Octave Generalization and Chroma	262
V.	Conclusions and Caveats	264
	A. Conclusions	264
	B. Caveats	264
	References	265

I. INTRODUCTION

In the vast majority of musical cultures, collections of discrete pitch relationships—musical scales—are utilized as a framework for composition and improvisation. In this chapter we will explore the perception of musical scales concentrating on the basic building block of scales, the musical interval. In addition, we will speculate on possible perceptual and/or physiological bases for scales. Among the questions to be addressed are the following: (1) Are scales necessary (i.e., why are only a relatively small subset of all possible pitch relationships utilized in music?)? (2) What evidence is there for the existence of "natural" intervals and scales? (3) What is the basis for the concept of octave generalization? and (4) What, if any, are the relationships between music perception and other facets of auditory perception, especially speech perception?

TABLE I

Interval Comparison in Different Mathematical Tuning Systems[a]

Interval name	Solfeggio	Letter notation	Pythagorean tuning (PT)			Just intonation (JI)			Equal temperament (ET)	
			Numerical origin	Frequency ratio	Cents	Numerical origin	Frequency ratio	Cents	Frequency ratio	Cents
Unison	DO	C	$1 : 1$	1.000	0.0	$1 : 1$	1.000	0.0	1.000	0
Minor second		D♭	$2^8 : 3^5$	1.053	90.2	$16 : 15$	1.067	111.7	1.059	100
		C♯	$3^7 : 2^{11}$	1.068	113.7	$16 : 15$	1.067	111.7	1.059	100
Major second	RE	D	$3^2 : 2^3$	1.125	203.9	$10 : 9$[b]	1.111	182.4	1.122	200
						$9 : 8$[c]	1.125	203.9		
Minor third		E♭	$2^5 : 3^3$	1.186	294.1	$6 : 5$	1.200	315.6	1.189	300
	MI	D♯	$3^9 : 2^{14}$	1.201	317.6	$6 : 5$	1.200	315.6	1.189	300
Major third		E	$3^4 : 2^6$	1.265	407.8	$5 : 4$	1.250	386.3	1.260	400
Fourth	FA	F	$2^2 : 3$	1.333	498.1	$4 : 3$	1.333	498.1	1.335	500
Tritone		G♭	$2^{10} : 3^6$	1.407	588.3	$45 : 32$	1.406	590.2	1.414	600
		F♯	$3^6 : 2^9$	1.424	611.7	$64 : 45$	1.422	609.8	1.414	600
Fifth	SO	G	$3 : 2$	1.500	702.0	$3 : 2$	1.500	702.0	1.498	700
Minor sixth		A♭	$2^7 : 3^4$	1.580	792.2	$8 : 5$	1.600	813.7	1.587	800
		G♯	$3^8 : 2^{12}$	1.602	815.6	$8 : 5$	1.600	813.7	1.587	800
Major sixth	LA	A	$3^3 : 2^4$	1.688	905.0	$5 : 3$	1.667	884.4	1.682	900
Minor seventh		B♭	$2^4 : 3^2$	1.788	996.1	$7 : 4$[d]	1.750	968.8	1.782	1000
						$16 : 9$[e]	1.777	996.1		
		A♯	$3^{10} : 2^{15}$	1.802	1019.1	$9 : 5$	1.800	1017.6	1.782	1000
Major seventh	TI	B	$3^5 : 2^7$	1.900	1109.8	$15 : 8$	1.875	1088.3	1.888	1180
Octave	DO	C	$2 : 1$	2.000	1200.0	$2 : 1$	2.000	1200.0	2.000	1200

[a] Adapted from Martin, 1962.
[b] Lesser.
[c] Greater.
[d] Harmonic
[e] Grave.

Since many readers may not be conversant with music theory and terminology, some of the relevant concepts of traditional Western music will be reviewed. A concept inherent in scale construction is that of the tonic (or keynote) of the scale: that tone to which the pitches of the other tones of the scale are referenced. The basic unit of the scale is the musical interval, which corresponds physically to the frequency ratio between two tones and perceptually to the pitch relationship between the tones. The adjective "harmonic" when describing musical intervals denotes that the two tones comprising the interval are presented simultaneously (regardless of whether or not the frequencies of the two tones are exact harmonics of a common fundamental frequency); the adjective "melodic" indicates that the two tones are presented sequentially. Also basic to Western theory is the concept of octave generalization (or tone chroma), which dictates that tones separated by an octave (frequency ratio of 2 : 1) are musically similar (have the same chroma), and, hence, a scale may be completely defined by specifying the intervals within an octave.

The present standard inclusive scale (i.e., the scale that includes all of the intervals used in Western music) is the 12-tone chromatic scale of equal temperament. This scale divides the octave into 12 equally spaced intervals. The basic interval unit (i.e., the smallest interval and the spacing between adjacent intervals) is called a *tempered semit* (or *semitone*) and corresponds to a frequency ratio of $2^{1/12} : 1$. (A useful unit for measuring frequency ratio is the cent: 1 cent = $2^{1/1200} : 1$; hence, a semit contains 100 cents and an octave contains 1200 cents.) Table I gives the name, solfeggio (vocal mnemonic), letter notation (assuming a tonic of C), frequency ratio, and cent value of the 12 intervals comprising the equally tempered scale. (The Just and Pythagorean scales are contenders for the title of "natural scale" and will be discussed in Section IV,A.) In Western music the absolute frequencies of the tones are also specified by defining a standard reference frequency (presently, "middle A" = 440 Hz) and using one of various schemes to notate octave ranges (Olson, 1952). Most compositions in Western music do not employ all of the intervals of the chromatic scale but are based on seven-interval subsets of the chromatic scale called *diatonic scales*, in which the interval between adjacent tones is either one or two semits (e.g., the diatonic major scale consists of the intervals, 200, 400, 500, 700, 900, 1100, and 1200 cents).

II. ARE SCALES NECESSARY?

Given that present Western music utilizes a relatively small set of discrete pitch relationships, an obvious question occurs: Is this use of discrete intervals universal? That is, are there musical cultures that employ continuously variable pitches, analogous, for example, to the rising or falling tones of some tone languages? The evidence from ethnomusicological studies indicates that the use of discrete pitch relationships is essentially universal. The only exceptions appear to be certain primitive musical styles—for example, "tumbling strains" (Sachs, 1961) or "indeterminate-pitch chants" (Malm, 1967)—which are found in a few tribal cultures. Of course, pitch glides—glissandos, portamentos, trills, etc,—are used as embellishment and ornamentation in most musical cultures. However, they are not an essential part of the structure of these musics. The concept of octave similarity, although far from universal in early and primitive music (e.g., Nettl, 1956; Sachs, 1962), also seems to be common to more advanced musical systems.

A related question follows: Does the 12-note chromatic scale represent a norm or a limit to the number of usable pitch relationships per octave? Several Western composers have written compositions in quartertone (i.e., 24 approximately equal intervals per octave) and other microtonal scales, but none of these scales have gained wide acceptance. There are numerous cultures whose scales contain less than 12 notes per octave. There are, however, apparently only two musical cultures that, in theory, utilize more than 12 intervals per octave: the Indian and the Arab–Persian. Both musical systems of India (Hindustani and Karnatic) are, according to tradition, based on 22 possible intervals per octave. They are not equal (or approximately equal) intervals, however. The basic structure of the inclusive scale is essentially the same as that of the Western 12-interval chromatic scale, and the microtones ("shrutis") are (theoretical) small variations of certain intervals, the exact values of which are dependent on the individual melodic framework ("raga") being played. There is evidence that in actual musical practice these theoretical variations are not played as discrete intervals but are denoted by a purposefully induced variability in intonation (e.g., a slow vibrato). (Jhairazbhoy & Stone, 1963; Callow & Shepherd, 1972).

The one system that may utilize true quartertones (i.e., intervals that bisect the distance between the Western chromatic intervals) is the Arab–Persian system. In this system there are various claims as to the number of possible intervals (ranging from 15 to 24) and some controversy as to whether they are true quartertones or, as in the Indian system, merely microtonal variations of certain intervals (e.g., Zonis, 1973). The limited data on measured intonation in this system are ambiguous as to how accurately these quartertones are produced in practice (e.g., Caron & Safvate, 1966; Spector, 1966). It is clear, however, that neither the Indian nor Arab–Persian scales are chromatically microtonal. That is, the quartertones (or microtones) are never played contiguously but only as alternative versions of certain larger intervals.

Thus, the evidence indicates that the 12-interval chromatic scale may, indeed, reflect some sort of limit on the number of intervals per octave that are of practical use in music or, at least, that the semit is probably the smallest usable separation between successively played tones. If we assume this limitation exists, is there any obvious perceptual basis for it or for the use of discrete intervals in general? Authors of books on musical perception often contrast the number of just noticeable differences (JNDs) in frequency to the step-size in the chromatic scale—from 20 to 300 JNDs per semit, depending on the frequency range and experimental paradigm—and point out the apparent discrepancy between the number of tones that can be "distinguished" and the number actually used in music. There are several reasons why this is not a meaningful contrast.

First, it is evident from music theory, from everyday musical experience, and from a number of experiments (e.g., White, 1960; Attneave & Olson, 1971) that frequency ratio, rather than frequency per se, is the primary mediator of melodic information.

Hence, frequency ratio JNDs, rather than frequency JNDs, are the more relevant comparison with scale step-size. Frequency-ratio JNDs for highly trained observers are an order of magnitude greater than frequency JNDs obtained in the same frequency region, using equivalent psychophysical paradigms (see Section III,C). Trotter (1967) has also pointed out that there is little correlation between the inability to perceive interval or melodic relationships ("tone deafness") and frequency discrimination ability.

The second, and probably more important, reason for the apparent discrepancy between JND magnitude (whether frequency or frequency ratio) and scale step-size is the limitation on the processing of information by sensory systems that is imposed by higher level processing (e.g., involving attention and memory). One useful concept in this regard (although certainly not the complete explanation for a complex experience such as music with its cultural and experiential overlays) is that of information theory, in which information is related to the uncertainty and complexity of the stimuli, and information transmitted is related to the reduction in uncertainty. The JNDs mentioned above were determined in minimal-uncertainty (i.e., low information) psychophysical procedures and, as such, probably reflect (at least for the case of frequency JNDs) the resolving power of the peripheral auditory system rather than any limitations imposed by higher level processing. The effect of stimulus uncertainty is illustrated in experiments by Watson, Kelly, and Wroton (1976), in which frequency JNDs were increased by a factor of 30 by paradigm manipulations that presumably increased stimulus uncertainty. Numerous studies have indicated (e.g., Estes, 1972) that when faced with high information signals and/or high information rates, observers tend to encode the information into categories as a means of reducing the information load. It is probable that such factors have dictated both the use of discrete pitch relationships (rather than continuous glides and sweeps, for example) and the number of practical discrete categories.

In a classic paper Miller (1956) reviewed experiments that tested the ability of observers to categorize stimuli in several sensory modalities. He concluded that for stimuli varying on a single physical dimension, the information transmitted to observers (i.e., their information channel capacity) was on the order of 2.8 bits in all modalities. That is, they were only able to place the stimuli, without error, into a maximum of about $2^{2.8}$ categories ("the magic number 7 ± 2"). This was contrasted with the ability of observers to discriminate several thousand stimuli along the same continuum in forced-choice discrimination tasks. The discrepancy between the magnitude of frequency ratio JNDs and the minimum interval size in musical scales thus appears to be just another example of this classic discrepancy between resolution in identification and discrimination tasks.

A number of investigators have formulated perceptual models based on differential modes of memory operation that predict this discrepancy. One example is the model of auditory intensity resolution proposed by Durlach and Braida (1969). This model, which is basically a version of Thurstone's "law of categorical judgment," divides the noise that limits resolution into three factors: sensation noise (dependent only on the properties of the stimulus) and two paradigm-dependent components of memory noise (corresponding to two modes of memory operation). In the "sensory-trace" mode the observer is assumed to attempt to retain an image of the stimulus, and the noise in this mode is related to (a primarily time-dependent) interference with this memory trace. In the "context-coding" mode the subject attempts to remember an imprecise verbal code of the relationship of the individual stimulus to the context of stimuli in the experiment (e.g., the use the stimuli at the extremes of the range as perceptual anchors). The noise associated with this mode is assumed to be dependent only on the range of stimuli. For single- (temporal) interval paradigms (e.g., absolute identification) the subject is assumed to operate in the context-coding mode. The model assumes that in a two-interval discrimination paradigm the subject operates in the mode (or combination of modes) that optimizes performance. The improved resolution in the typical two-interval, two-alternative discrimination task relative to a one-interval, multi-alternative identification task is predicted by this model on the basis of the relative dominance of context-coding noise for the usual experimental parameter values.

III. MUSICAL INTERVAL PERCEPTION

A. Identification of Isolated Musical Intervals

1. Absolute Identification

One obvious exception to Miller's 7 ± 2 rule for categorization is the performance of "possessors" of absolute pitch (i.e., persons who have the ability to identify the pitch of a single tone—usually in terms of musical scale categories or keys on a piano). The best subjects (see Chapter 14 by Ward and Burns) are able to identify perfectly about 75 categories (roughly 6.2 bits of information) over the entire auditory range compared to about 5 categories (2.3 bits) for nonpossessors (Pollack, 1952).

It would also appear that musicians who have relative pitch—the ability to identify frequency ratios in terms of musical interval categories—are also exceptions to the 7 ± 2 rule. Clearly, most competent musicians can recognize perfectly the 12 intervals of the chromatic scale in either harmonic or melodic modes (Plomp, Wagemarr, & Mimpen, 1973; Killam, Lorton, & Schubert, 1975). In informal experiments we have found that many musicians can identify perfectly the ascending and descending melodic intervals from unison to major tenth (32 categories). However, in light of octave generalization, it is not clear how these results should be interpreted. For example, Pollack (1953) has shown that adding independent dimensions increases the information transfer. Therefore, if chroma and tone height are indeed independent dimensions (see Section IV,D,1), information transfer for identification of frequency ratios exceeding an octave would not be expected to follow the 7 ± 2 rule for identification or unidimensionally varying stimuli. A similar problem of interpretation exists for identification of ascending and descending melodic intervals.

2. Category Scaling

Another apparent exception to the type of identification performance reported by Miller is performance in category-scaling paradigms using certain kinds of stimuli, primarily stimuli for which the observers possess highly-overlearned familiar labels. The most widely reported experiments of this type are those in which stimuli varying along a single acoustic dimension are categorized by observers in terms of phonemic labels from their native language. Observers in these experiments show very sharp category boundaries and high test-retest reliability (see Studdert-Kennedy, Liberman, Harris, & Cooper, 1970). More importantly, their perceptual categories are much less susceptible to contextual effects characteristic of stimuli that obey the 7 ± 2 rule (see Parducci, 1974; Lim, Berlinder, & Braida, 1977), although they are not completely immune from such effects (see Brady & Darwin, 1978; Diehl, Elman, & McCusker, 1978).

A number of experimenters have obtained category-scaling identification functions for melodic intervals spaced in increments of 10 to 20 cents, over ranges of 2 to 5 semits, where the labels are the relevant intervals from the chromatic scale (Burns & Ward, 1974, 1978; Rakowski, 1976; Siegel and Siegel, 1977a,b). Results for a typical musically trained subject (Burns & Ward, 1978) over the range from 250 to 550 cents (category labels: minor third, major third, and fourth) are shown in the lower graph of Fig. 1 (see p. 248). The form of the identification functions shows the sharp category boundaries that are also characteristic of the results of speech-token category-scaling experiments.

In contrast to the type of identification functions shown in Fig. 1, Siegel and Siegel (1977a) report data obtained from musically untrained observers in a similar task that show inconsistent, often multimodal, identification functions with large category overlap and poor test-retest reliability. The only stimuli categorized consistently are those at the extremes of the stimulus range. Siegel and Siegel also measured the effect on categorization of a contextual change (shift in the stimulus range); they found a large effect for the nonmusicians and essentially no effect for the musicians. This contextual independence was also evident in some data reported by Burns (1974).

Some general findings evident in the data of all experimenters are: (1) a tendency for observers to hear narrow intervals (intervals less than a fourth) as perceptually wider (i.e., a compression of the scale relative to equal temperament) and to hear wide intervals (greater than a fourth) as perceptually narrower (i.e., a stretch of the scale), and (2) large but reliable idiosyncratic differences between observers in their perception of the relative width and placement of interval categories. These effects appear for both ascending and descending intervals. Observers are not, in general, able to categorize reliably the stimuli to a finer degree than chromatic semits. For example, they are not able to identify consistently quartertones between chromatic semits (Burns, 1977; Burns & Ward, 1978) or to label consistently stimuli as "low," "pure," or "high" tokens of a single interval (Burns & Ward, 1974; Rakowski, 1976) even when the stimuli are limited to a very narrow range (Szende, 1977). (Bimodal distributions

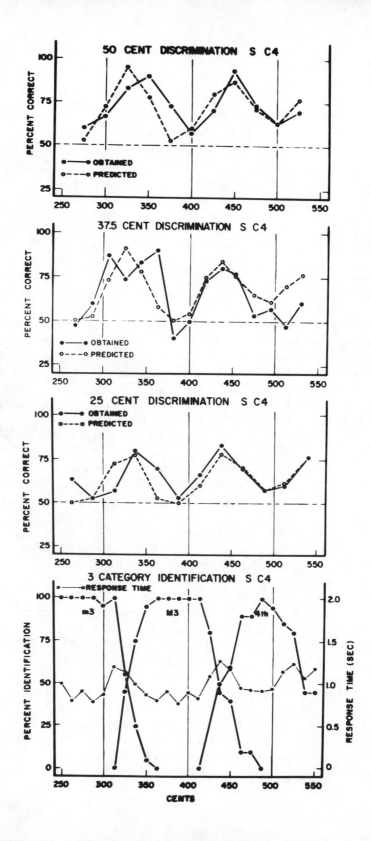

for "low" and "high" are not uncommon.) This inability to categorize the isolated intervals more precisely is also true of Indian musicians (Burns, 1974a, 1977), whose scales theoretically include microtonal variations of certain intervals. The above-mentioned category-scaling results were all obtained for melodic intervals composed of sinusoids. Similar identification functions have been obtained for harmonic intervals (Halpern & Zatorre, 1979).

3. Magnitude Estimation

Magnitude estimation procedures (i.e., identification with unlimited categories) have also been used to assess musical interval perception (Siegel & Siegel, 1977b). The magnitude estimation functions of musicians typically are step-like. That is, frequency ratios over a small range are estimated to have the same magnitude; then there is an abrupt transition to another estimate. The ranges over which the estimate is constant correspond roughly to semits. In addition, the function relating the standard deviation of repeated magnitude estimates to frequency ratio has a multimodal character, in which the modal peaks correspond to the regions between the plateaus of the magnitude estimation function. These functions are unlike those found for magnitude estimation of stimuli obeying the 7 ± 2 rule, which are typically smooth, monotonically increasing functions of stimulus magnitude both for magnitude estimates and for standard deviation of repeated estimates (see, e.g., Stevens, 1976). The results do, however, resemble those found for certain speech stimuli (Vinegrad, 1972) and will be further discussed in Section III,C.

B. Adjustment of Isolated Musical Intervals

Adjustment procedures have also been extensively used to study the perception of musical intervals, primarily the octave (Ward, 1953, 1954; Walliser, 1969; Terhardt, 1969; Sundberg & Lindquist, 1973; Burns, 1974b) but also other intervals (Moran & Pratt, 1926; Rakowski, 1976). In the typical paradigm the subject is presented with pairs of tones (either sequential or simultaneous), one of which is fixed in frequency and the other under the control of the subject. The subject is instructed to adjust the frequency of the variable tone so that the pitch relationship of the two tones corresponds to a specific musical interval. It should be noted that this is a one- (temporal) interval procedure because the subject is adjusting to some internal standard. Thus, these experiments are akin to the identification experiments discussed in Section

---

Fig. 1. Lower graph: Identification functions obtained from a musically trained subject for category scaling of isolated melodic musical intervals. Upper graphs: Discrimination functions (solid lines) obtained from the same subject in a roving-level melodic-interval discrimination experiment for interval separations of 25, 37.5, and 50 cents. (Percent correct discrimination is plotted at the mean value of the two intervals in a discrimination trial). Also shown are the discrimination functions (dashed lines) predicted from the identification functions assuming categorical perception (see text) (Burns & Ward, 1978).

III,A, not to the usual psychophysical adjustment experiment—in which the subject adjusts the variable stimulus to equal some physically presented standard and which is essentially a two- (temporal) interval discrimination experiment.

For repeated adjustments of intervals individual subjects typically show quite small variability relative to that obtained in magnitude production experiments for 7 ± 2-type stimuli (Stevens, 1976). The average standard deviation of repeated adjustments of sequential or simultaneous octaves composed of sinusoids is on the order of 10 cents (Ward, 1953, 1954; Terhardt, 1969). It is slightly less for octaves composed of complex tones (Walliser, 1969; Terhardt, 1969; Sundberg & Lindquist, 1973). A range of average deviations from 14 to 22 cents for adjustments of the other intervals of the chromatic scale (simultaneous presentation) has been reported by Moran and Pratt (1926). Rakowski (1976) reports variability—in interquartile ranges—of 20 to 40 cents for both ascending and descending melodic versions of the 12-chromatic intervals. Other general trends evident from the results of adjustment experiments are (1) a small but significant day-to-day variability in intrasubject judgments, (2) significant intersubject variability, and (3) a tendency to "compress" smaller intervals (adjust narrower than equal-tempered intervals) and "stretch" wider intervals (adjust wider). All of these trends have counterparts in the category-scaling results (see Section III,A,2).

C. Musical Interval Discrimination and Categorical Perception

There have been only a few attempts to measure frequency-ratio resolution using the two- (temporal) interval, two-alternative forced-choice (2I-2AFC) discrimination paradigms typically employed to determine resolution for other auditory stimulus[*] parameters, such as frequency and intensity. In one such experiment Houtsma (1968) obtained estimates of frequency ratio JNDs for melodic intervals composed of sinusoids using a 2I-2AFC task (i.e., subjects were asked to judge which of two melodic intervals was larger). The average JND for three subjects (based on the 75% correct point of the psychometric function) at the physical octave was 16 cents. The JNDs for other ratios in the immediate vicinity of the octave were not significantly different. The JNDs at the ratios corresponding to the (just-tempered) intervals of the chromatic scale were also determined for one subject. They ranged from 13 to 26 cents. The ordering of JND magnitude with interval magnitude indicates a general tendency for smaller JNDs for narrower intervals—a tendency also shown in the dispersion data for Rakowski's (1976) adjustment experiment. However, this ordering also roughly corresponds to smaller JNDs (or less variability) for the intervals that show the highest frequency of occurrence in melodies (e.g., Zipf, 1949).

The other experiments in which 2I-2AFC discrimination data for melodic musical intervals were obtained were those reported by Burns and Ward (1974, 1978). Before these data are reviewed, however, it is necessary to discuss the context in which they were obtained. The series of experiments comprised a study of *categorical perception*. The term "categorical perception" was coined by the speech-perception group at

Haskins Laboratories (see e.g., Studdert-Kennedy *et al.*, 1970) to describe the results of experiments in the perception of certain speech tokens that varied along a single acoustic continuum. The concept is defined by Studdert-Kennedy *et al.* according to two criteria: (1) the subjects' identification functions show sharp and reliable category boundaries when stimuli along the continuum are categorized in terms of phonetic labels (this result was discussed in Section III,A,2) and (2) the subjects' discrimination performance for stimuli equally spaced along the continuum can be correctly predicted from their identification functions if it is assumed that they can discriminate two stimuli only to the extent to which they can differentially identify them. This was contrasted by Studdert-Kennedy *et al.* with the usual situation in psychophysics (discussed in Section II in terms of the 7 ± 2 rule) in which subjects' resolution in 2I-2AFC discrimination tasks is much better than their resolution in single- (temporal) interval, multi-alternative identification tasks—a situation that Studdert-Kennedy *et al.* call *continuous perception*.

Results indicative of categorical perception were at first obtained only with speech stimuli and formed the basis of a portion of the rationale for speech-specific models of speech perception (Studdert-Kennedy *et al.*, 1970). However, a number of experiments showing results indicative of categorical perception for nonspeech stimuli were reported later (e.g., Locke & Kellar, 1973; Miller, Wier, Pastore, Kelly, & Dooling, 1976), including the original experiments of Burns and Ward (1974) on musical interval perception. These results forced an extension of the concept of categorical perception to signals other than speech.

One experiment in the Burns and Ward (1978) study was a musical-interval-discrimination experiment designed to duplicate closely the conditions of the typical speech-perception experiment. The basic paradigm was similar to that used by Houtsma (1968) except that the two melodic intervals to be discriminated on a given trial were adjacent ones chosen at random from a set of melodic intervals separated by an equal step-size in cents over a 300 cent range (i.e., roving-level discrimination) rather than two intervals that were fixed over a block of trials (i.e., fixed-level discrimination). The results of one subject for step-sizes of 25, 37.5, and 50 cents, over the range from 250 to 550 cents, are shown in the upper graphs in Fig. 1. Also shown are the discrimination functions predicted from the identification functions (discussed in Section III,A,2; see lower graph). The agreement between the obtained and predicted discrimination functions in Fig. 1 is comparable to that shown by categorically perceived speech stimuli. Thus, according to the criteria stated by Studdert-Kennedy *et al.*, musical intervals were perceived categorically in this experiment.

Siegel & Siegel (1977b) have interpreted the correlation between category boundaries in the category-scaling identification functions and the modal peaks in the magnitude-estimation, standard-deviation functions of their subjects as indicative of categorical perception of melodic intervals. Halpern and Zatorre (1979) have obtained results for the perception of harmonic musical intervals similar to those found by Burns and Ward (1978) for melodic intervals. Locke and Kellar (1973) also obtained results indicative of categorical perception for a harmonic triad varying from minor to major.

To obtain results indicative of categorical perception for musical intervals, one must use musically trained subjects who are able to reliably label the stimuli. Non-musicians have significantly poorer performance and show no evidence of categorical perception (Burns & Ward, 1978; Siegel & Siegel, 1977b; Locke & Kellar, 1973). For example, the lower graph in Fig. 2 shows the average performance of four musicians and four nonmusicians in a 50-cent roving-level discrimination experiment (Burns &

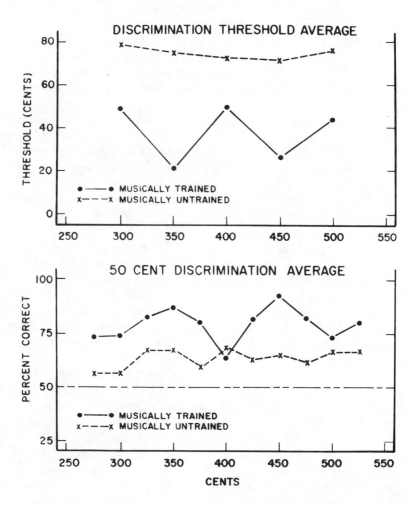

Fig. 2. Upper graph: The average melodic-interval JND estimates of four musically trained (points connected by solid lines) and four musically untrained subjects (points connected by dashed lines) obtained in a fixed-level discrimination experiment. Lower graph: Average discrimination functions (50 cent interval separation) of four musically trained (solid lines) and four musically untrained (dashed lines) subjects obtained in a roving-level discrimination experiment (Burns & Ward, 1978).

Ward, 1978). The discrimination function of the musicians shows the typical "peak–trough" form associated with categorical perception; the discrimination function of the nonmusicians shows significantly poorer performance with no evidence of categorical perception.

This evidence indicates that when equivalent paradigms are used, musical intervals are perceived as "categorically" as speech tokens. However, the usefulness and validity of the concept of categorical perception have become the focus of considerable controversy. Categorical perception almost certainly does not define the limits of perceptual ability, as most speech perception literature implies. This is clearly shown by another experiment (Burns & Ward, 1978) in which frequency-ratio-JND estimates were obtained for melodic intervals corresponding to "within category" and "between category" points on the identification functions, using a fixed-level 2I-2AFC adaptive paradigm. The results for one subject are shown in the upper graph of Fig. 3. JND estimates obtained from the initial adaptive run show the form that would be expected for categorically perceived stimuli (i.e., larger JNDs for "within-category" stimuli compared to "between-cateogry" stimuli). However, after subjects had reached asymptotic performance (the numbers by the data points indicate the number of adaptive runs necessary to reach asymptotic performance), the JND estimates for all ratios were roughly equal and comparable to those of Houtsma's (1968) subject for the same range. Furthermore, roving-level discrimination functions obtained after subjects had reached asymptotic performance in the adaptive paradigm still show the typical peak–trough form associated with categorical perception (see lower graph Fig. 3). Similar results for a speech continuum have been obtained by Carney, Widin, & Viemeister (1977). Thus, whether or not certain stimuli are perceived categorically depends to a large extent on the experimental paradigm. The increased stimulus uncertainty induced by a roving-level procedure is apparently a major factor in eliciting categorical perception.

These discoveries suggest that categorical perception and magic number 7 ± 2 results are not dichotomous phenomena but different manifestations of the processing of high information signals. This processing can probably be modeled by a slightly more general form of the Durlach–Braida model discussed in Section II. For example, using the criteria that discrimination resulution be equivalent to identification resolution, the model already predicts categorical perception for two special cases: (1) somewhat trivially, when both context-coding noise and trace noise are small and sensation noise limits performance and (2) when both context-coding noise and trace noise are high, relative to sensation noise, but trace noise is dominant (for example, for very long-time delays in a 2I-2AFC task) and, hence, optimum discrimination is accomplished by comparing context-coding representations. If it is assumed that there is a more precise form of the context-coding mode for highly overlearned, complex stimuli (such as speech tokens or musical intervals) that is not dependent on the immediate context of the stimuli in the experiment but is based on long-term experience, and if it is further assumed that sensory-trace-mode noise is inherently high due to the more complex nature of the stimuli, then sensory-trace noise would be expected

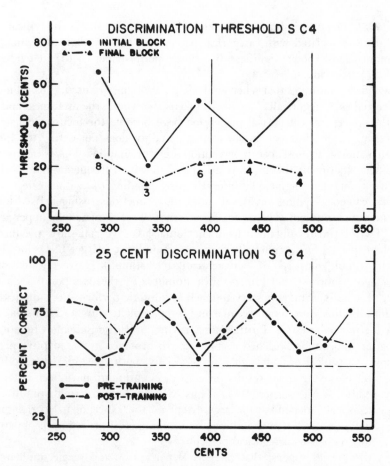

Fig. 3. Upper graph: Melodic-interval JND estimates obtained from a musically trained subject using a fixed-level adaptive discrimination paradigm. The solid lines connect estimates obtained in the initial adaptive run at each condition. The dash–dot lines connect estimates obtained after asymptotic performance was reached. Lower graph: Discrimination functions (25 cent interval separation) obtained from the same subject using a roving-level discrimination task. The functions plotted as solid lines were obtained prior to, and the functions shown as dash–dot lines were obtained after, the fixed-level discrimination experiment (Burns & Ward, 1978).

to dominate except for minimal uncertainty procedures. Under these assumptions optimum performance would be obtained in the context-coding mode for most paradigms, and categorical perception (i.e., equivalence of identification and discrimination) would be the norm. The fact that the standard deviation of repeated adjustments of musical intervals (an identification procedure) is of the same order of magnitude as the frequency ratio JND determined in a minimal-uncertainty 2I-2AFC discrimination procedure supports the idea of a precise context-coding mode in the case of musical intervals.

IV. NATURAL INTERVALS AND SCALES

A. Natural Intervals and Their Possible Basis

Given the assumption, based on the discussion in Part II, that practical music is limited to a relatively small set of discrete pitch relationships, how are the specific values of these relationships chosen? That is, are there "natural" frequency ratios inherent in the manner in which the auditory system processes tonal stimuli, which are perceptually salient or unique and, as such, define the intervals of the scale? According to traditional Western music theory, such natural intervals do exist. They are associated with the concept of consonance (and its inverse, dissonance) and are defined by small-integer frequency ratios. For example, the ratio 2:1 (octave) is the most consonant interval, the ratio 3:2 (fifth) is the next most consonant, and so on—consonance decreasing with increasing ratio complexity. It should be noted that the concept of consonance discussed in this section is defined, somewhat circularly, by music theory as the sensation associated with simultaneously presented small-integer frequency ratios. This (see Section IV,C) may or may not be synonymous with consonance as measured in psychophysical procedures that are designed to minimize any bias due to musical training. The origin of the concept of consonance in terms of small-integer ratios is usually attributed to the Greek scholar Pythagoras. However, the preference of the ancient Greeks for small-integer ratios was probably based more on metaphysics than on psychophysics.

There are essentially three current explanations of the concept of consonance and its association with small-integer frequency ratios [for an excellent review of the historical development of theories of consonance, see Plomp and Levelt (1965)] and, hence, three theories of the basis of natural intervals. The first is based on the fact that most tones in music (and in voiced speech) are complex periodic tones whose partials are (approximately, at least) harmonically related to the fundamental. This explanation states that we learn to recognize the relationships between the harmonic partials of complex tones and to consider those relationships consonant or natural. Terhardt (1974a, 1977, 1978) is a current proponent of this explanation of natural-interval categories (although he calls this concept "harmony" and divorces it from "sensory consonance", see Section IV,C,2).

The second explanation is also based on the harmonic structure of complex tones. For simultaneously presented complex tones, relatively more of the harmonics of the tones, as well as the primary nonlinear distortion products resulting from interaction between harmonics, will coincide in frequency to the extent that the tones are related by small-integer ratios. For example, if two tones are related by an octave, all of the harmonics of the higher frequency tone coincide with harmonics of the lower frequency tone resulting in a smooth (consonant) sound. Conversely, if complex tones are slightly mistuned from small-integer ratios, the interaction between nearly coinciding harmonics will create a sensation of beating or roughness, which is presumed to be related to dissonance. This explanation is usually attributed to Helmholtz (1954).

The third explanation is based on the assumption that the brain prefers combinations of frequencies whose neural-firing patterns contain a common periodicity. This extension of an old idea (e.g., Lipps, 1883; Meyer, 1898) is currently championed by Boomsliter and Creel (1961) and Roederer (1973). It essentially predicts the existence of small-integer-frequency-ratio "detectors."

The latter two explanations were both originally based on simultaneously presented tones. The argument is often made that since scales containing these natural intervals predate harmony and polyphony, explanations of scale development based on simultaneous presentation of tones are inappropriate. This argument is somewhat questionable as accompaniment in parallel octaves and fifths, as well as other intervals, is prevalent in many tribal music systems (see Sachs, 1961; Nettl, 1956). In any case, both explanations have been extended to melodic intervals. The "beats" explanation is extended via what one might term the "Flintstone hypothesis" (e.g., Wood, 1961)—that early music was played in highly reverberant caves that provided pseudosimultaneous presentation. The modern version of this hypothesis is currently promoted by Benade (1976), who assumes that cues provided by the (reverberant) interference between mistuned harmonics are the primary intonation criteria used by musicians in actual performance situations. Similarly, the neural-pattern explanation has been extended to melodic intervals by assuming some sort of "neural reverberation" (Boomsliter & Creel, 1971; Roederer, 1973). The explanation based on learning the harmonic relationships of complex tones is obviously equally applicable to melodic intervals. In Section IV,C some experimental evidence relevant to these explanations for the propensity for small-integer frequency ratios will be examined.

B. Natural Scales and Temperament

There are numerous versions of the natural scale based on these natural intervals, however, two general forms are usually distinguished. One is the scale of just intonation (JI), in which the intervals within an octave are determined, in essence, by choosing the smallest possible whole-number frequency ratios relative to the tonic [i.e., the most consonant intervals, for example: 3:2 (fifth), 4:3 (fourth), 5:4 (major third), etc.]. This process is fairly straightforward for choosing the intervals of the diatonic major scale (do, re, me, fa, so, la, ti, do; see Table I). However, attempts to "fill in" the remainder of the octave to give 12 approximately equally spaced intervals result in fairly complex frequency ratios, and there are a number of alternative candidates for some of the intervals. Although JI is the scale most often cited as being "the" natural scale, its importance is a direct result of the development of harmony in Western music, especially the prominence of the major triad in harmony. One of the characteristics of JI is that the tonic, dominant, and subdominant triads (do, mi, so; so, ti, re; and fa, la, do—respectively) are all tuned in the exact ratios of 4:5:6.

The other prominent form of the natural scale, and the historically precedent one (allegedly devised by Pythagoras himself), is Pythagorean tuning (PT). PT is an attempt to construct a scale using only the so-called perfect consonances (2:1, octave;

3:2, fifth; and 4:3, fourth). This is accomplished by cyclic application of the fifth (and fourth) and the reduction of the resultant intervals to within an octave: for example, $(3/2 \times 3/2) = 9/4 = (2/1 \times 9/8)$ (major second); $(9/8 \times 3/2) = 27/16$ (major sixth); etc. If this process is repeated 12 times, the approximate original starting point is reached. However, since powers of three can never be an exact multiple of two, there is a discrepancy. If the original starting note was C, this resultant is the enharmonic equivalent of C, B♯, which is sharp by a Pythagorean comma (24 cents). One way to avoid this is by proceeding downward in fifths (or equivalently, upward in fourths) for half of the intervals, thereby introducing the discrepancy at the tritone (F♯ = 612 cents or G♭ = 588 cents.). It can be seen in Table I that the main differences between JI and PT are in the major and minor thirds and major and minor sixths.

If the ratios between adjacent intervals in the diatonic JI or PT scales are calculated (see Table I), it will be seen that there are three values for JI (two whole tones 10/9 and 9/8 and a semit 16/15) and two values for PT (a whole tone of 9/8 and a semit 256/242, which is not half the whole tone). This is one manifestation of the major problem with either of the natural tuning systems: key modulations on fixed-tuning instruments require an inordinate number of intervals per octave (at least 30 in the case of JI) since the same note will have a number of different values depending on the key in which it is derived. (For example, if D in the diatonic just scale of C major is used as a keynote to derive a new diatonic major scale, the notes E and A in the new scale will have slightly different frequencies than the notes E and A in the old scale.) In an effort to reduce all of these discrepancies, various temperament systems (i.e., methods of "adjusting" the natural intervals, such as "meantone tuning") were devised. With the exception of equal-temperament, these systems are of only historical interest and will not be discussed here. (For a review of various temperaments and tunings, see Barbour, 1951.)

The scale of equal temperament (ET), discussed in Section I, which divides the octave into 12 equal intervals, was devised as a compromise that would permit modulation in any key but keep fifths, fourths, and thirds as close as possible to small-integer ratio values. Many musicians claim that ET has destroyed the "inherent beauty" of the natural scales and that performers unencumbered by fixed tuning will tend to play in one of the natural scales. We will review some of the evidence regarding the perception and production of natural intervals and scales in the next section.

C. Experimental Evidence Relevant to Natural Intervals and Scales

1. Measured Intonation

a. Non-Western Scales. Three of the major non-Western musical systems (Indian, Chinese, and Arab–Persian) have inclusive scales approximately equivalent to the Western 12-interval scales and, hence, have the same propensity for the "perfect" consonances (octaves, fourths, and fifths). There are, however, a number of musical cultures that apparently employ approximately equally tempered 5- and 7-interval scales (i.e., 240 and 171 cent step-sizes, respectively) in which the fourths and fifths are significantly mistuned from their natural values. Seven-interval scales are usually associated with Southeast Asian cultures (Malm, 1967). For example, Morton (1974) reports measurements (with a Stroboconn) of the tuning of a Thai xylophone that "varied only ±5 cents" from an equally tempered 7-interval tuning. (In ethnomusicological studies measurement variability, if reported at all, is generally reported without definition.) Haddon reported (1952) another example of a xylophone tuned in 171-cent steps from the Chopi tribe in Uganda. The 240-cent step-size, 5-interval scales are typically associated with the "gamelan" (tuned gongs and xylophone-type instruments) orchestras of Java and Bali (e.g., Kunst, 1949). However, measurements of gamelan tuning by Hood (1966) and McPhee (1966) show extremely large variations, so much so that McPhee states: "Deviations in what is considered the same scale are so large that one might with reason state that there are as many scales as there are gamelans." Another example of a 5-interval, 240-cent step tuning (measured by a Stroboconn, "variations" of 15 cents) was reported by Wachsmann (1950) for a Ugandan harp. Other examples of equally tempered scales are often reported for preinstrumental cultures (although in these cases, the concept of scales may be of doubtful validity). For example, Boiles (1969) reports measurements (with a Stroboconn, "±5 cents accuracy") of a South American Indian scale with equal intervals of 175 cents, which results in a progressive octave stretch. Ellis (1965), in extensive measurements of melodies in Australian aboriginal pre-instrumental cultures, reports pitch distributions that apparently follow arithmetic scales (i.e., equal separation in Hz).

Thus, there seems to be a propensity for scales that do not utilize perfect consonances and that are in many cases highly variable, in cultures that either are pre-instrumental or whose main instruments are of the xylophone type. Instruments of this type produce tones whose partials are largely inharmonic (see Rossing, 1976) and whose pitches are often ambiguous (see De Boer, 1976).

b. Intonation in Performance.   A number of measurements have been made of the intonation of musicians playing variable-tuning instruments under actual performance conditions (e.g., Greene, 1937; Nickerson, 1948; Mason, 1960; Shackford, 1961, 1962a,b). The results of these measurements have been summarized by Ward (1970). They show a fairly large variability for the tuning of a given interval in a given performance—ranges of up to 78 cents, interquartile values of up to 38 cents. The mean values of interval tunings, in general, show no consistent tendency to conform to either JI or PT in either melodic or harmonic situations. The general tendency seems to be to contract the semit and slightly expand all other intervals relative to ET. There is also some evidence of context-dependent effects [e.g., to play F♯ sharper than G♭ (Shackford, 1962a,b)]. Those results mirror, to a certain extent, the results of the adjustment and identification experiments using isolated intervals (discussed in Sections III,A and III,B), which showed a tendency to compress the scale for small intervals and stretch the scale for large intervals, in both ascending and descending modes of presentation.

The above measurements were obtained for Western classical music, but the same general tendencies are evident in measurements of intonation from a military band (Stauffer, 1954), Swedish folk musicians (Fransson, Sundberg, & Tjernland, 1970), and jazz saxophonists (Owens, 1974). Measurements of intonation in performance for Indian (Hindustani) classical music (Jhairazbhoy & Stone, 1963; Callow & Shepard, 1972) show similar variability. There are even large variations in the intonation (ranges of up to 38 cents) of a given interval in the single performance of a composition by one musician. Callow and Shepard analyzed these variations in terms of melodic context and found no significant correlations. Large variability (±50 cents) was also found in the intonation of a Thai vocalist whose frame of reference was presumably an equally tempered 7-interval scale (Morton, 1974).

There is no evidence from any of these studies that suggests that the performers tend to play intervals corresponding to exact small-integer ratios, either with reference to the tonic or to preceding notes, for either melodic or harmonic situations.

2. Sensory Consonance and Dissonance

As mentioned in Section IV,A, the degree of consonance of musical intervals is defined by music theory in terms of the simplicity of frequency ratios; hence, any attempt to rate consonance or dissonance of intervals by musicians who are able to identify the intervals is obviously subject to bias. Therefore, recent attempts to determine the physical parameters corresponding to the sensations of consonance and dissonance have employed musically naive observers. For example, van de Geer, Levelt, and Plomp (1962) showed that for naive observers the term consonance is synonymous with beautiful or euphonious, and, conversely, the term dissonance is synonymous with ugly or noneuphonious. Using such synonyms, when necessary, Plomp and Levelt (1965) and Kameoka and Kariyagawa (1969a,b) had musically naive observers scale the consonance of simultaneous stimulus pairs composed of both pure and complex tones. Both groups of experimenters found that for pure tones consonance first decreases as a function of frequency-ratio magnitude, reaching a minimum at a value corresponding roughly to one quarter of a critical band (a measure of the frequency resolving power of the ear) and then increases as a function of increasing frequency ratio. For complex-tone ratios, however, consonance shows maxima at small-integer frequency ratios (i.e., at those ratios dictated as consonant by music theory). Similarly, the results of a nonverbal triadic-comparison technique (Levelt, Van de Geer, & Plomp, 1966) implied that subjects order both pure- and complex-tone ratios in terms of ratio magnitude but that complex tones are additionally ordered along a dimension corresponding to simplicity of frequency ratio.

Other experimenters have shown that for pure-tone ratios the term "dissonance" is essentially synonymous with "roughness" (Plomp & Steeneken, 1968; Terhardt, 1974a, 1977, 1978), a quality which is highly correlated with the degree of amplitude modulation of the stimulus. The roughness of simultaneous pure-tone pairs as a function of frequency separation is limited at low frequencies by the frequency resolution of the ear and at high frequencies by the limits of the ear's ability to follow rapid amplitude modulations (Terhardt, 1974b). Plomp and Levelt (1965) and Kameoka and Kariyagawa (1969b) have shown that the dissonance of a complex-tone interval can be accurately predicted by adding the dissonances associated with the interaction of individual partials of the two tones. Slaymaker (1970) and Pierce (1966) have demonstrated that these considerations also predict the relative dissonance of inharmonic complex tones. These results are in essential agreement with Helmholtz's original hypothesis regarding the basis of consonance and dissonance.

3. Musical Interval Identification and Discrimination

The results of three harmonic-musical-interval absolute identification experiments have been analyzed in light of presumed small-integer-ratio natural categories. The rationale involved in the interpretation of these results is that the similarity of intervals is related to their confusability in absolute identification tasks (Plomp et al., 1973; Killam et al., 1975)—or to the response time in deciding whether a given interval is the same as an expected token (Balzano, 1977)—and the existence of small-integer-ratio detectors should result in a similarity based on ratio simplicity. The results of all three experiments show, however, that interval similarity is based primarily on interval width. That is, maximum confusions were made between adjacent intervals, or, equivalently, response time for "different" determinations was inversely proportional to difference in interval width. There were slight additional tendencies in all three experiments to consider equivalent name categories (e.g., major and minor third) and inversions (e.g., minor second, major seventh) as being more similar, but no general tendency for confusion between small-integer ratios. This, surprisingly, was true even for the case in which the intervals were composed of complex tones: Plomp et al. hypothesize that the short durations of the intervals used in their experiment prevented observers from using roughness cues for complex-tone pairs.

Contrary to the opinion of some authors (e.g., Husmann, 1953; cited in Schügerl, 1970), absolute identification of harmonic intervals does not require interaction of the two tones on the basilar membrane. Identification performance is essentially equivalent whether the two tones are presented in the same or in opposite ears (Burns & Ward, 1976).

These absolute identification results are consistent with the results of the category-scaling and interval-adjustment experiments (Sections III,A,2 and III,B, respectively), which show, in general, unimodal distributions of interval categories along the dimension of frequency-ratio magnitude. In addition, the large idiosyncratic differences, day-to-day variability, tendencies to stretch and compress the scale, and the apparent inability of musically untrained observers to categorize frequency ratios, shown in the category-scaling and adjustment experiments also argue against the existence of frequency-ratio detectors.

The results of melodic-musical-interval discrimination experiments (Section III,C) also show little evidence for small-integer-ratio detectors. Houtsma (1968) found no difference between frequency ratio JNDs at the exact octave (2:1) and at nearby ratios. Burns and Ward (1978) found essentially equal frequency ratio JNDs at five different ratios over a range of 250 cents with musically untrained observers showing JNDs an order of magnitude larger than those shown by musicians (see upper graphs in Figs. 2 and 3).

4. Conclusions: Learned versus Innate Categories

The evidence presented thus far implies that musical-interval categories are learned rather than are the direct result of characteristics of the auditory system. This evidence includes: (1) the variability found in measured scales and intonation, even when possible contextual effects are taken into account; (2) the intrasubject variability, large intersubject variability, and consistent deviations from small-integer-ratio categories found in category-scaling and adjustment experiments; (3) the absence of small-integer-ratio singularities in frequency-ratio-JND functions and absence of small-integer-ratio confusions in absolute-identification experiments; and (4) the relative inability of musically untrained subjects to perform musical interval identification or discrimination experiments. Although temporally coded information exists that might be utilized to discriminate exact from nonexact small-integer ratios of low-frequency simultaneous pure tones in a minimal-uncertainty psychophysical task (e.g., Plomp, 1967), this information is apparently of little use, or is ignored, as an intonation cue in actual musical situations. Similarly, there is no indication that possible roughness cues provided by the interaction of reverberant and ongoing complex tones are used as intonation cues in most musical situations.

Assuming, then, that the intonation of individual musicians is based on their ability to reproduce learned categories, there are basically three alternative hypotheses for the origin of these categories: (1) the categories are learned from the scales of a given culture, the intervals of which were originally chosen at random; (2) the categories are learned from the scales of a culture, the intervals of which were originally derived from considerations of sensory consonance (e.g., Plomp & Levelt, 1965); or (3) the categories are based on the early unconscious learning of relationships between the partials of environmental sounds—primarily voiced speech (Terhardt, 1974a, 1977, 1978).

Given the fairly universal occurrence in scales of perfect consonances, especially the octave (Section IV,C,1), hypothesis 1 seems untenable. The variability of scales in pre-instrumental music or music whose major instruments produce inharmonic tones is consistent with either hypothesis 2 or 3. One problem with Terhardt's "unconscious learning" hypothesis, however, is that this hypothesis predicts that even observers without musical training possess a sense of the basic musical intervals (e.g., octave, fifth). The evidence from a number of the experiments discussed in Sections II,C and III,D (e.g., Siegel & Siegel, 1977b; Locke & Kellar, 1973; Burns & Ward, 1978) indicates that this is not so. In fact, even the concept of octave-unison similarity appears to be a function of musical training (Allen, 1967; Thurlow & Erchul, 1977). There also appears to be evidence that young children do not possess an innate interval sense (Frances, 1968; Zenatti, 1969; cited in Risset, 1978).

Thus, on the basis of the available evidence, the most likely possibility seems to be that natural intervals, as dictated by sensory consonance, have influenced the determination of the scales of most cultures, but that the intonation of individual musicians is primarily a function of their acquired ability to reproduce the learned interval categories of these scales.

D. Octave Generalization and Chroma

1. Introduction

As was mentioned in Section I, the scales of Western music are predicated, in part, on the concept of octave generalization (i.e., that tones separated by an octave are in some sense musically equivalent, and thus scales are uniquely defined by specifying the intervals within an octave). Octave generalization appears to be farily universal for advanced musical cultures (see Section IV,C). Octave circularity of relative pitch is inherent in the conceptualizations of pitch as having two aspects: (1) pitch height, which is correlated with absolute frequency and (2) chroma, which is correlated with relative position within an octave. This idea has often been graphically represented by a helix or torus (see Chapters 9, 11, and 14, this volume).

2. Possible Explanations for Octave Generalization

There are several possible explanations for the uniqueness of the octave as the basis for an assumed circularity of relative pitch. In the discussion of sensory consonance in Section IV,C,2, it was pointed out that for simultaneous musical intervals composed of complex tones whose partials are harmonically related, the exact octave is unique in that all of the partials of the tones will coincide exactly. Therefore, the octave interval will be no more dissonant than the lower-frequency complex tone alone.

Another explanation is a consequence of the perception of the pitch of complex tones. Current models of complex-tone-pitch perception (e.g., Gerson & Goldstein, 1978; Terhardt, 1974a) assume that complex-tone-pitch perception is a pattern recognition process in which a "central pitch processor" attempts to match the partials of the complex tone with the best-fitting harmonic series. A consequence of this type of operation will be a certain amount of octave ambiguity in the model predictions of fundamental pitch. For example, a complex tone consisting of all harmonics of 200 Hz might also be estimated as the even harmonics of 100 Hz. Such ambiguity has, indeed, been found in complex-tone-pitch-perception experiments (see, e.g., Gerson & Goldstein, 1978; Houtsma, 1979).

3. Psychophysical Evidence Regarding Octave Generalizstion

The bidimensional representations of pitch imply that manifestations of octave equivalence should be found in experiments for which musical training is not a prerequisite. Two experiments often cited as providing such evidence for octave generalization are the conditioning experiments of Blackwell and Schlosberg (1943) using rats and Humphreys (1939) using humans. Both experiments, however, have methodological problems, primarily in the form of stimulus distortion, and have apparently never been replicated.

Other evidence appears to derive from the experiments of Shepard (1964), employing complex tones whose partials consist of octaves of the fundamental. These complex tones are, in essence, passed through a bandpass filter that serves to keep average tone height constant regardless of fundamental frequency. The objective experiments—which have recently been expanded upon by Pollack (1978)—show that judgments of the pitch relation between tones of this type with differing fundamental frequencies are based on the relative proximity of harmonics rather than on absolute fundamental frequency differences. These results—which can be explained either by relative pitch judgments between proximal harmonics or between the dominant "residue" pitches of the complex tones (see DeBoer, 1976)—essentially separate relative pitch from pitch height and are not unexpected. The surprising result is when a set of tones of this type, whose fundamental frequencies cover the range of an octave in semit steps, are played cyclically—with a sufficient time delay between individual tones—the impression is one of constantly rising (or falling) pitch without the octave jumps one would expect (and which are indeed heard if sufficient delay between the tones is not provided). This illusion is often cited as evidence for circularity of relative pitch based on octave equivalence. However, recent experiments (Burns, 1981) show that octave separation of partials is not a prerequisite for eliciting the illusion. An equally salient illusion obtains from cyclically repetitive sequences of tones composed of inharmonic partials (e.g., stretched or compressed octaves). In addition, experiments in which observers judge the similarity of both pure or complex sequential tones provide conflicting evidence (Allen, 1967; Thurlow & Erchul, 1977); in general, only musically trained observers give results indicative of octave similarity.

Another aspect of octave perception is the perceptual stretch of sequential octaves (which seems to reflect a general tendency to stretch all of the wider intervals; see Section III) in which exact octaves are perceived as being too small. This also seems to be fairly universal across musical cultures (Ward, 1954; Hood, 1966; Burns, 1974b). Terhardt's (1974a) hypothesis (see Section IV,C,4) of unconscious learning of the relationship between harmonics provides an explanation for this phenomenon. It is based on the fact that the pitches of the individual components of a complex tone are slightly altered by the presence of other components—in general a downward pitch shift for the lower components and an upward shift for the higher components—resulting in a wider subjective interval between components (Terhardt, 1971). However, this argument is based on purely circumstantial evidence and does not appear to be a completely satisfactory explanation. It does not, for example, explain the relative amount of stretch or compression of intervals other than the octave.

Our conclusion is that octave generalization is a learned concept that has its origins in the octave's unique position in the range of sensory consonance of complex-tone intervals. However, resolution of the question of the basis for octave generalization awaits further research, particularly on the Shepard illusion.

V. CONCLUSIONS AND CAVEATS

A. Conclusions

On the basis of the evidence reviewed, the following conclusions regarding the perception of musical intervals and scales seem justified.

1. The use of a relatively small number of discrete pitch relationships in music is probably dictated by inherent limitations on the processing of high information-load stimuli by human sensory systems.

2. Natural intervals, in the sense of intervals that show minimal sensory dissonance (roughness) for simultaneous presentation of complex tones, have probably influenced the evolution of the scales of many musical cultures, but the standards of intonation for a given culture are the learned interval categories of the scales of that culture. A corollary of this is that the intonation performance of a given musician is primarily determined by his or her ability to reproduce these learned categories and is little influenced, in most situations, by any psychophysical cues (e.g., roughness, beats of mistuned consonances, etc.).

3. The concept of categorical perception, also related to the limitations on processing of high information-load stimuli, is probably a reasonable description of the way in which intervals are perceived in all but minimal-uncertainty situations, an analogous situation to the perception of phonemes in speech.

4. Quartertone music might be theoretically feasible given sufficient exposure to it, but the present 12-interval Western scale is probably a practical limit. Any division of the octave into intervals smaller than quartertones is perceptually irrelevant for melodic information.

5. Octave generalization is probably a learned concept with its roots in the unique position of the octave in the spectrum of the sensory consonance of complex-tone intervals.

B. Caveats

The perception of isolated melodic musical intervals may have little to do with the perception of melody. As several of the chapters in this volume will indicate, there is considerable evidence that melodies are perceived as Gestalts or patterns, rather than as a succession of individual intervals, and that interval magnitude is only a small factor in the total percept. There is also an analogy here with speech perception, but the perception of individual musical intervals may be even less relevant to the perception of music than the perception of individual phonemes is to the perception of speech. The ability to label individual intervals is certainly not crucial to the perception of, or even the production of, music. Many amateur musicians who learn and accurately reproduce melodies "by ear" cannot identify isolated intervals. Categorical perception, at least as it is usually defined (i.e., in terms of the relationship between identification and discrimination), may only be relevant when musicians are listening "analytically"—for example, in order to transcribe a melody. There is obviously a need for experiments in the perception of the intonation of individual notes in familiar and unfamiliar melodic phrases.

ACKNOWLEDGMENTS

The authors would like to thank the following colleagues for commenting on a previous version of this manuscript: Lawrence Feth, Adrian Houtsma, Ernst Terhardt, and David Woods.

REFERENCES

Allen, D. Octave discriminability of musical and non-musical subjects. *Psychonomic Science*, 1967, 7, 421–422.

Attneave, F., & Olson, R. Pitch as a medium: A new approach to psychophysical scaling. *American Journal of Psychology*, 1971, *84*, 147–166.

Balzano, G. On the bases of similarity of musical intervals: A chronometric analysis. *Journal of the Acoustical Society of America*, 1977, *61*, S51 (A).

Barbour, J. M. *Tuning and temperament*. East Lansing, Michigan: Michigan State College, 1951.

Benade, A. *Fundamentals of musical acoustics*. London and New York: Oxford University Press, 1976.

Blackwell, H. R., & Schlosberg, H. Octave generalization, pitch discrimination, and loudness thresholds in the white rat. *Journal of Experimental Psychology*, 1943, *33*, 407–419.

deBoer, E. G. On the "residue" and auditory pitch perception. In W. Keidel and W. Neff (Eds.), *Handbook of sensory physiology*. (Volume V/3) Berlin and New York: Springer-Verlag, 1976.

Boiles, J. Terpehua thought-song. *Ethnomusicology*, 1969, *13*, 42–47.

Boomsliter, P., & Creel, W. The long pattern hypothesis in harmony and hearing. *Journal of Music Theory*, 1961, *5*, 2–31.

Boomsliter, P., & Creel, W. Toward a theory of melody. Paper presented to *Symposium on Musical Perception. Convention of the AAS, December 28, Philadelphia, Pennsylvania*, 1971.

Brady, S. A., & Darwin, C. J. Range effect in the perception of voicing. *Journal of the Acoustical Society of America*, 1978, *63*, 1556–1558.

Burns, E. M. In search of the Shruti. *Journal of the Acoustical Society of America*, *56*, Supplement, 1974, S26 (A). (a)

Burns, E. M. Octave adjustment by non-Western musicians. *Journal of the Acoustical Soceity of America*, Supplement, Fall, *56*, 1974, S25–26 (A). (b)

Burns, E. M. The perception of musical intervals (frequency ratios). Unpublished doctoral thesis, University of Minnesota, 1977.

Burns, E. M. Circularity in relative pitch judgments for inharmonic complex tones: The Shepard demonstration revisited, again. *Perception & Psychophysics*, 1981, *30*, 467–472.

Burns, E. M., & Ward, W. D. Categorical perception of musical intervals. *Journal of the Acoustical Society of America*, 1974, *55*, 456 (A).

Burns, E. M., & Ward, W. D. Perception of monotic and dichotic musical intervals. *Journal of the Acoustical Society of America*, 1976, *59*, 552 (A).

Burns. E. M., and Ward, W. D. Categorical perception—phenomenon or epiphenomenon: Evidence from experiments in the perception of melodic musical intervals. *Journal of the Acoustical Society of America*, 1978, *63*, 456–468.

Callow, G., & Shepherd, E. Intonation in the performance of North Indian classical music. Paper presented at the *17th Annual Meeting of the Society for Ethnomusicology, November 30–December 3, Toronto, Canada, 1972*.

Carney, A. E., Widin, G., & Viemeister, N. Noncategorical perception of stop consonants differing in VOT. *Journal of the Acoustical Society of America*, 1977, *62*, 961–970.

Caron, N., & Safvate, D. *Les traditions musicales, Iran*. Correa, France: Buchet/Chastel, 1966.

Diehl, R. L., Elman, J. L., & McCusker, S. B. Contrast effects on stop consonant identification. *Journal of Experimental Psychology*, 1978, *4*, 599–609.

Durlach, N. I., & Braida, L. D. Intensity perception I. Preliminary theory of intensity resolution. *Journal of the Acoustical Soceity of America*, 1969, *46*, 372–383.

Ellis, C. Pre-instrumental scales. *Ethnomusicology*, 1965, *9*, 126–144.

Estes, W. K. An associative basis for coding and organization in memory. In A. W. Melton and E. Martin (Eds.), *Coding processes in human memory*. Washington, D.C.: Winston, 1972. Pp. 161–190.

Frances, R. *La perception de la musique*. Paris: Vrin, 1958.

Fransson, F., Sundberg, J., & Tjernlund, P. Statistical Computer Measurements of the Tone-Scale in Played Music. STL-QPSR 2-3/1970. Department of Speech Communication, KTH, Stockholm.

Gerson, A., & Goldstein, J. L. Evidence for a general template in central optimal processing for pitch of complex tones. *Journal of the Acoustical Society of America*, 1978, *63*, 498–510.

Greene, P. C. Violin intonation. *Journal of the Acoustical Society of America*, 1937, *9*, 43–44.

Haddon, E. Possible origin of the Chopi Timbila xylophone. *African Music Society Newsletter*, 1952, *1*, 61–67.

Halpern, A. R., & Zatorre, R. J. Identification, discrimination, and selective adaptation of simultaneous musical intervals. *Journal of the Acoustical Society of America*, 1979, *65*, 540 (A).

Helmholtz, H. *The sensations of tone*. Translated from the 1877 German edition. New York: Dover, 1954.

Hood, M. Slendro and Pelog redefined. *Selected Reports in Ethnomusicology, Institute of Ethnomusicology, UCLA*, 1966, *1*, 36–48.

Houtsma, A.J.M. Discrimination of frequency ratios. *Journal of the Acoustical Society of America*, 1968, *44*, 383 (A).

Houtsma, A.J.M. Musical pitch of two-tone complexes and predictions by modern pitch theories. *Journal of the Acoustical Society of America*, 1979, *66*, 87–99.

Hymphreys, L. F. Generalization as a function of method of reinforcement. *Journal of Experimental Psychology*, 1939, *25*, 361–372.

Husmann, H. *Vom Wesen der Konsonanz*. Heidelberg: Verlag Müller-Thiergarten, 1953.

Jhairazbhoy, N., & Stone, A. Intonation in present day North Indian classical music. *Bulletin of the School of Oriental and African studies, University of London*, 1963, *26*, 118–132.

Kameoka, A., & Kuriyagawa, M. Consonance theory part I: Consonance of dyads. *Journal of the Acoustical Society of America*, 1969, *45*, 1451–1459. (a)

Kameoka, A., & Kuriyagawa, M. Consonance theory part II: Consonance of complex tones and its calculation method. *Journal of the Acoustical Society of America*, 1969, *45*, 1460–1469. (b)

Killam, R. N., Lorton, P. V., & Schubert, E. D. Interval recognition: Identification of harmonic and melodic intervals. *Journal of Music Theory*, 1975, *19.2*, 212–234.

Kunst, J. *Music in java*. (Volume II) The Hague: Martinus Nyhoff, 1949.

Levelt, W., Van de Geer, J., & Plomp, R. Triadic comparisons of musical intervals. *British Journal of Mathematical & Statistical Psychology*, 1966, *19*, 163–179.

Lim, J. S., Berliner, J. E., & Braida, L. D. Revised perceptual-anchor model for context coding in intensity perception. *Journal of the Acoustical Society of America*, 1977, *61*, S89 (A).

Lipps, T. *Psychologische Studien*. Heidelberg: Weiss, 1883. Pp. 92–161.

Locke, S., & Kellar, L. Categorical perception in a non-linguistic mode. *Cortex*, 1973, *9*, 355–368.

Malm, W. P. *Music cultures of the Pacific, the Near East, and Asia*. Englewood Cliffs, New Jersey: Prentice-Hall, 1967.

Martin, D. W. Musical scales since Pythagoras. *Sound* 1962, *1*, 22–24.

Mason, J. A. Comparison of solo and ensemble performances with reference to Pythagorean, Just, and equi-tempered intonations. *Journal of Research of Music Education*, 1960, *8*, 31–38.

McPhee, C. *Music in Bali*. New Haven, Connecticut: Yale University Press, 1966.

Meyer, M. Zur Theorie der Differenztöne and der Gehorseempfindungen überhaupt. *Beitr. Akust. Musikwiss*, 1898, *2*, 25–65.

Miller, G. A. The magical number seven, plus or minus two: some limits on our capacity for processing information. *Psychological Review*, 1956, *63*, 81–96.

Miller, J., Wier, C., Pastore, R., Kelly, W., & Dooling, R. Discrimination and labeling of noise-buzz sequences with varying noise-level times: An example of categorical perception. *Journal of the Acoustical Society of America*, 1976, *60*, 410–417.

Moran, H., & Pratt, C. C. Variability of judgements of musical intervals. *Journal of Experimental Psychology*, 1926, *9*, 492–500.

Morton, D. Vocal tones in traditional Thai music. *Selected reports in ethnomusicology*. (Volume 2) Los Angeles, California: Institute for Ethnomusicology, UCLA, 1974. Pp. 88–99.

Nettl, B. *Music in primitive culture*. Cambridge, Massachusetts: Harvard University Press, 1956.

Nickerson, J. F. A Comparison of Performances of the Same Melody Played in Solo and Ensemble with Reference to Equi-tempered, Just and Pythagorean Intonation. Unpublished doctoral thesis, University of Minnesota, 1948.

Olson, H. *Musical engineering*. New York: McGraw-Hill, 1952.

Owens, T. Applying the melograph to 'Parkers Mood.' *Selected reports in ethnomusicology*. (Volume 2) Los Angeles, California: Institute for Ethnomusicology, UCLA, 1974. Pp. 166–175.

Parducci, A. Contextual effects; a range-frequency analysis. In E. C. Carterette and M. P. Friedman (Eds.) *Handbook of Perception*. (Volume II) New York: Academic Press, 1974.

Pierce, J. C. Attaining consonance in arbitrary scales. *Journal of the Acoustical Society of America*, 1966, *40*, 249 (L).

Plomp, R. Beats of mistuned consonances. *Journal of the Acoustical Society of America*, 1967, *42*, 462–474.

Plomp, R., & Levelt, W.J.M. Tonal consonance and critical band-width. *Journal of the Acoustical Society of America*, 1965, *35*, 548–560.

Plomp, R., & Steeneken, H.J.M. Interference between two simple tones. *Journal of the Acoustical Society of America*, 1968, *43*, 883–884.

Plomp, R., Wagemarr, W., & Mimpen, A. Musical interval recognition with simultaneous tones. *Acustica*, 1973, *29*, 101–109.

Pollack, I. The information in elementary auditory displays. *Journal of the Acoustical Society of America*, 1952, *24*, 745–749.

Pollack, I. The information of elementary auditory displays, II. *Journal of the Acoustical Society of America*, 1953, *25*, 765–769.

Pollack, I. Decoupling of auditory pitch and stimulus frequency: The Shepard demonstration revisited. *Journal of the Acoustical Society of America*, 1978, *63*, 202–206.

Rakowski, A. Tuning of isolated musical intervals. *Journal of the Acoustical Society of America*, 1976, *59*, S50 (A).

Risset, J. Musical acoustics. In E. C. Carterette and M. D. Friedman (Eds.), *Handbook of perception*. (Volume IV) New York: Academic Press, 1978.

Roederer, J. *Introduction to the physics and psychophysics of music*. Berlin and New York: Springer-Verlag, 1973.

Rossing, T. D. Acoustics of percussion instruments—part I. *The Physics Teacher*, 1976, *14*, 546–556.
Sachs, C. In J. Kunst (Ed.), *The wellsprings of music*. The Hague: Martinus Nyhofif, 1962.
Schügerl, K. On the perception of concords. In R. Plomp and G. Smoorenburg (Eds.) *Frequency analysis and periodicity detection in hearing*. Leiden: Sijthoff, 1970.
Shackford, C. Some aspects of perception. Part I. *Journal of Music Theory*, 1961, *5*, 162–202.
Shackford, C. Some aspects of perception. Part II. *Journal of Music Theory*, 1962, *6*, 66–90. (a).
Shackford, C. Some aspects of perception. Part III. *Journal of Music Theory*, 1962, *6*, 295–303. (b)
Shepard, R. N. Circularity in judgements of relative pitch. *Journal of the Acoustical Society of America*, 1964, *36*, 2346–2353.
Siegel, J. A., & Siegel, W. Absolute identification of notes and intervals by musicians. *Perception & Psychophysics*, 1977, *21*, 143–152. (a)
Siegel, J. A., & Siegel, W. Categorical perception of tonal intervals: Musicians can't tell sharp from flat. *Perception & Psychophysics*, 1977, 399–407. (b)
Slaymaker, F. Chords from tones having stretched partials. *Journal of the Acoustical Society of America*, 1970, *47*, 1569–1571.
Spector, J. Classical *Ud* music in Egypt with special reference to Maqamat. *Ethnomusicology*, 1966, *14*, 243–257.
Stauffer, D. *Intonation deficiencies of wind instruments in ensemble*. Washington, D.C.: Catholic University of America Press, 1954.
Stevens, S. S. In G. Stevens (Ed.), *Psychophysics: Introduction to its perceptual, neural and social prospects*. New York: Wiley, 1976.
Studdert-Kennedy, M., Liberman, A. M., Harris, K., & Cooper, F. S. The motor theory of speech perception: A reply to Lane's critical review. *Psychological Review*, 1970, 77, 234–249.
Sundberg, J., & Lindquist, J. Musical octaves and pitch. *Journal of the Acoustical Society of America*, 1973, *54*, 922–927.
Szende, O. *Intervallic hearing: Its nature and pedogogy*. Budapest: Akadémia Kiadó, 1977.
Terhardt, E. Oktavspreizung und Tonhöhen der Schiefbung bei Sinustonen. *Acustica*, 1969, *22*, 348–351.
Terhardt, E. Pitch shifts of harmonics, an explanation of the octave enlargement phenomenon. *Proceedings of the 7th International Congress on Acoustics*, 1971, *3*, 621–624.
Terhardt, E. Pitch, consonance and harmony. *Journal of the Acoustical Society of America*, 1974, *55*, 1061–1069. (a)
Terhardt, E. On the perception of periodic sound fluctuations (roughness). *Acustica*, 1974, *30*, 201. (b)
Terhardt, E. The two-component theory of musical consanance. In E. F. Evans & E. P. Wilson (Eds.), *Psychophysics and Physiology of Hearing* London, Academic Press, 1977.
Terhardt, E. Psychoacoustic evaluation of musical sounds. *Perception & Psychophysics*, 1978, *23*, 483–492.
Thurlow, W. R., & Erchul, W. P. Judged similarity in pitch of octave multiples. *Perception & Psychophysics*, 1977, *22*, 177–182.
Trotter, J. R. The psychophysics of musical intervals: Definitions, techniques, theory and problems. *Australian Journal of Psychology*, 1967, *19*, 13–25.
van de Geer, J. P., Levelt, W., & Plomp, R. The connotation of musical consonance. *Acta Psychologica*, 1962, *20*, 308–319.
Vinegrad, M. D. A direct magnitude scaling method to investigate categorical vs. continuous modes of speech perception. *Language & Speech*, 1972, *15*, 114–121.
Wachsmann, K. An equal-stepped tuning in a Ganda harp. *Nature (London)*, 1950, *165*, 40.
Walliser, U. Über die Spreizung von empfundenen Intervallen gegenüber mathematisch harmonischer Intervallen bei Sinustones. *Frequenzy*, 1969, *23*, 139–143.
Ward, W. D. The Subjective Octave and the Pitch of Pure Tones. Unpublished doctoral thesis, Harvard University, Cambridge, Massachusetts, 1953.
Ward, W. D. Subjective musical pitch. *Journal of the Acoustical Society of America*, 1954, *26*, 369–380.
Ward, W. D. Musical perception. In J. Tobias (Ed.), *Foundations of modern auditory theory*. New York: Academic Press, 1970.

Watson, C., Kelly, W., & Wroton, H. Factors in the discrimination of tonal patterns II. Selective attention and learning under various levels of stimulus uncertainty. *Journal of the Acoustical Society of America*, 1976, *60*, 1176-1186.

White, B. W. Recognition of distorted melodies. *American Journal of Psychology*, 1960, *73*, 100-107.

Wood, A. *The physics of music*. New York: Dover, 1961.

Zenatti, A. La développement génétique de la perception musicale. (Monographies Francaises de Psychologie No. 17). Centre National de la Recherche Scientifique, 1969.

Zipf, G. K. *Human behavior and the principle of least effort*. Reading, Massachusetts: Addison-Wesley, 1949.

Zonis, E. *Classical Persian music: An introduction*. Cambridge, Massachusetts: Harvard University Press, 1973.

9

The Processing of Pitch Combinations

Diana Deutsch

I.	Introduction	271
II.	Feature Abstraction	272
	A. Octave Equivalence	272
	B. Interval and Chord Equivalence	273
	C. Proposed Physiological Substrates	273
	D. Contour	277
	E. Interval Class	278
III.	Higher Order Abstractions	282
IV.	Alphabets and Hierarchies	287
V.	Memory Systems	291
	A. The System Retaining Absolute Pitch Information	292
	B. The System Retaining Interval Information	300
	C. Interactions between These Systems	301
	D. Memory for Hierarchically Structured Sequences	304
VI.	Conclusion	311
	References	312

I. INTRODUCTION

In this chapter the processing of pitch combinations is examined at several levels. First, we inquire into the types of abstraction that give rise to the perception of local features. Such features may be considered analogous to those of orientation or angle size in vision. We have developed sufficient understanding of sensory physiology to justify speculation concerning how such abstractions are achieved by the nervous system. Other low-level abstractions result in the perception of global features, such as contour. Next, we consider how combinations of such features are abstracted so as to give rise to perceptual equivalences and similarities. We then examine processing where these higher level abstractions are themselves combined according to various rules.

Investigations into mechanisms of visual shape perception have led to a distinction between an early process, where many low-level abstractions are passively carried out in parallel, and a later process, where questions are asked of these low-level abstractions based on hypotheses about the scene to be analyzed (Hanson & Riseman, 1978). This distinction between abstractions that are formed passively from "bottom-up" and those that result from a "top-down" process is important in music also. As we shall see, much of musical shape analysis occurs only when the context is such as to allow for the confirmation of expectations.

The final sections of the chapter are concerned with memory. It is clear that a musical sequence is retained simultaneously at different levels of abstraction and that the information at these different levels combines to influence memory judgments. Interactions occurring within the different memory systems are examined, as are the ways the outputs of these systems interact during retrieval.

II. FEATURE ABSTRACTION

A. Octave Equivalence

It is clear that a strong perceptual similarity exists between tones separated by octaves—that is, whose fundamental frequencies stand in the ratio of 2:1 (or a power of 2:1). In the Western musical scale tones that stand in octave relation are given the same name so that a tone is specified first by its position within the abstracted octave and then by the octave in which it is placed (G_3, F_4, etc.). Octave duplications also occur in the scales of other cultures (Nettl, 1956).

Various experimental observations related to octave equivalence have been reported. Baird (1917) and Bachem (1954) have both found that listeners with absolute pitch may sometimes place a note in the wrong octave, even though they name it correctly. Experiments using conditioning procedures have demonstrated generalization of response to tones separated by octaves, both in people (Humphreys, 1939) and in animals (Blackwell & Schlosberg, 1943). Interference effects in memory for pitch have also been shown to exhibit octave generalization (Deutsch, 1973a).

Given the perceptual similarity between tones separated by octaves, it has been suggested that pitch be treated as a bidimensional attribute: the first dimension representing overall pitch level or *tone height*, and the second defining the position of a tone within the octave, or *tone chroma* (Meyer, 1904, 1914; Révész, 1913; Ruckmick, 1929; Bachem, 1948; Shepard, 1964). Contemporary music theorists make an analogous distinction between *pitch* and *pitch class* (Babbitt, 1961, 1965; Forte, 1973).

B. Interval and Chord Equivalence

When two tones are presented either simultaneously or in succession, there results the perception of a musical interval, and intervals are perceived as being the same size when the fundamental frequencies of their components stand in the same ratio. This principle forms an important basis for the traditional musical scale. The smallest unit of this scale is the semitone, which corresponds to a frequency ratio of approximately 1:1.06. Tone pairs separated by the same number of semitones are given the same name, such as major third, minor sixth, and so on. Contemporary music theory also treats tone pairs separated by the same number of semitones as perceptually equivalent.

Chords consisting of three or more simultaneous tones are also classified in part on the basis of the frequency ratios of their components. However, a simple listing of these ratios is not sufficient to define a chord. For example, a major triad and a minor triad both have as their components a major third (five semitones) and a minor third (four semitones) and a fifth (seven semitones). Thus, the fact that the minor third lies above the major third in the one instance and below it in the other is of perceptual importance, and needs to be taken into account in considering how chord abstraction might be achieved by the nervous system.

Given the principles of octave equivalence and interval equivalence, one might hypothesize that intervals whose components are placed in different octaves are also perceptually equivalent. This assumption is frequently made by contemporary music theorists who refer to such intervals as in the same *interval class*. However, traditional music theory assumes this equivalence for simultaneous but not for successive intervals. Simultaneous intervals whose components have reversed position by being placed in different octaves are termed inversions (Piston, 1948). Thus, a simultaneous interval of n semitones is considered perceptually equivalent to a simultaneous interval of 12-n semitones.

Laboratory evidence for the perceptual similarity of inverted intervals has been obtained. Plomp, Wagenaar, and Mimpen (1973) required subjects to identify intervals formed by simultaneous tone pairs, and they found that confusions occurred between intervals that were inversions of each other. Further evidence was provided by Deutsch and Roll (1974) and is discussed below.

For the case of intervals formed by successive tone pairs, the experimental evidence is complicated. As will be discussed below, it appears that interval class perception here occurs only indirectly through a process of hypothesis confirmation, where the features directly apprehended are pitch class and interval.

C. Proposed Physiological Substrates

Following Drobisch (1846, 1855), various psychologists have suggested that the phenomenon of the tone chroma (or pitch class) be accommodated by representing pitch as a helix, with tones separated by octaves lying most proximal within each turn of the helix. One can take this suggestion literally and propose that such a mapping of pitch exists in the auditory system, so that columns are formed of neural units that respond to tones spaced at octave intervals. Unfortunately, there is no physiological evidence for such columnar organization. On the other hand, units have been found that exhibit peaks of sensitivity at octave intervals. Such units could mediate the perceptual equivalence of tones standing in octave relation, and this hypothesis is described in detail below.

Various models for the perceptual equivalence of intervals and chords have been advanced. Pitts and McCulloch (1947) proposed that the auditory cortex is composed of layers, each layer containing a topographic projection of frequency-specific units. In each projection, units responding to frequencies related by equal intervals are spaced equal distances apart. These layers are arranged so as to produce columns of units that respond to the same frequencies. They further hypothesized the existence of fibers that traverse this columnar mass parallel to each other in a slantwise direction. Three such slanting pathways would therefore define a three-note chord. Such a mechanism could mediate transposition of simultaneous intervals and chords but could not mediate transposition of successive intervals nor the perceptual similarity of intervals and chords related by inversion.

Another mechanism, suggested by Boomsliter and Creel (1961), was based on the volley theory of pitch perception (Wever & Bray, 1930). They pointed out that when the components of two frequency combinations stand in the same ratio, these combinations should generate the same pattern of firing. That is, one pattern would be produced by the ratio 2:3, another by the ratio 4:5, and so on. They therefore proposed that the perceptual equivalence of simultaneous intervals is mediated by recognition of these patterns. This model would require an ability on the part of the nervous system to follow frequencies at much higher rates than has been established (Deutsch & Deutsch, 1973). A further difficulty for the model is that it cannot account for the perceptual equivalence of successive intervals and chords nor for the similarity of inverted intervals and chords.

Deutsch (1969) proposed a mechanism for the abstraction of first-order pitch relationships that accommodates both octave equivalence and also the equivalence of intervals and chords under inversion. This hypothesis was modeled on findings concerning the abstraction of low-order specific features by the visual system, such as orientation and angle size. It appears that such abstractions are accomplished in several stages (Hubel & Wiesel, 1962). Units with circular receptive fields[1] appear to project onto higher order units in such a way that units whose receptive fields taken together form straight lines converge onto the same higher order units. These higher order units respond to lines of specific orientation presented in a specific position in the visual field. It further appears that these higher order units project onto yet higher order units in such a way that those units responding to lines presented in a given

---

[1]The receptive field of a unit is that region which, when stimulated, causes a change in the activity of this unit.

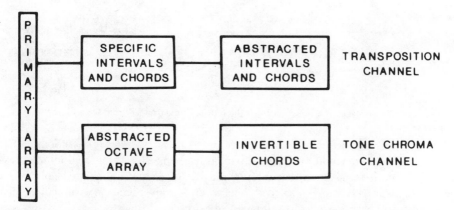

Fig. 1. Flow diagram for abstraction of pitch relationships. It is assumed that pitch information is simultaneously abstracted along two parallel channels, one mediating transposition phenomena and the other mediating octave equivalence effects (from Deutsch, 1969).

orientation but in different positions in the visual field converge onto the same unit. These units therefore respond to lines of specific orientation presented in different positions in the visual field.

The proposed mechanism for abstraction of first-order pitch relationships consists of two parallel channels along each of which information is abstracted in two stages (Fig. 1). Channel A mediates the perceptual equivalence of intervals and chords under transposition. In the first stage of abstraction along this channel, first-order units responding to tones of specific pitch are linked in groups of two and three to second-order units. These units therefore respond to specific intervals and chords (such as the combination of C_4, E_4 and G_4, or of D_5 and G_5). It is assumed that such linkages occur only between units underlying pitches that are separated by an octave or less. In the second stage of abstraction these second-order units are linked to third-order units in such a way that all units that are activated by tones standing in the same relationship are linked together. So, for example, all units activated by an ascending interval of four semitones (a major third) converge onto one unit, all units activated by a descending interval of seven semitones (a perfect fifth) converge onto another unit, all units activated by a major triad onto another unit, and so on (Fig. 2).[2]

Channel B mediates the equivalence of tones separated by octaves (tone chroma or pitch class). In the first stage of abstraction along this channel, first-order units responding to tones of specific pitch are linked in such a way that units underlying tones separated by octaves converge onto the same second-order unit. These units therefore respond to tones in a given pitch class regardless of actual pitch. In the second stage of abstraction, these second-order units converge in groups of two and

[2] Only intervals and chords formed out of elements of the 12-tone chromatic scale are described here, for the purpose of clarity. However, it is assumed that first-order units responding to tones that are not elements of the 12-tone scale are also linked to higher order units in this fashion. This theory therefore makes no assumptions about temperament.

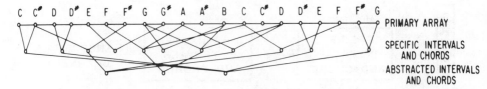

Fig. 2. Two stages of abstraction along the transposition channel (from Deutsch, 1969).

three onto third-order units, which therefore respond to pitch class combinations (Fig. 3). Such units would mediate the perceptual similarity of inverted intervals and chords. Since it is assumed that interval class is directly apprehended only where simultaneous intervals are concerned, this level of convergence is assumed to occur only for units that respond to simultaneously presented tones.

Although no attempt has been made to confirm this model at the neurophysiological level, some relevant findings may be cited. Suga, O'Neill, and Manabe (1979) describe neurons in the auditory cortex of the bat that showed facilitation when the first harmonic of a tone was delivered simultaneously with the second harmonic so that the combination formed a perfect fifth. Other units showed facilitation when the first and third harmonics were simultaneously presented, so that the combination formed an octave; yet others showed facilitation when the second and third harmonics were simultaneously presented, so that the combination formed a fourth. Such units often responded poorly to single tones in isolation but strongly and consistently when the appropriate tonal combination was presented. On the above model, units with such characteristics are hypothesized to occur at the first stage of abstraction along Channel A, i.e., the channel mediating interval and chord perception.

Evans (1974) reports the existence of neurons in the auditory cortex of the cat that exhibit peaks of sensitivity at more than one band of frequencies. Peaks spaced at octave intervals were commonly found. Also Suga and Jen (1976) note the presence of

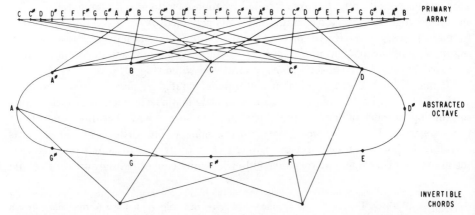

Fig. 3. Two stages of abstraction along the channel mediating octave equivalence effects (from Deutsch, 1969).

neurons in the auditory cortex of the bat that showed two peaks of sensitivity that were approximately harmonically related. They write: "since no neurons with a double peaked tuning curve were found at the periphery . . . it is evident that harmonically related components in acoustic signals are converging on some single neurons at higher levels in the auditory system." In the above model, units with these characteristics were hypothesized to occur at the first level of abstraction on Channel B, i.e., as mediating octave equivalence for single tones.

Units with other patterns of facilitation were also found in these neurophysiological studies. This is hardly surprising since the cat and the bat would not be expected to have the same mechanisms for abstraction of pitch relationships as humans. However, it is interesting that the two classes of neuron hypothesized on the model have been shown to exist, i.e., those with multiple peaks for single tones, and those that require the presentation of specific tones in combination to be securely activated. Furthermore, examples of neurons with characteristics as specifically hypothesized on the model were uncovered in these studies.

D. Contour

In recognizing a segment of music, we employ global as well as specific cues. These include, for example, overall pitch range, the distribution of interval sizes, the proportion of ascending versus descending intervals, and so on. The use of global cues has been best documented for the case of contour in the processing of linear sequence. As shown in the examples in Fig. 4 (taken from Schoenberg, 1967) melodies can be represented by their distinctive contours. We appear to be very sensitive to such information. For example, Werner (1925) found that listeners were able to recognize familiar melodies when these were transformed onto very small scales, so that the intervals were grossly distorted in size. Later, White (1960) found that listeners were able to recognize melodies to some extent when all the intervals were arbitrarily set to one semitone, so that the interval information was entirely removed, apart from the directions of pitch change. When the relative sizes of the intervals were retained, even though their absolute sizes were altered, performance was considerably enhanced. Recent studies by Dowling (1978), Dowling and Fujitani (1971), Idson and Massaro (1978), and Kallman and Massaro (1979) have confirmed and extended such findings.

Fig. 4. Contours from Beethoven piano sonatas as represented by Schoenberg. a. from Sonata in C minor, Op. 10/1-III, m 1–8. b. from Sonata in D, Op. 10/3-III, m 1–16 (from Schoenberg, 1967).

E. Interval Class

If different two-tone combinations form the same interval by appropriate octave displacement, these combinations are held to be in the same interval class. For example C_3 and D_5 in combination form the same interval class as G_2 and F_6. Whether interval class identity gives rise to perceptual equivalence is a matter for debate. As mentioned above, experimental evidence for such equivalence has been found where simultaneous intervals are concerned (Plomp *et al.*, 1973; Deutsch & Roll, 1974). Further compelling evidence is provided by the fact that we easily recognize root progressions of chords as abstractions.

Where successive intervals are concerned, however, the issue is complicated. If interval class were indeed a perceptual invariant, we should experience no difficulty in recognizing a melody when its component tones are placed in different octaves. This issue was examined experimentally by Deutsch (1972a). The first half of the tune "Yankee Doodle" was generated under various conditions. First, it was produced without transformation in each of three adjacent octaves. Then, it was generated such that each tone was in its correct position within the octave, but the choice of octave placement varied randomly between these same three octaves. And finally, the tune was generated as a series of clicks so that the pitch information was entirely removed but the rhythmic information retained. This was to provide a measure of identification performance on the basis of rhythm alone.

The different versions of the tune were played to separate groups of subjects, who were given no clues to its identity besides being assured that it was well known. Although the untransformed versions were universally recognized, recognition of the randomized octaves version was no better than for the version where the pitch information was removed entirely. However, when the subjects were later informed of the identity of the tune, and were again presented with the randomized octaves version, they now found they were able to follow the tune to a large extent. They were thus able to use octave generalization to *confirm* the identity of the tune, even though they had been unable to *recognize* it in the absence of prior information. It was concluded that this confirmation was achieved by the listeners' imagining the tune simultaneously with hearing the randomized octaves version. In this way they could match each note as it arrived with their auditory image and so confirm that the two were indeed in the same pitch class.

It would appear from this experiment that interval class can be perceived, but not as a first-order abstraction. Rather, perception occurs indirectly through a process of hypothesis testing in which the listener uses pitch class to transpose each tone to the appropriate octave, followed by perception of interval which enables the hypothesis to be confirmed or disconfirmed. By this line of reasoning, interval class, where successive intervals are concerned, is perceived through an active top-down process, in contrast with interval and pitch-class perception, which result from a passive bottom-up process. The extent to which interval class is perceived would then depend critically on the expectations of the listener.

Deutsch examined this issue again (1976, 1979), using a short-term recognition paradigm. Listeners were presented with a standard six-tone melody, followed by a comparison melody. The comparison was always transposed up four semitones from the standard. On half of the trials, this transposition was exact so that the set of intervals and their orders were preserved. On the other half, two of the tones in the transposed melody were permuted. The permuted tones were always a semitone apart in pitch, and no tones were permuted that were either at the beginning or the end of the melody or that were adjacent to each other. Thus, in the permuted sequences, four out of the five successive intervals were changed in size by a semitone; however, the contour of the melody'(as defined by the sequence of directions of pitch change) was unaltered regardless of whether or not the comparison melody was an exact transposition of the standard. (This invariance of contour was necessary to insure that contour could not be used as a basis for recognition judgments.)

There were four conditions in the experiment. In the first condition the standard melody was presented once, followed by the comparison melody. In the second condition the standard melody was repeated six times before presentation of the comparison melody. Here, all repetitions were exact. In the third condition the standard melody was again repeated six times, but now on half of the repetitions the melody was transposed in its entirety an octave higher and on the other half it was transposed an octave lower. In the fourth condition the standard melody was again repeated six times, but now on each repetition the individual tones in the melody were placed alternately in the higher and the lower octaves.

The results of the experiment are shown on Fig. 5. It can be seen that exact repetition of the melody produced a substantial improvement in comparison perfor-

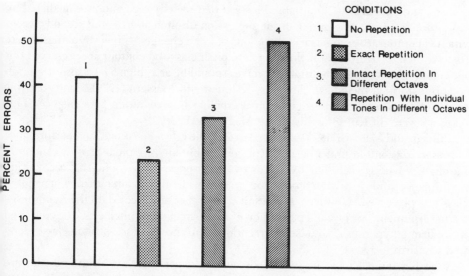

Fig. 5. Percent errors in different conditions of experiment studying the effects of octave displacement on consolidation of melodic information (from Deutsch, 1979).

mance, and an improvement also occurred when the melody was repeated intact in the higher and lower octaves. However, when the melody was repeated such that its component tones alternated between the higher and lower octaves, performance was significantly poorer than when the melody was not repeated at all. This experiment again strongly indicates that interval class cannot be treated as a first-order perceptual feature. Repetition of a set of successive intervals resulted in consolidation of memory for these intervals; however, repetition of a set of interval classes did not do so.

These findings are as expected on the model of Deutsch (1969), since this model assumes that the linkages that give rise to abstraction of successive intervals occur between units underlying specific pitches, and not between higher order units underlying pitch classes. Idson and Massaro (1978) proposed an alternative explanation. They argued that the placement of the tones in different octaves resulted in an alteration of melodic contour, and that this in turn acted to disrupt recognition performance. As evidence for this they point out that when the component tones of melodies were placed in different octaves but contour was preserved, recognition of these melodies was at a higher level than when contour was not preserved (Dowling & Hollombe, 1977; Idson & Massaro, 1978). However, preservation of contour would be expected to improve performance regardless of how interval calss is perceived, since contour alone has been shown to be a powerful cue in melody recognition (Werner, 1925; White, 1960, Dowling, 1978). Once the listener has guessed the identity of the melody on the basis of contour (or any other cue for that matter), he can then confirm or disconfirm his hypothesis by a process of matching each tone as it arrives with its octave equivalent (Deutsch, 1972a, 1978a). The findings on the preservation of contour are not, therefore, evidence against an explanation in terms of Deutsch's (1969) model.

Idson and Massaro (1978) proposed instead that melody recognition is mediated by two processes: first, recognition of the succession of pitch classes, and second, recognition of contour (the sequence of directions of pitch change). If their hypothesis were correct, then recognition of melodies where pitch class and contour are preserved but the component tones are in different octaves should be at as high a level as recognition of untransformed melodies. However, Kallman and Massaro (1979) found that this transformation resulted in a significant decrement in recognition performance. This poses a severe difficulty for Idson and Massaro's theory.

Kallman and Massaro (1979) also investigated the effect on recognition performance of preserving contour under octave displacement but altering pitch class by randomly raising or lowering each tone by one or two semitones. They found that recognition performance under this transformation was considerably poorer than where pitch class was preserved. However, this result would also be expected on the hypothesis-testing argument, for just as a perception of the correct set of pitch classes would tend to confirm a hypothesis, so would perception of an incorrect set of pitch classes tend to disconfirm it.

A further point should here be made. In the experiment by Idson and Massaro (1978), subjects were given the names of a small set of test melodies, and they were presented with these melodies under various transformations for hundreds of trials, allowing ample opportunity for hypothesis-testing. On the other hand Deutsch (1972a) and Kallman and Massaro (1979) presented subjects with each melody only once and did not inform them of the identities of these melodies so that hypothesis testing was much more difficult. In comparing the results from these two types of paradigm, we find that recognition performance where pitch class was preserved but octave placement was randomized was considerably better in the study of Idson and Massaro than in the other two studies. This difference would be expected on the theory that listeners recognize interval class through the mediation of hypothesis-testing, but provides a further difficulty for Idson and Massaro's model.

In this regard it is instructive to consider the use of octave jumps in traditional music. If the present line of reasoning is correct, such jumps can be made with impunity provided the musical setting is such that the displaced tone is expected by the listener. We should therefore suppose octave jumps to be limited to such situations. Indeed, this appears to be the case. In one such situation a melodic line is presented several times without transformation. A clear set of expectations having thus been established, a jump to a different octave occurs. The melodic line on Fig. 6a, for instance, occurs after this line has been presented several times with no octave jumps. Another such situation is where the harmonic structure is clear and unambiguous, so that again the displaced tones are highly probable to the listener. This is illustrated in the segment shown on Fig. 6b. It should also be observed that when octave jumps occur in traditional music, often the identical pitch class is quickly repeated in the new octave. This also occurs in the segment in Fig. 6b. According to the model of Deutsch (1969), this pitch class identity should be recognized directly. The repeated pitch class then provides a means of placing the tones in the new octave in correct relationship with the tones in the previous octave.

The technique of 12-tone composition employs very frequent octave jumps (see below). This raises the question of whether the listener does in fact recognize as perceptually equivalent two presentations of the same tone row under octave displacement. Given the evidence and arguments outlined above, such recognition

Fig. 6.   Two examples of the use of octave jumps. In these instances the jumps are readily processed. a. from Beethoven, *Rondo in C, Op. 5, No 1.* b. from Beethoven, *Sonata in C minor, Op. 10, No. 1.*

should be possible in principle, but only if the listener is very familiar with the material, or if its structure is such as to arouse strong expectations (see also Meyer, 1973).

III. HIGHER ORDER ABSTRACTIONS

Given that linkages are formed between first-order pitch elements, we may next inquire how higher order abstractions are further derived so as to lead to perceptual equivalences and similarities. We recognize visual shapes as equivalent when these differ in size, orientation, or position in the visual field. What transformations result in analogous equivalences in music?

Theorists have long drawn an analogy between perception of pitch relationships and of relationships in visual space (Helmholtz, 1859; Mach, 1906; Koffka, 1935). In contrast with visual space, however, pitch was conceived as represented along one dimension only. As Mach (1906) wrote:

> A tonal series occurs in something which is an analogue of space, but is a space of one dimension limited in both directions and exhibiting no symmetry like that, for instance of a straight line running from right to left in a direction perpendicular to the median plane. It more resembles a vertical right line. . . .

More recently, several investigators have shown that auditory analogues of visual grouping phenomena may be created by mapping one dimension of visual space into log frequency and the other into time (Van Noorden, 1975; Deutsch, 1975a; Bregman, 1978; Divenyi & Hirsh, 1978). In the visual representation of the sequence shown on Fig. 11 of Chapter 4, for example, the principle of proximity emerges clearly. We may therefore inquire whether auditory analogues also exist for perceptual equivalences found in vision (Julesz & Hirsh, 1972).

Von Ehrenfels (1890) in his influential paper on form perception, pointed out that a melody when transposed retains its essential form, the *Gestaltqualität*, provided that the relations among individual tones are unaltered. In this respect, he argued, melodies are similar to visual shapes. On our present intermodal analogy, transposing a melody would be like translating a shape to a different location in the visual field. Shapes may be moved in this way without destroying their perceptual identities (Deese & Grindley, 1947). Similarly, transposing melodies to different pitch levels may leave identification of these melodies unimpaired.[3]

We may next inquire whether further equivalences can be demonstrated for musical shapes that are analogous to their visuospatial counterparts. Schoenberg (1951)

---

[3]This is clear from everyday experience where long-term memory is concerned (Deutsch, 1969; Attneave & Olson, 1971) and also occurs in some short-term situations (Divenyi & Hirsh, 1978). However, short-term recognition of transposed melodies may be difficult (Attneave & Olson, 1971; Cuddy & Cohen, 1976; Dowling, 1978). This probably reflects the projection of interval information onto highly overlearned unequal-interval scales (Deutsch and Feroe, 1981).

argued that transformations similar to rotation and reflection in vision result in perceptual equivalences in music also. He wrote:

> The unity of musical space demands an absolute and unitary perception. In this space... there is no absolute down, no right or left, forward or backward.... Just as our mind always recognizes, for instance, a knife, a bottle or a watch, regardless of its position, and can reproduce it in the imagination in every possible position, even so a musical creator's mind can operate subconciously with a row of tones, regardless of their direction, regardless of the way in which a mirror might show the mutual relations, which remain a given quantity.

This statement may be compared with Helmholtz's (1844) description of imagined visuospatial transformations:

> Equipped with an awareness of the physical form of an object, we can clearly imagine all the perspective images which we may expect upon viewing it from this or that side (see Warren & Warren, 1968, p. 252).

On this basis, Schoenberg proposed that a row of tones may be recognized as equivalent when it is transformed such that all ascending intervals become descending intervals and vice versa ("inversion")[4], when it is presented in reverse order ("retrogression"), or when it is transformed by both these operations ("retrograde-inversion"). Figure 7 illustrates Schoenberg's use of his theory in compositional practice. As he wrote:

> The employment of these mirror forms corresponds to the principle of the absolute and unitary perception of musical space.

Schoenberg did not conceive of the vertical dimension of musical space simply as pitch, but rather as pitch class. That is, he assumed that octave displacement would not destroy the perceptual identity of a musical configuration. His assumptions of perceptual equivalence under transposition, retrogression, inversion, and octave displacement are fundamental to the theory of 12-tone composition (Babbitt, 1961, 1965). This compositional technique employs the following procedure. A given ordering of the 12 tones within the octave is adopted. This tone row is repeatedly presented throughout the piece; however, the above transformations are allowed on each presentation. It is assumed that the row as an abstraction is perceived in its different manifestations.

Whether such transformations indeed result in perceptual equivalences is debatable. In the visual case we must have evolved perceptual mechanisms that preserve the identities of objects regardless of their orientation relation to the observer. An analogous argument cannot be made for the case of inversion and retrogression of sound sequences. A second doubt is based on general experience. Sound sequences may be unrecognizable when reversed in time, as the reader can determine by attempting to decode a segment of speech played backward. Furthermore, many inverted three-note combinations are perceptually very dissimilar. For example, the major and minor

---

[4]The use of the term "inversion" as defined by contemporary music theorists should not be confused with the traditional use of the term defined earlier.

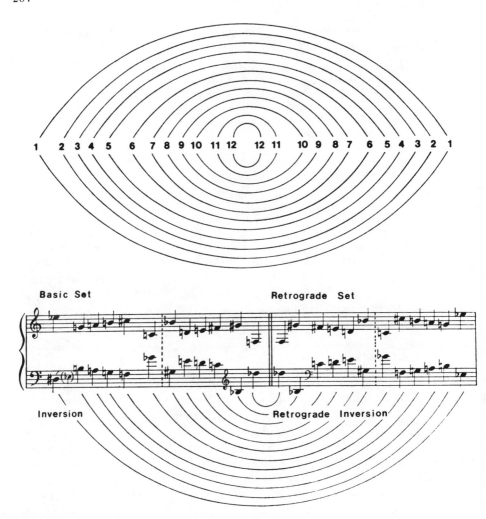

Fig. 7. Schoenberg's illustration of his theory of equivalence relations between pitch structures—taken from his *Wind Quartet, Op. 26* (from Schoenberg, 1951).

triads are inversions of each other; however, it appears quite implausible to regard them as perceptually equivalent. Rather it would seem that recognition of inverted and retrograde patterns is generally accomplished at a level of abstract coding equivalent to that which allows us to recite a segment of the alphabet backward, or to invert a sequence of numbers (Deutsch and Feroe, 1981).

At all events, a substantial body of music theory, aimed at defining equivalence and similarity relations between sets of pitches, is based on these assumptions of equivalence under retrogression and inversion, as well as the assumptions of pitch class and interval class identity. Although these theories are essentially concerned with stimulus structure, they do have implications about psychological representation.

A good example of this type of theory was provided by Chrisman (1971). He first defined the term "pitch-set" to refer to the set of elements derived from any collection of pitches, such that all members of a pitch class in the collection are represented by a unique element corresponding to that pitch class. In order to determine the intervallic relationships in a pitch-set, the elements of the pitch-set are given in ascending order, beginning with any pitch in the set. All members of the pitch-set are then contained within the octave above this initial pitch.

From any pitch-set whose elements have been placed in ascending order and within a single octave, one can construct an array which describes the intervallic structure of the set. Such an array consists of a linear succession of intervals and is termed a "successive-interval array." Each element of the array corresponds to the number of semitones between successive pitch-class representatives in the pitch-set. The array also includes the interval between the last note in the pitch-set and the first note an octave higher.

Cyclic reorderings of elements in each successive interval array are useful for determining intervallic relationships between pitch-sets with differing pitch contents. To take Chrisman's example, the pitch-sets S, T and V have different pitch contents and produce three different interval arrays: A, B, and C.

Pitch-Set	Interval-Array
S = C, C♯, E, F♯, G, A♯, B	A = 1-3-2-1-3-1-1
T = C, D♯, E, F, F♯, A, B	B = 3-1-1-1-3-2-1
V = C, D, D♯, F♯, G, G♯, A	C = 2-1-3-1-1-1-3

When the elements in these arrays are cyclically reordered, the arrays are shown to be equivalent.

$$A = 1\text{-}3\text{-}2\text{-}1\text{-}3\text{-}1\text{-}1$$

$$B = 3\text{-}1\text{-}1\text{-}1\text{-}3\text{-}2\text{-}1 \quad P_3(B) = 1\text{-}3\text{-}2\text{-}1\text{-}3\text{-}1\text{-}1$$
$$C = 2\text{-}1\text{-}3\text{-}1\text{-}1\text{-}1\text{-}3 \quad P_5(\overline{C}) = 1\text{-}3\text{-}2\text{-}1\text{-}3\text{-}1\text{-}1$$

The sets T and V are, thus by this definition, shown to be transpositions of the set S.

Another, much more elaborate formulation was proposed by Forte (1973). Forte was concerned not only with the conditions under which sets of pitches should be considered equivalent, but also with defining similarity relationships between pitch-sets. He used two measures of similarity, one based on pitch class intersection and the other on interval class intersection. For other work on pitch-sets see Howe (1965), Lewin (1960, 1962), Perle (1972, 1977), and Teitelbaum (1965).

The extent to which the structures defined by such theories are processed by the listener remains to be determined. As noted by Garner (1974), some structures that exist in a stimulus configuration are perceived readily, others with difficulty, and yet others not at all. A fundamental problem with this body of theory concerns the basic equivalence assumptions on which it rests. The issue of interval class is a thorny one, and the assumptions of equivalence under retrogression and inversion are also debatable. Reservations about these equivalence assumptions have also been raised recently by music theorists (Browne, 1974; Howe, 1974; Benjamin, 1974).

Other theorists have attempted to represent pitch relationships in terms of distances in a multidimensional space. Drobisch (1846, 1855) proposed that pitch be represented in three dimensions as a helix, with the vertical axis corresponding to pitch height, and tones separated by octaves lying closest within each turn of the helix. This representation reflects the perceptual closeness of the octave relationship. Shepard (Chapter 11) provides a detailed theoretical formulation that elaborates on this model.

Longuet-Higgins (1962a,b) has proposed that "tonal space" be represented as a three-dimensional array. Tones adjacent along the first dimension are separated by fifths, those adjacent along the second dimension by major thirds, and those adjacent along the third dimension by octaves. The intervals of tonal music then appear as vectors in this tonal space. If tones that are separated by octaves are treated as equivalent, an array is obtained such as shown on Fig. 8. Note that a closely related set of tones, such as comprise the C-major scale, forms a compact group, so that a key can be defined as a neighborhood in this space. Longuet-Higgins proposed that when presented with a segment of music, the listener initially selects a given region of space, thus attributing a key. However, if his choice forces him to engage in large jumps

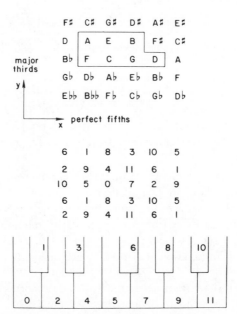

Fig. 8. Array hypothesized by Longuet-Higgins for the representation of "tonal space." See text for details (from Longuet-Higgins, 1978).

within this region, the listener abandons it and selects instead a region where the tones are more compactly represented, thus attributing a new key.

Another approach to the mapping of tonal space was taken by Krumhansl (1979). She performed an experiment in which subjects were presented with a set of context tones which were followed by two tones played in succession. The context tones were either the chord of the C-major triad or the C-major scale. Subjects judged on each trial how similar the first tone was to the second in the tonal system suggested by this context. Multidimensional scaling of the similarity ratings produced a three-dimensional conical structure around which tones were ordered according to pitch height. The components of the major triad formed a closely related cluster near the vertex of the cone; the remaining tones of the diatonic scale formed a less closely related subset that was further from the vertex; and the nondiatonic tones were widely dispersed, still further from the vertex. It is expected that different contexts would give rise to different patterns of similarity relationships using this technique. In the traditional music of our culture, the minor scale should produce a different configuration, and entirely different patterns would be expected from those familiar with other types of music. However, the study is important in demonstrating that pitch relationships are represented in a complex and well-defined fashion in a highly overlearned tonal context.

IV. ALPHABETS AND HIERARCHIES

We next consider a further level of abstraction, in which pitch information is mapped onto a relatively small set of highly overlearned alphabets. Although these differ from one culture to another, the use of such alphabets appears to occur cross-culturally. The invocation of a relatively small number of alphabets, each of which consists of a relatively small number of steps, allows for music of considerable complexity without the penalty of heavy processing load (Miller, 1956; Garner, 1974). In the tonal music of our tradition, the 12-tone chromatic scale forms a parent alphabet from which a family of subalphabets is derived, such as major scale, minor scale, major triad, and so on. Each of these subalphabets is itself a family of subalphabets that are related by transposition. Other alphabets involve chord progressions, such as progression along the cycle of fifths.

The ready mapping of musical sequences onto pitch alphabets is reflected in the finding that short-term transposition often tends to occur along such alphabets rather than in terms of exact interval sizes (Fig. 9). The consequent alterations in interval size do not produce an impression of musical "incorrectness." This contrasts with transposition in long-term situations, where exact intervals are generally preserved instead (Deutsch, 1969; Attneave & Olson, 1971). Short-term perceptual equivalences, therefore, appear to be more heavily influenced by pitch content than are long-term perceptual equivalences.

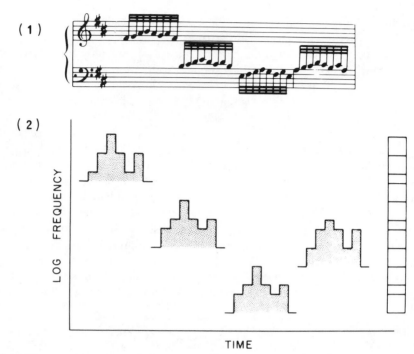

Fig. 9. Transposition along the alphabet of the scale. A given configuration is presented four times in succession at different positions along the scale. Since the scale has unequal intervals, there results a variation in the set of intervals involved. Ladder at right displays scale. From Bach, J. S. *The Well-Tempered Clavier, Book 1, Fugue V* (from Deutsch, 1977).

The invocation of scalar alphabets in short-term situations has been studied by several investigators. Francès (1958) found that listeners were better able to detect alterations in tonal than in atonal melodies. Similar conclusions were reached by Dewar (1974) and Dewar, Cuddy, and Mewhort (1977). Dewar also observed that for tonal melodies, when the altered tone was in the same diatonic scale as the other tones, discrimination accuracy was poorer than when the altered tone departed from this scale. Dowling (1978) further observed that listeners had considerable difficulty in distinguishing between exact transpositions of melodies to new keys and shifts along the same diatonic scale where intervals were not preserved.

The tonal music of our tradition is also composed of small segments that are systematically organized in hierarchical fashion. It is reasonable to suppose that such hierarchical organization reflects the ways in which musical information is abstracted and retained. As Greeno and Simon (1974) point out, many different types of information appear to be retained as hierarchies. In some instances, the information stored is in the form of concepts that refer to classes (Collins & Quillian, 1972). We also appear to retain hierarchies of rules (Gagné, 1962; Scandura, 1970), hierarchies of programs (Miller, Galanter, & Pribram, 1960), and hierarchies of goals in problem solving (Ernst & Newell, 1969). Visual scenes appear to be represented as hierarchies of subscenes (Winston, 1973; Palmer, 1975; Navon, 1977; Hanson & Riseman, 1978). The phrase structure of a sentence lends itself readily to hierarchical interpretations (Yngve, 1960; Miller & Chomsky, 1963).

Experiments by Restle and Brown (1970 and Restle (1970) have demonstrated that we readily acquire serial patterns as hierarchies that reflect the structures of these patterns. In their experiments, subjects were presented with a row of six lights, which came on and off in repetitive sequence, and their task was to predict which light would come on next. The sequences were structured as hierarchies of operators. For example, if the basic subsequence is X = (1 2), then the operation R ("repeat of X") produces the sequence 1 2 1 2; the operation M ("mirror-image of X") produces 1 2 6 5; and the operation T ("transposition +1 of X") produces 1 2 2 3. By recursive application of such operations, long sequences can be generated that have compact structural descriptions. For example, the sequence 1 2 1 2 2 3 2 3 6 5 6 5 5 4 5 4 can be described as M(T(R(T(1)))) and corresponds to the *structural tree* shown on Fig. 10.

Using sequences constructed in this fashion, Restle and Brown (1970) showed that the probability of error in prediction increased monotonically with the level of transformation along such a structural tree. For example, the highest probability of error in a sequence such as on Fig. 10 occurred at Locations 1 and 9, the next highest at Locations 5 and 13, and so on. From this and other evidence, it was concluded that the observer organizes information in accordance with such structures. Parallel theoretical developments by Simon and his colleagues (Simon & Kotovsky, 1963; Simon & Sumner, 1968; Simon, 1972) and by others (Leewenberg, 1971; Jones, 1974, 1978; Vitz & Todd, 1967, 1969) also utilized hierarchies of operators.

Deutsch and Feroe (1981) argue that sequences in tonal music have characteristics not reflected in the above formalisms, and they advance a model for the encoding of pitch sequences as hierarchies of operators, which takes these characteristics into account. In essence, the model may be characterized as a hierarchical network at each level of which, structural units are represented as organized sets of elements. Elements that are present at any one level are elaborated by further elements so as to form structural units at the next-lower level, until the lowest level is reached. It is also

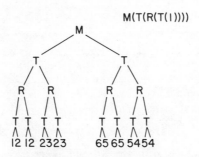

Fig. 10. Tree diagram of a long, regular binary pattern (from Restle, 1970).

assumed that Gestalt principles such as Proximity and Good Continuation contribute to organization at each hierarchical level.

The following are the rules for a simplified version of the system; however, the reader is referred to Deutsch and Feroe (1981) for a description of the full system:

1. A *structure* is notated by $(A_1, A_2, \ldots A_{l-2}, A_{l-1}, *, A_{l+1}, A_{l+2}, \ldots, A_n)$, where A_j is one of the operators n, p, s, n^i, or p^i. (A string of length k of an operator A is abbreviated kA.)

2. Each structure $(A_1, A_2, \ldots, *, \ldots, A_n)$ has associated with it an alphabet, α. The combination of a structure and an alphabet is called a *sequence* (or *subsequence*). This, together with the reference element r, produces a *sequence of notes*.

3. The effect of each operator in a structure is determined by that of the operator closest to it, but on the same side as the asterisk. Thus, the operator n refers to traversing one step up the alphabet associated with the structure. The operator p refers to traversing one step down this alphabet. The operator s refers to remaining in the same position. The two operators n^i and p^i refer to traversing up or down i steps along the alphabet, respectively.

4. The values of the sequence of notes $(A_1, A_2, \ldots, *, \ldots, A_n)$, α, r, where α is the alphabet and r the reference element, are obtained by taking the value of the asterisk to be that of r.

5. To produce another sequence from the two sequences $A = (A_1, A_2, \ldots, *, \ldots, A_m)$, α, and $B = (B_1, B_2, \ldots, *, \ldots, B_n)$, β, where α and β are two alphabets, we define the compound operator pr (prime). $A[pr]B;r$, where r is the reference element, refers to assigning values to the notes produced from $(B_1, B_2, \ldots, *, \ldots, B_n)$, such that the value of * is the same as the value of A_1, when the sequence A is applied to the reference element r. Values are then assigned to the notes produced from $(B_1, B_2, \ldots, *, \ldots, B_n)$, such that the value of * is the same as the value of A_2, and so on. This gives a sequence of length m × n. Other compound operators such as inv (inversion) and ret (retrograde) are analogously defined.

Fig. 11.   Example to illustrate the model of Deutsch and Feroe for the internal representation of pitch sequences (see text for details). Passage is from Bach's *Sinfonia 15*, BWV 801 (from Deutsch & Feroe, 1981).

To give a simple example of the use of the formalism, Sequence 1 of Fig. 16 is represented as

$$A = (*,3p)G_{tr}$$
$$B = (*,p,n)Cr$$
$$S = A[pr]B,G_5$$

where G_{tr} represents the G-major triad, Cr the chromatic scale, and G_5 the reference element.

It may be observed that this form of representation results in considerable parsimony of encoding. Further, the employment of distinct alphabets at different structural levels enables an encoding in terms of proximal relationships, so that the principle of proximity is upheld (see Chapter 4).

A more complex musical example is shown on Fig. 11 and is represented as on three structural levels as follows:

$$A = (*,4p)b_{tr}$$
$$B = (*,n,p)b_{tr}$$
$$S = A[pr](B,4(*))[inv,5pr](B,(*))D_5$$

So far we have considered the processing of a single melodic line. However, tonal music generally involves several such lines, and even where only one is presented a harmonic progression is often implied. It is assumed that such progressions may also be encoded in hierarchical fashion. The use of parallel linear sequences, which must themselves combine to form an acceptable harmonic sequence, places constraints on the choice of elements in each sequence, and this in turn serves to reduce processing load.

The present model may be related to characterizations of hierarchical structure in tonal music advanced by music theorists. The most important development in this field is that of Heinrich Schenker (1868–1935), who proposed a hierarchical system for tonal music that has points of similarity with the system proposed by Chomsky for linguistics (Chomsky, 1963). On Schenker's system music is considered as a hierarchy in which pitch events at any one level are considered "prolonged" by sequences of pitch events at the next-lower level. Three basic levels are distinguished in the system. First, there is the surface representation or *foreground*; second, there is the *middleground*; and third, there is the *background* or *Ursatz*. The *Ursatz* is itself considered a prolongation of the triad. For literature on Schenkerian analysis and related theoretical formulations, see particularly Lerdahl and Jackendorff (1977), Meyer (1973), Narmour (1977), Salzer (1962), and Schenker (1956,1973) and Yeston (1977).

V. MEMORY SYSTEMS

We assume that separate memory systems exist for retaining information at different levels of abstraction. Craik and Lockhart (1972) have made the general argument that the higher the level of abstraction, or "depth of processing" of information, the longer its persistence in memory. This may indeed be true of music. It is clear from general experience that memory for melodic and harmonic intervals persists for considerably longer than memory for absolute pitch values (Deutsch, 1969; Attneave & Olson, 1971); memory for higher order abstractions may well persist for longer still. Such differences in the persistence of memory would have the consequence that when retention of a musical sequence is examined following different time periods, it is likely to reflect different forms of encoding.

In previous sections we have examined the question of encoding in detail, and we now turn to a consideration of the influences acting on information in storage. This question has been explored in depth for the system retaining absolute pitch values, and a little is also known about the system retaining interval information, and the system retaining higher level abstractions.

A. The System Retaining Absolute Pitch Information

When listeners make pitch comparison judgments between tones that are separated by a silent retention interval, accuracy declines gradually as the retention interval is lengthened (Koester, 1945; Harris, 1952; Bachem, 1954; Wickelgren, 1966, 1969). However, the rate of memory deterioration here is very slow. For example, Harris (1952) found that following a retention interval of 15 sec, a difference of a small fraction of a semitone could still be reliably discriminated. This stands in sharp contrast to comparison performance when a sequence of extra tones is interpolated during the retention interval. In an experiment by Deutsch (1970a), listeners were selected for obtaining a score of 100% correct in comparing tone pairs that were separated by a six-second retention interval. The test tones were either identical in pitch or they differed by a semitone. When eight extra tones were then interpolated during this interval, the error rate rose to 40%, even though the listeners were instructed to ignore the interpolated tones. In a further experiment by Deutsch (1970b), this performance decrement was shown not to be due to attention distraction nor to a general memory overload, since only a minimal decrement occurred when spoken numbers were interpolated instead. This was true even when the subjects were simultaneously required to recall the interpolated numbers. It was concluded that pitch memory is subject to interference caused specifically by other tones.

Further experiments demonstrated that tones interact with each other in memory in an orderly and systematic fashion. Such interactions were shown to be a function of both the pitch relationships between the interacting tones and their closeness in serial position.

In one experiment, the effect of a tone that formed part of a sequence interpolated between two test tones was studied as a function of its pitch relationship to the first test tone (Deutsch, 1972b). Subjects compared the pitches of two tones that were separated by a five-second retention interval during which a sequence of six extra tones was interpolated. The test tones were taken from the 12-tone chromatic scale, and ranged from Middle C to the B above. In half of the sequences the test tones were identical in pitch; in the other half they differed by a semitone. The pitches of the intervening tones were also taken from the 12-tone chromatic scale and ranged from the F♯ below Middle C to the F an octave and a half above. The tones were chosen at random from this range with certain restrictions.[5]

The experiment consisted of eight conditions. In all conditions but the last, a tone whose pitch bore a critical relationship to the pitch of the first test tone was placed in the second serial position of the intervening sequence. The relationship between the critical intervening tone and the first test tone varied between identity to a whole-tone separation. A unique value of pitch separation was incorporated in each of the seven conditions, these values being placed at equal intervals of 1/6 tone within this whole tone range. However, in the eighth condition, the pitch of the tone in the second serial position was chosen in the same way as were the other pitches in the intervening sequence. This last ("null") condition therefore provided a baseline against which the effects of the critical interpolated tone could be evaluated.

It was found that the effect of the critical interpolated tone on memory for the test tone varied systematically as a function of their pitch relationship. When the critical interpolated tone was identical in pitch to the first test tone, memory facilitation occurred. With increasing pitch separation between the first test tone and the critical interpolated tone, the error rate rose progressively; it peaked at a separation of 2/3 tone and declined to baseline at roughly a whole tone separation.

Further experiments have reinforced and elaborated on these findings of specific interactions within the pitch memory system. One study investigated the effects of including in an intervening sequence a tone that was a semitone removed from the first test tone (Deutsch, 1973b). It was found that when the test tones were identical in pitch, including in the intervening sequence a tone that was either a semitone higher or a semitone lower, an increase in errors resulted. When both a tone a semitone higher and also a tone a semitone lower were included in the intervening sequence, a substantially greater increase in errors occurred than when only one of these was included. Further, when the test tones differed in pitch by a semitone, including in the intervening sequence a tone that was identical in pitch to the second test tone; there was a substantial increase in errors. An increase in errors that was however significantly smaller also occurred when the critical intervening tone was a semitone removed from the first test tone, but on the opposite side of the pitch continuum to the second test tone. When both of these tones were included in the same intervening sequence, a significantly greater increase in errors was produced than when only one of these was included.

This experiment demonstrated at least two separable disruptive effects in pitch memory. First, the inclusion of a tone that was a semitone removed from the tone to be remembered produced a small but significant disruptive effect which cumulated in size when two such tones, one higher and the other lower than this tone, were both included. Second, a significantly larger disruptive effect occurred when the test tones

---

[5]No sequences contained two tones of the same pitch class. Further, all tones were excluded from any sequence that lay within, and including, a whole tone range in either direction from the first test tone, or that were displaced by an octave from this range. This gap was necessary to prevent the random inclusion of tones in the critical range under study.

differed in pitch and the critical interpolated tone was identical in pitch to the second test tone.

To explain the second (and larger) of these two disruptive effects, the following hypothesis was advanced (Deutsch, 1972c). Memory for the pitch of a tone is laid down simultaneously both on a pitch continuum and also on a temporal or order continuum. As time proceeds, this memory distribution spreads in both directions, but particularly along the temporal continuum. As a result of this spread, when a tone of the same pitch as the second test tone is presented in the interpolated sequence, the subject sometimes concludes that this had been the first test tone. That is, errors of misrecognition result from the subject correctly recognizing that a tone of identical pitch to the second test tone had occurred, but being uncertain when it had occurred.

This hypothesis, which is described in detail in Deutsch (1972c), gives rise to various predictions. First, we should expect errors of misrecognition to be more numerous when the critical interpolated tone is placed early in the intervening sequence rather than late, since here there would be a greater chance of temporal or order confusion. That is, the closer the critical interpolated tone is to the first test tone, the more difficult it should be to discriminate their two positions along a temporal or order continuum and so the greater the number of misrecognition errors.

So, in a further experiment subjects made pitch recognition judgments between tone pairs that were separated by a sequence of six interpolated tones. In sequences where the test tones differed in pitch, a tone that was identical in pitch to the second test tone was sometimes placed in the second serial position of the intervening sequence, sometimes in the fifth serial position, and sometimes no such tone was included. It was found that the critical interpolated tone produced an increase in errors at both serial positions compared with sequences containing no such tone; however, the effect was much more pronounced when the critical tone was placed early in the intervening sequence rather than late (Deutsch, 1975b). This finding therefore corroborated the hypothesis.

Also in this experiment, in sequences where the test tones were identical in pitch, the effect was studied of including a tone that was a semitone removed from the test tone, as a function of its serial position in the interpolated sequence. No serial position effect was here found. So it seems that the first source of disruption, in contrast, does not depend on the serial position of the critical interpolated tone.

Given this large serial position effect based on interpolating a tone of identical pitch to the second test tone, we can ask whether this is due to a deterioration of information along a temporal continuum, or whether this effect is a function of order rather than time. An experiment was performed to investigate this question. Subjects compared the pitches of two tones that were separated by a sequence of six interpolated tones. In sequences where the test tones differed in pitch, a tone identical to the second test tone was placed either in the second serial position of the intervening sequence, or in the fifth serial position, or no such tone was interpolated. The experiment studied the effect of lengthening the pause following the first test tone, and also of lengthening the pause preceding the second test tone. The different temporal conditions are shown on Fig. 12. Now if this serial position effect were due simply to

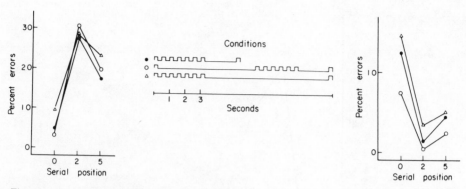

Fig. 12. Temporal parameters used in two experiments investigating the effects of unfilled delays on pitch recognition. Graph on left plots error rates in sequences where the test tones differed and a tone whose pitch was identical to the second test tone was placed in the intervening sequence. Graph on right plots error rates in sequences where a tone of identical pitch to the first test tone was interpolated. Numbers 2 and 5 indicate that the critical tone was placed in the second and fifth serial positions of the intervening sequence, respectively; "0" indicates that no such tone was interpolated.

interactions along a temporal continuum, we should expect substantial changes in the shape of the effect to result from such temporal manipulations. However, as shown on Fig. 14, the serial effect occurred under all temporal conditions. It would appear, therefore, that this deterioration of information takes place along an order continuum, which is not sensitive to temporal variations, at least in the range investigated here (Deutsch, in preparation).

There is a second prediction from the hypothesis of loss of temporal or order information. Suppose that we plotted errors precisely as a function of the pitch relationship between the first test tone and a critical interpolated tone, in 1/6 tone steps as described earlier, and we also varied the pitch difference between the two test tones. Then, in sequences where the critical interpolated tone and the second test tone are placed on the same side of the pitch continuum relative to the first test tone, the peak of errors should occur where the critical interpolated tone is identical in pitch to the second test tone. That is, a shift in the pitch of the second test tone, when the pitch of the first test tone is held constant, should result in a parallel shift in the peak of errors produced by the critical interpolated tone.

This prediction was tested in another experiment (Deutsch, 1975b). Here, when the test tones differed in pitch, this difference was either 1/3 tone, 1/2 tone, or 2/3 tone. Errors were plotted as a function of the pitch of a tone placed in the second serial position of an interpolated sequence, whose relationship to the pitch of the first test tone varied in 1/6 tone steps between identity and a whole tone separation. Whenever the second test tone was higher in pitch than the first, the critical interpolated tone was also higher; whenever the second test tone was lower, the critical interpolated tone was also lower. So, when the second test tone and the critical interpolated tone were separated from the first test tone by the same pitch distance, they were also identical in pitch to each other.

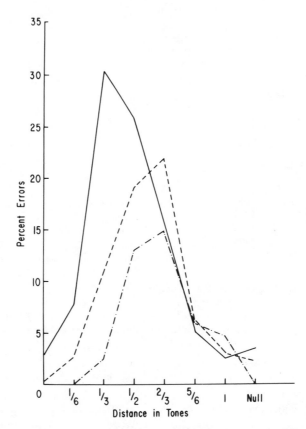

Fig. 13. Percent errors in pitch comparisons in sequences where the test tones differed in pitch, and the critical interpolated tone was placed on the same side of the first test tone along the pitch continuum. Errors were plotted as a function of the pitch relationship between the first test tone and the critical interpolated tone. (—) Test tones separated by 1/3 tone. (---) test tones separated by 1/2 tone. (-·-) test tones separated by 2/3 tone (from Deutsch, 1975b).

The results of this experiment are shown in Fig. 13. It can be seen that when the test tones were 1/3 tone apart, errors peaked when the critical interpolated tone was 1/3 tone removed from the first test tone, and so when it was identical in pitch to the second test tone. Similarly, when the test tones were 2/3 tone apart, errors peaked when the critical interpolated tone was 2/3 tone removed from the first test tone, and so again when it was identical in pitch to the second test tone. So, here a shift in the pitch of the second test tone relative to the first did indeed result in the predicted shift in the peak of errors produced by the critical interpolated tone. But note also that when the first and second test tones were a semitone apart, errors peaked not at a semitone but at 2/3 tone. This can be explained by assuming that the first source of disruption that peaks at 2/3 tone is superimposed on the present source of disruption produced by a relationship of identity or near identity between the second test tone and the critical interpolated tone.

In considering possible bases for this first source of disruption, two points should be noted. The first is that the relative frequency range over which this occurs corresponds well with the range over which centrally acting lateral inhibition has been found in physiological studies of the auditory system (Klinke, Boerger, & Gruber, 1969, 1970). Second, we can remember that the error rate cumulates when two such disruptive tones are interpolated, placed one on either side of the test tone along the pitch continuum (Deutsch, 1973b). There is an analogy here with lateral inhibitory interactions found in systems handling sensory information at the incoming level, where there is a cumulation of inhibition from stimuli placed on either side of the test stimulus (Ratliff, 1965). Evidence for lateral inhibition has been found in the system that handles pitch information at the incoming level (Carterette, Friedman, & Lovell, 1969, 1970; Houtgast, 1972). It was therefore theorized that elements of the pitch memory system are arranged as a recurrent lateral inhibitory network, analogous to those found in systems handling incoming sensory information. Elements of this system are activated by tones of specific pitch, and are organized tonotopically on a log frequency continuum (Deutsch & Feroe, 1975.)

Now, if this were so, we might hope to obtain an effect which would not be expected on other grounds. It has been found in physiological studies of peripheral receptors that when a unit that is inhibiting a neighboring unit is itself inhibited by a third unit, this releases the originally inhibited unit from inhibition. This phenomenon is known as disinhibition. Applying this to our present situation, we might expect that if a tone that was inhibiting memory for another tone were itself inhibited by a third tone, this could cause memory for the first tone to return. More specifically, in sequences where the test tones are identical in pitch, if two critical tones were interpolated—one always 2/3 tone removed from the first test tone and the other further removed along the pitch continuum—then the error rate should vary systematically as a function of the pitch relationship between the two critical interpolated tones. The error rate should be highest when these two tones are identical in pitch, decline as the second critical tone moves away from the first, dip maximally at a 2/3 tone separation, and then return to baseline. The curve produced should therefore be roughly the inverse of the curve plotting the original disruptive effect.

Accordingly, the following experiment was performed. Subjects compared the pitches of two test tones, which were separated by a sequence of six interpolated tones. A tone which was 2/3 tone removed from the first test tone was always placed in the second serial position of the interpolated sequence. Errors were then plotted as a function of the pitch of a further tone, which was placed in the fourth serial position, whose relationship to the tone in the second serial position varied in 1/6 tone steps between identity and a whole-tone separation. As can be seen in Fig. 14, a systematic return of memory was indeed obtained. The error rate in sequences where the second critical interpolated tone was identical in pitch to the first was significantly higher than baseline; further, the error rate where the two critical interpolated tones were separated by 2/3 tone was significantly lower than baseline. A first-order inhibitory function was also obtained experimentally, using subjects selected on the same criterion as for the disinhibition study. This function was then used to calculate the

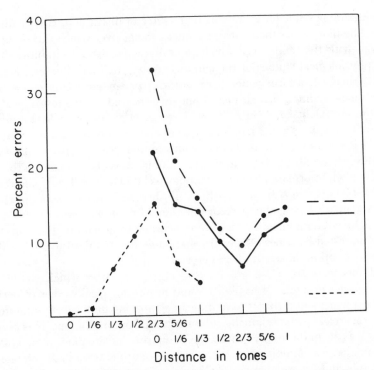

Fig. 14. Percent errors in pitch recognition obtained experimentally and predicted theoretically. Open triangles display percent errors in a baseline experiment that varied the pitch relationship between a test tone and a critical interpolated tone. (The open triangle at the right displays percent errors where no tones were interpolated in the critical range under study.) Filled circles display percent errors in an experiment where a tone that was 2/3 tone removed from the test tone was always interpolated. Errors are plotted as a function of the pitch relationship between this tone and a second critical interpolated tone that was further removed along the pitch continuum. Open circles display percent errors for the same experimental conditions predicted theoretically from the lateral inhibition model. (Filled and open circles at the right display percent errors obtained experimentally and assumed theoretically where no further critical tone was interpolated (from Deutsch & Feroe, 1975).

theoretical disinhibition function. As shown in Fig. 13, there is a good correspondence between the disinhibition function derived experimentally and that derived theoretically. This experiment provides strong evidence that pitch memory elements are indeed arranged as a lateral inhibitory network, analogous to those handling incoming sensory information.

1. Octave Generalization Effects

So far we have been considering interactions in memory between tones that are separated by less than an octave. We can now ask whether these effects take place along an array that is organized simply in terms of pitch, or whether an abstracted octave array, such as hypothesized on pp. 275–276, is also involved.

In one experiment (Deutsch, 1973a), subjects compared the pitches of two tones that were separated by a sequence of six interpolated tones. This experiment studied the effects of including in the interpolated sequence tones that bore the same relationships to the test tones as had been found earlier to produce disruption, but that were further displaced by an octave. In sequences where the test tones were identical in pitch, the effects were studied of interpolating two tones, one a semitone higher than the test tone and the other a semitone lower, except that the critical tones were also displaced an octave up or down. In sequences where the test tones differed, the effects were investigated of interpolating a tone of the same pitch as the second test tone, but that was also displaced an octave up or down. It was found that a substantial generalization of disruptive effect occurred from tones placed in the higher octave, and a weaker effect occurred from tones placed in the lower octave. However, the error rate was greatest when the critical tones were placed in the middle octave. From this pattern of results it was concluded that these disruptive effects take place along both a monotonic pitch continuum and also along an abstracted octave array.

2. Memory Consolidation

When a tone of identical pitch to the first test tone is included in an intervening sequence, the effect on memory is facilitatory rather than disruptive. In one experiment, subjects compared the pitches of two tones that were separated by a sequence of interpolated tones. In one condition, four tones were interpolated; in another, six tones were interpolated; in yet another, six tones were again interpolated, with a tone of identical pitch to the first test tone placed in the second serial position of the interpolated sequence. It was found that the error rate was lowest in sequences where the pitch of the first test tone was repeated, even compared with sequences containing fewer interpolated tones. We can conclude that the pitch memory system is subject to consolidation through repetition (Deutsch, 1975c).

However, in another experiment it was found that this consolidation effect is very sensitive to the serial position of the repeated tone. Here, subjects made pitch comparison judgments between tone pairs that were separated by a sequence of six interpolated tones. In some sequences a tone of the same pitch as the first test tone was placed in the second serial position of the interpolated sequence; in other sequences such a tone was placed in the fifth serial position; and in yet other sequences no such tone was interpolated. It was found that the facilitation effect was much more pronounced when the repeated tone was in the second serial position than in the fifth; indeed, this effect was statistically significant only for sequences where the repeated tone was in the second serial position (Deutsch, 1975c).

It was hypothesized that this consolidation effect results from the same process as produces the errors of misrecognition discussed above—namely, the spread of memory distribution along a temporal or order continuum. When two such distributions overlap, the overlapping portions sum, resulting in a stronger memory trace (Deutsch, 1972c). This again raises the question of whether this serial position effect is based on temporal factors, or whether it is simply a function of order. One might, for example, hypothesize that temporal proximity determines the amount of consolidation in pitch memory. If this were the case, then interpolating a long pause between the first test tone and the first interpolated tone should substantially reduce the consolidation effect. Alternatively, one might hypothesize that some mechanism tags the incoming stimuli in terms of order, and that consolidation takes place along such an order continuum, independent of temporal variations.

An experiment was therefore carried out to evaluate the effects of varying temporal parameters on the memory consolidation effect. Subjects compared the pitches of two tones that were separated by a sequence of six interpolated tones. A tone that was identical in pitch to the first test tone was placed either in the second serial position of the intervening sequence, or in the fifth serial position, or no such tone was included. The experiment studied the effect of lengthening the pause following the first test tone, and also of lengthening the pause preceding the second test tone. The different temporal conditions together with their error rates are shown on Fig. 12. These temporal manipulations did not significantly alter the consolidation effect as a function of serial position. It appears, therefore, that within this temporal range, consolidation takes place along a continuum that is organized in terms of order independent of time (Deutsch, in preparation).

B. The System Retaining Interval Information

We now briefly consider the influences acting on interval information in storage. Deutsch (1975d) proposed that memory for such information is based on a continuum whose elements are activated by the simultaneous or successive presentation of pairs of tones. Tone pairs that stand in the same ratio project onto the same elements and so onto the same point along the continuum; tone pairs standing in closely similar ratios project onto adjacent points; and so on. It was further hypothesized that interactive effects take place along this continuum that are analogous to those that occur within the system retaining absolute pitch values. Such effects would include consolidation through repetition and similarity-based interference.

An experiment was performed to test this hypothesis (Deutsch, 1978b). Subjects compared the pitches of two test tones that were both accompanied by tones of lower pitch. The test tones were either identical in pitch or they differed by a semitone. However, the tone accompanying the first test tone was always identical in pitch to the tone accompanying the second test tone. Thus, when the test tones were identical, the intervals formed by the test tone combinations were also identical. And when the test tones differed, the intervals formed by the test tone combinations also differed.

The test tone combinations were separated by a sequence of six interpolated tones. The tones in the second and fourth serial positions of the interpolated sequence were also accompanied by tones of lower pitch. It was found that when the intervals formed by the interpolated combinations were identical in size to the interval formed by the first test tone combination, the error rate was lower than when the sizes of the intervals formed by the interpolated combinations were chosen at random. Further, when the intervals formed by the interpolated combinations differed in size by a semitone from the interval formed by the first test tone combination, the error rate was higher than when the sizes of the intervals formed by the interpolated combinations were chosen at random.

This experiment, therefore, demonstrates the presence of both consolidation through repetition and also similarity-based interference in memory for harmonic intervals. This indicates that the system retaining such information is similar in organization to the system retaining absolute pitch values.

C. Interactions between These Systems

So far we have examined interactions that take place within a given memory system. We now turn to a consideration of how the outputs of the different systems interact in determining memory judgments. First, we examine ways in which abstracted information influences judgments of absolute pitch values. Then, we consider how information in the pitch memory system might in turn influence memory for pitch abstractions.

Since relational information is retained in parallel with pitch information, we might expect that judgments of sameness or difference in the pitches of two test tones would be biased by a sameness or difference in the relational context in which these test tones are placed. This possibility was investigated by Deutsch and Roll (1974). Subjects compared the pitches of two tones that were both accompanied by tones of lower pitch. The test tone combinations were separated by a retention interval during which six extra tones were interpolated. In some conditions the harmonic intervals formed by the test tone combinations were identical, and in others they differed; and these patterns of relationship were present both when the test tones were identical in pitch and also when these differed. It was found that relational context had a strong influence on pitch recognition judgments. When the test tones were identical but were placed in different relational contexts, there resulted an increased tendency for their pitches to be judged as different. Further, when the test tones differed in pitch, but were placed in an identical relational context, there resulted an increased tendency for their pitches to be judged as identical. It was further found that when the test tones differed, and the test tone combinations formed intervals that were inversions of each other, there also resulted an increase in errors of misrecognition. It was concluded that this misrecognition effect was based on the perceptual equivalence of the inverted intervals.

Deutsch (in press) performed an analogous experiment to study the effect of melodic relational context. Subjects compared the pitches of two tones that were each preceded by tones of lower pitch. The test-tone combinations were again separated by a retention interval during which six extra tones were interpolated. A strong effect of melodic context was demonstrated, analogous to that found for harmonic relational context.

Melodic relationships have been shown to influence pitch recognition judgments in another way. In listening to sequences, we process not only the individual tones, but also the melodic intervals between them. These intervals then provide a framework of pitch relationships to which the test tones can be anchored. Interpolated sequences forming melodic configurations that are more easily processed should then be associated with enhanced performance.

As described in Chapter 4, there is considerable evidence that melodic sequences are processed more effectively when these are composed of intervals of smaller size rather than larger (reflecting the operation of the principle of Proximity). One would therefore expect that interpolated sequences composed of smaller melodic intervals should be associated with higher performance levels than interpolated sequences composed of larger intervals. In an experiment by Deutsch (1978a), subjects compared the pitches of two tones that were separated by a sequence of six interpolated tones. Performance was studied under four conditions. In Condition 1 the interpolated tones were chosen at random from within a one-octave range, and they were ordered at random. Condition 2 was identical to Condition 1 except that the interpolated tones were arranged in monotonically ascending or descending order, with the result that the average size of the melodic intervals in the sequence was reduced. In Condition 3 the interpolated tones were chosen at random from within a two-octave range and were also ordered at random. Condition 4 was identical to Condition 3 except that the interpolated tones were arranged in monotonically ascending or descending order.

As shown on Fig. 15, the error rate was found to increase with an increase in the average size of the melodic intervals comprising the sequence. There was no evidence that monotonic ordering of the interpolated tones had any effect (apart from producing a smaller average interval size), though this might have been hypothesized from the principle of Good Continuation (see Chapter 4).

It has been shown that there is a striking cross-cultural tendency for the frequency of occurrence of a melodic interval to be inversely correlated with its size (Ortmann, 1926; Merriam, 1964; Fucks, 1962; Dowling, 1967; Jeffries, 1974; Deutsch, 1978d).

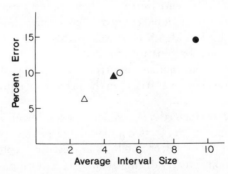

Fig. 15. Percent errors in pitch comparisons as a function of the average size of melodic interval in the sequence. Interpolated tones span a one-octave range: ▲ tones ordered at random; ● tones ordered monotonically. Interpolated tones span a two-octave range: ● tones ordered at random; O tones ordered monotonically (from Deutsch, 1978c).

One might hypothesize that this tendency is based on an increasing difficulty in the processing of melodic intervals as the sizes of these intervals increase. As indicated from the present experiment, this should in turn result in decreased accuracy in pitch recognition.

Two related studies should here be cited. Deutsch (1974) had subjects compare the pitches of two test tones that were separated by a sequence of eight interpolated tones. In one condition the interpolated tones were all drawn from the same octave as the test tones. In a second condition the interpolated tones were all drawn from the octave higher. In a third condition they were all drawn from the octave lower. In a fourth condition half of the interpolated tones were drawn from the octave higher than the test tones and the other half from the octave lower, the order of octave placement being random. It was found that when the interpolated tones were drawn from a single adjacent octave, the error rate was lower than when they were all drawn from the same octave. However, when the interpolated tones were drawn from both the octave higher and also the octave lower, the error rate was highest of all. In this last condition the average size of the intervals formed by successive tones in the sequence was considerably larger than in the other conditions, and it was concluded that these large jumps made it very difficult to make use of the melodic information in the interpolated sequence.

Another related study is that of Olson and Hanson (1977). They found, using several different paradigms, that increased errors in pitch recognition were associated with an increased pitch distance between the test tones and the interpolated tones. Since only three interpolated tones were used in this study, this increased pitch distance resulted in a significant increase in average interval size. These authors suggest an interpretation of their results that is very similar to the present line of reasoning.

Evidence for interactions based on more complex encodings has also been obtained. Krumhansl (1979) required subjects to compare the pitches of two test tones that were separated by a sequence of interpolated tones. Some of the sequences were constructed so as to suggest a tonality. It was found that for such sequences, when the first test tone was in the same scale as the interpolated tones, recognition performance was better than when it was outside this scale.

We should expect that interactions taking place within the pitch memory system would in turn affect memory for abstracted information. For example, given the memory consolidation effect produced by a repeated tone (Deutsch, 1975c), we should expect that sequences containing repeated tones would be better remembered, even in abstracted form, than sequences not containing repeated tones. Similarly, given the large disruptive effect produced by interpolating two tones, one a semitone higher than the tone to be remembered and the other a semitone lower (Deutsch, 1973b), we should expect that music composed in scales consisting mostly of semitonal steps would be more difficult to remember than music composed in scales consisting mostly of whole tone steps.

Erickson (1978) has argued that low-level effects, such as described here, have probably exerted a strong influence on the evolution of music systems. For example, it appears true cross-culturally that musical sequences tend to contain one or two tones that are repeated considerably more often than others. In our tonal system, for example, the first tone of the scale (the tonic) has this property. Given the finding of consolidation through repetition, we should expect that such repeated tones should be particularly well remembered. Second, it appears true cross-culturally that small melodic intervals occur considerably more often than large ones. We have also seen that recognition of the pitch of a tone is better in the context of a sequence consisting of small melodic intervals rather than of large ones (Deutsch, 1978c). When we consider these two low-order effects together, we can see that a considerable processing advantage is to be gained from a system in which there are a limited number of anchor tones—which are well remembered through repetition—surrounded by satellite tones which are linked to these anchor tones by pitch proximity. Thus, examination of these low-order effects enables us to develop an understanding of why musical systems have evolved as they did. Such systems should therefore not be considered as arbitrary sets of rules but rather as reflecting constraints imposed by our processing mechanisms.

D. Memory for Hierarchically Structured Tonal Sequences

We now turn to a consideration of memory for tonal information which is projected onto highly overlearned pitch alphabets, and which is organized in hierarchical fashion. Deutsch and Feroe (1981) have proposed that, at this level, tonal sequences are coded and retained as hierarchies of structures, each of which is associated with a given pitch alphabet. It is further proposed that such structures are encoded and retained as chunks, along with their associated alphabets and rules of combination. If this model is correct, then sequences that may be parsimoniously represented according to its rules should be better retained than those where such parsimonious representation is not possible.

An experiment was performed as a test of this hypothesis (Deutsch, 1980, 1981). In this experiment a second factor was also considered. It has been found in studies using strings of verbal materials that we tend to recall such strings in accordance with their temporal grouping (Mueller & Schumann, 1894; McLean & Gregg, 1967; Bower & Winzenz, 1969). This effect can be so powerful as to mask grouping by meaning, and so to obliterate the advantage incurred by such grouping (Bower & Springston, 1970). Analogous results have been obtained using nonverbal materials (Restle, 1972; Handel, 1973; Dowling, 1973). It was therefore expected that temporal grouping would have a strong effect on recall of these sequences also. Grouping in accordance with tonal structure was expected to result in enhanced performance, and grouping in conflict with tonal structure to give rise to performance decrements.

The experiment employed the following paradigm. Musically trained subjects were presented with sequences which they recalled in musical notation. The sequences employed are shown in Fig. 16. It can be seen that those in Fig. 16A each consisted of a higher level subsequence of four elements that acted on a lower level subsequence of

Fig. 16.   Sequences used in first experiment to study utilization of structure in recall. See text for details (from Deutsch, 1981).

three elements. The sequences in Fig. 16B cannot be represented in this parsimonious fashion. These eight sequences were each presented in three temporal configurations, which are illustrated in Fig. 17. In the first configuration (a), the tones were spaced at equal intervals; in the second (b), they occurred in four groups of three, so that segmentation was in accordance with tonal structure; in the third (c), they occurred in three groups of four so that segmentation was in conflict with tonal structure.

Table I shows the percentages of tones correctly recalled in their correct serial positions in the different conditions of the experiment. Large effects of tonal structure and temporal segmentation are apparent. For structured sequences that were segmented in accordance with tonal structure, the performance level was extremely high. For structured sequences that were unsegmented, the performance level was slightly lower, though still very high. However, for structured sequences that were segmented in conflict with tonal structure, the performance level was much lower. For unstructured sequences the performance level was considerably lower than for structured sequences that were segmented in accordance with tonal structure or that were

Fig. 17.   Types of temporal segmentation employed in first experiment to study utilization of structure in recall. a. Sequence unsegmented. b. Sequence segmented in groups of three, so that segmentation was in accordance with structure. c. Sequence segmented in groups of four, so that segmentation was in conflict with structure.

TABLE I

Utilization of Structure in Recall: Percent Correct Recall of Tones in Correct Serial Positions
in Experiment 1[a]

Condition	Percent correct
Sequences structured in groups of 3	
OS. Not temporally segmented	93.5
3S. Temporally segmented in groups of 3	99.3
4S. Temporally segmented in groups of 4	69.2
Sequences unstructured	
OU. Not temporally segmented	52.0
3U. Temporally segmented in groups of 3	63.2
4U. Temporally segmented in groups of 4	62.3

[a]From Deutsch (1981).

unsegmented, but in the same range as for structured sequences that were segmented
in conflict with tonal structure.

The serial position curves for the different conditions of the experiment are shown
on Fig. 18. Typical bow-shaped curves are apparent, and in addition, discontinuities
can be seen at the boundaries between temporal groups. This provides further evidence that temporal groups tend to be encoded as chunks and to be retained or lost
independently. This type of configuration is very similar to that obtained by others
with the use of verbal materials (Bower & Winzenz, 1969).

The transition shift probability (TSP) provides a further measure of interitem
association. This is defined as the joint probability of either an error following a
correct response on the previous item or of a correct response following an error on
the previous item (Bower & Springston, 1970). If groups of elements tend to be
retained or lost as chunks, we should expect the TSP values to be smaller for transitions within a chunk and to be larger for the transition into the first element of a
chunk. The TSP values for sequences segmented in temporal groups of three and four
are shown in Fig. 19A and B, respectively. It can be seen that the TSPs are larger on
the first element of each temporal group than on the other elements. This is as
expected on the hypothesis that temporal groups serve to define subjective chunks
that are retained or lost independently of each other.

Finally, a very strong sensitivity to musical alphabet was demonstrated in this
experiment. As shown in Fig. 16, four sequences employed only a triadic alphabet,
two employed a diatonic alphabet, and two employed other tones from the 12-tone
chromatic scale. Of the 12 subjects who participated in the experiment, 6 remained
entirely within the alphabet of the sequence they were notating. (For example, in
notating sequences 2, 4, 6, and 8, all their incorrect responses, as well as their correct
ones, were G, B, or D.) Of the remaining six subjects, five made between them a total
of only 15 responses that departed from the alphabet presented. This implies that the
subjects were retaining information concerning alphabet independently of structure.

Now in this experiment, the structured sequences all consisted of a higher level

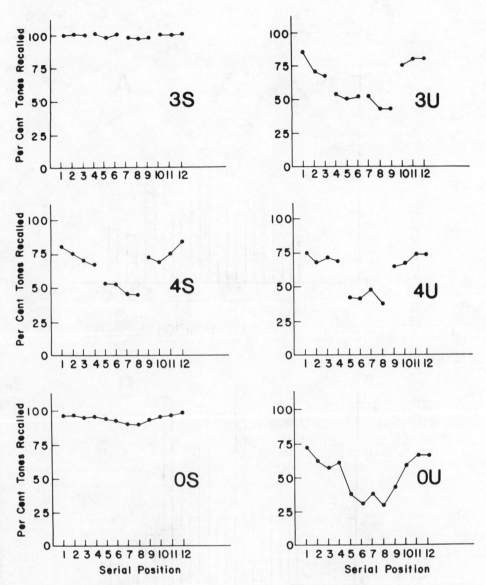

Fig. 18. Serial position curves for the different conditions of the first experiment to study utilization of structure in recall (from Deutsch, 1981).

subsequence of four elements that acted on a lower level subsequence of three elements. So compatible segmentation was always in groups of three and incompatible segmentation in groups of four. One might therefore argue that the enhanced performance found for structured sequences was due simply to an advantage conferred by the size of temporal group. A second experiment was designed to control for this.

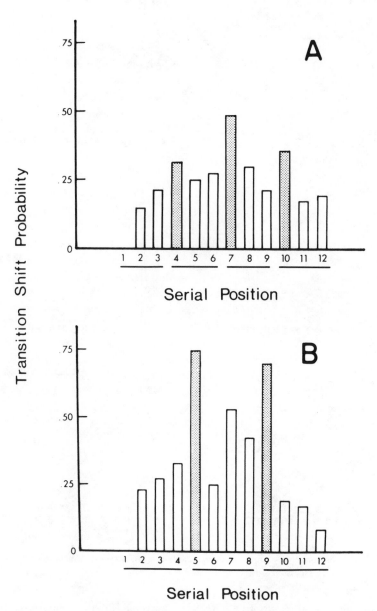

Fig. 19. (A) Transition shift probabilities for sequences segmented in temporal groups of three. (B) Transition shift probabilities for sequences segmented in temporal groups of four (from Deutsch, 1981).

Fig. 20. Sequences used in second experiment to study utilization of structure in recall. See text for details (from Deutsch, 1981).

Two types of tonal structure were employed, and these are shown in Fig. 20. In the first, shown in Fig. 20A, a higher level subsequence of four elements acted on a lower level subsequence of three elements. In the second, shown in Fig. 20B, a higher level subsequence of three elements acted on a lower level subsequence of four elements. Enhanced performance was expected where the number of elements in the lower level subsequence corresponded to the number within a temporal group, compared with sequences where these numbers did not correspond. In addition, segmentation in groups of two was examined. It was expected that where the lower level subsequence consisted of three elements, such segmentation would result in considerable performance decrements since it would conflict with tonal structure. However, where the lower level subsequence consisted of four elements, segmentation in group of two would be less disruptive since pauses would still be placed between tonal groups.

There were, therefore, six conditions in the experiment, shown in Table II. Also shown are the percentages of tones correctly recalled in their correct serial positions in these different conditions. It can be seen that performance levels were considerably lower when temporal segmentation was in conflict with structure. When pauses were

TABLE II

Utilization of Structure in Recall:
Percent Correct Recall of Tones in Correct Serial Positions in Experiment 2[a]

Condition	Percent correct
Sequences structured in groups of 3	
3–2. Temporally segmented in groups of 2	45.4
3–3. Temporally segmented in groups of 3	93.1
3–4. Temporally segmented in groups of 4	50.6
Sequences structured in groups of 4	
4–2. Temporally segmented in groups of 2	80.8
4–3. Temporally segmented in groups of 3	52.9
4–4. Temporally segmented in groups of 4	85.4

[a] From Deutsch (1981).

placed both between and within tonal groups (that is Condition 4-2), the performance level was slightly lower than when the pauses were placed only between groups, but considerably higher than when the pauses conflicted with tonal structure. The interaction between size of tonal unit and size of temporal unit was highly significant, reflecting the damaging effect of incompatible segmentation.

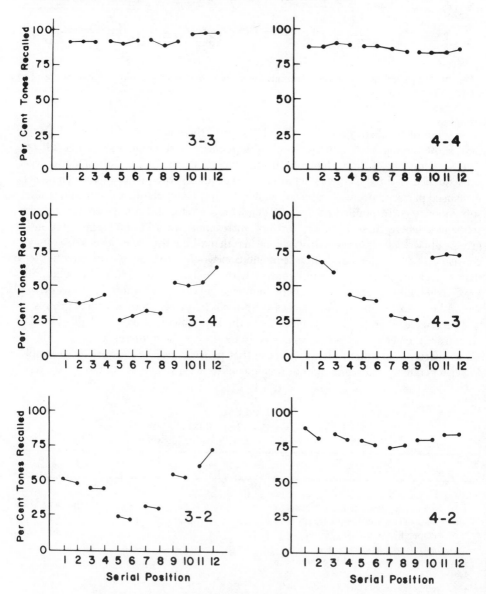

Fig. 21. Serial position curves for the different conditions of the second experiment to study utilization of structure in recall (from Deutsch, 1981).

Figure 21 displays the percentages of tones correctly recalled at each serial position in the different conditions of the experiment. It can be seen that again, discontinuities appear at temporal group boundaries, reflecting the formation of subjective chunks on the basis of temporal proximity.

These two experiments lead to several conclusions. First, they demonstrate that listeners perceive hierarchical structures that are present in tonal sequences and can utilize these structures in recall. For the structured sequences employed in this study, the listener need only retain two .chunks of three or four items each; but for the unstructured sequences no such parsimonious encoding was possible. The unstructured sequences therefore imposed a much heavier memory load, with resultant performance decrements. Second, the experiments demonstrate that temporal segmentation has a profound effect on perceived structure, as has been shown by others with different materials. On our present line of reasoning, when segmentation is in conflict with structure, there results a less parsimonious representation, which in turn leads to decrements in recall.

For example, Sequence 2 in Fig. 20 would be encoded in the absence of temporal segmentation as

$$A = (3n,*)G$$
$$B = (2n,*)G$$
$$S = A[pr]B,G_4$$

However, with temporal segmentation in groups of four, the same sequence would be encoded as

$$A = (2n,*)G_{tr}$$
$$B = (2n,p,*)G$$
$$C = (n,p,n,*)G$$
$$D = (p,2n,*)G$$
$$S = A[pr](B,C,D),G_4$$

Thus, four structures would need to be encoded and retained, together with their alphabets and rules of combination. A much heavier memory load would therefore be imposed.

VI. CONCLUSION

In the foregoing pages, we have considered the rules whereby abstractions based on pitch are formed and also how pitch information is retained at the different levels of abstraction. Where appropriate, we have considered underlying neurophysiological mechanisms, and we have also attempted to draw on insights provided by music theorists. The system that we are dealing with is clearly very complex, but an understanding of its operation is slowly developing.[6]

[6]This work was supported by United States Public Health Service Grant MH-21001.

REFERENCES

Attneave, F., & Olson, R. K. Pitch as a medium: A new approach to psychophysical scaling. *American Journal of Psychology*, 1971, *84*, 147–165.

Babbitt, M. Twelve-tone invariants as compositional determinants. *The Musical Quarterly*, 1960, *46*, 246–259.

Babbitt, M. The structure and function of musical theory. *College Music Symposium 5*, 1965, 10–21.

Bachem, A. Note on Neu's review of the literature on absolute pitch. *Psychological Bulletin*, 1948, *45*, 161–162.

Bachem, A. Time factors in relative and absolute pitch determination. *Journal of the Acoustical Society of America*, 1954, *26*, 751–753.

Baird, J. W. Memory for absolute pitch; Studies in psychology. In *Titchener commemorative volume*. Worcester, 1917. Pp. 69.

Benjamin, W. E. Review of Forte's *The structure of atonal music. Perspectives of New Music*, 1974, *2*, 170–211.

Blackwell, H. R., & Schlosberg, H. Octave generalization, pitch discrimination, and loudness thresholds in the white rat. *Journal of Experimental Psychology*, 1943, *33*, 407–419.

Boomslitter, P., & Creel, W. The long pattern hypothesis in harmony and hearing. *Journal of Music Theory*, 1961, *5*, No. 2, 2–30.

Bower, G. H., & Springston, F. Pauses as recoding points in letter series. *Journal of Experimental Psychology*, 1970, *83*, 421–430.

Bower, G., & Winzenz, D. Group structure, coding and memory for digit series. *Journal of Experimental Psychology Monographs*, 1969, *80*, No. 2, Part 2, 1–17.

Bregman, A. S. The formation of auditory streams. In J. Requin (Ed.), *Attention and performance*. (Volume VII) Hillsdale, New Jersey: Erlbaum, 1978.

Browne, R. Review of *The structure of atonal music* by A. Forte. *Journal of Music Theory*, 1974, *18*, 390–415.

Carterette, E. C., Friedman, M. P., & Lovell, J. D. Mach bands in hearing. *Journal of the Acoustical Society of America*, 1969, *45*, 986–998.

Carterette, E. C., Friedman, M. P., & Lovell, J. D. Mach bands in auditory perception. In R. Plomp & G. F. Smoorenburg (Eds.), *Frequency analysis and periodicity detection in hearing*. Sijthoff: Leiden, 1970.

Chrisman, R. Identification and correlation of pitch-sets. *Journal of Music Theory*, 1971, *15*, 58–83.

Collins, A. M., & Quillian, M. R. How to make a language user. In E. Tulving and W. Donaldson (Eds.). *Organization of memory*. New York: Academic Press, 1972.

Craik, F. I. M., & Lockhart, R. S. Levels of processing: A framework for memory research. *Journal of Verbal Learning and Verbal Behavior*, 1972, *11*, 671–684.

Cuddy, L. L., & Cohen, A. J. Recognition of transposed melodic sequences. *Quarterly Journal of Experimental Psychology*, 1976, *28*, 255–270.

Deese, V., & Grindley, G. C. The transposition of visual patterns. *British Journal of Psychology*, 1947, *37*, 152–163.

Deutsch, D. Music recognition. *Psychological Review*, 1969, *76*, 300–307.

Deutsch, D. The deterioration of pitch information in memory. Unpublished doctoral dissertation, University of California at San Diego, 1970. (a)

Deutsch, D. Tones and Numbers: Specificity of interference in short-term memory. *Science*, 1970, *168*, 1604–1605. (b)

Deutsch, D. Octave generalization and tune recognition. *Perception & Psychophysics*, 1972, *11*, 411–412. (a)

Deutsch, D. Mapping of interactions in the pitch memory store. *Science*, 1972, *175*, 1020–1022. (b)

Deutsch, D. Effect of repetition of standard and comparison tones on recognition memory for pitch. *Journal of Experimental Psychology*, 1972, *93*, 156–162. (c)

Deutsch, D. Octave generalization of specific interference effects in memory for tonal pitch. *Perception & Psychophysics*, 1973, *13*, 271–175. (a)

Deutsch, D. Interference in memory between tones adjacent in the musical scale. *Journal of Experimental Psychology*, 1973, *100*, 228–231. (b)

Deutsch, D. Generality of interference by tonal stimuli in recognition memory for pitch. *Quarterly Journal of Experimental Psychology*, 1974, *26*, 229–234.

Deutsch, D. Musical illusions. *Scientific American*, 1975, *233*, 92–104. (a)

Deutsch, D. The organization of short-term memory for a single acoustic attribute. In D. Deutsch & J. A. Deutsch (Eds.), *Short term memory*. New York: Academic Press, 1975. Pp. 107–151. (b)

Deutsch, D. Facilitation by repetition in recognition memory for tonal pitch. *Memory & Cognition*, 1975, *3*, 263–266. (c)

Deutsch, D. Auditory memory. *Canadian Journal of Psychology*, 1975, *29*, 87–105. (d)

Deutsch, D. Octave equivalence and the processing of melodic sequences. *Journal of the Acoustical Society of America*, 1976, *60*, S94.

Deutsch, D. Memory and attention in music. In M. Critchley & R. A. Henson (Eds.). *Music and the brain*, London: Heinemann, 1977. Pp. 95–130.

Deutsch, D. Octave generalization and melody identification. *Perception & Psychophysics*, 1978, *23*, 91–92. (a)

Deutsch, D. Interactive effects in memory for harmonic intervals. *Perception & Psychophysics*, 1978, *24*, 7–10. (b)

Deutsch, D. Delayed pitch comparisons and the principle of proximity. *Perception & Psychophysics*, 1978, *23*, 227–230. (c)

Deutsch, D. The psychology of music. In E. C. Carterette & M. P. Friedman (Eds.), *Handbook of perception*. (Volume X) New York: Academic Press, 1978. Pp. 191–218. (d)

Deutsch, D. Octave generalization and the consolidation of melodic information. *Canadian Journal of Psychology*, 1979, *33*, 201–204.

Deutsch, D. Recall of hierarchically structured melodic sequences. *Journal of the Acoustical Society of America*, 1980, *67*, 57.

Deutsch, D. The processing of structured and unstructured tonal sequences. *Perception & Psychophysics*, 1981, *28*, 381–389.

Deutsch, D. Facilitation and misrecognition effects in pitch memory as a function of serial position and temporal proximity. In preparation.

Deutsch, D. Effects of melodic context on pitch recognition judgment. *Perception and Psychophysics*, in press.

Deutsch, D., & Feroe, J. Disinhibition in pitch memory. *Perception & Psychophysics*, 1975, *17*, 320–324.

Deutsch, D., and Feroe, J. The internal representation of pitch sequences in tonal music. *Psychological Review*, 1981, *88* 503–522.

Deutsch, D., & Roll, P. L. Error patterns in delayed pitch comparison as a function of relational context. *Journal of Experimental Psychology*, 1974, *103*, 1027–1034.

Deutsch, J. A., & Deutsch, D. *Physiological psychology*. (2nd Ed.) Homewood: Dorsey, 1973.

Dewar, K. M. Context Effects in Recognition Memory for Tones. Unpublished doctoral dissertation. Queens University, Kingston, Ontario, 1974.

Dewar, K. M., Cuddy, C. L., & Mewhort, D. J. K. Recognition memory for single tones with and without context. *Journal of Experimental Psychology: Human Learning and Memory*, 1977, *3*, 60–67.

Divenyi, P. L., & Hirsh, I. J. Some figural properties of auditory patterns. *Journal of the Acoustical Society of America*, 1978, *64*, 1369–1385.

Dowling, W. J. Rhythmic Fission and the Perceptual Organization of Tone Sequences. Unpublished doctoral dissertation, Harvard University, 1967.

Dowling, W. J. Rhythmic groups and subjective chunks in memory for melodies. *Perception & Psychophysics*, 1973, *4*, 37–40.

Dowling, W. J. Scale and contour: Two components of a theory of memory for melodies. *Psychological Review*, 1978, *85*, 342–354.

Dowling, W. J., & Fujitani, D. S. Contour, interval and pitch recognition in memory for melodies. *Journal of the Acoustical Society of America*, 1971, *49*, 524–531.

Dowling, W. J., & Hollombe, A. W. The perception of melodies distorted by splitting into several octaves: Effects of increasing proximity and melodic contour. *Perception & Psychophysics*, 1977, *21*, 60–64.

Drobisch, M. W. *Uber die mathematische Bestimmung der musikalischen*. Intervalle, 1846.

Drobisch, M. W. *Abhandlungen der Sachsischen Wissenchaften math-phys*. C1.B.II. 1855, 35.

Erickson, R. Paper presented to Department of Music, University of California, San Diego, California, 1978.

Ernst, G. W., & Newell, A. *GPS: A Case Study in Generality and Problem Solving.* New York: Academic Press, 1969.

Evans, E. F. Neural processes for the detection of acoustic patterns and for sound localization. In F. O. Schmitt and F. T. Worden (Eds.), *The neurosciences, third study program.* Cambridge, Massachusetts: MIT Press, 1974. Pp. 131–147.

Forte, A. *The structure of atonal music,* New Haven, Connecticut: Yale University Press, 1973.

Francès, R. *La perception de de musique.* Paris, Vrin, 1958.

Fucks, W. Mathematical analysis of the formal structure of music. *Institute of Radio Engineers Transactions on Information Theory,* 1962, *8,* 225–228.

Gagné, R. M. The acquisition of knowledge. *Psychological Review,* 1962, *67,* 355–365.

Garner, W. R. *The processing of information and structure.* Hillsdale, New Jersey: Erlbaum, 1974.

Greeno, J. G., & Simon, H. A. Processes for sequence production. *Psychological Review,* 1974, *81,* 187–196.

Handel, S. Temporal segmentation of repeating auditory patterns. *Journal of Experimental Psychology,* 1973, *101,* 46–54.

Hanson, A. R., & Riseman, E. M. (Eds.) *Computer vision systems.* New York: Academic Press, 1978.

Harris, J. D. The decline of pitch discrimination with time. *Journal of Experimental Psychology,* 1952, *43,* 96–99.

Helmholtz, H. Von. *On the sensations of tone as a physiological basis for the theory of music.* (2nd English ed.) New York: Dover, 1954. (Originally published 1859).

Helmholtz, H. Von. The Origin of the Correct Interpretations of our Sensory impressions. *Zeitchrift für Psychologie und Physiologie der Sinnesorgane* 1894, *7,* 81–96.

Houtgast, T. Psychophysical evidence for lateral inhibition in hearing. *Journal of the Acoustical Society of America,* 1972, *51,* 1885–1894.

Howe, H. S. Some combinatorial properties of pitch structures. *Journal of Music Theory,* 1965, *4,* 45–61.

Howe, H. S. Review of Forte's *The structure of atonal music. Collectanea,* 1974, 118–124.

Hubel, D. H., & Wiesel, T. N. Receptive fields, binocular interaction and functional architecture in the cat's visual cortex. *Journal of Physiology,* 1962, *160,* 106–154.

Humphreys, L. F. Generalization as a function of method of reinforcement. *Journal of Experimental Psychology,* 1939, *25,* 361–372.

Idson, W. L., & Massaro, D. W. A bidimensional model of pitch in the recognition of melodies. *Perception & Psychophysics,* 1978, *24,* 551–565.

Jeffries, T. B. Relationship of interval frequency count to ratings of melodic intervals. *Journal of Experimental Psychology,* 1974, *102,* 903–905.

Jones, M. R. Cognitive representations of serial patterns. In B. H. Kantowitz (Ed.), *Human information processing: Tutorials in performance and cognition.* Hillsdale, New Jersey: Erlbaum, 1974.

Jones, M. R. Auditory patterns: Studies in the perception of structure. In E. C. Carterette and M. P. Friedman (Eds.), *Handbook of perception.* (Vol. VIII, Perceptual coding) New York: Academic Press, 1978.

Julesz, B., & Hirsh, I. J. Visual and auditory perception—An essay of comparison. In E. E. David and P. B. Denes (Eds.), *Human communication: A unified view.* New York: McGraw-Hill, 1972.

Kallman, H. J., & Massaro, D. W. Tone chroma is functional in melody recognition. *Perception & Psychophysics,* 1979, *26,* 32–36.

Klinke, R., Boerger, G., & Gruber, J. Alteration of afferent, tone-evoked activity of neurons of the cochlear nucleus following acoustic stimulation of the contralateral ear. *Journal of the Acoustical Society of America,* 1969, *45,* 788–789.

Klinke, R., Boerger, G., & Gruber, J. The influence of the frequency relation in dichotic stimulation upon the cochlear nucleus activity. In R. Plomp & G. F. Smoorenburg (Eds.), *Frequency analysis and periodicity detection in hearing.* Sijthoff: Leiden, 1970.

Koester, T. The time error in pitch and loudness discrimination as a function of time interval and stimulus level. *Archives of Psychology,* 1945, *297,* whole issue.

Koffka, K. *Principles of Gestalt psychology.* New York, Harcourt, 1935.

Krumhansl, C. L. The psychological representation of musical pitch in a tonal context. *Cognitive Psychology,* 1979, *11,* 346–374.

Leewenberg, E. L. A perceptual coding language for visual and auditory patterns. *American Journal of Psychology*, 1971, *84*, 307–349.

Lerdahl, F., & Jockendorff, R. Toward a formal theory of music. *Journal of Music Theory* 1977, *21*, No. 2, 111–172.

Lewin, D. The intervallic content of a collection of notes. *Journal of Music Theory*, 1960, *4*, 98–101.

Lewin, D. A theory of segmental association in twelve-tone music. *Perspectives of New Music*, 1962, *1*, 89–116.

Longuet-Higgins, H. C. Letter to a musical friend. *Music Review*, 1962, *23*, 244–248. (a)

Longuet-Higgins, H. C. Second letter to a musical friend. *Music Review*, 1962, *23*, 271–280. (b)

Longuet-Higgins, H. C. The perception of music. *Interdisciplinary Science Reviews*, 1978, *3*, 148–156.

Mach, E. *The analysis of sensations and the relation of the physical to the psychical.* (C. M. Williams, translator; W. Waterlow, review and supplement) New York: Dover, 1959. (Originally published in German, 1906)

McLean, R. S., and Gregg, L. W. Effects of induced chunking on temporal aspects of serial retention. *Journal of Experimental Psychology*, 1967, *74*, 455–459.

Merriam, A. P. *The anthropology of music.* Evanston, Illinois: Northwestern University Press, 1964.

Meyer, L. B. *Emotion and meaning in music.* Chicago, Illinois: University of Chicago Press, 1956.

Meyer, L. B. *Explaining music: Essays and explorations.* Berkeley, California: University of California Press, 1973.

Meyer, M. On the attributes of the sensations. *Psychological Review*, 1904, *11*, 83–103.

Meyer, M. Review of G. Révész, "Zur Grundleguncy der Tonpsychologie." *Psychological Bulletin*, 1914, *11*, 349–352.

Miller, G. A. The magical number seven, plus or minus two: Some limits on our capacity for processing information. *Psychological Review*, 1956, *63*, 81–97.

Miller, G. A., & Chomsky, N. Finitary models of language users. *Handbook of Mathematical Psychology*, 1963, *2*, 419–493.

Miller, G. A., Galanter, E. H., & Pribram, K. H. *Plans and the structure of behavior.* New York: Holt, 1960.

Mueller, G. E., & Schumann, F. Experimentelle Beitrage zur Untersuchung des Gedächtnisses. *Zeitschrift fur Psychologie und Physiologie der Sinnesorgane*, 1894, *6*, 81–190, 257–339.

Narmour, E. *Beyond Schenkerism.* Chicago, Illinois: University of Chicago Press, 1977.

Navon, D. Forest before trees: The precedence of global features in visual perception. *Cognitive Psychology*, 1977, *9*, 353–383.

Nettl, B. *Music in primitive culture.* Cambridge, Massachusetts: Harvard University Press, 1956.

Olson, R. K., & Hanson, V. Interference effects in tone memory. *Memory & Cognition*, 1977, *5*, 32–40.

Ortmann, O. On the melodic relativity of tones. *Psychological Monographs*, 1926, *35*, Whole No. 162.

Palmer, S. E. The effects of contextual scenes on the identification of objects. *Memory and Cognition*, 1975, *3*, 519–526.

Perle, G. *Serial composition and atonality.* (3rd ed.) Berkeley, California: University of California Press, 1972.

Perle, G. *Twelve-tone tonality.* Berkeley, California: University of California Press, 1977.

Piston, W. *Harmony.* (2nd ed.) London: Norton, 1948.

Pitts, W., & McCulloch, W. S. How we know universals. The perception of auditory and visual forms. *Bulletin of Mathematical Biophysics*, 1947, *9*, 127–147.

Plomp, R., Wagenaar, W. A., & Mimpen, A. M. Musical interval recognition with simultaneous tones, *Acustica*, 1973, *29*, 101–109.

Ratliff, F. *Mach bands: Quantitative studies of neural networks in the retina.* San Francisco, California: Holden Day, 1965.

Restle, F. Theory of serial pattern learning: Structural trees. *Psychological Review*, 1970, 77, 481–495.

Restle, F. Serial patterns: The role of phrasing. *Journal of Experimental Psychology*, 1972, *92*, 385–390.

Restle, F., & Brown, E. Organization of serial pattern learning. In G. H. Bower (Ed.), *The psychology of learning and motivation.* (Volume 4) New York: Academic Press, 1970. Pp. 249–331.

Révész, G. *Zur grundleguncy der tonpsychologie.* Leipzig: Feit, 1913.

Ruckmick, C. A. A new classification of tonal qualities. *Psychological Review*, 1929, *36*, 172–180.

Salzer, F. *Structural hearing.* New York: Dover, 1962.

Scandura, J. M. Role of rules in behavior: Toward an operational definition of what (rule) is learned. *Psychological Review*, 1970, 77, 516–533.

Schenker, H. *Neue musikalische theorien und phantasien: Der Freie Satz*. Vienna: Universal Edition, 1956.

Schenker, H. In O. Jonas (Ed. & Annotating), *Harmony*. (E. M. Borgese, Translator). Cambridge, Massachusetts: MIT Press, 1973.

Schoenberg, A. *Style and idea*. London: Williams & Norgate, 1951.

Schoenberg, A. In G. Strong (Ed.), *Fundamentals of musical composition*. New York: St. Martin's Press, 1967.

Shepard, R. N. Circularity in judgments of relative pitch. *Journal of the Acoustical Society of America*, 1964, 36, 2345–2353.

Simon, H. A. Complexity and the representation of patterned sequences of symbols. *Psychological Review*, 1972, 79, 369–382.

Simon, H. A., & Kotovsky, K. Human acquisition of concepts for sequential patterns. *Psychological Review*, 1963, 70, 534–546.

Simon, H. A., & Sumner, R. K. Pattern in music. In B. Kleinmuntz (Ed.), *Formal representation of human judgment*. New York: Wiley, 1968.

Suga, N., O'Neill, W. E., & Manabe, T. Harmonic-sensitive neurons in the auditory cortex of the mustache bat. *Science*, 1979, 203, 270–274.

Suga, N., & P. H-S. Jen. Disproportionate tonotopic representation for processing CF-FM sonar signals in the mustache bat auditory cortex. *Science*, 1976, 194, 542–544.

Teitelbaum, R. Intervallic relations in atonal music. *Journal of Music Theory*, 1965, 9, 72–127.

Van Noorden, L. P. A. S. Temporal coherence in the perception of tone sequences. Unpublished doctoral thesis. Technische Hogeschool, Eindhoven, Holland, 1975.

Vitz, P. C., & Todd, T. C. A model of learning for simple repeating binary patterns. *Journal of Experimental Psychology*, 1967, 75, 108–117.

Vitz, P. C., & Todd, T. C. A coded element model of the perceptual processing of sequential stimuli. *Psychological Review*, 1969, 76, 433–449.

Von Ehrenfels, C. *Uber Gestaltqualitäten Vierteljahrschrift fur Wissenschaftliche Philosophie*, 1890, 14, 249–292.

Warren, R. M., & Warren, R. P. *Helmholtz on perception: Its physiology and development*. New York: Wiley, 1968.

Werner, H. Uber Mikromelodik und Mikroharmonik. *Zeitschrift fur Psychologie*, 1925, 98, 74–89.

Wever, E. G., & Bray, C. W. The nature of the acoustic response; the relation between sound frequency and frequency of impulses in the auditory nerve. *Journal of Experimental Psychology*, 1930, 13, 373–387.

White, B. Recognition of distorted melodies. *American Journal of Psychology*, 1960, 73, 100–107.

Wickelgren, W. A. Consolidation and retroactive interference in short-term recognition memory for pitch. *Journal of Experimental Psychology*, 1966, 72, 250–259.

Wickelgren, W. A. Associative strength theory of recognition memory for pitch. *Journal of Mathematical Psychology*, 1969, 6, 13–61.

Winston, P. H. Learning to identify toy block structures. In R. L. Solo (Ed.), *Contemporary issues in cognitive psychology: the Loyola Symposium*. Washington, D. C.: Winston, 1973.

Yeston, M. (Ed.) *Readings in Schenker analysis and other approaches*. New Haven, Connecticut: Yale University Press, 1977.

Yngve, V. A model and an hypothesis for language structure. *Proceedings of the American Philosophical Society*, 1960, 104, 444–466.

10

Melodic Processes and the Perception of Music

Burton S. Rosner and Leonard B. Meyer

I. The Perception and Classification of Two Archetypal Melodic Processes 317
   A. Gap-Fill Melodies 323
   B. Changing-Note Melodies 325
II. Experimental Findings 326
   A. Purpose 326
   B. Method 327
   C. Results 330
   D. Discussion 335
III. Implications 339
   References 340

I. THE PERCEPTION AND CLASSIFICATION OF TWO ARCHETYPAL MELODIC PROCESSES

It is a familiar fact that we tend to understand and remember experience in terms of categories and classes. And this is as true of aesthetic experience as of other realms of human activity. In literature, for instance, narrative plots—that is, goal-directed *processes* implying probable outcomes—seem to form readily recognizable types: "boy-meets-girl" stories, "who-done-it" mysteries, "revenge" dramas, and so on. Such narrative processes are often complemented by commonly replicated *formal* plans—for example cyclic schemes, episodic successions, flashback structures, and the like. When they are considered to have transcended the confines of a particular cultural group or historical period, replicated kinds of processes and forms have frequently been referred to as *archetypes* (see, for instance, Frye, 1957, pp. 99–105 and *passim*)—a term we adopt here.

Archetypes are important for a number of reasons. They establish fundamental frameworks in terms of which culturally competent audiences (not only members of the general public but also creators, performers, critics, and scholars) perceive, comprehend, and respond to works of art. For what audiences enjoy and appreciate are neither the successions of stimuli *per se*, nor general principles *per se*, but the relationship between them as actualized in a specific work of art. Just as we can delight in the play of a particular football game only if we understand the constraints governing the action down on the field (the rules, strategies, physical conditions, etc.), so we can enjoy and appreciate the playful ingenuity and expressive power of works of art only if we know—and such knowledge may be tacit: a matter of ingrained habits and dispositions—the constraints that governed the choices made by the artist and, consequently, shaped the process and form of the particular work of art. Thus, archetypes are, in a sense, embodiments of fundamental stylistic constraints. As such, they connect understanding to other aspects of aesthetic experience.

For our appreciation and evaluation of a work of art involves not only understanding what is actually presented, but also what *might have been* presented given the constraints of the style. Put differently, a full appreciation of the significance of an actual patterning includes an awareness of possible alternatives that remain unrealized—what Eugene Narmour has called "implied structure" (Narmour, 1977, p. 212). For the sake of brevity, consider an example discussed at some length elsewhere (Meyer, 1979, pp. 33–38). The slow movement of Haydn's *Military* Symphony (No. 100) opens with a two-measure pattern that can without the slightest exaggeration be termed "archetypal" in the music of the eighteenth century (Fig. 1, first part). But the pattern belongs not to the class of *beginning* figures but to that of *closing* ones—as in the second and third parts of Fig. 1. One consequence of this anomalous usage is that the movement might have ended with the very same figure that it began with. (For other instances of movements that begin with a closing figure, see Meyer, 1973, pp. 212–217; and Levy, 1981, pp. 355–362). And, though Haydn did not choose this alternative, the competent listener's appreciation of the close of the movement includes some (perhaps unconscious) awareness that this option was a very real possibility. That this was indeed a possible alternative ending can, in this case, be convincingly documented. For the second movement of the *Military* Symphony is based almost in its entirety upon the slow movement of an earlier work by Haydn, his Concerto in G Major for Two Hurdy Gurdies and Orchestra. And in the Concerto, the movement closes with the same figure that it began with.

Similarly, our evaluation of works of art involves an awareness of the possibilities available to the composer in a specific set of stylistic cultural circumstances. Thus, to praise a work as being "perfect," "inevitable," or "exciting" is implicitly to assert that, given our knowledge of the constraints governing the composer's choices, the alternatives actually used were the most felicitous imaginable; while to deprecate a passage as being "awkward," "trite," or "bombastic" is to suggest that, considering existing constraints, more graceful, original, or convincing alternatives were available to the composer.

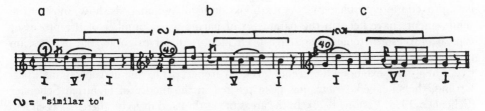

Fig. 1. Excerpts from (*a*) Haydn's Symphony no. 100 in G Major (*Military*), ii, mm 1–2; (*b*) Haydn's String Quartet in B flat, op. 64 no. 3, iii, mm 40–42; and (*c*) Mozart's Symphony no. 40 in G Minor (K. 550), iii, mm 40–42. Notice a similar melodic process in all three.

Because they are coherent, orderly, and simple, archetypes are easily learned and tend to be stable over time. For these reasons, they not only facilitate the appreciation and evaluation of particular works of art, but they also constitute an important means of cultural continuity. That is, they function as cognitive-mnemonic schemata—the replicated entities that Dawkins (1976) called "memes" because he considered them the cultural counterparts of the units of biological trait transmission. As such they may be an important basis for studying the histories of style of art.

As suggested earlier, archetypes may play a significant role in shaping aesthetic experience and fostering cultural continuity in the absence of any conscious conceptualization about their existence, nature, or kinds. Rather, they may be and usually are internalized as habits of perception and cognition operating within a set of cultural constraints. One of us, who has known the opera for many years, only recently recognized that the plot of Mozart's *Magic Flute* belongs to the archetypal class of quest-trial stories of which Dante's *Divine Comedy*, Bunyan's *Pilgrim's Progress*, and Cervantes' *Don Quixote* are celebrated members. And, as will soon be apparent, very familiar melodies may be members of archetypal classes without our being conscious of the fact.

Music, too, tends to be understood and remembered in terms of types and classes, some of which can, as Fig. 1 indicates, be thought of as archetypal. In the domain of musical form, this is abundantly clear. For though not usually so characterized, many of the forms described and labeled in books about musical analysis can be considered archetypal: for instance, strophic patterns (AA′A″ . . . A^n), exemplified in the theme and variation form; binary patterns (AB), the basis for many dance movements; bar forms (AA′B), the structural basis for countless melodies; ternary patterns (ABA), exemplified in *da capo* arias, many dance movements, and marches. Though formal organization is chiefly delineated by the syntactic processes of the primary parameters of music (melody, rhythm, and harmony), form is usually made particularly patent through the patterning of the secondary parameters (i.e., dynamics, tempi, register, instrumentation, sonority, and so on). The prevelance of such formal organizations has been amply documented both by theorists and historians of Western music and by ethnomusicologists.

The analysis and classification of the *processes* that complement such formal schemes have proved more problematic. As textbooks on form and analysis show, most of the achievements have been in the parameter of harmony. A number of the processes typical of Western tonal music have been identified: for example, the progression through the circle of fifths and characteristic cadences—authentic, plagal, and deceptive. On a more extended hierarchic level, an archetypal harmonic-contrapuntal patterning, the so-called *Ursatz*, has been posited in the theory of Heinrich Schenker (Schenker, 1956; Yeston, 1977). In the areas of rhythm and melody, there has been less success. Though there has been increasing interest in rhythm and meter in music and some typical groupings and patterns have been tentatively distinguished (Cooper & Meyer, 1960), little agreement has been reached (Komar, 1968; Yeston, 1976).

The difficulties encountered in the analysis of melodic processes, the concern of this study, result from a combination of conceptual, methodological and systemic problems. In the realm of human behavior, we tend to conceptualize and classify processes in terms of goals—and of the strategies devised for reaching them. Thus, reading a novel or seeing a play, we understand the succession of represented events in terms of the purposes of the protagonists: the union of boy and girl—despite her father's objections; the discovery of the criminal—despite his best efforts to avoid detection; the realization of revenge—despite obstacles of wealth or power. Because music is not well-suited to, or essentially concerned with, the representation of specific human actions, successive events in a composition cannot readily be related to one another in terms of such goals. Partly for this reason, melodic processes have resisted theoretical formulation and analysis.

A second difficulty is that while the formal plans, mentioned above, seem to be cross-cultural and atemporal, the syntactic processes generated by the primary parameters of melody, rhythm, and harmony are not. They are conventional: bound to a particular cultural context and limited to a specific historical epoch. The constraints governing melodic relationships and processes are not the same in Mozart's music as in Machaut's; nor are they the same in Western tonal music as in the music of Java. Put the other way around: it seems probable that we have a reasonably workable account of harmonic process precisely because what we have is *not* a fully general theory but one restricted to the practice of a particular culture and period—that of Western culture since the end of the Renaissance. If this observation has merit, then the search for "universal" principles may hinder the development of theories (*plural*) of melodic process.

The third difficulty, and perhaps the most important, is systemic. It arises because melodies are frequently hierarchically structured. As a result, the kind of patterning exhibited by a particular melody tends to change from one hierarchic level to the next; and so, of course, does the class of archetype involved. Consider, for instance, the melody of the opening measures of Mozart's Oboe Quartet (Fig. 2). As graph *a* of Fig. 2 shows, the foreground (note-to-note) level is characterized by rising and falling linear (scale) patterns. On the next level (graph *b*), rising and falling thirds create pairs of complementary diads. An archetypal changing-note pattern (F-G-E-F) arises on the third hierarchic level (graph *c*). And on the highest level, that resulting from the relationship created by phrase beginnings, the patterning is again linear—the first

Fig. 2. Mozart's Oboe Quartet in F Major (K. 370), i. mm 1–8. Graphs a, b, c, and d show analysis at increasingly higher levels of hierarchy. See text for explanation.

notes of a descending F-major scale, which continues beyond the music given in this figure.

If the kind of patterning changes from one hierarchic level to another within the same melody, which of the possible patterns should be the basis for classification? For instance, should the melody given in Fig. 2 be classed as linear on the basis of its foreground organization (graph *a*)? As two sets of complementary diads (graph *b*)? As a changing-note melody (graph *c*)? Or on the highest level, as again linear (graph *d*)?

The view adopted here is that melodic patterns are classified by listeners, as well as music theorists, in terms of the organization of the highest level on which significant closure is created by the parameters that shape musical relationships. Thus, Fig. 2 would be classed as a changing-note melody because that is the organization of the highest structural level when pattern closure occurs in measure 8. Had the closure that defines the limits of the whole melody (which lasts for 20 measures) been the basis for typology, then the pattern would have been classed as linear (graph *d*). For analysis of the whole melody, see Meyer (1973, pp. 192–195). In like manner, though the first half (AA′) of Fig. 3 consists of disjunct, triadic motion and the second (B)

Fig. 3. Mozart's Symphony in F Major (K. 112), ii, mm 1–4. Lower graph shows gap-fill process.

Fig. 4.   Mozart's Symphony no. 41 in C Major (K. 551), ii, mm 1–4. Lower graphs show analysis of alternative melodic structures. See text for explanation.

involves conjunct linear descent, the patterning of the highest level of closure creates what will be called a gap-fill melody.

Ease or difficulty of classification of melodic processes may be related to another sort of melodic complexity. Namely, the possibility that a single melody may contain two different strands of patterning on the *same* hierarchic level. For instance, the main pattern of the melody of the slow movement of Mozart's *Jupiter* Symphony is a changing-note figure (Fig. 4, graph *a*). But coordinate with this pattern is a subsidiary linear organization that is presented on weakbeats (graph *c*). To classify this melody, the listener must distinguish the two strands and discern which is the main one. As graph *b* indicates, the next level of this strand transcends the melodic and harmonic closure reached in measure 4. It is linear and implies continuation to a structural A (not shown in Fig. 4). Again, the basis for classification is the degree of closure. In measure 4 both the F (graph *a*) and the C (graph *c*) occur over stable, closed tonic harmony. But the F is more closed, both because it occurs on a stable, accented beat while the C comes on a mobile weakbeat, and because F is the stable tonic of the scale while C is the less stable fifth of the scale. As a result, the more closed changing-note pattern acts as the basis for melodic classification.

Of the primary parameters of music, melody has unquestionably been the most difficult to analyze and classify in terms of process. The paucity of practical and theoretical texts on the subject are evidence of this. So is the generally antitheoretical attitude expressed in the familiar maxim that since melody is a matter of native gift and inspiration, melodic processes cannot be "reduced" to principles or "forced" into artificial classes, and, consequently, melodic writing cannot be taught. Nevertheless, one of us (Meyer, 1973) has attempted to show that in the tonal music of Western culture, melodic processes can be separated into distinguishable classes on a particular hierarchic level—usually the level on which the pattern exhibits clear closure. Since two of these classes—gap-fill melodies and changing-note melodies—were investigated in an experiment described below, the characteristics of each class merit brief discussion.

A. Gap-Fill Melodies

Gap-fill melodies consist of two elements: (1) a disjunct interval or a succession of disjunct intervals moving in the same direction—the *gap* (or skip) and (2) a succession of conjunct (stepwise) intervals that "fill" the gap by presenting all or most of the notes previously skipped over. The relationship is one in which the incompleteness created by a gap implies subsequent completeness through a fill; and, generally speaking, the larger the gap, the stronger the sense of incompleteness and the implication of fill.

The subject of the fugue from Geminiani's Concerto Grosso in E Minor, Op. 3 No. 3, is an uncomplicated instance of a gap-fill melody (Fig. 5). As the graph (*a*) beneath the figure shows, the main gap consists of the octave from a low to a high E, and a subsidiary gap occurs from B up to E. This gap structure is immediately followed by conjunct motion—at first chromatic and then diatonic—that descends through the harmonic minor scale down to the tonic (E).

The same fundamental process, elaborated somewhat, forms the basis for the beginning of the chorus of the very familiar tune, "Over the Rainbow," by Harold Arlen (Fig. 6). Observe that whereas Geminiani's fugue subject has essentially only one skip (gap), followed by a fill that is slightly embellished by passing chromaticism, the generating gap of "Over the Rainbow" is reinforced by "auxiliary" gaps in measures 3 and 5; and most of the tones of the fill are prolonged through melodic-rhythmic elaboration. These differences affect formal structure. For instead of being a basically one-part form, as Geminiani's fugue subject is, "Over the Rainbow" is a bar form (AA'B), as indicated over Fig. 5. However, because the initial octave gap, the prime generating event, is immediately followed by the beginning of the fill, one thinks of the gap as being much shorter than the fill. Although most gaps are upward skips, downward skips may also function as gaps (see Narmour, 1977, pp. 76–77 for an example). And though upward skips are usually followed by descending fills and downward skips by rising fills, this is not necessarily the case: for instance, an ascending gap may be "filled" (completed) by a rising conjunct pattern. Moreover, the fill may be partly descending and partly ascending. For instance, in Fig. 6 the third gap (m. 5) is partly filled by the subsidiary ascending line shown in graph *b*.

But the gap part of a gap-fill process may be prolonged, so that the components of

Fig. 5. Geminiani's Concerto Grosso in E Minor, op. 3 no. 3, mm 1–4. Lower graph shows gap-fill process.

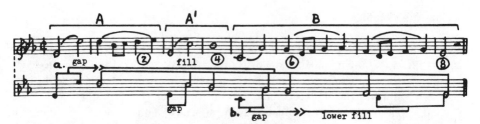

the whole melodic entity are roughly equal in length. This is true of the opening measures of the slow movement of Mozart's Symphony in F Major (K. 112) (Fig. 3). Thus, although the form (AA′B) is like that of Fig. 6, the first half of Mozart's melody is concerned with creating the gap; the fill takes place only in the second half. It should also be noted that, as in many cases, the pitches that define the full extent of the gap (the octave from low to high B♭) are not directly connected but are the end points of a triad.

Gap-fill patterns may also occur in conjunction with the quasi-strophic form AA′, called an antecedent-consequent period. The beginning of the Menuetto of Mozart's Flute Quartet in A Major (K. 298), illustrates this kind of process/form coupling (Fig. 7). In the antecedent phrase, a brief, anacrustic gap moves rapidly through the tonic triad from a lower to an upper fifth. The following fill descends conjunctly from the high A. However, before it is completed, a half cadence (IV–V) creates partial closure on the second degree of the scale, E (m. 4). The consequent phrase begins like the antecedent, reiterating the gap and the beginning of the fill. But the end of the fill is modified so that a full cadence occurs on the tonic D (m. 8). Though the melody never descends to the lower A, the gap is understood as being satisfactorily filled because the tonal/rhythmic closure at the end of the period (m. 8) is so decisive that whatever incompleteness might have been experienced is for the moment eclipsed.

Fig. 7. Mozart's Flute Quartet in A Major (K. 298), ii, mm 1–8. Lower graph shows gap-fill processes. Antecedent-consequent form indicated above.

B. Changing-Note Melodies

A changing-note melody is one in which the main structural tones of the pattern consist of the tonic (1), the seventh or leading tone of the scale (7), the second degree of the scale (2), and then the tonic again. As we have seen (Fig. 2), the order of the middle pitches may be reversed, resulting in the succession 1–2, 7–1. A variant of the changing-note process may occur beginning on the third degree of the scale, producing the succession 3–2, 4–3 (or 3–4, 2–3): an example is discussed in Meyer (1976). The pattern is always harmonized by a progression that moves from a tonic chord (I) to dominant harmony (V), and then from the dominant back to the tonic: that is, the progression is always I–V, V–I. Surrogates for these harmonies are possible: for example, vii for V, or vi for I. The form complementing the changing-note pattern is quasi-strophic, AA'. Thus, the basic plan can be diagramed as:

$$\frac{A}{I - V} : \frac{A'}{V - I}$$

It might be thought that the underlying regularity of a changing-note melody is really harmonic rather than melodic. However, since the same harmonic, and even formal, pattern may accompany other melodic processes—for instance, one that might be called a "sequential changing note pattern" (see Meyer, 1980)—the parameters are at least partially independent.

Any or all of the structural tones in a changing-note pattern may be extended—though ornamentation, triadic prolongation, etc. Consider, for instance, the beginning of the last movement of Beethoven's String Quartet in F Major, Op. 18 No. 1 (Fig. 8). In the first measure the tonic F is prolonged first through a turn involving lower and upper neighbor-notes and then through a linear descent. The leading tone E on the first beat of measure 2 is clearly structural despite the afterbeat G. In measure 3 a structural G, comparable in every way to the earlier F, is also prolonged, and then moves down by octave transfer to the tonic F followed by an afterbeat (A).

The cultural "potency" of this archetype seems evident in the fact that it acts as the basis for "Hinky Dinky, Parlee-voo," a tune that was enormously popular during the

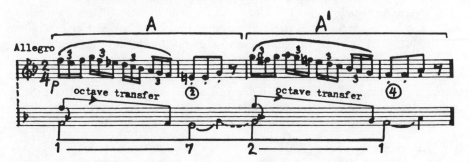

Fig. 8. Beethoven's String Quartet, op. 18 no. 1, iv, mm 1–4. Lower graph shows changing-note process and octave transfers. AA' form indicated above.

Fig. 9. (a) "Hinky Dinky, Parlee-voo," folk tune, mm 1–8, with analysis of changing-note process underlying it. (b) Notation of meter of (a) divided to conform to the meter of Fig. 8.

World War I (Fig. 9a). The similarity between the melodic process of this commonplace ditty and that of the last movement of Beethoven's Op. 18 No. 1 is evident enough. If the notation of its durational pattern is changed to conform to that of Fig. 8, then as Fig. 9b shows, the metric schemes are similar as well.

II. EXPERIMENTAL FINDINGS

A. Purpose

The preceding analysis of melodic processes raises an obvious psychological question. Do the different types of processes identified by musical theory play any role in the perception of music? If they do, a subject untutored in formal musical analysis should at least be able to place melodies into the classes which the analysis specifies. This argument can be tested by a concept identification experiment in which different types of melodic processes define the different classes of stimuli. The processes should be represented at the highest hierarchical level for each stimulus. A subject should be able to learn to associate different responses with the different classes. The subject then should successfully generalize the responses to a new sample of melodies.

We carried out such a concept identification experiment.[1] In this experiment, subjects had to learn to place gap-fill melodies into one class and changing-note melodies into another. The subjects were to respond to gap-fill instances by saying "A" and to changing-note instances by saying "B," without any explicit education in melodic analysis and without any didactic training about these two types of melodic processes. Training was conducted by merely informing the subject after each response what the correct response should have been. We used recordings of fully instrumented passages from the musical literature for this experiment, rather than

[1]The experiment grew out of a graduate seminar which we taught together in 1977. The students participated in the design of the experiment, selection of passages, and running subjects. We are grateful for their unusual help to James Copp, Erika Ellenberger, Christopher Foard, Robert Hopkins, Lief Laudamus, and Katherine Hirsch-Pasek. Scott Balthazar helped us to collect further necessary data and to organize the results.

melodies of our own devising. This choice rested on two grounds. First, we wanted to keep style as homogeneous as possible. We found that we could select sufficient material from works of the Classical period (ca. 1750–1827). Second, we feared that we could all too easily make the concept identification task trivial by composing our own melodies. We also rejected the procedure of abstracting melodies from the musical literature and having them played on a single instrument, such as a clarinet. We wanted to see whether classification of different types of melodic processes could emerge despite the presence of the many other parameters which are characteristic of music. Therefore, we used short passages of four to 15 measures' length chosen from works by Haydn, Mozart, Beethoven, and Schubert. Each passage reached significant closure and was an instance of either gap-fill or changing-note processes.

The results of this initial experiment suggested that subjects could indeed learn to place each melody into its appropriate class and could then generalize to new melodies. Inspection of the data, however, indicated that changing-note melodies generated fewer erroneous responses than did gap-fill ones. Subjects apparently carried out the task by learning to respond correctly first to the changing-note passages and then using the alternative response to all other passages. We could not conclude safely that the two types of melodic processes played more or less equal roles in the perception of music. Therfore, we redesigned the experiment as a two-part procedure. In one part, subjects heard gap-fill melodies along with some which represented a variety of different melodic processes other than gap-fill or changing-note. The subjects had to respond by saying "Type A" to the former and "Not type A" to the latter. A generalization test followed training. In another part of the experiment, subjects learned to respond to changing-note melodies by saying "Type B" and to melodies representing various processes other than changing-note or gap-fill by saying "Not type B." Again, a generalization test followed training. No passage used in one part of the experiment ever appeared in the other.

B. Method

1. Selection of Passages

Fifty-nine passages were selected for this experiment from the works of Haydn, Mozart, Beethoven, and Schubert. They represented parts of symphonies, chamber music, concertos for solo instrument and orchestra, and sonatas for piano or for piano and violin. Tables III and IV provide lists of the passages selected for the gap-fill and changing-note parts of the experiment, respectively. The tables show composer, work, movement, and measures. On request, we will provide details about the particular recordings used.

2. Gap-Fill versus Non-Gap-Fill (Part A)

Thirty passages were used in this part of the experiment. Eight gap-fill and eight non-gap-fill passages were used for training. Four of each type were of form AA'B and the other four were antecedent-consequent forms. In an AA′B form, the passage contains an initial motif, a repetition or a variation of it, and then a longer concluding motif (see Fig. 3). The antecedent-consequent form contains two related statements, the first of which does not resolve to the tonic while the second does (e.g., Fig. 7). There were two gap-fill passages of the form AA′B that ended on dominant harmony, and these were matched by a non-gap-fill passage of the same form that also ended on the dominant. In addition to the 16 training stimuli, two more gap-fill passages were chosen for introductory examples at the start of training. One was of form AA′B and the other was an antecedent-consequent passage. Since the non-gap-fill passages employed various melodic processes, no introductory examples of these selections were given. For the generalization test we chose six gap-fill and six non-gap-fill passages different from those used for training. Three gap-fill and three non-gap-fill passages had form AA′B. One of these ended on the dominant, and this was matched by a non-gap-fill passage that ended on the dominant. The other three gap-fill and the other three non-gap-fill passages were antecedent-consequent in form.

3. Changing-Note versus Non-Changing-Note (Part B)

Twenty-nine passages were used in this part of the experiment. All had form AA′ (see Fig. 8). Eight changing-note and eight non-changing-note passages served as training stimuli while an additional changing-note melody provided an introductory example at the start of training. A non-changing-note introductory example was not offered since passages in this category used a variety of melodic processes. The generalization test employed six changing-note and six non-changing-note passages different from those used in training.

4. Preparation of Tapes

Each passage was recorded on a master selection tape, from which it was rerecorded on separate segments of tape as many times as necessary. The segments then were spliced into the experimental tapes. There was a training and a generalization tape for each part (A and B) of the experiment.

For gap-fill training, the subject responded by saying "Type A" to all instances of gap-fill melodies and by saying "Not type A" to all non-gap-fill passages. The tape started with an announcer's voice stating, "This is an experiment in music perception. You will now hear an example of type A." The AA′B gap-fill introductory example then was played once. After a 10-sec pause, the announcer's voice stated, "This is another example of type A" and the antecedent-consequent gap-fill introductory example was then played. The two introductory examples never reappeared in the rest of the experiment. The announcer then said, "Now start responding." After a 2-sec delay, the first training passage was played. Ten sec after its termination, the announcer identified it by saying, "That was type A" or "That was not type A," as appropriate. The subject had to respond within the 10-sec interval between the end of the passage and the announcer's identification of it. Five sec after the identification, the announcer stated, "Next example," and another passage was begun 2 sec later and followed 10 sec after its conclusion by an identifying statement. The training tape continued, following this cycle of a warning of "Next example" 5 sec after termination of the previous identification, a 2-sec pause after the warning, a passage, a 10-sec pause for the subject to respond, and then identification of the type of selection just heard.

A single training trial consisted of one playing of each of the eight gap-fill passages and each of the eight non-gap-fill ones. The order of passages was randomized with the constraint that no more than three gap-fill or no more than three non-gap-fill selections could occur in sequence. One trial took about eight minutes. A different random order of the passages was used for different trials. The gap-fill training tape contained 12 trials, with no indication to the subject of where one trial ended and the next began. Our initial experiment had indicated that this would permit most subjects to reach a criterion of two successive trials with two errors or less on each.

The gap-fill generalization tape consisted of six gap-fill and six non-gap-fill passages in random order, with the constraint that no more than two of either type could occur in succession. The tape began with the message, "Now start responding." Two seconds later the first generalization passage began. It was repeated after a 2-sec pause. Then a 10-sec pause occurred, during which the subject was to respond. No information about correct identification was given. Instead, the announcer stated, "Next example," and after a 2-sec pause, two exposures to the next passage occurred. Ten seconds were then allowed for responding. The cycle of a warning, a 2-sec pause, two playings of a passage, and a 10-sec pause for responding continued throughout the gap-fill generalization tape. The entire tape ran for about 10 minutes.

The changing-note training tape was constructed exactly parallel to that for the gap-fill part of the experiment, with one minor exception. Since all passages were of form AA', only one example of a changing-note melody was played at the start of training. Subjects were supposed to respond with "Type B" to changing-note and with "Not type B" to non-changing-note passages. The introductory example on the training tape was preceded by the announcement, "This is an experiment in music perception. You will now hear an example of type B." Identifications after training passages were either, "That was type B" or "That was not type B." The changing-note generalization tape followed exactly the pattern of the gap-fill generalization tape.

5. Subjects

Twenty subjects were recruited individually by one of the experimenters from students taking music courses at the University of Pennsylvania. They included undergraduate and graduate students. Among the former were majors in music or in other subjects. The graduate students were all studying composition. No subject had received any exposure to analysis of melodic processes, although some were versed in more traditional aspects of musical theory, such as harmony, counterpoint, and musical form. Each subject received $6 at the end of two $1\frac{1}{2}$ hour sessions.

6. Procedure

Each subject underwent gap-fill training and generalization (part A) in one session and changing-note training and generalization (part B) in the other. Half the subject took part A first, and the other half took part B first. As they were recruited, subjects were assigned in alternation to one or the other initial condition. At the start of the first session, each subject filled out a questionnaire and a consent form. The questionnaire asked about academic status, previous training in musical performance, previous academic training in music, and current performance activities and listening habits.

The experimenter then read instructions to the subject and answered any questions. The instructions specified that subjects were to respond by saying "Type A" or "Not type A" for part A of the experiment (gap-fill) or "Type B" or "Not type B" for part B (changing-note). They also informed the subject that 10 sec were allowed for responding after the end of a passage and each failure to meet this requirement would result in losing 10 cents. The experimenter then started the appropriate training tape, which was reproduced at a comfortable listening level over an Akai model 400DS Mark II tape deck. The subject and the experimenter each listened to the tape over stereophonic earphones. After each passage had been played, the subject responded verbally. The experimenter marked correct responses on a specially prepared data sheet. At the end of each trial, the experimenter added up the number of errors and decided whether the subject had met the criterion for training: two successive trials with no more than two errors each. If criterion had not been met, the next training trial proceeded. If it had been met, the experimenter stopped the training tape, rewound it, removed it from the tape deck, and put the generalization tape on the deck. If the subject ran through 12 training trials without meeting criterion, the experimenter moved on to the generalization test nevertheless. The subject therefore had a brief rest between hearing the training and generalization tapes. The generalization tape was played and responses were recorded just as for the training tape. At the end of each subject's second session, the experimenter explained the purpose of the study to the subject and asked the subject not to discuss the experiment with any other participant.

C. Results

1. Gap-Fill (Part A)

During training, one subject failed to respond within the 10-sec limit to a single selection. Table I summarizes the results of part A of the experiment. Due to various exigencies, three Os did not complete part A of the experiment. Fourteen of the remaining 17 subjects met criterion in a median of 8.8 trials. They made a median of 37.0 errors in training and 4.7 errors out of a possible 12 in generalization. Three Os went 12 trials without meeting criterion. They had a median of 58.0 errors during

TABLE I

Results of Concept Identification Experiment

	Gap-fill (A)	Changing-note (B)
Os meeting criterion	14	12
Median trials	8.8	9.3
Median errors	37.0	43.0
Median errors in generalization	4.7	4.6
Os going 12 trials Without meeting criterion	3	4
Median errors	58.0	69.0
Median errors on last 2 trials	5.0	8.0
Median errors in generalization	4.0	4.3
Median errors in generalization for all Os	4.5	4.4

training, a median of only 5.0 errors out of a possible 32 on their final two training trials, and a median of 4.0 errors out of a possible 12 in generalization. All 17 Os together made a median of 4.5 errors during the generalization test. During generalization no O ever failed to respond within the 10-sec limit after the end of a passage.

We used the Kolmogorov-Smirnov test (Siegel, 1956) to determine whether subjects responded better than chance in the generalization test. If the subjects were just guessing throughout generalization, their errors would follow a binomial distribution. Table II shows the theoretical and the observed cumulative probabilities of error scores of at least a certain size. The observed cumulative probabilities are given for the 14 Os who met criterion and for all 17 who completed the gap-fill part of the experiment. The last two lines of the table show the maximum deviation of the observed from the theoretical probabilities and the associated significance level from the Kolmogorov-Smirnov text. The 17 subjects who completed part A of the experiment had fewer generalization errors than expected by chance; this difference was significant ($p = .05$). Therefore, these subjects acquired generalizable knowledge as a result of training. The 14 subjects who reached criterion showed the same trend in their generalization error scores, but the difference fell just short of significance. The results indicate that subjects who did not reach criterion during training still learned to classify the passages for the most part correctly and could generalize their knowledge to a new sample of selections.

Inspection of the data indicated that passages differed in their difficulty during training and possibly during generalization. Table III lists the individual selections used in part A of the experiment along with the errors made on them. Results are given separately for the Os who met criterion during training and for those who did not, along with total errors for all Os. The passages are separated into gap-fill and

TABLE II

Analysis of Number of Generalization Errors

Errors	Binomial cumulative probabilities	Gap-fill cumulative probabilities		Changing-note cumulative probabilities	
		Os meeting criterion ($n = 14$)	Os completing experiment ($n = 17$)	Os meeting criterion ($n = 12$)	Os completing experiment ($n = 16$)
12	1.0000	1.0000	1.0000	1.0000	1.0000
11	.9998	1.0000	1.0000	1.0000	1.0000
10	.9968	1.0000	1.0000	1.0000	1.0000
9	.9807	.9286	.9412	1.0000	1.0000
8	.9270	.9286	.9412	1.0000	1.0000
7	.8061	.9286	.9412	.9167	.9375
6	.6128	.7857	.8235	.9167	.9375
5	.3872	.7143	.7059	.9167	.9375
4	.1938	.5000	.5294	.5000	.5625
3	.0730	.3571	.3529	.4167	.3125
2	.0192	.1428	.1765	.3333	.2500
1	.0032	.0714	.0588	.2500	.1875
0	.0002	.0714	.0588	.0833	.0625
D_{max}		.3271	.3356	.5295	.5503
$p<$		.10	.05	.01	.01

non-gap-fill sets, for both training and generalization. If all passages within a set were equally difficult, the same number of errors would be made on each. We performed Friedman two-way analyses of variance (Siegel, 1956) on errors made during training in order to see whether passages differed in difficulty. The individual subjects were replicates and the different passages were the conditions. Tests were done on the gap-fill passages for subjects who met criterion, for those who did not, and for all Os combined. The results appear in Table III, which gives the values of χ_r^2 and their associated levels of significance. The results show that gap-fill training passages varied in difficulty. Three similar analyses on non-gap-fill training passages yielded no significant results, as Table III shows. Finally, chi square tests were made when possible on error data for individual selections during generalization. Tests were done on total errors per passage across all Os for gap-fill and non-gap-fill passages and for total errors per non-gap-fill passage across Os who met criterion. None of the results proved significant.

The data in Table III also suggest that subjects made more errors on non-gap-fill than on gap-fill passages. To test this hypothesis, we used the Wilcoxon signed-ranks test for matched samples (Siegel, 1956). The test was done on differences across subjects between total errors on gap-fill and total errors on non-gap-fill passages. Table III shows the results. Subjects who reached criterion and all Os combined who finished part A of the experiment made significantly more errors on non-gap-fill than

TABLE III
Errors on Gap-Fill Selections

Selection	Total errors		
	Criterion Os ($n = 14$)	Noncriterion Os ($n = 3$)	All Os ($n = 17$)
Training gap-fill			
Mozart: Piano Quintet in E-flat, K. 452 (III) mm. 1-8	19	16	35
Mozart: Flute Quartet in A, K. 298 (II) mm. 1-8	9	8	17
Beethoven: Violin Concerto (III) mm. 1-8	24	4	28
Mozart: Eine Kleine Nachtmusik, K. 525 (IV) mm. 1-8	13	9	22
Schubert: String Quartet in E-flat, op. 125 (D. 87) (II) mm. 1-8	41	16	57
Mozart: Symphony no. 18 in F, K. 130 (III) nm. 1-8	8	5	13
Beethoven: String Quartet in B-flat, op. 18 no. 4 (I) mm. 42-49	31	22	53
Beethoven: Piano Sonata in A, op. 2 no. 2 (III) Trio, mm. 1-8	36	10	46
Friedman χ_r^2	31.63	8.13	31.51
$p \leqslant$	.001	—	.001
Non-gap-fill			
Mozart: String Quartet in E-flat, K. 428 (IV) mm. 1-8	35	10	45
Mozart: String Quartet in D, K. 499 (II) Trio, mm. 1-8	52	4	56
Mozart: Symphony no. 41 in C, K. 551 (III) Trio, mm. 1-8	25	8	33
Beethoven: String Quartet in B-flat, op. 130 (II) mm. 1-8	35	11	46
Haydn: String Quartet in E-flat, op. 64 no. 6 (IV) mm. 1-4	35	14	49
Mozart: Piano Concerto in E-flat, K. 482 (III) mm. 1-8	44	11	55
Haydn: String Quartet, op. 33 no. 6 (III) mm. 1-8	50	17	67
Haydn: String Quartet in G, op. 64 no. 4 (II) mm. 1-4	19	10	29
Friedman χ_r^2	4.53	6.46	5.03
$p \leqslant$	—	—	—
A-NA Mdn	−7.5	—	6.5
T: $p \leqslant$	.01		.05
Generalization Gap-fill			
Haydn: Symphony no. 77 in B-flat (IV) mm. 72-80	6	0	6
Haydn: Symphony no. 79 (II) mm. 61-68	5	1	6

(Continued)

TABLE III (*Continued*)

Selection	Criterion Os $(n = 14)$	Noncriterion Os $(n = 3)$	All Os $(n = 17)$
		Total errors	
Mozart: Symphony no. 13 in F, K. 112 (II) mm. 1–5	2	1	3
Mozart: Symphony no. 24 in B-flat, K. 182 (II) mm. 1–8	3	2	5
Mozart: Sonata for Piano and Violin in G, K. 301 (II) mm. 1–6	2	0	2
Beethoven: String Quartet in B-flat, op. 18 no. 6 (IV) mm. 1–8	9	2	11
χ^2	—	—	9.0
$p \leqslant$			—
Non-Gap-fill			
Mozart: String Quartet in B-flat, K. 458 (III) mm. 1–8	8	0	8
Haydn: Symphony no. 104 in D (IV) mm. 3–10	6	1	7
Mozart: Symphony no. 35 in D, K. 385 (III) Trio, mm. 1–8	9	1	10
Haydn: Quartet op. 33 no. 3 in C, (IV) mm. 1–8	4	2	6
Mozart: Symphony in G, K. 45a (III) mm. 1–8	5	1	6
Haydn: String Quartet in G, op. 64 no. 4 (IV) mm. 1–4	4	1	5
χ^2	3.67	—	2.29
$p \leqslant$	—		—
GA-GNA Mdn	.4	—	.5
$T: p \leqslant$	—		—

on gap-fill training passages. No similar difference in difficulty between gap-fill and non-gap-fill selections occurred during generalization.

In summary, subjects learned to put gap-fill and non-gap-fill melodies into different classes, without explicit academic training in musical analysis. They subsequently proved able to classify new instances of each type of melody in a generalization test. During training, gap-fill passages differed among themselves in difficulty, but non-gap-fill ones did not. The gap-fill training passages were easier to identify correctly than were the non-gap-fill ones. Generalization passages showed no variation in difficulty either within or between types of passages.

2. Changing-Note (Part B)

Table I shows the results of part B of the experiment. During training, no subject ever failed to respond within the 10-sec limit. Due to various exigencies, four Os did not finish this part of the experiment. Twelve subjects met criterion in a median of 9.3

trials. They made a median of 43 errors during training and a median of 4.6 errors during generalization. Another four subjects underwent 12 training trials without meeting criterion, generating a median of 69 errors. They made a median of 8 errors on the last two training trials and a median of 4.3 errors during generalization. All 16 Os made a median of 4.4 errors during the generalization test. No O ever failed to respond within the 10-sec limit during generalization.

Table II shows the cumulative probabilities that subjects made error scores of at least a certain size. Results are given separately for Os who reached criterion and for all Os who completed part B of the experiment. Kolmogorov-Smirnov tests showed that subjects who met criterion made significantly fewer errors than expected by chance, as did all Os who completed part B. Subjects who met criterion and those who did not seemed to have acquired generalizable knowledge about changing-note melodies as a result of training.

Table IV shows the individual passages used in part B and the errors made on them. Results are given separately for the Os who met criterion, for those who did not, and for all Os combined who completed part B. The passages are separated into changing-note and non-changing-note sets, for both training and generalization. Friedman tests indicate that both the changing-note and non-changing-note passages varied among themselves in difficulty during training. The non-changing-note passages generated more errors than did the changing-note ones. Wilcoxon tests showed that this difference was statistically significant for Os who met criterion and for all Os combined. Chi square tests were made when possible on generalization error scores and gave no indication that changing-note or non-changing-note passages varied in difficulty. Nor was there evidence from Wilcoxon tests that the changing-note passages differed in difficulty from non-changing-note ones.

3. Gap-Fill versus Changing-Note

Of the 20 subjects who began the experiment, 10 managed to meet criterion in both parts A and B. Data from the latter subjects permit comparisons between the two parts of the experiment. During training, these subjects made a median of 6.0 more errors on gap-fill than on changing-note passages but took a median of .7 more trials to reach criterion on changing-note than on gap-fill passages. Wilcoxon tests showed that neither difference is significant. The 10 subjects also made a median of .8 more errors in generalization on changing-note than on gap-fill selections; again, the difference is not significant. In brief, we have no evidence of any difference in difficulty between the gap-fill and the changing-note parts of the experiment.

D. Discussion

Our experimental results indicate that at least two classes of melodic processes obtained from theoretical analysis can act as a basis for perceptual differentiation between melodic types. The melodic types, therefore, meet the minimal requirement

TABLE IV

Errors on Changing-Note Selections

	Total errors		
Selection	Criterion Os $(n = 12)$	Noncriterion Os $(n = 4)$	All Os $(n = 16)$
Training changing-note			
Mozart: Piano Sonata in E-flat, K. 282 (II) mm. 1–4	30	18	48
Mozart: Fantasy in D, K. 397 mm. 12–15	10	16	26
Mozart: Piano Quintet in E-flat, K. 452 (III) mm. 17–20	33	19	52
Beethoven: Piano Sonata in C, op. 10 no. 1 (I) mm. 1–8	14	17	31
Mozart: Oboe Quartet in F, K. 370 (I) mm. 1–8	26	24	50
Beethoven: String Quartet in F, op. 18 no. 1 (IV) mm. 1–4	22	10	32
Mozart: Symphony no. 39 in E-flat, K. 543 (III) Trio, mm. 1–8	24	10	34
Mozart: Piano Sonata K. 311 (I) mm. 7–10	10	16	26
Friedman χ_r^2	26.60	2.52	21.75
$p \leqslant$	.001	—	.001
Non-Changing-note			
Beethoven: Symphony no. 2 in D, op. 36 (III) mm. 85–92	27	13	40
Beethoven: Piano Sonata in G, op. 49 no. 2 (I) mm. 20–23	45	24	69
Mozart: Piano Quartet in G Minor, K. 478 (III) mm. 1–4	47	22	69
Mozart: String Quartet in A, K. 464 (I) mm. 1–8	49	25	74
Haydn: Symphony no. 94 in G (III) mm. 1–8	33	23	56
Beethoven: String Quartet, op. 18 no. 2, (III) mm. 1–8	29	16	45
Mozart: String Quartet in D Minor, K. 421 (IV) mm. 1–8	31	19	50
Haydn: String Quartet in D, op. 50 no. 6 (III) mm. 30–40	33	16	49
χ_r^2	13.83	5.92	16.97

for attributing psychological significance to them. Explicit training in musical analysis is not necessary for the types to form the basis of perceptual distinctions. Our findings, although encouraging, are merely an initial step. Further studies are necessary in order to specify just what sort of psychological reality different types of melodic processes may be said to possess, to determine the levels at which this reality is

TABLE IV (*Continued*)

Selection	Total errors		
	Criterion Os ($n = 14$)	Noncriterion Os ($n = 3$)	All Os ($n = 17$)
$p \leqslant$	—	—	.02
B-NB Mdn	−10.	—	−10.8
$T: p \leqslant$	.01		.01
Generalization changing-note			
Mozart: Piano Quartet in G Minor, K. 478 (I) mm. 1–8	6	0	6
Mozart: String Quintet in C, K. 515 (I) mm. 1–10	5	1	6
Mozart: String Trio in E-flat, K. 563 (III) mm. 1–8	2	1	3
Haydn: String Quartet, op. 64 no. 5 (I) mm. 1–8	3	2	5
Haydn: Symphony no. 46 in B (II) mm. 1–4	2	0	2
Mozart: Symphony no. 41 in C, K. 551 (II) mm. 1–4	9	2	11
χ^2	—	—	—
$p \leqslant$			
Non-changing-note			
Mozart: Sextet in F, K. 522 (III) mm. 1–4	2	1	3
Beethoven: String Quartet, op. 18 no. 2 (II) mm. 1–6	3	0	3
Haydn: Symphony no. 101 in D (IV) mm. 1–8	4	0	4
Haydn: Quartet, op. 33 no. 2 (II) Trio, mm. 1–8	3	1	4
Mozart: String Quintet in E-flat, K. 614 (I) mm. 1–8	9	2	11
Beethoven: Symphony no. 7 in A, op. 92 (III) mm. 149–163	5	2	7
χ^2	—	—	9.5
$p \leqslant$			—
B-NB Mdn	.0		.4
$p \leqslant$	—		—

represented, and to show the manner in which it operates. These tests will involve techniques such as direct judgments of similarity.

Training and generalization passages of every type in both parts A and B of the experiment differed among themselves in difficulty. One of the most important reasons for this variability is probably the hierarchic nature of the melodies themselves.

As observed earlier, hierarchically complex melodies exhibit different kinds of patterning on different levels. And the more hierarchic levels there are, the more likely that classification will be based upon the patterning of some level other than that of the highest level of closure. This may help to explain why our subjects found the melody of the first movement of Mozart's Oboe Quartet (Fig. 2) particularly difficult to classify. Not only are there at least four hierarchic levels, but the forceful linear motion of the highest level (Fig. 2, graph D) may well mask the changing-note melody that patterns the highest closural level. The whole melody is analyzed as being linear in Meyer (1973, pp. 192–195). The fourth movement of Beethoven's String Quartet in F Major (Fig. 8) is also a changing-note melody. But it is hierarchically simple and, despite octave transfers and potentially problematic afterbeats, our subjects found it relatively easy to classify. The preemptive force of a linear patterning that transcends the closure of a passage may also have made it difficult for subjects to recognize that the opening measures of Schubert's String Quartet in E-Flat create a gap-fill pattern (for an analysis of this passage see Meyer, 1973, pp. 234–238). But in both these cases, errors were probably a result of other problems as well. In the Mozart example, for instance, the changing-note pattern was unusual: instead of moving 1-7-2-1 as in the other instances of this archetype, it moves 1-2-7-1. And in the Schubert example, the gap is created by a downward skip rather than by the more usual upward one.

Inspection (as well as common sense) suggests more difficulty in learning to classify bilinear melodies, such as Fig. 4, compared to those consisting of just a single melodic strand. The degree of internal redundancy also seems to affect ease of classification. For instance, both the Andante from Mozart's Symphony in F Major (Fig. 3) and the last movement of Beethoven's String Quartet in B-Flat, op. 18 no. 6, are gap-fill melodies of the form AA'B. But the former, which is characterized by a high degree of internal redundancy (particularly, the first half involves repetition of a stable tonic triad), was generally classified correctly; the latter, which involves considerably less pitch and pattern repetition and is relatively unstable harmonically, proved much more difficult to classify. In this connection, it should be noted that while changing-note melodies occur in only one form (AA'), gap-fill melodies occur either in antecedent-consequent form (AA') or in so-called bar form (AA'B). The possibility of alternative forms may in part explain why subjects generally found it more difficult to classify gap-fill patterns than changing-note ones, although the difference was not statistically significant.

A review of passages in the light of differential error scores also suggests that secondary parameters—texture and tempo, dynamics and timbre—may significantly influence ease of classification. All else being equal, it seems probable that very rapid tempi and surprising changes in dynamics make melodies more difficult to classify. The organization of texture also seems to play a role in the ease with which the class of a melody is recognized. As one might expect, clear figure-ground division (as in a homophonic texture) facilitates the classification of melodies while textural intricacy makes it more difficult. For instance, though the Adagio melody from Mozart's Fantasy for Piano in D Minor is quite complex (for a discussion, see Narmour, 1977, pp. 89–95), our subjects seem to have learned its class quite readily. And perhaps they did so because the figure-ground relationship is very clear and the tempo is slow. It is possible, too, that familiarity facilitated classification in this case—and perhaps in some others as well. For Mozart's D-Minor Fantasy is often studied by beginning piano students, and it might have been known (and hence readily remembered) by some of our subjects.

Finally, in at least one case, the high number of errors can be attributed to the use of a passage that was not, properly speaking, a member of the class it was included to represent. The melody of the third movement of Mozart's Piano Quintet in E-Flat is indeed a changing-note melody; but instead of moving around the tonic (1-7-2-1), it moves around the third of the scale (3-4-2-3).

As the preceding discussion indicates, the ease or difficulty with which subjects classify a particularly melody is a result of the intricate interaction among *all* the features and parameters that make the patterning what it is. It cannot be sufficiently emphasized that the passages that our subjects were asked to classify were not invented abstractions or contrived simplifications but real music as it was really performed. Not only melodic organization on all hierarchic levels, but rhythmic and harmonic structure, texture, tempo and dynamics, at once shaped complex patterning and made the task of classification formidable. And because for each passage the relative importance of the various factors is different, general rules explaining how the resulting idiosyncratic relationships help or hinder classification are difficult, perhaps impossible, to discover.

III. IMPLICATIONS

Melodic archetypes, such as those considered in this experiment, make possible an almost infinite variety of particular instantiations. Our analysis suggests that unless the essential structural tones of a melodic process are kept intact, changing individual notes in a melody by one or several octaves at random should make recognition very difficult. Such octave shifts, for example, might transform a changing-note melody into something like an abortive gap-fill one. Deutsch (1972) found that octave displacements did interfere with recognition of a familiar tune. Dowling and Hollombe (1977) and Idson and Massaro (1978) have produced evidence that maintenance of contour can partly overcome the effects that Deutsch first reported. Having the undistorted tune available for comparison also facilitates recognition (see House, 1977 and Deutsch, 1978; Idson and Massaro also played undistorted tunes in their series). Therefore, maintenance of contour is only one factor that can oppose the effects of octave displacement. Other experimental work bears out the importance of contour in recognition of distorted melodies (Francès, 1958; White, 1960) and in perception of transpositions (Dowling & Fujitani, 1971).

We suspect that one of the crucial considerations for recognition in the face of variation is the presence or absence of hierarchic structuring. If hierarchic organization is present, pattern recognition is possible even when there is significant alteration *as long as* the structural tones that shape the essential process maintain their functions.

When these are changed, recognition should be increasingly difficult. And if the melodies used in an experiment are without hierarchic structure, it should make less difference which tones are altered—recognition should be more or less equally affected.

The idea of different types of melodic processes also illuminates other experimental findings on recognition of melodies. White (1960) found that retrograde variations on a familiar melody were particularly destructive of recognition. Dowling (1971, 1972) has examined the effects of inversion, retrograde, and retrograde inversion on recognition of short atonal sequences in an immediate memory paradigm. A sequence was presented on each trial, followed immediately by a variation on it or by some different sequence. Subjects had to say whether or not the second sequence was a transformation of the first. Dowling found that retrograde inversion made recognition most difficult. Because they are syntactic and create a sense of goal-directed motion, tonal melodies should be more difficult to recognize in inversion, retrograde and retrograde inversion than nontonal ones. The analysis of melodic process, however, suggests that the difficulty of recognizing a transformation will depend on the type of melody used. Changing-note melodies, for example, are more open to retrograde variation than are gap-fill ones. Different types of melodic processes will make one or another sort of transformation easier or harder to use while maintaining recognition. Generally, however, retrograde transformations are very likely to alter severely the process that underlies a particular melody and to render recognition harder. This fact gives some account of the findings\ f White and of Dowling.

Finally, some attention has been directed during the last 10 years to effects of interleaving two melodies, binaurally or dichotically (Deutsch, 1975; Dowling, 1973; Butler, 1979). Melodic interleaving is essential in the practice of polyphony. The analysis presented here suggests that some melodic types are probably better suited for polyphonic combination than others. For instance, because they quickly make clear the basic melodic process involved and employ motivically as well as functionally contrasting parts, gap-fill melodies—especially those with a patent initial skip and without complex hierarchic organization (see, for instance, Fig. 3)—provide a particularly good basis for polyphonic combination, as even a casual glance at the fugue subjects in Bach's *Well-Tempered Clavier* makes evident. Because they are quite different in these respects, changing-note melodies are not specially well-suited to polyphonic usage.

REFERENCES

Butler, D. A further study of melodic channeling. *Perception & Psychophysics*, 1979, *25*, 254–268.

Cooper, G. W., & Meyer, L. B. *The rhythmic structure of music*. Chicago, Illinois: University of Chicago Press, 1960.

Dawkins, R. *The selfish gene*. London and New York: Oxford University Press, 1976.

Deutsch, D. Octave generalization and tune recognition. *Perception & Psychophysics*, 1972, *11*, 411–412.

Deutsch, D. Two-channel listening to musical scales. *Journal of the Acoustical Society of America*, 1975, *57*, 1156–1160.

Deutsch, D. Octave generalization and melody identification. *Perception & Psychophysics*, 1978, *23*, 91–92.

Dowling, W. J. Recognition of inversions of melodies and melodic contours. *Perception & Psychophysics*, 1971, *9*, 348–349.

Dowling, W. J. Recognition of melodic transformations: Inversion, retrograde, and retrograde inversion. *Perception & Psychophysics*, 1972, *12*, 417–421.

Dowling, W. J. The perception of interleaved melodies. *Cognitive Psychology*, 1973, 5, 322–337.

Dowling, W. J., & Fujitani, D. A. Contour, interval, and pitch recognition in memory for melodies. *Perception & Psychophysics*, 1971, *9*, 524–531.

Dowling, W. J., & Hollombe, A. W. The perception of melodies distorted by splitting into several octaves: Effects of increasing proximity and melodic contour. *Perception & Psychophysics*, 1977, *21*, 60–64.

Francès, R. *La perception de la musique*. Paris: Vrin, 1958.

Frye, N. *Anatomy of criticism*. Princeton, New Jersey: Princeton University Press, 1957.

House, W. J. Octave generalization and the identification of distorted melodies. *Perception & Psychophysics*, 1977, *21*, 586–589.

Idson, W. L., & Massaro, D. W. A bidimensional model of pitch in the recognition of melodies. *Perception & Psychophysics*, 1978, *24*, 551–565.

Komar, A. *Theory of suspensions*. New York: Norton, 1968.

Levy, J. M. Gesture, form and syntax in Haydn's music. In J. P. Larsen, H. Serwer, & J. Webster (Eds.), *Haydn Studies*. New York: Norton, 1981. Pp. 355–362.

Meyer, L. B. *Explaining music: Essays and explorations*. Berkeley, California: University of California Press, 1973.

Meyer, L. B. Grammatical simplicity and relational richness: The trio of Mozart's G Minor symphony. *Critical Inquiry*, 1976, 2, 693–761.

Meyer, L. B. Toward a theory of style. In B. Lang (Ed.), *The concept of style*. Philadelphia, Pennsylvania: University of Pennsylvania Press, 1979.

Meyer, L. B. Exploiting limits: Creation, archetypes, and change. *Daedalus*, 1980, *109*, 177–205.

Narmour, E. *Beyond Schenkerism*. Chicago, Illinois: University of Chicago Press, 1977.

Schenker, H. *Der Freie Satz*. Vienna: Universal Edition, 1956.

Siegel, S. *Nonparametric statistics for the behavioral sciences*. New York: McGraw-Hill, 1956.

White, B. Recognition for distorted melodies. *American Journal of Psychology*, 1960, *73*, 100–107.

Yeston, M. *The stratification of musical rhythm*. New Haven, Connecticut: Yale University Press, 1976.

Yeston, M. (Ed.) *Reading in Schenker analysis*. New Haven, Connecticut: Yale University Press, 1977.

11

Structural Representations of Musical Pitch

Roger N. Shepard

I.	Introduction	344
II.	Unidimensional Approaches to Pitch	344
	A. The Purely Physical Approach	344
	B. The Psychophysical Approach	345
	C. The Cognitive–Structural Approach	346
III.	Potentially Multidimensional Approaches to Pitch	347
	A. A Purely Physical Approach	347
	B. A Psychophysical Approach	347
	C. A Cognitive–Structural Approach	349
IV.	The Spatial Representation of Pitch	350
	A. Foundations for Unidimensional Psychoacoustic Scales	350
	B. Foundations for Multidimensional Cognitive–Structural Representations	351
	C. The Form of the Data Required	354
	D. Constraints Inherent in Any Spatial Representation	355
	E. The Construction of the Implied Structure by Multidimensional Scaling	356
	F. The Construction of the Implied Structure by Euclidean Composition	357
	G. Considerations in Choosing Structural Components	357
	H. A Proposed Set of Component Structures	359
	I. Some Derivable Compound Structures	361
V.	Illustrative Analyses of Empirical Data	365
	A. Multidimensional Scaling (Using Individual Difference Scaling)	365
	B. Euclidean Composition (Using Linear Regression)	367
VI.	Discussion	369
	A. Is Pitch Really Multidimensional?	369
	B. Multidimensional Variation of the Pitch of Synthesized Tones	370
	C. Further Comments on Psychoacoustic versus Cognitive–Structural Representations	372
	D. Alternative Cognitive–Structural Representations of Musical Pitch	373
	E. The Two-dimensional Melodic Map	374

The Psychology of Music

343

F. The Two-dimensional Harmonic Map 376
G. Structural Properties of Musical Scales 378
H. Pitch as a Morphophoric Medium 380
I. The Problem of the Representation of Pitch within a Tonal Context 381
VII. Conclusions 384
References 385

I. INTRODUCTION

In this chapter I am concerned with the perceived relations between musical tones and with schemes for representing such tones as points in a geometrical structure (psychophysical scale, musical scale, or higher dimensional spatial model) in such a way that the perceptually important relations between the tones have direct counterparts in the geometrical structure (as relations of spatial proximity or, possibly, collinearity). I argue that the traditional psychoacoustic representations are inadequate for the representation of the relations between pitches that are perceived musically, and I propose some more complex structures that appear to capture more of these musically significant relations.

Throughout, I am concerned with relative pitch only, that is, with the perceived relations between two or more pitches. The ability to identify the absolute pitch of a single tone with accuracy, though of considerable interest in itself (Bachem, 1955; Ward, 1963), is quite rare even among musicians and may be essentially independent of the ability to discriminate differences in pitch (Oakes, 1955). For most listeners absolute identification of individual pitches—just as the absolute identification of individual loudnesses, brightnesses, durations, etc.—is comparatively crude and structurally impoverished. For ecological reasons we are quite generally more responsive to the relations and, particularly, to the ratios between physical quantities than we are to those physical quantities themselves (Shepard, 1978c). This appears to be true for the attributes of musical tones as well.

II. UNIDIMENSIONAL APPROACHES TO PITCH

A. The Purely Physical Approach

For the purposes purely of physical specification of an acoustic vibration, there is little reason to distinguish the pitch of the vibration from its physical correlate, frequency, if the vibration is a simple, sinusoidal vibration. For anyone concerned with the response of a listener, however, a distinction between psychological pitch and physical frequency becomes essential. For, whether the relationship between tones a and b is equivalent to that between two other tones c and d, as these tones are perceived by a human listener, is an empirical question. It can only be answered by determining such things as whether the listener will in fact accept the interval c–d as equivalent to the interval $a-b$, whether actual frequencies of error or latencies of response will in fact be equivalent in discriminating c and d as in discriminating a and b, and so on. As a result of internal transformations in the process of perceptual registration, psychological equivalence of these kinds is not ensured merely by equating physical differences in frequencies. Perhaps we should equate, instead, differences in log frequency or differences in some other nonlinear function of frequency.

An identification of pitch with physical frequency runs into further difficulties when more complex tones or combinations of tones are considered. A complex sound may be heard to have a well-defined pitch, and listeners may be able to adjust the frequency of a variable sinusoid to match that perceived pitch. Yet the sinusoidal frequency produced by such a match may not in some cases (such as that variously referred to as subjective pitch, residue pitch, or the missing fundamental) correspond to any physically measurable frequency in the originally presented sound (Schouten, 1938; see Plomp, 1976, pp. 112–114; Ward, 1954).

B. The Psychophysical Approach

The classical psychophysical approach, as originally proposed by Fechner (1860–1966) and most vigorously advocated in recent years by Stevens (1975), attempted to determine the mathematical form of the monotonic psychophysical function that would convert the physical value of a stimulus (its frequency, say, in the case of sinusoidal tone) into a corresponding psychological value (pitch). Pitch was thus treated in much the same way as other subjective variables, such as the loudness of a tone or brightness of a light, which were also regarded as monotonic functions of their corresponding physical variables (amplitude and luminance, respectively). By discovering the appropriate psychophysical function, it was hoped, the physical scale (in our case, frequency) would in effect be relatively stretched and compressed in different regions with the result that if tones a and b were separated by the same distance as tones c and d on the resulting transformed scale, the interval $a-b$ would be perceptually equivalent to the interval $c-d$. One example of such a scale for pitch is the *mel* scale developed by Stevens and his associates (Stevens & Volkman, 1940; Stevens, Volkman, & Newman, 1937; or, for a more recent variant, see Beck & Shaw, 1961, 1963).

At this point the question arises, however, whether a unique psychological scale of pitch results regardless of the particular choice of listeners, tones, tasks, or types of data collected. Not surprisingly, in view of the complexity and flexibility of the human organism and the multidimensional variety of tones that can give rise to an impression of pitch, the answer is negative. For example, if listeners who have not been especially selected for musical ability are presented with pure sinusoidal tones in the absence of any musical context, the resulting scale of pitch will tend to be compressed at the low-frequency end relative to a log frequency scale—reflecting the fact that the ear is less sensitive to differences between tones standing in the same frequency ratio when those tones are both at the low end of the continuum of audible frequencies. Indeed, successive octaves, which are equally spaced in log frequency (and on a piano keyboard), are for this reason more and more compressed as we move toward the low end of the mel scale of pitch. From the standpoint of the musician, however, such a representation is quite unsatisfactory. It fails to preserve the fact that in a musical context there is something unique about a particular musical interval, such as an octave, regardless of where the two tones separated by that interval fall—at least within a range for which musical intervals are well perceived as such, say between 100 and 4000 Hz (Attneave & Olson, 1971; Dowling, in press; Guttman & Pruzansky, 1962; Watt, 1917, p. 63).

C. The Cognitive-Structural Approach

In order to obtain data that are more reflective of the relations between tones as they are perceived musically, one needs to depart from traditional psychoacoustic practice. In particular, one needs (a) to present the tones in a more musical context in which, for example, the intervals between the tones are those of a standard musical scale and perhaps the tones themselves possess some of the upper harmonics whose absence renders pure sinusoids so lacking in musical interest and (b) to ensure that the listeners possess at least the minimum level of musical ability necessary to be responsive to musically significant intervals.

The point was forcefully demonstrated by Attneave and Olson (1971). They showed that when the task was one of judging whether the musical intervals in a short melody were or were not the same under various overall shifts of the melody in pitch height (i.e., were or were not correct transpositions), the psychologically equivalent intervals were those on the logarithmic scale rather than on previous psychophysical scales of pitch such as the mel scale. This leads to a fundamental distinction, which I develop more fully later in this chapter—a distinction between what I refer to as the psychoacoustic and the cognitive-structural approach to pitch.

Quite apart from this distinction there is, however, a fundamental limitation inherent in any purely unidimensional representation of pitch. Even if one chooses a scale such that a musically significant interval has the same size at all locations along that scale—that is, even if one chooses the log scale—there is no way in which such a unidimensional scale can represent the fact that under appropriately musical conditions, two tones separated by an especially significant interval, such as the octave (e.g., see Allen, 1967; Krumhansl & Shepard, 1979), are preceived to be more closely related than two tones separated by a slightly smaller interval, such as the major seventh. In order to accomodate an increse in similarity between all tones separated by any particular interval, the rectilinear scale of pitch must be deformed into some more complex structure requiring, as we shall later see, a higher-dimensional embedding space. (It is for this reason that the following approaches are characterized as "potentially multidimensional." However, an explicit consideration of the nature of the multidimensional geometry to which they lead will be deferred to a later section in this chapter.)

III. POTENTIALLY MULTIDIMENSIONAL
APPROACHES TO PITCH

A. A Purely Physical Approach

The motion that tones separated by certain intervals may actually have more in common than tones separated by somewhat smaller differences in log frequency has, in fact, a long history. Even for pure, sinusoidal tones the degree of musical significance of the relation between a pair of such tones has been recognized since the time of Pythagoras to be related to the simplicity of the numerical ratio between the two frequencies (or, more precisely, in the case of Pythagoras, between the lengths of the two vibrating strings)—with the octave first (with a ratio of 2:1), followed by the perfect fifth (3:2), the perfect fourth (4:3), the major third (5:4), and so on. However, it cannot be the simplicity of the numerical ratio of the frequencies, in any strict sense, that is the determining factor:

1. As Risset (1978) has remarked, ratios that are very close to simple ratios (e.g., 29,998:20,000) are highly complex and yet indiscriminable from the corresponding simple ratios (in this case 3:2).

2. In fact, the interval that listeners accept as the best octave is not the interval with a precisely two-to-one frequency ratio but one with a slightly larger and thus numerically much more complex ratio (Ward, 1954; also see Burns, 1974; Dowling, 1973b, in press; Elfner, 1964; Sundberg & Lindqvist, 1973; Ward & Martin, 1961 Chapter 10, this volume). And the frequencies of the tones actually produced by musicians or preferred by listeners as representative of other musical intervals, as well, often fail to conform to the predicted most simple ratios (Seashore, 1938; Ward & Martin, 1961; Van Esbroeck & Montfort—cited in Risset, 1978).

3. Preference ratings that listeners give for pairs of tones that do stand in the various simple frequency ratios tend to depart systematically from the orderings of those ratios predicted on the basis of what is usually taken to be their numerical simplicities—with, for example, the major third (5:4) often preferred to the numerically simpler perfect fourth (4:3) (e.g., Butler & Daston, 1968; Krumhansl & Shepard, 1979; see also Davies, 1978, p. 158; Fyda, 1975; Van de Geer, Levelt, & Plomp, 1962).

4. Despite numerological theories going back at least to Leibnitz (see Revesz, 1954, p. 50), to my knowledge no psychologically plausible mechanism has been offered to explain how a listener determines that two tones achieve or approximate a simple frequency ratio—particularly when the tones are pure sinusoids and are presented only successively.

B. A Psychophysical Approach

von Helmholtz (1862–1954) held that for musical and hence harmonically rich tones, it is the extent of actual coincidence between the upper harmonics rather than merely the simplicity of the frequency ratio of the fundamentals that primarily determines the degree to which two tones are perceived to have a harmonious relation. The rationale for this view is that failures of coincidence between harmonics of nearly the same frequencies tend to produce rapid, temporal pulsations or beats that, to the extent that they are audible, contribute to the perceived roughness, discord, or dissonance between simultaneously sounded tones. Although departures from strict coincidences between harmonics can be defined purely in terms of the physical stimuli, the importance of the audibility of the beats in producing perceptual roughness or discord ultimately leads to considerations of the response of the ear to small differences in relative frequency at various absolute levels of frequency, amplitude, and timbre—hence my characterization of this approach as psychophysical rather than as purely physical. This approach has more recently been developed in considerable quantitative detail by Plomp and Levelt (1965), Kameoka and Kuriyagawa (1969), and others. Although the degree of consonance predicted for two tones depends in general on the harmonic content of the tones (Kameoka & Kuriyagawa, 1969), for most musical tones the predicted ordering of the standard musical intervals is in approximate agreement with that predicted on the basis of the simplicity of the frequency ratios of the fundamentals—with the octave predicted to be the most harmonious (after the unison), followed by the perfect fifth, and so on.

However, it cannot be that the actual audibility of beats directly determines the perceived musical relation between tones in general. When the tones are pure sinusoids or are presented successively (as melodic rather than harmonic intervals), the same musical intervals are recognized or, under some conditions, are preferred (Krumhansl & Shepard, 1979), although audible beats will be largely or (in the case of successive presentation) completely absent. Moreover, even for simultaneously presented, harmonically rich tones, owing to the properties of the ear, the audibility of the beats for any given interval will depend, as I noted, on the timbre and the placement of the tones within the range of audible frequencies (Risset, 1978). But the significant musical intervals, as I have also noted, can be recognized and appreciated for what they are regardless of their transpositional locations within an appropriate musical range and across musical instruments of very different timbres.

Despite these and other difficulties (shortly to be considered), the psychophysical approach continues to be developed in attempts to deal (in various ways that are beyond the scope of this chapter) with perceived pitch relations between more complex sounds, inharmonic tones, combinations of tones, filtered noises, pulse trains, and the like (e.g., de Boer, 1976; Goldstein, 1973; Terhardt, 1974; Wightman, 1973). In general, the objective of the psychophysical approach to pitch is to formulate quantitative rules according to which perceived pitches of sounds are related to physically specifiable properties of those sounds. However, from the cognitive–structural standpoint taken here, any purely psychophysical approach has two related shortcomings: first, it does not by itself make sufficient provision for the apparently important role in the interpretation of musical tones of cognitive structures that the listener brings to the situation or that have been induced in the listener by a preceding musical context; second, although it may—in discriminating, for example, between "spectral" and "periodicity" pitch—imply that perceived pitch is multidimensional, in focusing on the relation between physical variables and perceptual responses, the psychophysical approach does not generally concern itself with the precise multidimensional form of the interpretative cognitive structures themselves (although these internal structures may constrain the perceptual response quite as much as the physically specified external stimuli).

C. A Cognitive-Structural Approach

There is in fact a growing body of empirical evidence that in the perception of tones in a musical context, what each externally presented tone gives rise to within the listener is not a percept that varies continuously with the physical parameters of that tone according to a fixed, though perhaps multidimensional, psychophysical function. Rather, a more apt description seems to be that by a kind of "categorical perception," each continuously variable tone activates the closest node in some discrete cognitive structure corresponding, for example, to a tonal framework or diatonic scale (Balzano, 1978, 1980; Dowling, 1978; Francès, 1958, p. 49; Ward, 1970), which may be explicitly established by a preceding musical context (Krumhansl & Shepard, 1979) or which may be induced by the musical relations between the test tones themselves (Blechner, 1977; Burns & Ward, 1978; Locke & Kellar, 1973; Siegel & Siegel, 1977a,b; Zatorre & Halpern, 1979). (For further indications of the importance of a tonal interpretive framework, see Cohen, 1978; Cuddy, Cohen, & Miller, 1979; Dewar, Cuddy, & Mewhort, 1977; Francès, 1958, Experiments III & IX.) Indeed, in agreement with expectations based on music theory (e.g., see Risset, 1978, p. 526), Krumhansl (1979) has obtained evidence, to which I shall later return, that the perception of the relation between tones separated by any given physical interval depends on the relation of the pair of tones to a contextually established tonal center (or "tonic") and, hence, can never be explained solely in terms of physical properties of the two presented test tones themselves—no matter how complex the specification of those properties may be.

It is understandable that psychophysical investigators, who have traditionally focused on the operating characteristic of sensory transducers, have tended to prefer simple physical stimuli—especially, in the case of the ear, sinusoidal tones varying on easily specified physical variables of frequency and amplitude—and have eschewed the cognitive complications that might arise in a musical context. It is only from the very different standpoint of the cognitive scientist—who is accustomed to working toward the characterization of the abstract mental structures that underlie our higher level perceptual, conceptual, and linguistic competencies—that an investigation of the abstract structural complexities that make possible the appreciation of a Bach fugue or a Beethoven quartet appears at all enticing.

The analogy with the study of language may be helpful here. The investigation of how the ear responds to carefully controlled acoustic events in the time–frequency domain is not irrelevant to the problem of the recognition of speech. But in order to

understand how the spoken sentences of a natural language are perceptually segmented, syntactically parsed, and semantically interpreted, we must concern ourselves even more with highly developed syntactic and semantic structures and rules,
which operate at a very different and physiologically less accessible level and,
perhaps, in a very different, more discrete and combinatorial mode (Chomsky, 1965;
Winograd, 1972).

More specifically, the "competence-performance" distinction that Chomsky enun-
ciated for language (see Chomsky, 1965) may have an instructive analogue for musical
cognition. Chomsky argued that our linguistic competence presupposes an implicit
knowledge of general algebraic rules of syntactic formation and transformation, even
though our actual linguistic performance in any concrete situation may be more or less
faulty, distorted, or incomplete—particularly in dealing with long, complex, or self-
embedded constructions—owing to limitations of short-term memory, failures of
lexical retrieval, difficulties of articulation, external distraction, and so on. Similarly,
our musical competence may presuppose an implicit knowledge of underlying structures (e.g., diatonic scales, hierarchies of tonal functions) and transformations (e.g.,
transpositions, inversions, and the like), even though for reasons of sensory, memory,
or motor limitations, we may fail on occassions to comprehend or to execute complex
musical passages.

In particular, I suggest that considerations of the sensory limitations of the input
transducer—such as the reduced efficiency of the ear in discriminating nearby amusi-
cal pitches at the low end of the continuum of audible frequencies, which such
psychophysical scales of pitch as the mel scale had been designed to represent—are
essentially irrelevant to the problem of the representation of the cognitive structures
that underlie the interpretation of musical sequences. In order to preserve the musically important structural relations between tones (the musical intervals of the octave,
fifth, and so on) and in order to preserve invariance under the musically important
transformations (e.g., transposition), the cognitive representation of musical pitch
must have properties of great regularity, symmetry, and transformational invariance.

The question of the representation of musical pitch then comes down to this: How
can we represent musical tones as points in a regular structure so that (a) all pairs of
tones separated by the same musical interval are separated by the same distance in this
structure and (b) tones separated by especially significant musical intervals (such as
the octave and perfect fifth) have corresponding special relations (e.g., of spatial
proximity) within this structure?

IV. THE SPATIAL REPRESENTATION OF PITCH

A. Foundations for Unidimensional Psychoacoustic Scales

Although the various unidimensional scales that psychophysicists have constructed
for the representation of pitch differ in detail, they all appear to presuppose certain

basic conditions. I suggest that the most essential of these can be set down roughly as follows:

1. *Unique correspondence.* Each pitch corresponds to a particular point in a metric space.
2. *Preservation of equivalence.* Pitches perceived to stand in the same psychological relation correspond to points separated by the same distance in the space.
3. *Monotonicity.* Pitches perceived to be more similar to a given pitch correspond to points that are closer in the space to the point corresponding to that given pitch.
4. *Unidimensionality.* The metric space is the one-dimensional Euclidean line.

The difference between the individual scales of pitch that have been constructed (such as those of Attneave & Olson, 1971; Beck & Shaw, 1961; Stevens & Volkman, 1940; Stevens, Volkman, & Newman, 1937) arise primarily from differences in how the investigators set about determining (in accordance with the second of these four conditions) which pitches "stand in the same psychological relation." Thus, if the determination was based on the discriminability of sinusoidal tones (just as much as if it were based on the discriminability of narrow bands of white noise) without any musical context, the points representing pitches an octave apart tended to be separated by smaller distances at the low end of the scale. Whereas if the determination was made on the basis of judgments of equivalence of intervals between musical tones under transposition (as by Attneave & Olson, 1971), the points for pitches an octave apart tended, over a suitable musical range, to be equally spaced (also see Dowling, 1978; Null, 1974; Ward, 1954; Burns and Ward, this volume, Chapter 8).

As I have already implied, however, the simultaneous satisfaction of all four of these conditions is not always possible. Particularly in the more musical context the fact that tones separated by special musical intervals (such as the octave) tend to be perceived as having more in common than tones separated by somewhat smaller intervals cannot simultaneously be reconciled with the conditions both of monotonicity (3) and of unidimensionality (4).

B. Foundations for Multidimensional Cognitive–Structural Representations

If the richer structural relations that apparently hold between the pitches of tones that are interpreted musically are to be fully captured in the spatial representation itself (apart, that is, from the mapping rules that relate that spatial representation to the set of possible pitches), it is the condition of unidimensionality rather than the condition of monotonicity that we should abandon. (Later, however, I consider the possibility of weakening in addition the monotonicity condition and of representing some special relations of pitch by colinearity rather than exclusively by proximity of points in the multidimensional space.) For the present, then, I take as the basis for a cognitive–structural representation of musical pitch, only the first three of the four stated conditions, and I suppose that the representational space may in general be multidimensional. If, now, tones separated by standard musical intervals are presented to musical listeners under appropriate conditions, all tones separated by the same interval should, I claim, be perceived as musically equivalent—except for tones that are so low or so high in pitch as to exceed the performance limitations of the sensory transducer (cf., again, Attneave & Olson, 1971; Dowling, in press; Guttman & Pruzansky, 1962; Watt, 1917, p. 63; and my present invocation of the competence-performance distinction). By the second of the three retained conditions, the points corresponding to such tones should be equally spaced in the geometrical structure. What, then, will be the form of this structure?

The equidistant, regular spacing of the points implies that the structure maps into itself under all distance-preserving transformations, including translations, reflections, and rotations. In fact, according to a geometrical theorem of classical kinematics, the most general rigid motion of three-dimensional space into itself is a rotation together with a translation along the axis of the rotation—that is, a helical or screwlike motion (Coxeter, 1961, pp. 101, 321; Goldstein, 1950, p. 124; Greenwood, 1965, p. 318; Hilbert & Cohn-Vossen, 1932/1952, pp. 82, 285). This theorem, properly generalized to higher-dimensional spaces and also to include reflections, implies that the structure we are looking for must be a generalized helical structure or some degenerate variant of such a structure—including, in the simplest cases, the straight line, if there is no rotational component, or the circle, if there is no translational component.

For example, as illustrated in Fig. 1, we can deform the usual rectilinear scale of pitch into a simple helix having one complete turn per octave and thus represent any increased similarity at the octave by a reduced distance of separation (e.g., by Path b versus Path a between C and C' in the figure). Indeed by varying the ratio of the rotational component (the circumference of the helix) to the translational component (the rectilinear height of one complete turn), we can move anywhere between the two degenerate cases of the helix: (1) that in which it is stretched back into a straight line and there is, therefore, no longer any increased similarity at the octave, and (2) that in which it is compressed all the way down into a circle and there is complete perceptual identity of all tones in the octave relation (such as C, C', C'', C''', etc.). It was in fact through this line of thought that I was originally led to the computer synthesis of a special set of tones as a concrete instantiation of the latter possibility of complete octave equivalence and, hence, complete circularity of pitch (Shepard, 1964b, 1970; Shepard & Zajac, 1965).

In the process of my earlier explorations of the possibilities of this simple helical representation for pitch, I soon discovered that in similar efforts to account for the increased similarity at the octave, variants of this helix had long before been proposed by other theorists (for example, by Drobish, 1855; Revesz, 1954; Ruckmick, 1929; also see Pickler, 1966, concerning Drobish's proposal and the related 1874 proposal of a planar spiral by Donkin). By now the implied rectilinear and circular components of the helical representation of pitch have become widely enough accepted to be generally referred to as *tone height* and *tone chroma*, respectively (Bachem, 1950; Revesz, 1954; Risset, 1978; also see Kallman & Massaro, 1979).

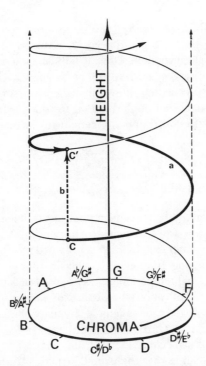

Fig. 1. The simple helix of pitch (relabeled from Shepard, 1965).

The distinction that I have urged between the cognitive–structural and the psychoacoustic approaches to pitch applies just as much to the multidimensional or helical as to the unidimensional or rectilinear representations. Thus, my arguments for equality of intervals and invariance under transposition in the perception of musical pitch imply that the helix must be a completely regular helix, falling on the surface of a right cylinder, with successive turns equally spaced with respect to the axis of the cylinder (just as I have previously portrayed the helix, e.g., see Shepard, 1965, p. 105). Only in this way will the helical structure map into itself (by a rigid helical motion consisting of a translation and/or a rotation) under musical transposition. This is in contrast to the helical representations proposed earlier from a more psychophysical standpoint by Drobish (1855) and Ruckmick (1929), in which the helix was intentionally distorted so that intervals (and hence successive turns of the helix) were, once again, relatively compressed toward the low end of the range of audible frequencies.

Of course, this simple helix in three-dimensional space, whether regular or distorted, cannot account for an increased similarity between tones separated by intervals other than the octave. Yet there are strong indications that there is indeed something special about other musical intervals, such as, for example, the perfect fifth or the major third—indications from music theory (e.g., Goldman, 1965; Schenker, 1954/1973), from psychoacoustic considerations (e.g., von Helmholtz, 1862/1954; Plomp & Levelt, 1965; Kameoka & Kuriyagawa, 1969), from group-theoretic arguments (see, especially, Balzano, 1978, 1980); and from recent empirical evidence (Balzano, 1977, in press; Butler & Daston, 1968; Krumhansl & Shepard, 1979). In order to generalize the helical model so that it will accommodate other special relations, in addition to the octave we have to move into a still higher dimensional embedding space. Before proceeding, however, we need first to consider a little more carefully the form of the data that might force us to adopt such a higher-dimensional representation and, then, the constraints inherent in any spatial representation of such data.

C. The Form of the Data Required

In the case of the musical pitch, we can simplify our problem by restricting consideration to the set of discrete musical tones corresponding to the equally tempered chromatic (12-tone or semitone) scale, which is obtained by dividing each octave into 12 steps that are equal in log frequency. (Later in this chapter I argue that the restriction to the scale of equal temperament, as opposed to some scale approximating "just intonation," with its implication of a distinction between the sharp of one scale degree and the flat of the degree above (e.g., C♯ versus D♭) as well as the choice of whether the octave is taken to correspond to a frequency ratio of exactly two-to-one or somewhat more, may be of little consequence from the present, cognitive standpoint.) Moreover, I propose to assume that the overall structure is determined by the perceived relations between tones at all intervals of an octave or less; that is, that the perceived relations between tones separated by more than an octave can be inferred from the relations between tones that are no more than an octave apart. As a first approximation this assumption seems reasonable on musical grounds, and it has the further virtue of simplifying geometrical considerations. However, it is an assumption that is susceptible to empirical evaluation and can subsequently be modified if necessary.

By my assumptions, then, the generalized helical structure of the set of chromatic pitches is to be determined from just 12 numbers, representing the perceived degrees of musical relations between tones separated by the 12 musical intervals within an octave—minor second, major second, minor third, major third, perfect fourth, tritone, perfect fifth, minor sixth, major sixth, minor seventh, major seventh, and octave (which more or less following others, e.g., Balzano, 1981; Balzano & Liesch, in press, I abbreviate as m2, M2, m3, M3, P4, T, P5, m6, M6, m7, M7, and O, respectively). Such data might be obtained from various sources, including subjective ratings of successive (melodic) intervals presented in a tonal context (Krumhansl, 1979; Krumhansl & Shepard, 1979) or of simultaneous (harmonic) intervals (e.g., Butler & Daston, 1968; also see Davies, 1978, p. 158), or under appropriate experimental conditions, from observed frequencies of confusion or latencies of discrimination between different intervals (e.g., Balzano, 1977; Balzano & Liesch, in press). For comparison, theoretical numbers might also be calculated on the basis of acoustic or psychoacoustic considerations (such as those presented by Kameoka & Kuriyagawa, 1969).

D. Constraints Inherent in Any Spatial Representation

The proposal to represent relations of pitch as relations of spatial proximity entails certain constraints on those pitch relations corresponding to constraints on distances in a metric space. Even in the case of the most general type of metric space, the distances are subject to the three standard axioms of distance, which for present purposes can be set down as follows (see Shepard, 1980):

$$d_{ij} \geq d_{ii} = 0 \quad \text{(positivity)}$$
$$d_{ij} = d_{ji} \quad \text{(symmetry)}$$
$$d_{ik} \leq d_{ij} + d_{jk} \quad \text{(triangle inequality)}$$

And for more specific types of spaces, still stronger constraints hold. In the case of n-dimensional Euclidean space—in particular, the three-point triangle inequality is expanded in effect into a related $(n + 2)$-point condition (see Blumenthal, 1938, pp. 55 ff.; Shepard, 1974, 1980a).

In the application to relations of pitch, the triangle inequality implies that the closer two tones are to any third tone, the closer those two tones must be to each other. As an example, since the two tones a major third away on either side of any given tone are necessarily a minor sixth from each other, we cannot represent major thirds by small distances without representing minor sixths by at least moderately small distances. Moreover, from the triangle inequality together with symmetry, it follows that the closer any two tones are to each other, the more nearly equal must be the distances from those two tones to any third tone. In particular, this implies that if tones separated by an octave are close together, any two intervals related to each other by an inversion in the octave must have a comparable (close or distant) relation. For example, closeness of tones separated by a perfect fifth would then entail moderate closeness of tones separated by a perfect fourth, remoteness of tones separated by a major seventh would entail moderate remoteness of tones separated by a minor second, and so on.

These geometrical constraints are not without some musical plausibility. For example, there are music-theoretic reasons and even some empirical data (Balzano, 1977, 1981; Balzano & Liesch, in press) supporting the expectation that pairs of intervals related by an inversion in the octave (e.g., P4 and P5, M3 and m6, m2 and M7, etc.) are to some extent related to each other—especially to the extent that octaves are treated as equivalent. Indeed, the fact that a musical listener can hear a sequence of normal musical tones ascending by major sevenths—either as rising by large, slightly less than octave steps in pitch height or as falling by small, minor second steps in chroma (to which I have previously called attention—Shepard, 1964b, p. 2346) is attributable to this phenomenon of partial octave equivalence and the consequent

partial equivalence of inversions. Nevertheless, empirical data on the perceived relations between tones may systematically depart, as we shall see, from even these quite
general geometical constraints. Accordingly, I shall consider in a later section how we
might accommodate such departures without abandoning a spatial representation, by
elaborating the mapping assumed to hold between that representation and the particular relations perceived between the pitches presented in a particular musical context.

E. The Construction of the Implied Structure by Multidimensional Scaling

Generally, data on the degree of perceived relations between tones separated by
different intervals cannot be directly interpreted as distances; they are measures
merely of "proximity"—that is, numbers related only monotonically to distances.
(This is an agreement with the monotonicity condition already stated.) However, as I
demonstrated in 1962, such measures of proximity are often sufficient to determine
the corresponding, unknown distances with considerable precision (Shepard, 1962,
1966). Accordingly, one who accepts the assumption that all tones separated by the
same musical interval are equivalent can appropriately enter copies of the empirically
obtained numbers for the 12 different intervals until all off-diagonal cells are filled in
the 13×13 square matrix giving the estimated proximity between each tone and
every other within one complete octave. (Each row or column of the completed matrix
will be identical to the preceding except for a circular shift by one cell.) Application of
nonmetric multidimensional scaling or "analysis of proximities" (Kruskal, 1964;
Shepard, 1962) should then yield the implied spatial structure for one octave in the
Euclidean space for the minimum number of dimensions needed to accommodate this
structure. In a later section I describe such an analysis using, however, a metric
variant of multidimensional scaling subsequently developed by Carroll and Chang
(1970) to take account of differences in the patterns of judgments made by different
individuals (in this case, listeners with different musical backgrounds).

One limitation of multidimensional scaling from the standpoint advocated here is
that there is no guarantee that the structure obtained in any particular number of
dimensions will realize the perfect symmetry and regularity that I take to be implied
by our musical competence. In particular, as we shall see, if the tones from just one
octave are scaled, the two ends of the octave-long structure may be somewhat distorted with the result that it cannot be extended into other octaves in such a way that
the entire structure is strictly invariant under transposition. One could collect data for
tones spanning two or more octaves, but this would require collecting data for intervals greater than an octave and analyzing a much larger matrix—that is $(12n + 1) \times$
$(12n + 1)$ for n octaves. Moreover, the structure, though considerably more regular,
might still be subject to some distortion—again, especially toward its two ends.
Fortunately, for certain kinds of data the desired structure can be synthesized in
another way that ensures complete regularity and transpositional invariance.

F. The Construction of the Implied Structure by Euclidean Composition

Just as a helical motion can be generated as a combination of two simple motions (a rotation and a translation along the axis of the rotation), a complex helical structure can be constructed out of simpler, circular and rectilinear components. According to a Euclidean rule of composition (Blackett, 1967, p. 213; Shepard, 1978a), the squared distances between n points in another structural component (a one-dimensional line, say) when added to the corresponding squared distances between n points in another structural component (a circle in a two-dimensional plane, say) yield the squared distances between n points in a resulting combined structure (in this case, a helix in three-dimensional space). In this type of "Euclidean composition" of complex structures out of simpler components, the number of points in the resultant structure is the same as the number in each of its structural components, but the number of dimensions needed to embed the resultant structure is the sum of the dimensions needed to embed each of the components (in the example given, $1 + 2 = 3$).

The additivity of the squared distances in Euclidean composition means that under the appropriate condition we can use methods of linear regression to estimate a set of weights—one weight for each of the proposed structural components—that will provide a best fit to the matrix of data. The appropriate condition is, of course, that we must be able to put or to transform the data into a form in which those numbers are, to a sufficient approximation, linearly related to squared distances. We have in effect thus traded the absence, in multidimensional scaling, of constraints to ensure the desired strict regularity and symmetry of the obtained representation for the imposition of stronger, metric assumptions about the data. In principle, extensions of existing methods should enable one either (a) to impose the desired regularity in the process of obtaining a representation by nonmetric multidimensional scaling (cf. Bentler & Weeks, 1978; de Leeuw & Heiser, 1979) or, equivalently, (b) to carry out the linear regression without using more than the ordinal properties of the data (cf. Kruskal, 1965; Kruskal & Shepard, 1974). But in practice the same overdetermination of the solution that makes nonmetric analyses possible should make the results of a standard linear regression relatively insensitive to departures from the assumed linearity (e.g., see Abelson & Tukey, 1963; Weeks & Bentler, 1979; Shepard, 1974).

G. Considerations in Choosing Structural Components

Precisely what set of structural components ought to be taken as the initial basis set for the proposed regression analysis is not immediately clear because the several conditions that such a set should satisfy must be balanced against each other. Principle among these conditions are, it seems to me, the following four:

1. There should be at least one component, analogous to the rectilinear dimension of pitch height in the previously proposed simple helix, that can provide for both (a)

the possibility of arbitrarily large distances between tones that are separated by arbitrarily large numbers of semitone steps and (b) the interpolation, when necessary, of additional tones (such as quartertones) within the standard semitone intervals of the chromatic scale.

2. For each musical interval, from the minor second to the octave, that might have a special perceptual relation (that is, a perceptual proximity not adequately provided for by a purely rectilinear component of pitch height), there should be a corresponding component in which the distance between all tones separated by that interval is as small as possible relative to the other distances in that component. An appropriately weighted combination of such components would then come as close as possible to realizing whatever pattern of proximities is indicated by a given set of data.

3. The components needed to fit the data should, however, be as parsimonious as possible—both with regard to the number of these components and with regard to the number of dimensions required for each component.

4. The assignment of positive weights to the components for intervals other than the octave, such as the perfect fifth, should not entail a positive increment in the distance corresponding to the interval of an octave in the overall structure. The motivation for this condition is that it is possible with musical listeners (Krumhansl & Shepard, 1979) or with specially contrived tones (Shepard, 1964b) to approach complete equivalence between all tones standing in the octave relation while at the same time maintaining an augmented proximity for certain other intervals such as the fifth.

If we had to satisfy only the first two conditions, we could choose as the structural component corresponding to the interval consisting of n semitone steps, an n-cornered regular simplex in $(n - 1)$-dimensional space. All tones differing from any given tone by the specified interval would then collapse into the same vertex of the simplex and hence would be separated by a distance of zero while any two tones that do not differ either by that interval or by any integer multiple of it would fall on different vertices and hence would be separated by some fixed, larger distance, say unity. However, the triangle inequality constrains us, in thus making the distance arbitrarily small for any specified interval, to make the distances comparably small for all multiples of that interval as well. One consequence is that for the interval of the minor second, the components as just described would collapse into a single point in which all intervals (being alike, integer multiples of the minor second) would be represented by a distance of zero. Hence, any differential proximities of minor seconds could not be achieved by the weighted addition of such a component but would, instead, have to be provided for by the rectilinear pitch-height component (in which, however, tones differing by a minor second are adjacent rather than coincident).

More seriously, the proposal to erect the generalized helical structure by combining the rectilinear component with simplexes of various dimensionalities fails to satisfy Conditions 3 and 4. Thus, in violation of Condition 3, the components for the large intervals—including, particularly, the all-important octave—are notably unparsimonious. While the minor and major third would require, respectively, the equilateral triangle and regular tetrahedron and hence embedding spaces of just two and three dimensions, the octave alone would require the 12-cornered regular simplex and hence an 11-dimensional embedding space. And in violation of Condition 4, since the octave is not an integer multiple of the perfect fifth, differential emphasis of the perfect fifth would entail a departure from octave equivalence. Yet the evidence indicates that it is just those listeners manifesting the strongest octave equivalence who also perceive the relation between tones separated by the perfect fifth to be very pronounced as well (Krumhansl & Shepard, 1979).

Another more parsimonious type of component is the simple helix, already proposed as a way of representing the octave relation. Thus, for each other interval we could take, as the corresponding structural component, the simple helix that completes one full turn in exactly that interval. The rectilinear subcomponent common to all of the component helices could then be factored out to yield (a) a single pitch-height component as required by Condition 1 and (b) a separate component in the form of a circle (or regular polygon) for each musically significant interval with the component for the interval consisting of n semitone steps represented by a circular n-gon with its n equally spaced vertices embedded in just two dimensions. (The representation for the minor second again becomes degenerate and, so, must be entirely provided by the common, rectilinear component.)

Condition 4 still remains unsatisfied, however. Neither of the so-called "perfect" intervals—the musically important fifth or the fourth (which is the inversion of the fifth in the octave)—can be evenly divided into the octave. Consequently, the positive weighting of the circular n-gons for either of these two intervals entails a departure from octave equivalence (even when the weight of the rectilinear component corresponding to pitch height is reduced to zero).

H. A Proposed Set of Component Structures

Taking as essential the ability to represent the limiting case of full octave equivalence, I propose simply to substitute, for the five- and seven-sided polygons already considered for the perfect fourth and fifth, the well-known (and 12-sided) circle of fifths—which, under octave equivalence and hence inversion in the octave, can as well be interpreted as a circle of fourths traversed in the opposite direction. Although tones differing by a fifth (or a fourth) are not strictly coincident in this structure, they are at least adjacent (i.e., nearest neighbors) around the circle—just as tones differing by a second, while never coincident, are nearest neighbors both along the rectilinear pitch-height component and around the chroma circle. Moreover, octaves do become coincident in this structure. Hence, they no longer prevent the simultaneous achievement of octave equivalence and a strong relation at the fifth.

Finally, a further major simplification immediately becomes possible. As is to be expected under octave equivalence, each structural component, except the rectilinear one for pitch height (which is itself inherently incompatible with octave equivalence), is invariant under inversion of intervals. That is, within any component the distance is the same for any interval as for its inversion in the octave. Therefore, we can reduce

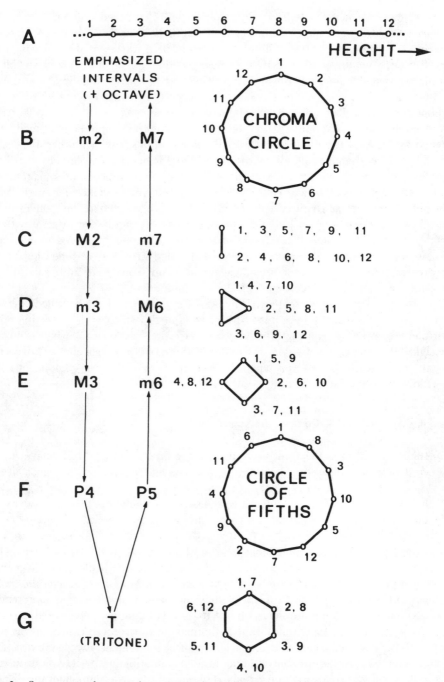

Fig. 2. Seven proposed structural components for the Euclidean synthesis of generalized helical representations for musical pitch.

our set of structural components to just the seven exhibited in Fig. 2: (A) a rectilinear component, which emphasizes both proximity of the minor second and large differences in pitch height; (B) the chroma circle, which emphasizes octave equivalence and proximities of both the minor second and its inversion, the major seventh; (C) the degenerate polygon, which emphasizes the major second and its multiples including its inversion, the minor seventh; (D) the triangle, which emphasizes the minor third and its multiples including its inversion, the major sixth; (E) the square, which emphasizes the major third and its multiples including its inversion, the minor sixth; (F) the circle of fifths, which emphasizes the perfect fifth and its inversion the perfect fourth; (G) the hexagon, which emphasizes the tritone, which being exactly half an octave is its own inversion. (The small numerals—1, 2, 3, . . . , 12—attached to the nodes of each of the components A through G represent successively higher semitones within any one octave. For example, if we begin on C, these numerals represent the tones C, C♯, D, . . . , B, respectively, and the next tone, 13 if it were included, would represent a return to C but one octave higher.)

The maximum number of dimensions that could be required using this basic set is given by the sum of the dimensions of the seven components. Since five of the components require two-dimensional embedding spaces, the overall number is 5(2) + 2(1) = 12 (which is, incidently, exactly the same as the number of distinct intervals in the octave). However, if some intervals (such as the tritone and perhaps the major second and minor third) turn out to have negligible weights, their corresponding components can be eliminated, yielding a considerable reduction in complexity and dimensionality of the overall structure.

The structural components displayed in the figure already contain some of the representations that have previously been discussed in connection with musical pitch—such as the rectilinear representation of pitch height in a one-dimensional embedding space (A), which corresponds to the log frequency scale of pitch advocated by Attneave and Olson (1971); the chroma circle in two-dimensional space (B), which has been proposed by a number of workers and was concretely instantiated in my computer-generated circular tones (Shepard, 1964b); and the circle (or "cycle") of fifths in two-dimensional space (F), which has played a central role in music theory (e.g., see Goldman, 1965; Schenker, 1954/1973).

I. Some Derivable Compound Structures

Weighted combinations of two or more of these structural components can yield a variety of more complex structures that show promise for the fuller representation of musical pitch. By combining A and B of Fig. 2, we obtain, as I have noted, a simple helix in three-dimensional space (Fig. 1) that is akin to the various helices that have previously been proposed to account simultaneously for the two factors of pitch height and similarity at the octave. Here, however, in accordance with my stipulation that the resulting structure should map strictly into itself under musical transposition, the helix generated by the proposed rule of composition will be completely regular

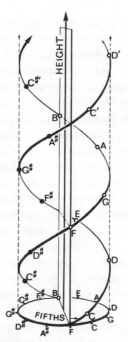

Fig. 3. The double helix of musical pitch in three dimensions (obtained by combining Components A and F of Fig. 2). As illustrated for C major, a vertical plane divides the tones in a key (white circles to right) from those not in that key (black circles to left).

and symmetrical rather than, for example, compressed at the low-frequency end. And, by combining other subsets of components, we can obtain other structures that I have more recently proposed for the still fuller representation of musical pitch (Shepard, 1978b, 1981a, 1982) as follows.

If we combine F (rather than B) with A, we obtain the "double helix of musical pitch" (Fig. 3) that I initially derived on the basis of rather different assumptions from those used here—including an assumption that successive steps of the diatonic scale can under some circumstances be heard as equivalent but not including any assumption about the importance of the perfect fifth itself (Shepard, 1978b). As a consequence of the fact that the circle of fifths is nevertheless present as one component, this three-dimensional structure has two related properties of some musical significance:

1. The tones included in any particular major diatonic key can be divided from the tones not in that key simply by passing a plane through the central axis of the double helix. Thus, as is illustrated, the plane passing through the diagonally opposite B and F in the base circle in the figure divides the tones (on the right) that are in the key of C major from the tones (on the left) that are not—indicated (in an analogy with a piano keyboard) by circles that are white and black, respectively.

2. Transpositions into the most closely related keys are achieved by the smallest

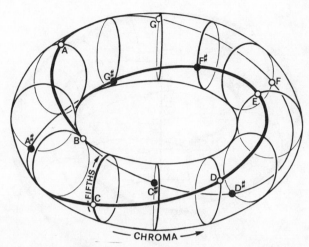

Fig. 4. The double helix wrapped around a torus in four dimensions (obtained by combining components B and F of Fig. 2).

angles of rotation of the dividing plane about the central axis. Thus, the two keys most closely related to the key of C are those of F and G—adjacent to C around the circle of fifths. (For convenience, in this and subsequent figures, the chromatic tones between adjacent C-major tones are indicated by sharps rather than by the equivalent flats—e.g., between C and D by C♯ rather than by D♭.)

If we combine F with B rather than with A, we obtain the double helix wound around a torus. This structure, generated as it is from a pair of two-dimensional components (the chroma circle and the circle of fifths), can only be isometrically embedded in four-dimensional space, where it realizes the full degree of symmetry required for transpositional invariance. A somewhat crude and distorted idea of its form can be gained from the sketch of a three-dimensional "projection" of this toroidal structure shown in Fig. 4. Since the points on the double helix of the earlier Fig. 3 fall on the surface of a right circular cylinder (the so-called "topological," "Cartesian," or "direct product" of the circle and the straight line—Blackett, 1967), one can think of the toroidal structure in Fig. 4 as having been obtained from that earlier structure by cutting a one-octave segment out of the cylinder and then bending the cylindrical segment around until its two free ends join to form the closed torus (the direct product of two circles). The move is exactly analogous to that of bending a one-octave segment out of the rectilinear scale of pitch height until the two free ends of that segment join to form the closed chroma circle in two-dimensional space. In both cases such a move would be required for the representation of tones, like my computer-generated circular tones (Shepard, 1964b), that achieve complete octave equivalence. Again, either of the two extremes can be approached in which either component completely dominates the other.

In order to obtain a more general representation, we can combine all three of these components, namely, the rectilinear pitch-height component (A), the chroma circle

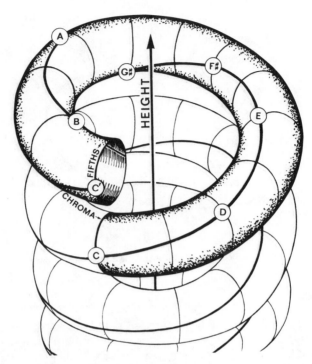

Fig. 5. The double helix wrapped around a helical cylinder in five dimensions (obtained by combining Components A, B, and F of Fig. 2).

(B), and the circle of fifths (F). The number of dimensions required to embed the resulting structure is five $(1 + 2 + 2)$, and, again, the intrinsic form of the structure can be no more than crudely suggested by the two-dimensional portrayal of a three-dimensional "projection" (as in Fig. 5). This structure, which is roughly describable as a double helix wound around a helical cylinder, should, however, go farther than any other that has previously been proposed to account for perceived relations of musical pitch. By varying the relative weights of the three components, one can account for (a) proximity in pitch height—that is, perceived similarity of tones separated by small intervals such as the major and particularly the minor second (as well, of course, as the even greater perceived similarities of any tones interpolated at microtonal steps within the semitone interval)—(b) heightened similarity at the octave, including the limiting case of complete octave equivalence, and (c) heightened similarity at the perfect fifth and (to the extent that octave equivalence is more heavily weighted than pitch height) its inversion, the perfect fourth. Moreover, much as I already explained for the double helix, tones in any major diatonic key remain linearly separable from tones not in that key with transpositions between the most closely related keys achieved by the smallest rotations of the hyperplane that separates them in five-dimensional space. (For some recent evidence for the psychological importance of closeness of relations between keys see Bartlett & Dowling, 1980.)

The most prominent musical interval that is not specifically provided for by the five-dimensional generalized helical structure of Fig. 5 is the major third. One can of course add the square component, E, and hence two more dimensions, if this proves necessary in fitting data. Note, also, that the previously considered alternative component for major thirds—namely, the three-dimensional regular tetrahedron—could also be introduced, even within the scheme shown in Fig. 2, by forming an appropriately weighted combination of components E and C. In the interest of parsimony, however, I hope that special components (C, D, and G) for the major second, minor third, and tritone (and their inversons) will prove to be dispensable.

V. ILLUSTRATIVE ANALYSES OF EMPIRICAL DATA

A. Multidimensional Scaling (Using Individual Difference Scaling)

As indicated earlier, many different types of data on the relations between musical tones differing in pitch might usefully be subjected to multidimensional analysis—including subjective judgments of degree of musical relation, actual frequencies of confusion or latencies of discriminative reaction, or (for comparison) acoustic data (whether empirically measured or theoretically calculated) concerning, for example, alignment of harmonics. Whatever the type of data, if the predominant effects include an overall dependence on pitch height (with tones separated by a very small number of semitones generally more closely related than tones separated by a very large number of semitones) and a strengthened relation between tones separated by the octave, the perfect fifth, and/or the perfect fourth, the pattern of those data should be approximated by the five-dimensional structure schematized in Fig. 5 or, if some of these effects are relatively weak, by one of its simpler limiting cases (depicted in Figs. 1, 3, or 4).

Purely for purposes of concrete illustration, I here present the results that we obtained by applying the multidimensional scaling method INDSCAL (Carroll & Chang, 1970) to the data that Krumhansl and I collected on the judged relatedness to the tonic of tones differing by each of the 12 intervals from the tonic within the octave (see Krumhansl & Shepard, 1979). INDSCAL, which is designed to capitalize on differences between individuals in their weightings of different dimensions (or, in this case, different components), seemed particularly suitable since we found by other analyses that the individual listeners differed widely. (The rows of the matrix were circularly displaced duplicates of each other, as described earlier.)

Figure 6 shows the four-dimensional solution projected onto the plane of Dimensions 1 and 2 and onto the orthogonal plane of Dimensions 3 and 4. As suggested by the added broken-line circle, the first projection, shown on the left, is essentially the chroma circle, going clockwise from C (through C♯, D, D♯, etc.) around to C′ one octave above. The configuration departs from the chroma circle, however, in that the spacing is wider near C and C′ and, particularly, in that C and C′ are separated from

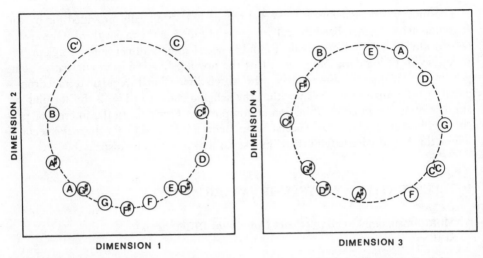

Fig. 6. Two orthogonal projections of the four-dimensional INDSCAL solution obtained from an analysis of Krumhansl and Shepard's (1979) data.

each other by a large gap, indicating nonequivalence of octaves on Dimension 1. Dimension 1 thus seems to combine one dimension of the chroma circle with the dimension of pitch height. The projection shown on the right, however, is an almost perfect circle of fifths, with C and C' nearly superimposed, indicating complete octave equivalence. Except for the gap between C and C' on Dimension 1, the four-dimensional configuration is precisely the double helix on the torus depicted in Fig. 4, which was generated by Euclidean composition from the chroma circle and the circle of fifths (B and F in Fig. 2).

Figure 7 displays the INDSCAL weights for each of the listeners on each of the four dimensions. The plot on the left shows that the listeners with the least extensive musical backgrounds (represented by the triangles) had the heaviest weights on Dimension 1, which separated the tones with respect to pitch height, while the plot on the right shows that the listeners with the most extensive musical backgrounds (represented by the circles) had the heaviest weights on Dimensions 3 and 4, which contained the circle of fifths and implied complete equivalence between octaves. Moreover, the fact that the points for all listeners fall on a 45-degree line in that right panel means that the circle of fifths emerges, to whatever extent that it does for any one listener, as an integrated whole and never one dimension at a time. That the points for Group 1 listeners also fall close to the (broken) 45-degree line in the left panel indicates that under the complete octave-equivalence characteristic of the most-musical listeners, the chroma circle, too, comes and goes as an integrated unit.

My interpretation of the obtained four-dimensional structure in Fig. 6 is as follows: It is essentially a one-octave piece of the endless five-dimensional theoretical structure portrayed in Fig. 5. But because it includes only one octave, the gap between the two ends, which should have been represented by a displacement in a separate fifth

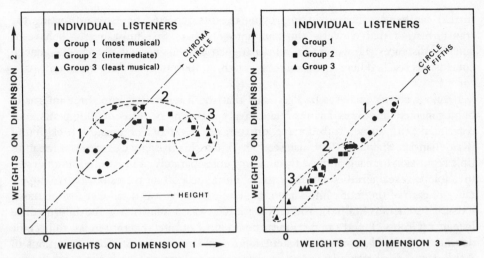

Fig. 7. Weights for individual listeners in Krumhansl and Shepard's experiment plotted against the four dimensions of Fig. 6. (Each broken curve encloses all points for listeners within one of the three groups.)

dimension, has (with a small distortion) been accommodated in the four dimensions of the embedding space of the torus generated from the circle of chroma and of musical fifths. In other words, the separation in pitch height between C and C' an octave above has been achieved by cutting through the torus in Fig. 4 at C and springing it slightly apart in that same four-dimensional space rather than, as in Fig. 5, in an orthogonal fifth dimension. My prediction is that if similar data were collected and analyzed for a range of tones spanning two or three octaves, the data could no longer be fit by a small distortion of this sort in the four-dimensional space, and thus the truer, five-dimensional structure would emerge.

Although this analysis is only intended to be illustrative and should be tried with other, more complete sets of data before definite conclusions are drawn, the results do suggest that the kind of higher-dimensional structures that I have been proposing here (and in Shepard, 1978b, 1981a,b, 1982) are not merely fanciful construction but are, to some degree, actually implied by empirical data.

B. Euclidean Composition (Using Linear Regression)

In a very preliminary exploration of the feasibility of accounting for the data, alternatively, in terms of Euclidean combinations of regular structural components, Shelley Hurwitz and I carried out a multiple linear regression of the data considered in the preceding section onto the squared interpoint distances in each of the four one-octave component configurations—A, B, F, and E of Fig. 2—that I thought to be most important for accounting for perceived relations in pitch—namely, those of height, chroma, fifths, and major thirds, respectively. (As I have already implied, further work may succeed in improving the fits reported here by estimating the transformation that converts the data into numbers that most nearly behave as squared distances. However, I doubt that such refinements will change the general conclusions reached here concerning the relative importances of the component structures.)

Previous cluster analyses had revealed that the listeners fell into three internally homogeneous subgroups having qualitatively different patterns of judgments and, correlated with those, considerable differences in extents of musical background (Krumhansl & Shepard, 1979; also see Fig. 7). For this reason we carried out the multiple regression for each of these three subgroups separately. The results, summarized in Table I, reveal a rather simple pattern. For almost all measures of relative importance of each of the four components, the circle of fifths was dominant for the most-musical listeners (Group 1), the chroma circle was dominant for the intermediate listeners (Group 2), and the rectilinear component of pitch height tended to become dominant for the least-musical listeners (Group 3). (The significant correlations in Table I are all negative because the data were measures of proximity rather than measures of distance—squared or otherwise.)

These results are quite compatible with the multidimensional scaling results discussed in the preceding section. Presumably by taking advantage of the greater con-

TABLE I

Krumhansl and Shepard's (1979) Data on the Relatedness of Pitches to a Tonal Center, Regressed on Proposed Components of Height, Chroma, Perfect Fifths, and Major Thirds—for Listeners with Three Levels of Musical Background[a]

Component	Height (A)[c]	Chroma (B)[c]	Fifths (F)[c]	Thirds (E)[c]
Group 1 (most musical)				
Variance explained[b]	.004	.205	.425	.194
Simple correlation	.061	−.454	−.705	−.566
Beta weight	−.098	−.338	−.606	−.448
F ratio	.417	4.847	16.551	9.036
Group 2 (intermediate)				
Variance explained[b]	.004	.359	.206	.157
Simple correlation	−.067	−.563	−.518	−.507
Beta weight	−.255	−.519	−.412	−.403
F ratio	1.774	7.178	4.973	4.586
Group 3 (least musical)				
Variance explained[b]	.310	.389	.081	.088
Simple correlation	−.557	−.463	−.321	−.354
Beta weight	−.742	−.576	−.252	−.301
F ratio	31.095	18.315	3.715	5.300

[a]The boxes enclose the largest entry in each row.

[b]"Variance explained" means the increment in multiple R-squared obtained by adding the indicated component to the components listed to its left.

[c] Designation in Fig. 2.

straints imposed here, however, the new results also go beyond the earlier results in providing support for some theoretically derived expectations that were not directly confirmed by multidimensional scaling. First, although from the generally high weighting of the two circular components of chroma (B) and fifths (F) we again see the emergence of the four-dimensional toroidal structure in Fig. 4, we now see the fifth dimension of pitch height (A) also emerging as an orthogonal component for the less-musical listeners (rather than manifesting itself merely as a distortional stretch-plus-gap in the four-dimensional torus). And, second, we see that the component emphasizing the harmonically important major thirds (E), although never the most important factor for any group of listeners, tends to be more important than the component of pitch height for the more-musical listeners (Groups 1 and 2).

Apart from the further dimensions that would be required by the addition of this further component for major thirds, the overall structure defined by the first three components—A, B, and F—is, of course, the five-dimensional structure schematically portrayed in Fig. 5. As expected, this structure systematically changes in its linear proportions between the different groups of listeners: For the most-musical Group 1, the two circular components are the largest components with the circle of fifths clearly dominant. For the intermediate Group 2, the same two circular components remain the largest, but it is the chroma circle that now dominates. And for the least-musical Group 3, pitch height and the chroma circle are the largest components with height generally dominant and with the circle of fifths (like the square of thirds) reduced essentially to naught.

VI. DISCUSSION

A. Is Pitch Really Multidimensional?

Psychoacoustic investigators who are accustomed to thinking of pitch as a function of a single physical attribute such as frequency may still be inclined to think that pitch itself must surely be unidimensional. Except for the dimension that I have referred to as pitch height, all the dimensions of pitch that I have been discussing, including those underlying the circles of chroma and of fifths, might from that standpoint be dismissed as existing (if at all) only at some higher level of cognitive interpretation that need not concern the psychophysical investigator and, perhaps, that should not even be subsumed under the term "pitch."

Such a view is encouraged, moreover, by the usual finding in psychoacoustic experiments that the principal determinant of the perceived relation between two tones separated in frequency is simply that separation (measured, for example, as a difference in log frequency). Seldom is there much indication of an increase in perceived similarity at any particular musical interval, except for the occasional finding of a relatively slight effect at the octave. Indeed, I myself have argued that the multidimensional scaling results of at least two psychophysical studies (including the one by Levelt, Van de Geer, & Plomp, 1966) that seemed to provide evidence for a degree of octave equivalence and even for the existence of two or more dimensions of pitch were artifacts of the scaling method used and that the data were entirely consistent with a purely one-dimensional interpretation (Shepard, 1974, pp. 387–388).

As I have noted, however, the failure to find evidence for a heightened perceptual relation at special musical intervals in most psychoacoustic experiments appears to have been a consequence of the typical avoidance in those experiments of conditions that might ensure an appropriately musical set in the listeners—that is, an avoidance of (a) a preceding musical context, (b) specifically musical intervals between the test tones, (c) harmonically rich, and hence musical, tones, and (d) the selection of listeners with at least some degree of musical background or ability. When instead of avoiding such conditions we intentionally arrange for them, the results become quite different and, indeed, the factor of the musical significance of each interval comes to dominate the factor of mere separation in pitch height (Krumhansl, 1979; Krumhansl & Shepard, 1979).

And, incidentally, the fact that individual listeners can be shown to differ not only widely (Seashore, 1938; Shepard, 1964b) but also in accordance with qualitatively different patterns (Krumhansl & Shepard, 1979; Shepard, 1981a; also see the present Fig. 7) implies that pitch must be multidimensional. If pitch were only a matter of separation in pitch height or log frequency, listeners would be expected to differ only in their fineness of discrimination of pitches that are more or less close to each other in log frequency. In fact, however, they also differ markedly in the extent to which they are sensitive to special musical relations such as the octave and the perfect fifth (Allen, 1967; Krumhansl & Shepard, 1979).

As I argue in the following section, even from the purely psychoacoustic standpoint the attempt to dismiss the existence of more than one dimension of pitch is untenable in the face of the following three psychoacoustic facts—which, by means of digital techniques for the additive synthesis of arbitrarily specified tones, can be demonstrated even with nonmusical listeners and in the absence of a musical context: First, tones separated by musically significant intervals such as the octave and fifth, whose augmented perceptual proximities must entail the deformation of a geometrical representation of pitch into a higher dimensional embedding space, can be made arbitrarily similar and, ultimately, indiscriminable. Second, the implied component dimensions of pitch such as height and chroma, which normally vary together in perfect correlation, can be made to vary independently and even in opposite directions simultaneously. And, third, between two fixed tones differing in pitch, a variable tone can be made to traverse different paths in pitch space—paths corresponding, for example, to a shift through height, a shift through chroma, or a shift through the circle of fifths.

B. Multidimensional Variation of the Pitch of Synthesized Tones

The first of the three just listed facts is most simply illustrated by my original computer synthesized tones, in which all tones standing in the octave relation to each other were made identical, thereby collapsing the (helical) continuum of pitch into the endlessly repeating circle of chroma (Shepard, 1964b). More recently, I have synthesized an analogous continuous variation around the circle of fifths, which (as portrayed in Figs. 4 and 6) may be another component of pitch. Each tone consisted of 12 equally spaced sinusoidal components per octave extending throughout the audible range with the amplitudes adjusted so that for a given tone, say C, all components in the octave relation to any C (considered as the fundamental or first harmonic for that chroma) had the highest amplitudes; the components closest to the chroma of the next harmonic with a different chroma (G) had the next highest amplitude; the components closest to the chroma of the next harmonic with yet a different chroma (E) had the next highest amplitude; and so on, according to an essentially exponential decay for succeeding harmonics that did not correspond to previously used chromas. In addition, these amplitudes were weighted, as in my original circular tones, by a fixed, bell-shaped spectral envelope that fell away to below-threshold amplitudes for low and high frequencies. Taking advantage of the great overlap, already noted, between the harmonics of tones differing by a perfect fifth, I effected the shift through a fifth simply by linear interpolation between the amplitudes of components of the same frequencies (Shepard, 1978b).

The second of the listed facts is also illustrated by my original circular tones and subsequently developed variants of them. For, by rigidly displacing, up or down in log frequency, either the bell-shaped spectral envelope with the frequencies of all the sinusoidal components held fixed or the frequencies of all the sinusoidal components with the spectral envelope held fixed, we can produce a variation either in pitch height or around the chroma circle, respectively. It appears arbitrary to maintain that only one of these two orthogonal variations is a variation in pitch when listeners are quite ready to characterize both variations in this way. Particularly arbitrary would be the claim that only the pitch-height variation of the spectral envelope is a variation in pitch, because the other, circular variation in chroma is generally more salient for a small displacement of a given size in log frequency. The possibilities inherent in this scheme for independent variation of height and chroma have been most fully demonstrated by Risset (1971, 1978) who was, for example, the first to vary these two components simultaneously in opposite directions—producing a tone that is heard as continuously ascending in pitch but is paradoxically heard, at the end, to be much lower in pitch than it was at the beginning.

The third of the listed facts is also illustrated by these sorts of computer-generated tones. In my original circular tones, the very same sequence consisting of one tone followed by a second that is on the opposite side of the chroma circle (for example, C followed by F♯) can be heard in either of two distinctly different ways—as a tritone shift up or a tritone shift down—but never as something between or as both at once (Shepard, 1964b). This implies the existence of at least two alternative paths for moving between these two tones differing in pitch. In this case the paths, though in opposite directions, are both around the chroma circle. However, the paths traversed between two tones can also be carried out over quite different dimensions of pitch. Thus, with the aid of my more recent scheme for effecting shifts around the circle of fifths, we can continuously shift between the very same C and G, for example, in either of two ways: by passing around the chroma circle (and hence through the intermediate chromas C♯, D, D♯, E, and F) or directly between these two adjacent tones on the circle of fifths without passing through any of those intermediate chromas.

C. Further Comments on Psychoacoustic versus Cognitive-Structural Representations

If pitch does have more than a single degree of freedom even when approached from the psychoacoustic standpoint, psychoacoustic pitch as well as musical pitch cannot be represented by a one-dimensional line without losing information about the relations and possible paths of transition between tones. (Not even topological structure is preserved under dimensional reduction.) This raises the question of what multidimensional representation would be appropriate from the standpoint of the psychoacoustic investigator, who is more interested in modeling the transducing properties of the sensory system than in modeling the cognitive-structural properties underlying musical interpretation. From what has been said about the possibility of achieving arbitrary degrees of similarity between synthesized tones separated by special musical intervals such as the octave or fifth, it appears that similar, generalized helical representations are still appropriate. The extreme cases of a one-dimensional rectilinear scale or some sort of collapsed circular or toroidal structure would then be approached, even in the absence of a musical context, as the extreme situations are arranged, in which, on the one hand, the tones are pure sinusoids and are presented successively or in which, on the other, the tones either are especially synthesized to maximize equivalence at octaves or fifths or are harmonically rich and presented simultaneously.

The purposes of a psychophysical endeavor might be best served by representations of this kind that allow for systematic distortion in which, for example, the structure is relatively more compressed at the low end of the pitch-height continuum. For these purposes, standard multidimensional scaling (whether metric or nonmetric) might be the most appropriate type of data-analytic method since, as I noted, that method allows for deviations of this kind from a completely regular structure. By contrast, for the fundamentally different purposes of representing the higher-level structure presumed to underlie musical competence, I have argued that we want the regularity that will ensure invariance under transposition. And, in this case, data-analytic methods based on some variant of Euclidean composition seem more suitable.

From the psychoacoustic standpoint, what is of interest about musical tones is how the representation of those tones changes with continuous variation in the parameters of the physical stimuli. From this standpoint one is concerned with such questions as (a) whether what is perceived as the best octave corresponds to a strict 2-to-1 frequency ratio or to a somewhat larger ratio, (b) whether the favored ratio systematically changes at low or at high frequencies, and (c) whether other standard musical intervals are most preferred when they correspond to steps of equal temperament (and, so, are designed to preserve equal steps in log frequency) or some scheme of so-called just tuning (and, thus, are designed to maintain numerically simple frequency ratios). However, from the cognitive–structural standpoint these psychophysical concerns are of little importance. Once the tones are categorically mapped into the discrete nodes of an internal representation that is functionally regular, it is the structural properties inherent in that regular representation that are important. Thus, the fact that all tones in octave relations to a given tone are separated by multiples of a fixed distance (and, perhaps, are colinear as well) is essential; but whether the frequency ratio that corresponds, physically, to that fixed psychological unit of octave distance is equal to or greater than 2-to-1 or, indeed, whether it changes somewhat toward low or high frequencies is no longer relevant. For the same reason, from this cognitive–structural standpoint, the long-standing psychophysical concern over the fact that it is mathematically impossible to construct a scale in which all the intervals exactly realize simple frequency ratios (e.g., see the appendix in Westergaard, 1975) is quite irrelevant also.

D. Alternative Cognitive–Structural Representations for Musical Pitch

Even for the purposes of representing the cognitive structure of musical pitch, alternative representations are possible. This is because different representations that preserve the topological structure can be adopted as long as we compensate for any information-preserving change in the representation by an appropriate change in the rules taken to relate the representation to the data (cf., Shepard & Carroll, 1966; and for a related tradeoff between representation and process in cognitive theory, see Anderson, 1978; Shepard, 1981b).

In the present connection we can use the simple helix (Fig. 1) and the double helix (Fig. 3) to illustrate two alternative ways in which an increased similarity at any particular interval—say the octave—might be accounted for in terms of the spatial representation. In the simple helix, all tones standing in the octave relation to each other have two special geometrical relationships within the spatial representation: such tones are closer to each other than they would be without the deformation into the regular helix, and they are also colinear. In the double helix of Fig. 3, however, the tones standing in the octave relation to each other have only one special geometrical property in common: they are colinear. This is why, in attempting to represent the octave relation solely in terms of proximity, we had to bend the double helix (Fig. 3) around to form a higher order helix (Fig. 5) or, in the limiting case of complete octave equivalence, a toroidal structure (Fig. 4).

So far I have made use only of the relation of proximity. In part this is because the relation of proximity has the advantage of being continuously variable; by changing the degree of the compression of the helix, we can bring tones an octave apart as close together as we choose (until, in the limit, we achieve complete identity of octaves and, hence, complete degeneration of the helix into the chroma circle or torus). By contrast, the relation of colinearity is all or none: either the tones in a particular set fall on a certain line or they do not.

Still there is evidence to support the notion of Revesz (1954) and Bachem (1950) that (at least within, again, a suitable musical range) musical listeners hear tones differing by multiple octaves as having some discrete feature (or chroma) in common regardless of the number of intervening octaves (e.g., see Dowling & Hollomb, 1977; Idson & Massaro, 1978; Kallman & Massaro, 1979; Thurlow & Erchul, 1977; and, for comparison, Deutsch, 1972). This is quite analogous to the fact, in the visual domain, that (for example) bars at a certain angle share the analyzable property of that certain orientation, regardless of large differences in their sizes (Shepard, 1964a). In the present, auditory case this suggests that chroma may act as an attribute of tones that is "analyzable" (Shepard, 1964a) or "separable" (Garner, 1970). If so, there is good reason for representing the perceptual equivalence of all tones in the multiple-octave relation to a particular tone by a coincidence of the corresponding points with a certain chroma line regardless of their distance of separation in the spatial model. Such coincidence could also provide for a sharper tuning to the octave relation than could plausibly be provided purely by proximity in the helix (where increased closeness at the octave must imply increased closeness at the neighboring major seventh and minor ninth as well). Only further study will reveal whether all special pitch relations can adequately be represented solely by spatial proximity or whether the extent and sharpness of tuning to other special relations will require the use of other geometrical relations such as colinearity as well.

Possibly, different forms of representation will prove to be more suited for bringing out the relations between pitches that are most salient in different situations—such as those of simultaneous presentation (harmony), immediate succession (melody), or longer-range shifts of tonality (modulation of key). Moreover, even when the alternative forms of representation are essentially isomorphic, some forms may be more accessible to visual grasp by the human mind. As a case in point, the difficulty of picturing structures in spaces of more than three dimensions, such as the structures depicted in Figs. 4 and 5, motivates the search for lower dimensional "maps" of those structures that preserve, if not all the relations, at least the relations that are most important for particular purposes.

E. The Two-dimensional Melodic Map

In each of the structures portrayed in Figs. 3, 4, and 5, one octave is represented by a double helix wound around a two-dimensional surface that is, alternatively, a straight cylinder in three dimensions (Fig. 3), a cylinder curved into a closed torus in four dimensions (Fig. 4), or the same torus cut through again and twisted apart into an orthogonal, fifth dimension (Fig. 5). The surface in which the double helix is embedded in each case, being itself two-dimensional, has a flat "topological map" (Blackett, 1967) that is obtained by (a) cutting out a one-octave segment of the tube, (b)

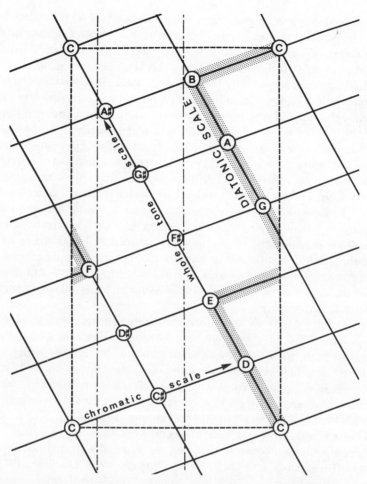

Fig. 8. The two-dimensional melodic map obtained by unwrapping the double helical structure of Figs. 3, 4, and 5. (The structure of a diatonic scale is illustrated for the key of C major.)

cutting along the length of the straightened one-octave tube (whether it was initially straight, curved into itself, or twisted), and (b) opening the cylindrical surface out into a flat rectangle, like that illustrated in Fig. 8. The fact that the original surface was unbounded in each case can be represented in the topological map by replicating the rectangle endlessly in all directions within the plane, as indicated in the figure. The two-dimensional map contains an infinite lattice in which adjacent nodes, representing the tones, are related by minor seconds (semitones) running in one diagonal direction, and by major seconds (whole tones) running in the other diagonal direction. (The whole-tone scales, running in the latter direction, correspond to the two opposite edges of the original double helix.)

The fact that in the original curved representations (of Figs. 3, 4, and 5), tones in a particular diatonic key are linearly separable by a hyperplane with closely related keys obtainable by small rotations of the hyperplane has a direct analog in this two-dimensional map: Tones in a particular key fall within a narrow vertical band (demarcated for the key of C major by the vertical broken lines in Fig. 8), and the most closely related keys are obtained by the smallest horizontal shifts of this band. Notice that the tones falling within such a band always form a characteristic zig-zag pattern (illustrated by the stippled strip for the key of C major). Indeed any rigid translational motion of this zig-zag pattern into another set of nodes—whether horizontally, vertically, or diagonally—will again fall in such a band and will therefore yield another diatonic key. Moreover, the relative minor and all the so-called church modes are also represented by this same pattern and differ from each other only with regard to which of the seven distinct nodes included within each octave of the key is designated as the primary focal tone or tonic. Finally, the most common pentatonic scales are represented by the very similar five-tone zig-zag patterns that form the complements of these seven-tone diatonic sets. In the following subsection, I shall return to a consideration of the musical significance of the fact that the most common musical scales have these particular zig-zag structures. For the moment, it is sufficient to notice that all such scales, as well as the chromatic and whole-tone scales, have compact, orderly representations in this space.

Not surprisingly, since they are constructed within the frameworks of such scales, tunes or melodies also have generally compact representations within this lattice. Indeed, quite apart from any consideration of the underlying scales, statistical analyses of the melodies occurring in popular, folk, and classical music have substantiated the generalization that most intervals between successive tones in such melodies are minor or major seconds with larger intervals relatively less common (Dowling, 1978, p. 352; Fucks, 1962; Merriam, 1964; Philippot, 1970, p. 86). The reason for the preponderance of small melodic intervals seems to be that the perceptual integration of successive tones into a coherent unit depends especially strongly on proximity in pitch height (Bregman & Campbell, 1971; Deutsch, 1978; Dowling, 1973a; Jones, 1976; McAdams & Bregman, 1979; Van Noorden, 1975)—a dependence that can be seen as a manifestation of a much more general principle of proportionality between time and distance known, in connection with visual apparent motion, as "Korte's Third Law" (see Shepard, 1981b). In any case, because adjacent nodes in the two-dimensional lattice of Fig. 8 are separated by the predominant intervals in melodies (minor and major seconds), I have proposed to refer to this two-dimensional topological map of the double helix as *melodic space* (Shepard, 1978b, 1980a, 1981a,b).

F. The Two-dimensional Harmonic Map

Although tones that differ by minor or major seconds typically follow each other in melodic sequences, they are dissonant when sounded simultaneously. Accordingly, the harmonic intervals that make up the most common chords are not the dissonant minor and major seconds but the larger, consonant intervals of the minor and major thirds. As a consequence, whereas melodic sequences are compact in the two-dimensional lattice of Fig. 8, chords tend to be spread out in that representation. The major and minor triads, for example, form two triangles with a common longer side (corresponding to the perfect fifth) and hence together form an elongated parallelogram in Fig. 8. From the C in the lower left corner of the rectangular map for one octave in that figure, this parallelogram extends diagonally up to the G, the perfect fifth that is to the right and above that C. The other two vertices of that parallelogram are formed by E, for the major third, and E♭ (labeled D♯), for the minor third.

However, because no other standard musical tone falls within this parallelogram, all such elongated parallelograms can be compressed into compact, more nearly square configurations by a single affine transformation consisting of a linear compression of the whole two-dimensional space along the long (C-to-G) axis of the parallelogram considered—with, if desired, a compensating expansion in some other, more-or-less orthogonal direction. This affine transformation of the two-dimensional map corresponds, in the torus, to the transformation achieved (a) by cutting through the torus in the direction orthogonal to the cut needed to open the torus back into a one-octave cylinder, and (b) by giving the resulting cylinder two complete torsional twists, and (c) by reattaching the torsionally twisted ends to form an altered torus. The resulting, affinely transformed two-dimensional map is displayed in Fig. 9. As is illustrated for the key of C, the set of other tones that are consonant with the tonic of any key (represented here by the double-circled C) does now have compact representations. The same is true for any of the most common chords, whether major or minor, augmented or diminished. Thus, although none of the structures incorporating the double helix (Figs. 3, 4, 5, and 8) were explicitly based on musical thirds, those structures are nevertheless related by a simple transformation to a structure that

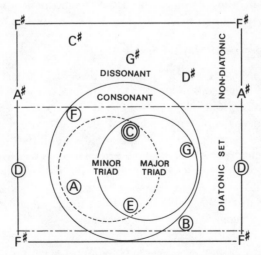

Fig. 9. The two-dimensional harmonic map obtained by an affine transformation of the melodic map. (Relations of consonance and a diatonic set are illustrated for an arbitrarily selected tone, C.)

does emphasize thirds—including the major third, which according to Table I does play a significant role in the perception of musical pitch.

Spaces that are essentially isomorphic to this harmonic space have previously (and often independently) been proposed by many theorists, including Balzano (1978, 1980), Hall (1974), Lakner (1960), Longuet-Higgins (1962, 1979), and O'Connell (1962). What I presume to be new, here, is the demonstration of a simple affinity (in the literal mathematical sense) between this space and the melodic space (Fig. 8) that I have derived from my double helical representation for pitch. In an especially promising development, Krumhansl and Kessler (1982), extending the probe tone technique of Krumhansl and Shepard (1979), have now shown that essentially this toroidal structure can also represent the set of major and minor tonalities, with chord progressions moving the listener's momentary tonal center around on the two-dimensional surface.

I am not claiming that the different components or alternative representations for pitch that I have proposed here or the different musical intervals that each of these emphasizes, all operate on the same level of the hierarchically organized perceptual system. On the contrary, the ways in which individual listeners differ in their relative sensitivities to these components (see Fig. 7 and Table I) suggest that the smallest intervals, the thirds, and the perfect fifths may operate at three different, increasingly cognitively structured levels. By analogical extension of my earlier remarks about proportionality of time and distance, we might conjecture that the time constants should be greater for successively higher, more complexly structured levels of the system (cf. Powers, Clark, & McFarland, 1960). Such a conjecture appears to be consonant with the observation that I, as well as some of my colleagues (Balzano, 1980; Krumhansl, Bharucha, & Kessler, 1981), have recently made; namely, that in tonal music, shifts from one tone to the next of a melody are usually the most rapid, followed by somewhat slower shifts in harmonic accompaniment with modulations of key or tonal center occurring, when they do, at a still slower rate.

G. Structural Properties of Musical Scales

The asymmetrical zig-zag character that the principal musical scales have in the two-dimensional melodic space of Fig. 8 is fundamental in tonal music. The alternating pattern of three and four whole-tone steps between semitone shifts (3-4-3-4-3-4-...) that characterizes the diatonic scales and the similar alternating pattern of two and three whole-tone steps between one-and-a-half-tone shifts (2-3-2-3-2-3-...) that characterizes the pentatonic scales have the essential property that each scale degree has a unique relation (in terms of numbers of intervening semitone steps) to all other tones in that scale. As has been emphasized particularly by Zuckerkandl (1956, 1972) and, recently, by Balzano (1978, 1980), it is this property that confers on each scale degree its unique "dynamic quality" (Zuckerkandl, 1956, 1972) or "tonal function" (Meyer, 1956; Piston, 1941; Ratner, 1962) and, hence, that enables the listener to have, at every moment, a clear sense of where the music is with respect to a fixed tonal framework. Only with respect to such a framework can there be such things as motion or rest, tension and resolution, or, in short, the underlying dynamisms of tonal music. By contrast, the complete symmetry and regularity of the chromatic and whole-tone scales means that every tone has the same status as every other. The fact that for such scales there can be no clear sense of location and, hence, of motion is, I believe, the reason that such scales have never enjoyed wide or sustained popularity as a basis for music.

The idea is often expressed, whether explicitly or by implication, that the diatonic as well, perhaps, as the complementary pentatonic scales, which are so pervasive in the music of the Western world are arbitrary and probably rather recent cultural conventions and that in Eastern cultures scales have developed with entirely different structures and even with octaves divided into quite different and sometimes much larger numbers of steps than the traditional 12 of Western music. However, this idea should be evaluated in view of the following points.

First, as Balzano (1978, 1980) in particular has shown, quite apart from the psychoacoustic considerations usually invoked to justify the diatonic scale (such as that it permits an especially good approximation to the simplest frequency ratio for the perfect fifth), there are deep cognitive–structural justifications of a group-theoretic character both for the division of the octave into 12 parts and for the selection from the resulting set of tones of the diatonic (or the pentatonic) subsets of seven (or five) tones to constitute a particular scale. One such justification is the already noted achievement, in these particular asymmetric subsets of the unique tonal function of each tone corresponding to its unique structural relation to the contextually established scale (also see Rothenberg, 1978a,b).

Second, far from being a recent Western invention, the diatonic scale has in fact been traced back to the most ancient tuning systems so far deciphered from archaeological records (Kilmer, Crocker, & Brown, 1976).

Third, although different tuning systems continue to be used in other cultures and although some (e.g., Indian and Indonesian) scales require the division of each octave into as many as 22 parts, a subset of five or seven focal tones, corresponding to something more or less akin to a Western pentatonic or diatonic scale, usually plays the central role in a particular piece of music—with the additional, microtonal steps used more for subtle melodic decorations or ornamentations around these focal tones (e.g., see Dowling, 1978, in press). Indeed, just as may be the case for different natural languages (Chomsky, 1965), what is more significant about the scales used in different cultures may be their deep structural similarities rather than their superficial differences:

1. Virtually all such scales are based on the octave (whether or not it corresponds to an exactly 2-to-1 frequency ratio) with every octave divided up in the same way (Dowling, 1978, in press).

2. Nearly all assign a central role to the so-called perfect intervals, the fifth and its inversion in the octave, the fourth (Sachs, 1943).

3. And as I have already noted, most select a subset of either five or seven tones from each octave as the principal or focal tones, and these focal tones quite generally

have a definite, irregular or asymmetric spacing much like that in the diatonic or pentatonic scales in order, I believe, to confer a unique status on each tone of the scale.

Finally, and presumably for the same deep group-theoretic reasons, in some (e.g., West African) cultures in which rhythmic structure has evolved a complexity comparable to that of Western tonal structure, the basis of rhythmic variations has recently been seen to be isomorphic, in the time domain, to the diatonic system in the pitch domain (Pressing, 1979).

Within Western tonal music, incidentally, the hierarchical organization of the levels of musical interpretation noted in the preceding section—in addition to having different associated time constants—contributes different and sometimes recursive levels of dynamism to the music. Thus, even after a melody has itself come to a stable resting point, the harmony may maintain tension by delaying resolution to the tonic; and even after the harmony and the melody have both subsequently resolved to the locally defined tonic, an implicit tension may remain at a deeper level until that locally established tonic finally modulates back to the initially instated global tonic of the piece as a whole. The forward momentum of music (as of life, generally) is thus maintained by a hierarchy of subgoals within subgoals (cf. Hofstadter, 1979, p. 612).

H. Pitch as a Morphophoric Medium

I believe that there is a fundamental reason why pitch and time, among the potentially variable attributes of tones (including such others as loudness, timbre, and perceived spatial location of source), have always played the most essential roles in music. The two attributes of pitch and time appear to be unique in the auditory modality in the extent to which they are capable of bearing form or, to adopt Attneave's term, are "morphophoric" (see Attneave, 1972; Attneave & Olson, 1971). The essential property of the continua of pitch and time is that musical objects— namely, melodies and chords—preserve their perceived structural identities under rigid transformations of transposition in pitch or displacement in time—just as visual objects preserve their structural identities of shape under rigid transformations of translation and rotation. At present, there is little evidence that perceived patterns of loudnesses, timbres, or spatial locations (any more than perceived patterns of colors in the visual modality) will preserve their structural identities to the same extent under transformation in those continua.

The distinction appears to be intimately connected with the distinction that Kubovy (1981) has recently drawn between "dispensable" and "indispensable" attributes. According to this distinction, time is an indispensable attribute in both the visual and the auditory modalities; but whereas space is a second indispensable attribute in the case of vision, it is pitch and not literal space that is the second indispensable attribute in the case of audition. To use a variant of the example by means of which Kubovy illustrates these concepts: if two projected spots of light, one red and one blue, are superimposed on each other in the same spatial location, they are perceived to merge into a single spot, purple in color; hence, the original difference in spatial location of the two spots was indispensable to their separate identities. If, however, the two spatially separated spots are made the same color, purple, they will still be perceived to be two in number; hence, the difference in color was dispensable in Kubovy's sense. The situation is the other way around in the auditory domain. If two sound sources, one emitting middle C and the other emitting E, are superimposed in space, the two tones will still retain their individual identities as two tones separated by a major third; hence, the difference in spatial location was dispensable. If, however, the two spatially separated tones are brought to the same pitch, say the intermediate D, they will be heard to be a single tone of that pitch centered between the two sources; hence, the difference in pitch was indispensable.

I. The Problem of the Representation of Pitch within a Tonal Context

I have claimed that the context of a particular musical key (whether explicitly presented or only implied by a musical passage) induces an internal cognitive framework or hierarchy of tonal functions within a musical listener and that this cognitive framework plays, in turn, an essential role in the perceptual interpretation of each succeeding tone or chord. But how is the dependence of this contextually induced cognitive framework on a particular key to be represented with respect to the underlying geometrical structures that I have proposed for musical pitch? Throughout this chapter I have argued for an invariant underlying representation in which all tones separated by the same musical interval correspond to points separated by the same spatial distance and, hence, a representation that maps into itself under rigid transformations. Principally, the contrast that I have emphasized in this connection has been with alternative psychoacoustic proposals that the perceptual relations corresponding to particular intervals might systematically change toward the low or the high ends of the continuum of audible frequencies. The departures from a strictly regular representation that are suggested by considerations of cognitive interpretation within a tonal context are quite different. Departures of this latter sort would not accumulate over global shifts in pitch height; rather, they would operate differentially at the local level in exactly the same way within each octave.

Such departures, unlike those of the former, psychoacoustic kind, necessarily imply that the psychoacoustic goal, pursued since the time of Helmholtz, of accounting for the perceived musical relations between tones entirely in terms of the physical properties of the two tones making up that interval can never be achieved. The perception of musical intervals would then depend, as well, on the cognitive framework within which those physical stimuli are categorically interpreted by a musical listener.

At the same time, such departures appear to be inconsistent with the kind of invariant cognitive–structural representation proposed here—that is, one in which all tones separated by the same interval have the same distance of separation in the underlying structure. Accordingly, we need to consider some of the kinds of evidence for—and implications of—these apparent departures from strict structural regularity and symmetry.

First, the most easily disposed of, is one phenomenon that I already claimed to hold, at least for some musical listeners; I mean that in which the successive steps of a diatonic scale—do, re, mi, etc.—can be heard as in some sense equal, or at least more equal than one would expect from the fact that two of these steps (namely, mi-fa and ti-do), being semitone intervals, are just half the physical size of the remaining (whole-tone) steps (Fig. 8). For as I have shown elsewhere (Shepard, 1978b, 1982), there exists a relative weighting of the circle of fifths (Component F in Fig. 2) such that the distances corresponding both to minor and to major seconds are all equal to each other in the resulting combined structure. Listeners who do not claim to hear the successive steps of a diatonic scale as equal, then, would presumably be those characterized by a different weighting of the circle of fifths relative to the chroma circle and to height. (See the individual variation in such weights indicated in Fig. 7.)

Of greater concern is another cognitive phenomenon, which is already well known to students of music theory (see, for example, illustrations discussed by Rosen, 1971). Here, I expand on the example given by Risset (1978, p. 526); the same physical interval, whether it is called F-B or F♯-B, may be differently perceived in different contexts. In C-major it is the upper tone in the interval that is interpreted as the leading tone, and, hence, the interval is perceived as tending to resolve to the interval E-C. In F♯-major, however, it is the lower tone that is interpreted as the leading tone, and, hence, the interval is in this case perceived as tending to resolve to the different interval F♯-A♯. Correspondingly, musicians may actually execute such an interval differently in the two cases (e.g., see Shackford, 1961, 1962; Small, 1936). Indeed, in experiments with listeners in the psychological laboratory, Krumhansl (1979) has now provided evidence that the perceived relation between tones separated by the very same interval depends systematically on the relation between that interval and the contextually established tonic. Her listeners judged the relation between two tones separated by a particular interval to be greatest when the two tones were selected from the tonality-defining major triad, next greatest when the two tones were selected from other tones that still belonged to the associated key, and least when the two tones were selected from the remaining tones not belonging to that key.

Clearly, Krumhansl's findings pose a major challenge to the psychoacoustic goal of accounting for perceived relations between tones solely in terms of physical properties of those tones. From the present standpoint, however, we should perhaps be cognizant of the possibility that the judged relatedness of tones in a contextually established key might be a reflection of the differential saliencies of the individual tones relative to that key rather than a reflection of a true alteration of the perceived distances between those tones. As Tversky (1977) has shown, in comparison with one pair of stimuli, a pair of perceptually richer or more salient stimuli may be judged to be more similar if the judgment is in terms of similarity, but also more different if the judgment is in terms of difference. (Also see Krumhansl, 1978.) Thus, in order to substantiate the claim that the minor third is actually represented by a smaller cognitive distance when that minor third is a part of the contextually established major triad (that is, when it is E-G in the key of C major) than when it falls entirely outside that key (e.g., when it is D♯-F♯), it may be necessary to show that this same result is obtained whether the judgments are of similarity or of dissimilarity.

I presume, in any case, that the multidimensional scaling results obtained by Krumhansl (1979; also see Krumhansl et al., 1980) are subject to the end-distortion that I have already said is to be expected when data are scaled for a single octave only. Neither the two- nor the three-dimensional solutions obtained by Krumhansl, as they stand, can be strictly prolonged into additional octaves. Just as in the case of the left panel of the present Fig. 6, however, a slight torsional distortion into an additional dimension will permit the structures to be extended in this way, and, indeed, they then become helical, as we should expect. The precise form that such a helix might ultimately take and, in particular, the extent to which it might correspond to any of the completely regular forms illustrated in the present Figs. 3, 4, and 5 would depend, in part, on the resolution of the similarity–dissimilarity issue just raised.

No matter how that particular issue is eventually resolved, a prevailing tonal framework nevertheless does appear to exert a powerful influence on the interpretation of tones within a musical context. Thus, even the data of Krumhansl and Shepard (1979), which the present Figs. 6 and 7 and Table I have already shown to provide support for the proposed geometrical representations of pitch at the global level, manifest systematic deviations from those structures at the local level. The most striking and consistent pattern in these deviations is this: As the condition of complete octave equivalence is approached—as it is for the most musical listeners (see Fig. 7)—pairs of intervals that are related to each other by an inversion in the octave (namely, m2 and M7, M2 and m7, m3 and M6, and M3 and m6 in Fig. 2) do not become equivalent as predicted by the geometrical model. Instead, some of these intervals—particularly M2 and M3—strongly dominate their inversions even in the limit of complete octave equivalence (see Fig. 3 in Krumhansl & Shepard, 1979).

As of this writing I can think of three possible ways in which these various tonal asymmetries may eventually prove to be reconcilable with the kinds of regular representations for pitch proposed here.

First, as I have already suggested, some of the asymmetries might be handled, without altering the underlying distances between the tones, simply by assigning to each individual tone a weight or salience representing how central that tone is in the prevailing tonal context. Perceived relations between tones, including asymmetries of these relations, would then be explained in terms of these weights operating in conjunction with the fixed underlying distances—perhaps in a manner similar to that proposed by Tversky (1977).

Second, one could go further and propose that a tonal context does invoke a fixed, asymmetric internal representation of the corresponding diatonic scale and its associated hierarchy of tonal functions quite independent of the underlying regular representation of pitch considered in abstraction from any particular musical key.

Under the prevailing tonal context, then, each succeeding tone would be mapped from a node in the underlying regular structure into the closest node in the fixed, asymmetric representation for that diatonic key. Hence, although all tones related by the same interval would be separated by the same distance in the former, helical structure, such tones might be separated by different and even asymmetric distances in the latter structure—depending on the tonal function of each tone in that tonal structure. Very generally, some analogy between melodies and sentences might even be discerned here. That is, somewhat as each noun phrase in a sentence is represented, at a deep level, as having a certain function of grammar (subject, direct object, indirect object, etc.) or of case (agentive, instrumental, locative, etc.—see Fillmore 1970, 1977), each tone in a melody may be represented as having a definite tonal function (tonic, dominant, subdominant, leading tone, etc.).

Third, the mapping of the underlying abstract, invariant structure into the particular asymmetric structure for a particular tonality might in some way be regarded, still more specifically as a kind of "projection." Thus, much as the concrete visual representation of a three-dimensional object must always be from a particular spatial point of view (Metzler & Shepard, 1974; Shepard, 1981b), the concrete musical representation of the underlying abstract helical structure of pitch must always be from a particular tonal point of view. Although the precise rules that might govern such projections remain unspecified, consideration of the structures shown in Figs. 3, 4, and 5 has indicated that change of viewpoint (i.e., change of tonality) corresponds—just as in the visual case—to a rotation (see Shepard & Cooper, 1982, Ch. 16).

VI. CONCLUSIONS

1. Pitch is multidimensional. A one-dimensional rectilinear representation of pitch is incompatible with the facts (a) that under appropriately musical conditions, tones separated by certain intervals (especially the octave and perfect fifth) are perceived to have heightened musical relations and (b) that between two tones differing in perceived pitch a synthesized tone can be continuously varied from one to the other over distinctly different paths (in pitch height, in chroma, or even around the circle of fifths). The heightened perceptual relations between tones separated by these special musical intervals implies a generalized helical structure for pitch. In order to fit empirical data for more than a single octave, an embedding space of at least five dimensions will be required for this structure (including one dimension for a rectilinear component of pitch height and two dimensions for each of two circular components: the chroma circle and the circle of fifths).

2. For psychophysical purposes of characterizing the relations between musical tones as they are transduced by the sensory system, this generalized helical structure may be allowed to assume a globally distorted form in which, for example, the component of height is relatively compressed toward the low end of the range of audible pitch. In this way we can represent such facts about the ear as that it is less effective in discriminating differences in pitch at low frequencies. In order to extract

such a globally distorted helical structure from empirical data, multidimensional scaling appears to provide a potentially useful tool.

3. For purposes of characterizing the cognitive structure of pitch as interpreted within a musical setting, however, the helical structure should have exactly the same conformation within each octave. Only within such a regular representation will musical objects—principally, melodies and chords—retain their unique structural identities under transposition. In order to extract such a regular structure from empirical data, a different method of Euclidean composition appears to be more promising.

4. Still remaining to be fully elucidated are the rules of projection that map such an abstract, symmetrical structure into the more concrete and perhaps asymmetrical structure representing the perceived relations between tones within the context of a particular musical key—between, that is, the unique tonal functions (tonic, dominant, subdominant, leading tone, etc.) relative to that key.

ACKNOWLEDGMENTS

This chapter is based on research supported by National Science Foundation Grants BNS 75–02806 and BNS 80–05517 and by a Sabbatical Award from the James McKeen Cattell Fund. The chapter represents in part a recasting of ideas developed in a previously written paper (Shepard, 1982). I undertook this recasting in June 1980, while I was a visiting scientist at the *Institute de Recherche et Coordination Acoustic/Musique* (*IRCAM*) of the *Centre Georges Pompidou*, Paris. My interest in the possibility of regular geometrical representations for the structure of musical pitch, dormant since 1964 (when I had explored the single helix for pitch), was reawakened by a demonstration by Gerald Balzano, while he was still a graduate student at Stanford, of the group-theoretic basis of the diatonic system. My own geometrical developments, presented here, have benefited from the ideas and information contributed by a number of colleagues and associates both in the United States and in France, including (in addition to Balzano) Carol Krumhansl, Michael Kubovy, Stephen McAdams, Jean-Claude Risset, and David Wessel. In addition, I am indebted to Shelley Hurwitz for technical assistance in the analyses of the data and to Teresa Putnam for her part in the preparation of the final manuscript.

REFERENCES

Abelson, R. P., & Tukey, J. W. Efficient utilization of nonnumerical information in quantitative analysis: General theory and the case of simple order. *Annals of Mathematical Statistics*, 1963, *34*, 1347–1369.

Allen, D. Octave discriminability of musical and non-musical subjects. *Psychonomic Science*, 1967, 7, 421–422.

Anderson, J. R. Arguments concerning representations for mental imagery. *Psychological Review*, 1978, *85*, 249–277.

Attneave, F. The representation of physical space. In A. W. Melton and E. Martin (Eds.), *Coding processes in human memory*. Washington, D.C.: Winston, 1972. Pp. 283–306.

Attneave, F., & Olson, R. K. Pitch as a medium: A new approach to psychophysical scaling. *American Journal of Psychology*, 1971, *84*, 147–165.

Bachem, A. Tone height and tone chroma as two different pitch qualities. *Acta Psychologica*, 1950, 7, 80–88.

Bachem, A. Absolute pitch. *Journal of the Acoustical Society of America*, 1955, 27, 1180–1185.

Balzano, G. J. Chronometric studies of the musical interval sense. Doctoral dissertation, Stanford University, 1977. *Dissertation Abstracts International*, 1977, *38*, 2898B (University Microfilms No. 77-25, 643).

Balzano, G. J. The structural uniqueness of the diatonic order. In R. N. Shepard (Chair), *Cognitive structure of musical pitch.* Symposium presented at the meeting of the Western Psychological Association, San Francisco, California, April 1978.

Balzano, G. J. The group-theoretic description of twelvefold and microtonal pitch systems. *Computer Music Journal,* 1980, *4,* 66–84.

Balzano, G. J. Musical versus psychoacoustical variables and their influence on the perception of musical intervals. *Bulletin of the Council for Research in Music Education,* 1981. (In press).

Balzano, G. J., & Liesch, B. W. The role of chroma and scalestep in the recognition of musical intervals in and out of context. *Psychomusicology.* (In press).

Bartlett, J. C., & Dowling, W. J. Recognition of transposed melodies: A key-distance effect in developmental perspective. *Journal of Experimental Psychology: Human Perception and Performance.* 1980, *6,* 501–515.

Beck, J., & Shaw, W. A. The scaling of pitch by the method of magnitude estimation. *American Journal of Psychology,* 1961, *74,* 242–251.

Beck, J., & Shaw, W. A. Single estimates of pitch magnitude. *Journal of the Acoustical Society of America,* 1963, *35,* 1722–1724.

Bentler, P. M., & Weeks, D. G. Restricted multidimensional scaling models. *Journal of Mathematical Psychology,* 1978, *17,* 138–151.

Blackett, D. W. *Elementary topology.* New York: Academic Press, 1967.

Blechner, M. J. Musical skill and the categorical perception of harmonic mode. Status Report on Speech Perception SR-51/52. New Haven, Connecticut: Haskins Laboratories, 1977. Pp. 139–174.

Blumenthal, L. M. Distance geometries. *University of Missouri Studies,* 1938, *13,* No. 2.

Bregman, A. S., & Campbell, J. Primary auditory stream segregation and the perception of order in rapid sequences of tones. *Journal of Experimental Psychology,* 1971, *89,* 244–249.

Burns, E. M. Octave adjustment by non-Western musicians. *Journal of the Acoustical Society of America.* 1974, *56,* 525. (Abstract)

Burns, E. M., & Ward, W. I. Categorical perception—phenomenon or epiphenomenon: Evidence from experiments in the perception of melodic musical intervals. *Journal of the Acoustical Society of America,* 1978, *63,* 456–468.

Butler, J. W., & Daston, P. G. Musical consonance as musical preference: A cross cultural study. *Journal of General Psychology,* 1968, *79,* 129–142.

Carroll, J. D., & Chang, J.-J. Analysis of individual differences in multidimensional scaling via an N-way generalization of Eckart-Young decomposition. *Psychometrika,* 1970, *35,* 283–319.

Chomsky, N. *Aspects of the theory of syntax.* Cambridge, Massachusetts: MIT Press, 1965.

Cohen, A. J. Inferred sets of pitches in melodic perception. In R. Shepard (Chairman), *Cognitive structure of musical pitch.* Symposium presented at the meeting of the Western Psychological Association, San Francisco, California, April 1978.

Coxeter, H.S.M. *Introduction to geometry.* New York: Wiley, 1961.

Cuddy, L. L., Cohen, A. J., & Miller, J. Melody recognition: The experimental application of musical rules. *Canadian Journal of Psychology,* 1979, *33,* 148–157.

Davies, J. B. *The psychology of music.* London: Hutchinson, 1978.

de Boer, E. On the "residue" and auditory pitch perception. In W. D. Keidel & W. D. Neff (Eds.), *Handbook of sensory physiology* (Vol. V/3, *Auditory system: Clinical and special topics*). New York: Springer-Verlag, 1976. Pp. 479–583.

de Leeuw, J., & Heiser, W. Multidimensional scaling with restrictions on the configuration. In P. R. Krishnaiah (Ed.), *Multivariate Analysis* (Volume 5). Amsterdam: North Holland Publ., 1979.

Deutsch, D. Octave generalization and tune recognition. *Perception & Psychophysics,* 1972, *11,* 411–412.

Deutsch, D. Delayed pitch comparisons and the principle of proximity. *Perception & Psychophysics,* 1978, *23,* 227–230.

Dewar, K. M., Cuddy, L. L., & Mewhort, D.J.K. Recognition memory for single tones with and without context. *Journal of Experimental Psychology: Human Learning and Memory.* 1977, *3,* 60–67.

Dowling, W. J. The perception of interleaved melodies. *Cognitive Psychology,* 1973, *5,* 322–337. (a)

Dowling, W. J. The 1215-cent octave: Convergence of Western and Nonwestern data on pitch-scaling. *Journal of the Acoustical Society of America,* 1973, *53,* 373A. (Abstract) (b)

Dowling, W. J. Scale and contour: Two components of a theory of memory for melodies. *Psychological Review*, 1978, *85*, 341–354.

Dowling, W. J. Musical scales and psychophysical scales: Their psychological reality. In T. Rice & R. Falck (Eds.) *Crosscultural approaches to music.* Toronto: University of Toronto Press. (In press)

Dowling, W. J., & Hollombe, A. W. The perception of melodies distorted by splitting into several octaves: Effects of increasing proximity and melodic contour. *Perception & Psychophysics*, 1977, *21*, 60–64.

Drobish, M. W. *Uber musikalische Tonbestimmung und Temperatur. Abhandl Math. Phys. Kl. Konigl. Sachs, Ges. Wiss.* 1855, *4*, 1–120.

Elfner, L. Systematic shifts in the judgment of octaves of high frequencies. *Journal of the Acoustical Society of America*, 1964, *36*, 270–276.

Fechner, G. *Elements of psychophysics.* New York: Holt, 1966. (Original publication in German, 1860)

Fillmore, C. J. The case for case. In E. Bach & R. T. Harms (Eds.), *Universals in linguistic theory.* New York: Holt, 1970. Pp. 1–90.

Fillmore, C. J. The case for case reopened. In P. Cole & J. Sadock (Eds.), *Syntax and Semantics.* (Volume 8, Grammatical relations) New York: Academic Press, 1977. Pp. 59–81.

Francès, R. *La perception de la musique.* Paris: Vrin, 1958.

Fucks, W. Mathematical analysis of formal structure of music. *IRE Transactions on Information Theory*, 1962, *8*, 225–228.

Fyda, M. C. Perception and Internal Representation of Musical Intervals. M. A. Thesis, Michigan State University, East Lansing, Michigan, 1975.

Garner, W. R. The stimulus in information processing. *American Psychologist*, 1970, *25*, 350–358.

Goldman, R. F. *Harmony in Western music.* New York: Norton, 1965.

Goldstein, H. *Classical mechanics.* Reading, Massachusetts: Addison-Wesley, 1950.

Goldstein, J. L. An optimum processor theory for the central formation of the pitch of complex tones. *Journal of the Acoustical Society of America*, 1973, *54*, 1496–1516.

Greenwood, G. D. *Principles of dynamics.* Englewood Cliffs, New Jersey: Prentice-Hall, 1965.

Guttman, N., & Pruzansky, S. Lower limits of pitch and musical pitch. *Journal of Speech and Hearing Research*, 1962, *5*, 207–214.

Hall, D. E. Quantitative evaluation of musical scale tunings. *American Journal of Physics*, 1974, *42*, 543–552.

Hilbert, D., & Cohen-Vossen, S. *Geometry and the Imagination.* New York: Chelsea, 1952. (Original publication in German, 1932)

Hofstadter, D. R. *Gödel, Escher, Bach: An eternal golden braid.* New York: Basic Books, 1979.

Idson, W. L., & Massaro, D. W. A Bidimensional model of pitch in the recognition of melodies. *Perception & Psychophysics*, 1978, *24*, 551–565.

Jones, M. R. Time, our lost dimension: Toward a new theory of perception, attention, and memory. *Psychological Review*, 1976, *83*, 323–355.

Kallman, H. J., & Massaro, D. W. Tone chroma is functional in melody recognition. *Perception & Psychophysics*, 1979, *26*, 32–36.

Kameoka, A., & Kuriyagawa, M. Consonance theory Part II: Consonance of complex tones and its calculation method. *Journal of the Acoustical Society of America*, 1969, *45*, 1460–1469.

Kilmer, A. D., Crocker, R. L., & Brown, R. R. *Sounds from silence: Recent discoveries in ancient Near Eastern music.* Berkeley, California: Bīt Enki Publication, 1976.

Krumhansl, C. L. Concerning the applicability of geometrical models to similarity data: The interrelationship between similarity and spatial density. *Psychological Review*, 1978, *85*, 445–463.

Krumhansl, C. L. The psychological representation of musical pitch in a tonal context. *Cognitive Psychology*, 1979, *11*, 346–374.

Krumhansl, C. L., Bharucha, J. J., & Kessler, E. J. Perceived harmonic structure of chords in three related musical keys. *Journal of Experimental Psychology: Human Perception and Performance*, 1981, in press.

Krumhansl, C. L., & Kessler, E. J. Tracing the dynamic changes in perceived tonal organization in a spatial representation of musical keys. *Psychological Review*, 1982, in press.

Krumhansl, C. L., & Shepard, R. N. Quantification of the hierarchy of tonal functions within a diatonic context. *Journal of Experimental Psychology: Human Perception & Performance*, 1979, *5*, 579–594.

Kruskal, J. B. Multidimensional scaling by optimizing goodness of fit to a nonmetric hypothesis. *Psychometrika*, 1964, *29*, 1–27.

Kruskal, J. B. Analysis of factorial experiments by estimating monotone transformations of the data. *Journal of the Royal Statistical Society, Series B*, 1965, 27, 251–263.

Kruskal, J. B., & Shepard, R. N. A nonmetric variety of linear factor analysis. *Psychometrika*, 1974, *39*, 123–157.

Kubovy, M. Concurrent pitch-segregation and the theory of indispensable attributes. In M. Kubovy & J. R. Pomerantz (Eds.), *Perceptual organization*. Hillsdale, New Jersey: Lawrence Erlbaum, 1981.

Lakner, Y. A new method of representing tonal relations. *Journal of Music Theory*, 1960, *4*, 194–209.

Levelt, W.J.M., Van de Geer, J. P., & Plomp, R. Triadic comparisons of musical intervals. *British Journal of Mathematical and Statistical Psychology*, 1966, *19*, 163–179.

Locke, S., & Kellar, L. Categorical perception in a nonlinguistic mode. *Cortex*, 1973, *9*, 355–369.

Longuet-Higgins, H. C. Letter to a musical friend. *Music Review*, 1962, *23*, 244–248.

Longuet-Higgins, H. C. The perception of music (Review Lecture). *Proceedings of the Royal Society, London, Series B*, 1979, *205*, 307–332.

Merriam, A. P. *The anthropology of music*. Evanston, Illinois: Northwestern University, 1964.

McAdams, S., & Bregman, A. Hearing musical streams. *Computer Music Journal*, 1979, *3*, 26–44.

Metzler, J., & Shepard, R. N. Transformation studies of the internal representation of three-dimensional objects. In R. Solso (Ed.), *Theories in cognitive psychology: The Loyola Symposium*. Potomac, Maryland: Lawrence Erlbaum, 1974. Pp. 147–201.

Meyer, L. B. *Emotion and meaning in music*. Chicago, Illinois: University of Chicago Press, 1956.

Null, C. Symmetry in Judgments of Musical Pitch. Unpublished doctoral dissertation. Michigan State University, 1974.

Oakes, W. F. An experimental study of pitch naming and pitch discrimination reactions. *Journal of Genetic Psychology*, 1955, *86*, 237–259.

O'Connell, W. Tone spaces. *Die Reihe*, 1962, *8*, 34–67.

Philippot, M. *L' Arc, Beethoven*, No. 40, 1970.

Pickler, A. G. Logarithmic frequency systems. *Journal of the Acoustical Society of America*, 1966, *39*, 1102–1110.

Piston, W. *Harmony*. New York: Norton, 1941.

Plomp, R. *Aspects of tone sensation: A psychophysical study*. New York: Academic Press, 1976.

Plomp, R., & Levelt, W.J.M. Tonal consonance and critical band width. *Journal of the Acoustical Society of America*, 1965, *38*, 548–560.

Powers, W. T., Clark, R. K., & McFarland, R. L. A general feedback theory of human behavior: Parts I & II. *Perceptual & Motor Skills*, 1960, *11*, 71–88, 309–323.

Pressing, J. Cognitive isomorphisms in pitch and rhythm in world musics: West African, the Balkans, Thailand and Western tonality. Unpublished manuscript, Department of Music, La Trobe University, Bundoora Victoria, Australia 3083, 1979.

Ratner, L. G. *Harmony: Structure and style*. New York: McGraw-Hill, 1962.

Revesz, G. *Introduction to the psychology of music*. Norman, Oklahoma: University of Oklahoma Press, 1954.

Risset, J. C. *Paradoxes de hauteur: le concept de hauteur sonore n'est pas le meme pour tout le monde*. Proceedings of the 7th International Congress on Acoustics. Budapest, 1971, Paper 20510.

Risset, J. C. Musical acoustics. In E. C. Carterette & M. P. Friedman (Eds.), *Handbook of perception*. (Volume 4, Hearing) New York: Academic Press, 1978. Pp. 521–564.

Rosen, C. *The classical style: Haydn, Mozart, Beethoven*. New York, Viking Press, 1971.

Rothenberg, D. A model for pattern perception with musical applications. Part I: Pitch structures as order-preserving maps. *Mathematical Systems Theory*, 1978, *11*, 199–234. (a)

Rothenberg, D. A model for pattern perception with musical applications. Part II: The information content of pitch structures. *Mathematical Systems Theory*, 1978, *11*, 353–372. (b)

Ruckmick, C. A. A new classification of tonal qualities. *Psychological Review*, 1929, *36*, 172–180.

Sachs, C. *The rise of music in the ancient world, East and West*. New York: Norton, 1943.

Schenker, H. *Harmony*. Cambridge, Massachusetts: MIT Press, 1973. (Translated from original 1954 Edition)

Schouten, J. F. The perception of subjective tones. *Proceedings Kon. Ned. Akad. Wetensch.*, 1938, *41*, 1086–1093.

Seashore, C. E. *Psychology of music*. New York: McGraw-Hill, 1938.

Shackford, C. Some aspects of perception. I. *Journal of Music Theory*, 1961, *5*, 162–202.

Shackford, C. Some aspects of perception. II. *Journal of Music Theory*, 1962, *6*, 66–90.

Shepard, R. N. The analysis of proximities: Multidimensional scaling with an unknown distance function, I & II. *Psychometrika*, 1962, 27, 125–140, 219–246.

Shepard, R. N. Attention and the metric structure of the stimulus space. *Journal of Mathematical Psychology*, 1964, *1*, 54–87. (a)

Shepard, R. N. Circularity in judgments of relative pitch. *Journal of the Acoustical Society of America*, 1964, *36*, 2346–2353. (b)

Shepard, R. N. Approximation to uniform gradients of generalization by monotone transformations of scale. In D. I. Mostofsky (Ed.), *Stimulus generalization*. Stanford, California: Stanford University Press, 1965, Pp. 94–110.

Shepard, R. N. Metric structures in ordinal data. *Journal of Mathematical Psychology*, 1966, *3*, 287–315.

Shepard, R. N. Shepard's tones. In M. V. Mathews, J. C. Risset *et al.*, *The voice of the computer*. Decca Record DL 710180, 1970.

Shepard, R. N. Representation of structure in similarity data: Problems and prospects. *Psychometrika*, 1974, *39*, 373–421.

Shepard, R. N. The circumplex and related topological manifolds in the study of perception. In S. Shye (Ed.), *Theory construction and data analysis in the behavioral sciences*. San Francisco: Jossey-Bass, 1978. Pp. 29–80. (a)

Shepard, R. N. The double helix of musical pitch. In R. N. Shepard (Chair), *Cognitive structure of musical pitch*. Symposium presented at the meeting of the Western Psychological Association, San Francisco, California, April 1978. (b)

Shepard, R. N. On the status of "direct" psychophysical measurement. In C. W. Savage (Ed.), *Minnesota studies in the philosophy of science*. (Volume IX) Minneapolis, Minnesota: University of Minnesota Press, 1978. Pp. 441–490. (c)

Shepard, R. N. Multidimensional scaling, tree-fitting, and clustering. *Science*, 1980, *210*, 390–398.

Shepard, R. N. Individual differences in the perception of musical pitch. In *Documentary report of the Ann Arbor symposium: Applications of psychology to the teaching and learning of music*. Reston, Virginia: Music Educators National Conference, 1981. Pp. 152–174. (a)

Shepard, R. N. Psychophysical complementarity. In M. Kubovy & J. R. Pomerantz (Eds.), *Perceptual organization*. Hillsdale, New Jersey: Lawrence Erlbaum Associates, 1981. Pp. 279–341. (b)

Shepard, R. N. Geometrical approximations to the structure of musical pitch. *Psychological Review*, 1982. (In press).

Shepard, R. N., & Carroll, J. D. Parametric representation of nonlinear data structure. In P. R. Krishnaiah (Ed.), *Multivariate analysis: Proceedings of an international symposium*. New York: Academic Press, 1966. Pp. 561–592.

Shepard, R. N., & Cooper, L. A. *Mental images and their transformations*. Cambridge, Massachusetts: The MIT Press/Bradford Books, 1982.

Shepard, R. N., & Zajac, E. *A pair of paradoxes*. Murray Hill, New Jersey: Bell Telephone Laboratories, 1965. (A computer-generated 16-mm sound film.)

Siegel, J. A., & Siegel, W. Absolute identification of notes and intervals by musicians. *Perception & Psychophysics*, 1977, *21*, 143–152. (a)

Siegel, J. A., & Siegel, W. Categorical perception of tonal intervals: Musicians can't tell *sharp* from *flat*. *Perception & Psychophysics*, 1977, *21*, 399–407. (b)

Small, A. M. An objective analysis of violin performance. *University of Iowa Studies in the Psychology of Music*, 1936, *4*, 172–231.

Stevens, S. S. *Psychophysics: Introduction to its perceptual, neural and social prospects.* New York: Wiley, 1975.

Stevens, S. S., & Volkman, J. The relation of pitch to frequency: A revised scale. *American Journal of Psychology*, 1940, *53*, 329-353.

Stevens, S. S., Volkman, J., & Newman, E. B. A scale for the measurement of the psychological magnitude of pitch. *Journal of the Acoustical Society of America*, 1937, *8*, 185-190.

Sundberg, J.E.F., & Lindqvist, J. Musical octaves and pitch. *Journal of the Acoustical Society of America*, 1973, *54*, 922-929.

Terhardt, E. Pitch, consonance, and harmony. *Journal of the Acoustical Society of America*, 1974, *55*, 1061-1069.

Thurlow, W. R., & Erchul, W. P. Judged similarity in pitch of octave multiples. *Perception & Psychophysics*, 1977, *22*, 177-182.

Tversky, A. Features of similarity. *Psychological Review*, 1977, *84*, 327-352.

Van de Geer, J. P., Levelt, W.J.M., & Plomp, R. The connotation of musical intervals. *Acta Psychologica*, 1962, *20*, 308-319.

Van Noorden, L.P.A.S. Temporal Coherence in the Perception of Tone Sequences. Unpublished doctoral dissertation. Technishe Hogeschool, Eindhoven, Holland, 1975.

von Helmholtz, H. *On the sensations of tone as a physiological basis for the theory of music.* New York: Dover, 1954. (Original publication in German, 1862)

Ward, W. D. Subjective musical pitch. *Journal of the Acoustical Society of America*, 1954, *26*, 369-380.

Ward, W. D. Absolute pitch (Parts I & II). *Sound*, 1963, *2*, 14-21, 33-41.

Ward, W. D. Musical perception. In J. V. Tobias & E. D. Hubert (Eds.), *Foundations of modern auditory theory.* (Volume 1) New York: Academic Press, 1970. Pp. 407-447.

Ward, W. D., & Martin, D. W. Psychophysical comparison of just tuning and equal temperment in sequences of individual tones. *Journal of the Acoustical Society of America*, 1961, *33*, 586-588.

Watt, H. J. *The psychology of sound.* London & New York: The University of Cambridge Press, 1917.

Weeks, D. G., & Bentler, P. M. A comparison of linear and monotone multidimensional scaling models. *Psychological Bulletin*, 1979, *86*, 349-354.

Westergaard, P. *An introduction to tonal theory.* New York: Norton, 1975.

Wightman, F. L. The pattern-transformation model of pitch. *Journal of the Acoustical Society of America*, 1973, *54*, 407-416.

Winograd, T. Understanding natural language, *Cognitive Psychology*, 1972, *3*, 1-191.

Zatorre, R. S., & Halpern, A. R. Identification, discrimination, and selective adaptation of simultaneous musical intervals. *Perception & Psychophysics*, 1979, *26*, 384-395.

Zuckerkandl, V. *Sound and symbol.* Princeton, New Jersey: Princeton University Press, 1956.

Zuckerkandl, V. *Man the musician.* Princeton, New Jersey: Princeton University Press, 1972.

12

Musical Ability

Rosamund Shuter-Dyson

I.   Concepts of Musical Ability 391
II. Correlational and Factorial Studies of Musical Ability 393
     A. General Considerations 393
     B. Pitch Perception 396
     C. Tonal Memory 397
     D. "Feeling for Tonal Center" 399
     E. Harmony and Polyphony 400
     F. Appreciation Tests 401
     G. Rhythmic Abilities 402
     H. Kinesthetic Perception 403
     I. Summary 404
III. Musical Ability and Other Intellectual Abilities 404
     References 408

I. CONCEPTS OF MUSICAL ABILITY

The term *musical ability* is "the broadest and safest" in that it suggests the power to act but indicates "nothing about the heritability or congenitalness of inferred potentiality" (Farnsworth, 1969, p. 151). However, Gordon (1979) points out the words *ability* and *talent* include, and thereby confuse, aptitude and achievement. Certainly a broad distinction should, where possible, be drawn between *aptitude* (potential to learn) and *achievement* (what has been learned). The earlier view that it is possible to test innate capacity needs modification by the recognition that all aptitude tests are to some extent achievement tests just as all achievement tests necessarily reflect the initial aptitude that the individual can bring to the learning situation. However, attainment depends not only on aptitude but also on the teaching received and the child's interest in music and willingness to learn. Colwell (1970, pp. 72–73) suggests that it is useful to regard musical aptitude as referring to those qualities that develop over a long period and may cease to improve beyond a certain level in spite of further training. For example, tonal memory improves slowly and is possessed in widely varying degrees that do not seem to be directly related to length of experience with music. Differentiating between the major and minor modes may be learned at any period of life and within a relatively short time and hence may appropriately be measured in an achievement test.

A useful analogy may be drawn with intelligence. As Vernon (1968) noted in a paper on "Potential Ability," we need to recognize the existence of genetic differences between individuals in their capacities for building up neural and mental schemata, what Hebb (1949) called "Intelligence A." The psychologist can, however, only observe the effectiveness of present behavior or thinking through the interaction of the genes and the stimulation offered by the environment (i.e., Intelligence B). This is culturally conditioned by the environment provided by the ethnic group into which the child is born, especially by the child's home and his or her leisure pursuits. Vernon also notes the effects of physiological conditions before and shortly after birth, Cattell's (1965) *Constitutional Intelligence*. The results of intelligence tests, Intelligence C, are of considerable predictive value because they sample useful mental skills.

The term *musicality* is used by Revesz (1953) to denote "the ability to enjoy music aesthetically." The ultimate criterion is the depth to which a person, listening and comprehending, can penetrate the artistic structure of a composition. As Zuckerkandl (1973, Chapter 1) points out, music is equated with the compositions that have evolved in the Western world over the past thousand years, characterized by their tonal polyphony. Composing and interpreting have become the business of experts, whose works seem to demand special sensitivity to comprehend them. Hence, a distinction between "musical" and "unmusical" comes to be drawn, even though conceived as a continuum rather than a dichotomy.

A different concept of musicality implies that all men *qua* men are music makers. Blacking (1971), for example, proposes that human beings possess musical competence similar to the linguistic competence postulated by Chomsky and that "average musical ability" is as universal as average linguistic competence.

For example, the Venda in Africa assume that everyone is capable of music making, even deaf persons having the ability to dance. However, the Venda recognize that some persons perform better than others do. Exceptional musical ability is indeed expected of children born into certain families. Only a few may actually become exceptional musicians; if they do, what is considered to set them apart is not that they can do what others cannot but that they devote more time and effort to music.

Important evidence on the inherent music-making potential of humans comes from exploratory studies conducted at the Bioacoustic Laboratory in Pennsylvania. In neonates, the effects of multidimensional signals, whether tonal sequences or synthetic speech sounds, produce distinctive overt reactions whatever the state of prior arousal (Eisenberg, 1976, p. 137). Such responses occurred, for example, to descending versus ascending sequences (2000 down to 500 Hz versus 500 up to 2000 Hz). Moog (1976, p. 113) noted that up to the age of about 3 the development of a response to music is determined by innate ability and by the musical stimuli presented to the child more or less haphazardly. But he reported from his investigation of some 500 children that "by the end of the third year all children are capable of imitative singing" (p. 97), even if only some groups of notes are sung correctly.

Certain of Moog's results are of special interest: 16% of 2-year-olds did not sing words but hummed or sang something similar to the rhythm and pitch of Moog's tests (p. 83). Singing before speaking seems to be one characteristic of children with conspicuous musical talent. For example, Erwin Nyiregyhazy, a prodigy whose talents were studied by Revesz (1925), could reproduce correctly melodies sung to him in his second year; at the beginning of his fourth year, he began to play on the piano everything he heard; and by seven could analyze complicated chords with great accuracy. Many such children are born into families of musicians, even if not distinguished ones. Others are born into families with only modest musical abilities. Conversely, highly talented parents may produce children with little aptitude or interest in music. Such "anomalies" suggest more strongly than do family resemblances the likely action of hereditary factors (Shuter, 1968, p. 112).

In one sense, then, the ability to make and apprehend music is inherent in all humans, but in another sense aptitude varies among individuals and may set a limit on ultimate achievement, no matter how favorable the environmental influences nor how highly motivated the person.

II. CORRELATIONAL AND FACTORIAL STUDIES OF MUSICAL ABILITY

A. General Considerations

A fair variety of material from which tests might be constructed has been examined over the last 70 years. The best of the published tests, in spite of various imperfections, have proved successful in helping to identify the relative status of individuals to an extent that makes them useful in music education. Detailed information on such tests is readily available elsewhere (Lundin, 1967; Colwell, 1970; Whybrew, 1971). All the more reputable batteries were subjected to several years of experimentation before they were published, thus throwing light on what subtests are the most efficient. Allowance has to be made for the limitations imposed by the group testing situation: tests of vocal or instrumental performance have lagged behind perceptual ones since they need to be administered individually.

It is as research tools that tests are to be considered in this paper. In assessing the meaningfulness of correlation and factor analytic studies, we must bear in mind the reliability and the validity of the tests used and their suitability for the groups tested.

Tests naturally reflect differences in their authors' concepts of musical ability. Seashore (1938, p. 3) believed that the sensory capacities measured in his laboratory and eventually presented in his *Measures of Musical Talent* (1919) were basic to musical aptitude, could be sharply defined, and could be present or absent in the individual to varying degrees. Correlation studies of the *Measures* rarely produce zero correlations. Teplov (1966, pp. 62–64) tabulated the intercorrelations from 14 early studies of the *Measures*. The average of these ranged from .22 (intensity-rhythm) to .52 (pitch-tonal memory). Some of the agreement is probably due to intelligence. But after partialing out intelligence, Drake (1939) found a common factor and two group factors in a study of 163 13-year-old boys. He concluded that even when a special attempt is made to measure independent capacities, it is seldom entirely successful. While the revised version of the *Measures* (1939 and 1960) appears to have improved reliability (rising to .8 at least in the case of pitch, intensity, and tonal memory), the relevance of sensory capacities to functional music activities has been repeatedly questioned (Mursell, 1937; Wing, 1948; Lundin, 1967).

Wing (1948) experimented with 25 tests that were eventually reduced to seven: three of ear acuity (chord analysis, pitch, and melodic memory) and four of appreciation. They became the Wing Standardised Tests of Musical Intelligence (1961). One criterion for including a test in the short series was a satisfactory, but not too high, correlation with the total for the whole battery. This was justified, he believed, since his factorial studies had shown a general factor existed in a wide variety of tests. Though these studies were carried out on small groups by present standards, the results produced a general factor having 40% of the variance with positive saturations throughout. Minor factors separated tests and persons into "analytic" and "synthetic" types, and those depending mainly on harmony as opposed to melody. How far any common factor is evidence of the unitariness of musical ability obviously depends on how successfully the tests used cover all aspects of the ability. In Wing's case this depends essentially on how valid is his claim that "no vital test is missing from the short series" (Wing, 1948, p. 49). The battery is certainly comprehensive for one limited to an hour; its reliability and validity, at least taken as a whole as Wing intended, are good.

The Gordon *Musical Aptitude Profile* (*MAP*) (Gordon, 1965) consists of three parts: tonal (melody and harmony); rhythm (tempo and meter), and musical sensitivity (phrasing, balance, and style). The intercorrelations of the tonal with the rhythm subtests range from .45 to .65 (Gordon, 1965, pp. 56–57) and from .35 to .70 (Tarrell, 1965). Since these values were lower than the reliabilities of the subtests, Gordon (1965, p. 51) claims that this "constitutes evidence although somewhat indirect, of the multidimensional nature of musical aptitude." However, he also states (p. 9) that in music "rhythm and melody interact in an inseparate way." Considerable evidence has been reported on the reliability and validity of the MAP and its subtests (Gordon, 1967). His new *Primary Measures of Music Audiation* (*PMMA*) (Gordon, 1979) has separate tonal and rhythm subtests, since he considers that a sense of meter to be on a par with that of tonality. Intended for children kindergarten through grade 3, reliability and validity are most promising.

The first battery devised primarily for children aged 7/8 to 14 was the *Measures of Musical Abilities* (*MMA*) (Bentley, 1966a). Bentley (1966b, pp. 89–92) stated that, though the functions measured by his tests may overlap and seem to be working together, they are in fact separate. Certainly the test of rhythmic memory correlates rather weakly with the rest of the tests in both his and Young's (1973) research.

The results of factor analyses depend in part on the method used and on whether and how the factors are rotated. Unlike Wing (1941) and McLeish (1950), who were content with unrotated solutions, Karlin (1941, 1942), Franklin (1956) and Holmstrom (1963) rotated their factors. Computer programs are now producing objectivity in rotations and giving several "primary" factors of more nearly equal importance.

Whellams (1971) reanalyzed many previous correlation and factorial studies by principal components, followed by varimax rotation, to investigate how far the various diverse studies might confirm or deny similar results. In the reanalyses of 16 studies of the Seashore *Measures*, three factors recurred, all seeming to involve tonal memory. Three rather similar factors emerged with the Kwalwasser–Dykema (K-D) (1930) tests, plus a fourth factor of tonal movement and rhythm imagery. Factorizing five correlation matrices of the MAP produced only two significant factors: tempo/meter and phrasing/style. Ten studies of the Wing tests produced five significant factors. In all, 15 factors of some significance were extracted. The tentative interpretations of these were summarized by Whellams thus:

Significant[a] Factors		Tests loaded	Interpretation	P.A.M.A. factor
Perceptual				
I, VI, XI	(23)	Pitch, tonal memory	Factor for pitch imagery	pi
II, V	(11)	Rhythm, tonal memory	Dynamic or kinesthetic factor for the development of pitch perception	kp
III, XV	(12)	Consonance, chords, harmony, memory	Factor for harmonic ability	h
X	(10)	Chord analysis, harmony	Tonal separation factor	t
VIII	(4)	Tempo, meter	Rhythmic ability	r
IV	(3)	Tonal movement, memory	Experience factor	xp1
VII	(2)	Rhythm imagery, tonal movement	Experience factor	xp2
Appreciation or judgment				
IX	(3)	Phrasing, style	Musical judgment factor	j
XII	(7)	Intensity	Wing test factor	j1
XIII	(6)	Phrasing	Wing test factor	j2
XIV	(4)	Rhythm	Wing test factor	j3

[a] Numbers in parentheses are the number of studies in which the factors appeared.

From nonorthogonal primary factors second-order factors may be extracted by further analysis. For example, Cattell (1963) proposed two second-order factors of intelligence—one representing the crystallization of intellectual potential through acculturation (Gc) and one representing the capacities of intellect that have remained relatively "fluid" immune to acculturation influences (Gf). So far, only Horn and Stankhov seem to have tried to extract second-order factors from auditory tests. They carried out an extensive exploration of auditory and visual functions, using the Seashore battery, Drake's Rhythm tests, and the Wing tests 1–3, as well as visual tests and auditory tests devised to correspond to the visual ones. Their subjects were 241 men, aged between 16 and 54, inmates of a state penitentiary. Results indicated six primary auditory abilities: auditory reasoning (Ra), temporal reordering (Tr), nonsymbolic recognition memory (Mr), detection of distorted speech (DDS), masked speech comprehension (MSC), and rhythm (Ry) (Horn, 1973). Later analyses of the data (Stankov & Horn, 1980; Horn & Stankov, in preparation) include the extraction of a second order factor of general auditory functioning (Ga) and one of auditory acuity (Ac).

B. Pitch Perception

Pitch discrimination is widely acknowledged to be an essential part of musical perception. It appears in some form in most test batteries and in many experimental studies of the development of musical ability (e.g., Andrews & Deihl, 1967). Pitch tasks are among the most difficult for younger children, though it is sometimes not clear how far this is due to a lack of understanding of "higher" and "lower" as applied to music.

Quite strong intercorrelations are typically found between tests that explore discrimination of fine pitch differences by means of oscillator-produced tones (Seashore and Bentley) and also between these and Wing's test where the pitch change is masked within two piano chords. Examples are

Seashore–Wing	.63 (McLeish, 1966)
	.49 .67 .62 (Franklin, 1956, pp. 184–185)
	.53 (Faulds, 1959)
Bentley–Wing	.46 (Donat, 1964)
	.26 (Whellams, 1971)

Closely allied to pitch discrimination are interval tests. Lundin (1944, 1949) required his subjects to judge whether a second melodic interval moved up or down. Faulds (1959) slightly modified the test and found that the Seashore pitch test correlated .58 and the Wing pitch test .76 with it.

The work of the Siegels (Siegel & Siegel, 1977b) provides a different perspective on the perception of pitch by musicians, who appear to categorize pitches in a way similar to the categorization of consonants in language. One group of six musicians, whose participation in music averaged 53 hours a week, identified in-tune intervals with a 95% accuracy. In one experiment they were asked to identify 13 tonal intervals ranging from 20 cents below a perfect fourth by 20-cent steps to 20 cents above a perfect fifth by pressing buttons labeled perfect fourth, augmented fourth, and perfect fifth. All examples of a musical category were perceived as equivalent, variability being least at the center of the category and most at each boundary. Intermediate stimuli were heard to "pop" one way or the other, not as halfway between two musical intervals. Siegel and Siegel had previously (1977a) found that subjects chosen for their lack of musical experience made inconsistent judgments largely influenced by context in this type of experiment. For a further experiment (J. Siegel, 1976), the six musicians were joined by a performer of Indian music who was also experienced in Western music; his score on in-tune intervals was 100%. Subjects were now required to judge whether intervals (minor third, fifth, and octave) were in-tune, sharp, or flat. In one type of stimuli, all were out of tune, with sharp and flat examples occurring equally often; in another, half were in tune, 25% flat, and 25% sharp; and in a third all the intervals were in tune. The flat/sharp intervals deviated by .25 of a semitone from accuracy. As the percentage of in-tune intervals increased from 0 to 100%, the percentage of in-tune judgments increased only from 47 to 62%. Flat intervals were detected more accurately than sharp or in-tune ones. In spite of their many years of musical training, no subject approached perfect performance, two reaching only chance level. The performer of Indian music fell in the middle of the group. In a musical context he might have scored better. Citing Seashore's (1938, p. 269) conclusions from his acoustic measurements of the deviations from exact pitch in the performances of well-known artists, Siegel and Siegel (1977b) concluded that "categorical perception allows one to recognize the melody, even when the notes are out of tune, and to be blissfully unaware of the poor intonation that is characteristic of good musical performance." When, however, a musician was given an untimed production task, emulating the tuning of an instrument, he was very accurate at adjusting the frequency of an oscillator to a value corresponding to musical notes (W. Siegel, 1976).

C. Tonal Memory

Drake (1939) believed that memory acts to knit together specific capacities such as discrimination of pitch, time, and rhythm. Bugg and Herpel (1946) investigated whether the intercorrelations of the various Seashore tests would drop substantially when tonal memory was partialed out. Partialing out the results of testing 181 subjects with the Seashore *Measures* did lead to reduced intercorrelations, but the differences were not great.

The Seashore tonal memory test contains 3-, 4-, and 5-tone items, which are repeated with one tone changed, the task being to detect which tone has been altered. Wing's test ranges from 3 to 10 notes and includes a rhythmic content but is based on the same principle. The Drake Musical Memory Test (Drake, 1957) is rather different. Two-bar melodies have to be remembered and compared for possible changes of time, key, or notes. The testee has to detect what element (if any) has been changed. As the test progresses, up to 7 variations follow the original, considerably increasing the memory load. Gaston (1957) included in his Test of Musicality seven items built on the same principle as the Drake except that the testee must identify change of note or rhythm from a repetition. This was the most discriminating of all the tests used by Bentley (1955) in an investigation contrasting the scores of 110 noninstrument-playing high-school students with 110 instrument-playing music students, matched on the bases of sex, IQ, grade placement, and socioeconomic status on music tests, including the Wing battery.

The intercorrelations of the various tests of tonal memory are quite strong:

Seashore–Wing	.74 (McLeish, 1966)
	.64 and .75 (Franklin, 1956, pp. 184–185)
Seashore–Drake	.56 (Lundin, 1958)
	.55 (Farnsworth, 1969)
	.61 (Rainbow, 1965)

Davies (1971) sought to devise a new type of test material that would place emphasis on memory for entire sequences rather than for single elements. First, a tonal sequence of three or four tones was presented, then a longer sequence (from 4 to 8 tones). Sometimes the short sequence was contained intact in the longer one. The testees were asked whether or not the long sequence contained the short one and also in what part of the longer sequence it was located. The sequences were derived from statistical approximations to music upon the analogy with Miller and Selfridge's (1950) experiments with verbal material. The Davies test had reliabilities as high as .7 even for children as young as 7. The items were based on the equal-tempered scale; sequences based on a scale not common to any culture might also be produced.

The above mentioned tests could be subsumed under "Short-Term Memory." Long-term memory is obviously crucially involved in musical ability, as was recognized by Seashore: "Hearing is not a mere registering of sounds. It is a positive active process of reconstruction in the mind of the listener (1938, p. 168)." He also speaks of auditory imagery "the capacity to hear music in recall, in creative work, and to supplement the actual physical sounds" as perhaps the most outstanding mark of the musical mind (p. 161). Gordon (1977, p. 2) uses the term "audiation" to designate hearing music through recall or creation, in the absence of the physical sound, and thereby deriving musical meaning, as opposed to musical perception/conception when the music is actually being performed by others.

At least in the early stages of learning, auditory imagery seems to need to be supported by kinesthetic imagery (see Section II,H). Gordon recognizes this when he speaks of the person who is tonally audiating as singing silently and of rhythmic audiation requiring covert, if not overt, eurhythmic functioning. Agnew (1922) found most of 200 musicians rated their auditory image of "America" as played on the piano, "as clear as the actual hearing" or "very clear." Eighty-nine psychologists rated their auditory imagery as low and needing kinesthetic support. Curiously, a study of self-rated musical imagery produced with naive subjects a sizable association with a pitch identification test but none with Drake's memory test (Bergan, 1967).

D. "Feeling for Tonal Center"

Even now that much contemporary music is atonal or polytonal, the ability to feel the presence or absence of a tonal center is to be considered important (Colwell, 1969, p. 112; Gordon, 1977, p. 1). Yet the melodies children spontaneously sing do not seem to relate to any observable tonal center, at least not one found in Western music (Moorhead and Pond, 1942, p. 14). Gordon (1979) suggests that a sense of tonality develops simply out of the child audiating the resting tone. A notable feature of the tonal part of his *PMMA* test is that the tonic is found in at least one of the patterns of the pair (which the child is required to judge as "same" or "different") and is included in both in strategically located items. All the patterns used had in an extensive previous research been found to be "easy," differences in difficulty in the test being attained by the pairings of the patterns for comparison. Gordon considers the sense of tonality to be basic to the development of musical understanding, for example, in the ability to follow modulations.

Just as one criterion of linguistic ability is the child's acquisition of a command of his or her native language, it is reasonable to expect musical aptitude to manifest itself in acquisition of feelings for tonality. Zenatti's experiments (1973, 1975) were concerned with comparisons between the perception and discrimination of tonal (or pentatonic) melodies as compared with atonal ones. Not until the age of 7 or 8 were tonal melodies perceived better than atonal ones above a chance level. Success with tonal as opposed to atonal melodies improved with age, though in the case of three-note tasks, when the children were either very good or very bad at discrimination, it made little difference whether the phrases were tonal or atonal. In the case of four-tone phrases, the better the discrimination score, the greater was the difference between tonal and atonal perception (Zenatti, 1969, Chapter III). Even adults perceived a change of note on a second playing more surely with tonal as opposed to atonal phrases (Francès, 1958, pp. 81–90).

One of the most valid of the K–D tests is on tonal movement, in which the testee hears an incomplete pattern of four tones and is asked to indicate whether the tone needed to complete the sequence should move "up" or "down" from the fourth tone. Drake (1931) found that few could succeed in this test but not on tonal memory, but that many could make good scores on tonal memory but not on tonal movement (i.e., "judgement, an entirely different operation from memory, is yet impossible without the latter"). Franklin (1956) based his Tonal Musical Talent (TMT) test on the principle that if a short two-part melody is interrupted immediately before the final tone, the subject who could sing the tonic would thereby demonstrate his sense of tonality. The TMT correlated .43 and .55 with Wing's pitch test, .55 with Wing's memory test, and .40 with Wing's harmony test, and .60 and .55 with Seashore's memory test but only .18 and .40 with Seashore's pitch test.

From his factor analyses of his test, the Wing battery and Seashore's pitch and memory tests, Franklin found two factors of special interest to him: (1) "mechanical-acoustic" pitch discrimination (of fine differences, as required by Seashore) and (2) "judicious-musical" pitch discrimination, the ability to deal with pitch changes in a musical context, as in his TMT and the Wing tests. Franklin argued that judicious pitch would be the most important aspect of any general music factor that might be found. Holmstrom (1963) pointed out that fine pitch discrimination is likely to help rather than hinder pitch tasks in a musical context. Holmstrom's own analyses yielded two pitch factors: "alpha" had a loading on intensity, had possibly a physiological basis, and might be only slightly influenced by experience with music; "beta" had greater loadings on tonal memory and seemed to be more salient among older children with varied experience of music. In Whellams' more comprehensive studies (see Section II,A), the pi factor does not overshadow all others. His interpretation of pi seems more comparable to Holmstrom's beta. Pi seemed to be influential in sight-singing and to improve with length of training.

E. Harmony and Polyphony

Franklin (1956) concluded from the researches of Rupp and of Brehmer that the establishment of an ear for tonality is preceded by a stage in which an ear for pitch and an ear for consonance and dissonance may exist but not for simultaneous horizontal and vertical listening. However, an acquisition of a sense of tonality is no guarantee of an appreciation of suitable harmonizations (on the criterion of conventional Western harmony) (Teplov, 1966, Chapter VI). Teplov cites the interesting case of a subject who found the "good" harmonization more pleasant but the discordant one less distracting from perceiving the melody. Though Zenatti (1969, Ch. II) found children between 8 and 10 began to be able to recognize a well-known tune presented fugually, even children up to 12 had difficulty perceiving the bass part.

The *MAP* harmony test is concerned with "like/different" judgments about the lower of two-part melodies. The Wing test is concerned with the judgment of the better harmonization. This test tends to be linked with the Wing pitch and memory tests, but a harmony (h) factor as distinct from a tonal separation factor was revealed in Whellams' reanalyses of the Wing and Seashore batteries. In his own study of children around 9, in which both the Wing and the Bentley chord analysis tests were included but not the Wing harmony test, a combined h:t factor emerged. In McLeish's analysis (1966) the Wing chord analysis and the harmony test loaded similarly (.66 versus .65) on the "musical cognition" factor. With professional students of the Eastman School of Music, the harmony test proved too easy, but the chord analysis test successfully separated the good from the very good student (Shuter, 1968, pp. 35–36).

Experiments with cadences have provided valuable data on the growth of musical ability. Imberty (1969, p. 216) showed that 10-year-old subjects understood both perfect and imperfect cadences, but if the third degree of the scale was used for the tonic chord, a feeling of surprise was created (i.e., judgment was still essentially melodic). Yet, a cadence test devised by Wing (1948, p. 16, 48), in which the melodic line of two cadences to be compared for their feeling of finality was kept as similar as possible, proved too easy for his subjects. It would seem to be true that at certain stages of musical development (using the criterion of age or of level of aptitude) an appreciation of appropriate harmonization is salient; at others, the analysis of chords appears to be more discriminative.

F. Appreciation Tests

Among tests of appreciation of music that are commercially available are the Indiana–Oregon Music Discrimination Test, the last four tests of the Wing battery, and the third part of the *MAP*. Indiana–Oregon, developed by Long, was based on the original Hevner–Landbury test. The principle remains the same: an original excerpt is paired with a "distorted" version. The testee has to state which version he or she prefers and which element—rhythm, harmony, or melody—has been changed. Wing presents an original along with an impoverished version but uses these to make separate tests of rhythm, harmony, intensity, and phrasing. A criticism of such a procedure is that testees who recognize the music are at an advantage. But, as Wing (1948, Chapter VI) makes clear, scores made on known tunes were no higher than unrecognized tunes. When Wing was devising his tests (in the late 1930s), the music of Wagner and Ireland proved too strange to be useful as test material. In Martin's (1976) research and in McLeish's (1950), the Wing appreciation tests do not correlate conspicuously with the Oregon.

Gordon's approach to establishing the "better" version was to begin by asking professional musicians which of two interpretations of a specially composed item they preferred. Only when high consensus (9 out of 10) was reached, and this was confirmed by experimental field trials, were the items incorporated into the final version of the test. [Hoffren (1964) also used a "consensus" judgment on which to base a test of expressive performance of music that would resemble as closely as possible the judgment required in an actual musical situation.] Consensus is obviously based on value judgments that may change with time—such tests may need to be updated.

An early statement of the relationship between Seashore's tonal memory test and the Oregon was that they correlated .65 (Bugg & Herpel, 1946). This finding was confirmed by McLeish (1950). The Oregon test proved to be highly related to the Wing battery, especially to the memory, pitch and harmony tests, and to Seashore's tests of pitch and tonal memory. In fact, the judgment of "Which element changed?" received the highest loading (.86) on McLeish's musical cognition factor. The correlations between Gordon's sensitivity tests and the Seashore *Measures* are much lower (Gordon, 1969). Gordon himself takes the view that musical appreciation depends on musical understanding, which depends on awareness of basic aural elements (Gordon, 1977, p. 1).

Swanick (1973), too, believes that much cognitive activity is involved in esthetic response to music and that the intensity and quality of any emotional response depends on this. His experiments were based on setting up an experimental subculture, a pair of alternating notes in a metric scheme as a basic unit as a repeated norm against which a deviation could be located. (See Fig. 1). The various musical events included

Basic Unit   Event

Fig. 1.   From Swanick (1973).

change of tonality, of tempo, of direction of melody. The subjects were simply asked, "What happens in the music just before the end?" and to record their responses on semantic differential scales such as active/passive, light/heavy, and happy/sad. Even small changes carried for all subjects, even for those as young as 7, a clear and specific meaning, and there was a strong consensus of opinion. He concluded that, in addition to perceptual and memory abilities, three more musical abilities are central to the processes of understanding music: (1) the ability to locate piece and style norms, (2) the ability to understand the flux of "meaning" embodied in ongoing music, and (3) the ability to make predictions as to what may follow so that deviations arouse surprise and excitement.

Scherer and Oshinsky (1977) manipulated acoustic cues with electronically synthesized tone sequences; these produced in their naive judges systematic emotional effects—results which seem to confirm Swanick's.

G. Rhythmic Abilities

Wing (1948, p. 47) justified the inclusion of only one rhythm ability in his short series on the grounds that the correlation between time-pattern dictation and appreciation of rhythm was very high, hence one could be regarded as redundant. Drake's rhythm tests are concerned with the ability to maintain a steady beat, in the case of Form B against a faster or slower distracting beat. Tanner and Loess (1967) reported intercorrelations of .37 between Seashore's time and rhythm tests, .56 between Seashore's rhythm test and Drake A and .38 with Drake B, .38 between Seashore's time test and Drake A and .43 with Drake B. Very low correlations were found between the Wing rhythm test and all these tests. Horn (1973) reported a correlation of .69 between the two versions of the Drake tests and a loading of the Seashore rhythm test on a rhythm factor. However, the Seashore rhythm test had a higher correlation with a factor largely involving other Seashore tests than it had with the rhythm factor. It therefore seemed more a function of nonsymbolic recognition memory (Mr) than a function of capacity to continue an established rhythm—Whellams might have interpreted this as a kp factor (See Section II,H). Hiriartborde (1964) found a factor that had high loadings on the Wing and Seashore memory tests, the Wing intensity and phrasing test, as well as on a test of synchronization. The factor that showed the highest variance, 28%, involved motor coordination and control of movement as well as tonal memory and pitch. A factor concerned with the ability to structure rhythmic groups had a loading on the Seashore rhythm test.

For his study of the rhythmic abilities of adults, Thackray (1969) devised tests of rhythmic perception, rhythmic performance, and rhythmic movement. He later adapted the perception and performance tests for use with children (Thackray, 1972). He noted that inability to memorize some of the longer items was an important reason for low scores (1969, p. 29)—again suggesting a kp linkage between rhythm and memory. His own factor analyses (unrotated) suggested that there was a general factor, though this was complex. With adult physical education students, the following intercorrelations were found: perception and performance .63, perception and movement .55, and performance and movement .59. With child groups performance tests seemed superior to tests of perception as a means of testing general rhythmic ability. Ability to maintain a steady tempo appeared to be a highly specific rhythmic ability. Igaga (1974) compared the rhythmic abilities of Ugandan with those of English children. The Ugandan children tended to excel on the Thackray performance tests. In particular, the Ugandan girls were superior to the boys by 10 points on perception and 8 on performance—perhaps because Ugandan girls participate from their earliest years in domestic activities, accompanied by rhythmic music.

H. Kinesthetic Perception

Whellams' (1971, p. 240) kp factor seems to span the tonal memory and rhythmic aspects of music, to have a large genetic component, and to suggest the kind of overall musical talent envisaged by Wing. It is interesting in drawing attention to the muscular component in auditory perception that is in line with contemporary feedback models of skilled behavior. From validation experiments on the Seashore tests, Whellams (p. 239) suggests that kp has a positive influence on harmonic attainments, that its connection with rhythmic ability goes beyond mere recognition of meter or time, that it is indeed an important central activity influencing the development of various kinds of overt musical behavior and of the higher level aural imagery required for tasks such as written harmony and dictation. A factorizing of Gordon's (1969) data comparing the MAP with the Seashore produced a first factor heavily loaded on MAP melody (.80), MAP harmony (.77) which also had sizable loadings on MAP tempo (.46) and meter (.41) and on Seashore pitch (.59) and memory (.30). This, too, Whellams reasonably considered a kp factor.

Mainwaring (1933) found that children and Training College students tended to translate auditory into kinesthetic processes in order to recall tunes they had listened to well enough to answer questions about them. He also cites the disturbance to recall in an experienced singer who had been forbidden to sing a tune to herself while it was being played to her. Vernon (1931, p. 126) noted the importance of the kinesthetic aspects of music in making perception of music definite but believed that at the level of the highly trained musician, many can listen in purely auditory and intellectual terms. Sergeant too (1969, p. 434) agrees that childhood perception of pitch is first facilitated by a vocal scheme but believes that kinesthetics is not an important factor in adult perception and reports that subjects who do not possess absolute pitch are more likely to have recourse to kinesthetic sensations than those who do. Joyner (1969) and Gould (1969) both worked on the assumption that improving pitch perception and the singing voice requires a kinesthetic approach. [See Shuter (1974) for a review of such studies.] An extensive investigation by Kyme (1967) demonstrated the value of performing in an orchestra or a choir as the prime means of developing musicality (capacity to grasp in its completeness and detail a musical idea that has been heard).

The disruptive effects of DAF seem to operate on a music performance task as with verbal tasks (Gates, Bradshaw, & Nettleton, 1974).

Some evidence on the role of gross bodily movements on rhythmic perception was obtained by Moog (1978). He tested children, aged 10 to 11 (1) with serious physical handicaps, (2) with mental handicaps, and (3) normal children (IQ 80–118). Limitation of movement since earliest childhood reduces rhythmic perception nearly as much as does low intelligence. Children with physical handicaps tend to use pitch rather than rhythmic perception to discriminate rhythmn patterns that may (or may not) be presented in a melodic context. The question of whether some individuals are attentive to pitch structure and others to rhythmic structure, Moog believes, needs further research.

I. Summary

Davies (1978, pp. 154–155) is right to say that a more open-ended approach to testing is now needed. Some older tests do not reach current recording standards. The greater exposure to music of all kinds may require an updating of norms (Tomita and Kurosu, 1976). New tests, such as Davies' (1971), seem to show up the possibilities of using "nonmusical" material that might minimize the effects of experience of music. Attempts like Vaughan's to parallel in music "creativity" tests, such as those of Torrance, need to be given due regard (Vaughan, 1977). Karma's (1975, 1978) test based on the ability to structure acoustic material would seem just the kind of culture-fair test that might throw light on "fluid musical ability."

III. MUSICAL ABILITY AND OTHER INTELLECTUAL ABILITIES

The correlations between the results of testing musical ability with other intellectual abilities in the case of some 16,000 subjects, as tabulated by Shuter (1968), were almost without exception positive but low. Both Wing (1954) and Kwalwasser (1955) refer to .30 as being about the correlation to be expected with ordinary, unselected subjects. Wing observed that there was usually good agreement between low intelligence and low scores on his test, but that disagreement occurred when a high IQ was accompanied by a low musical ability score. Edmunds (1960) studied 118 children, aged 12 and 13, in a mixed-ability school. He concluded that once a certain level of intelligence is reached (approximately IQ 90), intelligence no longer plays a significant part in level of musical ability. A large proportion of the correlations tabulated by Shuter refer to college students for whom intelligence would not be likely to be important in success with musical ability tests. Whellams (1971 p. 299) reported that correlations between the Wing tests 1–3 and the Bentley tests as compared with nonmusical tests frequently exceeded .5 and some were greater than .6 with his young subjects whose test scores on nonverbal tests were about average, but whose reading ages were about two years lower than the norms. If one applies Edmunds' formula to children of 10, the equivalent mental age would produce an IQ of 108. Zenatti (1975) found that the acuity of perceptive discrimination and tonal acculturation among 396 subnormal children approximated to that of normal children of the same *mental age*.

However, the correlations between the *PMMA* and intellectual tests are low. For example at kindergarten level, with Metropolitan Readiness Tests Level 2, tonal correlated .29 with language and .24 with quantitative; rhythm .16 with language and .15 with quantitative. At grade 1, correlations with the Stanford Reading and Mathematics Achievement Test range from .24 and .37; at grade 3, correlations with the Lorge–Thorndike Intelligence Tests (verbal and nonverbal) range from .19 to .30.

In the case of those Achievement in Music Tests that are largely tonally based, correlations with intellectual tests are also low. For 1400 fourth-grade students, the Musical Achievement Test (MAT) (Colwell, 1969) correlated .23 with the Iowa Tests of Basic Skills (Colwell, 1969, p. 80). Intercorrelations among scores on the Iowa Tests of Musical Literacy (ITML) (Gordon, 1970) and the verbal Lorge–Thorndike Intelligence tests fell around .3 (Gordon, 1970, p. 116). On the other hand, grades on theory of harmony and musical history can be predicted by verbal intelligence tests (Holmstrom, 1969). Mursell (1937, pp. 336–339) pointed up the close association between educational attainments and musical ability when the criteria employed are teachers' estimates of student ability. It is hard to judge how far the student's incentive to work hard and the "halo" effect of success in other school work may contaminate such results.

The statistic used in the above research was usually the correlation coefficient. Sergeant and Thatcher (1974), however, consider that analysis of variance provides a more useful result. They investigated the interrelationships among the Cattell Culture Free Scale B, ratings of the sociocultural and -economic characteristics of the family, and the abilities of 75 children, aged 10 to 11, to perform a rhythmic and a melodic task. Highly significant relationships were found among all the variables, the trends being linear. In the case of the rhythmic task quadratic and cubic trends were also significant. Phillips (1976) carried out a careful study of the scores made on Wing tests 1–3 and five of the Thackray Rhythmic Perception tests by 194 children from four contrasting schools. Highly significant differences were found among the variables whether classified by music scores, musical background or the Thorndike–Hagen Cognitive Abilities Test.

Pedagogically, it is of importance that children from disadvantaged homes (and probably with relatively low IQs) can, given suitable opportunities to learn a musical instrument, equal or surpass the achievements of a heterogenous group both when the former's *MAP* scores were superior and when they were average. A potent motive was probably a desire to compensate for their limited academic attainments (Gordon, 1975).

That certain persons of low mental ability can show capacities for music far superior to their general intellectual functioning is exemplified by the so-called idiot-savants. Typical musical accomplishments show some similarities to those of infant prodigies, they can, for example, often play a tune by ear after hearing it only once or twice (Shuter, 1968, pp. 98–102). Feats of memory are certainly commonly reported. Blind Tom was able to memorize a piece after one hearing (Drake, 1940); a blind imbecile girl could play a new and difficult piece after hearing it only once (Rife & Snyder, 1931); *XY* had good pitch discrimination and a good tonal memory, being able to play by sight or by ear, though he produced no original compositions (Minogue, 1923; Rife & Snyder, 1931). One idiot-savant described by Rife and Snyder could play on the piano any tune sung to him, using harmonically correct chords, though he had never received any training in music. *L* showed remarkable interest and ability in music, rhythm, and counting in his third year and was apt to acquire long-lasting obsessive interest in certain music—like an aria from *Otello*, the words of which he learned to sing in Italian phonetically (Scheerer, Rothmann, & Goldstein, 1945). Current theorists on hemisphere bilaterity might postulate left-hemisphere malfunctioning. A subject (*S*) with a Binet IQ of only 67 but a WAIS verbal score of 92 was eventually taught to speak through the medium of lyrics; he became good at sight-reading and played the piano at rehearsal for a chamber music orchestra. He too had an outstanding rote memory, being able to reproduce a two-and-a-half-page article verbatim after a single silent reading, but without being able to grasp the social significance of the passage (Anastasi & Levee, 1960).

As Horn (1973) points out one of the problems of investigating the relationship between auditory abilities and intelligence is that existing intelligence tests fail to do justice to input through the auditory modality.

Musical ability must involve temporal integration, "perhaps," according to Hearnshaw (1951) "the most basic intellectual skill." In Stankov & Horn's researches on the temporal integration and reasoning aspects of auditory functions, they found two factors: Tr and Ra (Horn, 1973). A test that particularly defined Tr was one which required a subject to retain awareness of a sound while listening to determine when the same sound occurred again in a series. Seashore's time test correlated .27 with this factor. Stankov (1980) has investigated this factor, now called Tc (Temporal Tracking), further. To study the reasoning processes involved in tasks of auditory input, Stankov and Horn devised tasks parallel to visual reasoning tasks such as analogies and classifications. For example, a chord of three notes was followed by four sets of three notes played individually, the subject having to select the one that contained the same three notes that were in the original chord. Such tests came together in the Ra factor. This was also defined by variables selected to indicate closure, in their attempt to test the hypothesis that auditory and visual flexibility and speed of closure might represent similar mental functions. A test designed to imitate the Gottschaldt figures test loaded .49 on the Ra factor and the Wing chord analysis test, .42. The Gottschaldt tonal test required the subject to choose one of four pairs of piano notes that had been embedded in a previously present chord.

Perhaps the test most successful in producing a clear-cross modality measurement was called "hidden tunes" (a test similar to Davies' described in Section II,D). In White's (1954) study it correlated .66 with "embedded figures" (its visual counterpart) and sizably with three other visual tests. Fleishman, Roberts, and Freidman (1958) found that "hidden tunes" had a major loading (.62) on a factor that involved tests of ability to detect the dots and dashes of the Morse code. Since it also loaded .56 on the Seashore rhythm test, they interpreted it as a factor of auditory rhythm perception.

Horn's (1973) factorization of the intercorrelations among the auditory and visual primary factors produced four second-order ones. In the first, Mr, Tr, and Ra appeared with five visual primaries. Horn interpreted this as a factor indicating fluid intelligence. Factor 2 reflected a crystallized form of intelligence also manifested in visual primaries and in Ra, Tr, and DDS. A third factor was concerned with visualization. The fourth was almost wholly defined by the auditory primaries. Mr had the most prominent correlation with this broad auditory Ga factor, followed by MSC (comprehension of speech distorted—e.g., by masking) with a correlation of .74. The loadings of Ra, DDS, and Tr, each of which had prominent loadings on the Gf or Gc factors, were .59, .49, and .43, respectively.

It seemed that the distinction between Gf and Gc was manifested in the auditory as well as in the visual realm. However, the auditory tests contained a systematic variance of their own. The perception keenness and retention represented by MSC and Mr suggested to Horn these were more important than temporal ordering in his Ga factor. However, his musically unselected adults may well have been operating at a rather basic "melodic" rather than "harmonic" level. It would be interesting to investigate whether different results would be found among trained musicians. For a more detailed discussion of researches of Horn and Stankov and their implications for music, see Shuter-Dyson and Gabriel (in press).

Two areas to which musical ability might seem to be especially associated are mathematical/spatial abilities and ability in the other arts. Shuter (1968) discussed the difficulties of proving or disproving the traditional view of a connection between musical and mathematical abilities. More recently, the view that some musical abilities and some mathematical or spatial abilities are more efficiently processed in the right cerebral hemisphere might give renewed credence to their association. In his earlier research Karma's test did seem to be more highly correlated with spatial abilities than with verbal (Karma, 1978). He hypothesized that some persons (perhaps females) might process musical stimuli verbally and others (perhaps males) spatially. His later research with a revised form of his test, however, pointed to the tentative conclusion that the essential difference between "verbal" and "spatial" types of musical processing is the amount of musical training. For a review of studies of musical training and lateralization, see Shuter-Dyson and Gabriel (in press, Chapter 18).

The parents of great musicians have often been distinguished in the other arts (Feis, 1910). However, attempts to obtain empiric evidence of a relationship through testing

have been disappointing. Guilford (1957)—while considering that the ability to produce and express ideas in the graphic arts was distinct from the ability to produce and
express ideas in music—suspected that there might be something in common among
the parallel factors in the different arts.

It is possible that connections between the arts exist on a personality rather than on
a cognitive level. At least one of the Cattell 16 PF factors, apart from "B" (intelligence) has been consistently found in a number of studies of personality and musical
abilities (Cattell, Eber, & Tatsuoka, 1970; Shuter, 1975). This is the "I" (tender-
mindedness) factor. This factor was shown both by musical children and professional
music students, but it did not clearly distinguish them from nonmusical groups;
rather it was common to all whose interests lay in the arts (Martin, 1977). Beldoch
(1964) found highly significant correlations among sensitivity to emotional expressions in speech (recognition of emotion expressed by the voice, given a neutral
verbal content), in graphic art (abstract representations of the same 10 emotions), and
music (short compositions depicting the same emotions). Though verbal intelligence
was related to all three measures, significant intercorrelations remained after intelligence had been partialed out. This result Beldoch interpreted with reference to
Langer's (1942, 1953) theory of discursive and nondiscursive symbols. On the general
question of the personality structure of the musician, Kemp (1981) reports the results
of an extensive investigation.

In summary, however valuable intelligence may be in the development of musical
ability, mere intellectual efficiency, however highly oriented to music, will not make
a musician. During the later years of the twentieth century, music is likely to become
an important leisure interest, one for which education should be provided. Perhaps
test producers may be induced to accord auditory/musical abilities a more prominent
place in their batteries. If a second-order factor (or factors) were to be extracted from
the results of testing, it would account nicely for the existence of a number of musical
abilities in varying degrees in individuals and also for the need for an overall, *coordinated* level of efficiency for success in music whether as listener, performer, or composer.

REFERENCES

Agnew, Marie. A comparison of auditory images of musicians, psychologists and children. *University of
    Iowa Studies in Psychology*, 1922, *8*, 268–278.
Anastasi, Anna, & Levee, R. E. Intellectual defect and musical talent. *American Journal of Mental Deficiency*,
    1960, *64*, 695–703.
Andrews, Frances M., & Deihl, N. C. *Development of a technique for identifying elementary school children's
    musical concepts*. Washington, D.C.: U.S. Office of Education Project 5-0233, 1967.
Beldoch, M. Sensitivity to expression of emotional meaning in three modes of communication. In J. R.
    Davitz (Ed.), *The communication of emotional meaning*. New York: McGraw-Hill, 1964.
Bentley, A. *Measures of musical ability*. London: Harrap, 1966. (a)
Bentley, A. *Musical ability in children and its measurement*. London: Harrap, 1966. (b)
Bentley, R. R. *A critical comparison of certain aspects of musical aptitude test*. Doctoral thesis, Univ. Southern
    California. 1955.

Bergan, J. R. The relationship among pitch identification, imagery for music sounds, and music memory. *Journal of Research in Music Education*, 1967, *15*, 99–109.

Blacking, J.A.R. Towards a theory of musical competence. In E. DeJager (Ed.), *Man: Anthropological essays in honour of O. F. Raum*. Cape Town: Struik, 1971.

Bugg, E., & Herpel, L. The significance of tonal memory for musicality. *Journal of General Psychology*, 1946, *35*, 3–15.

Cattell, R. B. Theory of fluid and crystallized intelligence: A critical experiment. *Journal of Educational Psychology*, 1963, *54*, 1–22.

Cattell, R. B. *The Scientific Analysis of Personality*. Baltimore: Penguin. 1965.

Cattell, R. B., Eber, H. W., & Tatsuoka, M. M. *Handbook for the Sixteen Personality Factor Questionnaire (16 PF)*. Champaign, Illinois: Institute for Personality & Ability Testing, 1970.

Colwell, R. *MAT Music achievement tests 1 and 2, Interpretive Manual*. Chicago, Illinois: Follett, 1969.

Colwell, R. *The evaluation of music teaching and learning*. Englewood Cliffs, New Jersey: Prentice Hall, 1970.

Davies, J. B. New tests of musical aptitude. *British Journal of Psychology*, 1971, *62*, 557–565.

Davies, J. B. *The Psychology of music*. London: Hutchinson, 1978.

Donat, Kinga. *Testing Musical Ability*. Unpublished paper, University of London, Institute of Education, 1964.

Drake, R. M. *Tests of musical talent*. Ph.D. thesis, University of London, 1931.

Drake, R. M. Factorial analysis of music tests by the Spearman-Tetrad-Difference technique. *Journal of Musicology*, 1939, *1* (1), 6–16.

Drake, R. M. The relation of musical talent to intelligence and success at school. *Journal of Musicology*, 1940, *2*, No 1.

Drake, R. M. *Manual for the Drake Musical Aptitude Tests*. (2nd ed.) Chicago, Illinois: Science Research Associates, 1957.

Edmunds, C. B. *Musical ability, intelligence and attainment of secondary modern and E.S.N. children*. Thesis, University of Leeds, 1960.

Eisenberg, Rita B. *Auditory competence in early life*. Baltimore, Maryland: University Park Press, 1976.

Farnsworth, P. R. *The social psychology of music*. (2nd ed.) Ames: Iowa State University Press, 1969.

Faulds, B. D. *The perception of pitch in music*. Princeton, New Jersey: Educational Testing Service, 1959.

Feis, O. *Studien über die Genealogie und Psychologie der Musikers*. Wiesbaden: Bergmann, 1910.

Fleishman, E. A., Roberts, N. H., & Freidman, M. P. Factor analysis of aptitude and proficiency measures in radio-telegraphy. *Journal of Applied Psychology*, 1958, *42*, 127–137.

Francès, R. *La perception de la musique*. Paris: Vrin, 1958.

Franklin, E. *Tonality as a basis for the study of musical talent*. Göteborg: Gumperts Förlag, 1956.

Gaston, E. T. *A test of musicality*. Lawrence, Kansas: Odell's Instrumental Service, 1957.

Gates, Anne, Bradshaw, J. L., & Nettleton, N. C. Effect of different delayed auditory feedback intervals on a music performance task. *Perception & Psychophysics*, 1974, *15*, 21–25.

Gordon, E. *Musical aptitude profile*. Boston, Massachusetts: Houghton Mifflin, 1965.

Gordon, E. *A three-year longitudinal predictive validity study of the musical aptitude profile*. Iowa City, Iowa: University of Iowa Press, 1967.

Gordon, E. An investigation of the intercorrelation among musical aptitude profile and Seashore measures of musical talent subtests. *Journal of Research in Music Education*, 1969, *17*, 263–271.

Gordon, E. *Iowa tests of music literacy*. Iowa City, Iowa: Bureau of Educational Research and Service, 1970.

Gordon, E. Fourth-year and fifth-year final results of a longitudinal study of the musical achievement of culturally-disadvantaged students, *Experimental Research in the Psychology of Music: Studies in the Psychology of Music*, 1975, *10*, 24–52.

Gordon, E. E. *Learning sequence and patterns in music*. Chicago, Illinois: G.I.A., 1977.

Gordon, E. E. *Primary measures of music audiation*. Chicago, Illinois: G.I.A., 1979.

Gould, A. O. Developing specialized programs for singing in the elementary schools. *Bulletin of the Council for Research in Music Education*, 1969, No 17, 9–22.

Guilford, J. P. Creative abilities in the arts. *Psychological Review*, 1957, *64*, 110–118.

Hearnshaw, L. S. Exploring the intellect. *British Journal of Psychology*, 1951, *42*, 315–321.

Hebb, D. O. *The organization of behavior*. New York: Wiley, 1949.

Hiriartborde, E. *Les aptitudes rythmiques.* Paris: Dactylo-Sorbonne, 1964.

Hoffren, J. The construction and validation of a test of expressive phrasing in music. *Journal of Research in Music Education,* 1964, *12,* 159–164.

Holmstrom, L-G. *Musicality and prognosis.* Uppsala: Almqvist & Wiksells, 1963.

Holmstrom, L-G. Intelligence vs. progress in music education. *Journal of Research in Music Education,* 1969, *17,* 76–81.

Horn, J. L. Theory of functions represented among auditory and visual test performances. In J. R. Royce (Ed.), *Multivariate analysis and psychological theory.* London: Academic Press, 1973. Pp. 203–239.

Horn, J. L. & Stankov, L. Auditory and visual factors in intelligence. In preparation, 1981.

Igaga, J. M. *A comparative developmental study of the rhythmic sensitivity of Ugandan and English schoolchildren.* Ph.D. thesis, University of London, 1974.

Imberty, M. *L'acquisition des structures tonales chez l'enfant.* Paris: Klincksieck, 1969.

Joyner, D. R. The monotone problem. *Journal of Research in Music Education,* 1969, *17,* 115–124.

Karlin, J. E. Musical ability. *Psychometrika,* 1941, *6,* 61–65.

Karlin, J. E. A factorial study of auditory function. *Psychometrika,* 1942, 7, 251–279.

Karma, K. *The ability to structure acoustic material as a measure of musical aptitude.* Helsinki: Institute of Education, Research Bulletin, No 43, 1975.

Karma, K. Musical, spatial and verbal abilities. Paper to the *7th International Seminar on Research in Music Education, Bloomington, Indiana,* 1978.

Kemp, A. The personality structure of the musician. I. Identifying a profile of traits for the performer. *Psychology of Music,* 1981, *9(1),* 3–14. II. Identifying a profile of traits for the composer. *Psychology of Music,* 1981, *9(2),* (in press).

Kwalwasser, J. *Exploring the musical mind.* New York: Coleman-Ross, 1955.

Kwalwasser, J., & Dykema, P. W. *Kwalwasser-Dykema Music tests.* New York: Fischer, 1930.

Kyme, G. H. A study of the development of musicality in the junior high school and the contributions of musical composition to this development. *Bulletin of the Council for Research in Music Education,* 1967, No 10, 15–23, No 11, 36–45.

Langer, Susanne K. *Philosophy in a new key.* Cambridge, Massachusetts: Harvard University Press, 1942.

Langer, Susanne K. *Feeling and form.* New York: Scribners, 1953.

Long, N. H. *Indiana-Oregon Music Discrimination Test.* Bloomington, Indiana: Midwest Music Tests, 1978.

Lundin, R. W. A preliminary report on some new tests of musical ability. *Journal of Applied Psychology,* 1944, *28,* 393–396.

Lundin, R. W. The development and validation of a set of musical ability tests. *Psychological Monograph,* 1949, *63(305),* 1–20.

Lundin, R. W. What next in the psychology of musical measurement? *Psychological Record,* 1958, *8,* 1–6.

Lundin, R. W. *An objective psychology of music.* (2nd ed.) New York: Ronald Press, 1967.

McLeish, J. The validation of Seashore's measures of musical talent by factorial methods. *British Journal of Psychology (Statistical section),* 1950, *3,* 129–140.

McLeish, J. The factor of musical cognition in Wing's and Seashore's Tests. Paper represented to *Music Education Research Conference, Reading University,* 1966.

Mainwaring, J. Kinaesthetic factors in the recall of musical experience. *British Journal of Psychology,* 1933, *23,* 284–307.

Martin, P. J. *Appreciation of music in relation to personality factors.* Ph.D. thesis, University of Glasgow, 1976.

Martin, P. J. The personalities of musicians. Paper to the *9th Conference of the Society for Research in Psychology of Music and Music Education, Cambridge,* 1977.

Miller, G. A., & Selfridge, J. A. Verbal content and recall of meaningful material. *American Journal of Psychology,* 1950, *63,* 176–185.

Minogue, B. A case of secondary mental deficiency with musical talent. *Journal of Applied Psychology,* 1923, 7, 349–352.

Moog, H. *The musical experience of the pre-school child.* London: Schotts, 1976.

Moog, H. The perception of rhythmic forms by physically handicapped children and those of low intelligence in comparison with non-handicapped children. Paper to the *7th International Seminar on Research in Music Education, Bloomington, Indiana,* 1978.

Moorhead, G. E., & Pond, D. *Music of Young Children: II General observations*. Santa Barbara, California: Pillsbury Foundation Studies, 1942.

Mursell, J. L. *The psychology of music*. New York: Norton, 1937.

Phillips, D. An investigation of the relationship between musicality and intelligence. *Psychology of Music*. 1976, *4*(2), 16-31.

Rainbow, E. L. A pilot study to investigate the constructs of musical aptitude. *Journal of Research in Music Education*, 1965, *13*, 3-14.

Revesz, G. *The psychology of a musical prodigy*. New York: Harcourt, 1925.

Revesz, G. *Introduction to the psychology of music*. London: Longmans, Green, 1953.

Rife, D. C., & Snyder, L. H. A generic refutation of the principles of behavioristic psychology. *Human Biology*, 1931, *3*, 547-559.

Scheerer, M., Rothmann, E., & Goldstein, K. A case of "idiot savant": an experimental study of personality organization. *Psychological Monographs*, 1945, *58*, No 4.

Scherer, K. R., & Oshinsky, J. Cue utilization in emotion attribution from auditory stimuli. *Motivation & Emotion*, 1977, *1*, 331-346.

Seashore, C. E. *Seashore Measures of Musical Talent*. Chicago, Illinois: Stoelting, 1919. Revised and retitled *Measures of Musical Talents* 1939 and 1960. *Revised Manual* New York: The Psychological Corporation, 1960.

Seashore, C. E. *The psychology of music*. New York: McGraw Hill, 1938.

Sergeant, D. C. *Pitch perception and absolute pitch—a study of some aspects of musical development*. Ph.D. thesis, University of Reading, 1969.

Sergeant, D. C., & Thatcher, G. Intelligence, social status and musical abilities. *Psychology of Music*, 1974, *2*(2), 32-57.

Shuter, Rosamund. *The psychology of musical ability*. London: Methuen, 1968.

Shuter, Rosamund. Singing out of tune: A review of recent research on this problem and its educational implications. *Scientific Aesthetics*, 1974, *9*, 115-120.

Shuter, Rosamund. The relationship between musical abilities and personality characteristics in young children. In New Zealand Council for Educational Research, Studies in Education No 25, *Music education for the very young Child*, Wellington, 1975. P. 30.

Shuter-Dyson, Rosamund, & Gabriel, C. *The psychology of musical ability*. 2nd edition. London: Methuen (in press).

Siegel, Jane A. Judgment of intonation by musicians: Further evidence for categorical perception. London: University of Western Ontario Research Bulletin, No. 375, 1976.

Siegel, Jane A., & Siegel, W. Absolute identification of notes and intervals by musicians. *Perception & Psychophysics*, 1977, *21*, 143-152. (a)

Siegel, Jane A., & Siegel, W., Categorical perception of tonal intervals: musicians can't tell *sharp* from *flat*. *Perception & Psychophysics*, 1977, *21*, 399-407. (b)

Siegel, W. The paradox of pitch categories. London: University of Western Ontario Research Bulletin No. 373, 1976.

Stankov, L. Ear differences and implied cerebral lateralization in some intellective auditory factors. *Applied Psychological Measurement*, 1980, *4*, 21-38.

Stankov, L., & Horn, J. L. Human abilities revealed through auditory tests. *Journal of Educational Psychology*, 1980, *72*, 19-42.

Swanick, K. Musical cognition and aesthetic response. *Psychology of Music*, 1973, *1* (2), 7-13.

Tanner, J., & Loess, H. Correlations among rhythm tests. *Perceptual & Motor Skills*, 1967, *25*, 721-726.

Tarrell, V. V. An investigation of the validity of the musical aptitude profile. *Journal of Research in Music Education*, 1965, *13*, 195-206.

Teplov, B. M. *Psychologie des aptitudes musicales*. Paris: Presses Universitaires de France, 1966.

Thackray, R. *An investigation into rhythmic abilities*, Music Education Research Papers No 4. London: Novello, 1969.

Thackray, R. *Rhythmic abilities in children*, Music Education Research Papers No 5. London: Novello, 1972.

Tomita, M., & Kurosu, M. A preliminary study on the assessment of musical aptitude. Tokyo: Waseda University Psychological Report 8, 1976.

Vaughan, M. M. Musical creativity: Its cultivation and measurement. *Bulletin of the Council for Research in Music Education*, 1977, No 50, ,72-77.

Vernon, P. E. The psychology of music with especial reference to its appreciation. Ph.D. dissertation, University of Cambridge, 1931.

Vernon, P. E. What is potential ability? *Bulletin of the British Psychological Society*, 1968, *21*, 211-219.

Whellams, F. The aural musical abilities of junior school children: A factorial investigation. Ph.D. thesis, University of London, 1971.

White, B. W. Visual and auditory closure. *Journal of Experimental Psychology*, 1954, *48*, 234-240.

Whybrew, W. E. *Measurement and evaluation in music* (2nd ed.) Dubuque: Brown, 1971.

Wing, H. D. A factorial study of musical tests. *British Journal of Psychology*, 1941, *31*, 341-355.

Wing, H. D. Tests of musical ability and appreciation. *British Journal of Psychology, Monograph Supplement*, No 27, 1948.

Wing, H. D. Some applications of test results to education in music. *British Journal of Educational Psychology*, 1954, *24*, 161-170.

Wing, H. D. *Standardised tests of musical intelligence*. Windsor, England: N.F.E.R., 1961.

Young, W. T. The Bentley Measures of Musical Abilities: A congruent validity report. *Journal of Research in Music Education*, 1973, *21*, 74-79.

Zenatti, Arlette. *Le développement génétique de la perception musicale*, Monographies Françaises de Psychologie 17, Paris: CNRS, 1969.

Zenatti, Arlette. Etude de l'acculturation musicale chez l'enfant dans une épreuve d'identification mélodique. *Journal de Psychologie normale et pathologique*, 1973, *4*, 453-464.

Zenatti, Arlette. Melodic memory tests: A comparison of normal children and mental defectives. *Journal of Research in Music Education*, 1975, *23*, 41-52.

Zuckerkandl, V. *Man the musician*. Princeton, New Jersey: Princeton University Press, 1973.

13
Melodic Information Processing and Its Development
W. Jay Dowling

I. Introduction 413
II. Development 415
   A. Infancy 415
   B. Childhood 416
   C. Training 419
   D. School-Age Years 420
III. Adult Memory 420
   A. Melodic Features 421
   B. Immediate Memory 421
   C. Tonality 423
   D. Long-Term Memory 424
IV. Contour versus Interval 426
V. Summary 427
   References 427
                                       428

I. INTRODUCTION

In this chapter I review what we presently know about humans' processing of pitch information in melodies. The time has come for such a summary because in the 25 years since Francès' (1958) classic work an increasingly clear picture of how adults hear and remember melodies has been emerging, along with a clearer picture of how those abilities develop. I will start by following the developmental pattern from infancy to adulthood, and then I will analyze the adult behaviors in more detail.

Melodies have properties that musicians and psychologists can vary more or less independently of one another. The pitches of a melody may be preserved when it is

Fig. 1. Examples of types of stimuli described in the text. At the top is the first phrase of a familiar melody, "Twinkle, Twinkle, Little Star." Following it are (a) an exact repetition; (b) a transposition to another key; (c) a tonal imitation in the key of the original; (d) an atonal imitation; and (e) a melody with a different contour.

repeated exactly (Fig. 1A), but it is more usual for melodies to be repeated at a variety of pitch levels. In such cases the identity of the melody is preserved as long as the pitch *intervals* between notes have been preserved through transposition to a new *key* along a logarithmic scale of frequency (Fig. 1B). A further change, one that does not preserve the identity of the melody though it does result in something similar, is to preserve the melodic *contour* (the pattern of ups and downs of pitch) while allowing the interval sizes to change (a tonal imitation, Fig. 1C). Examples 1A and 1C share melodic contour and key (tonality) but not interval sizes. Fig. 1D shows the result of taking the same contour but changing the intervals even more radically so that the result lies outside any tonal scale and is *atonal*. Finally, Fig. 1E displays the result of altering the contour, leaving only the rhythmic pattern of the original song and whatever nonspecific features it might have, such as general pitch range, tempo, and instrumental timbre. These latter features are nonspecific in that they might be properties of whole families of similar songs.

The kinds of features preserved through the transformations of Fig. 1 evoke different patterns of response in adults asked to recognize similarities and differences among them. And in the developmental sequence the child's abilities to utilize these different sorts of stimulus invariance stabilize at different ages. In early infancy the child can reproduce single pitches and can notice a change of melodic contour (but not of key). It is not until the age of 5 or 6, however, that the child develops a stable sense of tonality; that is, until he or she can detect when the key of a melody has been changed and distinguish tonal from atonal melodies. It is still later that the child becomes sensitive to small changes of interval sizes in familiar songs—that is, to the differences between examples 1A and 1C. The developmental sequence is one of going from the baby's ability to distinguish gross features such as contour and pitch level, to the 5-year-old's grasp of tonal scales and ability to discriminate key changes, to the adult's ability to detect small changes of interval size. There seems to be a hierarchy of features, and the sequence of human development follows that hierarchy closely (Pick, 1979). I will now review the evidence in more detail.

II. DEVELOPMENT

A. Infancy

Infants 5 months old notice changes in melodic contour while treating transpositions of melodies as equivalent. Melson and McCall (1970) demonstrated the first of these results, finding dishabituation of the baby's heartrate response when the temporal positions of all eight notes of an eight-note pattern were changed. And Kinney and Kagan (1976) found the same effect with 7-month-olds when the contour *and rhythmic pattern* of a melody were altered. Chang and Trehub (1977a) demonstrated both aspects with 5-month-olds. They presented babies with six-note melodies played at a rate of 2.5 notes/sec. The melodies were atonal and had rather large pitch intervals between notes. The pitches lay in a two-octave range covering the treble staff from the C below to the C above (262 to 1048 Hz). One melody was played 30 times over a 5.5 min period, during which the baby's heart rate habituated to the melody. (Only babies showing initial heartrate deceleration followed by habituation were used— about half the babies tested). After the 30 repetitions the pattern was switched to either an exact transposition of the first melody (up or down a minor third) or a permutation of the notes of the transpostion that destroyed the contour of the original. (Note that the transposition left the test melody in more or less the same pitch range as the original except that all the particular pitches had been changed.) Chang and Trehub found that the babies showed dishabituation—a reappearance of the heartrate deceleration "startle" response—to the melody with the altered contour, but not to the transposed melody. That is, for infants as for adults the transposition sounds like the same old melody again while the different-contour melody sounds new. (In a related study Chang and Trehub (1977b) also found dishabituation to a change in rhythmic pattern.) Thus, Chang and Trehub demonstrated both the noticing of melodic discrepancy (contour changes) and the acceptance of melodic similarity (transposition).

Vocal play in which infants explore the pitch range accessible to their voices has often been observed (Ostwald, 1973), and some infants even tried to match pitches they heard (Révész, 1954, p. 171; Shuter, 1968, p. 67). In a more controlled study,

Kessen, Levine, and Wendrich (1979) have demonstrated that with a few brief training sessions babies under 6 months of age can learn to match pitches, singing back the pitches sung to them. Using test pitches from the minor triad D-F-A, the experimenters found that the babies sang successful matches two-thirds of the time, and a large proportion of these hits were very nearly in tune. According to Kessen *et al.*, the babies enjoyed the task and worked hard at it. Apparently the singing of specific pitches is something that the 6-month-old is ready and willing to learn. In both noticing contour changes and matching pitches, the infant's behavior is already like that of the adult. But in still another way it is very adultlike: in Chang and Trehub's task in which absolute pitch level was irrelevant to the identity of the melody the infants ignored changes in pitch. Yet they were quite capable of discriminating pitches when the task required it, as Kessen *et al.* demonstrated. Of course, the infant is insensitive to many dimensions accessible to the adult, including tonality and interval size, and so I will continue the story.

B. Childhood

During their second year children begin to recognize certain melodies as stable entities in their environments. My daughter at 18 months would run to the TV set when she heard the "Sesame Street" theme come on but not for other melodies. At 20 months, after a week or so of going around the house singing "uh-oh" rather loudly to a descending minor third, she responded with the spoken label "uh-oh" when I played the pattern on the piano. Especially after 18 months the child begins to generate recognizable, repeatable songs. As Ostwald (1973) says, "Song patterns become more coherent." Songs for a child around the age of 2 years often consist of brief phrases repeated over and over. The rhythm of these phrases is coherent, and their contour is replicable, but the pitch wanders. The same contour is repeated at different pitch levels, usually with different intervals between the notes. An example from a 24-month-old[1] consisted of a descending phrase with the words "Duck on my house" repeated 10 or 12 times at different pitch levels with small intervals within the phrase and a leap up to the start of a new phrase. The song was repeated by the child over a period of two weeks at which point it disappeared. (The contour was probably borrowed from the "E-I-E-I-O" phrase of "Old MacDonald," which the child also sang.) Such spontaneous songs have a systematic form and display two essential features of adult singing: they use discrete pitch levels, and they use repetition of rhythms and melodic contours as a formal device. They are unlike adult songs, however, because they lack a framework of stable pitches (a scale) and use a very limited

---

[1]This observation and following ones are drawn from tape recordings of the singing of 21 children: four of age 2; six of age 3; five of age 4; and six of age 5; with between 5 and 32 "songs" collected from each. Such sampling does not lend itself to statistical analysis, and the results reported are intended as illustrative. I have usually used examples that find substantiation elsewhere in the literature. And as with all such observations the ages mentioned should not be taken as normative in a rigid sense since children vary immensely in the age at which they display these behaviors.

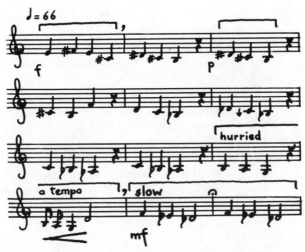

Fig. 2. A child's spontaneous song at 32 months. Each note was vocalized to the syllable "Yeah." Brackets indicate regions of relatively accurate intonation. Elsewhere intonation wandered.

set of contours in one song—usually just one or two. A more sophisticated construction by the same child at 32 months can be seen in Fig. 2. The pitch still wanders but is locally more coherent within phrases. Here three replicable phrases are built into a song structure that begins to be meaningful for the adult listener in a way that the "Duck on my house" song is not. The child has moved from Frank Zappa somewhat in the direction of the Beatles.

The above observations are in general agreement with those of Gardner, Davidson, and McKernon (1981) on spontaneous singing by 2-year-olds. Gardner *et al.* extended their observations by teaching a simple song to children across the preschool age range. Two- and three-year-olds generally succeeded in reproducing the contours of isolated phrases. As they got older they were able to concatenate more phrases in closer approximation of the model. It was only very gradually that the interval relationships of the major scale began to stabilize. Four-year-olds could stick to a stable scale pattern within a phrase but would often slip to a new key for the next phrase. It was not until after 5 that the children could hold onto a stable tonality throughout the song. Further, with a little practice the 5-year-olds were able to produce easily recognizable versions of the model. My own observations suggest that the typical 5-year-old has a fairly large repertoire of nursery songs of his or her culture. This phenomenon appears when children are asked to sing a song and can respond with a great variety of instances as well as when they are asked to perform short-term recognition-memory tasks and do better with familiar materials than with novel, randomly generated melodies.

A converging line of evidence on the 5-year-old's acquisition of a stable scale structure, of tonality, is provided by a study by Bartlett and Dowling (1980, Experiment 4). That study explored subjects' ability to distinguish between transpositions of familiar melodies (Fig. 1B) and tonal imitations retaining the same contour but with changes of interval size (Fig. 1C). On each trial of the experiment the first phrase of a familiar melody would be presented, followed shortly afterwards by a comparison stimulus that was either a transposition or a tonal imitation. The comparison was either in a nearly related (or the same) key as the standard or in a distant key. Near keys share many overlapping pitches in their scales; distant keys share few. For example, starting with the key of C major (CDEFGABC), we could move to the hear key of G (GABCDEF♯G) that shares every note with C but the F♯ or to the far key of B major (BC♯D♯EF♯G♯A♯B) that shares only two pitches with C: the B and E. Table I summarizes the results in terms of the tendency to say "Same" when presented with the various types of stimulus pair. The responses of nonmusician adults are presented for comparison. Note that the adults are highly accurate in saying "Same" to transpositions (over 90%) and not saying "Same" to imitations (under 10%). The pattern for the 5-year-olds is very different: they tend to say "Same" to near key comparisons whether transpositions or imitations and to avoid "Same" responses to far-key items. That is, the 5-year-olds have one component of the adult behavior pattern—the ability to distinguish near from far keys—but not the other component—the ability to detect changes of interval sizes in the tonal imitations. Note that both components are reflected in the adults' better performance in rejecting far-key (as opposed to near-key) imitations, a result that Bartlett and I obtained in a series of experiments using a variety of materials and that we call a *key-distance* effect (Bartlett & Dowling, 1980). Note also that as the child grows older, the pattern of response changes markedly in the adult direction so that the 8-year-old child accepts near-key *imitations* less often than far-key *transpositions*. Both cognitive strategy components are clearly visible in the 8-year-olds' data: they can use both key distance and interval changes to reject a comparison stimulus.

As with all of these ages, 5 years of age should not be taken as rigidly normative but as an approximate guideline for when stable tonal structures appear, depending on how the experimenter tests for them. Zenatti (1969, Chap. 3), for example, found that with the rather difficult task of saying *which* note of a three-note sequence has been altered in pitch, 5-year-olds perform at about chance level with both tonal and atonal

TABLE I

Probabilities of Responding "Same" to Transpositions and Tonal Imitations in Near and Far Keys[a]

Age group (yr)	Transpositions		Imitations	
	Near	Far	Near	Far
5.6	.67	.58	.63	.55
6.9	.58	.54	.60	.36
8.6	.70	.62	.50	.35
29.4	.91	.92	.11	.02

[a] After Bartlett and Dowling, 1980.

melodies, and only with 6- and 7-year-olds does superior performance with tonal melodies appear. And in keeping with the result of Bartlett and Dowling (1980), Imberty (1969, ch. 4) found that 7-year-olds could notice sudden changes of key in the middle of familiar tunes and that 8-year-olds could tell when a melody had been switched from the major mode to the minor, an effect very similar to that produced by creating a tonal imitation in the above sense.

The 5- or 6-year-old's grasp of stable tonal centers fits other results in the literature. For example, in a series of studies Riley and McKee (1963; Riley, McKee, & Hadley, 1964; Riley, McKee, Bell, & Schwartz, 1967) found that first graders have an overwhelming tendency to respond to pitch-interval comparison tasks by choosing the same pitch rather than the same interval. This tendency to respond to the pitch tasks in terms of a stable frame of reference contrasted with the same children's ability to respond to loudness-comparison tasks in terms of *relative* (not absolute) loudness. And the emergence of tonal scale relationships among the child's cognitive structures has implications for the conduct of research. The fact that Chang and Trehub (1977a) used atonal materials had little impact on their results since babies do not respond to tonal scale structures as such. But Wohlwill's (1971) use of atonal and (to the adult ear) rather strange sounding melodies very probably led to his result that first graders could distinguish targets from different-contour lures at a level barely better tban chance (in a long-term memory task). When first graders are asked to perform a short-term memory task with tonal materials in which they have to distinguish between repetitions of the target and lures containing the same pitches but in permuted order (that is, with different contour), they get about 65% correct compared with a chance level of 50% (Dowling & Goedecke, in preparation). At any rate, Wohlwill's (1971, p. 228) conclusion that "The establishment of pitch as a directional dimension is a relatively late phenomenon" could not possibly be true in the light of Chang and Trehub's result. What is true is that first graders have trouble with their language descriptions of pitch direction, as Zimmerman and Sechrest (1970; Pflederer & Sechrest, 1968) and Hair (1977) have documented. Words like "up" and "down" are very difficult for children of 5 or 6 to learn to apply to pitch in the way we adults do.

C. Training

As with the development of any information processing skill, it is useful to know about the impact of training at various ages. Dowling and Goedecke (in preparation) studied first and third graders who had been in an instrumental music program for 6 to 8 months, as compared with children who were on the waiting list for the program but could not participate. The music program was designed to emphasize auditory information processing skills (as distinct from other skills such as reading music). Each child performed two short-term recognition memory tasks: one in which repetitions of a brief, novel, tonal melody were contrasted with melodies different in both their contours and in the pitches they contained; and another in which repetitions were contrasted with different-contour melodies containing the same pitches but in different order. This second task, which was harder than the first, was designed as a test of the child's ability to conserve the temporal order of a series of auditory events. On the first task, untrained first graders got about 75% correct (chance was 50%). After training, however, performance was around 90% correct. (This task was quite easy for the third graders—with training their performance went from somewhat under to somewhat over 90%.) Thus, first graders seem quite ready to learn more skills involving the discrimination of melodic contour. With the more difficult task in which lures contained the same pitches as targets, training had less effect on the first graders with their performances going from about 65% to about 70%. Unlike the first task this task did not benefit from simple maturation: untrained third graders performed in the same range as the first graders. However, with training, the third graders improved dramatically to around 80% correct. As with other materials it appears that there are periods in the child's life when he or she can benefit more than at other times from training that focuses attention on relevant aspects of auditory materials.

D. School-Age Years

The period between early school years and adulthood has not been studied much. One study that helps fill this gap is Zenatti's (1969), mentioned above. Zenatti studied short-term memory for sequences of three, four, and six notes with subjects ranging in age from 5 years to adulthood. On each trial a standard melody was presented at 1.5 notes/sec, followed by a comparison melody in which one of the notes of the standard had been changed by one or two semitones. The subject had to say which of the notes had been changed—as I said before, a very difficult task. With four-note atonal sequences adults got only 75% correct (versus chance of somewhere between 20 and 40%).[2] In comparison, subjects in Dowling and Fujitani's (1971, Experiment 1) study performed above 90% (with chance at 50%) on five-note, atonal melodies at a rate of 6.0 notes/sec, where they had only to say "same" or "different," but not specify the difference. What makes this task difficult is in part an effect observed by Guilford and Nelson (1937), that when one note of a melody has been altered in pitch, it sounds as though temporally adjacent notes had been changed as well. For this reason Zenatti's results cannot be compared directly with the results of studies in which essentially easier tasks were used. However, she obtained a qualitative result of great interest. For the three-note sequences, 5-year-olds perform at about chance level with both tonal and atonal stimuli. From ages 6 through 10 the results for tonal and atonal se-

[2]The appropriate baseline comparison rate is difficult to arrive at for adults. The *a priori* chance level is .20, and this is empirically validated in the younger children's data. However, for adults I believe the lowest score that we are likely to obtain really lies somewhere between 20 and 40%. This is because the task has two components: the relatively easy task of discriminating one fifth of the trials in which the melodies are the same from four fifths the trials in which they are different; and the more difficult task of saying which of the four notes was changed. Dowling and Fujitani (1971) obtained performance better than 90% on the former task. At the extremes, pure guessing on both tasks gives 20% correct while perfect performance on the former task and pure guessing on the latter would lead to 40% correct. Unfortunately, Zenatti does not provide a further breakdown of her data beyond the percent correct.

quences diverge, with the children doing better on the tonal sequences. Then around ages 12 or 13 processing of the atonal sequences catches up with the tonal. For four- and six-note sequences the same pattern appears, but the tonal and atonal difference remains across all age groups except for the most proficient adults. This result is qualitatively very similar to the "word superiority effect" in reading, in which the youngest readers take just as long to analyze nonword letter strings as they do to analyze real words while experienced readers process real words faster (Juola, Schadler, Chabot, & McCaughey, 1978). Experience with language and orthography leads the reader to recognize more efficiently stimuli that follow the well-learned patterns, processing them on a more holistic level (LaBerge, 1976). Similarly, experience with the tonal scale system leads people to improve on recognition of tonal melodies but not atonal. If the stimuli are simple, in the three-note melodies, atonal performance catches up; but the tonal system still confers an advantage on the longer sequences. The superiority of recognition performance with tonal materials has been observed several times with adults (Francès, 1958; Dowling, 1978). It is clear from Zenatti's study that the effect can be observed early in development and can be used as an index of the internalization of the scale structures of the culture.

In summary, the development of melody-processing skills can be seen as a progression from the use of gross, obvious features to the use of more and more subtle features. Babies can distinguish pitch contours and produce single pitches. Around the age of 5 the child can organize songs around stable tonal centers (keys) but does not yet have a stable tonal scale system that can be used to transpose melodies accuratley to new keys. The scale system develops during the elementary school years and confers on tonal materials an advantage in memory that remains into adulthood.

III. ADULT MEMORY

A. Melodic Features

The same features of melodies determine adult behavior that we have seen gradually emerging in the developmental sequence. These features arrange themselves into the more global types that pertain to whole phrases and melodies and the local types that describe individual notes and note pairs (LaBerge, 1981). The more global features include the melodic contour, the rhythmic pattern, and the tonal scale of a melody. Local features include pitches and durations of individual notes and the intervals between them. The basic questions of melodic information processing concern what features will be perceived, what features will be stored in memory, and what features can be retrieved from memory. The answers to these questions vary with the context in which the features appear and with the task we give the listener.

From the point of view of music theory, the choices of features in a particular melody are not independent of each other. At the global level, in Western music the contour and the mode of the scale (for example, major versus minor) can be chosen independently, though this is not true of numerous other musical cultures. For exam-

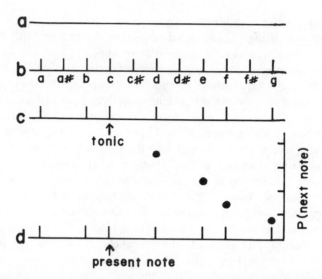

Fig. 3. A schematic outline of levels of pitch analysis relevant to melodic information processing: (a) the psychophysical pitch continuum, (b) tonal material used in a culture's music, (c) a tuning system and modal scale, and (d) the imposition of a melodic contour and probability distribution of interval sizes.

ple, in the music of India choosing a particular *rāg* means choosing a modal scale and at the same time limiting the choice of characteristic melodic patterns (Jairazbhoy, 1971). But even when they are independent of each other, scale and contour taken together limit the choice of individual pitches in much the same way as the global features of a word limit the choice of individual letters. The process by which this happens may be visualized in Fig. 3. All the pitches people can perceive fall on a psychophysical continuum as in Fig. 3A. This continuum is not divided into discrete steps—all the pitches of a fire siren or a baby's cry are represented.[3] The tonal material (Fig. 3B) a culture uses in its music constitutes a subset of all the possible pitches of the psychophysical continuum. In Western music the tonal material consists of the chromatic scale represented by all the notes on the piano. Choosing a tuning system and modal scale (Fig. 3C) involves selecting a subset of the pitches of the tonal material (for example, the white notes on the piano) and establishing a tonal hierarcy (for example, by selecting the scale of C major with C as tonic). When a contour is chosen, it limits further the choice of each succeeding pitch (Fig. 3D). Given the pitch of the present note of the melody, the direction of the particular

---

[3]This analysis draws on a more detailed description of levels of pitch coding elsewhere (Dowling, in press). The present model differs from the one Deutsch (1975) applies to similar phenomena. The main differences are as follows: (1) I include two levels of feature abstraction (namely, raw waveform data and psychophysical pitch) more primitive than her "primary array"; or, more precisely, the primary array collapses into one level what I prefer to divide into three. (2) For Deutsch, intervals are extracted directly from the primary array in a level corresponding to my "tonal material." I believe intervals *can* be so obtained, but that it is difficult. I think intervals are much more easily abstracted from the encoding level of the modal scale.

interval in the contour eliminates half the possible pitches of the next note. And the distribution of interval sizes in Western melodies (as in other cultures) favors small intervals over large, further restricting the choice (Dowling, 1968, 1978). The interdependence of global and local stimulus features could also have been described from the other direction since the choice of notes in a melody determines scale and contour. But this interdependence of features in the stimulus does not necessarily carry over to perception. It is an empirical question whether melodic contour, for example, might be stored and remembered under circumstances in which pitches and intervals are forgotten, or vice versa.

B. Immediate Memory

I will begin my description of the listener's processing of the above sorts of features from the local end and proceed to the more global. When a person hears a sound, his or her auditory system registers an enormous amount of raw data concerning its waveform. Figure 3A represents sounds as already coded into perceived pitches, but a wealth of information is available in the stimulus that may or may not be encoded into perceived pitches, as Kubovy and Howard (1976) have demonstrated. Kubovy and Howard presented listeners with tone complexes of ambiguous pitch. Certain pitches could be disambiguated by presentation of a second-tone complex, and the disambiguating information was hidden in the fine structure of the waveform—namely in the interaural time disparity of the waveform of the target tone versus the other tones in the complex. (Interaural time disparity translates perceptually into spatial position.) Kubovy and Howard found that they could delay something like 1 sec before presenting and disambiguating tone complex, and more than half their listeners could detect the pitch relationship of the two. (One subject could wait almost 10 sec.) This means that information from the first complex remained in some sort of immediate storage without being encoded into a "perceived" pitch (of the kind represented in Fig. 3A) until the second complex arrived, a length of time that might vary considerably depending on task conditions and the listener's prior experience. It would be interesting to see how much of this information can be transformed into the perceptual features of pitch, timbre, and rhythm without mutual interference. The psychomusicological question here is, can the listener attend to the beauty of the soloist's tone and at the same time make accurate judgments about her intonation?

When pitches are coded at the psychophysical level or the level of tonal material outside of a tonal context, listeners find it difficult to integrate them into higher order units. The pitches can be remembered in and of themselves very accurately, but higher order features such as the intervals between them are difficult to extract. When Attneave and Olson (1971) presented isolated intervals to subjects and asked them to transpose them to other pitch ranges, subjects were not very successful. This contrasts with subjects' performance in the same study when asked to transpose a familiar tonal melody, which they did very well. Dowling and Fujitani (1971) found that when subjects were asked to distinguish between exact repetitions of brief atonal melodies and imitations in which the pitches had been changed, they achieved better than 90% correct. But when subjects tried to distinguish between exact transpositions and imitations at a new pitch level having the same contour but different intervals, their performance was little better than chance. The intervals of atonal melodies—melodies in which the set of pitches is restricted to those of Fig. 3B but not to those of Fig. 3C—are hard for subjects to encode accurately. Deutsch (1979) replicated Dowling and Fujitani's result and went on to find that repeating the target melody several times at the same pitch level helps in the recognition of a transposition (as opposed to a same-contour imitation), boosting the proportion correct to 75%. Repetitions transposed to other octaves did not help as much while repetitions that destroyed melodic continuity by assigning successive pitches of the melodies to different octaves ("octave scrambling") actually hurt performance. Taken together, these results suggest that as a rule, only very specific information about pitch is extracted from atonal melodies encoded at the tonal material level. Intervals between notes are hard to encode, though exact repetition helps. The pitches and intervals of atonal melodies seem especially hard to learn. When they are remembered, it is in a relatively specific way and not easily generalized to a new context.

C. Tonality

Intervals are easier to abstract from melodies that can be encoded in terms of a tonal scale. In an experiment similar in design to the preceding, Dowling (1978) asked subjects to distinguish between exact transpositions of novel tonal melodies and atonal, same-contour imitations (that is, between Figs. 1B and 1D). Performance was much better than that obtained by Dowling and Fujitani with atonal melodies. Moderately experienced adults achieved almost 80% correct on the task. Further, Bartlett and Dowling (1980, Experiment 2) found subjects could distinguish transpositions from far-key tonal imitations at the 75% level. This suggests that melodic intervals, difficult to encode with atonal materials, are encoded relatively well with tonal melodies so that they are recognized in transposition. Performance was still better with familiar melodies (of the sort actually shown in Fig. 1). Bartlett and Dowling (1980) found adults' performance to be better than 90% with such materials. (Some of the data are in Table I.) This agrees with the result of Attneave and Olson (1971) who found that subjects found it much easier to transpose a familiar tonal melody (the NBC chimes) than to transpose isolated intervals.

In considering the accuracy of people's memory for interval sizes, we should consider alternative ways of looking at the problem. A formal description of the "Twinkle, Twinkle" standard melody in Fig. 1 could, in terms of intervals, read:

$$\text{unison, up perfect fifth, unison, up major second, unison,} \quad \text{down major second} \tag{1}$$

which could be written in semitones as follows:

$$0, +7, 0, +2, 0, -2 \tag{2}$$

Alternatively, "Twinkle, Twinkle" could be written in terms of degrees of the major scale as

$$Do, Do, Sol, Sol, La, La, Sol \qquad (3)$$

or using numbers for the diatonic scale steps as

$$1, 1, 5, 5, 6, 6, 5 \qquad (4)$$

Expressions (2) and (4) are formally equivalent at the level of music theory. But it remains an empirical question which of them might be closer to what people actually store in their memory when they learn a new melody. In an earlier article (Dowling, 1972) I argued on the basis of the relative difficulty subjects have with performing pitch-time transformations (such as inversion and retrograde) that their memory representations for brief melodies were more like (4) than (2). It may well be that representations of the quasi-solfeggio sort, like (4), are typical of most memory storage of tunes.

One way of summarizing the preceding series of results would be to say that exact interval sizes are remembered to the degree that the diatonic scale values of the notes are remembered. The key distance effect referred to above is best seen from this point of view. That is, in evaluating accuracy of transposition of a comparison melody, the listener typically attempts to base his or her judgment on a match to the contour of the standard and on the compatibility of the pitches he or she hears with those of the scale of the standard. Suppose the comparison were the tonal imitation of Fig. 1C. In intervals it would be represented as

$$0, +7, 0, +1, 0, -1 \qquad (5)$$

In scale steps it would be

$$3, 3, 7, 7, 1, 1, 7 \qquad (6)$$

retaining the scale framework of the standard in (4). With novel, tonal melodies (not "Twinkle, Twinkle"), listeners accept tonal imitations of this type as accurate transpositions provided they are in the same (or nearly the same) key as the standard (Bartlett & Dowling, 1980). Though the listener is able to match the sequence of signs of expressions (2) and (5) (the contour), he or she does not succeed well in matching the quantities (the interval sizes). Further, the listener seems to evaluate the acceptability of (6) on the basis of its sharing of pitches with the 1, 2, 3, 4, 5, 6, 7, 1 scale of (4). When the comparison melody is in a more distant key from the standard, fewer pitches are shared between the two scales and the listener is not misled by this second source of similarity. Presumably the listener is then forced to reinterpret (6) and (5) as beginning on 1 of a new mode. Bartlett and Dowling (1980, Experiment 1) found that listeners could discriminate transpositions from far-key tonal imitations with about 60% accuracy as contrasted with approximately chance performance with near-key imitations. This indicates that subjects had *some* information regarding interval sizes available in their memories but were easily misled by comparison trials that did not force them to change their key and scale frame of reference.

D. Long-Term Memory

Contour information is easily encoded in memory, and subjects perform very well when tested immediately for contour information (Dowling & Fujitani, 1971; Dowling, 1978; Bartlett & Dowling, 1980). Interval information is difficult to encode, and subjects are easily confused about it in immediate tests, as the above results show. However, it seems that interval (or scale step) information, once stored in memory, fades slowly. Dowling and Bartlett (1981, Experiment 4) contrasted immediate tests with delayed tests for the same set of brief, novel, tonal melodies. They found that though both interval information and contour information were more difficult to retrieve with delayed testing, discrimination of true transpositions from tonal imitations did not decline with delay. Moreover, when stimuli were more "natural" brief excerpts of Beethoven quartets and subjects were instructed to respond positively *only* on the basis of contour, they were unable to do so. With delayed testing subjects could hardly discriminate same-contour imitations from different-contour lures (Fig. 1C versus 1E) while they could recognize exact repetitions with about 75% accuracy (Dowling & Bartlett, 1981, Experiments 1 & 2). It may be that the additional musical context of the "natural" stimuli facilitated interval encoding. Nevertheless, contour information is generally the easiest to encode.

A different aspect of the key distance effect appears under different testing conditions. If the listener's task is to detect the alteration in pitch of one of seven notes of a novel tonal melody, performance is better with transposition to a near (versus far) key. Cuddy, Cohen, and Miller (1979) found performance in detecting the altered note to be especially good when the alteration departed from the tonal scale of the comparison stimulus and when the stimuli provided a firm tonal-scale context. This shows that when subjects must shift keys to evaluate a comparison stimulus differing in only one pitch from the standard, they do so more easily to a near than to a far key.

One reason I have for preferring representations like (4) over those like (2) as descriptions of what listeners store in memory is that listeners are able to recognize melodies in cases in which the intervals of (2) but not the scale steps of (4) have been destroyed. One way to destroy the interval sizes is to interleave foreign pitches between the notes of a familiar melody (Dowling, 1973, Experiment 3). Thus, every other note the subject hears is from a target melody he or she is trying to detect, and every other note is irrelevant. When such sequences are presented rapidly (8 to 10 notes/sec), subjects perform almost perfectly in detecting the target melodies. It is as though the listener were able to hold a template like (4) up to the sequence consisting of every other note of the stimulus and evaluate a match. Another situation in which the interval sizes from note to note are destroyed while the list of scale steps is preserved (given octave-equivalence) is when melodies are scrambled so the successive pitches fall in different octaves. Deutsch (1972) demonstrated that such scrambling makes familiar tunes difficult to recognize. Dowling and Hollombe (1977) and Idson and Massaro (1978) showed that where both contour and tone-chroma (scale-step) information are available, recognition performance improves. However, this last result seems to depend critically on the presence of scale-step information. Kallman and Massaro (1979) found that if the chromas of notes in octave-scrambled melodies were altered slightly, recognition performance was very poor even when contour was preserved. It seems as though contour can be used to narrow the set of possibilities in recognition, but that final verification of a match is done with reference to the chroma (scale-step) information of representations like (4).

IV. CONTOUR VERSUS INTERVAL

From the above review it appears that contour information is very important to melody recognition under certain circumstances—especially when tonal context is weak (as with atonal melodies) or confusing (as with tonal imitations). Contour is less important with familiar melodies stored in long-term memory or even novel melodies remembered over periods of minutes. Meaningful musical context seems to aid memory for interval and/or scale-step information and not contour information. Contour is easy to extract from a melody but no easier to remember than intervals. Finally, contour information seems useful as an idexical device to access melodies in long-term storage, but recognition of such melodies seems critically dependent upon scale-step information.

One further aspect of adult behavior remains to be explored—namely, the effects of training on the processing of the various features of melodies. Even persons with little or no musical training perform at near-perfect levels when reproducing (Attneave & Olson, 1971) or recognizing (Bartlett & Dowling, 1981, Experiment 3) the intervals of familiar melodies. It is when dealing with novel materials that differences between trained and untrained people appear. ("Training" here refers to minimal training—usually two or more years of music lessons.) Training facilitates discrimination between tonal and atonal comparison melodies (Dowling, 1978). Untrained subjects do not find contour recognition much more difficult than trained subjects (Dowling, 1978) but do find interval recognition more difficult (Cuddy & Cohen, 1976; Bartlett & Dowling, 1980, Experiment 1). Trained listeners are much more sensitive to the tonal scale structure than untrained listeners when making judgments about how well various pitches fit a tonal context (Krumhansl & Shepard, 1979). It is safe to conclude from this evidence that one effect of training is to enhance the importance of the tonal scale system in information processing of melodies. The intervals of the scale system are firmly embedded in the minds of even untrained listeners. Training facilitates the application of that system to new materials.

V. SUMMARY

The same hierarchy of melodic features—pitch, contour, tonality, and interval size—appears in adult behavior as in the developmental sequence. The psychological reality of these feature types is attested by their differential importance at different developmental stages, and the ways they can be manipulated in context to produce independent effects on the behavior of adults.

ACKNOWLEDGMENTS

I wish to thank James Bartlett, Kirk Blackburn, and Darlene Smith for their help in developing this article.

REFERENCES

Attneave, F., & Olson, R. K. Pitch as a medium: A new approach to psychophysical scaling. *American Journal of Psychology*, 1971, *84*, 147–166.

Bartlett, J. C., & Dowling, W. J. The recognition of transposed melodies: A key-distance effect in developmental perspective. *Journal of Experimental Psychology: Human Perception & Performance*, 1980, *6*, 501–515.

Chang, H-W., & Trehub, S. Auditory processing of relational information by young infants. *Journal of Experimental Child Psychology*, 1977, *24*, 324–331. (a)

Chang, H-W., & Trehub, S. Infants' perception of temporal grouping in auditory patterns. *Child Development*, 1977, *48*, 1666–1670. (b)

Cuddy, L., & Cohen, A. J. Recognition of transposed melodic sequences. *Quarterly Journal of Experimental Psychology*, 1976, *28*, 255–270.

Cuddy, L., Cohen, A. J., & Miller, J. Melody recognition: The experimental application of musical rules. *Canadian Journal of Psychology*, 1979, *33*, 148–157.

Deutsch, D. Octave generalization and tune recognition. *Perception & Psychophysics*, 1972, *11*, 411–412.

Deutsch, D. The organization of short-term memory for a single acoustic attribute. In J. A. Deutsch & D. Deutsch (Eds.), *Short-term memory*. New York: Academic Press, 1975. Pp. 107–151.

Deutsch, D. Octave generalization and the consolidation of melodic information. *Canadian Journal of Psychology*, 1979, *33*, 201–205.

Dowling, W. J. Rhythmic fission and the perceptual organization of tone sequences. Unpublished Ph. D. Thesis, Harvard University, 1968.

Dowling, W. J. Recognition of melodic transformations: Inversion, retrograde, and retrograde inversion. *Perception & Psychophysics*, 1972, *12*, 417–421.

Dowling, W. J. The perception of interleaved melodies. *Cognitive Psychology*, 1973, *5*, 322–337.

Dowling, W. J. Scale and contour: Two components of a theory of memory for melodies. *Psychological Review*, 1978, *85*, 341–354.

Dowling, W. J. Musical scales and psychophysical scales: Their psychological reality. In T. Rice & R. Falck (Eds.), *Cross-cultural perspectives on music*. Toronto: University of Toronto Press, in press.

Dowling, W. J., & Bartlett, J. C. The importance of interval information in long-term memory for melodies. *Psychomusicology*, 1981, *1*, 30–49.

Dowling, W. J., & Fujitani, D. S. Contour, interval, and pitch recognition in memory for melodies. *Journal of the Acoustical Society of America*, 1971, *49*, 524–531.

Dowling, W. J., & Goedecke, M. The impact of a Suzuki-based instrumental music program on auditory information-processing skills of inner-city school children. (in preparation)

Dowling, W. J., & Hollombe, A. W. The perception of melodies distorted by splitting into several octaves: Effects of increasing proximity and melodic contour. *Perception & Psychophysics*, 1977, *21*, 60–64.

Francès, R. *La perception de la musique*. Paris: Vrin, 1958.

Gardner, H., Davidson, L., & McKernon, P. The acquisition of song: A developmental approach. In *Documentary Report of the Ann Arbor Symposium*, Reston, Virginia: Music Educators National Conference, 1981.

Guilford, J. P., & Nelson, H. M. The pitch of tones in melodies as compared with single tones. *Journal of Experimental Psychology*, 1937, *20*, 309–335.

Hair, H. I. Discrimination of tonal direction on verbal and nonverbal tasks by first-grade children. *Journal of Research in Music Education*, 1977, *25*, 197–210.

Idson, W. L., & Massaro, D. W. A bidimensional model of pitch in the recognition of melodies. *Perception & Psychophysics*, 1978, *24*, 551–565.

Imberty, M. *L'acquisition des structures tonales chez l'enfant.* Paris: Klincksieck, 1969.

Jairazbhoy, N. A. *The rāgs of North Indian music.* Middletown, Connecticut: Wesleyan University Press, 1971.

Juola, J. F., Schadler, M., Chabot, R. J., & McCaughey, M. W. The development of visual information processing skills related to reading. *Journal of Experimental Child Psychology,* 1978, *25,* 459–476.

Kallman, H. J., & Massaro, D. W. Tone chroma is functional in melody recognition. *Perception & Psychophysics,* 1979, *26,* 32–36.

Kessen, W., Levine, J., & Wendrich, K. A. The imitation of pitch in infants. *Infant Behavior & Development,* 1979, *2,* 93–99.

Kinney, D. K., & Kagan, J. Infant attention to auditory discrepancy. *Child Development,* 1976, *47,* 155–164.

Krumhansl, C. L., & Shepard, R. N. Quantification of the hierarchy of tonal functions within a diatonic context. *Journal of Experimental Psychology: Human Perception & Performance,* 1979, *5,* 579–594.

Kubovy, M., & Howard, F. P. Persistence of a pitch-segregating echoic memory. *Journal of Experimental Psychology: Human Perception & Performance,* 1976, *2,* 531–537.

LaBerge, D. Perceptual learning and attention. In W. K. Estes (Ed.), *Handbook of learning and cognitive processes* (Vol. 4). Hillsdale, New Jersey: Erlbaum, 1976. Pp. 237–273.

LaBerge, D. Perceptual and motor schemas in the performance of music. In *Documentary Report of the Ann Arbor Symposium,* Reston, Virginia: Music Educators National Conference, 1981.

Melson, W. H., & McCall, R. B. Attentional responses of five-month girls to discrepant auditory stimuli. *Child Development,* 1970, *41,* 1159–1171.

Ostwald, P. F. Musical behavior in early childhood. *Developmental Medicine & Child Neurology,* 1973, *15,* 367–375.

Pflederer, M., & Sechrest, L. Conservation-type responses of children to musical stimuli. *Bulletin of the Council for Research in Music Education,* 1968, No. 13, 19–36.

Pick, A. D. Listening to melodies: Perceiving events. In A. D. Pick (Ed.), *Perception and its development: A tribute to Eleanor J. Gibson.* Hillsdale, New Jersey: Erlbaum, 1979. Pp. 145–165.

Révész, G. *Introduction to the psychology of music.* Norman, Oklahoma: University of Oklahoma Press, 1954.

Riley, D. A., & McKee, J. P. Pitch and loudness transposition in children and adults. *Child Development,* 1963, *34,* 471–482.

Riley, D. A., McKee, J. P., Bell, D. D., & Schwartz, C. R. Auditory discrimination in children: The effect of relative and absolute instructions on retention and transfer. *Journal of Experimental Psychology,* 1967, *73,* 581–588.

Riley, D. A., McKee, J. P., & Hadley, R. W. Prediction of auditory discrimination learning and transposition from children's auditory ordering ability. *Journal of Experimental Psychology,* 1964, *67,* 324–329.

Shuter, R. *The psychology of musical ability.* London: Methuen, 1968.

Wohlwill, J. F. Effect of correlated visual and tactual feedback on auditory pattern learning at different age levels. *Journal of Experimental Child Psychology,* 1971, *11,* 213–228.

Zenatti, A. Le développement génétique de la perception musicale. *Monographies Françaises de Psychologie,* 1969, whole no. 17.

Zimmerman, M. P., & Sechrest, L. Brief focused instruction and musical concepts. *Journal of Research in Music Education,* 1970, *18,* 25–36.

14

Absolute Pitch

W. Dixon Ward and Edward M. Burns

I.	Introduction	431
	The Pitch Helix	432
II.	Genesis of AP	434
III.	Measurement of AP	436
	A. Extraneous Cues	436
	B. Absolute Piano	436
	C. Relative Pitch	437
	D. Accuracy of AP	438
	E. Information Transfer in an Expert Possessor	440
IV.	Stability of the Internal Standard	444
V.	Learning AP	445
VI.	The Value of AP	447
	References	449

I. INTRODUCTION

The ultimate in musical endowment is commonly regarded by musicians to be the possession of "absolute pitch" (AP), also called "perfect pitch" or "positive pitch": the ability to identify the frequency or musical name of a specific tone, or, conversely, the ability to produce some designated frequency, frequency level, or pitch without comparing the tone to any objective reference tone (i.e., without using relative pitch).

Suppose we present to an individual the following sequence of frequencies: 260, 260, 290, 330, 260, 330, 290 Hz and ask "What was that?" Individuals who are "tone-deaf" [or better, "melody-deaf" (Trotter, 1967)] are apt to answer with something no more specific than "a bunch of tones." The median American nonmusician will probably answer "Yankee Doodle" (identification of tune), although many may remember enough from grade school to add that it was "do, do, re, mi, do, mi, re" (identification of solfeggio). The typical performing musician can do all of that and may add that "the sequence of successive intervals was unison, ascending major second, another ascending major second, descending major third, ascending major third, and descending major second" (identification of intervals). But only the person with AP is able to answer "Middle C, C, D, E, C, E, D" (identification of the musical designation of individual components).

The Pitch Helix

Musically educated persons with good relative pitch behave as though they have developed an internal scale of pitch, a movable conceptual template that is permanently calibrated in terms of the pitch relations among the notes in our musical scale (i.e., in subjective octaves, each of which is further subdivided into 12 equal parts called subjective semitones or semits). Because corresponding semit markers within the octaves are given the same name, this template can be represented in the form of a pitch helix: a spiral that ascends the shell of an invisible vertical cylinder (Fig. 1). This schema allows several aspects of pitch to be simultaneously represented: the projection of a point on this pitch spiral on the vertical axis determines its "tone-height" in mels, the angle involved in its projection on the horizontal plane indicates its "chroma" (the scale note—A, A♯, B, etc.—or its solfeggio), and its octave designation depends on which coil of the helix it lies on, the coils being numbered in succession from low to high frequency. If the individual with good relative pitch is presented a reference tone X and told what its chroma and octave number are, the pitch engendered serves to tie one point on this pitch helix to all other pitches. The pitch helix is mentally rotated until the corresponding subjective semit marker coincides with this "anchor" pitch, and the musician can now auralize all other pitches on the scale. The musician is now prepared to make judgments of the musical interval (a concept that corresponds to distance along the spiral) that separates the anchor from some other frequency. Such judgments have been shown in Chapter 8 to be categorical in nature, involving a labeling process that is analogous to that used in the discrimination of speech sounds. So, when next given tone Y, this listener will categorize the interval between X and Y, and by using knowledge of the number of semits in that interval, the listener can indicate the musical pitch (chroma plus octave number) that tone Y must have.

However, in the foregoing case the helix is, so to speak, free-floating. That is, there are no *permanent* labels attached that serve to tie this subjective template to the objective world; there are only temporary ones. Thus if we were to present the person with relative pitch a tone of 440 Hz followed by one of 525 Hz, there might be a rapid recognition of the interval as a minor third, but only if our musician was told that the first one was A4 would he or she call the second C5. Indeed, we could say that the *first* one was C5, and the individual would then indicate that the second was D♯5 or E♭5.

Such deception would not succeed if the person has AP, however. Here the helix apparently has permanent labels attached; given the sequence 440 Hz, 525 Hz, the

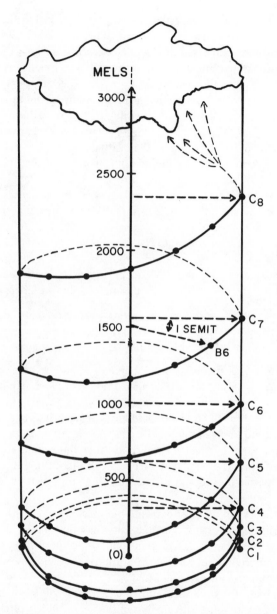

Fig. 1. The pitch spiral. The chroma of any point on the surface of the cylinder is determined by its projection on the XZ plane and its tone-height by its projection on the Y axis. Thus, for example, all Cs are shown to lie at 0° azimuth; since C6 is shown as having a tone-height of 1000 mels (which is, by definition, the pitch of a 1000-Hz sinusoid), this orientation of the pitch spiral assumes a physical A4 of about 420 Hz rather than 440 Hz. Chroma tends to become impalpable for tone-heights above 2500 mels or so (sinusoids above 5000 Hz), so the upper boundaries of both the spiral and the axis are left vague and irregular.

musician would immediately recognize A4 and C5, and if told that the first was C5, would merely snap, "Nonsense."

This ability has been subjected to scientific scrutiny for about a century (Stumpf, 1883), and we now know quite a bit about the characteristics of AP. Still an enigma, however, is the genesis of the ability: why do some people identify pitches with no apparent effort while others must engage in strenuous training to develop AP? Indeed, there was doubt that it was even possible to "learn" AP until Paul Brady did so in 1970. For this reason, its possession was for many years regarded with pride, as if it indicated that its owner were mysteriously gifted.

Yet a bit of reflection should convince one that, viewed in comparison to other sensory modalities, AP is not so strange after all. We learn labels for colors, smells, and tastes—indeed, for speech sounds, voices, and instrumental timbres. Why not also pitches? Stimuli that fall along any metathetic continuum should be labelable, one would think, and not require the comparison between stimuli either present or in short-term memory that is involved in relative-pitch judgments. One does not need to look at a rainbow in order to see that a rooster's comb is red nor take a whiff of camphor to identify a nearby skunk. Viewed in this light, the real question is why everyone does not have AP: Why cannot some people put labels on pitches?

II. GENESIS OF AP

There are four major theories of AP: heredity, on the one hand, and learning, unlearning, and imprinting on the other. The *heredity* viewpoint, espoused most vigorously by possessors such as Revesz (1913) and Bachem (1937), contends that AP is a special innate ability that one either inherits or not, that those who do inherit the trait will demonstrate pitch-naming ability as soon as an appropriate situation arises, regardless of their early musical training, and that those who are not so genetically blessed can never attain the degree of excellence in identifying pitch displayed by the chosen few, no matter how much instruction they are given or how diligently they practice naming tones.

The *learning* theory, in its most extreme Skinnerian form, is the exact antithesis of the heredity position, asserting that heredity has nothing to do with the matter. Instead, the development of AP depends on some more or less fortuitous set of circumstances whereby the individual is reinforced for trying to put labels on pitches. Oakes (1951) postulates, for example, that "an examination of the total history of the interactions involving the organism and tonal stimuli will show a complex series of events, some gross and some extremely subtle, from which pitch-naming reactions evolved or did not evolve—depending on factors in the history itself." Just to make sure that his position cannot be disproved, he adds: "In explaining whether or not pitch-naming reactions did develop, it is necessary that we take into account every contact of the organism and tonal stimuli, and we also must consider setting and situational factors in each of the interactions." The implication, in short, is that anyone can develop AP under the "right"—but, alas, unknown—circumstances.

A variant of the learning theory is the *unlearning* viewpoint expressed by Abraham (1901) in the first extensive monograph on AP, who pointed out that most musical experience is not conducive to the development of AP. For example, a given tune may be heard in many different keys. How can a child develop absolute recognition of a particular frequency, say 261 Hz, if it is called "do" today and "sol" tomorrow or if it is heard when he presses "the white key just left of the two black keys in the middle of the piano" at home but a completely different key (perhaps even a black one) at grandfather's house? Considering all the factors that conspire to enhance the development of relative pitch at the expense of AP, Abraham suggested that perhaps an inborn potential for developing AP was relatively widespread, but that it is simply trained out of most of us. Watt (1917) pursued Abraham's line of reasoning to its ultimate and proposed that perhaps AP is initially universal: "In some favoured persons it is acquired early and more or less unwittingly and never lost. Perhaps these persons have some special refinement of hearing. . . . Or perhaps a highly favoured auditory disposition gives them the power to maintain their absoluteness of ear in spite of the universality of musical relativity. In that case we should all naturally possess absolute ear and then proceed to lose it or to lose the power to convert it into absolute nomenclature."

Abraham had also commented that pitch-naming ability was relatively easy to develop in children. Copp (1916) pursued this idea and on the basis of her own experience suggested that something like the modern concept of "imprinting" may be involved. Claiming that 80% of all children can be taught to produce middle C when asked and to recognize it when played or sung by others, she insisted that this is so only if they begin musical training at an early age. The notion here that AP can be developed only in children, possibly as the result of some crucial incident, may be related to the comparative ease with which children develop accent-free speech in foreign tongues.

The nature–nurture debate in this particular arena essentially ended with the death in 1957 of Bachem, who had been the most eloquent exponent of inheritance despite the lack of any convincing supportive scientific evidence. On the other hand, advocates of learning have made only slight headway either. Although Meyer (1899) indicated that he and a colleague brought themselves up to "60 and 64% terminal proficiency" after a heroic regimen of training, this improvement soon disappeared when practice was discontinued. Other later attempts to train AP [Gough (1922); Mull (1925); Wedell (1934)—and no doubt several that remained unreported] were equally unsuccessful. Wellek (1938), in a study of 27 of the best possessors in Vienna, Prague, Dresden, Leipzig, and Hamburg, noted a correlation of .80 between the age at which AP behavior appeared and number of errors on an identification test, and Sergeant (1969) has recently reported a similar result. So there is little doubt that *early* learning is important, though not all-important: Brady (1970), after months of practice, was able as an adult to achieve a degree of pitch-naming ability that was indistinguishable, in terms of error score or reaction time, from four possessors who had had the ability from childhood (Carroll, 1975). The evidence, then, favors the learning theory, although learning is clearly easier in childhood. And, of course, a genetic component can never be ruled out completely unless some technique for teaching AP is developed that will succeed with everyone, or at least all children.

III. MEASUREMENT OF AP

A. Extraneous Cues

If we accept AP as the ability to attach labels to isolated auditory stimuli on the basis of pitch alone, tests for AP should not involve extraneous cues such as loudness, timbre, duration, or any other attribute. As an extreme example, nobody would take seriously as an AP test one in which stimulus #1 was a taped record of someone singing "Number One" on C3, stimulus #2 was someone else singing "Number Two" on C♯3, and so on.

There are two ways to ensure the nonuse (or at least ineffective use) of these other attributes. One is to try to hold constant all attributes except pitch. In this case, the set of tones to be judged would have to be balanced in advance by each listener to give a constant loudness, timbre, and duration. This is a tedious process, however, and even after it was finished, the tones would still differ in density and volume.

The second alternative is therefore better, to wit: vary the extraneous attributes randomly over a small range, presenting a given frequency now with one intensity and duration, next time with different ones. Under these conditions, although many parameters are varying, the only one that will provide the correct cue is pitch. Theoretically, of course, one should determine equal-pitch contours over the range of intensities to be used so that all stimuli that are supposed to be labeled A4, for example, could be adjusted in frequency as intensity is changed so that they would actually have the same pitch for that listener. However, the change of pitch with intensity over a moderate range is ordinarily negligible (Ward, 1954; Cohen, 1961), so this factor can generally be ignored. Timbre and tonal envelope could also be varied randomly, but it is practicable to hold these particular parameters constant; indeed, if anything but pure tones (sinusoids) are used, one will be in the position of presenting the listener with *several* pitches and then asking him what *one* pitch he hears (a question that has been asked all too often, despite its patent absurdity, in the field of musical perception).

B. Absolute Piano

From the very beginning of the study of AP, it was abundantly clear to the more astute experimenters that piano tones are extraordinarily poor stimuli from the point of view of extra cues (von Kries, 1892). Abraham (1899) discusses the effect of timbre differences, nonmusical elements such as strike noises, and inharmonic partials at some length, concluding that of all instruments, tones from the piano are probably the easiest to identify because of the myriad extraneous cues that exist. On the other hand, if the piano is struck with great force, the relative intensity of the partials may change considerably so that note identification becomes more difficult, particularly in the lowest octave or two. Thus not all of the characteristics of the piano make identification easier. The net effect is, however, that we are never quite certain just what role pitch alone plays in the identification of piano tones.

Nevertheless, a major portion of the literature on AP is based on studies using piano tones, simply because pianos are abundant. Furthermore, despite the shortcomings of the instrument, some aspects of the results are applicable to the more general picture. So, in order to avoid throwing the baby out with the bath, studies using the piano need not be completely ignored, although it must be kept in mind that "absolute piano" may not be quite the same as "absolute pitch."

C. Relative Pitch

Much more difficult than extraneous cues to eliminate from the AP testing situation is the relative-pitch ability of a good musician. If the tones to be identified are all members of an ordinary musical scale (i.e., are separated by whole numbers of semits), it is not much of a challenge for such a listener, knowing what any one of a series is, to compare the next with it and make the second judgment agree with the estimated interval between them. Obviously, such relative-pitch judgments are likely to increase if feedback is provided on each item (e.g., Terman, 1965; Fullard, Snelbecker, & Wolk, 1972; Fulgosi & Zaja, 1975).

Various procedures have been used in attempts to destroy the short-term memory trace of preceding items on which such judgments are based. Stumpf (1883) used conversation interjected between successive stimuli, Abraham (1899) "unusual modulations" on the piano, Mull (1925) a "short period of auditory distraction," Petran (1932) reading aloud, Hartman (1954) a burst of white noise, and Hurni-Schlegel and Lang (1978) an unrelated interval-comparison task. Strangely enough, no one has yet conducted a systematic study of some of these "pitch erasers" in which subjects are *encouraged* to "cheat" and use relative pitch so that the relative efficiency of the distractors could be assessed, although a few studies have addressed the question of the effect of intervening tonal sequences on short-term memory per se—i.e., the ability to tell whether a preceding tone and a subsequent tone were the same or different (Deutsch, 1973; Siegel, 1974). Indeed, some experimenters merely rely on a blank interval of a minute or as little as 10 sec to destroy memory of a tone (Lundin & Allen, 1962; Heller & Auerbach, 1972; Carroll, 1975), apparently on the basis of a study of two possessors and two nonpossessors by Bachem (1954) in which he reported that comparison judgments deteriorated in the nonpossessor groups after as short an interval as 15 sec. However, no details of procedure or results were given by Bachem, and a recent study by Rakowski (1972) indicates that even nonpossessors can hold pitches in short-term memory over periods as long as 5 minutes.

Fortunately, there is some evidence that relative pitch is seldom used in AP experiments. Petran (1932), after a thorough review of the literature on AP at that time, did an experiment in which each of 16 subjects was asked to identify a single piano tone as soon as he or she awoke on each of 50 days; then at the end of that time, the same 50 tones were tested at a single session. There were no significant differences between the two tests in either the number or degree of errors, which certainly suggests that in the latter case no judgments were made on the basis of relative pitch. Perhaps those who think they "have" AP feel no need for additional cues, and those who do not are seldom confident enough of any particular judgment (in the absence of feedback) to make estimating the interval between that stimulus and the next one worthwhile.

Given that there is no proven "pitch eraser," the best way of testing whether or not relative pitch was used in any given experiment is to examine the pattern of each subject's responses. If an error of say +2 categories is followed by an error of the same magnitude on the next two or three stimuli, it is likely that relative pitch was being utilized (again, a no-feedback condition is assumed). Appropriate statistical tests will allow one to determine the probability that the particular pattern of errors observed is a chance one. However, even this is not completely infallible. As Petran (1932) points out, subjects with poor relative pitch may be trying to use it but failing so that "even though there may be no trace of correct interval judgments in the results of a series test for absolute pitch, yet incorrect interval judgments may be there in numbers." This dilemma seems to have no solution.

Relative pitch may also enter into AP studies in other ways. If listeners are permitted to hum and whistle at will, many of them can come quite close to the correct pitch from knowledge of the highest or lowest note in their range (although the stability of either of these is not outstanding). Others, even without making any sound, perform as if they have AP for a single tone. That is, some violinists are apparently able to auralize A4 at will and can, given time, compare any pitch to this single internal standard. Bachem (1937) calls this type of AP "quasi-absolute pitch."

A special type of quasi-AP exists in those individuals who are afflicted with a permanent tinnitus of fixed pitch. Stumpf (1901) was one such person: he had, in essence, a built-in tuning fork whose pitch level was very nearly that of a 1500-Hz tone, so it was not necessary for him to auralize some internal standard—it was always there for the listening. There would seem to be no way to discriminate individuals with "true" AP from those with quasi-AP on the basis of error scores, although one might search for differences in the time required to make judgments, which would be expected to be greater for those with quasi-AP because they must make a relative pitch estimate (except, of course, when the stimulus is the same as their internal standard). No one has recently studied persons with quasi-AP in depth.

D. Accuracy of AP

From this discussion of some of the pitfalls of procedure and caveats of interpretation, it appears that for the least equivocal results, one should use for the study of AP only pure-tone stimuli whose intensity and duration are varied randomly over a narrow range. Let us turn, then, to specific procedures that have been used to measure AP. As the original definition implies, AP is manifested either by accurate production of a designated note or by correct categorization of a presented tone. The problem of course is deciding on how to define "accurate" and "correct" in the two cases, respectively. "Accuracy" in production is perhaps the easier to define, as only one psychophysical method is applicable—the method of adjustment. Even then, though, one can argue over the relative merits of "absolute accuracy" and "relative accuracy." Absolute accuracy would be measured by calculating the difference between frequencies based on A4 = 440 Hz and those produced by the subject. The subject's usefulness as an animate tuning fork in setting the pitch for a chorus would depend on absolute accuracy. However, such a procedure is in a sense "unfair" to an individual who grew up with a piano tuned a semit or so flat or who has suffered "paracusis": a change in the pitch aroused by a specific frequency (Ward, 1954), presumably due to a more or less localized disturbance on the basilar membrane. So if our interest is not so much in the practical aspects of AP as in the theoretical basis of absolute identification, the important statistic would be relative variability, as manifested in the distribution of repeated adjustments. From this point of view constant errors should be ignored; the "best" absolute pitcher is the individual with the lowest variance.

There is, however, yet another problem: what to do about "octave errors." Suppose that the subject, told to adjust an oscillator to A4, gives successive values of 444, 432, 449, 438 and 882 Hz. To say unthinkingly that the mean of these judgments is 529 Hz or that the SD is 177 Hz would clearly be misleading since the last judgment, in terms of the pitch helix, was within a few Hz of the correct chroma but was one octave off in tone-height. Although we may be in the position of trying to average apples with oranges, the most accepted solution to the problem here has been to consider only chroma. In the example given, the 882 Hz would be dropped an octave to 441 Hz, making the mean now also 441 Hz with a standard deviation of 5.7 Hz. (A more rigorous procedure would be to determine the frequency that actually appeared to be one octave lower than 882 Hz and use this value in calculating the mean, but ordinarily the difference between the subjective octave and the physical octave will be small enough—Ward, 1954—that its determination would not be worth the considerable effort involved.)

Identification techniques, although greater in variety, have the same problems as pitch production, plus a few more. Not only must one deal with octave errors and constant errors, but now the categorization process also confuses the issue. It becomes difficult to test the ability of subjects to identify quartertones because half of the stimuli will have no "name" in our diatonic scale. This problem is attacked by asking the subject to learn a new set of labels—that is, arbitrary numbers assigned to specific frequencies. One can then apply information-transfer analysis to an experiment in which a subject attempts to identify a series of stimuli consisting of some number of items from this fixed set. In theory, such a procedure, when used not only for testing but also for training, might also be a method of discovering persons with "latent

AP"—that is, individuals who can make absolute judgments but have never learned the names of the notes of the scale. However, to our knowledge there is in the literature no instance of such a person being "discovered" in this fashion.

E. Information Transfer in an Expert Possessor

In 1952 Pollack published the first study of the information transmitted by pitch in average (unselected) listeners, finding that the maximum information that could be transmitted by pitch was only about 2.7 bits (i.e., $2^{2.7} = 7$ different pitches spread over the entire frequency range could just be named correctly by his best listener). However, it was clear that these subjects used only tone-height in their judgments: none had AP. For this reason an intensive study of one particular listener JL was undertaken (Ward, 1953). Although these data are nearly 30 years old, as far as we know no one has demonstrated greater facility at pitch-naming than JL, so the experiments will be reported here in detail.

In each of the experiments of this study, each of a set of 10 (or, for some tests, 20) frequencies was presented to the left ear of JL one at a time together with its number in that series, and JL was instructed to write on a card with the appropriate numbers anything that would help her identify number 1, number 2, and so on. After the entire list had been presented twice, a set of 100 items, 10 of each category, was judged. The intensity was varied randomly over a 20-dB range around 50 phons. JL responded vocally to each test item with a number; no feedback was given. The order of stimuli was semirandom: each subset of 20 stimuli contained two of each of the categories, the only rule of succession being that there could not be three of the same category in a row, even at the subset boundary. A confusion matrix was constructed for each test, and by means of standard formulas the information transmitted was determined. From this, the number of categories over this range that could have been correctly distinguished on a consistent basis was calculated. No attempt was made to erase the short-term memory effect via interfering tones, conversation, or noise; as will be seen, however, this was not a serious mistake because her pattern of errors indicated little if any serial dependence in her responses. JL was seated in an anechoic chamber while the experimenter was outside; communication took place via intercom.

The sequence of tests with the experimental outcome is shown in Fig. 2. The first test employed 10 stimuli from C4 (262 Hz) to A7 (3520 Hz). Successive stimuli were separated by a musical fourth (i.e., C4, F4, B♭4, etc.) so that there was no duplication of chroma (a move designed to minimize octave errors) yet with large degrees of difference in tone height. JL made no errors on this test, although the ordinary musician without absolute pitch will indicate transfer of only about 2.4 bits of information, implying that five categories could have been distinguished nearly perfectly (we routinely use this test to screen for possessors of AP in groups of listeners).

In Test 2, again the stimuli had different names, but this time they were separated only by one semit (A5 to F♯6, or 880 Hz to 1480 Hz). Again JL made no errors.

Next, a situation that would maximize the possibility of octave confusions was

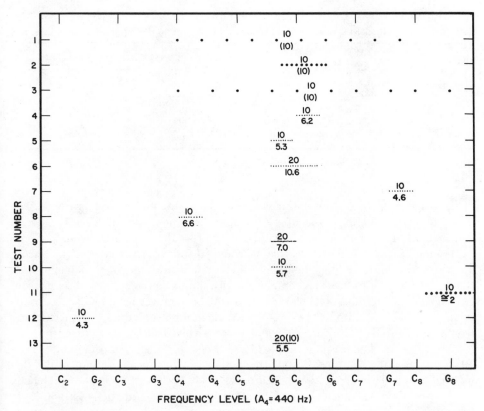

Fig. 2. Graphic representation of pitch identification tests on subject JL. For each test the upper number indicates the number of different stimuli involved, the dots show their frequency level, and the lower number represents the information transmitted in the form of the number of stimuli in the range concerned that could have been identified without error.

developed. In Test 3, five Cs and five Gs were used: from C4 (262 Hz) to G8 (6270 Hz). In this test JL made three mistakes: number 7 (C7) was called number 5 (C6) twice and 5 was called 7 once. However, this is still very close to perfect transmission of information; besides, the errors all occurred in the first half of the test battery, which suggests that a slight amount of learning was necessary. This result reinforces the hypothesis that octave errors are largely an artifact of using piano tones or other complex stimuli that of course *do not have* a single pitch.

Because earlier experiments on persons with AP had indicated that the best performers could distinguish quartertones with 95% accuracy (Abraham, 1901; Petran, 1932; van Krevelen, 1951; for a detailed summary of this early literature see Ward, 1963a,b), Test 4 involved 10 stimuli spaced by 50 cents from C6 to E6+50 (1046 to 1357 Hz). With this set of tones JL finally made some errors, dropping to 80% correct. The pattern of these errors is shown in Table I, which is a horizontal version

TABLE I

Responses Made to Each Stimulus in Test 4 (C6 to E6+50 cents)

Stimulus minus response	Stimulus Number									
	1	2	3	4	5	6	7	8	9	10
+1		6	1	1		2				
0	10	4	7	9	8	7	8	9	9	9
−1			2		2	1	2	1	1	1

of the diagonal of the confusion matrix. In this case the information transmitted I_T was 2.64 bits, implying a potential error-free discriminability of 6.2 categories, a value slightly greater than the 5.5 semits spanned by the range employed.

One might conclude from this that JL could just identify perfectly tones 1 semit apart over the entire auditory range. However, it was next necessary to demonstrate that if one range of frequencies contained X discriminable categories and an adjacent range contained Y, the results of a test involving both ranges would indicate a transmission of information of $X + Y$ categories. Therefore, in Test 5, 10 quartertones from G5 − 25 to B5 + 25 were used, and Test 6 involved all 20 quartertones from G5 − 25 to E6 + 25. The reason for using G5 − 25, G5 + 25, etc., instead of G5, G5 + 50, etc., was that a test for AP using the method of adjustment had shown that JL's internal template was about 25 cents flat re A4 = 440 Hz (Ward, 1954); her pitch helix was apparently tuned much closer to the old "physical" standard pitch based on C4 = 256 Hz.

Test 5 gave an I_T of 2.39 bits (5.2 categories), and Test 6 indicated 3.41 bits (10.6 categories). Based on Tests 4 and 5, the expected value of distinguishable categories in Test 6 was 6.2 + 5.3, or 11.5, so one category was lost, as it were, in the process of doubling the number of alternatives. Perhaps this effect is due to elimination of a boundary.

The implication that error-free performance was limited to conventional semit categories was checked by two more 10-quartertone tests: Test 7 showed 2.20 bits transmitted (4.6 categories) in the range of G7 − 25 to B7 + 25, and Test 8 gave 2.71 bits (6.6 categories) from C♯4 ≠ 25 to F♯4 − 25. In the latter test, stimuli 8, 9, and 10 (F4 − 25, F4 + 25, and F♯4 − 25) were correctly identified all 10 times.

In order to make sure that the last fragment of information was being extracted from JL, Test 9 used categories separated by only 25 cents. The range was the same as for Test 5 (G5 − 25 to B5 + 25) but there were 20 stimuli at 25-cent intervals. Results showed a slight improvement over Test 5, as I_T rose to 2.8 bits (7.0 categories). That this improvement was more than a learning effect was shown by Test 10, which was simply a repetition of Test 5 and which gave nearly the same result: 2.5 bits, 5.7 categories.

In order to determine the limits of JL's identification range, Test 11 was designed to investigate the area from D8 to B8 in 100-cent (semit) steps. However, the test was terminated after 30 trials because JL became upset at being unable to perform accurately; her last nine responses were all either 8, 9, or 10, even though the stimuli were actually 3, 7, 6, 2, 5, 8, 2, 5, 3. JL thus displayed the "chroma fixation" reported by Bachem (1948): an inability to name notes much above 4000 Hz. This was somewhat surprising because JL, who was also serving as a subject in a study of relative pitch (Ward, 1954), had learned to make octave judgments in this range; that is, given a reference tone of A7, she would consistently set a variable tone to about A8 + 50. However, her experience with these high-frequency tones was apparently too limited to affect her ability to identify them on an absolute basis.

Performance is somewhat degraded at extremely low frequencies also. Test 12 (D2 + 25 to G2 − 25, 75 to 91 Hz, in 50-cent steps) gave I_T = 2.1 bits, 4.3 categories. On the final test JL was told that it was to be a repetition of Test 9 (20 stimuli at 25-cent intervals); however, only stimuli 1, 3, 5, . . . , 19 were actually presented. The results were essentially the same as for Tests 5 and 10: I_T was 2.45 bits, implying 5.5 discriminable categories. JL was unaware that half of the possible categories had never been presented.

In all these tests, when errors were made, they usually occurred at random. That is, there was never the long run of errors in the same direction that would be expected if JL were attempting to use relative pitch (i.e., if she were comparing stimulus N with the memory of stimulus N − 1). So in her case the use of a short-term-memory eraser was unnecessary. It may also be mentioned that errors occurred as often on the weaker stimuli as on the stronger (recall that the range of intensities was 20 dB).

One can infer from these data that JL should be able to identify without error some 70 to 75 pitches in the auditory range, which is about the number of semits from 60 to 4000 Hz, and that quartertones can be discriminated well above chance. Indeed, if one uses the criterion for AP proposed by Bachem—that is, ignoring errors in which the correct category was only missed by one semit—JL would be considered able to name quartertones accurately (e.g., Table I). However, that seems to be about the limit, as 25-cent intervals transfer only slightly more information than 50-cent intervals.

A test of "absolute loudness" on JL (1000-Hz tone, 10 intensities from 10 to 100 dB SPL in 9-dB steps) showed I_T to be 2.69 bits (6.5 categories), so one could contend that there are, for JL, about 500 pure tones that can be completely distinguished. Unfortunately, this extrapolation was not tested directly (or perhaps fortunately, from the point of view of the sanity of JL). Even now, apparently only one experiment has attempted to have subjects judge pitch and loudness categories simultaneously (Fulgosi et al., 1975), and since none of the subjects in that study had AP, the total information transmitted by both loudness and pitch was only 3.85 bits rather than 9, implying something on the order of only 14 separable pure tones—and this in a situation in which the subjects were given feedback, scored their own results, and revealed their scores to their classmates. Truly, possessors of AP are different.

IV. STABILITY OF THE INTERNAL STANDARD

All pitch-frequency relations, both in possessors and in nonpossessors of AP, are apparently established early in life and cannot be changed. If something happens to disturb the normal hydromechanical or neurophysiological processes at one particular area of an ear so that a given frequency no longer affects exactly the same receptors and associated neural elements, the pitch in this region is shifted and the listener has "musical paracusis." (And, if the two ears are not affected equally, "binaural dip-lacusis" will exist.) However, no learning takes place; that is, musical paracusis does not gradually disappear as one "relearns" that a 3500-Hz tone arouses a percept formerly associated with a 3700-Hz tone.

Only a possessor of AP, however, will become aware of a change in the *entire* tuning of the auditory system. If, for some reason, *all* pitches were shifted by the same percentage, the individual with only relative pitch ability would hear nothing amiss. The possessor of AP, though, would complain that everything is in the "wrong" key—that all music sounds as though it has been transposed.

Interestingly enough, several possessors do indeed make this specific complaint. After age 50 or so, music was heard one or even two semits sharp from what it "ought" to be. Triepel (1934) reported that this occurred in himself, his father, and his brother. Vernon (1977) noticed about age 52 that keys were shifted about a semit. This was particularly distressing because, as a result, he heard the overture to *Die Meistersinger* in C♯ instead of C and for him C is "strong and masculine" while C♯ is "lascivious and effeminate." Now, at age 71, he hears everything *two* semits high (which at least brings Wagner away from the sauna parlor, although Vernon fails to indicate the nature of "D-ness" for him). Beck (1978) experienced a 1-semit sharping at 40 years of age that progressed to 2 semits at age 58; although he finds it somewhat disconcerting to watch a trumpet player performing in B♭ but to hear it in C, he indicates that if he can watch the score, "the eyes and ears lock in synchrony" and everything sounds all right.

It is possible that some possessors have experienced this shift without being consciously aware of it. For example, Corliss (1973) reports that she was surprised to find that when she plays Chopin's Prelude in A Major (op. 28, no. 7) from memory (pitch memory, not motor memory), she performs it in G♯. Although she attributes this to the fact that she originally learned the piece as a child on an old piano that was more than a quartertone flat, it may be that she, too, has a hearing mechanism that has aged by 1 semit. Apparently, at any rate, one aspect of presbyacusis (the change in hearing with age) may be a gradual shift of the excitation on the basilar membrane in the direction of the oval window. However, not everyone experiences this change, it would seem. Wynn (1973), for example, tells us that Carpenter's (1951) subject claims that his A4 has not changed from 435 Hz in 50 years.

Shorter term changes in tuning have also been reported in tests using the method of adjustment. Abraham (1901) indicates that his A4 varied, over a three-month period, from 451.3 to 442.8 Hz in a random manner, though consistent on a single day. Wynn (1971, 1972) tested his wife's ability to sing A4 on demand over a period of three months, during which time the frequency produced rose from about 440 Hz in the first two weeks to 462 Hz in the last month (and has remained there six months later). Wynn sees in his data a slow cyclical change in the mean that is associated with the menstrual cycle; however, that particular evidence is far from compelling. More significant, though inexplicable, is the fact that his wife's internal standard seems to have gone *flat* by nearly a semit (since she had to raise the frequency to sound "right").

V. LEARNING AP

Various methods have been proposed for improving proficiency at pitch naming up to the level displayed by JL. The first attempt was made by Max Meyer and Heyfelder in 1895 (Meyer, 1898). Beginning with 10 different pitches (both piano tones and tuning forks were used), they gradually increased the number to 39. Although details of procedure are not given, Meyer states that by the time they abandoned the experiment, they had achieved 64 and 60% proficiency. He also indicates that at the time he was writing the article (three years later), he had lost the increased facility.

Gough (1922) reports that the average error of nine graduate students dropped from 5 semits to about 1.5 after a year of practice on identification of piano tones. A study by Mull (1925) also produced a slight improvement in the ability to recognize one particular tone after nine months of practice (one hour weekly). Her technique, apparently designed to develop quasi-AP, consisted of presenting middle C steadily for 15 minutes (!) and then having the listener try to pick middle C from a series of tones within a two-octave range. As soon as a subject responded, the experimenter told him whether or not he was correct; then middle C was again presented (happily, only 5 sec this time), followed by another random series of tones, etc. At the end of this training, a series of tests was performed in which no correction was given. In this series the nine stimuli used were 232 to 296 Hz in 8-Hz steps (i.e., somewhere around quartertone separation); in a long series of tones, the subject was asked to indicate the occurrence of each middle C (256 Hz at this time). The percent correct identification in four successive sessions was 43, 47, 64, and 57, respectively, which is hardly evidence that AP has developed.

Wedell's (1934) study was the first to use response categories other than musical-scale values. The range of frequencies from 50 to 7500 Hz was divided in order to provide 5, 9, 13, 17, 25, or 49 stimuli separated by approximately equal values of pitch extent (tone height)—actually, by equal numbers of just-noticeable differences: 333, 167, 111, 84, 55, and 28, respectively. All were presented at a loudness level of 40 phons. The subject had a chart on which was printed a list of the frequencies used in that particular test.

In the first part of his experiment, he measured in four subjects the learning of the 25-category series. In each daily experimental session, each tone was first presented once, and the subject was asked to identify each, without correction. Then three complete series were presented with feedback. Significant improvement was shown from day 1 to day 4 on session 1, but little thereafter (a total of 20 sessions were run). The average error dropped from about 2.5 categories (125 DLs) to just over 1 category (60 DLs). After a three-month rest, he retrained the subjects on the 25-category series; then he ran two sessions using the 49-item series. The average error remained at 60 DLs (about 3 semits) although this was now more than a two-category separation. No subjects came close to 100% correct identification. A second experiment in which listeners were first trained to identify 5, then 9, then 13 different stimuli also produced only slight improvement; none could get 100% correct on the 13-item series.

Lundin and Allen (1962) report improvement of performance in both possessors and nonpossessors using a 24-button voting board that provided feedback automatically. Lundin (1963) indicates that with this apparatus, learning was even more facilitated by starting with a few tones and gradually increasing their number but gives no details.

A variant of Mull's "learn a single reference" method was proposed by Cuddy in 1968. Here, listeners were required to respond either "A" or "not A" to a series of semits ranging from E4 to D♯5 in which A4 occurred very often during the early training, gradually dropping in later sessions; all six subjects showed improvement with practice. Brady (1970) employed this procedure in the unique development of his ability to name pitches. Using a computer, he presented himself various tones from 117 to 880 Hz in which there was a high proportion of Cs; as training progressed, the proportion gradually dropped to the "chance" 1/12. Although he admits using relative pitch at the beginning of the experiment, he reports that gradually (i.e., no sudden "revelation") he became able to recognize any C immediately. In tests using Petran's (1932) technique for confirming his ability (that is, having his wife play a single note chosen at random every morning for 57 days), he made two 2-semit errors, 18 1-semit errors, and was correct 37 times. As indicated earlier, Carroll (1975) tested Brady's ability, finding that he responded as accurately and as swiftly as four individuals who claimed AP without any formal training. However, Brady himself points out that, unlike them, he does not identify the key of a piece instantly.

Cuddy (1970, 1971) has recently extended the single-standard method to three standards. In the first study, which can be called the nonmusical experiment, she tried to get subjects to classify stimuli as low, medium, or high in pitch, and then to further subclassify each of the three areas into three specific pitches: L−, L, L+; M−, M, M+; H−, H, H+. Two types of spacing were compared: equal mels (nine stimuli from 290 to 3000 Hz spaced at 200-mel intervals), and grouped mels (500, 600, 700; 1100, 1200, 1300; 1700, 1800, 1900 mels). Half of the subjects were given training using a gradually decreasing proportion of L, M, and H (the "standards") beginning at 14/16 and progressing to 8/13, while the other half were given series in which all nine stimuli were equally probable. Spacing proved to be irrelevant (the grouping did not help); although musicians improved more with "standards" training, nonmusicians succeeded better with the equal-probability series. Performance, however, was not noteworthy—the best average I_T was 1.91 bits (in musicians, after three-standard training).

Cuddy's other study (1971) was an improvement in that she used musical stimuli and exploited musical skills. The stimuli in the main experimental group were all the Fs, As, and Cs from F3 to C7 (175 to 2093 Hz); this is called *triad spacing*. Ability to learn to identify these 12 stimuli was compared to learning to identify (1) 12 tones over the same range separated by 3 or 4 semits with no repetition of chroma or (2) 12 tones with essentially equal arithmetic spacing. All series included A4. Training led to great improvement in the musicians using triad spacing; indeed, three listeners finally achieved 100% scores (3.59 bits). Of course, this is a fairly unique "kind" of AP; the listener had only to identify the octave in which the tone occurred. Because all tones were members of the ordinary F triad, she had only to remember this triad in order to decide whether it was the tonic (F), the third (A), or the fifth of the chord (C).

Heller and Auerbach (1972) examined the importance of the type of feedback during training. Using semit stimuli from F4 to D5, they developed a series of 4 training tapes in which the proportion of A4s was successively 40, 30, 20 and 10%. One group of subjects was told whether each tone was A or not A while the other group received full feedback. Improvement in ability to identify all tones in a no-feedback trial was the same for both groups. They conclude that the single-standard procedure is not crucial. However, the improvement was only from 27% correct to 37%, and this may merely represent learning to utilize relative pitch more efficiently. In view of this equivocal result, the issue can hardly be regarded as closed.

VI. THE VALUE OF AP

Thousands of hours have been spent trying to develop AP, yet only one person has been able to achieve as an adult the proficiency that seems to come so naturally to most possessors. One may well ask whether or not AP is worth that much effort. What are the advantages of AP? The most obvious, of course, is that if the pitch pipe is lost, an *a cappella* performance can still be started by a possessor on the correct pitch—an absolute necessity in some songs such as the American national anthem that require an octave and a half of vocal range. Beck (1978) writes me that he can tell his speed on a particular road from the pitch of his tires, McCleve (1979) judges his car's RPM from the motor whine, and Corliss (1973) indicates that identification of elements in a chord is easier for possessors because each element is recognized as such. However, outside of these few instances in which the frequency of a tone is important, the alleged advantages are mostly incapable of confirmation. For example, Bachem (1955) enthuses that "Particular characteristics of certain keys, e.g., the brilliancy of A major, the softness of D-flat major, can only be appreciated fully through absolute pitch." Although he apparently would agree with Vernon on pieces played in C♯ (unless he would maintain that C♯ is different from D♭), we can only take his word that that is how things sounded to him. As recently as 1976 nonsensical claims such as the following are still appearing despite a lack of corroborative evidence: "Absolute pitch is generally an asset to a musician because it helps in playing an instrument in tune, in sight-singing easily and accurately, and in knowing what a piece of music will sound like simply by reading the musical score" (Eaton & Siegel,

1976). These are all skills displayed by nonpossessors of AP as well as by possessors. There is also little evidence that there is much of a correlation between AP and other musical traits such as the ability to improvise (Weinert, 1929) or to make judgments of relative pitch (Ward, 1954; Baggaley, 1974).

Indeed, one would predict that if persons with AP cannot help categorizing notes, they might well be at a disadvantage in certain relative-pitch tasks. For example, in experiments dealing with categorization of intervals such as those described by Burns and Ward (Chapter 8), four tones are presented, and a subject is asked to compare the musical-pitch distance between the first and second tones to that between the third and fourth. The results (Burns and Ward, 1974, 1978) imply that in this task, as in all categorization tasks, some information is sacrificed when categorization occurs. The effect is as if the memory trace of the interval defined by the first pair of tones shifts toward the "best" interval in that category. If an analogous process occurs in AP, it would seem that the possessor might be subject to double jeopardy in this particular situation because he may be making not two but four categorical judgments. Consider the sequence A + 40, C − 40,; D − 40, E + 40 as an extreme example. The person using relative pitch will easily recognize the first interval of 220 cents (i.e., from A + 40 to B + 60) as a major second and the second interval of 280 cents as a minor third and will conclude that the second interval was the larger. On the other hand, if a possessor of AP were unable to avoid categorizing each note and had an internal pitch helix tuned to A4 = 440 Hz, he would perceive the sequence as being A, C; D, E and would therefore say that the *first* interval was the larger. The question, obviously, is how well the possessor can suppress the tendency to categorize individual tones.

Perhaps when the tones are in rapid succession even the most zealous possessor can attend to the intervals as such—can shift from the reference tonality established by the first tone (for judging the distance to the second) to the new reference tonality associated with the third tone, which of course is necessary if the pitch distance between the third and fourth tones is to be accurately evaluated. With longer insterstimulus intervals, however, possessors of AP might find their memory trace of A + 40 gradually slipping to A, etc., leading to the confusion described above for certain pairings of frequencies. At the moment nobody has yet studied the ability of possessors to make relative interval judgments using these "off-frequency" tones (i.e., mistuned relative to the possessor's internal scale), although Siegel and Siegel (1977) were on the brink of such an experiment: they studied interval categorization in nonpossessors and single-stimulus pitch categorization in possessors but not interval discrimination in possessors. So how much of a handicap AP provides in such a situation (admittedly only peripherally related to musical experience) remains to be seen.

One situation that puts possessors at a disadvantage has recently been devised by Cuddy (1977). The task was to identify whether two 7-tone sequences (melodies) were identical or differed on one of the tones by half a semit (3%). Performance of nonpossessors was independent of whether the sequence was tonal or atonal (i.e., used only the 7 major tones of the scale or, instead, all 12) or whether the tones used were separated by equal ratios or by equal steps of linear frequency (log and linear scales, respectively). Possessors were like nonpossessors in two of the tasks but showed significantly poorer performance when judging atonal sequences in the linear scale while simultaneously displaying significantly superior skill at distinguishing tonal sequences in the log scale. That is, possessors were better at picking out a single mistuned tone from a sequence, but when many of the tones were already mistuned (from the viewpoint of standard scales), they were unable to determine whether or not an additional 50-cent change had occurred. They are, it appears, less flexible—less able to learn a new scale.

In any event, AP is not an unmixed blessing. It remains a fascinating phenomenon, although its fascination, for many of us, lies in the question of why so many people do not have the ability rather than why a few do. Any situation in which one particular frequency is to be discriminated from all others, as in testing for "frequency generalization" in experimental animals, is a type of AP experiment; and although the literature is not completely unequivocal, there is evidence that a high degree of discrimination of tones separated by long intervals of time is indeed found in lower organisms such as the dog (Andreyev, 1934) or rat (Blackwell & Schlossberg, 1943), though perhaps it is not highly developed in the cat (Thompson, 1959).

Interestingly enough, mentally retarded teenagers apparently have AP. Paulson, Orlando, and Schoelkopf (1967) trained three of these retardates to tap rapidly on a lever when a 1455-Hz tone was present in order to receive bits of candy, and then the experimenters tried to measure "generalization" to tones of 1100 and 1855 Hz. To the surprise of the experimenters, they got hardly any responses to the new tones in two of their subjects. One of these was therefore tested further with tones spaced at 100-Hz intervals, and even with such small separations, only 1455 Hz was able to elicit a response. Clearly, this illustrates AP in these subjects (assuming, of course, that there was not something unique about the acoustic effects of the 1455-Hz tone in that particular situation that provided an unwanted cue, such as some object that resonated at that frequency). Paulson et al., however, were not overjoyed to find this; rather than rejoicing that the children had AP, they bemoan the results as being "indicative of a broad deficit in generalization processes" of retardates. It appears that AP is typical of either musical precociousness or mental retardation. So if you have it, be sure it is for the right reason.

REFERENCES

Abraham, O. Das absolute Tonbewusstsein. *Sammelbde. International Musikges*, 1901, 3, 1–86.

Andreyev, L. A. Extreme limits of pitch discrimination with higher tones. *Journal of Comparative Psychology*, 1934, 18, 315–332.

Bachem, A. Various types of absolute pitch. *Journal of the Acoustical Society of America*, 1937, 9, 146–151.

Bachem, A. Chroma fixation at the ends of the musical frequency scale. *Journal of the Acoustical Society of America*, 1948, 20, 704–705.

Bachem, A. Time factors in relative and absolute pitch determination. *Journal of the Acoustical Society of America*, 1954, 26, 751–753.

Bachem, A. Absolute pitch. *Journal of the Acoustical Society of America*, 1955, 27, 1180–1185.

Baggaley, J. Measurement of absolute pitch: A confused field. *Psychology of Music*, 1974, *2-2*, 11-17.

Beck, J. F. Personal communication, May 1978.

Blackwell, H. R., & Schlosberg, H. Octave generalization, pitch discrimination, and loudness thresholds in the white rat. *Journal of Experimental Psychology*, 1943, *33*, 407-419.

Brady, P. T. Fixed-scale mechanism of absolute pitch. *Journal of the Acoustical Society of America*, 1970, *48*, 883-887.

Burns, E. M., & W. D. Ward. Categorical perception of musical intervals. *Journal of the Acoustical Society of America*, 1974, *55*, 456.

Burns, E. M., & W. D. Ward. Categorical perception—phenomenon or epiphenomenon: Evidence from experiments in the perception of melodic musical intervals. *Journal of the Acoustical Society of America*, 1978, *63*, 456-468.

Carpenter, A. A case of absolute pitch. *Quarterly Journal of Experimental Psychology*, 1951, *3*, 92-93.

Carroll, J. B. Speed and Accuracy of absolute pitch judgments: Some latter-day results. Research Bulletin (preprint). Princeton, New Jersey: Educational Testing Service, Ocotber 1975.

Cohen, A. Further investigation of the effects of intensity upon the pitch of pure tones. *Journal of the Acoustical Society of America*, 1961,*133*, 1363-1376.

Copp, E. F. Musical ability. *Journal of Heredity*, 1916, 7, 297-305.

Corliss, E. L. Remark on "fixed-scale mechanism of absolute pitch." *Journal of the Acoustical Society of America*, 1973, *53*, 1737-1739.

Cuddy, L. L. Practice effects in the absolute judgment of pitch. *Journal of the Acoustical Society of America*, 1968, *43*, 1069-1076.

Cuddy, L. L. Training the absolute identification of pitch. *Perception & Psychophysics*, 1970, *8*, 265-269.

Cuddy, L. L. Absolute judgement of musically-related pure tones. *Canadian Journal of Psychology*, 1971,*25*, 42-55.

Cuddy, L. L. Comment on "Practice effects in the absolute judgment of frequency" by Heller and Auerbach. *Psychonomic Science*, 1972, *28*, 68.

Cuddy, L. L. Perception of structured melodic sequences. Paper given at *Conference on Musical perception in Paris, France, July 10-13, 1977.*

Deutsch, D. Octave generalization of specific interference effects in memory for tonal pitch. *Perception & Psychophysics*, 1973, *13*, 271-275.

Eaton, K. E., & M. H. Siegel. Strategies of absolute pitch possessors in the learning of an unfamiliar scale. *Bulletin of the Psychonomic Society*, 1976, *8*, 289-291.

Fulgosi, A., Bacun, D., & Zaja, B. Absolute identification of two-dimensional tones. *Bulletin of the Psychonomic Society*, 1975, *6*, 484-486.

Fullard, W., Snelbecker, G. E., & Wolk, S. Absolute judgments as a function of stimulus uncertainty and temporal effects: Methodological note. *Perception & Motor Skills*, 1972, *34*, 379-382.

Gough, E. The effects of practice on judgments of absolute pitch. *Archives of Psychology, New York*, 1922, 7, No. 47, 93.

Hartman, E. B. The influence of practice and pitch distance between tones on the absolute identification of pitch. *American Journal of Psychology*, 1954, *67*, 1-14.

Heller, M. A., & Auerbach, C. Practice effects in the absolute judgment of frequency. *Psychonomic Science*, 1972, *26*, 222-224.

Hurni-Schlegel, L., & Lang, A. Verteilung, Korrelate und Veränderbarkeit der Tonhöhen-Identifikation (sog. absolutes Musikgehör). *Schweizerische Zeitschrift fur Psychologie & Anwendungen*, 1978, 37, 265-292.

von Kries, J. Über das absolute Gehör. *Zeitschrift fur Psychologie & Physiology Sinnesorg*, 1892, *3*, 257-279.

van Krevelen, A. The ability to make absolute judgments of pitch. *Journal of Experimental Psychology*, 1951, *42*, 207-215.

Lundin, R. W. Can perfect pitch be learned? *Music Education Journal*, 1963, 49-51.

Lundin, R. W., & Allen, J. D. A technique for training perfect pitch. *Psychology Record*, 1962,*12*, 139-146.

McCleve, D. E. Personal communication, March 1979.

Meyer, M. Is the memory of absolute pitch capable of development by training? *Psychological Review*, 1899, *6*, 514-516.

Mull, H. K. The acquisition of absolute pitch. *American Journal of Psychology*, 1925, *36*, 469-493.

Oakes, W. F. An alternative interpretation of "absolute pitch." *Transactions of the Kansas Academy of Sciences*, 1951, *54*, 396-406.

Paulson, D. G., Orlando, R., & Schoelkopf, A. M. Experimental analysis and manipulation of auditory generalization in three developmental retardates by discriminated-operant procedures. IMRID Papers and Reports 4, No. 13, 1967. (Institute on Mental Retardation and Intellectual Development, George Peabody College for Teachers, Nashville, Tennessee 37203.)

Petran, L. A. An experimental study of pitch recognition. *Psychological Monograph*, 1932, *42*, No. 6.

Pollack, I. The information of elementary auditory displays. *Journal of the Acoustical Society of America*, 1952, *24*, 745-749.

Rakowski, A. Direct comparison of absolute and relative pitch. *Symposium on Hearing Theory, Eindhoven, Netherlands*, sponsored by IPO, June 22-23, 1972.

Revesz, G. *Zur Grundlegung der Tonpsychologie*. Veit, Leipzig, 1913.

Riker, B. L. The ability to judge pitch. *Journal of Experimental Psychology*, 1946, *36*, 331-346.

Sergeant, D. Experimental investigation of absolute pitch. *Journal of Research in Music Education*, 1969, *17*, 135-143.

Siegel, J. A. Sensory and verbal coding strategies in subjects with absolute pitch. *Journal of Experimental Psychology*, 1974, *102*, 37-44.

Siegel, J. A., & W. Siegel. Absolute identification of notes and intervals by musicians. *Perception & Psychophysics*, 1977, *21*, 143-152.

Stumpf, C. *Tonpsychologie*. Herzel, Leipzig, 1883.

Stumpf, C. Beobachtungen über subjective Töne und über Doppelthören. *Beitrage zur Akustik & Musik*, 1901, *3*, 30-51.

Terman, M. Improvement of absolute pitch naming. *Psychonomic Science*, 1965, *3*, 243-244.

Thompson, R. F. The effect of training procedure upon auditory frequency discrimination in the cat. *Journal of Comparative & Physiology Psychology*, 1959, *52*, 186-190.

Triepel, H. Zur Frage des absoluten Gehörs. *Archiv für die Gesamte Psychologie*, 1934, *90*, 373-379.

Trotter, J. R. The psychophysics of melodic interval: Definition, techniques, theory and problems. *Australian Journal of Psychology*, 1967, *19*, 13-25.

Vernon, P. E. Absolute pitch: A case study. *British Journal of Psychology*, 1977, *68*, 485-489.

Ward, W. D. Information and absolute pitch. *Journal of the Acoustical Society of America*, 1953, *25*, 833.

Ward, W. D. Subjective musical pitch. *Journal of the Acoustical Society of America*, 1954, *26*, 369-380.

Ward, W. D. Absolute pitch. Part I. *Sound*, 1963, 2 (3), 14-21. (a)

Ward, W. D. Absolute pitch. Part II. *Sound*, 1963, 2 (4), 33-41. (b)

Watt, H. J. *The psychology of sound*. London and New York: Cambridge Univ. Press, 1917.

Wedell, C. H. The nature of the absolute judgment of pitch. *Journal of Experimental Psychology*, 1934, *17*, 485-503.

Weinert, L. Untersuchungen über das absolute Gehör. *Archiv. für die Gesamte Psychologie*, 1929, *73*, 1-128.

Wellek, A. Das absolute Gehör und seine Typen. *Zeitschrift für Angewandte Psychologie & Charakterkunde-Beihefte*, 1938, *83*, 1-368.

Wynn, V. T. "Absolute" pitch—a bimensual rhythm. *Nature (London)*, 1971, *230*, 337.

Wynn, V. T. Measurements of small variations in "absolute" pitch. *Journal of Physiology*, 1972, *220*, 627-637.

Wynn, V. T. Absolute pitch in humans, its variations and possible connections with other known rhythmic phenomena. In G. A. Kerkut and J. W. Phillis (Eds.), *Progress in neurobiology*, Vol. 1, Part 2. Oxford: Pergamon, 1973. Pp. 111-149.

15

Neurological Aspects of Music Perception and Performance

Oscar S. M. Marin

I. Introduction 453
II. Amusia 454
    A. Amusia with Aphasia 455
    B. Aphasia without Amusia 461
    C. Amusia without Aphasia 462
III. Auditory Agnosia and Verbal Deafness 462
IV. General Comments 466
    A. Neuroanatomical Basis of Musical Functions 466
    B. Perspectives for a Neuropsychological Study of Disorders of Musical Function 469
    References 473

I. INTRODUCTION

An article dealing with the neurology of music should include two levels of inquiry: (a) description of the dissociations and clinical deficits in music perception or performance found in patients with localized or diffuse damage to the nervous system and, on the basis of this data, (b) analysis of normal and abnormal psychological, physiological and anatomical functions, in order to determine the principles and modes by which the brain stores, codifies, or processes music.

Clinical descriptions of abnormalities of musical perception or performance abound in the neurological literature, particularly that of the second half of the last century and the early part of this one. It is significant, however, that in the last 20 years the confident enthusiasm with which clinical deficits were related to functional localization in the brain have become increasingly restrained. This restraint is largely due to a realization that in dealing with brain processes, one can no longer accept the simplistic concept that the central nervous system can be represented merely as a mosaic of complex mental faculties. One should reject the idea that it is possible to give an adequate account of verbal, musical, or any other complex behavior by anatomically describing a handful of fiber interconnections among a few perceptual or executive functional components. Of even more fundamental importance has been the realization that one cannot study the neuropsychology of complex behavior without a prior understanding of the cognitive structures of the systems involved.

Despite this awareness, progress in the field of neurology of music has been slow. Until recently, a similar simplistic approach controlled the study of the neurology of speech and language; and it still prevails to a large degree in understanding the agnosias and disorders of motor behavior. Disillusionment with the whole mental faculty approach caused a shift to the opposite extreme and emphasized instead the minute analysis of the hardware. This is as if in order to understand the plot of a television program, we analyze the details of the television circuit or the trajectory of the electronic beam projected onto the screen. But behavioral reductionism also had its hour, and most would now agree that from the cognitive standpoint, music is a hierarchical function that requires processing at many interacting levels.

Because some useful information on auditory perceptual processing has begun to emerge from the study of auditory agnosias and verbal deafness, these clinical syndromes will be analyzed here despite the fact that there is still little known concerning the way in which disorders of music perception relate to such cases. Because neuropsychological studies of language and speech have proven their value in the analysis of cognitive processes and because these functions are related to music, we shall frequently use neurolinguistic and psycholinguistic experience as points of reference.

The clinical characteristics of disorders of musical function will be described, but a summary of these clinical experiences will not yet provide a neuropsychologically coherent interpretation in terms of information processing, or localization in the nervous system. Rather, these clinical descriptions will be used as points of departure for critical comments on issues that await preliminary study before fruitful research in this area can proceed.

II. AMUSIA

Amusia is a generic term used to designate acquired clinical disorders of music perception, performance, and reading or writing that are secondary to organic brain damage. These disorders, like other syndromes of higher cortical function—such as agnosias, aphasias, or apraxias—should represent fairly well-circumscribed disabilities and not be the result of a diffuse decay of overall mental capacity as observed in dementia, psychosis, or mental retardation.

The classical literature describing amusia has been reviewed many times in recent years. Of special value are the works of Benton (1977), Jellinek (1956), and Wertheim (1963, 1969, 1977) in English, and of Barbizet (1972), Dorgeuille (1966), and Grison (1972) in French. The German speaking authors have sustained interest in the subject with works ranging from highly theoretical speculative essays to clinical or anatomo-clinical reviews. Notable are the works of Edgren (1895), Feuchwanger (1930), Henschen (1920, 1926), Jellinek (1933), Kleist (1928, 1962), Ustveldt (1937), and Walthard (1927).

While the agnosias (i.e., auditory agnosia, visual agnosia) are clinical nosological terms used to designate modality specific disorders of perception, the amusias are terms referring to attempts to group together a variety of disabilities related to musical function. Some amusias are specifically perceptual in nature; some involve symbolic systems of reading and writing or are based on previously acquired knowledge, while still others comprise complex executive vocal or manual motor activities. We should also note that the degree of proficiency and automatization with which each of these tasks was performed before illness varies considerably in individual patients. It can be anticipated that such a heterogeneous assortment of dysfunctions will not enable us to determine whether basic musical mechanisms are related to consistent lesional topographies. Consequently, as also noted by others (Ustveldt, 1937; Wertheim, 1977), the nosological term amusia is too general; and is thus essentially meaningless for describing, and useless for explaining, the brain mechanisms that may be involved in music functions.

Efforts to improve and clarify the main issues relating to disorders of music perception or performance have utilized four main approaches:

1. Nosological studies attempting subclassifications of the amusias into clinical syndromes that are more closely related to the impairment of basic mechanisms of musical functions (Dorgeuille, 1966; Henschen, 1920; Kleist, 1934; & Wertheim, 1963, 1969).

2. Attempts to define the relationships between disturbances of speech and language (aphasias) and those of music by comparing the clinical syndromes, documenting the clinical coexistence or segregation of these syndromes in individual patients, and correlating the anatomoclinical findings of both disorders.

3. Improvements in methods of assessing premorbid material skill and knowledge in amusic patients that would serve as a reliable base line for the evaluation of deficits (Grison, 1972).

4. Improvement and systematization of the methods of clinical investigation of musical disorders (Dorgeuille, 1966; Jellinek, 1956; Wertheim & Botez, 1959; Wertheim, 1969).

A. Amusia with Aphasia

It has been stressed that music is a "language" and, consequently, that amusia and aphasia are likely to be closely linked in their neuroanatomical substrates (Feuchtwanger, 1930). Thus, the *criteria* required for their documentation and even their nosological subclassification would be expected to be closely related (Weissenburg & McBride, 1935). Musical disabilities that are predominantly receptive (receptive or sensory amusias) would somehow parallel the receptive and sensory aphasias of

Wernicke; disorders that are predominantly expressed in terms of an inability to vocalize or sing would be somewhat equivalent to Broca's aphasia; disorders of musical writing would parallel agraphias; disorders of musical reading would correspond to alexias; while the inability to remember a familiar tune would be similar to an anomia. Nonparalytic difficulties in playing an instrument would constitute a musical apraxia.

A strong clinical association between aphasias and amusias would have important implications for the anatomical localization of musical functions, since speech and language are strongly lateralized to the dominant cerebral hemisphere (for distribution of speech and language functions, see Marin, Schwartz, & Saffran, 1979). If, on the other hand, the association is only partial or inconsistent, a conclusion that language and music share only some processes or may even be totally independent functions, would be suggested. In this respect, one should remember that neuropsychological similarities between these two functions do not necessarily mean that they must share a common physiological or anatomical substratum. The evolutionary tendency of the central nervous system is toward the assignment of task-oriented neural subsets (Simon, 1967). This subspecialization for speech and music would result in independent neural operators of greater efficiency.

It is not possible to evaluate with certainty the frequency with which aphasias and amusias occur in association. Most of the published clinical cases were preselected, examined only from the standpoint of either aphasia or amusia. Cases of amusia have been analyzed for aphasia more often than cases of aphasia have been analyzed for amusia. Feuchtwanger (1930) found various degrees of aphasia in each of his observations of amusia, and on the basis of his findings suggested that the neurolexical substrates of music and language were intimately related. Since then, a growing number of cases have shown dissociations between the two functions. Dorgeuille (1966), in his study of 26 observations, found 11 cases of amusia with aphasia and two examples of isolated amusia. In reviewing the observations of a large number of clinical articles on amusia, we were able to collect 87 case reports with fairly complete clinical descriptions. Aphasia and amusia coexisted in 33 of these cases. Well-documented examples of amusia without aphasia were found in 19 cases. Amusia and general auditory agnosia were reasonably well-documented in four cases, and there were at least five cases of amusia associated with verbal deafness with only minor or nonexistent signs of auditory agnosia. There were one or possibly two cases of auditory agnosia with a possible musical perceptual disorder but without verbal deafness or aphasia (Nielsen, 1962; Spreen, Benton, & Fincham, 1965).

No attempt will be made here to review the large number of cases already recorded by others. Examples will be selected because they represent dissociations that are clinically characteristic, or because they offer an opportunity to discuss special aspects of the neuropsychological structure of music or cognitive function in general.

The existence of fairly distinct disorders of music perception (receptive amusia) are well recognized. Their association with similar deficits in language perception and comprehension is not exceptional (Feuchtwanger, 1930), but the two functions may often be dissociated (Ustvedt, 1937). Kohl and Tschabitscher (1952) describe a patient with left hemisphere damage, expressive aphasia, normal comprehension, and predominantly receptive amusia. Wertheim and Botez (1961) also describe the case of a 40-year-old professional violinist who, after developing a sudden right-sided sensorimotor hemiparesis and a mixed but predominantly receptive aphasia, showed a number of difficulties in musical processing. While the patient previously had absolute pitch, he now consistently makes errors in identifying and naming isolated sounds. However, his pitch discrimination was normal even for intervals smaller than a semitone, and vocal and instrumental reproduction were correct. In contrast, recognition and identification of work, composer, and even style of well-known musical themes were incorrect. He was capable of identifying differences in melodies and chords, and to recognize faulty performances of a melody (including errors in tonal modulation); however, he was unable to identify and name intervals in melodic or harmonic contexts. Identification of rhythmic measures, motor reproduction, and dictation of rhythms were also poorly performed. Music reading was impossible in sequence, but the patient was able to name notes in isolation. Reading of musical symbols was normal but rendition of their meaning was often faulty. Singing of isolated sounds or familiar melodies was often incorrect, while evaluation of major and minor scales was usually correct. Some errors were made in copying or transcribing melodies.

This case, summarized in some detail, shows the clinical complexity of some of the deficits and, at the same time, shows the variances in the cognitive nature of the errors made by the patient, even given unvarying exploration of pitch, rhythm, melody, or chord perception. It is interesting to observe that most of the tasks that involved simple perceptual discriminations were apparently performed more successfully than similar tasks that required identification or naming. In this respect, it is of significance to note that the residual aphasic disorder of this patient was also predominantly a lexical difficulty in the form of anomia. The deficits exhibited by this patient could well have been due to a basic lexical disorder common for language and music.

This case illustrates the need to distinguish between specifically perceptual defects, and disorders related to the "linguistic" or symbolic lexical level of the organization of the musical system. A further distinction between musical perceptual and auditory sensory levels will be made later in this paper when observations of auditory agnosias and verbal deafness are discussed. Souques and Baruk (1930) describe a patient with severe Wernicke's aphasia due to extensive left temproal damage. The patient was unable to recognize familiar melodies but was able to play spontaneously pieces of music at the piano, as well as to play major and minor scales. This patient was able to detect minute errors in the instrumental execution of others, and his music reading and writing was preserved. Here again we observe disabilities in the higher level functions of identification and naming, while other musical perceptual functions were intact.

Bernard (1881), cited by Dorgeuille (1966), describes the case of a professional piano teacher who was affected by a severe mixed expressive-receptive aphasia and alexia and was unable to read or recognize music. Despite this, she was able to sing the melody and lyrics of a famous song, and she did so repetitively and automatically.

Benton (1977) cites a similar description by Dalin (1745) of an aphasic patient who was nevertheless still capable of singing with words. Other such cases were reported by Gowers (1875), Knoblauch (1888), and Proust (1866). This contrast between normal and automatic performance of overlearned familiar tasks and an inability to execute new sentences or new motor acts or to sing new melodies is a well-known aspect of the neurological disintegration of behavior.

A dissociation between what Jackson called automatic and propositional behavior can be observed in practically all functions (speech and language, movements, singing). It reminds us of the critical problem that any distinct motor or language task, or any ostensive behavior, may correspond to varying levels of processing depending on an individual's previous experience and the context in which it appears. While a patient may be unable to name an object voluntarily (i.e., a drinking "glass"), he or she may a few minutes later request, "Give me the glass. I am thirsty." When one of our demented patients, whom we have studied over a prolonged period (Schwartz, Marin, & Saffran, 1979) was recently reexamined, we found that her spontaneous speech had totally disappeared. Her spontaneous vocalizations consisted only of iterative sounds that she said in sentence-like sequences with appropriate sound contours to express her emotions and intentions. She was now totally unable to name spontaneously any object, and only exceptionally did she vaguely approximate the phonology of certain words. However, when asked to count aloud, after some prompting by the examiner, she could count perfectly normally, in sequence and in pronounciation, up to 32. This woman, who is suffering from a diffuse bilateral cortical atrophy, was also able to sing, without the lyrics, the entire national anthem with perfect rhythm, intonation, and prosody. The usual explanation given in such cases is that abnormal functions reflect the effect of the damaged left cortical areas while those that are preserved are based on normal right anatomical substrata. But in this case of diffuse cortical damage such an explanation is not determinative, since there is no good reason to believe that her right cerebral cortex was functioning any better than her left language sustaining hemisphere. The researcher must accept that, depending on the automatism acquired in the performance of different tasks or skills, a patient can develop alternative representations at multiple cortical or subcortical loci or perhaps that representations become resistant to anatomical pathological simplification resulting from cortical atrophy by virtue of their widespread anatomical substrates.

Ethological literature is rich with examples of centrally programmed and complex behaviors of long duration that are stored and performed as wholes. Neurophysiology has only recently found similar examples of behavior in higher vertebrates whereas clinical neurology hardly recognizes their importance in clinical situations.

The hypothesis that under special circumstances of automatism or overlearning, a cognitive task may escape the complexity of its original function and may operate in relative independence provides another explanation for the evolutionary specialization of neural subsets. Such a hypothesis should have importance for neuropsychological theory as well as for theories of cognition and cognitive development. Although speech is a learned function in both its receptive and productive aspects, there is evidence that in adult life this phonological-articulatory loop can function with incredible precision in isolation from the rest of the linguistic cognitive organization. In fact, lesions that isolate the speech areas of the left hemisphere may originate a clinical syndrome of echolalia characterized by automatic ability to repeat faithfully any heard speech (Geschwind, Quadfasel, & Segarra, 1965). In such patients there is no evidence of understanding of language, and, in fact, the semantic–linguistic disconnection seems to be partly responsible for the phonological-articulatory automatic independence (Marin et al., 1979; Marin & Gordon, 1979a,b). A similar, but less frequent, phenomenon can be observed in some patients who continuously repeat gestures or movements made by others (echopraxia). Although these examples are taken from pathology, they show how functionally specialized subsets can detach themselves from the original cognitive roots that nurtured their development.

An aphasic patient described by Finkelnburg (1870) was able to play melodies on his violin, but was unable to do so on the piano, which was a less familiar instrument. In music, as in language, such automatisms are of enormous importance and may explain the sparing of some complex musical tasks while others that appear to be more basic and simple are lost. Perhaps the best example of this is seen in the motor skills of instrumentalists or in instrumental musical improvisation. In both cases, success depends to a large extent on the ability to create central programs of long duration based on tactual-motor loops. Performance, thus, demands a minimal requirement of higher cognitive control whereby the motor system performs with almost total independence, allowing the musician's mind to occupy itself with the higher level of musical aesthetic controls. Sudnow (1978), discussing his experience in jazz improvisation, wrote: "My hands have come to develop an intimate knowledge of the piano keyboard, ways of exploratory engagement with routing through its spaces, modalities of reaching and articulatory, and now I choose to go in the course of moving from place to place as a handful choosing."

A frequent and perhaps predictable association is that of verbal and musical alexia: Case 9 of Bouillaud (1865) was agraphic, alexic, and musically alexic, as were the cases of Brazier (1892), Dejerine (1892a,b), Dupre and Nathan's Case 2 (1911) and those of Jellinek (1953) and Wertheim and Botez (1961). Dorgeuille (1966) found disturbances of music reading in six of his collected cases, but only three of these were associated with verbal alexia. Jossmann's case (1927) was unable to read music or to sing but was not aphasic, and his lesion was in the right hemisphere.

Here again, we are confronted with a function, reading, which in no way may be considered simple, and a deficit, which does not correspond to a single altered mechanism or to a well-defined lesional topography. Music reading does not depend only on the ability to recognize the symbolic lexical nature of specific graphic designs such as in Fig. 1A and the assignment to each of them of a referential meaning (symbolic-semantic level). Thus, a study of music reading demands consideration of other processes involved in the perception of the lexical elements of music. Perceptual defects (visual agnosia) may account for some cases of musical alexia. Ballet (cited by Dorgeuille, 1966) tells us, for example, of one of Charcot's patients who suddenly developed an inability to read music because he became incapable of "deciphering" the notes that he saw but could not "understand" any longer.

An element of fundamental importance in reading music is the fact that the script is displayed in a highly bisymmetrical space. For music reading we have to deal not only with the perceptual recognition of elements as in Fig. 1B as such but also with the spatial problems of discriminating them from elements such as in Fig. 1C. Consequently, music reading might be simpler than verbal reading in terms of the number of lexical-semantic items represented in the musical "dictionary." However, verbal reading is more ambiguous in terms of perceptual features of object identification and more complex in terms of its visuospatial organization. The discrimination in music reading of perceptual orientation and symbolic-referential aspects may have important neuropsychological implications for the varieties of musical alexias and their possible anatomoclinical correlates.

There is an important neuropsychological, physiological, and comparative anatomical literature which indicates that form perception, and spatial orientation are two different aspects of vision (Schneider, 1969; Weiskrantz, Warrington, Sanders, & Marshall, 1974). This literature will not be reviewed here, but its implications are obvious: It cannot be expected that music reading depends on a single anatomical substrate or even that its various components will overlap entirely with those of verbal reading whether this be syllabic or ideographic. The greater role of the parietal cortex of the minor hemisphere, so significant in visuospatial functions, seems to be clear in the case of music reading as opposed to verbal reading. If reversals and other disturbances of spatial orientation are prominent abnormalities in cases of developmental dyslexias, one can easily imagine the importance of these factors in the case of music reading. There is, in fact, some evidence that relatives of dyslexic children, who are not dyslexic themselves, often have great difficulties in learning to read music (E. Saffran, personal communication).

One of the earliest reports of amusia is Case 9 of Bouillaud (1865). This was a woman who suffered a sudden right hemiplegia, associated with aphasia. Her articulatory defects ("sort d'ataxie verbale . . ."), possibly a word order syntactic defect, her agraphia and acalculia, were accompanied by a peculiar inability to read music. Occasionally, she was able to play some passages correctly, but she frequently made mistakes in the sequential ordering of the music. The case is remarkable because this ' disorder allows for various alternative interpretations. On the one hand, it may be due to the association of a language and a musical disorder that is the manifestation of a common cognitive defect: abnormality in the language syntactic word order and abnormality in the sequence of the musical execution of a tune. On the other hand, the same music reading defect could be explained by a visual spatial disorganization and attentional disorder, similar to the type of verbal reading abnormality observed by Shallice and Warrington (1977). In such circumstances, there is a perceptual disorder in relation to selective visual attention that results in an attenuation of the perceived order of a sequence of letters or words.

Proust (1872) described the case of another woman who became aphasic and who was also unable to vocalize music. The patient could, however, name notes, recognize familiar tunes, and sign musical scales. Although the author did not give details of the patient's language disorder, one can be reasonably sure that comprehension was relatively well preserved and that language production was predominantly affected. In this case, the speech disability was accompanied by a corresponding defect in vocalization, an association not at all uncommon. Similar cases have been reported by Botez and Wertheim (1959), Brazier (1892), Cramer (1891), and Jellinek (1933).

It is not unusual to find cases of severely aphasic patients that are able to sing with normal intonation and rhythm but without lyrics. One of our patients with Broca's aphasia was a very well-educated woman who, despite her severe expressive disorder, was able to sing a number of themes of the classical symphonic repertoire and to sing songs without the lyrics. The dissociation in performance between verbal and melodic tasks gives strong support to the contralateral localization of these expressive functions (Barbizet, 1972).

B. Aphasia without Amusia

There are at least 12 documented cases of aphasia in professional or amateur musicians in whom musical abilities were not noticeably affected. These cases of total dissociation are of particular interest because they decisively contradict the hypothesis that language and music must share common neural substrates.

Perhaps the most remarkable case is the one reported by Luria, Tsvetkova, and Futer (1963). The patient was a well-known composer and professor of music at the Moscow Conservatory who suffered a cerebrovascular accident that damaged the left temporal and temporal-parietal regions leaving him with a severe sensory aphasia. This patient, despite the aphasia, was able to resume his work as a composer successfully, creating works that were considered by other professional musicians as excellent in quality. Other cases of aphasia without amusia have been reported by Assal (1973), Bouillaud, (1865), Brazier (1892), Charcot (1886, cited by Dorgeuille 1966), Henschen (1926), Lasegue (1872, cited by Dorgeuille, 1966), and Proust (1866). These cases indicate that the neurological substrates of the left hemisphere that are responsible for aphasia do not sustain, to any significant degree, the musical functions of these patients.

C. Amusia without Aphasia

Cases of amusia unaccompanied by language impairment support the hypothesis of independence of musical and verbal processes. At least 19 such clinical examples have been recorded. A significant number of cases in which there is satisfactory information concerning the site of lesion show damage to the right hemisphere, notably affecting temporal regions. The clinical symptoms are diverse, but the majority of them, as expected, are related to defects in music perception, discrimination, or memory. Dorgeuille (1966) found in his series of 26 patients, eight examples of alterations in memory for melodies, four of disorders of rhythm, and seven musical perceptual defects. In two of the four cases of specific melodic perceptual defects, there was also avocalia. The rest of his music patients had complex combinations of perceptual deficits, disorders of instrumental sound recognition, or disturbances of music reading or writing. Despite Dorgeuille's careful review, no clear nosological picture emerges from his efforts that could be interpreted in terms of basic neuropsychological mechanisms. The correlation between clinical deficits and morbid anatomy is inconclusive. The involvement of the temporal lobes on both sides, including the anterior portions, were, however, prominent anatomical features.

III. AUDITORY AGNOSIA AND VERBAL DEAFNESS

Auditory agnosia constitutes the auditory perceptual disorder par excellence: in such instances, the association of abnormal perception of noises, speech, and animal sounds with that of music is not at all surprising. Unfortunately, it is common to find that reported cases of auditory agnosia have been only cursorily explored for their musical perceptual abilities. The syndrome usually results from bilateral cortical damage to the temporal cortex of the primary acoustic area of Heschl and surrounding fields (Albert, Sparks, von Stockert, & Sax, 1972; Jeger, Weikers, Shorbrough, & Jeger, 1969; Kogerer, 1924; Laignel-Lavastine and Alajouanine, 1921; Misch, 1928; Pötzl, 1939; Pötzl and Uiberall, 1937; Reinhold, 1948). There are recorded cases in which the syndrome resulted from a unilateral lesion in the right hemisphere. Here, the abnormal perception of nonverbal sounds contrasted with the preservation of normal speech perception and absence of aphasia (Nielsen, 1962; Spreen et al., 1965).

Disorganization of speech perception (verbal deafness or word agnosia) with preservation of normal nonverbal discrimination is well known and is usually the result of localized damage to the acoustic and paracoustic cortical fields of the dominant speech hemisphere.

Typically, patients with auditory agnosia are not truly deaf, but in fact continuously experience chaotic sounds from the environment as well as auditory acoustic illusions and hallucinations. Many patients complain that noises, voices and sounds have become too loud and unpleasant (Arnold, 1943); that sounds are like crackling noises running against each other and creating indistinct, blurred noises; that sounds are incomprehensible and do not "register" in their minds; that they resound in unpleasant echoes, vibrating or oscillating in intensity, even becoming painful to hear. For example, one of our patients constantly complained that the hinges of the doors needed oiling because they emanated constant unpleasant squeaky noises. Others heard human voices or their own thoughts. Such patients have great difficulty in distinguishing between real and illusory noises, sounds or voices; and like patients with other cortical cognitive disorders (i.e., hemiplegia, cortical blindness, somatoagnosic defects), they have difficulty in gaining full awareness of the extent of their perceptual deficits. One of our patients with visual agnosia insisted on driving his car. Another patient with an auditory agnosia that had lasted for years still insisted on calling and answering the telephone, thus renewing each time his frustration at not being able to comprehend the voices of speakers or the noises produced by the apparatus. The essential deficit here therefore does not seem to be one of threshold perception but rather one of discrimination and pattern organization.

Systematic and thorough studies of auditory deficits are practically nonexistent. This is due not only to extreme difficulties in achieving meaningful communication with such patients but also to their unusual irritability and anxiety. Communication by gestures is usually unsatisfactory and full of ambiguity, and laborious written communication is their only option. In typical cases, reading and writing are normal with only occasional paralexic errors. In some cases, spontaneous speech may show paraphasic errors. Occasionally, there is a tendency to talk too loudly and in a rather forced high pitch. One of our patients developed, together with his auditory agnosia, a high pitch falsetto voice. Another patient had completely incomprehensible utterances mostly consisting of iterative fast repetition of single syllables (i.e., da-da-da, or sh-sh-sh) or combinations that in no way resembled anarthric or typical paraphasic speech. The same patient was unable to sing, imitate animal sounds, or repeat vocal rhythms with syllables. By contrast, his written communication was perfect.

It is difficult to be sure what the relationship is between this abnormality of speech production and the auditory defect, but one cannot fail to remember the importance of acoustic templates for the production of songs in birds (Marler, 1976; Nottebohm, 1975), the effect of the delayed auditory feedback on speech perception (Yates, 1963), or the studies of jargon aphasia (Alajouanine and Lhermitte, 1961, 1964). Auditory agnosics have great difficulty with a number of sound discriminations. Although many of them have absolute thresholds for tones that are only slightly higher than normal, intensity discrimination thresholds are quite poor. Often, noises or sounds are either not heard at all, or they appear at a loud and uncomfortable level. In general, patients have no difficulty in determining whether or not a stimulus has been turned on. Very often, however, they are unable to detect the off-change, and they declare that the stimulus has terminated before its actual end. In successive on–off trials, patients soon lose track of the changes and the direction in which the stimulus operates. This on–off confusion has also been observed by us in intermittent visual stimulations of patients with visual agnosia. Temporal distribution of stimuli and temporal clusters (rhythm) are very poorly discriminated. Patients exhibit total inability to distinguish, describe, or reproduce rhythmic patterns. Binaural sound localization is usually quite abnormal. Recognition of timbre and of complex sounds is usually hopelessly defective. One of our patients thought that the barking of a dog was a "kind of music," while a locomotive noise was interpreted as human singing, and typewriter tapping as "children playing." Patients often say that they can hear, but that they cannot make sense of the sound.

One patient, who was extensively studied by Albert *et al*. (1972) commented after hearing a bird singing: "I hear the sound but I can't seem to associate it with any of these pictures" (pictures that represented possible sources of the stimuli). Whether these patients have some clear internal auditory representation of the stimulus to which they are exposed is an important but yet incompletely answered question. One patient was exposed to the ticking noise of an alarm clock. We observed that despite the fact that she went so far as to declare that the object made a kind of a "tic tac, tic tac" noise, she was unable to identify the object from among a group of objects that were presented visually or to choose it from a list of alternative names. No other type of naming disorder was present in this patient. Another of our patients could not determine with certainty if a spoken sound "ai" corresponded to the picture of an "eye" or that of a "tie." However, he always pronounced the name of the picture of these or other objects correctly. This same patient was totally unable to provide words that rhymed with a given word or with the name of an object or picture of an object. In this task, despite our efforts to give written instruction and multiple examples, the enormous difficulty encountered by the patient raised doubts as to whether the concept of rhyming itself was still present in the patient's mind.

Many authors have attempted to differentiate levels of perceptual disorganization. From a broad perspective, Vignolo (1969) studied auditory perception in cases of right or left hemisphere damage. He devised tests that would in some cases discriminate the acoustic properties of a stimulus among distractors and in other cases identify the source or the nature of the stimulus. This allowed the author to separate auditory-perceptual from semantico-referential aspects; levels of processing previously suggested by Kleist (1928). Vignolo found that patients with damage to the left hemisphere performed well in the discriminatory tasks and worse in the identification tasks, whereas patients with damage to the right hemisphere performed poorly in the discrimination of meaningless sounds. Albert *et al*. (1972) were impressed that their patient was always correct in selecting the title of a popular tune just heard among multiple choices, but was only 30% correct in producing spontaneously the name of the tune. It is therefore an open question whether Vignolo's left hemisphere damaged patients failed in the identification task because of a semantic referential disorder or because of difficulties in retrieving the verbal lexical tags of the stimuli.

Studies reflecting this dichotomy between identification and discrimination have been performed in the area of language perception by a number of authors (Basso, Casati, & Vignolo, 1977; Blumstein, 1973, 1977). The studies suggest the existence of multiple stages in the auditory perceptual process, a notion that may have important implications for the neurological aspects of music percpetion. Therefore, it seems useful to review briefly what has been observed in the field of verbal deafness—a perceptual auditory disorder that specifically involves a hierarchically organized system. Today this entity is well recognized as resulting from a unilateral lesion of the dominant hemisphere that isolates the auditory association areas from the primary auditory projections (Lichtheim, 1885). This syndrome has been described and analyzed in a long series of reports by Albert and Bear (1974), Barrett (1910), Hemphill and Stengel (1940), Klein and Harper (1956), Richter (1957), and Saffran, Marin, and Yeni-Komshian (1976). Saffran *et al.*, made a detailed study of a right-handed, 37-year-old patient who very likely suffered an embolic infarction in the left temporal lobe. As is usually the case with such patients, his illness began with a clincial picture that corresponded to a Wernicke's aphasia including defective comprehension and paraphasic speech. Later on, his speech production improved to normal levels, but the abnormalities of his auditory comprehension remained unchanged. The findings can be summarized as follows:

1. Monaural presentation of previously rehearsed or familiar names resulted in correct perception through either ear.

2. Dichotic presentations of similar words resulted in perception of the stimuli presented in the left ear with total unawareness of the stimuli presented in the right. An increase in intensity of an order of 20 or more dB to the right ear was needed to make the patient aware of the presence of the stimulus. Dichotic presentation of vowel sounds and consonant-vowel combinations gave a strong extinction effect in the right ear. When presented with natural and synthetic speech sounds (vowels and stop consonants), there was severe and complex disorganization of the expected discrimination and identification of these sounds. The picture that emerged was one of a considerable reduction in the number of items that could be identified with some certainty. This reduction involved overextension of some categories relative to others. There were parallelisms between these identification difficulties and errors made in purely discriminative tasks, suggesting that these two phenomena are, at least, closely interdependent. The patient was able to make discriminations and identifications of nonverbal sounds without difficulty. He was also well able to distinguish intonation contours, changes in types of voices, and the number of voices speaking simultaneously. He was quite alert in detecting when a speaker changed without transition from one language to another (English–German–Spanish) despite the fact that he was unable to understand any of these utterances, and all sounded to him as "kind of Greek." A number of tests demonstrated that the patient's speech comprehension was very sensitive to semantic, syntactic, and other contextual factors with occasional impressive improvements in understanding.

The analysis of this case emphasizes aspects of perceptual processing that are currently subject to active research and discussion in the realm of speech and language but that could be equally valid for our study of music:

1. There is strong evidence that speech sounds are decoded by a specialized perceptual apparatus. This specialization relates to the peculiar acoustical composition of speech sounds.

2. Certain parts of speech (consonants) are categorically identified and perceived. There is evidence that perceptual categorical boundaries may be present before babies begin to hear significant amounts of spoken language and well before they start uttering speech (Eimas, 1971, 1974; Eimas & Corbit, 1973). Categorical learning, however, is not restricted to speech sounds but is applicable to other acoustic events as well: bow-pluck sounds (Cutting & Rosner, 1974), chords (Locke & Kellar, 1973), and musical intervals (Burns & Ward, 1973; Siegel & Sopo, 1975, also see Chapter 8, this volume). Further, categorical perceptual boundaries are present in other modalities (Miller & Morse, 1976), and in the acoustic mode they are present for speech sounds in nonspeaking animals (Morse & Snowden, 1975; Sinnott, Beecher, Moody, & Stebbins, 1976, Walter & Wilson, 1976).

All this suggests that categorical perception is a property of the perceptual cognitive apparatus that is extensively utilized in the codification of information originating in the surrounding world. Its prevalence in speech is a consequence of the consistency and universality of human speech sounds, all of which have developed in accordance with pre-established neural mechanisms.

Perception of speech sounds seems to be hierarchically organized, as many other types of perception (Palmer, 1977). In the case of speech, one can distinguish initially between two levels of analysis: auditory and phonetic (Studdert-Kennedy, 1974). Auditory analysis extracts basic psychophysical parameters of pitch and intensity. For this, no specialized lateralization of perceptual apparatus is necessary. Phonetic analysis, closely lateralized, identifies and analyzes information in terms of phonetic features. Verbal deafness represents a disorganization of this later level with at least a relative preservation of the auditory analysis. Still higher perceptual units and processing levels are operative in speech analysis. Semantic, lexical, and syntactical contexts facilitate perception by limiting the number of possible alternatives and by allowing the listener to predict likely outcomes. Perception in this sense becomes largely a problem of recognition, by matching the incoming stimuli with internal templates (analysis by synthesis) (Neisser, 1967). One can easily see how similar phenomena could be operative in music at levels of motives, thematic, rhythmic configurations, harmonic patterns, musical forms, the stylistic characteristics.

IV. GENERAL COMMENTS

A. Neuroanatomical Basis of Musical Functions

With regard to the localization of lesions in cases of disorders of music perception and performance, the following generalizations may be proposed: sensory and perceptual disorders seem to be related to lesions in the temporal lobe of either hemisphere (for a recent review, see Ullrich, 1978). Pure cases of sensory amusia without aphasia are likely to correspond to right-sided lesions. The neuropsychological structure for sensory and perceptual deficits varies. Damage to the left side often generates combinations of aphasia and amusia in which amusia shows a neuropsychological structure that varies from perceptual to symbolic or lexical musical disorders. Musical abnormalities that are usually called expressive have a neuropsychological structure of greater complexity and, as is the case with language production, involve complex perceptual, mnemonic, lexical, and programmative tasks of greater variety and temporal duration. Correlation with locus of lesion is uncertain, and lesions may invo;ve temporal as well as frontal and even parietal regions. To the extent that musical disorders affect temporally organized programs and the nature of the task is related to linguistic functions or vocalization, lesions tend to predominate in the left hemisphere.

In many professional and even amateur musicians, overlearned and automated tasks are frequently spared. These are tasks performed by the average individual only through careful analysis or orderly sequential programming, which in musicians are partially automatisms. This may have important implications in terms of the neural substrates involved.

Some authors have suggested that deficits in music perception are related to right hemisphere lesions whereas deficits in musical expression are more often due to left-sided damage (Wertheim, 1969). This view needs to be examined further: lateralization of functions has developed not only because they are primarily expressive or receptive but rather because required operations need neural substrata "wired" or "programmed" so specifically as to make them impossible to be shared with other functions. Lateralization, as well as physiological or anatomical localization, is the *consequence of specialization*, and this in turn becomes gradually less compatible with sharing. In some cases, specialization and functional segregation result from an expansion in the amount of data to be processed, while in other cases these may be the result of the peculiar nature of the computation that needs to be performed (i.e., temporal order as opposed to spatial distribution). Nonverbal auditory perception may not require detailed exploration in terms of serial order processing. Instead, great effort may be required to extract the components of the stimulus and to decipher its configuration and cognitive *content*.

Despite the fact that all music displays itself "in time," the temporal perceptual task of the listener who hears the recurring rhythmic clusters of a popular tune is quite simple: it consists in merely discovering and identifying a musical segment of very short duration that consists of repetition of a rhythmic, melodic or timbral pattern with hardly any harmonic, instrumental, or contrapuntal complexity. Hardly any analysis of the information is needed, and usually the perceptual task is performed by analysis-by-synthesis as well as by comparing the incoming information against previously stored and familiar abstract models (Deutsch, 1978). Perceptual tasks of this degree of complexity and variability can be performed by units of configurations that are performed well by the right hemisphere. However, perception of more elaborate music requires a greater awareness of the temporal articulation and relation of musical components. One must be aware of thematic elements required to be stored in memory; of melodic, rhythmic or harmonic developments; of contrapuntal relation of voices; of tonal modulations that shift the tonal resting point; of subtle changes in instrumentation; and of the harmonic and formal structure of the total work of music. As suggested by dichotic listening studies several perceptual operations of this higher degree of complexity in music are preferentially performed by the right ear, left hemisphere processes. Bever (1980) has reached similar general conclusions with regard to the factors that determine lateralization of functions. Studying the operations involved in language and music perception and discriminating holistic from operational ones, he concludes that these correspond better with their right or left preferential processing than by assignment of the total function to either hemisphere.

Executive functions (i.e., singing, complex rhythmic tasks) are fundamentally dependent on serial temporal and *sequential* organization and may depend on processing systems that were lateralized very early (Divenyi & Efron, 1975).

Trained musicians tend to regard music as an ongoing series of interrelated events over longer periods of time (Bever & Chiarello, 1974; Gordon, 1978; Johnson, 1977; Locke & Keller, 1973). This perception requires short- and long-term memory (Deutsch, 1977), internal perceptual representations (Warren, 1974), and strategies of temporal organization similar to that that we observe in motor skills or verbal syntax. When this indepth analysis is required, the evidence indicates that trained musicians tend to process music with their dominant hemisphere (Bever & Chiarello, 1974; Locke & Kellar, 1973; but also Zatorre, 1979).

Thus, it is plausible to hypothesize that in the process of learning musical tasks that involve sequential programs, analogous to most of language, speech or praxis, there would be an initial tendency to share specialized neural processors with most of the other functions. Thus, the preferential left hemisphere *lateralization* found in musicians would be due both to the cognitive "linguistic" structure of classical music, the need for *their* processing along *syntactical algorithms* and in general to cognitive operations that imply related computations and prelearned internal representations.

However, it is also plausible to hypothesize that when such musical programmatic activities are to be developed to a still greater degree (as could be the case in professional composers), new conflicts in processing would arise, and the neurobiological tendency would then be for the development of specialized musical processors that become totally independent from other functions. This often happens to each of us with respect to speech and language. Although in this case there are important genetic, functional, and even anatomical preadaptations (Lenneberg, 1967, 1975; Geschwind & Levitsky, 1968; Marin et al., 1979), it is clear—as demonstrated by the vicarious function of the minor hemisphere following lesions of the dominant hemisphere in infancy and early childhood—that the anatomical substrates to be assigned are not fixed until the function begins to develop. The variability in the degree of separation of the various specialized musical processors in individuals with different degrees of musical sophistication may explain the equal variability in the *lateralization* of musical functions as reflected by cases of severe aphasia unaccompanied by any noticeable alteration of musical abilities. (For a more extensive discussion of neurobiological issues in relation to lateralization of language and cognition, see Marin, 1976; Marin and Gordon, 1979a,b.)

B. Perspectives for a Neuropsychological Study of Disorders of Musical Function

The optimistic view of classical neurology that musical functions are clearly localized has not been verified. Not only are fixed anatomical representations unattainable for the various aspects of musical perception, memory, or performance, but even basic musical operations—such as chord or melody perception and identification, music reading, or vocalization—seem to be fairly complex processes that are manifested with considerable individual variability (Barbizet, Duizabo, Enos, & Fuchs, 1969; Deutsch, 1978; Dowling, 1972, 1978; Gordon, 1970, 1974). The uncertainty surrounding the field of neuropsychology of music has been attributed to various factors. Many authors comment that because of the lack of standards for musical ability in the normal population as compared with those for speech and language, writing, or reading, one cannot anticipate whether a particular musical discrimination or performance should be expected in an otherwise normal individual. Not only is it difficult to evaluate the capacities of the musically unsophisticated, but in the amateur musician, or even in the professional, it is difficult to obtain strict criteria for normal performance. Experience with professional musicians reveals the uneven distribution of musical talents, acquired skills, or even understanding of the rules of music as a combinational system of perceptual forms. It is not at all clear that the same musical problem is processed by all musicians in the same way with equal depth or even that the problem would be solved by different musicians following similar and consistent cognitive strategies.

Some authors hope that the neuropsychological study of music will advance when studies employ more systematic and sophisticated methods of examination. Improvements have been proposed by many authors (Dorgeuille, 1966; Grison, 1972; Jellinek, 1956; Ustveldt, 1937; Wertheim and Botez, 1959). No essential argument against this approach can be made; however, it should be noted that when a similar approach was adopted in early studies of aphasia, no real progress was achieved merely by sharpening the details of examination. Real progress in the study of aphasia was not forthcoming until we began to uncover the basic structure of language (see for instance, Head, 1926; Weisenburg & McBride, 1935). Just as an elaborate study of phonetic discrimination would in itself fail to provide a better understanding of speech and language production, it is also unlikely that exhaustive psychophysical analysis of rhythmic interval, perception, or intensity discrimination will tell us anything meaningful about musical processing. Substantial headway in the neuropsychology of music can be achieved only with the study of those levels of perception and memory that are truly musical and could serve as a basis for musical information processing schemas. Recent reviews (Deutsch, 1978) and the results of research reported in the present volume indicate that a sufficient basis exists for undertaking such neuropsychological studies. Even so, this progress does not necessarily indicate that a better understanding of musical neuropsychology will delineate "musical centers" or even less well-delineated anatomical substrates for music. Music can be conceived as a communication between composer and listener through an interpreter.

The musical message contains both a *cognitive* and an *emotional* component, and the full effect of such communication is achieved only if what was conceived by the composer is reproduced in the listener's mind. The *medium* is a construction of acoustic configurations of diverse complexity and duration. The basic *cognitive structures* are abstract mental auditory forms that the composer creates and combines, following rules imposed by stylistic traditions. The *acoustic realization* is a performance that is sometimes modified by the idiomatic constraints of various modes of musical expression. As is the case in other branches of aesthetics, the degree of emotional arousal achieved by different individuals has little to do with the formal complexity or subtlety of the music heard. For the unsophisticated person, cognitive complexity of music has no significant correlation with its enjoyment and even less with the emotional changes that the music may induce. People tend to enjoy music more when it is familiar and when its rules of organization are balanced between that which can be predicted with some degree of accurate anticipation and some modest ingredient of novelty (Pribram & Melges, 1969).

Correlation between enjoyment of music and its cognitive complexity is functional for the musically initiated individual. For such an individual, musical language is fully discriminated and is allowed to interact with the individual's own prelearned internal models, thus extending the individual's enjoyment to a gamut of emotions that involve the whole of his or her cognitive experience (Meyer, 1956; Berlyne, 1971). But more often, all that is required for musical familiarity and enjoyment is the simple repetition of easy-to-recognize melodies or rhythmic patterns. Rules of organization and cognitive structure are important ingredients of music, but this degree of complexity is a matter that solely concerns and satisfies the composer, the intellectual, or sophisticated interpreter, or the analytical musicologist who sees in the musical medium an increasingly complex linguistic-like system. The universality of music is a function of its ability to arouse emotions through some organized system of sound patterns, but the complexity of a musical structure may or may not add to its function in communicating emotion. Esthetic pleasure may depend on perceptual cognitive forms and relations, but the emotional effect is largely incorporated into the musical message by a number of expressive changes in the sound that are interpreted culturally by the listener in very much the same way as are other nonverbal modes of communication (e.g., gestures, mimicry). As in speech, the emotional content of music depends greatly on dynamic changes, contour emphasis, agogic accents, vibrato, rubato, changes in intensity and speed, and even on tasteful exploitation of the inaccuracies and idiomatic limitations of the instruments of expression. All these factors add to the cognitive musical structure an intentiality that permits the listener to detect an emotional meaning (Blumenthal, 1977). Notice that in this process of musical performance, the discrepancy between the abstract musical model and its realization can be substantial (Deutsch, 1978).

Music differs radically from language and speech in the following way: linguistic complexity, in phonological lexical or syntactic terms, is directly related to the effect of the communicative message. Full production of the verbal message is achieved by complete programming of all the cognitive linguistic structures. Furthermore, aside from rules that regulate the temporal flow in which a linguistic message needs to be encoded (syntax), language is largely a stable referential symbolic system that represents our knowledge of the world. Lexical items (words) are symbols that exist not only by themselves in phonological terms, but also as representatives for their referents. So far as these lexical-referential linkages are fixed and the combinatory rules (syntax) are constant and universal for all languages, one can predict that its computations are made through a similarly stable series of psychological processes. From this we would predict some regularity in the corresponding physiological substrates of these processes (Marin, 1976; Marin & Gordon, 1979a,b).

This is not the case in music: Here we are dealing with a system of communication in which each piece of music consists of a few nonreferential items that are combined according to the prevailing stylistic "syntactic" rules of harmony, melody, timbre, rhythm, or musical form. Music is thus a game of combinatory acoustical constructs that the brain of the composer can conceive and that the listener should be able to learn or discover. For the latter, the intelligence of the communication resides in processing the musical message in such a way as to gain conscious or unconscious access to the rules and its forms (Rozin, 1976). Contemporary music, by making use of new combinatory rules and the great novelty of its acoustical units and clusters, obliges the listener to expend greater effort in perceptual preparation and learning. The cognitive challenge in these circumstances require perceptual learning, and it is similar to that which Warren (1974) has described for other nonverbal sound sequences (see Chapter 4).

If neuropsychologists studying language have found it increasingly difficult to confirm the fixed anatomical localizations predicted by classical neurological models, one should anticiapte that the instability of formal musical units and their combinatory rules might make such precise localizations essentially impossible. These fixed anatomical representations are concepts of the past, because the progress that is being made in the structural psychology of music (reviewed extensively in this volume) offers new approaches for the study of the neurological basis of perception of musical structures.

A review of the types of disorder of musical function due to localized cortical lesions reveals that the traditional clinical classifications are too broad. Grouping symptoms of differing complexity under the same nosological clinical heading does not facilitate an understanding of the neuropsychological processes involved in musical function. For this purpose, musical deficiencies could instead be arranged in a hierarchical order. By borrowing some basic principles from the neuropsychology of language and the psychology of music to establish this order, we can distinguish disorders of psychological, categorical, perceptual, lexicosymbolic, and programmative types. Such a classification would distinguish:

1. *Disorders at the acoustical-psychophysical level:*
   perception of stimulus onset and offset
   perception of changes in intensity
   perception of changes in pitch
   sound localization

perception of arousal, orienting response, habituation
perception of sound spectra or timbre
perception of temporal auditory features (Divenyi & Efron, 1979; Hirsch, 1959)
2. *Disorders of precategorical auditory perception:*
perception of transition changes (Tallal & Newcomber, 1978)
interval perception
chord perception (Gordon, 1970)
pitch discrimination
intensity discrimination, agogic, and dynamic changes
visual perception (for music reading)
visual spatial orientation (for music reading)
timbre discrimination
3. *Disorders of categorical perception of musical elements:*
categorical identification of intervals (Burns & Ward, 1973; Siegel & Sopo, 1975)
categorical identification of chords (Deutsch, 1969; Locke & Kellar, 1973)
perception of melodies (Ward, 1970)
categorical perception of octaves and semitonal subdivision of octaves
scale perception
octave equivalence
perception of rhythmic patterns
4. *Disorders of perception of musical configurations:*
melody perception (Dowling, 1979), identification of motives and themes chord
    articulation
melodic cluster perception (Deutsch, 1978), melodic transformation (Dowling,
    1972)
tonal and modal changes, modulation
timbre recognition and identification of instruments
rhythmic discrimination and motor reproductions of rhythm
5. *Symbolic musical processes:*
apprehension of meaning of musical symbols
naming of notes, solfeggio
identification and naming of intervals, chords, and rhythms
singing with vocalization
6. *Learning complex musical perceptual or executive functions:*
harmonic spatial orientation (in the sense of Schenker), harmonic pivots, har-
    monic rhythms (Piston, 1948), sequences, and harmonic changes
thematic melodic and rhythmic transformations (Dowling, 1972), thematic
    hierarchy and developments
recognition of musical form
stylistic characteristics of melodies, rhythm, use of harmonic functions, use of
    instruments
recognition of characteristics of individual composers
recognition of individual musical
tactile-praxic loop automatisms (Sudnow, 1978)

This tentative outline would not serve the pragmatic goals of the clinician who searches for a nosology of clinical or anatomical predictive value. A neurological grid systemization would only offer a tentative frame for a process oriented study of musical abnormalities.

REFERENCES

Alajouanine, T., & Lhermitte, F. Les désorganizations des activités expressives du langage dan l'apahsie. Report at the *VIIth International Congress of Neurology, Rome, 1961.*

Alajouanine, T., & Lhermitte, F. Aphasia and physiology of speech. In *Disorders of communications*, Proceedings of the Association Research Nervous and Mental Disorders, Vol. 42. Baltimore, Maryland: Wilkins, 1964.

Albert, M. L., Sparks, R., von Stockert, T., & Sax, D. A case study of auditory agnosia: Linguistic and non-linguistic processing. *Cortex*, 1972, *8*, 427-443.

Albert, M. L., & Bear, D. Time to understand: a case study of word deafness with reference to the role of time in auditory comprehension. *Brain*, 1974, *97*, 373-384.

Arnold, G. Cortikale Hörstorung bei Leitungsaphasie. *Monatschrift Ohrenheilkunde*, 1943, *79/80*, 11-27.

Assal, G. Aphasie de Wernicke chez un pianiste. *Revue Neurologique*, 1973, *29*, 251-254.

Barbizet, J. Role de l'hémisphère droit dans les perceptions auditives. In J. Barbizet, M. Ben Hamida, & P. Duizabo (Eds.), *Le monde de l'hémiplégie gauche*. Paris: Masson, 1972.

Barbizet, J., Duizabo, Ph., Enos, G., & Fuchs, D. Reconnaisance de messages sonores: bruits familiers et airs musicaux familiers lors de lésions cérébrales unilatérales. *Revue Neurologique*, 1969, *121*, 624-630.

Barrett, A. A case of pure word-deafness with autopsy. *Journal of Nervous and Mental Disease*, 1910, *37*, 73-92.

Basso, A., Casati, G., & Vignolo, L. A. Phonemic identification defect in aphasia. *Cortex*, 1977, *13*, 84-95.

Benton, A. L. The Amusias. In M. Critchley & R. A. Henson (Eds.), *Music and the brain*. Springfield, Illinois: Thomas, 1977.

Berlyne, D. E. *Aesthetics and psychobiology*. Appleton, New York, 1971.

Bever, T. G., & Chiarello, R. J. Cerebral dominance in musicians and non musicians. *Science*, 1974, *185*, 537-539.

Bever, T. G. Broca and Lashley were right: Cerebral dominance is an accident of growth. In D. Caplan (Ed.), *Biological studies of mental processes*. Cambridge, Massachusetts: MIT Press, 1980.

Blumenthal, A. L. *The process of cognition*. Englewood Cliffs, New Jersey: Prentice-Hall, 1977.

Blumstein, S. E. *A phonological investigation of aphasic speech*. The Hague: Mouton, 1973.

Blumstein, S. E. The perception of speech in pathology and ontogency. In A. Caramazza & E. B. Zurif (Eds.), *The acquisition and breakdown of language: Parallels and divergencies*. Baltimore, Maryland: Johns Hopkins University Press, 1977.

Bouillaud, J. B. Sur la faculté du langage articulé. *Bulletin de l'Academie de Medicine*, 1865, *30*, 752-768.

Botez, M. I., & Wertheim, N. Expressive aphasia and amusia. *Brain*, 1959, *82*, 186-202.

Brazier, M. Du trouble des facultés musicales dans 1-aphasie. Etude sur les représentations mentales des sons et des symboles musicaux. *Revue de Philosophie*, 1892, *34*, 337-368.

Burns, E. M., & Ward, W. D. Categorical perception of musical intervals. *Journal of American Acoustical Society of America*, 1973, *54*, 596.

Cramer, K. Zur Lehre der Aphasie. *Archiv fur Psychiatrie & Nervenheilkunde*, 1891, *22*, 141-160.

Cutting, J. E., & Rosner, B. S. Categories and boundaries in speech and music. *Perception & Psychophysics*, 1974, *16*, 564-570.

Dalin, O. Betattelse om en dumbe som kan slunga. K. Swenka Wetensk. *Academia Hand inguar*, 1745, *6*, 114 (cited by Benton, 1977).

Déjèrine, J. Sur la localisation de la cécité verbale avec intégrité de l'écriture spontanée et sous dictée; cécité verbale pure. *Semaine médicale*, 1892, , 88-89. (a)

Dejerine, J. Des variétés de cécité verbale. *Memoires de la Societé de Biologie*, 1892, 27, 1. (b)

Deutsch, D. The Psychology of Music. In E. C. Carterette & M. P. Friedman (Eds.), *Handbook of perception*, Vol. X, Perceptual Ecology. New York: Academic Press, 1978. Pp. 191-224.

Deutsch, D. Memory and attention in music. In M. Critchley & R. A. Henson (Eds.), *Music and the brain*. London: Heinenmann, 1977.

Divenyi, P. L., & Efron, R. Spectral versus temporal features in dichotic listening. *Cortex*, 1979.

Dorgeuille, C. *Introduction a l'étude des amusics*. Thesis, Faculty of Medicine of the University of Paris, France, 1966.

Dowling, W. J. Recognition of melodic transformations: Inversion, retrograde and retrograde-inversion. *Perception & Psychophysics*, 1972, *12*, 417-421.

Dowling, W. J. Scale and Contour: Two components of a theory of memory for melodies. *Psychological Review*, 1978, *35*, 341-354.

Dupre, E., & Nathan, M. *Le langage musical: étude médicopsychologique*. Paris: Alcan, 1911.

Edgren, J. G. Amusie (musikalische Aphasie). *Deutsche Zietschrift der Nervenheilkunde*, 1895, *6*, 1-64.

Eimas, P. D., Signeland, E. R., Jusczyk, P., & Vigorito, J. Speech perception in infants. *Science*, 1971, *171*, 303-306.

Eimas, P. D., & Corbit, J. D. Selective adaptation of linguistic feature detectors. *Cognitive Psychology*, 1973, *4*, 99-109.

Eimas, P. D. Auditory and linguistic processing of cues for place of articulation by infants. *Perception & Psychophysics*, 1974, *16*, 513-521.

Feuchtwanger, E. *Amusie. Studien zur Psychologie der akustischen Wahrnehmung und Vorstellung und ihrer Strukturgebiete besonders in Musik und Sprache*. Berlin: Springer, 1930.

Finkelnburg, F. C. Asymbolie. *Berliner klinishe Wochenschrift*, 1870, *7*, 449-451.

Geschwind, N., Quadfasel, F., & Segarra, J. Isolation of the speech area. *Neuropsychologia*, 1965, *6*, 327-340.

Geschwind, N., & Levitsky, W. Human brain: left-right asymmetries in temporal speech region. *Science*, 1968, *161*, 186.

Gordon, H. W. Hemispheric asymmetries in the perception of musical chords. *Cortex*, 1970, *6*, 387-398.

Gordon, H. W. Auditory specialization of the right and left hemispheres. In M. Kinsbourne & W. L. Smith (Eds.). *Hemispheric disconnection and cerebral function*. Springfield, Illinois: Thomas, 1974.

Gordon, H. W. Left hemisphere dominance for rhythmic elements in dichotically-presented melodies. *Cortex*, 1978, *14*, 58-70.

Gowers, W. R. On a case of simultaneous embolism of central retrieval and middle cerebral arteries. *Lancet*, 1875, *2*, 794-796.

Grison, B. *Étude sur les alterations musicales an cours des lesions hémisphèriques*. Doctoral Thesis. University of Paris, Faculty of Medicine de Creteil, 1972.

Head, H. *Aphasia and kindred disorders of speech*. London and New York: Cambridge University Press, 1926.

Hemphill, R. E., & Stengel, E. A study on pure word-deafness. *Journal of Neurology and Psychiatry*, 1940, *3*, 251-262.

Henschen, S. E. *Klinische und anatomische Beiträge zur Pathologie des Gehirns*. Teil 5: Ueber Aphasie, Amusie und Akalkulie. Stockholm, Nordiska Bokhandeln, 1920.

Henschen, S. E. On the function of the right hemisphere of the brain in relation to the left in speech, music and calculation. *Brain*, 1926, *49*, 110-126.

Hirsh, I. J. Auditory perception of temporal order. *Journal of the Acoustical Society of America*, 1959, *31*, 759-767.

Jeger, J., Weikers, N. J., Sharbrough, F. W., & Jeger, S. Bilateral lesions of the temporal lobe: A case study. *Acta Oto-Larygngologica Supplement*, 1969, *258*.

Jeger, J., Lovering, L., & Wertz, M. Auditory disorder following bilateral temporal lobe insult: Report of a case. *Journal Speech and Hearing Disorder*, 1972, *37*, 523-535.

Jellinek, A. Zur Phäna menologie der Amusie. *Jahrbuch fur Psychiatry & Neurologie*, 1933, *50*, 115-127.

Jellinek, A. Amusia. *Folia Phonetica*, 1956, *8*, 124-149.

Johnson, P. R. Dichotically-stimulated ear differences in musicians and nonmusicians. *Cortex*, 1977, *13*, 385-389.

Jossmann, P. Die Beziehungen der motorischen Amusie zu den apraklischen Storungen. *Monatshrift für psychiatrie und Neurologie*, 1927, *63*, 239–274.

Klein, R., & Harper, J. The problem of agnosia in the light of a case of pure word deafness. *Journal of Mental Sciences*, 1956, *102*, 112–120.

Kleist, K. Gehirupathologische und localisatorische Ergebrisse über Hörstörungen, Geräuschtaubheiten und Amusien. *Monatschrift fur Psychiatrie und Neurologie*, 1928, *68*, 853–860.

Kleist, K. *Gehirnpatologie*. Leipzik: Johann Ambrosius Barth, 1934.

Kleist, K. *Sensory aphasia and amusia, the Myeloarchitectonic Basis* (English translation by F. J. Fisch & J. B. Stanton). Oxford: Pergamon, 1962.

Knoblauch, A. Ueber Störungen der musikalischen Leistungs-fähigkeit infolge von Gehirnläsionen. *Deutsches Archiv für Klinische Medizin*, 1888, *43*, 331–352.

Kogerer, H. Worttaubheit, Melodientaubheit, Gebärdenagnosie. *Zeitschrift für Neurologie und Psychiatrie*, 1924, *92*, 469–483.

Kohl, G. G., Tschabitscher. Uber einen Fall von Amusie. *Wiener Zeitschrift für Nervenheilkunde*, 1952, *6*, 219–230.

Laignel-Lavastine, M. M., & Alajouanine, T. Un cas d'agnosie auditive. *Revue Neurologique*, 1921, *37*, 194–198.

Lenneberg, E. H. *Biological Foundation of Language*. New York: Wiley, 1967.

Lenneberg, E. H. In search of a dynamic theory of aphasia. In E. H. Lenneberg and E. Lenneberg (Eds.), *Foundation of language development: A multidisciplinary approach*, Vol. 2. New York: Academic Press, 1975.

Lischtheim, M. L. On aphasia. *Brain*, 1885, 7, 433–484.

Locke, S., & Kellar, L. Categorical perception in a non-linguistic mode. *Cortex*, 1973, *9*, 355–369.

Luria, A. R., Tsvetkova, L. S., & Futer, D. S. Aphasia in a composer. *Journal of Neurological Science*, 1965, 2, 288–292.

Mahoudeau, D., Lemoyne, J., Dubrisay, J., & Caraes, J. Sur un cas d'agnosie auditive. *Revue Neurologique*, 1956, *95*, 57.

Mahoudeau, D., Lemoyne, J. F., Foncin, J. F., & Dubrisay, J. Considérations sur l'agnosie auditive. *Revue Neurologique*, 1958, *99*, 454–471.

Marchand, M. L. Surdi-mutité par lésion symétrique du lobe temporal. *Bulletin de la Societé Anatomique de Paris*, 1904, *6*, 473–475.

Marin, O.S.M. Neurobiology of Language: An overview. *Annals of the New York Academy of Sciences*, 1976, *280*, 900–912.

Marin, O.S.M., & Gordon, B. Neuropsychologic Ascpects of Aphasia. In H. R. Tyler & D. M. Dawson (Eds.), *Current neurology*, Vol. 2. Boston, Massachusetts: Houghton Mifflin, 1979. (a)

Marin, O.S.M., & Gordon, B. The production of language and speech from a clinical neuropsychological perspective. In G. E. Stelmach (Ed.), *Tutorials in motor behavior*. NATO Advanced Study Institute of Motor Learning and Control, June, 1979, Sénanque, France. Amsterdam: North Holland Publ., 1979. (b)

Marin, O.S.M., Schwartz, M. F., & Saffran, E. M. Origins and distribution of language. In M. S. Gazzaniga (Ed.), *Neuropsychology*, Vol. 2. New York: Plenum Press, 1979.

Marler, P. An ethological theory of the origin of vocal learning. *Annals of the New York Academy of Sciences*, 1976, *280*, 386–395.

Meyer, L. B. *Emotion and meaning in music*. Chicago, Illinois: University of Chicago Press, 1956.

Miller, C. L., & Morse, P. A. The heart of categorical speech discrimination in young infants. *Journal of Speech & Hearing Research*, 1976, *19*, 578–589.

Misch, W. Über Corticale Taubheit. *Zeitschrift der Neurologie & Psychiatrie*, 1928, *115*, 567–573.

Morse, P., & Snowdon, C. An investigation of categorical speech discrimination by Rhesus monkeys. *Perception & Psychophysics*, 1975, *17*, 9–16.

Neisser, V. *Cognitive psychology*. New York: Appleton, 1967.

Nielsen, J. M. Agnosia. In A. B. Baker (Ed.), *Clinical neurology*, Vol. 1. New York: Harper, 1962.

Nottebohm, F. A. A zoologist's view of some language phenomena with particular emphasis on vocal learning. In E. H. Lenneberg & E. Lenneberg (Eds.), *Foundations of language development*, Vol. 1. New York: Academic Press, 1975.

Palmer, S. E. Hierarchical structure in perceptual representation. *Cognitive Psychology*, 1977, 9, 441–474.

Piston, W. *Harmony* (2nd ed.) New York: Norton, 1948.

Pötzl, O. Zur pathologie der Amusie. *Zietschrift fur Neurologie & Psychiatrie*, 1939, 165, 187–194.

Pötzl, O., & Uiberall, H. Zur Pathologie der Amusie. *Wiener Klinical Wochenschrift*, 1937, 50, 770–775.

Pribram, K. H., & Melges, F. T. Psychophysiological basis of emotion. In P. J. Vinken and G. W. Bruyn (Eds.). *Handbook of clinical neurology*, Vol. 3, Disorders of higher nervous activity. Amsterdam: North Holland Publ., 1969.

Proust, A. De l'aphasia. *Archives Generales Medicine*, 1872, 1, 147.

Proust, A. Archives generales de Medicine. Cited by Henschen (1920), 1866.

Quensel, F., & Pfeifer, R. A. Über reine sensorische Amusie. *Zeitschrift für der Gesamte Neurologie & Psychiatrie*, 1923, 81, 311–330.

Reinhold, M. A case of auditory agnosia. *Brain*, 1948, 73, 203–223.

Reinhold, M. An analysis of speech perception in word deafness. *Brain & Language*, 1976, 3, 209–228.

Richter, H. E. Akustischer Funktionswandel bei Sprachtaubheit. *Archiv Psychiatrie & Nervenkrankheiten*, 1957, 196, 99–113.

Rozin, P. The evolution of intelligence and access to the cognitive unconscious. In *Progress in Psychobiology & Physiological Psychology*, Vol. 6. New York: Academic Press, 1976.

Saffran, E. M., Marin, O.S.M., & Yeni-Komshian, G. H. An analysis of speech perception in word deafness. *Brain & Language*, 1976, 3, 209–228.

Schneider, G. E. Two visual systems. *Science*, 1969, 163, 895–902.

Schwartz, M. F., Marin, O.S.M., & Saffran, E. M. Dissociations of language functions in dementia: A case study. *Brain & Language*, 1979, 7, 277–306.

Shallice, T., & Warrington, E. K. The possible role of selective attention in acquired dyslexia. *Neuropsychologia*, 1977, 15, 31–41.

Siegel, W., & Sopo, R. Tonal intervals are perceived categorically by musicians with relative pitch. *Journal of the Acoustical Society of America*, 1975, 57, 511.

Simon, H. A. The architecture of complexity. *Proceedings of the American Philosphical Society*, 1967, 106, 467–482.

Sinnott, J. M., Beecher, M. D., Moody, D. B., & Stebbins, W. C. Speech sound discrimination by monkeys and humans. *Journal of the Acoustical Society of America*, 1976, 60, 687–695.

Souques, A., & Baruk, H. Autopsie d'un cas d'amusie (avec aphasie) chez un professeur de piano. *Revue Neurologique*, 1930, 37, 545–556.

Spreen, O., Benton, A. L., & Fincham, R. W. Auditory agnosia without aphasia. *Archives of Neurology*, 1965, 13, 84–92.

Studdert-Kennedy, M. The perception of speech. In T. Sebeock (Ed.), *Current trends in linguistics*, Vol. 12. The Hague: Mouton, 1974.

Sudnow, D. *Ways of the hand*. Cambridge, Massachusetts: Harvard University Press, 1978.

Tallal, P., & Newcombe, F. Impairment of auditory perception and language comprehension in dysphasia. *Brain & Language*, 1978, 5, 13–24.

Ulrich, G. Interhemispheric functional relationships in auditory agnosia. *Brain & Language*, 1978, 5, 286–300.

Ustvedt, H. I. Über die untersuchunghen musikalischen Functionen bei Patienten mit Gehir leiden, besonders bei Patienten mit Aphasie. *Acta Medica Scandinava Suppl.* 1937, 86.

Vignolo, L. A. Auditory agnosia: a review and report of recent evidence. In A. L. Benton (Ed.), *Contributions to clinical neuropsychology*. Chicago, Illinois: Aldine, 1969.

Walthard, L. Bemerkungen zum Amusie-Problem. *Schweizer Archiv fur Neurologie & Psychiatrie*, 1927, 20, 295–315.

Ward, W. D. Musical perception. In J. Y. Tobias (Ed.), *Foundations of modern auditory theory*, Vol. 1. New York: Academic Press, 1970. Pp. 407–447.

Warren, R. M. Auditory temporal discrimination by trained listeners. *Cognitive Psychology*, 1974, 6, 237–256.

Waters, R., & Wilson, W. Speech perception by Rhesus monkeys: The voicing distinction in synthesized labial and velar stop consonants. *Perception & Psychophysics*, 1976, *19*, 285–289.

Weisenburg, T. H., & McBride, K. E. *Aphasia*. New York Commonwealth Fund, 1935.

Weiskrantz, L., Warrington, E. K., Sanders, M. D., & Marshall, J. Visual capacity in the hemianopic field following a restricted occipital ablation. *Brain*, 1974, *97*, 709–728.

Wertheim, N., & Botez, M. Plan d'investigation des fonctions musicales. *L'Encèphale*, 1959, *48*, 246–254.

Wertheim, N., & Botez, M. I. Receptive Amusia: A clinical Analysis. *Brain*, 1961, *84*, 19–30.

Wertheim, N. Disturbances of the musical functions. In L. Halpern (Ed.), *Problems of dynamic neurology*. Jerusalem: Jerusalem Press, 1963.

Wertheim, N. The amusias. In P. J. Vinken & G. W. Bruyn (Eds.), *Handbook of clinical neurology*, Vol. 4. Amsterdam: North-Holland Publ., 1969.

Wertheim, N. Is there an anatomical localization for musical faculties? In Critchley, M. & Henson, R. A. (Eds.), *Music and the brain*. Springfield, Illinois: Thomas, 1977.

Yates, A. J. Delayed auditory feedback. *Psychological Bulletin*, 1963, *60*, 213–232.

Zatorre, R. J. Recognition of dichotic melodies by musicians and non-musicians. *Neuropsychologia*, 1979, *17*, 607–617.

16

Music Performance

John A. Sloboda

I.   Introduction 479
II. The Nature of Performance Plans 480
III. Acquisition of Performance Plans 483
     A. Memorization 483
     B. Improvisation 483
     C. Transcription 484
IV. The Role of Feedback in Performance 488
V.   Social Factors in Performance 491
VI. Summary 494
     References 494

I. INTRODUCTION

This review examines four central questions about music performance. First, how do we best characterize what it is that someone knows when he or she is able to perform a piece of music? Second, how does this person acquire that knowledge? Third, what use does the performer make of perceptual feedback in controlling his or her performance? Fourth, how is music performance affected by social and situational factors? These questions are central for two reasons. First, they relate to all varieties of music performance, regardless of music type, production mode, or cultural setting. Second, they reflect general psychological concerns that are fundamental to the study of any human skill. Several authors (e.g., Martin, 1972; Shaffer, 1976) have argued that music performance can be seen as a member of a family of skills that includes speech and typing, and whose underlying mechanisms share important features.

II. THE NATURE OF PERFORMANCE PLANS

Whenever someone performs a piece of music, he or she is translating a mental representation or plan of the music into action. We all have such plans. They allow us to sing or hum tunes we know as we go about our daily affairs. What kind of plan is necessary to execute these everyday acts? One possibility would be a list of actions in a specific order and of specific durations. A gramophone record could be seen as one embodiment of such a plan. Each execution of that plan by the same reproduction equipment results in exactly the same performance. Most human beings, however, do not perform music in exactly the same way on each occasion. They are capable of effecting substantial, systematic, and controlled variation in performance. For instance, most people are able to sing a known tune from any starting note within their range (Attneave & Olson, 1971) and are able to comply with requests to sing faster or louder. In addition, someone who knows a piece of music well enough to sing it can usually, without relearning, thereby whistle, hum, or transfer it to an instrument on which he or she is competent, and, if literate, write it down in musical notation.

These observations suggest that a performer's basic plan is something more abstract than a list of actions to be executed and that this plan can be realized in an indefinite number of ways. It seems that the diversity of outputs that can result when a person decides to perform a tune closely resembles the diversity of inputs from which a person can recognize the same tune. Thus, performance theories are constrained in similar ways to theories of recognition (D. Deutsch, 1969). Given these constraints, we could take the performer's plan to be a list of items in which the pitch, duration, and intensity of each note is specified *relative* to other notes. Before such a plan could result in action, absolute values of these dimensions would need to be assigned to the plan, and the appropriate motor actions would then be determined by reference to knowledge about the specific performance mode being used (voice, instrument, etc.).

The performance variations described so far have a common property, that of *context-free* application. In other words, each variation applies in the same way to each note. When a tune is sung faster, each note is shortened by the same proportion; when a tune is sung in a different key, the pitch of each note is raised or lowered by the same proportionate amount, and so on. Some of the most significant variations in music performance are, however, highly *context-sensitive*. These variations are often called *expressive* and include such techniques as rubato, pitch fluctuation, variations in attack, and timbre. It is these variations that prevent performances from appearing "deadpan," and performers are generally able to vary the degree of expressiveness to suit the requirements of a situation.

For instance, a professional musician practicing a piece to improve his or her technical grasp of it will probably use less expression than in concert, even though overall speed and intensity remain the same. The point about expressive variations is that they cannot be applied either to all notes in a piece of music or to a randomly chosen subset of notes.

Rubato is a deviation from strict tempo, but not any deviation comprises true rubato.

It matters both which notes rubato is applied to and also what kind of deviation is effected (i.e., whether the note comes earlier or later than it should and by how much). The classical conception of rubato is of a variation in tempo that, while bending the basic metrical pulse, does not destroy it (Schoenberg, 1964, pp. 25–40). Thus, for instance, rubato is probably more effectively applied to subsidiary stresses rather than main stresses. Similarly, expressive sharpening or flattening should probably be avoided on notes that are crucial for determining the tonality of a passage. A performance plan that is adequate as a basis for effective expressive variation must therefore contain information about the rhythmic and tonal structure of the music. In such a plan individual notes cannot be thought of as simply separate items standing in some fixed relationship to other individual notes. Rather they must be thought of as elements within superordinate structures whose nature determines the functions of the items. It is hard to see how a musician could perform expressively, except by rote-learning a set of expressive "tricks" for each new piece, unless his or her knowledge of the music were couched in terms of these structures. Sight-reading an unedited score expressively would certainly be impossible.

The view that abstract structural representation is fundamental to musical cognition has motivated work in artificial intelligence by Longuet-Higgins (1972, 1976), Steedman (1977), and Winograd (1968); and some empirical consequences of this view have been explored by Martin (1972) and Shaffer (1976).

Shaffer (1976) discusses keyboard playing in particular, when the two hands play separate notes simultaneously. Keyboard music (e.g., a Bach fugue) is often best described in terms of two or more independent but temporally overlapping, melodic lines whose structures are to a certain extent dissociated from one another, although they will share superordinate features such as meter and tonality. If a performer organizes his or her playing on the basis of a plan that reflects these structures, this performer should, for instance, be able to apply expressive variation to the several lines independently. Certainly expert performers give the impression of being able to do this, while novices tend to apply variation indiscriminately to all simultaneously played notes. Shaffer (1981) presents the first results of a research program examining these specific issues.

Empirical studies on performance variations of this kind are few despite the long availability of the technical means for accurately recording such variations (Seashore, 1938). A difficulty with Seashore's (1938) methods is that they produce visual records by mechanical means. These records must be analyzed by eye before any useful quantitative data can be obtained. More recently methods have been developed of transferring performance details directly to computer, thus making complex analysis much easier (Liberman, Olive, & Zukofsky, 1977; Michon, 1974; Shaffer, 1981). Michon (1974) reports a finding of some interest. He recorded four performances of Eric Satie's *Vexations*, a piece in which the same short motif is played 840 times in succession. He found considerable within-subject variation in the speed at which the motif was played. There was also considerable deviation from strict metricality. He found a "clearcut relationship" between speed and the nature of the deviation from metricality, although the relationship is not described in detail. The result shows, however, that alterations in speed are *not* achieved simply by altering the absolute durations of notes whose relative durations are specified in the performance plan. Rather, relative durations must be altered for different performing speeds if the same *rhythmic* pattern is to be communicated.

Gabrielsson (1973) analyzed the performances of three expert musicians asked to perform notated rhythms with strict metricality. He discovered certain regular deviations from strictness. For instance, when two eighth-notes appeared in a sequence of quarter-notes, the duration of the first note was always shorter than the second. Liberman *et al.* (1977) argue that such deviations are inevitable if a performer is to communicate rhythmic information to a listener. How else, for example, is a listener to tell whether a sequence of six equally intense notes is to be thought of as two groups of three notes or as three groups of two notes? Notation often answers such questions for a music reader (Gregory, 1978; Sloboda, 1978b), but the reader–performer must translate his or her perceptions into distinctive actions if a listener is to achieve the same perception. The communicative effectiveness of such actions by pianists of varying standards is currently being studied by this author.

Although many facts about music performance demand the existence of a highly abstract performance plan, it would be a mistake to look for such a plan in every instance of music performance. Sometimes the degree of performance variation is less than that that an abstract plan would allow. For instance, a musician competent on two instruments (say flute and oboe) need not always be able to transfer a piece of music from one instrument to the other without some specific practice, in which fingerings were worked out, and so on. Sometimes instrumental performers seem to learn complex fast passages as highly integrated movement patterns that "fall to pieces" if taken at a different speed. Pianists experience considerable difficulties if asked to transpose a piece learned in one key to a new key (Moore, 1962, Chapter 26). Their knowledge of specific motor actions seems to interfere with their transposition efforts. One could multiply such examples indefinitely. What they suggest is a hierarchy of levels of abstraction such that, according to circumstance or accomplishment, performance plans can exist at a higher or lower level in the hierarchy.

In general, what we would call "musicianship" seems to entail the ability to mobilize the higher, more abstract levels in a wide variety of circumstances. "Technique" would, then, be the elimination of "noise" in the transformation of the plan through successively lower levels. For instance, rubato is only possible for performers who both know where they want variation and also have achieved fine enough control over the timing of finger movements to effect this variation accurately.

The above considerations make unclear the extent to which musicological descriptions of musical structure (e.g., Cooper & Meyer, 1960; Forte, 1962) also describe psychological structures in the perception and performance of music (Laske, 1975; Perkins & Howard, 1974). They should certainly be able to provide a rich source of hypothesis to direct future empirical research. It must not, however, be assumed that they have psychological reality for all performers in all situations.

III. ACQUISITION OF PERFORMANCE PLANS

The ways in which performance plans are acquired can be divided into three broad categories: memorization, improvisation, and transcription.

A. Memorization

Very often memorization is a seemingly passive process. One hears a tune several times, and then one is able to reproduce it. Most people have experienced the phenomenon of having a snatch of melody "running around in the head." It is sometimes such an inconsequential fragment that they wish they could forget it. On other occasions, the memorization is more deliberate: conscious strategies are invoked to commit the music to memory. In the case of a lengthy work, such a process may take a musician many months. This process has not been studied in depth by psychologists, even though it is of intense interest as an example of a highly complex cognitive achievment. Nonetheless, there exists some incidental data on errors and transformations in musical memory that shed a little light on the memorization process. For instance, ethnomusicologists have shown that tunes handed on by oral tradition suffer significant transformations over geographical and temporal distance (Cohen & Cohen, 1973; Kolinski, 1969; Seeger, 1966; Sundberg & Lindblom, 1976). Such studies show that contour and overall tonality are often preserved while chromatic notes and passing notes are often removed or added. Furthermore, tunes that migrate from one culture to another are often transformed so as to conform with special harmonic and other formal conventions of that culture. It seems that Bartlett (1932) might well have used serial reproduction of tunes rather than of stories to demonstrate the thesis that memory is a constructive process in which people bring their internal schemata to bear on material presented to them (Dowling, 1978).

Errors that show such transformations occurring in the individual can be found in the performances by young children of songs they have learned. For instance, they frequently make the intervals smaller than they should be, while preserving rhythm and contour (Moog, 1976), although it is not clear how many of these errors are attributable simply to poor voice control. A rather different example of a memorization error will be well known to musically literate churchgoers. The hymn tune "St. Denio" contains a line that, in standard hymn books, is notated as shown in Fig. 1(a). Arguably, every competent church organist therefore plays it this way. Every congregation, however, sings it as in Fig. 1(b), unless they have been specifically drilled not to. It seems that their cognition of the melodic structure is such that they "infer" the added passing note (marked *).

B. Improvisation

Improvisation is analogous to spontaneous speech. In improvisation a novel piece of music is generated according to an underlying set of rules that constrain the final form

Fig. 1. The hymn "St. Denio" (a) as written and (b) as usually sung.

to a greater or lesser degree. This characterization seems to fit musical improvisation no matter what cultural setting is involved. It applies equally to Western jazz (Ostransky, 1977, Chapter 3), the singing of Yugoslavian epic poetry (Lord, 1960; Parry, 1971) and Indian sitar music (Menuhin, 1976, pp. 257–260). Excellence in improvisation results from having "at one's fingertips" a large repertoire of procedures or options for accomplishing some end result within a limited time. In this respect it resembles fluent public speaking, or rapid mental calculation (Hunter, 1979). In such performances, one can often not know the best step to take unless one has determined the result of the previous step. For instance, one may not be able to choose an appropriate closing sequence in a jazz improvisation until one knows where the previous sequence will lead and how much time is available to get "back to base." In mental calculation one can often only take a certain short cut if one can determine that the result of a certain operation will have a certain property, say that of being divisible by 11. The door-to-door sales representative must find rapid answers to novel objections, and so on. Thus, it is clearly not enough for an improviser to know how his or her performance must be structured (e.g., that he or she must negotiate a given chord sequence in a given time); the improviser must have rapid access to a large and well-organized body of knowledge.

Typically, the mediocre improviser solves "real time" problems by choosing "moves" from a restricted and unadventurous set of options, producing a result that is repetitive and uninventive. Even the expert improviser will have a distinctive "style" that reflects the way his or her improvisatory repertoire is chosen from the infinitely large set of possible options (Stewart, 1973).

As with memorization, the complexity of improvisatory skill seems to have inhibited experimental investigation and psychological theorizing. Most workers have chosen to examine a more tractable task, that of transcription.

C. Transcription

Transcription is the name given to the family of activities in which presentation of musical material in one mode (auditory or visual) is immediatly followed by production in another mode (written, vocal, or instrumental). Transcription from auditory input usually occurs only within the context of formal tests of musical attainment. For instance, most college music students are examined in their ability to write down or sing a melody played over once or twice. It is also widely used as a method of teaching songs in the classroom: the teacher will sing a phrase of the song and get the class to sing it back (Franklin, 1972, pp. 89–97). Nonetheless, it is not used to any great extent in real performing situations. Transcription from written or printed text, however, is widely used in music performance. Many contemporary professional musicians perform from text to the near exclusion of any other form of performance.

No definite line can be drawn between transcription and memorization since there is always *some* time lag in transcription between input and output. Also many music readers use printed text to augment existing long-term knowledge of the music acquired from previous exposure to it. It is not uncommon to observe professional performers glance at their music only once or twice each page. In such cases, the text seems to be assisting recall rather than providing new information.

The auditory transcription task approximates to the standard short-term memory paradigm in experimental psychology. Most published research on musical short-term memory, however, has used recognition, rather than recall, measures. This literature has been reviewed by Deutsch (1977) and Dowling (1978) and goes a considerable way towards establishing the salient dimensions along which listeners discriminate and classify melodies. It does not necessarily provide a basis for understanding how listeners asked to recall melodies will memorize them. Unpublished recall data obtained by this author suggests that unskilled adults seldom retain the contour, pitch ratios, or tonality of the original in any simple way. Rather, fragments of a melody are distorted and recombined in complex ways to make up a response that is often, on any simple analysis, quite unlike the original. A method is needed of capturing unfocused intuitions about recall in a formal description procedure before any real sense can be made of such data. The recent explosion of methods for analyzing prose recall (e.g., Bower, 1976; Kintsch, 1976; Harris & Terwogt, 1979) offers some encouragement in this direction.

Transcription from text is usually continuous so that the performer is reading one note while executing another note read earlier. Typically, a good sight-reader will execute a note about 2 sec after reading it. This estimate is derived from studies of the eye–hand span (EHS) in proficient instrumental performance (Sloboda, 1974a, 1977). In these studies subjects were asked to read melodies at predetermined speeds. On each trial the text was removed at a precise point in the performance known in advance to the experimenter only. Subjects had to continue playing until they had executed all the music read up to that point in time. The EHS of each subject was obtained by counting the number of notes played after the text was removed. The EHS of good readers was typically six or seven notes while that of poorer readers was only three or four notes. In addition, EHS was affected by the nature of the material being read. It decreased for meaningless (atonal) material and showed a tendency to expand or contract to coincide with phrase boundaries. It was hypothesized, therefore, that the greater span of fluent readers is related to the ability to perceive superordinate structures in the text. If, indeed, knowledge of such structures is necessary for forming adequate performance plans, it follows that psychologically effective units in the melodies used must comprise six notes or less on average since the reader would need to identify at least one whole unit before starting to perform it.

Evidence confirming the importance of structural units in reading comes from studies of eye movements in piano sight-reading carried out by Weaver and his associates (Van Nuys & Weaver, 1943; Weaver, 1943). They showed that the sequence of fixations is to some extent determined by the nature of the music. Contrapuntal music, in which horizontal sequences of notes are structurally significant, elicited more horizontal fixation sequences. Homophonic music, in which vertical chords are structurally significant, elicited more vertical fixation sequences. Thus, proficient readers tend to take in a complete musical unit in a series of successive fixations rather than sample from two or more units concurrently. This is an optimal strategy for performance if it is important to identify the next structural unit as quickly as possible.

Transcription errors also reveal something about the performance plan. Although some errors are clearly due to "peripheral" factors (indistinct text, tremor, miscalculated leaps, etc.) a substantial body of sight-reading errors can be explained only by recourse to structural considerations. Wolf (1976) describes one case in which a misprint in a frequently played piano score went unnoticed for many years. Most readers unconsciously substituted the musically correct note for the misprint. It was only when a poor reader actually played what was printed and was criticized for so doing, that the misprint was brought to light. Sloboda (1976b) studied this "proofreaders' error" in an experiment where little-known, highly conventional classical keyboard pieces were rewritten so as to introduce a large number of deliberate notational pitch errors. These errors were distributed equally between the two staves and between various positions in musical phrases. Subjects were proficient readers whose instructions were to play the pieces exactly as written. Not a single subject was able to comply with this request. All restored some errors to their original pitch without noticing it. In addition, on a second playing of the same pieces, subjects made even more unconscious restorations. So, it seems that sight-readers' performance plans are not simple transcriptions of the printed page; rather they also take account of musical "grammar" in order to allow a musically correct performance to result from a musically incorrect score. Another finding was that most restorations occurred in the middle of musical phrases. Exact transcription was most likely at beginnings and ends of phrases. It may be argued that, in this type of music, beginnings and ends of phrases carry most information, whereas middles are, to a certain extent, determined by the surrounding context and the rules of music. Thus, proficient readers seem to have developed selective strategies for transcribing text that correspond to structural constraints in the music.

Written transcription of pitch notation has been studied in several experiments by Sloboda (1976a, 1978a). Subjects were presented with briefly exposed arrays of pitch symbols on staves that they then had to attempt to reproduce onto blank staves. Since the basic transcription skill can be taught in a few minutes, this procedure allowed the comparison of music readers with musical illiterates. Two main results were ob-

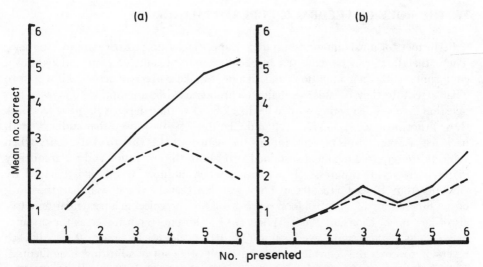

Fig. 2. Mean number of notes correctly reported as a function of number of notes displayed (a) at an exposure duration of 2 sec and (b) at an exposure duration of 20 msec. Full lines are musicians; dashed lines are nonmusicians. Adapted from Sloboda (1974a).

tained. When exposure duration was as long as 2 sec, a gross superiority in exact recall was shown by the musicians (Fig. 2a). For instance, when six items were presented, many musicians recalled all six correctly while many nonmusicians recalled one or none correctly. Second, when exposure duration was as short as 20 msec, there was no difference between subject groups in the number of notes correctly recalled [Fig. 2(b)], but musicians were significantly better at preserving the contour of the stimulus pattern. These results suggest that musicians are employing two types of coding procedure not available to nonmusicians. First is a rapid identification of contour (which could be useful in performance, for example, when planning direction of hand movement). Second is a slower identification of the exact position of component notes that allows access to abstract musical codes for holding the notes in memory. These processes allow musicians to overcome memory limitations that prohibit nonmusicians from transcribing much more than one note at a time.

Indirect confirmation that pitch symbols are coded in different ways by musicians and nonmusicians comes from laterality studies by Oscar-Berman, Blumstein, & De Luca (1976) and Salis (1980). In both studies musicians displayed right visual field superiority for report of tachistoscopically presented musical notation. In contrast, report of dot patterns (which would include pitch symbols as seen by nonmusicians) typically shows left-field superiority (McKeever & Hulig, 1970; Salis, 1977). Thus, a shift in hemispheric involvement seems to result from the processing of visual patterns in a musical mode, suggesting mobilization of different cognitive mechanisms. This resembles shifts found when visual material is coded verbally (Cohen, 1977, Chapter 8). Other analogies between language and music reading are discussed more fully by Sloboda (1974a, 1978b).

IV. THE ROLE OF FEEDBACK IN PERFORMANCE

Performers of music intend to produce a specific auditory experience in listerners. They, therefore, can be expected to check that the results of their actions are in conformity with their intentions and, if not, to take corrective action. How and to what extent do they do this? A major technique used in attempting to answer this question involves disrupting normal feedback by providing delayed auditory feedback (DAF). For instance, J. A. Deutsch and Clarkson (1959) showed that auditory feedback has a crucial role in determining the nature of the vibrato that occurs when subjects are required to sing a sustained note. Both the amplitude and the frequency of pitch change is progressively increased when auditory feedback is delayed by amounts from .10 sec up to .50 sec: They postulate that the vibrato is in part the result of the functioning of a control loop serving to keep the voice on a particular note (see also Clarkson & Deutsch, 1966). When DAF is absent, pitch traverses the distance between its highest and lowest value (one half-cycle) about every .10 sec. If each reversion towards the central pitch is the result of a control adjustment, as Deutsch and Clarkson argue, these adjustments must be made every .10 sec. Rostron (1976, 1978) has argued that such control of the vibrato should be increasingly disrupted by DAF of up to .10 sec and should show no systematic effect with longer delays. He failed to find any effect of DAF below .10 sec and argues that the data are more consistent with an "envelope" theory of pitch control in which less frequent pitch adjustments (about every .50 sec) are superimposed on vocal tremor produced independently of the control loop (e.g., by "physiological wobble" or intensity fluctuations).

However, as Clarkson and Deutsch (1978) point out, the conditions under which DAF is presented are crucial for determining whether the subject will actually use it to control his or her performance. For instance, subjects are less likely to do so if they can still hear their own immediate auditory feedback (IAF) or if the DAF is distorted. Since different methodologies were used in the two laboratories, it is hard to know whether DAF was functioning equivalently in the two situations. However, an observation by Rostron (1978) suggests that the dispute may not have great relevance to most music performance situations. When a sung note is initiated, pitch fluctuation is extreme for the first .50 sec until it reaches the "steady state" studied above. In much vocal music many notes do not last significantly longer than .50 sec, and some last for much less time. Since these initial fluctuations appear to settle rapidly on the intended note, singers must be making control corrections considerably earlier than .50 sec after note onset. Thus, the dispute outlined above turns on whether a rapid control loop is switched off after about .50 sec and not on whether the control loop exists.

A more realistic performance situation has been studied by Gates, Bradshaw, and Nettleton (1974). Keyboard players learned to perform pieces as fast as they were able under normal feedback conditions. They were then required to play the pieces with IAF and DAF presented simultaneously. It was found that total playing time increased for all delays between .10 and 1.05 sec, although the maximum increase occurred at about .20 sec. One cause of the increased playing time was the tendency to repeat individual notes or to insert an extra note that, for instance, extended a scale passage one note beyond its correct conclusion. The fact that insertions and repetitions never comprised more than a single note suggests that auditory feedback is, in this instance, applied to the level of performance organization in which motor commands for playing individual notes are specified rather than to higher levels in which performance units or groups are specified. If the latter were the case, one might expect repetitions or disruptions of whole groups of notes.

Gates and Bradshaw (1974) had subjects play on the keyboard of an electronic instrument whose speakers could be switched off to eliminate IAF. This condition produced performance indistinguishable from one in which IAF was provided, although both these conditions were superior to conditions in which DAF was present. This is an important result since, if it does not matter whether or not subjects obtain IAF when DAF is absent, the disruption caused by DAF can hardly be due *simply* to interference with IAF. The situation must also make it impossible to use whatever cues are used in the absence of IAF (i.e., kinesthetic or visual feedback). One possible explanation for the effect would be that "auditory capture" operates such that whenever a discrepancy arises between feedback from hearing and some other modality, hearing dominates. It would be interesting to know whether vision dominates over touch in the absence of auditory feedback. This could be tested by presenting delayed visual feedback through a television monitor. There is reason to suppose that vision *is* important for performance, even when auditory feedback is available.

An indirect argument in favor of the importance of vision is that performers who cannot inspect the movements responsible for sound production (i.e., singers) seem to be at a particular disadvantage to other performers (i.e., instrumentalists) when it comes to the acquisition of technique. Singing teachers are more prone than most to resort to prescriptions (e.g., "try to sing more in the head") that turn out to have no meaningful physical or physiological basis (Sundberg, 1974). These prescriptions may, nevertheless, be necessary psychological aids for the singer in conceptualizing his or her actions.

More direct evidence for the importance of vision is provided by studies that show that augmented visual feedback can have quite striking effects on the acquisition of technical skills. For instance, Tucker, Bates, Frykberg, Howarth, Kennedy, Lamb, and Vaughan (1977) describe a computer based interactive aid for musicians that allows a passage played on the keyboard of an electronic organ to be displayed visually in a modified notation that reflects the exact duration of the notes played. With the aid of this feedback, a pianist of concert standard improved his performance of a triple trill quite dramatically within minutes (Fig. 3). Similarly, Basmajian and Newton (1974) showed that with visual electromyographic biofeedback, wind players learned within minutes to suppress or activate specific parts of the buccinator muscle in the cheek. Singers can also be helped in a similar way (Fourcin & Abberton, 1971).

One important aspect of performance that musicians must control is the intensity of sound produced. Composers do not often specify absolute values for intensity, but they establish relative levels of intensity through the use of conventional dynamic instructions. The most frequently used, in order from softest to loudest, are pianis-

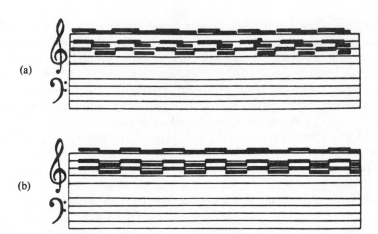

Fig. 3. Triple trill played by concert-standard pianist (a) when first played and (b) as played within minutes of visually and aurally interacting with the system. From Tucker *et al.* (1977).

simo, piano, mezzopiano, mezzoforte, forte, and fortissimo. Such a classification demands that a performer be able to perform with at least six discriminable levels of intensity. Patterson (1974) describes some studies of the intensity ranges of professional symphony orchestra players. It appears that intensity changes of as much as 5 decibels go unnoticed in musical performance; therefore, performers need to span an intensity range of at least 30 decibels if they are to get the six basic dynamic levels across to listeners. Such a range is certainly within the capability of most instruments. However, in a sample of professional bassoonists asked to produce their loudest and softest comfortable notes, the largest difference found was 17 decibels, a range capable of encompassing only three dynamic levels. In defense of these players, it has sometimes been claimed that performers achieve perceptible changes between dynamic levels by altering the quality (timbre) rather than the intensity of their sound, at least in some situations. This could not be the case in the studies described by Patterson since listeners were unable to distinguish between notes produced under differing dynamic instructions when playback intensity was equal for each note. Thus, it appears that professional players may not be making effective dynamic changes at points where the composer demands it. This suggests *either* that their own use of auditory feedback is more sensitive than that of most listeners, that they are using inappropriate feedback (such as how hard they feel themselves to be blowing), or that they are simply not using feedback at all. Lack of dynamic range among performers of all standards is such a common phenomenon that it seems unlikely that the difficulty is technical. It could be that, for some reason, intensity is not a highly salient dimension of feedback for performers.

A final type of feedback relates to ensemble playing, where performers need to keep their playing in synchrony with that of other performers. In rigidly metrical music, this problem is, maybe, not serious, but in music in which the speed fluctuates (as in a rallentando) the performer needs to make complex predictions about when the next note of a colleague is going to come on the basis of previous notes. For example, a pianist accompanying a singer may well find that the singer introduces different degrees of tempo fluctuations in successive performances of the same song. The expert accompanist is rarely "thrown" by this. Experimental studies of synchronization are at present being carried out by Vos.[1] In these studies a human subject and a computer attempt to tap in synchrony with one another. By varying the models on which the computer bases its attempts at synchrony, it is hoped to discover which one "fits" the human performer most precisely.

V. SOCIAL FACTORS IN PERFORMANCE

Very often a musician is performing with or for other people. The performance situation and the musician's perception of that situation can have a profound effect on the performance itself. Perhaps the most well-known example of this is the phenomenon of "stage fright," an unpleasant state of nervousness experienced before and during public performance by many musicians. This state can have physiological correlates that are highly detrimental to the skilled motor control required in many performance situations (e.g., muscle tremor, excessive sweating). Bochkaryov (1975) studied contestants in international music competitions and found that although the less successful contestants displayed more anxious behavior and reported feeling more nervous than successful contestants, they did not appear to show more arousal (as measured by galvanic skin response, temperature, and heart rate). Rather, the distinctive feature of the successful contestants was a heightened arousal *during* the performance as compared to just prior to performance. In contrast, less successful contestants showed little difference in before performance and during performance measures. Bochkaryov hypothesizes that successful contestants are those who are able to mobilize arousal specifically for their performance, whereas the less successful suffer from a nonspecific arousal that they cannot control and that manifests itself as stage fright.

Since the physiological correlates of stage fright seem mainly a result of the action of the sympathetic nervous system and since these very correlates often confirm the performer's feeling of impending failure thus increasing anxiety further, it has occurred to some that the circle might be broken by the use of drugs that inhibit the action of the sympathetic nervous system while leaving central nervous system functions unimpaired. A suitable drug for this purpose would be one of the β-adrenoceptor-blocking drugs such as oxprenolol (Turner & Hedges, 1972). James, Griffith, Pearson, and Newbury (1977) administered either oxprenolol or a placebo at random to 24 music students just before a stressful public performance. On the

---

[1]Vos, P. G. Synchronization in duo tapping tasks. Paper in preparation. Psychologisch Labatorium, Katholieke Universiteit, Erasmuslaan 16, Nijmegen, The Netherlands.

second day of testing, those who had received the placebo on the first day now received the drug and vice versa. The performances were rated by two professional musicians who did not know which subjects had received the drug. It was found that oxprenolol caused a significant improvement in performance over the placebo condition. It also caused a significant fall in pulse rate measured immediatly before performance. Finally, the subjects who received the drug reported feeling calmer before the recital and happier with their performance.

It appears, then, that oxprenolol has a double effect on performance. One is purely physiological: it affects mechanisms associated with detrimental phenomena such as tremor. The other is cognitive (and resembles the effect described by Schacter and Singer (1966) but in reverse). Because performers perceive themselves to be less "trembly" than usual, they conclude that they are less worried about their performance and are able to set about the performance with greater confidence. The existence of drugs such as oxprenolol is bound to raise ethical problems for performers, especially in competitive situations, since it can be argued that those who resort to drugs have an unfair advantage over those who attempt to control nervousness consciously. On the other hand, there may be constitutional factors that make the control of nervousness easier for one performer than for another. In this case, the naturally placid performer has the unfair advantage.

In many performing situations there is not just one performer "pitted against" a more or less threatening audience; there is instead a group of performers involved in a cooperative effort, and, so, the performers themselves can have an effect on one another. The focal point of many Western performing groups is a conductor who rehearses the performers and provides cues for timing, intensity, and expressive playing during the performance itself. A study of the attitudes of professional symphony orchestra players towards their conductors by Faulkner (1973) illustrates the need of a conductor to communicate effectively with and gain the respect of his or her players. Players are very rapidly aware when a conductor is inadequate (although less able to characterize that inadequacy precisely) and respond with sloppy playing and lowered work effort. Effective conductors use a rich array of verbal and nonverbal gestures to guide and respond to their players. Razhnikov (1973) has described and quantified some of the major rehearsal techniques used by a small sample of professional conductors, but little attempt has been made to articulate the nature of the two-way interaction between conductor and players. That a two-way interaction is essential is evident from a remark of one of Faulkner's (1973) subjects:

> They (the poorer conductors) don't communicate. They are of no use to us. And then maybe they're too distant, you can never tell whether you're doing it right or wrong; they never respond when you respond to them. I guess after a while you stop watching them, you stop paying attention to what they're doing.

One of the only studies to examine conductor behavior experimentally (Yarbrough, 1975) yields results that appear to be at odds with the perceptions of Faulkner's (1973) subjects. In Yarbrough's experiment a variable named "conductor magnitude" was manipulated. The "high-magnitude" conductor maintained eye contact with performers, used expressive gestures and facial expressions of approval and disapproval while the "low-magnitude" conductor never looked at individuals and used no expressive gestures or expressions. Each conductor took the same group of singers through an equivalent amount of material chosen from different parts of the same work. It was found that although performers preferred the high-magnitude conductor, there was no effect of magnitude on attentiveness or on performance of the music. Yarbrough concludes that the conductor "is not the source of reinforcement that maintains the appropriate behaviour. Instead it is suggested that music itself functions as the reinforcement which maintains appropriate behaviour."

The reason for this apparent discrepancy is probably that neither the subjects nor the situations in the two studies are really comparable. Yarbrough's subjects were college students in amateur choirs who attended by choice and who were learning new music under a conductor whom they were required to endure for a few minutes only. On the other hand, Faulkner's typical subject was a seasoned professional whose presence at a rehearsal was a contractual obligation, playing music he or she had probably played many times before, under a conductor whom he or she would probably have to endure for many months. It is hardly surprising that the motivations and effective reinforcements for the two groups were rather different. In addition, it is a common feature of amateur singers that they fail to attend to nonverbal cues from a conductor, especially when learning new music. They tend to "bury their heads" in the score and have not learned the trick, second nature to professionals, of looking at the conductor "over the top of their copy." In such circumstances, it is hardly surprising that conductor behavior has so little effect on them.

One of the most elegant demonstrations of the effect of social factors on music performance is a study by Weick, Gilfillian, and Keith (1973). Two jazz bands of equivalent standard were asked to rehearse two new pieces (A and B). These pieces were by the same arranger and were of similar difficulty and style. The crucial experimental manipulation was the description of each piece given to performers prior to the rehearsal. Players were told that they had been invited to try out two pieces that a major publishing company was thinking of promoting. Each piece was accompanied by one of two press releases incorporating a "serious" or a "nonserious" description of the arranger. The serious release imputed high prestige and relevant experience to the arranger while the nonserious release imputed low prestige and little relevant experience to the arranger. In one band, piece A was accompanied by the serious press release and piece B by the nonserious one. In the other band, the press releases were exchanged. The results showed that for both bands, the nonserious piece was less well performed, liked, and remembered. This finding suggests that a significant proportion of the hostility displayed by performers and listeners alike to, for instance, certain styles of contemporary music stems, not from the music itself, but from the perceptions of the credibility of such styles established before hearing the music. And, of course, if performers, through their own attitudes towards a piece of music, perform it badly, the listener is provided with an objective reason for rejecting the music. In other words, performers' evaluations of music are liable to act as self-fulfilling prophecies.

VI. SUMMARY

An adequate theory of music performance must account both for the range of variations in output that a performer can display on successive occasions of executing the same piece of music and also for the limitations on these variations that specific situations impose. The performance plans that most people formulate must be couched, at least in part, in abstract tonal and rhythmic form rather than in terms of specific motor sequences or even sequences of items related by relative pitch and duration. This has consequences for the way in which performance plans are acquired. For instance, memorization and transcription errors can often be accounted for by reference to abstract structural properties of the music. Musical text appears to be read in structural "chunks," and improvisation displays structural regularity. As in all purposive sequential behavior, music performers make frequent checks that their intentions are actually being realized. Delayed auditory feedback disrupts this process while various types of augmented feedback improve performance. Performance plans are not executed in isolation from the rest of the performer's mental apparatus. Optimum levels of attention and arousal are determined by the performer's situation and perceptions of his or her situation. To achieve the best possible performance, a musicians need to avoid the excessive arousal of stage fright while having a positive enough view of their coperformers and the music being performed to allocate adequate attention and effort to their performance.

REFERENCES

Attneave, F., & Olson, R. K. Pitch as a medium: A new approach to psychophysical scaling. *American Journal of Psychology*, 1971, *84*, 147–166.

Bartlett, F. C. *Remembering*. London & New York: Cambridge University Press, 1932.

Basmajian, J. V., & Newton, W. J. Feedback training of parts of buccinator muscle in man. *Psychophysiology*, 1974, *11*, 92.

Bochkaryov, L. L. The psychological aspects of musicians' public performance. *Voprosy Psikhologii*, 1975, *21*, 68–79.

Bower, G. H. Experiments on story understanding and recall. *Quarterly Journal of Experimental Psychology*, 1976, *28*, 511–534.

Clarkson, J. K., & Deutsch, J. A. Effect of threshold reduction on the vibrato. *Journal of Experimental Psychology*, 1966, *71*, 706–710.

Clarkson, J. K., & Deutsch, J. A. Pitch control in the human voice: a reply to Rostron. *Quarterly Journal of Experimental Psychology*, 1978, *30*, 167–169.

Cohen, A., & Cohen, N. Tune evolution as an indicator of traditional musical norms. *Journal of American Folklore*, 1973, *86*, 37–47.

Cohen, G. *The psychology of cognition*. London & New York: Academic Press, 1977.

Cooper, G. W., & Meyer, L. B. *The rhythmic structure of music*. Chicago, Illinois: Chicago University Press, 1960.

Deutsch, D. Music recognition. *Psychological Review*, 1969, *76*, 300–307.

Deutsch, D. Memory and attention in music. In M. Critchley & R. A. Henson (Eds.), *Music and the brain*. London: Heinemann, 1977.

Deutsch, J. A., & Clarkson, J. K. Nature of the vibrato and the control loop in singing. *Nature (London)*, 1959, *183*, 167–168.

Dowling, W. J. Scale and contour: Two components of a theory oa memory for melodies. *Psychological Review*, 1978, *85*, 341-354.

Faulkner, R. R. Orchestra interaction: Some features of communication and authority in an artistic organization. *The Sociological Quarterly*, 1973, *14*, 147-157.

Forte, A. *Tonal harmony in concept and practice.* New York: Holt, 1962.

Fourcin, A. J., & Abberton, E. First applications of a new laryngograph. *Medical and Biological Illustration*, 1971, *21*, 172.

Franklin, E. *Music Education: P ychology and Method.* London: Harrap, 1972.

Gabrielsson, A. Performance of rhythm patterns. *Scandinavian Journal of Psychology*, 1974, *15*, 63-72.

Gates, A., & Bradshaw, J. L. Effects of auditory feedback on a musical performance task. *Perception & Psychophysics*, 1974, *16*, 105-109.

Gates, A., Bradshaw, J. L., & Nettleton, N. C. Effect of different delayed auditory feedback intervals on a music performance task. *Perception & Psychophysics*, 1974, *15*, 21-25.

Gregory, A. H. Perception of clicks in music. *Perception & Psychophysics*, 1978, *24*, 171-174.

Harris, P. L., & Terwogt, M. M. A network account of synoptic processes in story recall. In M. M. Gruneberg, P. E. Morris & R. Sykes (Eds.), *Proceedings of the international conference on practical aspects of memory.* New York: Academic Press, 1979.

Hunter, I. M. L. Memory in everyday life. In P. Morris & M. Gruneberg (Eds.), *Applications of memory.* New York: Academic Press, 1979.

James,.I. M., Griffith, D.N.W., Pearson, R. M., & Newbury, P. Effect of Oxprenolol on stage-fright in musicians. *The Lancet*, 1977, *2*, 952-954.

Kintsch, W. Memory for prose. In C. N. Cofer (Ed.), *The structure of human memory.* San Francisco, California: Freeman, 1976.

Kolinski, M. "Barbara Allen": Tonal versus melodic structure, part II. *Ethnomusicology*, 1969, *13*, 1-73.

Laske, O. E. On psychomusicology. *International Review of the Aesthetics and Sociology of Music*, 1975, *6*, 269-281.

Liberman, M. Y., Olive, J. P., & Zukofsky, P. Studies of metric patterns. *Journal of the Acoustical Society of America*, 1977, *62*(supplement no. 1), 44.

Longuet-Higgins, H. C. Making sense of music. *Proceedings of The Royal Institution of Great Britain*, 1972, *45*, 87-105.

Longuet-Higgins, H. C. Perception of melodies. *Nature (London)*, 1976, *263*, 646-653.

Lord, A. B. *The singer of tales.* Cambridge, Massachusetts: Harvard University Press, 1960.

Martin, J. G. Rhythmic (heirarchical) versus serial structure in speech and other behavior. *Psychological Review*, 1972, *79*, 487-509.

McKeever, W. F., & Huling, M. D. Right hemisphere superiority in graphic production of briefly viewed dot figures. *Perceptual & Motor Skills*, 1970, *31*, 201-202.

Menuhin, Y. *Unfinished Journey.* London: Macdonald and Jane's, 1976.

Michon, J. A. Programs and "Programs" for sequential patterns in motor behaviour. *Brain Research*, 1974, *71*, 413-424.

Moog, H. *The musical experience of the pre-school child.* London: Schott, 1976.

Moore, G. *Am I too loud? The memoirs of a piano accompanist.* London: Hamish Hamilton, 1962.

Oscar-Berman, M., Blumstein, S., & DeLuca, D. Iconic recognition of musical symbols in the lateral visual fields. *Cortex*, 1976, *12*, 241-248.

Ostransky, L. *Understanding jazz.* Englewood Cliffs, New Jersey: Prentice-Hall, 1977.

Parry, M. *The making of homeric verse.* London and New York: Oxford University Press, 1971.

Patterson, B. Musical Dynamics. *Scientific American*, 1974, *233*, 78-95.

Perkins, D. N., & Howard, V. A. Toward a notation for rhythm perception. *Interface*, 1976, *5*, 69-86.

Razhnikov, V. G. The formation and the reproduction of conductor's intention. *Voprosy Psikhologii*, 1973, *19*, 55-66.

Rostron, A. B. Pitch control in the human voice. *Quarterly Journal of Experimental Psychology*, 1976, *28*, 305-310.

Rostron, A. B. What can you do with your larynx? A rejoinder to Clarkson and Deutsch. *Quarterly Journal of Experimental Psychology*, 1978, *30*, 171-174.

Salis, D. L. Laterality effects with visual perception of musical chords and dot patterns. *Perception & Psychophysics*, 1980, *28*, 284-294.

Schacter, S., & Singer, J. E. Cognitive, social, and physiological determinants of emotional state. *Psychological Review*, 1962, *69*, 379-399.

Schoenberg, H. C. *The great pianists*. London: Gollancz, 1964.

Seashore, C. *The psychology of music*. New York: McGraw Hill, 1938.

Seeger, C. Versions and variants of the tunes of "Barbara Allen." *Selected Reports, UCLA Institute of Ethnomusicology*, 1966, *1*, 120-167.

Shaffer, L. H. Intention and Performance. *Psychological Review*, 1976, *83*, 375-393.

Shaffer, L. H. Performances of Chopin, Bach, and Bartok: Studies in motor programming. *Cognitive Psychology*, 1981, *13*, 326-376.

Sloboda, J. A. Music reading and prose reading: Some comparisons of underlying perceptual processes. Unpublished Ph.D. Thesis, University of London, 1974. (a)

Sloboda, J. A. The eye-hand span: An approach to the study of sight reading. *Psychology of Music*, 1974, *2*, 4-10. (b)

Sloboda, J. A. Visual perception of musical notation: registering pitch symbols in memory. *Quarterly Journal of Experimental Psychology*, 1976, *28*, 1-16. (a)

Sloboda, J. A. The effect of item position on the likelihood of identification by inference in prose reading and music reading. *Canadian Journal of Psychology*, 1976, *30*, 228-236. (b)

Sloboda, J. A. Phrase units as determinants of visual processing in music reading. *British Journal of Psychology*, 1977, *68*, 117-124.

Sloboda, J. A. Perception of contour in music reading. *Perception*, 1978, 7, 323-331. (a)

Sloboda, J. A. The psychology of music reading. *Psychology of music*, 1978, *6*, 3-20. (b)

Steedman, M. J. The perception of musical rhythm and metre. *Perception*, 1977, *6*, 555-570.

Stewart, M. L. Structural development in the jazz improvisational technique of Clifford Brown. Unpublished Ph.D. Thesis, University of Michigan, 1973.

Sundberg, J. Articulatory interpretation of the "singing formant." *Journal of the Acoustical Society of America*, 1974, *55*, 838-844.

Sundberg, J., & Lindblom, B. Generative theories in language and music descriptions. *Cognition*, 1976, *4*, 99-122.

Tucker, W. H., Bates, R. H. T., Frykberg, S. D., Howarth, R. J., Kennedy, W. K., Lamb, M. R., & Vaughan, R. G. An interactive aid for musicians. *International Journal of Man-Machine Studies*, 1977, *9*, 635-651.

Turner, P., & Hedges, A. An investigation of the central effects of Oxprenolol. In D. M. Burley, J. H. Frier, R. K. Rondel, & S. H. Taylor (Eds.), *New perspectives in beta-blockade*. Horsham, England: Ciba Laboratories, 1973.

Van Nuys, K., & Weaver, H. E. Memory span and visual pauses in reading rhythms and melodies. *Psychological Monographs*, 1943, *55*, 33-50.

Weaver, H. E. A study of visual processes in reading differently constructed musical selections. *Psychological Monographs*, 1943, *55*, 1-30.

Weick, K. E., Gilfillian, D. P., & Keith, T. A. The effect of composer credibility on orchestra performance. *Sociometry*, 1973, *36*, 435-462.

Winograd, T. Linguistics and the computer analysis of tonal harmony. *Journal of Music Theory*, 1968, *112*, 3-49.

Wolf, T. A cognitive model of musical sight reading. *Journal of Psycholinguistic Research*, 1976, *5*, 143-171.

Yarbrough, C. Effect of magnitude of conductor behavior on students in mixed choruses. *Journal of Research in Music Education*, 1975, *23*, 134-146.

17

Social Interaction and Musical Preference

Vladimir J. Konečni

I. Introduction 497
II. Effects of Social Stimulation on Aesthetic Choice 502
III. Effects of Information Load and Arousing Nonsocial Stimulation on Aesthetic Choice.... 505
IV. Effects of Listening to Melodies Differing in Complexity on Emotional States and
    Social Behavior 507
V. Listeners' Sequencing and "Chunking" of Musical Materials and the Use of Music for
    Mood Optimization 511
    References 516

I. INTRODUCTION

Studies of aesthetic preference and of the process of appreciation have always represented a major aspect of experimental aesthetics and of the psychology of music and art (e.g., Child, 1969). Experimental work on, and theorizing about, preference for both authentic pieces of music and visual art, on one hand, and for stimulus patterns synthesized specifically for experimental purposes, on the other, have been going on at least since Fechner's (1876) *Vorschule der Ästhetik*, and have had a major boost in the 1960s and 1970s through Berlyne's "new experimental aesthetics" (Berlyne, 1971, 1974) and other influential developments (e.g., Arnheim, 1966; Farnsworth, 1969; Francès, 1958, 1968; Kreitler & Kreitler, 1972; Meyer, 1956). Numerous studies of musical preference have been carried out both early in the century (e.g., Gilliland & Moore, 1924; Moore, 1914) and more recently (e.g., Bragg & Crozier, 1974; Crozier, 1974; Heyduk, 1975; Konečni & Sargent-Pollock, 1976; Overmier, 1962, Simon & Wohlwill, 1968; Steck & Machotka, 1975; Vitz, 1966), and there have been several good reviews and theoretical integrations, which, though greatly varying in breadth, are all helpful for a better understanding of preference (e.g., Berlyne, 1971; Child, 1978; Madsen, 1973; Meyer, 1956; Walker, 1973).

The sheer size of the literature on music preference sometimes obscures the existence of a serious imbalance in terms of the amount of experimental and theoretical attention that has been devoted to various topics that can be reasonably regarded as falling within this area. For example, a great deal of effort seems to have been invested in discovering the exact shape of the function relating preference (in terms of ratings of pleasingness and interestingness, listening time, and various choice measures) to the complexity of authentic and synthesized musical materials (e.g., Berlyne, 1971; Steck & Machotka, 1975; Heyduk, 1975). By comparison, other issues have been almost completely ignored. For example, the vast majority of research studies and most of the theoretical attempts have treated aesthetic preference and choice as if they, and the process of appreication itself, normally occur in a social, emotional, and cognitive vacuum, as if they were independent of the contexts in which people enjoy aesthetic stimuli in daily life. In contrast, one of the main contentions of the present chapter is that a thorough understanding of aesthetic behavior cannot be achieved without examining how it changes as a function of its immediate social and nonsocial antecedents, concurrent cognitive activity, and resultant emotional states (cf. Cantor & Zillman, 1973). Before I examine these points in more detail, it seems useful to speculate about the reasons for the fact that social, emotional, and cognitive context factors have been so consistently ignored.

One possible reason is that psycho-aestheticians have underestimated or failed to grasp the significance of the extent to which music appreciation has been radically altered by the technological and social changes in the twentieth century. Consider first the conditions prevailing in the eighteenth and nineteenth centuries, when non-folk music was performed almost exclusively in the salons of the wealthy and later in the concert halls and opera houses accessible only to the privileged few. Enjoyment of music was a special occasion, something carefully planned in advance, each performance a unique, fleeting event. Contrast that with our times. There is wide availability of relatively low-cost, high-quality equipment for the recording and reproduction of music. There are excellent recordings of an astonishing range of musical pieces. In most large cities of the Western world, there are numerous radio stations specializing in every conceivable type of music and making it available on a 24-hour basis. Consider the amount of time in an average day that so many people spend listening to music—in their homes, offices, and automobiles (even while walking or roller skating!).

As a function of all of these factors taken collectively, a veritable revolution in music appreciation has occurred. Music of all types has become a major part of the lifestyle of a very large number of people.[1] Gone are the days when only the elite could hear high-quality music, while the rest had to await weddings and harvest

---

[1]Although perhaps not quite to the same extent, the advent of television has analogously revolutionized the appreciation of theatrical performances, opera, and ballet, and vastly increased the number of viewers.

festivities to hear any music at all (unless they produced it themselves or were content with bird songs). This situation has been replaced by the penetration of music into every corner of people's lives, literally and metaphorically. Entire generations of youngsters have been brought up on rock-'n'-roll. Social mini-movements and subcultures revolve around music and its association to other mood-optimizers, such as drugs and alcohol.[2] The most frequent, prototypical situations in which people listen to music have shifted from specialized locations, such as opera houses and concert halls, into the informal settings like the home and the automobile.

Perhaps related to this notable disregard for the technological and social changes affecting music appreciation are the prevailing elitist views of what constitutes "serious" music and, especially, which types of music are worthy of serious attention by psycho-aestheticians. Commonly ignored in both the experimental and theoretical work in the psychology of music are even the best examples of the jazz, rock-'n'-roll, and rhythm-and-blues idioms. The typically given reasons why these forms of music are not worthy of study are quite feeble when one considers the imprecision and arbitrariness of the existing formal definitions of what constitutes "serious music," the extent of the disagreement in value judgments among the critics, aestheticians and aesthetes themselves, and the extent to which all definitions and evaluations are culture- and period-bound. Above all, the exclusion of, say, rock-'n'-roll from the pool of music worthy of scientific attention blatantly ignores the obvious fact that it brings a great deal of pleasure to an immense number of people. These people's aesthetic preference and choice are presumably at least as important as those of the minority preferring "serious" music—if one is interested in developing a general theory of music appreciation. Moreover, major aspects of the aesthetic experience (in terms of both the factors affecting choice behavior and the hedonic effects of the music) may well be more similar for the appreciators of Palestrina, Stravinsky, and Led Zeppelin, respectively, than is generally believed.[3]

What seems needed is a broader perspective on music appreciation, one that transcends the narrow, elitist, and arbitrary definitions of what constitutes good and serious music and also takes into account the reality of music appreciation in our time. From this perspective, one of the most important by-products of the dramatic changes in the dominant modes and locations of music appreciation is the fact that music is nowadays so frequently enjoyed in a great variety of *social* contexts. More-or-less

---

[2]The following quotation from a film review by Carol Olten (the *San Diego Union*, 23 Oct. 1980) illustrates this point well, if casually:

> It is doubtful if anyone will truly define how or why rock 'n' roll or the entire area of pop music began to change the fabric of our lives. A groupie—probably a third-generation groupie—in *One-Trick Pony* . . . comes close to some explanation. "Rock 'n' roll kept me sane when I was a child. We were always moving around the country changing houses, changing schools. But on the road I could always turn on the radio and there would be the same rock 'n' roll song playing. It kept me sane, I tell you, sane." Softly, she begins to hum the first few lines of "Me and Bobby McGhee": "From the Kentucky coal mines to the California sun . . ."

[3]Introspections by a subject in an informal study ($N = 1$, myself, and an appreciator, incredibly, of both Bach and the Rolling Stones) have "confirmed" this.

active listening to music has become fully imbedded in the stream of daily life of ordinary men and women. People listen to music while working, talking, eating, engaging in sexual intercourse. That this fact has been ignored by psycho-aestheticians, and that they have continued to think of preference as a process largely unrelated to social situations, is quite remarkable. What music does to people at different times, why they choose to listen to it so much, why they choose a particular type of music while engaged in a particular activity—all of these are important and unanswered questions. They cannot be answered by "speculative aesthetics" (Berlyne, 1971), by philosophical treatments of the "social function" of music and art, or by the hitherto popular types of studies of aesthetic preference. One needs to analyze preference with at least some reference to the typical situations in which music is appreciated, in social contexts, in the presence of friends, lovers, and family members, in the stream of daily life.

Whereas an average person probably rarely goes to a concert of any kind and probably never attends an operatic performance, ordinary days are filled with countless aesthetic micro-episodes—numerous conscious decisions to listen to some type of music by turning on the radio, putting on a record, and so on, and then proceeding to listen. One of the main contentions of this chapter is that the nature of these aesthetic choices, which music people decide to listen to, and for how long are to a very high extent affected by the social context in which the listening occurs. The social activity the listeners are engaged in, whom they are with, and what emotions and moods they are experiencing as a function of the social stimulation emanating from others in their environment are very likely to affect the type of music that is chosen. Furthermore, effects on choice among musical pieces (including computer-generated "melodies" synthesized for research purposes) differing on various stimulus dimensions (e.g., complexity, novelty, surprisingness) can also be reasonably expected to be a function of the nature, difficulty, information-processing requirements, and arousingness of tasks and activities in which a person is concurrently engaged. In short, what I am suggesting is that musical preference and choice may be highly affected by the social, emotional, and cognitive factors leading to, and in, the listening situation.

This point logically leads to another issue largely ignored in the psychology of music. Despite a considerable amount of interesting theoretical work on the relationship between music appreciation and emotion (e.g., Langer, 1942; Meyer, 1956, 1957), there have been few experimental investigations of the very real possibility that not only the listeners' emotional states but also their social behavior and their treatment of others in numerous everyday social micro-episodes may be perceptibly and differentially affected by music. That both subtle and major changes in social behavior may occur as a function of listening to music is another contention of the present chapter.

The two basic propositions made so far are complementary and can be related to each other within the same theoretical framework as components of a prototypical "aesthetic episode." The model assumes that music, and aesthetic stimuli in general—specialized and highly valued as they are—are simply another aspect of a person's acoustic (or visual) environment and that they are chosen largely for the purpose of mood- and emotion-optimization. The model regards a person as being engaged in a constant exchange with the social and nonsocial environment, of which the acoustic stimuli are a part. The social behavior of others—and I am referring to the ordinary, everyday behavioral sequences unambiguously interpreted as indicating social support, love, antagonism, and so on—is assumed to have a profound effect on a person's emotional states, which, in turn, affect aesthetic choices, including the choice of music, that a person will make in a given situation.[4] The degree of enjoyment of the chosen piece presumably varies as a function of the concurrent social and nonsocial micro-environmental conditions (which also may affect the probability of that particular piece being chosen in the future).[5] Listening to music is further assumed to produce changes in the listener's emotional state and thereby affect his or her behavior toward others in the situation. Since social behavior is by definition interactive, it is safe to assume that the behavior directed toward the listener by others will also change, leading to a further modification in the listener's emotional state, and possibly to different subsequent musical choices. The model thus contains a feedback-loop feature representing the ongoing nature of a person's interaction with the social and musical environment—a series of aesthetic episodes mediated by changes in emotional state and mood.

I do not mean to imply that the factors discussed above are likely to override completely the basic individual differences in the preference for different types of music produced by, say, early exposure (see footnote 4). However, these factors can perhaps account for a respectable amount of variance in the choice behavior within the broad preference domains (e.g., classical versus rock-'n'-roll) and also increase the understanding of the reasons for the occasional choice switches across these domains.

Also the aesthetic episodes and musical choices I have been discussing clearly may well be far removed on several dimensions from the profound effects of hearing for the first time a great piece of music, be it Mozart's *Don Giovanni* or the Who's *Tommy*. But how often do such experiences occur, and how many people have them? Music clearly plays an important role in human life, but one is not likely to understand this role and develop a reasonably general theory of music preference, choice, and enjoyment by consistently ignoring the music-related behaviors of the vast majority of listeners. Indeed, a good argument can be made that further progress in the psychology of music hinges on the success of investigations of *mundane* types of aesthetic appreciation and choice, those preceded and accompanied by routine social behaviors and common emotional states.

[4]I am not denying the importance of other factors that may affect aesthetic choice, including availability and the appropriateness of listening to a particular piece of music in a given situation and, of course, a person's basic liking ("musical taste") for different types of music that is presumably affected by a host of factors in the person's upbringing, exposure, cultural conditions, musical education, peer pressure, and so on.

[5]This type of context effect in which aspects of the social environment are assumed to affect the basic liking (preference for a piece of music has been discussed by others—e.g., Child, 1978) and is, of course, a part of the folklore surrounding music preference. Child's example was of a not particularly musically inclined couple who attended a concert while falling in love and found the music divine.

My collaborators and I have so far carried out a number of experiments relevant to the various stages of aesthetic episodes. We have used different experimental paradigms, induced a variety of emotional states in our subjects, and explored the subjects' preferences and choice behavior for pieces of music ranging from computer-generated melodies to authentic musical pieces from the eighteenth, nineteenth, and 20th century, as well as contemporary rock-'n'-roll. These experiments and the analogous studies using visual aesthetic stimuli (e.g., Konečni & Sargent-Pollock, 1977; Sargent-Pollock & Konečni, 1977) should be regarded as only the first tentative steps toward the elucidation of the various components of aesthetic episodes. For one thing, although they examined the relationship between music-related behaviors and some of the social, emotional, and cognitive factors discussed above, they have so far all been laboratory experiments. Putting some of the ideas presented so far to the test, however, should facilitate subsequent field investigations, both those paralleling the laboratory studies and others designed to collect normative data. Such field investigations could perhaps be profitably organized around the basic question of how people's everyday aesthetic choices are influenced by the setting (house, automobile), emotional state (elation, anxiety, depression), information load (conversation, manual work, reading, eating), physical state (fatigue, illness), the type of other people present (family members, other intimates, co-workers), even by atmospheric conditions.

The remainder of this chapter will consist of a brief review of some of our experiments. With a few exceptions, these studies have been previously published; so the main purpose here is to convey the flavor of the research and present some of the conclusions.

II. EFFECTS OF SOCIAL STIMULATION ON AESTHETIC CHOICE

In one study (Konečni, Crozier, & Doob, 1976; also see Konečni, 1979, Section II,A), the subjects were, in the first part of the experiment, repeatedly insulted in the course of working on a task by an accomplice of the experimenter, posing as a subject. Pilot work had shown that this procedure significantly increases various psychophysiological indices of arousal and that, moreover, subjects invariably report themselves as experiencing considerable anger. In the second part of the experiment, seemingly quite unrelated to the first, the subjects, now alone in the room, chose on each of many trials to listen to 10 sec of one of two types of melodies. Both types of melodies were computer-generated; they differed considerably from each other in both objective complexity (or "uncertainty," measured in information-theory terms) and subjective complexity (measured by verbal ratings in pilot studies). The two particular complexity levels were chosen because the normally aroused subjects, experiencing no pronounced emotion, chose to listen to them about equally in pilot studies. Indeed, in the experiment proper, a control group of subjects who had not been insulted by the accomplice showed roughly equal preference for the two types of melodies over trials.

In sharp contrast, subjects who had been insulted chose the simpler of the two types of melodies about 70% of the time, shunning the more complex type. In the third experimental condition, insulted subjects were given an opportunity to retaliate behaviorally against the accomplice prior to the choice measure. In line with predictions from prior research (e.g., Hokanson & Shetler, 1961; Konečni, 1975a), which had shown that retaliation by angry people may reduce arousal level, these subjects' choice behavior was very similar to that of the noninsulted controls.

The pattern of results that was obtained had been predicted on the basis of a great deal of prior research relating arousal, anger, aggression, and collative variables, such as complexity. From the perspective of the present chapter, however, the findings are important insofar as they show that a socially induced change in a listener's emotional state may strongly affect that person's aesthetic choice (i.e., choice between musical stimuli varying in complexity—the first stage of the proposed prototypical aesthetic episode. Moreover, to the extent that the insulted subjects' preference for the simpler type of melody was reduced, brought down to "normal," by retaliation (presumably because this behavior had decreased the level of arousal and the degree of anger), the finding in that condition is also relevant for the feedback-loop aspect of the proposed model regarding the relationship between overt behavior and internal states. A person's socially induced emotional state affects his or her social behavior toward other people; in addition, the execution of actions directed at social targets affects the actors emotional state, which, in turn, regulates subsequent behavior, and so on.

Aesthetic factors fit in this feedback loop in two related ways. First, to the extent that choice between musical stimuli varying on certain dimensions (such as complexity) is affected by fluctuations in emotion and arousal, it follows that the performance or nonperformance of behaviors (such as aggression) that are seemingly totally unrelated to musical preference would turn out to be very relevant (because such behaviors seem to affect emotions and arousal). Second, insofar as listening to musical stimuli varying in complexity may itself differentially affect arousal and emotional state, it follows that music would play an important part in the behavior/internal state/behavior causal sequence.

Some of these hypotheses were further investigated in another experiment involving simple and complex computer-generated melodies, anger, and retaliatory aggression (Konečni, 1979, Section II,B). After being either insulted by an accomplice of the experimenter or neutrally treated by this person, the subjects participated in another task involving the same accomplice in the course of which, on each of many trials, they had the choice of either punishing or rewarding the accomplice by pressing the appropriate button. Unlike the situation in the experiment described earlier, the *aesthetic* consequences *for the subjects* were inextricably linked, on each trial, on their punishment versus reward choice. In the study as a whole, across all seven experimental conditions, there were three possible aesthetic consequences for the subjects: a simple melody, a complex melody, and silence. Different permutations of these three consequences were operative in different experimental conditions. For example, in one of the conditions, whenever a subject pressed the punishment button (supposedly physically hurting the accomplice), he or she heard—for as long as the button was pressed—an example of the simple melody, whereas whenever the subject pressed the reward button, he or she heard—for as long as the button was pressed—an example of the complex melody. In another condition the pairing of the aesthetic consequences with the two behaviors in question was reversed. In still another condition pressing the punishment button yielded silence; this pairing was reversed in a further condition, and so on.

In making the predictions, we found several reasonable assumptions, based on other studies in my laboratory and elsewhere, helpful. One assumption was that in comparison to the noninsulted subjects, the insulted ones would be significantly more inclined to press the punishment button. Another assumption, more relevant to one of the components of the hypothesized aesthetic episode, was that angry subjects would prefer simple to complex melodies both in absolute terms and in comparison to the noninsulted subjects and that their preference for the no-melody (silence) consequence would fall in between.

When these assumptions are put together with other ideas presented so far, quite precise predictions can be made concerning the subjects' aesthetic-choice behavior (i.e., punishment versus reward behavior, since the aesthetic consequences for oneself and behavioral consequences for the social target, the accomplice, where inextricably linked in this experiment). The clearest preference for simple melodies (i.e., the least preference for complex melodies) should be displayed by the insulted subjects for whom listening to simple melodies is linked with the punishment of the accomplice, whereas listening to complex melodies is linked with the reward of the accomplice. At the other extreme should be the insulted subject for whom exposure to simple melodies is linked with the reward of the accomplice, and listening to complex melodies with the punishment of the accomplice. In the former condition, the two motivations (to listen to simple melodies and to punish when angry—an internal and an external consequence of the same behavior) were experimentally made maximally congruent whereas in the latter condition they were maximally divorced. The exact pattern of data for the experiment as a whole would, of course, depend on the relative strengths of the two motives (i.e., their relative strengths as manipulated in this particular experiment) and on the degree of preference for the "silence" consequence, relative to the other two consequences, for the insulted and neutrally treated subjects, respectively.

On the whole the findings closely followed the predictions and thus gave a considerable amount of support to the underlying assumptions that had been based on the previous studies and, more importantly, on the feedback aspect of the aesthetic-episode formulation. The choice between melodies differing in complexity does indeed seem to be affected both by the socially induced emotional states and by the feedback effects on such states from overt actions directed at social targets.

Another way of looking at the results would lead one to stress, perhaps with some surprise, the extent to which the performance of a socially (and presumably biologically) very important behavior—retaliatory aggression—can be modulated by the seemingly subtle differences in the musical consequences for the listener (i.e., aggressor). For example, whereas the insulted subjects who heard a simple melody whenever they punished the accomplice (and a complex melody whenever they rewarded that person) chose the punishment button on 26.6 of the 50 trials on the average, the mean for the equally insulted subjects who heard a complex melody whenever they pressed the punishment button (and a simple melody whenever they rewarded the accomplice) was only 18.8—and this was a statistically highly significant difference. The difference between these two groups in terms of the mean duration of punishments to the accomplice was no less than about 3.8:1.

III. EFFECTS OF INFORMATION LOAD AND AROUSING NONSOCIAL STIMULATION ON AESTHETIC CHOICE

Just as the social aspects of music appreciation have been largely neglected in the psychology of music so far, so has the "cognitive context" in which choice and listening occur. Yet, it would seem clear that in many situations involving listening to music, not all of a listener's attention or processing capacity (Broadbent, 1958; Moray, 1969; Treisman, 1964) is devoted solely to the appreciation of the chosen piece of music. As often as not the person may be concurrently engaged in other intellectual activities or motor tasks. In addition to being intrinsically interesting, the issue of how various intellectual and motor activities affect aesthetic choice seems worthy of investigation for another important reason.

The reason is that there is a possibility that the effect of the socially induced emotional states on aesthetic choice (observed in the experiments discussed so far) is mediated by fluctuations in arousal level. If so, a further question arises. How do gross changes in the arousal system affect the subtle operations presumably involved in aesthetic choice? The missing link may be found through an extension of the views that high levels of arousal impair cue selection and lead to a "narrowing" of attention (e.g., Broadbent, 1971; Easterbrook, 1959). After all, in the experiments described so far as well as in real-life choice situations involving different pieces of music, people do not simply choose one piece over another but actually then proceed to listen to the chosen piece for a time. It is reasonable to assume that listening to a piece of music requires cognitive work; it requires that the components of which the piece of music consists be analyzed and processed, and that their meaning be extracted (e.g., Berlyne, 1971; Günzenhauser, 1962; Moles, 1958; Morris, 1957; Perkins and Leondar, 1977). In the experiments discussed earlier, subjects were well aware before each choice of the information-processing demands of the two types of melodies. In other words, they had a fairly good idea of how much their processing capacity would be taxed in the 10 sec following a particular choice. Similarly, in daily life, when people choose between various pieces of music or between radio stations, they are aware from prior experience of the general characteristics of the piece of music about to be listened to, including its complexity and information-processing requirements. Therefore, it could be hypothesized that the experimental subjects experiencing anger shun complex melodies because these melodies' information content exceeds the subjects' currently available processing capacity (which had been reduced by the elevation of arousal characteristic of anger and other pronounced emotional states).

It therefore seemed of interest to us to examine within the same experiment the effects on aesthetic choice of both high arousal per se (induced by an information-free loud tone) and of cognitive tasks carried out simultaneously with the listening to the chosen melody on each trial where the tasks varied in (a) the processing effort demanded and (b) arousingness (Konečni & Sargent-Pollock, 1976).

Prior to each block of choice trials (the previously described simple and complex melodies were the choice alternatives), some subjects were exposed to bursts of a very loud squarewave tone, which considerably raised their arousal level (measured by the common psychophysiological indices), especially in the first half of the choice trials, whereas other subjects heard bursts of the same tone at a much lower loudness level.

The second experimental variable was the type of task on which the subjects worked while listening to the chosen melody on each trial. During each block of choice trials (between two exposures to the tone), one group of subjects worked continuously on the "digit-symbol" task (which requires the continuous processing of information with little fluctuation in processing difficulty over time), pausing only to press one of the two choice buttons every 10 sec and thus hear either a simple or a complex melody on that trial. Because the digit-symbol task involves not only the processing of information but also rapid writing—which by itself may raise arousal level—a number of additional conditions were included. In one of these ("contour-tracing"), subjects were asked to trace, as fast as possible, the contours of the symbols that had already been written in on the worksheets given to them. Thus, these subjects engaged in at least as much rapid writing as the digit-symbol group but were required to process far less information. In another condition, subjects were asked to watch slides of paintings closely during the choice trials and to memorize as many details as possible for a supposed subsequent test. The active storage of information involved in this task presumably required a great deal of processing effort but contained few elements of "conceptual conflict" (Berlyne, 1960), which the digit-symbol task—a series of mini-problems—may contain and which may itself raise arousal level (Blatt, 1961). In a further condition, subjects saw the same slides but without the memorization instructions, meaning that they would probably process less information during the choice trials. In the final control condition, subjects did not work on any task while choosing and listening to the melodies.

The results of the experiment were quite clear. The subjects' choice behavior was strongly affected by the task in which they were engaged while choosing and processing the melodies. Being required to work on the digit-symbol and slides-memorization tasks, both of which involved a considerable amount of information processing (and thus presumably decreased the subjects' processing capacity), sharply reduced the choice of complex melodies. The contrast of these two conditions with the remaining three accounted for virtually all of the variance due to the type of task. More processing capacity was presumably allocated to these congitively more demanding tasks (cf. Kahneman, 1973); since complex stimuli are more difficult to process than simple stimuli and given that the option existed, subjects chose to listen to the less demanding additional stimulation, simple melodies.

If we turn to the arousal aspects of the results, several observations are worthy of mention. First of all, being exposed to a loud tone prior to a block of choice trials significantly increased the level of arousal and decreased the percentage of choices of complex melodies in comparison to the control condition. However, the arousal aspects of the cognitive tasks themselves were quite irrelevant. Even though the slides-memorization subjects were physiologically far less aroused than were the rapidly writing digit-symbol subjects, they chose as few complex melodies. Furthermore, the digit-symbol subjects were no more aroused physiologically than were the contour-tracing ones, but they chose significantly fewer complex melodies. These and other aspects of the findings clearly showed that the processing-capacity factors, unmediated by the arousal-level fluctuations, had a direct and powerful effect on the choice between melodies. This finding does not prove that the effect on choice of high arousal (due to a loud tone or anger) is itself mediated by a decrease in processing capacity, but it does make such an explanation tenable.

Experiments discussed so far show that the socially induced emotional states, nonsocially-induced high arousal (due to a loud tone), and processing requirements of the concurrently performed cognitive tasks, all affect choice between melodies differing in complexity. In addition, they suggest a plausible mediational chain, one which runs from the actions of other people directed at the listener, via the listener's interpretation of these actions, his or her labelling of the emotional state, and arousal fluctuations, to the change in processing capacity and its effect on choice behavior.[6]

IV. EFFECTS OF LISTENING TO MELODIES DIFFERING IN COMPLEXITY ON EMOTIONAL STATES AND SOCIAL BEHAVIOR

In the introductory section I suggested that any treatment of aesthetic appreciation that aspires to some degree of completeness must deal not only with the antecedents of

---

[6]Perhaps we are now a step closer to understanding why a person enraged by someone, thinking hard about the details of the encounter and simultaneously maneuvering his automobile through noisy, rush-hour traffic, seems likely to tune his car radio away from his favorite classical station playing, say, Stravinsky's *Rite of Spring* (though it seems already a relatively tame, traditional piece) and tune in, volume reduced, to the local "mellow" station or switch off the radio altogether.

It is also of considerable interest to explore the effects on musical preference of variables that fall, on the social–nonsocial dimension, somewhere between impersonal bursts of an aversive squarewave tone and verbal insults from a stranger in a face-to-face situation. In an experiment designed by Sigrid Flath-Becker and presently being carried out by her in my laboratory, subjects are differentially aroused by being repeatedly and sternly told by the experimenter to be faster while working on demanding cognitive tasks and subsequently informed that they did either very poorly or very well in different experimental conditions. (There are several additional control conditions.) Flath-Becker is investigating the effect of such manipulations on subjects' preference for different rhythmic structures (regular, ostinato, syncopated, complex) in piano (Bach, Debussy, Bartok, Schönberg, respectively), orchestral (Bach, Ravel, Bartok, Schönberg), and percussion (Baker, Fink, Fink, Cage) compositions.

preference and choice but also with the consequences of the choice and exposure to aesthetic materials. Yet, this issue has been almost completely ignored in the psychology of art [with the honorable exception of a vintage study by Gilliland and Moore (1924)]. The prevalent, if unstated, attitude has been that the domain of interest does not extend beyond the period of exposure (unless one takes seriously the metaphysical speculations on the enrichment of the soul and spirit and the taming of savage beasts by music). However, to the extent that music may affect moods and emotions (a point that everyone readily agrees with) and given the social context in which music is so often appreciated, it would be very surprising if people's exposure to aesthetic stimuli, including music, would not have quite considerable effects on their social behavior. Paradoxically, this would also suggest that perhaps some of the most important effects of music (in terms of the sheer frequency of their occurrence in the life of average people) may be quite transient in that they are primarily mediated by emotional changes that ordinarily dissipate quite quickly.

Unfortunately, it is extremely difficult to study the ways in which the quality of people's interactions with their intimates is affected by the type of music they listen to in their homes and automobiles, at work, or on a picnic. Perhaps this will be possible in the future. So far, however, I have been forced to remain in the laboratory, but the inclusion of many of the features of the experiments to be described in this section has been inspired by the broader picture of music appreciation in social contexts.

Does listening to melodies varying in complexity differentially affect the amount of subsequent aggressive behavior? If so, does the effect of the melodies combine with that of anger? Also, does the loudness level at which the melodies are presented play a part in determining the amount of aggression that ensures? These were among the questions dealt with in an experiment by Konečni (1975b; also see Konečni, 1979, Section III,A).

In the first part of the experiment, some of the subjects were treated in an insulting, rude way by the accomplice of the experimenter whereas others were treated neutrally. All subjects then had an opportunity to administer supposedly painful "electric shocks" to the accomplice on each of many trials. With the exception of a control group that heard no melodies at any point in the experiment, the subjects listened to a 10-sec computer-generated melody on each trial while making the decision whether or not to shock the accomplice. Some subjects listened to a simple melody played at a comfortable listening level on each of the trials whereas others also heard simple melodies on all trials except that they were played at a very high listening level. Still other groups of subjects heard a complex melody on each trail, either at a comfortable or very high listening level, depending on the experimental condition. This experimental design allowed a detailed comparison of the effects on aggressive behavior of three quite different experimental treatments each of which, however, independently produced differences in arousal level. Pilot work had shown that listening to complex melodies in comparison to simple ones may raise the level of arousal; however, listening to these complex melodies is not, by any criterion, aversive for the normally aroused subjects. On the other hand, listening to melodies at a very high listening level (close to 100 dB-A) in comparison to listening to these melodies at a comfortable listening level is both arousing and aversive. Finally, prior work had shown that being rudely insulted by an accomplice in a face-to-face situation is arousing, aversive, and leads subjects unequivocally to label themselves angry.

On the basis of such information, rather precise predictions could be made. It was hypothesized that the melodies themselves—whether complex or simple and whether heard at a high or low listening level—would have little, if any, effect on aggressive behavior. The subjects would be differentially aroused and find the experimental situation differentially aversive, but this would presumably not be quite enough to produce differences in a highly important, high-consequence social behavior, such as aggression. In contrast, it was predicted that the aggressive behavior of subjects who had been made angry by the accomplice's insults would be further augmented by the melodies they were forced to listen to while making the choice of whether or not to punish the accomplice on each trial. The more arousing and/or aversive the melodies, the greater the increment over the baseline established by anger alone. The highest amount of aggression was thus expected to occur in the condition in which angry subjects listened to complex melodies at the high listening level on each trial.

The pattern of results that was obtained largely corroborated these predictions with some interesting exceptions. Subjects who had not been insulted generally displayed a low level of aggressive behavior that varied little as a function of the type of melody and loudness level. The one exception to this was the noninsulted subjects who had been repeatedly exposed to complex melodies at the high listening level: these subjects' aggressive behavior was only somewhat less pronounced, and statistically not different, from the amount of aggression displayed by the insulted controls who had heard no melodies whatsoever. It would thus seem that there is at least some tendency for the arousing complex melodies when they are played at a very high listening level to incline the subjects toward aggression. One could well imagine a situation in which people aroused by loud complex music would tend to overreact to relatively slight additional provocations that would ordinarily be brushed aside.

The pattern of results for the insulted subjects was quite different. As predicted, angry people who had been exposed to loud complex melodies displayed the greatest amount of aggression in the experiment, significantly more than the angry subjects who had heard no melodies. The insulted subjects who had heard complex melodies at a low listening level and those who had heard simple melodies at a high listening level displayed an intermediate amount of aggression. The one result that did not fit well in this general pattern but was not altogether unanticipated [on the basis of a study using visual aesthetic stimuli by Konečni and Sargent-Pollock (1977)] was the amount of aggression displayed by the insulted subjects who had repeatedly heard simple melodies at a low listening level. These people's aggressive behavior was significantly lower than that of the insulted subjects who had heard no melodies at all; it was, in fact, lower (though not significantly so) even than the aggressive behavior of some noninsulted subjects (those who had heard complex melodies at a high listening level). It thus seems that simple, soft melodies may have been actively soothing—perhaps by virtue of reducing the level of arousal and the degree of anger faster than was the case in the condition involving insulted subjects who had heard no melodies.

The experiment was thus a tentative demonstration that the exposure to melodies varying in complexity could have a differential effect on an important (anti)social behavior—both directly, insofar as it may combine with the effects of anger, and indirectly, in that it may raise arousal level and create a disposition to aggress. It was also shown that the loudness at which the melodies are heard is important, but it remains to be seen whether loudness would have a similar effect with authentic musical pieces and nonmusical acoustic patterns.

The apparently soothing effect of simple melodies presented at a comfortable listening level was tested by a different procedure in another experiment (Konečni, 1979, Section III,B). In the key condition of this complex experiment, subjects were rudely treated by the experimenter as soon as they walked into the laboratory, blamed for "being late" in a hostile and arrogant manner, and told that being late for important appointments implied irreponsibility and immaturity.[7] Next, subjects listened to simple melodies for three minutes continuously. The hypothesized effect of listening to simple melodies at this point was that the melodies would accelerate the decrease in the subjects' anger over and above the rate of recovery that would have been produced by homeostatic processes acting alone. Following the listening period, subjects rested for 15 minutes, after which they were insulted again by a different person, an accomplice of the experimenter using a different angering procedure.

In the final part of the experiment, the dependent measures were collected. These were the number and duration of simple-melody choices to which the subjects decided to listen, and the number and duration of punishing blasts of noise supposedly delivered to the accomplice in the context of a task. Subjects were told that every time a light of a particular color came on, they could press a button, which would expose them to a simple melody, and that the melody would go on for as long as the button was pressed. They were also told that when a light of a different color came on, they could press another button for as long as they wished, which would deliver a blast of noise to the accomplice (a plausible pretext was devised and presented to subjects).

There were several sets of control conditions that can be characterized by the following: (a) no listening to melodies following the first anger induction; (b) no initial anger induction; and (c) no second induction of anger. (There were additional conditions that are of little interest from the perspective of the present chapter.)

The major experimental hypothesis was that the subjects whose recovery from a high degree of anger was accelerated in the first part of the experiment by listening to the soothing melodies—presumably a relatively favorable state of affairs in that people can be reasonably expected to prefer a fast rate of diminution of a pronounced negative emotional state—would be particularly prone to listen to simple melodies following the second anger induction. In comparison to various control groups, the simple melodies had, for these subjects, proved their usefulness in alleviating a negative emotional state. In contrast, the same melodies had accomplished no such outcome for

---

[7]The reader may assume that at the end of all experimental sessions involving the insult procedure, subjects are thoroughly debriefed about the purpose of the experiment, the nature of the procedures, and reassured about their performance.

subjects who had listened to them in the first part of the experiment without being angry. Similarly, subjects who had been made angry in the first part of the experiment, but not given the opportunity to listen to the simple melodies at that time, could not have been as sure, following the second anger induction, of the melodies' positive impact on anger. Finally, subjects who were not angered the second time, just before the collection of the dependent measure, presumably did not experience at that time a negative emotional state that needed to be diminished.

The actual results confirmed these hypotheses, in terms of both the frequency and duration of listening to simple melodies and the frequency and duration of blasts of noise to the accomplice (the choice of melodies and the decision to deliver a blast of noise to the accomplice were independent, nonredundant measures). This experimental outcome and the data from an analogous experiment involving the emotion of fear (Konečni, 1979, Section III,C) suggest that listening to simple melodies, paired with negative emotional states, can have a powerful effect on the subjects' behavior at the time of the second anger induction. Subjects who had experienced that simple melodies can successfully decrease their anger (faster than simply the passage of time) resorted to listening to such melodies a great deal when angered again. These subjects were less prone to engage in aggression at that time.

In summary, the experiments presented in this section, taken together, seem to suggest—even if with regard to a very restricted range of musical materials and social behaviors—that listening to melodies varying on certain fundamental stimulus dimensions may differentially affect subsequent behavior of the listeners toward other people and that they may learn to seek actively the melodies with certain properties to alleviate negative emotional states. This question, the use of musical materials for the purpose of mood optimization, is further pursued in the next section.

V. LISTENERS' SEQUENCING AND "CHUNKING" OF MUSICAL MATERIALS AND THE USE OF MUSIC FOR MOOD OPTIMIZATION

Given a range of musical materials to which they are asked to listen, how do people plan their "musical environment"—that is, how do they program their exposure to the materials in terms of the listening sequence and the duration of the individual "chunks"? If there is some truth to the idea that music is consciously used for the purpose of mood optimization or an emotional boost, would this extend to the active use of certain pieces of music (characterized by a given level of pleasingness, soothingness, and so on) in order to offset the effects of an aversive event (e.g., exposure to a very loud tone)? In other words, what type of music do people choose to listen to immediately after exposure to aversive auditory stimulation? These and related questions were systematically investigated in a series of previously unpublished experiments conducted in my laboratory (Allen, Hammerbeck, & Konečni, 1978; Allen, Breckler, & Konečni, 1980), in which an entirely different aesthetic-choice research paradigm was used.

In the main experiment subjects were first acquainted with the range of musical materials by hearing for 30 sec an example of each of the following: (1) eighteenth century "serious" music; (2) twentieth century "serious" music; (3) "mellow" rock'-n'-roll; (4) "hard" rock'-n'-roll; (5) computer-generated simple melodies (similar to those in the experiments previously described); (6) computer-generated complex melodies; and (7) intermittent bursts of a highly aversive 350-Hz squarewave tone at 95 dB-A. The musical selections that the subjects heard had undergone a considerable amount of pretesting. From a much larger pool of musical pieces, three pieces were chosen to represent each of the four types of music, such that within each type the pieces were homogenous with regard to the ratings (by pilot subjects) of arousingness, soothingness, pleasingness, interestingness, and complexity. In addition, the eighteenth century selections (by Bach, Haydn, and Vivaldi) were rated as highly similar to the "mellow" rock selections (by Genesis, Mott the Hoople, and Linda Ronstadt) on the arousingness, soothingness, and complexity scales. Also, these two types of music had been rated as far less arousing and complex and more soothing than the twentieth century "serious" pieces (by Bartok, Prokofiev, and Skriabin) and the "hard" rock selections (by Montrose, Outlaws, Scorpions) while the latter two types had been rated as equal to each other on these three dimensions. However, on the dimensions of pleasingness and interestingness, the four types of music (or, rather, the particular selections that were decided upon on the basis of pretesting) had been rated as fairly comparable to each other, although there was a certain preference, on the pleasingness scale, for "mellow" rock, followed by the eighteenth century "serious" music—a very stable finding that held across a wide variety of selections and could not be eliminated, at least for the population studied (UCSD students).

In the pretest, subjects also rated the computer-generated melodies and the loud squarewave tone. The simple and complex melodies were rated both significantly less pleasing and less interesting than any of the authentic musical pieces but significantly more pleasing and interesting (by about 4 points on a 10-point scale) than the squarewave tone. The mean ratings of the aversive squarewave tone on both the arousingness and soothingness scales were at the very extremes of the scales, at the expected scale ends.

In the main experiment, after they heard a 30-sec example of each of the seven types of auditory stimuli, subjects were seated in front of a console on which seven keys were arranged in a circle and told that they would have to listen to two minutes of each of the seven types of stimuli. Every 15 sec subjects were to choose one of the seven (and keep track of the choices on a tally-sheet provided) until all seven types had been heard for two minutes. The order in which subjects were to hear the different types of stimuli was completely up to them. At one extreme, subjects could choose the same type eight times in a row, thus exhausting that type, and then move on to the next type, and so on. At the other extreme, subjects could switch from type to type every 15 sec in a more-or-less random fashion.

Subjects heard the stimuli over headphones with musical selections and computer-generated melodies at 73 dB-A and the squarewave tone at 95 dB-A. The tracks with each of the four types of music were prepared in such a way that four minutes of each of three selections within a type were recorded in a random succession for a total of 36 minutes per track.

There were also a number of variations of this basic experimental condition. In one of these, subjects were asked to write a hypothetical program of 15-sec choices without actually listening to any of the stimuli after making the choices. In addition, there were experimental conditions involving only six (no squarewave tone), five (no simple or complex computer-generated melodies), and four (no squarewave tone or simple and complex melodies) types of stimuli. The basic seven-types condition and these additional three with fewer types of stimuli can be thought of as a 2 × 2 design with the squarewave tone (present or absent) and simple and complex melodies (present or absent) as the two factors.

The results were interesting and will be briefly summarized here. In the five-types and seven-types conditions, both of which involved the aversive squarewave tone, there was a very strong tendency for subjects to choose the loud squarewave tone very early in the session. The aversive tone was heard in relatively short "runs" (in terms of sequential 15-sec choices), interspersed with runs of both simple and complex computer-generated melodies (when these, as well as the tone, were available in the seven-types condition). These chunks of exposure to various stimuli of relatively low pleasingness early in the session were followed by longer runs of the type of music that the subject liked *second* best, which for the majority of subjects in the experiment proper, as in the pretest, was the soothing, nonarousing eighteeth century "serious" music. (Since the ratings on the five dimensions described above were available from subjects in the main experiment, it was possible to do the various analyses on the basis of each subject's individual order of preference for the various types of music, as opposed to the group means from the pretest.)

Thus, in what seems to have been a disconfirmation of what one would reasonably predict from most versions of the general learning theory, subjects chose to get the aversive stimulation over with early in the session, rather than delay the aversive experience as long as possible. They "chose to suffer" in small "doses" and apparently made the whole experience more palatable by listening immediately afterward to the type of music that pleased them considerably (though not their most favorite type). These results gave further support to the notion that people actively seek different types of music at different times in order to optimize their mood or, as in the present case, to offset the impact of aversive stimulation.

In the condition with six available types of auditory stimulation (no aversive squarewave tone), an analogous pattern of results was obtained. Subjects tended first to listen to a great deal of both types of computer-generated melodies (thus, again getting the exposure to the least liked stimulation over with early in the session), which was interspersed with chunks of the second best-liked music. However, for this type of choice behavior and listening strategy to occur, a certain threshold of aversiveness apparently has to be exceeded; namely, in the four-types condition, in which the squarewave tone and both type of computer-generated melodies were absent, subjects tended to begin the session by a considerable amount of listening to the second best-liked music, rather than by listening to the less pleasing types. (In the pretest the least liked type of authentic music, the twentieth century "serious" pieces, still received a relatively high mean rating of 6.2 on a 10-point pleasingness scale in comparison to 3.4 for complex computer-generated melodies and 7.1 for the most pleasing music, "mellow" rock.)

In all the conditions, whether there were four, five, six, or seven types of stimulation available, the majority of the subjects reserved the end of the session for long runs of listening to the most pleasing music, which was—both in the pretest and in the experiment proper—"mellow" rock. With the proverbial liver and spinach eaten—in small bites—subjects helped themselves to mouthfuls of chocolate mousse at the end. (An irresistible, though imprecise, analogy in that the spinach/mousse sequence is influenced by factors other than preference.) This particular mood-optimization strategy was convenient for us as experimenters concerned with the subjects' welfare: it insured that subjects left the experiment happy.

The middle part of the session tended to be filled with listening to the two least preferred types of music, "hard" rock and twentieth century "serious" pieces. Even these types of music, however, were listend to in longer runs than were the squarewave tone and computer-generated melodies.

Perhaps the most parsimonious explanation of the subjects' overall listening strategy links mood-optimizing to subjects' efforts to keep arousal level within a certain range and avoid getting overaroused, while experiencing a controlled variety of arousal fluctuations through a sequence composed of: arousing squarewave tone; soothing eighteenth century "serious" music; arousing "hard" rock and twentieth century "serious" pieces; and, finally, soothing "mellow" rock—an alternating arousing/soothing sequence vaguely reminiscent of the order of fast and slow movements in certain musical compositions (cf. Berlyne, 1971, for a discussion of arousal-related musical "devices" used by composers).

It is somewhat surprising that subjects almost never chose to listen to a full two minutes of the same type of music, even in the 4-types condition. Since the selections within each type were all recorded in four-minute segments, there would have been a good chance for a subject to hear a pleasant piece of music uninterrupted by either other types of stimuli or to change from one to another selection within a type. It is possible that the nature of the experimental procedure favored relatively frequent alternations between types. Also, the fact that a choice had to be made every 15 sec, even if of the same type of music repeatedly, may have disturbed the subjects' perception of continuity of a piece. Interestingly enough, if the latter reason is important, the subjects were apparently unable to predict that this is how they would feel; namely, in the previously mentioned experimental variation in which subjects prepared a hypothetical listening program without actually listening to any auditory stimulation, there were far longer runs of the music of the same type.

The experiments described in this section seem to provide additional information about the use of music for the purpose of mood optimization. Moreover, the major finding has now been replicated with visual nonartistic stimuli. In the course of the experimental session, subjects had to view five different sets of slides that vastly differed in rated pleasingness. Although the subjects had to view all slides within all sets for a fixed length of time, the order in which they viewed the slides was completely up to them. Subjects generally viewed the least pleasing slides (those belonging to the set of gory slides of accident victims) early in the session, interspersed with the second most-liked slides, those from the set of humorous cartoons. As was the case in the experiment involving musical stimuli, these subjects—who were male—left the most pleasing slides, of *Playboy* nudes, for the end. Again, it seemed to us that subjects left the laboratory quite content.

In summary, it seems that both the idea that music is used for the purpose of mood optimization and a theoretical framework with feedback features based on the concept of an aesthetic episode could be of heuristic value. The experimental steps taken so far have been tentative and relatively narrow in scope, but they can perhaps help develop a psychology of music that recognizes the role of social, emotional, and cognitive factors in music appreciation as well as the conditions under which music of all kinds is enjoyed in daily life.

REFERENCES

Allen, R. B., Hammerbeck, J. A., & Konečni, V. J. *Planning an auditory aesthetic environment: Listeners' sequencing of musical and non-musical stimuli.* Paper presented at the 58th Annual Convention of the Western Psychological Association, San Francisco, California, 1978.

Allen, R. B., Breckler, S., & Konečni, V. J. *Sequencing and chunking of musical and visual stimuli.* Unpublished manuscript, University of California, San Diego, California, 1980.

Arnheim, R. *Toward a psychology of art.* Berkeley, California: University of California Press, 1966.

Berlyne, D. E. *Conflict, arousal and curiosity.* New York: McGraw-Hill, 1960.

Berlyne, D. E. *Aesthetics and psychobiology.* New York: Appleton, 1971.

Berlyne, D. E. The new experimental aesthetics. In D. E. Berlyne (Ed.), *Studies in the new experimental aesthetics.* New York: Wiley, 1974.

Blatt, S. J. Patterns of cariac arousal during complex mental activity. *Journal of Abnormal and Social Psychology*, 1961, *63*, 272–282.

Bragg, B.W.E., & Crozier, J. B. The development with age of verbal and exploratory varying in uncertainty level. In D. E. Berlyne (Ed.), *Studies in the new experimental aesthetics.* New York: Hemisphere Publ., 1974.

Broadbent, D. E. *Perception and communication.* Oxford: Pergamon, 1958.

Broadbent, D. E. *Decision and stress.* New York: Academic Press, 1971.

Cantor, J. R., & Zillmann, D. The effect of affective state and emotional arousal on music appreciation. *Journal of General Psychology*, 1973, *89*, 97–108.

Child, I. L. Esthetics. In G. Lindzey & E. Aronson (Eds.), *The handbook of social psychology* (Vol. 3) (2nd ed.). Reading Massachusetts: Addison-Wesley, 1969.

Child, I. L. Aesthetic theories. In E. C. Carterette & M. P. Friedman (Eds.), *Handbook of perception* (Vol. 10). New York: Academic Press, 1978. Pp. 111–131.

Crozier, J. B. Verbal and exploratory responses to sound sequences varying in uncertainty level. In D. E. Berlyne (Ed.), *Studies in the new experimental aesthetics.* New York: Wiley, 1974.

Easterbrook, J. A. The effect of emotion on cue utilization and the organization of behavior. *Psychological Review*, 1959, *66*, 183–201.

Farnsworth, P. R. *The social psychology of music* (2nd ed.). Ames, Iowa: Iowa State University Press, 1969.

Fechner, G. T. Vorschule der Ästhetic. Lipzig: Breitkopf & Härtel, 1876.

Francès, R. Le perception de la musique. Paris: Vrin, 1958.

Francès, R. *Psychologie de l'esthétique* Paris: Presses Universitaires de France, 1968.

Gilliland, A. R., & Moore, H. T. The immediate and long-time effects of classical and popular phonograph selections. *Journal of Applied Psychology*, 1924, *8*, 309–323.

Gunzenhäuser, R. *Ästhetisches Mass and Ästhetische Information*. Quickborn bei Hamburg, West Germany: Schnelle, 1962.

Heyduk, R. G. Rated preference for musical compositions as it relates to complexity and exposure frequency. *Perception & Psychophysics*, 1975, *17*, 84–91.

Hokanson, J. E., & Shetler, S. The effect of overt aggression on psysiological arousal level. *Journal of Abnormal and Social Psychology*, 1961, *63*, 446–448.

Kahneman, D. *Attention and effort*. New York: Prentice-Hall, 1973.

Konečni, V. J. Annoyance, type and duration of postannoyance activity, and aggression: The "cathartic effect." *Journal of Experimental Psychology: General*, 1975, *104*, 76–102. (a)

Konečni, V. J. The mediation of aggressive behavior: Arousal level vs anger and cognitive labeling. *Journal of Personality and social Psychology*, 1975, *32*, 706–712. (b)

Konečni, V. J. Determinants of aesthetic preference and effects of exposure to aesthetic stimuli: Social, emotional and cognitive factors. In B. A. Maher (Ed.), *Progress in experimental personality research* (Vol. 9). New York: Academic Press, 1979. Pp. 149–197.

Konečni, V. J., & Sargent-Pollock, D. Choice between melodies differing in complexity under divided-attention conditions. *Journal of Experimental Psychology: Human Perception and Performance*, 1976, *2*, 347–356.

Konečni, V. J., & Sargent-Pollock, D. Arousal, positive and negative affect, and preference for Renaissance and 20th century paintings. *Motivation & Emotion*, 1977, *1*, 75–93.

Konečni, V. J., Crozier, J. B., & Doob, A. N. Anger and expression of aggression: Effects on aesthetic preference. *Scientific Aesthetics/Sciences de l'Art*, 1976, *1*, 47–55.

Kreitler, H., & Kreitler, S. *Psychology of the arts*. Durham, North Carolina: Duke University Press, 1972.

Langer, S. *Philosophy in a new key*. Cambridge, Massachusetts: Harvard University Press, 1942.

Madsen, K. B. Patterns of preference and models of motivation. In D. E. Berlyne & K. B. Madsen (Eds.), *Pleasure, reward, preference*. New York: Academic Press, 1973.

Meyer, L. B. *Emotion and meaning in music*. Chicago, Illinois: University of Chicago Press, 1956.

Meyer, L. B. Meaning in music and information theory. *Journal of Aesthetics and Art Criticism*, 1957, *15*, 412–424.

Moles, A. *Théorie de l'information et perception esthétique*. Paris: Flammarion, 1958.

Moore, H. T. The genetic aspects of consonance and dissonance. *Psychological Monographs*, 1914, *17* (2, whole No. 73).

Moray, N. *Attention*. London: Hutchinson Educational, 1969.

Morris, C. Significance, signification and painting. In R. Lepley (Ed.), *The language of value*. New York: Columbia University Press, 1957.

Overmier, J. B. Auditory pattern preference as a function of informational context. Unpublished M. A. thesis, Bowling Green State University, 1962.

Perkins, D., & Leondar, B. *The arts and cognition*. Baltimore, Maryland: Johns Hopkins University Press, 1977.

Sargent-Pollock, D., & Konečni, V. J. Evaluative and skin-conductance responses to Renaissance and 20th century paintings. *Behavior Research Methods and Instrumentation*, 1977, *9*, 291–296.

Simon, C. R., & Wohlwill, J. F. An experimental study of the role of expectation and variation in music. *Journal of Research in Music Education*, 1968, *16*, 227–238.

Steck, L., & Machotka, P. Preference for musical complexity: Effects of context. *Journal of Experimental Psychology: Human Perception & Performance*, 1975, *1*, 170–174.

Treisman, A. Selective attention in man. *British Medical Bulletin*, 1964, *20*, 12–16.

Vitz, P. C. Affect as a function of stimulus variation. *Journal of Experimental Psychology*, 1966, *71*, 74–79.

Walker, E. L. Psychological complexity and preference: A hedgehog theory of behavior. In D. E. Berlyne & K. B. Madsen (Eds.), *Pleasure, reward, preference*. New York: Academic Press, 1973.

18

New Music and Psychology

Robert Erickson

I. Introduction 517
II. Music Theory and Music 519
III. Understanding Tonality 520
IV. Music and Perceptual Streaming 523
V. Fused Sounds in Music.. 529
VI. Music Theory and Experimental Science.. 534
References 535

I. INTRODUCTION

There has always been a problem of communication between disciplines. The languages often seem incommensurable and the goals different. When music is involved there is a double barrier, a large one between musical practice and music theory and another between music theory and those disciplines that touch music at some point or other—acoustics, psychoacoustics, cognitive psychology, and others. Nevertheless, developments in these fields over the past 20 years have led scientific investigators increasingly toward musical problems. Theoretically minded musicians are turning to experimental psychology for useful concepts and better underpinnings for their theoretical constructs.

The first wave of musical interest came with the electronic technology that followed World War II. The tape recorder, electronic generation of sound by means of oscillators, and its manipulation by filters, gates, and modulators—were quickly taken up by composers in Europe, Asia, and America. Problems of electronic music and music reproduction provided the initial common ground for new music developments in psychophysics, psychology, and other disciplines. Periodicals such as *Die Reihe* and *Gravesaner Blätter* provided a forum in which possible musical uses for an approach through information theory were explored by W. Meyer-Eppler and A.A.

Moles; acoustics and psychoacoustics by W. Burck, E. Leipp, and F. Winckel; practical and theoretical music utilizing concepts from acoustics, psychoacoustics, and information theory by Pierre Schaeffer, Karlheinz Stockhausen, and others.

The R.C.A. music synthesizer, installed at the Columbia/Princeton Electronic Music Center, could be more precisely controlled than other electronic music devices of its time through programming by means of punched tape. Informal experiments carried out in the early 1960s indicate the kinds of questions that needed musically useful answers. At a meeting of the International Folk Music Council, Babbitt (1964) presented some findings, starting from musical notation and its relation to a performer.

> The solution of the apparently innocent problem of musical notation thus carries one to the central problems of musical perception, and onto the same path as that upon which the composer finds himself when he becomes aware that the responsible use of the electronic medium involves him, formally and informally, in acoustical and psycho-acoustial research. He must specify his compositional decisions with an accuracy and completeness that have been unnecessary and impossible in the past and he must discover the answers to questions that have never been posed before and which never could have been answered before. These questions can now be answered with the aid of electronic media and must be answered if these media are to be employed to the full of their singular capacities.... The examples presented included instances of:
>
> (1) Identical specifications of frequency that, for different spectra and *only* for durations of less than one-tenth of a second, produce what are identified as different, yet individually unambiguous pitches. This provides an unprecedented case of one–many relations between the frequency and pitch domains and of the variance of pitch with regard to duration. The "threshold" durational values at which such frequency specifications produce pitch identity (equivalently, it appears, the 'normal' frequency–pitch correlations) appear to be a non-trivial function of the characteristics of respective spectra and the absolute value of the frequency. (2) The threshold of identification of frequency succession as demonstrated in the presentation of a succession in which each of the components is of the same duration and loudness, at a speed at which only about half of the components can be identified. (Each component's duration is about one-thirty-second of a second.) The speed is then reduced in a number of stages. This is comparable with tachistoscope tests in visual perception to provide a reasonable criterion of 'simplicity.' These speed tests indicate the importance of pitch extrema in the perception of succession. (3) The effect of quantitative time factors on the identification of qualitative temporal relations. Certain successions, identical in every respect except in the *order* of the components, are perceived as totally identical, whereas others are not so perceived. Similarity of interval succession appears to be the basis of such misidentification. (4) The increase of the threshold duration for the identification of succession as the registral span is increased. (5) The greater accuracy of durational judgments when the durations are associated with "specific" pitches rather than with "indefinite," percussion instrument-like pitches. (6) The dubious status of certain "time-order errors" of classical psychophysics, when presented in musical terms to trained musicians; this includes both protensity judgements and loudness judgements as a function of the time interval between the phenomena to be compared. (7) The apparent alteration of timbral characteristics resulting from an alteration of the temporal relations between component timbres in an "ensemble" appears to depend on, for example, the coincidence of peaks between trills. (8) The "misidentification" of timbral families and the inability to identify components in a complex as a result of the precise synchronization of attacks of the component frequencies. (9) The dependence of frequency discrimination on the duration of the presented frequencies. (10) The dependence of durational identification on timbral characteristics.

Even such modest, if novel attempts to determine the correspondence between input specification and perceived outputs in time-dependent phenomena serve, at least, to indicate the critically limited nature of our knowledge in this field.

Significantly, Babbitt stresses the interrelatedness of the musical dimensions. Pitch, timbre, rhythm, tempo have startling effects upon each other in perception. As a composer Babbitt saw clearly that musically significant studies must deal with these complexities, and it seems certain that investigations of music perception must be prepared to study musical phenomena in contexts that are fully musical.

Also in 1963, Max Mathews, director of the Behavioral Research Laboratory at Bell Telephone Laboratories, published "The Digital Computer as a Musical Instrument" (Mathews, 1963). He and his colleagues had developed a program for producing sound from numbers, and had used it for generating speech sounds and other stimuli for use in experimental work. Mathews and J.R. Pierce realized that the computer could be used as a completely generalized musical instrument, and his paper describes how it may be so used. Mathews, like Babbitt, puts psychoacoustic questions in the foreground when he writes:

Our musical studies with the computer indicate that, in this area, the major problem to be overcome by a composer concerns the relation of the physical description of the sound waves to the psychoacoustic effects which he desires.... Our experience has shown how little we now know about the relation of the quality of sound to various features of the waveform. A new body of psychoacoustic data is necessary. These data should relate the properties of the acoustic waves of music to perceived qualities of sound. Part of the task of assembling these data can, of course, be given to the composer, and part of the data can be supplied by interested psychologists. An increase in knowledge in this field is bound to be of value and interest in other fields, including those of speech and hearing.

This is more sharply formulated than Babbitt's remarks. Mathews' idea is that we need to know more so that we can find the numbers to generate the needed waveform. On the surface it may look more congenial to experimenters familiar with the methods of modern psychophysics. Nevertheless, the need for musical context is there, in the suggestion of cooperation between composers and psychologists. I believe this cooperation between disciplines is essential if we are to have a solidly based psychology of music, and the burden of this paper will be to show why I believe this to be true.

II. MUSIC THEORY AND MUSIC

The remarks by Babbitt and Mathews about the need for a new body of psychoacoustic data make some sort of cooperation a practical necessity. Interdisciplinary work is taking place now. Psychologists and composers do occasionally meet, often near a computer terminal. More than a few psychologists are working directly on problems that are basic to a psychology of music. Nevertheless, there are problems, important ones, difficult to surmount; for example, the major problem in music is the chasm between thinking about it and doing it. It is one thing to know when and how and where to pass the thumb in fingering the C-major scale on the piano, and altogether another thing to do it smoothly at moderate and fast tempos. Theoretical ideas—say Rameau's theories about the roots of triads, or those of Boethius about musical numbers, or Hindemith's groupings of more and less dissonant chords—are like knowing when to pass the thumb in that scale—not exactly irrelevant, but very distant from the composing process. The chasm between music theorizing and music making has not been narrowed at all since Plato. It has probably widened, largely because theory has increasingly been perceived as prescriptive. The purpose of a proper music theory should be to help us to think more clearly about musical problems and only that. An important arena is the common ground between the physical world of sound and our perception, cognitive processing and mental organizing of ordered sounds. Theory cannot tell us what to do, but it can help us explain to ourselves what we have done.

Theorizing about music has been going on for so long, 2000 or 3000 years, that it is no surprise that it is a very confusing body of knowledge. Theorists of any particular time have written on topics of local interest, usually promoting them to the level of universal validity. The history of music theory can be read as a tale of ingenious special pleading for this or that musical style. That must be changed. We need a music theory that is not style bound, that is valid for world music, not its European, Chinese, or Indonesian varieties. We need to know what things in music are a matter of culture and what things belong to our common humanity. The tools of modern cognitive psychology seem appropriate for this task.

III. UNDERSTANDING TONALITY

Much of the music theory of the past 100 years has been built upon a theory of tonality, "loyalty to a tonic." Early in this century a controversy arose over a new kind of music composed by Schoenberg, Berg, and Webern, dubbed "atonal" by polemicists. The controversy has not subsided. As Salzer (1952) wrote:

> Today's musical crisis centers on the problem of tonality. Tonality, new tonality, atonality, polytonality, twelve-tone music, new-classicism, impressionism—all these terms may symbolize various and often conflicting currents, but they vitally concern the substance of musical language (p. 5). . . . Our period, however, is completely at odds about basic conceptions of musical utterance and coherence (p. 6).

Theoretical ideas about tonality are bound up with stylistic ideas about music and what music should be. Tonality has been understood to require chords and chord progression. The edifice of chord construction rested upon appeals to the harmonic series, the "chord of nature." Schoenberg was concerned to show that his music was "pantonal" rather than "atonal," a word he considered meaningless; and he used the harmonic series (Schoenberg, 1934) to sketch an evolution in musical perception from the simpler diatonicism found in the lower harmonics to the chromatic scale that could be extracted from higher harmonics. "It is certain that the more perceptible overtones sound more familiar to the ear than those it hears but faintly; these last therefore remain strange to it. For that reason the chromatic scale is a somewhat more complicated tonal form than the major" (p. 171).

He also suggested that tonality is a product of art rather than a product of the nature of sound. (One must infer that the harmonic series is somehow only important for scale construction and for the construction of chords, unless he is changing his ground here) (p. 175):

> Now then, since tonality is not something which the composer unconsciously achieves, which exists without his contribution and grows of itself, which would be present even if the composer willed the opposite; since, in a word, tonality is neither a natural nor automatic consequence of tone combinations and therefore cannot claim to be the automatic result of the nature of sound and so an indispensible attribute of every piece of music, we shall probably have to define tonality as the art of combining tones in such successions and such harmonies or successions of harmonies, that the relation of all events to a fundamental tone is made possible.

Schoenberg is certainly right in saying that a tonality is constructed, but he *has* shifted his ground, because earlier in the paper, leading up to his discussion of overtones, he had been quite clear about relationships between tones: "How, after all, can two tones be joined one with another? My answer is that such a juxtaposition of tones, if a connection is to be brought about from which a piece of music may be the result, is only possible because a relation already exists between the tones themselves" (p. 169). He continues: "To elucidate the relationship between tones one must first recall that every tone is a compound sound, consisting of a fundamental tone (the strongest sounding one) and a series of overtones. We may now make the statement, and to a great extent test and prove it, that all musical phenomena can be referred to the overtone series so that all things appear to be application of the more simple and more complex relationships of this series" (pp. 169–170). The implication here is that atonal music, highly chromatic, can be referred to the upper reaches of the harmonic series. Intervallic relationships are therefore validated by the harmonic series; the creation of a tonality is a matter of art.

Working in Vienna at the same time, Heinrich Schenker used the harmonic series to serve a somewhat different theory. Schenker's ideas and his method of analysis by reductive graphing of music have gained wide support in the United States. Modern definitions of tonality tend to cluster around his notion of a triad unfolding in time. Here is a short description of his essential theory by Kalib (1975) (p. 3).

> Stated in most succinct, nut-shell form, Schenker views the musical work of art as the stage-upon-stage artistic unfolding of the triad of nature in time. The tone upon which this triad is based is viewed as reproducing, in the sense of procreating, other tones in the order in which they occur in the overtone series. Due to the limitations of the ear in perceiving more distant overtones, music, as a human art, avails itself of no more than the first five partials of the overtone series, or composites, thereof.

Both Schoenberg and Schenker appear to make chords a requirement of tonality. Each makes statements about the relation between the perceptibility of harmonics and musical structures. Each believed that ancient music and medieval monophonic and polyphonic music (modal music) was somehow deficient and primitive compared to the developed systems of eighteenth and nineteenth century—chiefly German—music. The basic idea of tonality, loyalty to a tonic, is dealt with in the following way: the root of the unfolding triad is for Schenker the tonic of the composition and the fundamental of the harmonic series. Schoenberg leaves more room for maneuver by deriving the triads on I, IV, and V from the harmonic series (p. 170):

> The origin of the main fundamental tones is explained by the fact that each one occurs as the third overtone of the one lying a fifth below it. So that C is the third overtone of F, just as G is the third overtone of C. In this manner G:C = C:F; And it is evident that C attracts the tones related to it through G, just as F and its related tones do with the complex of C.

For both theorists it appears that tonality rests ultimately upon an appeal to the harmonic series; and if we ask, "Why do we feel loyalty to a tonic?"—the ultimate answer would presumably be that it is the fundamental of the harmonic series, the "chord of nature."

This answer is unsatisfying from a world music standpoint. There are cultures whose music appears to have little relationship to the harmonic series. Worldwide there is a multiplicity of scales and harmonies hardly expressible in the small number ratios that might relate them to the harmonic series, even roughly equidistant scalar schemes, and harmonies that owe no allegiance to the triad, that entity so prominent in the thinking of Schenker and Schoenberg. Yet many of these musics exhibit the characteristic of loyalty to a tonic. Some analysts are finding tonal centers in the very music by Schoenberg, Berg, and Webern that was previously described as atonal. Modern discussions, such as that in the second edition of the Harvard *Dictionary of Music*, have tried to take account of this fact:

> TONALITY. Loyalty to a tonic, in the broadest sense of the word. One of the most striking phenomena of music is the fact that, throughout is evolution—in non-Western cultures, in Gregorian chant, and in harmonized music—practically every single piece gives preference to one tone (the tonic) making this the tonal center to which all other tones are related.

Travis (1959), working within the tradition of Schenker's formulations, has proposed a view that could encompass both non-Western musics and some aspects of atonal and other contemporary music: "Music is tonal when its motion unfolds through time a particular tone, interval, or chord. It is this tone, interval, or chord, called the tonic, which identifies the tonality" (p. 261).

A final definition in this long parade, couched in up-to-date music-theoretic language, is by Berry (1976). It specifically allows for tonal music of all times and places, and has the additional merit of leaving the relation between system and perception ready for empirical research (p. 27):

> Tonality may be broadly conceived as a *formal system in which pitch content is perceived as functionally related to a specific pitch-class or pitch-class-complex of resolution*, often preestablished and preconditioned, as a basis for structure at some understood level of perception. The foregoing definition of tonality is applicable not just to the "tonal period" in which the most familiar conventions of tonal function are practiced (roughly the eighteenth and the nineteenth centuries), but through earlier modality and more recent freer tonal applications as well. (The terms *pitch class* and *pitch-class-complex* are used to denote pitch independent of specific registral occurrence, or a complex of such pitches generically understood).

All of these definitions posit the idea of a pitch center of some sort as basic. Cognitive psychologists could use empirical methods to investigate the question: Is there centering? If it can be established that centering is one of our cognitive strategies then, in my view, music theorists would have a firmer base for definitions of tonality than those that require adherence to the limited and limiting harmonic series. There are easy starting points for experiments in monophonic music: beginning and ending pitches; long notes ornamented by other notes, especially upper and lower neighbors; repetition of significant pitches; upper and lower extrema, among others. Ethnomusicologists have accomplished an enormous amount of analysis of the melodies of various peoples by counting pitch occurrences, extracting weighted scales, and submitting large masses of material to statistical analyses. If cognitive psychologists worked from the other end, we would soon have a body of musical and psychological information about monophonic music that could provide a floor upon which we could build (and test) theories of monophonic, homophonic, polyphonic, and heterophonic music.

Work by Deutsch (1975a), who examined recognition of the pitch of a tone following a sequence of interpelated tones, has shown that repetition of the tone results in substantially improved memory. Such laboratory investigation provides converging evidence for the concept of centering.

A further concept of importance is the more ready processing of pitch combinations that are proximal. Van Noorden (1975) has suggested the idea of pitch motion detectors, hypothesizing that these operate on pitch combinations that are relatively closely related. Deutsch (1979), using her paradigm described above compared the pitches of two tones that were separated by six interpolated tones and found that error rates were lower when the interpolated sequences were composed of smaller melodic intervals, and argued that such sequences formed a more effective framework of pitch relationships to which the test tones could be anchored. Now melodies the world over appear to use a great many narrow intervals and fewer skips, and it is likely that this reflects a musical and perceptual universal. Is there a limit to the size of an interval that can be perceived as a step? Studies of centering would find that information useful. It might also prove fruitful to look into the finding (Bilsen, 1977; Fastl, 1971) that the pitch of bandpass noise is correlated with the center frequency when the bandwidth is small, roughly less than 1/5 of an octave, whereas for larger bandwidths pitches are correlated with the low and high cutoff frequencies. Upper and lower neighbors of a tone in tempered tuning will fill up a minor or a major third, 300 and 400 cents, respectively. A fifth of an octave is 240 cents, bigger than our common whole step of 200 cents but not quite our minor third. It is poised between being a step and being a skip.

IV. MUSIC AND PERCEPTUAL STREAMING

The phenomenon of perceptual channeling is fundamental to an understanding of melody, and it goes a long way toward demonstrating perceptual phenomena that must underly melodic patterning and certain kinds of polyphony, both old and new.

The formation of perceptual streams or channels was first investigated by Miller and Heise (1950). They found that a rapid trill broke into two separate streams when the frequency distance exceeded about 1/7 of an octave in musical ranges. They named the region of transition the *trill threshold*. Warren, Obusek, Farmer, and Warren (1969) found that in listening to a tape loop of four sounds (40 Hz square wave, 1000 Hz sine wave, the vowel "ee," white noise burst) played at a rate of 200 msec for each of the four items, their subjects had great difficulty in judging the order of the sounds. The four different sounds tended to form separate perceptual channels unless played very slowly. Bregman and Campbell (1971) suggested that stream formation is a primary auditory phenomenon, and Bregman and his associates have performed a number of later experiments relating to the perception of melodic matters in quasi-musical situations. Van Noorden (1975) related phenomena of fission and temporal coherence to music and to certain rules of counterpoint and musical composition stemming from the Classic and Baroque eras.

Bregman and Campbell (1971) defined a stream as "a sequence of auditory events whose elements are related perceptually to one another, the stream being segregated perceptually from other co-occuring events. We assume that attention cannot be paid to more than one such stream at a time, i.e., that the *apparent* simultaneous streams produced by this process have the same properties as actual simultaneous streams sent to separate ears."

Van Noorden (1975) made it clear that, within limits, our listening strategy is important, and he determined those limits experimentally (p. 10).

> The *temporal coherence boundary* is the boundary between temporal coherence and fission when the observer is trying to hear temporal coherence. The *fission boundary* is the boundary between temporal coherene and fission when the observer is trying to hear fission. ... At tone intervals above the temporal coherence boundary fission is observed no matter what the observer's attentional set, and at tone intervals below the fission boundary there is always temporal coherence; we may thus speak here of *inevitable* fission and *inevitable* temporal coherence, respectively.

The connection between auditory stream segregation and music can be shown vividly in certain movements of sonatas for solo instruments by J.S. Bach, where the single string of tones often breaks up into two, sometimes three, lines of melody, as shown in Fig. 1. The music for solo violin is shown on the top staff, and on the three lower staves, I have parsed it into its streams.

Bach's Finale from his C Major solo violin sonata displays three streams, from the beginning of the excerpt to measure 18, and two streams, in measures 19 through 22. The streams are well maintained in perception, even when there are quite long times between events in a stream; streaming is further facilitated by well-defined pitch registers for each of the streams.

The changes in texture from one to two to three streams are particularly interesting. For example, the downward scale passage on the last two quarter note beats of measure 18 dissolves the earlier established three voice scheme ("erases" it) and clears the perceptual field for the setting up of a two voice texture from measure 19 to the end of the example.

Fig. 1

My layout of the music sometimes shows a particular pitch belonging to two channels simultaneously (measure 16) to indicate a real ambiguity of channel. More often pitches shown in two channels will have one marked in parenthesis to show an ambiguity more easily resolved in listening. Especially at these points, the way we listen (our "set") can affect our perception of the music; viewed musically, these are pivots for changes between one channel and two, or between two channels and three.

The product of this sort of compound melodic line, as it is usually called by musicians, is polyphonic music. A two-part or three-part texture is easily heard. It is probably impossible for one to hear this as music without breaking the string of pitches into streams. Moreover, one hears an implied chordal skeleton with a harmonically meaningful bass line, and normal voice leading in all the virtual voices.

In none of his solo sonatas does Bach use more than three streams. Is three the upper limit? Informal experiments carried out by students in my timbre seminar at the University of California, San Diego, indicate that it is very difficult for musicians to maintain more than three in perception, when the material is disposed in alternating schemes such as those in the Bach solo sonata. Would a wider pitch range facilitate formation of more streams? At furthest stretch, using all musical resources of pitch, timbre, melodic and rhythmic patterning, how many simultaneous streams can we attend to, in the sense of being aware of their identity as streams? More than three? If so, would additional perceptual strategies be involved? Throughout the Bach excerpt in Fig. 1, there are surely musical grounds for "vertical" listening, especially at measures 21 through 22, where we can easily hear the music in terms of a dominant chord. With four or more streams, vertical listening may be even more likely because possible elements of melodic lines would be perceived more easily as elements of a vertical configuration.

Some music is directly related to the rapidly alternating tones design used by Van Noorden and Bregman and his associates, and most other investigators. But more often, the situation in music is mixed, with slower alternation, with some pitches held over to create real rather than virtual polyphony, and with other sorts of stream formation mixed together with those aspects of stream formation relating to pitch. Nevertheless, the model is of great value for our understanding of traditional music concepts. It can extend and even change some of them, and in the case of some contemporary music, this kind of music may be a necessity. The term in music for alternation of this sort is *hocket*. Traditionally, it means the breaking up of a melodic line between two or more singers, each singing a single note or a very few notes; a hocket among instruments is thought of as the same sort of distribution among instruments. It is a very general term, but its root notion is that one participant sings or plays while the other rests. In that way, the melody may be distributed among a group of performers.

There are not very many examples of written hocket in Western medieval music, but it is thought by some scholars that liturgical singers introduced hocketed passages into music notated otherwise. Beethoven's late quartets have many hocketed passages, some of dazzling complexity. In our century a most original development of hocket can be found in the music of Anton Webern. Hocket is common in the music of various peoples of Africa and Indonesia and, in fact, can be found in one form or another all over the world. Performance of hocket is difficult for Western musicians. Our whole system of notation and performance developed toward different musical goals. The performance of hocket appears to need a highly developed sense of community, in which each performer knows all the parts intimately and is able to contribute his or her single note at exactly the right moment. Hockets performed by BaBenzélé and Ituri forest pygmies show how complex communal performance can be.

In contemporary music the idea of hocket appears most usually in relation to *klangfarbenmelodie*. Webern distributed melodic elements among many instruments to bring out the motivic detail of the music. His orchestration of the Bach "Ricercar" from the Musical Offering (Erickson, 1975) looks in the score like a partially completed jigsaw puzzle but when heard it makes very good sense indeed, even though individual instruments often play only a few notes (but always a significant motivic element) at a time. All of Webern's music makes use of this breaking up of the traditional linking between instrument and melodic line and makes the following questions of more than passing interest. When do we follow timbre, and when do we follow pitch when the link between single melody/single sound source is broken?

In order to learn more about this question, I made an informal experiment (Erickson, 1974) using six instruments and a repeating melodic sequence. I reasoned that if, for example, I had a six-tone sequence performed by five players with each instrument playing a single note in the manner of a hocket, each pitch of the melodic pattern would eventually be played by a different instrument, averaging out, so to speak, qualitative differences of individual instruments in relation to the various pitches of the repeating melodic sequence. The instruments used were those I had available to me: flute, clarinet, saxophone, bassoon, trumpet, and marimba. The marimba is a foreigner among the other instruments, all winds. Nevertheless, I felt that I could at least make gross judgments about the effects of pitch versus timbre on the formation of perceptual streams. In Fig. 2 the repeating melodic figure is six tones long, printed at the top of the score. The individual parts for the instruments are below, transposed for the transposing instruments.

Clearly, one is able to listen to this delicious confusion in more than one way:

1. One may follow the tune through its changes of timbre.

2. One may begin to form perceptual streams on a pitch basis. In this kind of listening the C/B♭ patterns of the high line and the E♭/D♭ patterns of the low line are clearest.

3. One may follow the line of a single instrument (marimba is easy; clarinet is more difficult).

4. One may listen—and this is most likely—in a mixed manner, using (1) or (2) or (3), depending upon the detailed musical situation at any particular moment and depending also upon ones "set."

With fewer instruments one might expect the channeling to be stronger because each instrument is heard with fewer rests between appearances. Therefore, some segments of my LOOPS experiment employ only three instruments. It might be very slightly easier to follow an individual instrumental line when three instruments are employed, but not much. The following of an instrument appears to depend here

Fig. 2

more upon the special characteristics of the instrument, especially its attack quality, in relation to the total group or subgroup, surely reflecting the importance of context to any understanding of how timbre works in music.

Melodic sequences of from 5 to 13 pitches were used, over spans of up to three octaves, and a variety of schemes were devised to cycle the six instruments over these patterns. Rigid schemes were sometimes modified by compositional intuitions, and certainly LOOPS can be thought of as an experiment only in the vague sense that it was not conceived as a musical composition. Nevertheless, it does answer the fundamental musical question: Is this sort of disposition of material worth bothering about for music? And the answer is certainly yes—difficult, very difficult for the players, but worth the effort.

In the light of the LOOPS experiment, it appears that the answer to the question, can a melodic figure be preserved while undergoing radical changes of instrumental timbre is yes—but. The *but* includes matters such as the total range of the melodic pattern, the tempo, the particular instruments involved, their timbres at the specified pitches, and the type of articulation of the attack and decay. It is easy, by allowing only slight overlaps of sound, to turn a precariously sequential melodic formation into something clearly polyphonic.

How strong is the effect of the timbre pattern versus the melodic pattern? Strong—but no general statement is possible. The subpatterns produced by the competition between pitch channeling and timbre channeling are local effects but controllable and full of compositional potential, not least in the area of rhythm. It is of great interest that in spite of the meter of the counting process, the patterning is chiefly a result of tonic accent, loudness of the various notes in an instrument's repertory, and articulation of attack and decay. Timbral distinctiveness or vividness (Dowling, 1973) appears important, perhaps crucial, to the formation of the sub-groupings and, therefore, to the rhythm and the higher levels of the musical organization.

Why is the number of effective perceptual categories often less than six, even when all instruments are playing? This certainly could be investigated experimentally, but it is of musical interest, too, because confusions among clarinet, saxophone, and bassoon in certain contexts of LOOPS mean that there are different perceptual contrast relationships in different musical situations. The distinctiveness of a timbre, and therefore its contrast potential, is different in different registers (or even different pitches not very far apart) in a nonsimple way. We cannot think merely in terms of gross contrast—clarinet, trumpet, saxophone, etc.—but must always consider the timbre of the instrument at whatever particular pitch it is playing. Now, if certain instruments can be composed in such a way that either they can be made to tend toward homogeneity or confusability of sound or toward diversity and distinctiveness of sound, there is a possibility for structural interplay between timbre and pitch that could be of use to composers today.

If all this seems inconclusive, part of the reason is certainly the vagueness of the concept of timbre. We have come a long way from the time when timbre was identified chiefly with the spectrum of a stationary sound. We can now analyze time varying complex individual instrument sounds and synthesize convincing replicas through the computer music technology started by Mathews and Pierce (Grey, 1975; Moorer, 1975). These replicas and the potential for their controlled modification by the experimenter should make possible an approach to musical timbre and its perception that could benefit both music and science. Timbre itself has been a tangle of puzzles. Timbre in music may need many different models. That of streaming is certainly important, exactly because principles of streaming can be applied to the understanding of both timbre and pitch. We may be able to learn more about what we call pitch by learning more about timbre.

V. FUSED SOUNDS IN MUSIC

If we ask questions about how we are able to recognize the various instruments in an ensemble, certain musical/perceptual ways of thinking about timbre are uncovered. Helmholtz (1859–1954) was close to Gestalt concepts in this passage (pp. 59–60):

Now there are many circumstances which assist us first in separating the musical tones arising from different sources, and secondly, in keeping together the partial tones of each separate source. Thus when one musical tone is heard for some time before being joined by the second, and then the second continues after the first has ceased, the separation in sound is facilitated by the succession of time. We have already heard the first musical tone by itself, and hence know immediately what we have to deduct from the compound effects for the effect of this first tone.... All these helps fail in the resolution of musical tones into their constituent partials. When a compound tone commences to sound, all its partial tones commence with the same comparative strength; when it swells, all of them generally swell uniformly; when it ceases, all cease simultaneously.... Hence we have no reason to be surprised that the resolution of a compound tone into its partials is not quite so easy for the ear to accomplish...

These remarks have been a springboard for several investigators. Van Noorden (1975) showed that in a fast alternating sequence of a pure tone and a complex tone of the same pitch but without any contiguous frequency components among its partials, we can hear two streams. Temporal coherence is heard when the frequency components of complex tones are contiguous. Noncontiguous frequency components produce fission. A musician would say that we are making the two streams on the basis of timbre differences.

Rasch (1977, 1978) took up another Helmholtz cue: that we are able to distinguish the instruments because they never play in absolute synchrony. In a series of elegant experiments, he found that asynchronies of up to 30 msec were still perceived as simultaneous and that this "asynchronization is an important factor in the perception of the various parts or voices in music."

Bregman and Pinker (1978) and Dannenbring and Bregman (1978) responded to Helmholtz's remarks from another viewpoint:

> There are two principles embedded in Helmholtz's speculation: they could be referred to as "continuation" and "common fate." Both of these are principles that have been studied by the Gestalt psychologists, e.g. Koffka (1935). The first principle states that if an element of a perceptual array forms a simple continuation of another series, it should be treated as part of that series. In audition, if a set of frequency components, not yet assigned to stream A, are a good continuation of components of a stream, they should be assigned to that stream.
>
> The second principle is that of "common fate," sets of sensory elements that change in parallel ways will be perceived as whole and distinct entities.... In audition, the principle might apply to the movement of pure tone components over time. If two of them change in amplitude together (e.g., come on at the same time) or are frequency modulated together, they should fuse into a single stream with a timbre determined by the set of fused components (Bregman & Pinker, 1978).

The method they used in some of their experiments, in which the listener makes judgments about "richness," may be open to criticism; additional experiments (Dannenbring & Bregman, 1978) explore other aspects such as intensity and onset/offset asynchrony. There is, therefore, considerable experimental data to support their striking assertion (Bregman & Pinker, 1978): "Timbre seems to be a perceptual description of a stream, not of an acoustic waveform." They conclude that "sequential and simultaneous grouping effects can compete... frequency separation is a strong determinant of the sequential effect... onset/offset synchrony is an important determinant of the simultaneous effect (perceptual fusion)." They view the distinction between the sequential and the simultaneous as applying to music, in which the distinction is expressed as that between melody and timbre; and they view that the two together play their role in ordinary listening situations, parsing the input waveform to find the meaningful sources: "The sequential effect hooks frequency components into streams. The simultaneous effect, by selecting which harmonics to fuse, determines the acoustic quality (timbre) of each moment of each stream." A related experiment on the effects of stimulus asynchrony on streaming was performed by Deutsch (1979). She used a paradigm in which melodic sequences were distributed between ears and presented these with a drone pitch in several conditions. She found that onset/offset asynchrony produces less input to the two ears and that such asynchrony resulted in an increased tendency to treat this input as emanating from different sources.

In another experiment Deutsch (1975b) presented two simultaneous sequences of tones, one to each ear. The sequences formed ascending and descending scales such that when a note from the ascending scale was in one ear, a note from the descending scale was in the other ear and successive notes in each scale alternated from ear to ear. She found that this sequence was perceptually reorganized by the listeners so that (in the majority of cases) a sequence corresponding to the higher tones appeared to be coming from one earphone and a sequence corresponding to the lower tones from the other. Butler (1979) studied the effect of presenting the Deutsch scale sequence to students in a school of music through speakers as well as through earphones and found that the same perceptual reorganization occurred. He also studied the effect of introducing differences in timbre between the stimuli presented through the different earphones. Although all listeners heard an overall change of quality that pervaded the sequences, this seemed to emanate from both earphones or both speakers.

If further experimental work supports these hypotheses, musicians will have ways of thinking about timbre that go beyond those of psychophysics. The basic discoveries of psychophysics are solidly in place, and what is needed for theoretical thought about music is more work that deals with the ways in which we mentally process musical information. Experiments with fusion of vertical elements and onset and offset may give us further insight into the meaning of simultaneity in music. Musicians know that the idea of "together" is a very complex one: the onset characteristics of the instruments in an orchestra are vastly different; players must compensate for these differences and consider the further the factor is irreducible human variability; sounding "together" is a matter of context, musical context, with important components contributed by tempo, isolation by silence, register, pitch variability, vibrato, among others. There is also the fascinating fact for musicians that the bigger the ensemble the wider the "together" time window. Why should this be true?

Anything we can learn about fusion processes in audition will be especially valuable to music theory. Much contemporary music uses fused masses of sound for its musical effect—for example, György Ligeti's *Atmospheres*, in which there are no melodies, no profiled rhythms, no "voices." What is presented is a subtle play of timbre mixtures and changing textures. Textures here are good analogies to those of visual perception, but music theory is poor in concepts dealing with textures of this sort. The usual musical distinctions are between monophonic, polyphonic, and homophonic types with additional distinctions as to the number of voices and the relations, primarily rhythmic and harmonic, between important foreground and background events.

For new music since the 1950s, two ideas about musical texture, massing and layering, are especially prominent. Dense agglomerations of pitches can sometimes be perceived as totalities, textures, sound blocks. They can be contrasted with each other sequentially, or they can be superimposed in various ways. They are objects in the sense that they have perceived beginnings and endings and are disposed cohesively by means of pitch, timbre, tempo and articulation. Nevertheless, their integrity is likely to be perceptually precarious, and that is what makes them interesting. In discussing the musical consequences for 1950s serialism, Ligeti (1965) introduced the notion of permeability: "Let us take an illuminating analogy: playing with plasticine. The distinct lumps of the various colours gradually become more dispersed the more you knead the stuff; the result is a conglomeration in which patches of the colours can still be distinguished, whereas the whole is characterized by lack of contrast." He discusses how a musical organization of these global configurations might be accomplished with a serialist ideology without an accompanying greying out of contrast:

> The function of shaping the form, which was once restricted to individual melodic lines, motifs, or chordal shapes, has been handed over in serial music to more complex categories, such as Groups, Structures or Textures, and, because of this, the way these are woven now takes over a very eminent role in the compositional design. It is possible to distinguish various "aggregate-conditions" of the material. One can see most clearly how such conditions articulate the form in compositions where the diverse types of "weave" are accompanied by considerable differences in timbre and density, and are thus even more clearly differentiated. In Stockhausen's "Gruppen," for example, the backbone of the form is given by contrasted types—hacked, pulverized, melted, highly condensed—and their gradual transformations and mixtures one with another. In this method of composition it is vitally important to pay attention to the available degrees of permeability. The two extreme types enjoy exceptionally good mutual permeability: a dense, gelatinous, soft and sensitive material can be penetrated *ad libitum* by sharp hacked splinters. Their mutual indifference is so great that the layers can get considerably "out" in time, and enjoy fields of inexactitude of considerable latitude.... "Soft" materials are less permeable when combined with each other, and there are places in Stockhausen's "Gruppen" of an opaque complexity beyond compare.

Cone (1972) has presented an interesting view of the sudden breaks and interruptions characteristic of Stravinsky's music from the time of *Rite of Spring* onward.

> On examination, the point of interruption proves to be only the most immediately obvious characteristic of a basic Stravinskyan technique comprising three phases, which I call stratification, interlock, and synthesis. By stratification I mean the separation in musical space of... musical areas, juxtaposed in time; the interruption is the mark of this separation. The resultant layers of sound may be differentiated by glaring contrast.... The effect may be much more subtle.... In almost every case, however, there is at least one element of connection between successive levels...

Interrupted streams characterized by register, rhythm, timbre, and sometimes by tempo can be understood as layers. Cone's concepts, interlock and synthesis, are more difficult to relate to primary cognitive processes and may belong to different analytical levels. In Stravinskian strata pitch separation of each stratum is essential; though melodic, rhythmic and timbral organizations certainly facilitate their formation. The rather strict isolation by register makes them easy to hear and to follow throughout the interruptions.

Music theory does not have a very sharply formulated conception of what an object might be, probably because it has been concerned largely with melodic and harmonic processes in which the notion of an object can become very slippery. Nevertheless, it would be of value for an understanding of what Ligeti calls "types of material" and what other writers have referred to as "sound blocks" to look into perceptual aspects of musical phenomena that may be related to our object perception in the visual domain.

Informal experiments, many of them in seminars at the University of California, San Diego, have uncovered a few criteria that lead to agreement among musicians. Isolated sounds (surrounded by silence) can most easily be heard as objects. Compact sounds are good candidates: the beginning of the sound should be clearly defined so that it does not allow the listener to break it apart into two or more components. The end of the sound must disappear smoothly; otherwise, a listener will perceive a break and therefore another object. The law of common fate is involved here. Things that begin and end together have a good chance of being perceived as belonging together. If there are perceptible interruptions, the sound may break apart into two or more objects. If the sound lasts very long, musicians are likely to listen to component frequencies, noise components, beats, and other elements; and the object will lose its holistic identity.

Experiments were made with the sorts of concatenations that Ligeti referred to as aggregates and textures, asking the question, when can an aggregate or a texture be an object; further informal experiments demonstrated that an object could glide in pitch without losing its single object quality. These informal experiments and demonstrations—carried out by means of electronic generation, electronic manipulation, tape speed changes, and shaping with filters—as well as with musical instruments indicate that if scientific studies were to proceed along this line, the results would be of value for musicians and might have some interest for those who are studying the fusion of sounds in the real world.

Similar informal experiments and demonstrations were carried out in relation to layering and stratification, asking the question, how many layers can we hear at the same time. Remembering that melodic fission appeared to offer no musical examples of more than three streams, we wondered if layers of sounds had a similar limitation.

Segments of layered sound were presented in units from 2 to 3 sec long. Some of these had 6 or 7 levels known to the experimenter, but musicians were rarely able to hear more than 3 or 4 layers, even when the layers were distributed across seven octaves of pitch. Apparently we fuse the sounds when times are short; if more time is available, we follow streams of sound. All musicians who heard these sounds were sure that they could hear more layers if the sounds extended longer in time.

Helmholtz mentioned in the passage quoted earlier in this essay that we are helped in our identification of instruments by the fact that they rarely begin together. Com-

posers have been keenly interested since the time of Berlioz, if not before, in composing for instruments in such a way that the sound of the individual instruments are lost
in an ensemble timbre. From a musical point of view we may assume that whether we
are likely to hear a compound ensemble sound as a single fused timbral entity or as
discrete pitches of a chord depends overwhelmingly on the musical situation: how
long the sound lasts, whether players begin and end together, the pitch disposition,
whether it can be more easily understood as a vertical formation or as individual
instrumental parts, whether the component instrumental sounds are steady or un-
steady, whether the instruments are balanced in loudness, the characteristics of the
hall, and the placement of the instruments. In spite of these hurdles musicians are
sometimes able to produce ensemble timbres that sometimes fuse for listeners in a
concert hall. It is as though one were hearing an unknown new instrument rather than
a group. Brilliant instances are to be heard in the music of Varese, but composers of
instrumental music and composers of computer music are equally interested in this
musical possibility.

Texture may be related to musical pitch perception, too. The choric effect, the
difference between the sound of one violin and a section of 16 or more, can best be
thought of as a texture. Investigators have found the choric effect to be acoustically
complex and do not know enough about it; but it is musically remarkable that the
same passage played by single instruments of an ensemble, say a chamber group of
single string instruments, is harder to get acceptably in tune than the same passage
played by multiples of those same instruments. Is it because listeners are able to select
the "in-tune-ness" from the section sound, which must in fact be a pitch band of
substantial width, and are unable to use that strategy with single instruments?

VI. MUSIC THEORY AND EXPERIMENTAL SCIENCE

I believe that the answers to questions such as this can be addressed with the
methods and conceptual framework of experimental cognitive psychology. They are
mostly fundamental questions about perceptual processes and strategies, and it is on
that level that they intersect with music.

There cannot be a very large number of classes of strategy for the processing of
auditory information. The work of the last 15 years indicates that there may be only a
few. Viewed from outside, modern cognitive psychology appears to be giving the
rules of Gestalt psychology a solid empirical base. These findings intersect with
music consistently. Music can be well understood in all its dimensions in terms of
grouping—the dividing of the sound world. The complexity comes not from a multiplicity of strategies but from interactions between pitch, timbre, rhythm, texture, and
other dimensions, especially interactions on the microlevel that has been so little
addressed in music theory.

The problem for music theory is to discover the musical level or levels at which
these processes function. I have tried to confine my remarks to those levels where a
definite connection between music and perceptual processing can be demonstrated. It

is possible, even probable, that relationships between higher levels of cognition and musical organization can be shown by experiment and supported by empirical work with pseudomusical models. If that is to take place, it appears to me that it can succeed only if there is continuous close interaction between musicians and scientific investigators. There are many barriers to cross before this can be accomplished—the difficulty of communication across disciplines, the belief on the part of musicians that nothing of value to music can be learned from science, the skepticism of scientists about the vague and confusing terminology of music, especially contemporary music, and the scientist's own prejudices about what music is. In reading scientific literature that refers to music, I have found over and over that the implied definition of music within which the writer has conducted his or her discussion has been so primitive, so narrow, that it could only have been formed in childhood, probably during a period of study of some instrument, commonly the piano. If interaction with sophisticated musicians can be of value in helping scientists to expand and refine their ideas about what music has been and what it could be, it will at the same time help to erase the impression of many musicians that scientists are people who wear white coats and produce prescriptive final answers.

Both scientists and musicians may feel that my expectations from science for music are too modest. I do not think that the findings of cognitive psychology are in themselves music theory. They are (should be) the substrate upon which theories of various aspects of music can be erected. A music theory that does not take into account our perceptual processing and perceptual strategies cannot possibly be related to any real-world musical activity no matter how ingenious its superstructure.

Neither science nor music theory is of any great value to the practicing musician when performing or composing. Theory is a separate and distinct world that exists to satisfy our curiosity. Making music is a unitary process. Imagination, invention, and memories of sounds are mixed with thinking, and the thinking is not like theoretical thinking or the thinking that goes into science. That is why prescriptive music theory is so annoying to those musicians who actually make music. Consequently, I see the value of science as providing the substrate of ideas upon which a proper music theory may be erected. The task of that theory is to rationalize what musicians do.

REFERENCES

Babbitt, M. The synthesis, perception and specification of musical time. *Journal of the International Folk Music Council*, 1964, *16*, 92–95.

Berry, W. *Structural functions in music*. Englewood Cliffs, New Jersey: Prentice-Hall, 1976.

Bilsen, F. A. Pitch of noise signals: Evidence for a "central spectrum." *Journal of the Acoustical Society of America*, 1977, *61*, No. 1, 150–161.

Bregman, A. S., & Campbell, J. Primary auditory stream segregation and perception of order in rapid sequences of tones. *Journal of Experimental Psychology*, 1971, *89*, No. 2, 244–249.

Bregman, A. S., & Pinker, S. Auditory streaming and the building of timbre. *Canadian Journal of Psychology*, 1978, *32*, 20–31.

Butler, D. A further study of melodic channeling. *Perception & Psychophysics*, 1979, *25*, 264–268.

Cone, E. T. Stravinsky: The progress of a method. In B. Boretz & E. Cone (Eds.), *Perspectives on Schoenberg and Stavinsky*. New York: Norton, 1972.

Dannenbring, G. L., & Bregman, A. S. Streaming vs. fusion of sinusoidal components of complex tones. *Perception & Psychophysics*, 1978, *24*, No. 4, 369–376.

Deutsch, D. Facilitation by repetition in recognition memory for tonal pitch. *Memory & Cognition*, 1975, *3*, 263–266. (a)

Deutsch, D. Two-channel listening to musical scales. *Journal of the Acoustical Society of America*, 1975, *57*, 1156–1160. (b)

Deutsch, D. Binaural integration of melodic patterns. *Perception & Psychophysics*, 1979, *25*, No. 5, 399–405.

Dowling, W. J. The perception of interleaved melodies. *Cognitive Psychology*, 1973, *5*, 322–337.

Erickson, R. LOOPS; An informal timbre experiment. Center for Music Experiment, University of California, San Diego (with tape of musical examples). Q-037, U.C.S.D., La Jolla, California 92093, 1974.

Erickson, R. *Sound structure in music*. Berkeley, California: University of California Press, 1975.

Fastl, H. Ueber Tonhohenempfindungen bei Rauschen. *Acustica*, 1971, *25*, 350–354.

Grey, J. An exploration of musical timbre. Report No. STAN-M-2, Department of Music, Stanford University, 1975.

Helmholtz, H.L.F. *On the sensations of Tone* (Translated by A. J. Ellis). New York: Dover, 1954.

Kalib, S. *Thirteen Essays from the Three Yearbooks "Das Meisterwerk in der Musik"*, 1975, *1*, 73–30, 626.

Ligeti, G. Metamorphosis of musical form. *Die Reihe*, 1965, 7, 5–19.

Mathews, M. V. The digital computer as a musical instrument. *Science*, 1963, *142*, 553–557.

Miller, G. A., & Heise, G. A. The trill threshold. *Journal of the Acoustical Society of America*, 1950, *22*, 637–638.

Moorer, J. A. The synthesis of complex audio spectra by means of discrete summation formulae. Report No. STAN-M-5, Department of Music, Stanford University, 1975.

Rasch, R. A. The perception of simultaneous notes such as in polyphonic music. Abstract, p. 15. *IRCAM Symposium sur la Psychoacoustique Musicale, Paris*, July 1977.

Rasch, R. A. The perception of simultaneous notes such as in polyphonic music. *Acustica*, 1978, *40*, No. 1, 21–31.

Salzer, F. *Structural hearing*. Vol. 1. New York: Charles Boni, 1952.

Schoenberg, A. Problems of harmony. *Modern Music*, 1934, *11*, No. 4, 167–187. Translated by A. Weiss.

Travis, R. Towards a new concept of tonality? *Journal of Music Theory*, 1959, *3*, No. 2, 257–284.

Van Noorden, L.P.A.S. Temporal Coherence in the Perception of Tone Sequences. Published Ph.D. thesis, Institute for Perception Research, Eindhoven, Holland, 1975.

Warren, R. M., Obusek, C. J., Farmer, R. M., and Warren, R. P. Auditory sequences: Comparisons of patterns other than speech or music. *Science*, 1969, *164*, 586–587.

Index

A

Absolute pitch
  accuracy, 438–440
  and heredity, 434
  and imprinting, 435
  and information transfer, 246, 440–443
  and learning, 434, 445–447
  and relative pitch, 344, 432, 337–438, 448
  and the piano, 436–437
  and timbre, 436–437
  and unlearning, 435
  disabilities relating to, 457
  octave errors, 272, 439, 440–441
  quasi-absolute pitch, 438, 445, 446
  stability, 444–445
  the value of, 447–449
Accent, *see also,* Loudness
  in musical performance, 173
  relation to rhythmic groups, 157, 159
Aesthetics, 318ff
  aesthetic episode, 500ff
  and culture, 317–320
  and emotion, 500–502, 507–511
  and mood optimization, 513–515
  and musical idioms, 498–500
  and technology, 498–499
  choice and attention, 505–507
  choice and social factors, 499–501, 502–505
  effects of complexity on emotion and behavior, 507–511
  music appreciation testing, 401–402
  phrasing and emotion in singing, 91–94
  planning of music sequences, 511–515
Agnosia, relation to amusia 456, 462–466
Amusia, 454ff
Aphasia, relation to amusia, 455–462, 466–468
Archetypes, 317ff
Arrhythmia, 150, 165–167
Attention, *see also* Channeling
  automaticity, 458–459, 467
  dual task, 218–220
  effects on aesthetic choice, 505–507
  shifts in, 215–216
  voluntary attention and grouping, 127–130

B

Bach, 171ff, 524–526
Bartok, 172
Basilar membrane, 52, 260
Beat, 182ff
Beats, 14–16, 91, 255–256, 348
Beethoven, 119, 171, 172, 325–326, 327ff, 526
Berg, 520
Berlioz, 534
Bottom-up processes, 272, 278
Boulez, 50

C

Categorical perception, 250–254, 349, 384, 396–397, 432, 465–466
Channeling, *see also* Grouping
  of rapid sequences of tones, 43, 48, 118ff, 523ff
  of sequences of simultaneous tones, 526, 533
Chopin, 172, 175
Chords, 273, 377, 394, 400–401, *see also* Harmony, inversions
  and tonality, 520–523
  disabilities relating to, 457
  physiological substrata, 274–277
Circular tones, 54, 263–264, 352, 358, 361, 370–372
Cochlea, 4
Combination tones, 8, 17–19
Composition, 514
Conducting, 492–493
Consonance, 19–21, 348, 376, 400
  of complex tones, 20–21
  sensory consonance, 19–21, 259–262
  small integer ratios, 255–256
Critical band, 5, 6, 15, 19, 28–29, 76, 259

D

Debussy, 50, 172
Definition, 137, 141–142, 145–146
Development
  comparisons with adults, 416, 418
  of absolute pitch, 435
  of interval sense, 262

of musical ability, 392–393, 394–395, 399,
    400–401
of rhythm, 161, 415, 416
Direct sound, 135
Dissonance, 19–21, 255–256, 348, 376, 400
    of complex tones, 260
    sensory dissonance, 19–21, 259–262
Duration, *see also* Intervals of time
    accuracy and pitch, 518
    and channel capacity, 168
    and emotion, 93
    and grouping, 159–160
    and rhythmic patterns, 165–167
    comparisons with interval fractions, 220–223
    of interval markers, 216–217
    of notes, 482
    subjective duration, 183–184

E

Echoes, 104, 114, 136
Echogram, 138–140
Emotion, 91–94, 470, 501, 507–511
Euclidean composition, 357, 367–369, 372

F

Factor analysis, 137, 140, 141, 143, 174, 176,
    393–396
Feedback, 403–404
    and absolute pitch, 446, 447
    and vibrato, 488
    delayed auditory feedback, 404, 488–489
    immediate auditory feedback, 488–489
    in judgment and production, 200–203, 225–226
    social feedback, 501, 503, 504
Fission boundary, 118, 120, 128, 524
Formants, 27–28, 36, 61–63, 66–69, 69–71, 74, 79,
    82–84
Fourier analysis, 4–5, 26–27, 44, 50–52
Fraction names, 185
Fractional, intervals 184
Frequency, *see* Pitch
Frequency analysis by the ear, 4–5, 26–27, 52
Frequency glide, 54, 124, 127

G

Gestalt psychology, 7, 100–101, 116, 158, 161, 282,
    529–530, 534
    common fate, 7, 101, 107, 530, 533
    good continuation, 100–101, 102–103, 120, 124,
        161, 290, 302, 530

proximity, 100, 102, 105ff, 118, 161, 282, 302,
    290–291
similarity 100, 124–125, 161
Gregorian chant, 175
Grouping
    and kinesthetic response, 158
    and pause, 159–160, 168
    and repetition, 120–122
    and tonality, 304–311
    by amplitude, 126, 162
    by frequency, 102–104, 109–110, 112, 118–123ff,
        160–162, 527
    by spatial location, 102, 105–107, 108ff
    by timbre, 124–125, 128, 160, 527, 529–534
    duration of groups, 157–158
    fission boundary, 118, 120, 128, 524
    handedness correlates, 114–116
    melodic invariance under timbral change, 526–529
    pitch versus timbre, 529, 530
    scale illusion, 102–104, 114–115, 127–128, 531
    temporal coherence boundary, 119–120, 128, 524
    temporal relationships, 104–108, 113–114,
        122–123, 126–127, 304–311
    the octave illusion, 108–116, 122, 128

H

Harmonic series, 520–523
Harmonics, 4–5, 7–10, 13–14, 26–29, 60, 255–256,
    347
Harmony, 243, *see also* Chords, inversions
    and categorical perception, 251
    and culture, 320
    choric effect, 534
    harmonic map 376–378
    testing for harmonic appreciation, 400–401
Haydn, 318–319, 327ff
Helix of pitch, 274, 286, 352–354, 361, 373,
    432–434
Hocket, 128, 526–529

I

Idiot–savants, 406
Illusions
    octave, 108–116, 122, 128
    scale, 102–104, 114–115, 127–128, 531
Improvisation, 483–484
Indirect sound, 136ff
Indirect/direct ratio, 140, 143, 144
INDSCAL, 365–367
Interaural differences, 101–118, 144
Intervals

of pitch, *see also* Octave, pitch
    absolute identification, 260–261
    adjustment procedure, 249–250, 260
    and category-scaling, 247–249, 251, 260
    and context-coding, 245–246, 253–254
    and culture, 302–303
    and information transfer, 245–246
    and loudness, 518
    children's perception of, 418–419
    comparison with speech discrimination, 251ff
    contextual independence, 247
    critical band, 5, 6, 15, 19
    discrimination, 250–254, 260–261
    frequency ratio detectors, 260–261
    harmonic intervals, 243, 246, 251, 258–259,
        260, 273, 274, 276, 278, 300–301, 348
    interval and chord equivalence, 273
    interval class, 273, 278–282, 286
    interval size and tonality, 523
    interval succession, 518
    learned versus innate categories, 261–262
    magnitude estimation, 249
    melodic intervals, 243, 246, 274–249, 250–251,
        258–259, 261, 273, 277, 278, 302, 347, 348
    memory for, 300–304
    natural intervals, 255–262
    size of intervals, 302–304
    small frequency ratios, 347
    successive-interval, array 285
    transposition, 274–275, 279, 285, 287ff, 346,
        414, 415–416, 417–418, 423–424
of time
    and spontaneous tapping, 157
    dependence on duration versus fraction,
        220–223
    full-concatenation model, 208, 213
    imitation of, 207ff
    judgment of, 187ff, 215–223, 457
    onset and offset marking, 216–217
    partial-concatenation model, 213
    production of, 198ff, 224–229, 457
Inversion, 283–284, 286, 425
Inversions of chords, 260, 273, 355–356, 361, 379,
    383
    interference in memory, 301
    physiological substrata, 274–277

J

Judgment function, 185, 187

K

Kinesthetic perception, 398, 403–404

L

Lateralization, 467–468
Ligeti, 531–533
Linear predictive coding, 37, 46–47, 51
Liszt, 175
Loudness, 10–12
    absolute loudness, 443
    and channeling, 110ff
    and classification of melody, 338
    and duration, 160
    and emotion, 93
    and formant tuning, 63–66
    and grouping, 162
    and room acoustics, 136–137, 140
    and spectrum, 12
    children's perception of, 419
    in performance, 489–490
    phone scale, 11
    sone scale, 11
    thresholds, 463

M

Melody, *see also* Grouping
    and culture, 421–423
    and interval class, 278–281
    and phase-shifted tones, 116–117
    and tonality, 399
    ascending melody, 246, 250
    changing-note melodies, 325–326, 326ff
    channeling of rapid sequences, 43, 48, 118ff, 523ff
    concept-identification experiments, 326–340
    contour, 111–112, 277, 279, 414, 415, 416–418,
        419–420, 421–423, 424–427
    descending melody, 246, 250
    difficulties in analyzing, 320–322
    disabilities relating to, 457, 459, 462, 464
    gap-filled melodies, 322–324, 326ff
    handedness correlates, 114–116
    hierarchical structure, 290–291, 320–322,
        337–338
    hocket, 526–529
    interdependence of features, 422–423
    melodic space, 375–376
    melody perception in childhood, 416–421
    melody perception in infants, 415–416
    memory for, 118–119, 279–281, 301–302,
        304–311, 397–398, 423–427, 485
    recognition of, 278–280
    semitone versus tonal representation, 424–425, 426
    testing of melodic ability, 394ff
    the scale illusion, 102–104, 114–115, 127–128, 531
    transposition, 116

two-channel listening, 101–118
Memorization, 406, 483
Memory
  and interval size, 245–246
  and lateral inhibition, 297–298
  and organization of a sequence, 158, 294–300
  for absolute pitch, 292
  for hierarchical tonal sequences, 304–311
  for interval sizes, 424–425
  for melody, 118–119, 279–281, 301–302,
    304–311, 397–398, 423–427, 485
  for melody in children, 416–417, 419–420,
    420–421
  for pitch, 245–246, 292–304, 397–398, 437–438
  for waveform data, 423
  interactions between pitches, 292–300
  interactions between systems, 301–304
  interference and octaves, 272
  octave generalization effects, 298–299
Meter, 171–173
Modulation transfer function, 142
Morse code, 168, 169
Mozart, 318–320, 322, 324, 327ff
Multidimensional scaling, 14, 33, 47–49, 138, 174,
    287, 356, 365–367, 372
Music and psychoacoustics, 517ff
Music appreciation, see Aesthetics
Music reading, disabilities, of 457, 459–461
Music theory and psychology, 517ff, 534–535
Music and culture, 520, 522, 526–527
Musical ability, and intelligence 394, 404–408
Musical achievement, 391–393
Musical aptitude, 391–393
Musical training, 419–420, 427

O

Octave, 346ff, see also Pitch, intervals of pitch
  adjustment procedure, 249–250
  and culture, 244, 263, 272
  and sensory consonance, 262
  octave errors, 439
  octave generalization, 246, 262–264, 272,
    274–277, 278–281, 298–299, 346ff, 426
  physiological substrata, 274–277
  the octave illusion, 108–116, 122, 128

P

Paisiello, 119
Palestrina, 499
Partials, see Harmonics
Perceptual restoration, 127

Performance, 223, 480ff
Personality, 408
Pitch, see also Octave
  alphabets and hierarchies, 287–291, 304–311
  analogy with vision, 274, 282–283
  and bandwith, 523
  and duration, 518
  and frequency, 6–10, 243, 344–345, 369
  and inharmonic partials, 9
  as a morphophoric medium, 380–381
  children's understanding of tonality, 415, 416,
    417–419, 420–421
  chroma, 246, 262–264, 272, 273–277, 278–282,
    283–287, 298–299, 426–427, 432, 439, 433,
    352, 359–364, 365–369, 371, 374
  circle of fifths, 287, 320, 359–364, 365–369, 371,
    382
  circular tones, 54, 263–264, 352, 358, 361,
    370–372
  cognitive-structural approach to, 346, 349–350,
    372–374
  combination tones, 8, 17–19
  component structures, 357–361
  disabilities relating to, 457ff
  discrimination, 244–246, 396, 399–400
  discrimination in infants, 416
  dominance region, 8–9
  effect on time interval judgments, 215–216
  feature abstraction, 272ff
  helix of pitch, 274, 286, 352–354, 361, 373,
    432–434
  low pitch, 7–10, 349
  mel scale, 6–7, 345, 433
  memory for, 245–246, 292–304, 397–398,
    437–438
  microtones, 244, 248–249, 439
  multi-dimensional representations of, 286–287,
    347–369, 369–384
  of complex tones, 7–10, 262–264, 345, 348, 371
  pitch accuracy in singing, 89–91
  pitch class, 272, 273–277, 278–282, 283–287,
    298–299, see also Chroma
  pitch height, 246, 262–264, 272, 352, 357ff,
    365–369, 370, 371, 432, 439
  pitch-set, 285
  relation to rhythmic groups, 157, 160–161, 163
  spatial representation of, 350–369
  testing of pitch perception, 396–397ff
  transcription of pitch notation, 486–487
  variance of pitch and duration, 518
  vibrato, 35, 54, 84–89, 488
  volley theory of perception, 274
Pitch-synchronous, analysis, 31

Plans in performance, 480–487
Plato, 150–151
Polyphony, 400–401, 521–522, 523ff
Polyrhythm, 170
Power functions, 205–207
Preference, 498ff
  and complexity, 498, 502–504, 505–507
  for frequency ratios, 347
Production function, 185
Psychometric function, 3, 188–189, 194–198, 233, 234–236
Psychophysical methods, 2–4, 137–140, 231–237
Psychophysical scaling, 11–12, 143, 187ff, 345
Pythagoras, 255, 347

R

Reaction time, 154–155, 203–205
Residue, 8
Retrogression, 283–284, 286, 425
Reverberation, 104, 114, 135–136, 141, 143
Rhythm, *see also* Grouping
  and arrhythmia, 150, 165–167
  and biological clocks, 152
  and culture, 380
  and development, 415, 416
  and lateralization, 467–468
  and melody, 278
  and movement, 150, 152ff, 174, 403–404
  and runs, 163–164
  and spatial patterns, 167–168
  and spontaneous tempo, 151–156
  disabilities of, 462, 463
  musical rhythms, 170–174
  polyrhythm, 170
  subjective rhythmization, 155–156
  testing of rhythmic ability, 393, 394, 402–403, 404, 405
Rock music, 499
Room acoustics, 136ff
Roughness, 14–16, 32–33, 53, 76, 255, 259–260, 348
Scales, 378–380
  and culture, 243–244, 257–258, 261, 379–380, 421–423
  and temperament, *see* Tuning
  chromatic scale, 243, 244, 287, 306, 323, 376, 379, 422, 520–521
  diatonic scale, 102, 243, 257, 287, 288, 306, 323, 362, 376, 378–380, 382, 383–384, 425, 520–521
  discrepancy between step size and JND, 244–246
  natural scales, 376, 378–379, 399

pentatonic scale, 376, 378–379, 399
  scale illusion, 102–104, 114–115, 127–128, 531
  whole-tone scale, 375, 379
Schemata, 319
Schenker, 291, 521–522
Schoenberg, 50, 277, 283–284, 520–522
Schubert, 327ff
Shadowing, 129–130
Sight-reading, 486
Singing
  acoustics, 60–62
  and heredity, 393
  and masking by orchestra, 63–66, 69, 70–71
  and vowel intelligibility, 66–69, 72–73, 83–84
  coloratura, 89–90
  comparison of alto and tenor, 75–76, 77
  comparison of bass, baritone, and tenor, 73–75
  comparison of male and female voices, 73–76
  disabilities of, 457, 458, 461, 463
  falsetto, 79–82
  female singing, 62–69, 78–79
  in childhood, 416–417
  loudness, 63–66, 69, 77
  male singing, 67, 69–73, 79–82
  phonation, 76–82
  phrasing and emotion, 91–94
  pitch accuracy, 89–91
  range of fundamental frequency, 62, 69, 73
  register, 78–82
  resonatory aspects, 62–76
  respiration, 60
  the singer's formant, 69–73, 75
  vibrato, 80, 82–89
  vocal effort and pitch, 77–82
  vocal play in infants, 415–416
  voice classification, 73–76
  voice synthesis, 36–37, 43–44
Social factors in performance, 491–493
Space, 109, 114–115
Spaciousness, 142–146
Stockhausen, 532
Stravinsky, 172, 499, 532–533
Streaming, *see* Channeling
Synchronization, 154–155, 170, 198–199, 490–491
Synthesized music, 29ff, 517–519
  and musical phrases, 42–44
  signal representations, 50–54
Synthetic sound fields, 138–139

T

Tchaikowsky, 104
Tempo

and classification of melody, 338
and patterns in time, 164
and rhythmic organization, 151
and temporal coherence, 119–120
preferred tempo, 153–154ff
rubato, 489–481
spontaneous tempo, 153–154, 168
Temporal coherence boundary, 120, 128, 524
Texture, 531–534
Timbre 12–14, 26ff
    acoustic modeling, 41–42
    additive synthesis, 30–36, 37–39, 53
    and classification of melody, 338
    and frequency shift, 27–29
    and grouping, 124–125, 128
    and intensity, 32
    and musical phrases, 42–44
    and pitch registers, 529
    and reflections, 145
    and room acoustics, 29, 42
    and the scale illusion, 103
    and trills, 518
    attack transients, 30, 48, 53
    brightness, 28, 43, 48
    cross-synthesis, 36–37, 47
    disabilities relating to, 464
    distinguishing instruments, 531–534
    inharmonicity of partials, 35
    intensity, 530–531
    nonlinear distortion, 32
    onset/offset asynchrony, 530–531
    onsets, 13–14, 32–33, 35, 42, 518
    presence, 28
    recognition of instruments and distortion, 29
    roughness, 14–16, 32–33, 53, 76, 255, 259–260, 348
    subtractive synthesis, 39–41
    the classical view, 26–29
    the effect of context, 42–44
    the use of analysis–synthesis models, 45–47

timbral richness, 84
timbral space, 14, 47–49
voice synthesis, 36–37, 43–44
Time delays, 136–137, 141–142
Timing, process model of, 212–215
Tonality, 243, 303, 322, 326, 378–379, 381–384, 399–400, 424–425, 520–523
Tone deafness, 245, 431
Top-down processes, 272, 278
Transcription, 484–487
Transposition, 274–275, 279, 285, 287ff, 376, 414, 415–416, 417–418, 423–424
Trill threshold, 524
Tuning
    equal temperament, 242–243, 257ff
    intonation in performance, 258–259, 261
    just intonation, 242–243, 250, 256–257ff, 354
    Pythagorean tuning, 242–243, 256–257ff
Twelve-tone composition, 281–282, 283–284, 520

U

Ursatz, 291, 320

V

Varese, 50, 534
Verbal deafness, 464–466
Vibrato, 35, 54, 84–89, 488
Voice source, 60, 77ff

W

Wagner, 64–65, 141, 175
Webern, 520, 526–527

Y

Yankee Doodle effect, 278ff, 339, 426

ACADEMIC PRESS
SERIES IN COGNITION AND PERCEPTION

SERIES EDITORS:
Edward C. Carterette
Morton P. Friedman
Department of Psychology
University of California, Los Angeles
Los Angeles, California

Stephen K. Reed: *Psychological Processes in Pattern Recognition*

Earl B. Hunt: *Artificial Intelligence*

James P. Egan: *Signal Detection Theory and ROC Analysis*

Martin F. Kaplan and Steven Schwartz (Eds.): *Human Judgment and Decision Processes*

Myron L. Braunstein: *Depth Perception Through Motion*

R. Plomp: *Aspects of Tone Sensation*

Martin F. Kaplan and Steven Schwartz (Eds.): *Human Judgment and Decision Processes in Applied Settings*

Bikkar S. Randhawa and William E. Coffman: *Visual Learning, Thinking, and Communication*

Robert B. Welch: *Perceptual Modification: Adapting to Altered Sensory Environments*

Lawrence E. Marks: *The Unity of the Senses: Interrelations among the Modalities*

Michele A. Wittig and Anne C. Petersen (Eds.): *Sex-Related Differences in Cognitive Functioning: Developmental Issues*

Douglas Vickers: *Decision Processes in Visual Perception*

Margaret A. Hagen (Ed.): *The Perception of Pictures, Vol. 1: Alberti's Window: The Projective Model of Pictorial Information, Vol. 2 Dürer's Devices: Beyond the Projective Model of Pictures*

Graham Davies, Hadyn Ellis and John Shepherd (Eds.): *Perceiving and Remembering Faces*

Hubert Dolezal: *Living in a World Transformed: Perceptual and Performatory Adaptation to Visual Distortion*

Gerald H. Jacobs: *Comparative Color Vision*

Diana Deutsch (Ed.): *The Psychology of Music*

in preparation

John A. Swets and Ronald M. Pickett: *Evaluation of Diagnostic Systems: Methods from Signal Detection Theory*

Trygg Engen: *The Perception of Odors*

C. Richard Puff (Ed.): *Handbook of Research Methods in Human Memory and Cognition*